SEVENTH EDITION

Rules

for

Writers

Diana Hacker
Nancy Sommers

Brief Menu

SEVENTH EDITION

Rules for Writers

with Writing about Literature

Diana Hacker

Nancy Sommers
Harvard University

Contributing ESL Specialist
Marcy Carbajal Van Horn
St. Edward's University

Consulting Editor
Joseph Bizup
Boston University

Bedford/St. Martin's   Boston ◆ New York

For Bedford/St. Martin's

Executive Editor: Michelle M. Clark
Senior Development Editor: Barbara G. Flanagan
Senior Development Editor: Mara Weible
Senior Production Editor: Rosemary R. Jaffe
Assistant Production Manager: Joe Ford
Senior Marketing Manager: Marjorie Adler
Editorial Assistant: Kylie Paul
Copyeditor: Linda McLatchie
Indexer: Ellen Kuhl Repetto
Permissions Manager: Kalina K. Ingham
Senior Art Director: Anna Palchik
Text Design: Claire Seng-Niemoeller
Cover Design: Marine Miller
Composition: Nesbitt Graphics, Inc.
Printing and Binding: Quad/Graphics Taunton

President: Joan E. Feinberg
Editorial Director: Denise B. Wydra
Editor in Chief: Karen S. Henry
Director of Marketing: Karen R. Soeltz
Director of Production: Susan W. Brown
Associate Director, Editorial Production: Elise S. Kaiser
Managing Editor: Elizabeth M. Schaaf

Library of Congress Control Number: 2010941562

Manufactured in the United States of America.

6   5   4   3   2   1
f   e   d   c   b   a

For information, write: Bedford/St. Martin's, 75 Arlington Street,
Boston, MA 02116   (617-399-4000)

ISBN: 978-0-312-64795-7

Acknowledgments

*Acknowledgments and copyrights can be found at the back of the book on pages 680–
83, which constitute an extension of the copyright page. It is a violation of the law to
reproduce these selections by any means whatsoever without the written permission
of the copyright holder.*

Preface for instructors

Hacker handbooks have long been recognized as the most innovative and practical college references — the handbooks that respond most directly to student writers' questions and challenges. Over the past six editions, students and instructors have relied on *Rules for Writers* for its comprehensive instruction and affordable price. As a classroom teacher, I know how important a trusted handbook is in helping students make the most of their writing experiences in college and beyond. The more students rely on their handbook and learn from its lessons, the more powerful and effective they become as writers. And more than a million college students have become confident writers with the practical and straightforward guidance of *Rules for Writers*.

My goal in revising the seventh edition was to create an even more useful handbook for today's college writers. With this goal in mind, I traveled to more than forty-five colleges and universities to observe how students use their handbooks and how instructors teach from them. I listened, everywhere, for clues about how to make *Rules for Writers* an even more valuable companion for students throughout their academic careers and an even stronger resource for the teachers guiding their writing development. Throughout my travels, I heard students talk about the challenges of applying the handbook's lessons to their own writing. All of the seventh edition's new features are designed to make this task easier for students. For instance, you'll find a series of writing prompts — *As you write* — to help your students connect key lessons of the handbook to their ongoing drafts. These prompts ensure that *Rules for Writers* will be even more useful — and of greater value — for students as they compose their way through college and into the wider world.

As you look through the seventh edition, you'll discover practical innovations inspired by conversations with teachers and students — content crafted to increase the handbook's ease of use in and out of the classroom. An innovative feature I'm particularly excited about is *Revising with comments*. During my travels, I asked students about the comments they receive most frequently and asked instructors to show me the comments they write most frequently on their students' drafts. The answers to these questions, combined with my own research on responding to student writers, shaped this feature, which helps students and instructors make the most of revising and commenting. In keeping with the Hacker tradition, this new feature teaches one lesson at a time — how to revise an unclear thesis, for instance — and directs students to specific sections of the handbook to guide and inform their revision strategies.

In *Rules for Writers*, Diana Hacker created a handbook that looked squarely at the writing problems students face and offered students practical solutions. Diana took everything she knew from her thirty-five years of teaching and put it to work on every page of *Rules for Writers*. It has been one of the great pleasures of my teaching career to build on that foundation and carry on this tradition. And I'm happy to extend the tradition of offering practical solutions by including new material for instructors in this edition. I hope that you and your colleagues find this edition more useful for your classroom teaching than ever before.

As coauthor, I am eager to share this handbook with you, knowing that in the seventh edition you'll find everything that you and your students trust and value about *Rules for Writers*.

Features of the seventh edition

What's new?

More choices add flexibility.

- a **Classic** edition of *Rules for Writers*, spiral-bound with coverage of writing, research, and grammar
- a **tabbed** spiral-bound edition of *Rules for Writers*, with all of the Classic content *plus* coverage of writing about literature and easy navigation with eight tabbed sections

A more practical Instructor's Edition.   For your own teaching, the IE will come in handy; it features classroom activities, help for integrating the handbook into your course and promoting student use of the handbook, and answers to exercises.

New help that prompts students to use their handbook

- *New writing activities* — called *As you write* — help students apply handbook content to their own writing. (See p. 17.)
- *New* **Making the most of your handbook** *boxes* help students pull together the advice they need from different parts of the book to complete writing assignments. (See p. 4.)
- *New student-friendly terms (main idea, flow, representing the other side)* help students find advice using language they recognize. (See p. 93.)

Concrete strategies that help students revise

- *New* Revising with comments *pages, based on Nancy Sommers's research* with students at two- and four-year schools, help students understand feedback and give them strategies for revising in response to comments on their drafts — comments like "narrow your introduction" and "be specific." (See p. 30 for an example.)

- *A new stepped-out process for revising thesis statements* helps students identify a problem in a draft thesis, ask relevant questions, and then revise. (See pp. 28–29.)

More emphasis on key academic writing and research skills

- *New coverage of synthesis* — with illustrated examples — helps writers understand sources, put sources in a conversation, and then figure out what new angle they bring to that conversation. (See 58c and 63c.)

- *New advice for writing an annotated bibliography*, a common college assignment, features a sample entry in the handbook (see p. 449) along with two full annotated bibliography models on the companion Web site.

- *More than eighty-five new documentation models*, many annotated, help students cite sources in MLA and APA style — with special attention to new types of sources like podcasts, online videos, and blogs.

- *A new student argument essay* models effective reasoning, use of evidence (including visual evidence), use of counterargument, and proper MLA-style formatting.

What's the same?

Comprehensive coverage of grammar, academic writing, and research. A classroom tool and a reference, the handbook is designed to help students write well in any college course. This edition includes nearly one hundred exercise sets, many with answers in the back of the book, for plenty of practice.

A brief menu and a user-friendly index. Students will find help fast by consulting either the brief list of contents on the inside front cover or the user-friendly index, which works even for writers who are unsure of grammar terminology.

Citation at a glance. Annotated visuals show students where to find the publication information they need to cite common types of sources in MLA and APA styles.

Quick-access charts and an uncluttered design. The seventh edition has what instructors and students have come to expect of a Hacker handbook: a clear and navigable presentation of information, with charts that summarize key content.

What's on the companion Web site?
hackerhandbooks.com/rules

Grammar, writing, and research exercises with feedback for every item. More than 1,800 items offer students plenty of extra practice, and our gradebook gives instructors flexibility in viewing students' results.

Annotated model papers in MLA, APA, *Chicago*, CSE, and USGS styles. Student writers can see formatting conventions and effective writing in traditional college essays and in other common genres: annotated bibliographies, literature reviews, lab reports, business proposals, and clinical documents.

Research and Documentation Online. This award-winning resource, written by a college librarian, gives students a jump start with research in over thirty academic disciplines.

Resources for writers and tutors. Checklists, hints, tips, and helpsheets are available in downloadable format.

Resources for ESL and multilingual writers. Writers will find advice and strategies for understanding college expectations and completing writing assignments. Also included are charts, exercises, activities, and an annotated student essay.

Language Debates. Twenty-two brief essays provide opportunities for critical thinking about grammar and usage issues.

Access to premium content. The print handbook can be packaged with premium content: The *Rules for Writers e-Book*, a series of online video tutorials, and a collection of resources that includes games and activities. The activation code for premium content is free when packaged with a new copy of *Rules for Writers*.

Supplements for instructors

Practical

Teaching with Hacker Handbooks: Topics, Strategies, and Lesson Plans

Rules for Writers instructor resources (at hackerhandbooks.com/rules)

Professional

Teaching Composition: Background Readings
The Bedford Guide for Writing Tutors, Fifth Edition
The Bedford Bibliography for Teachers of Writing, Sixth Edition

Supplements for students

Print

Developmental Exercises for Rules for Writers
Working with Sources: Research Exercises for Rules for Writers
Research and Documentation in the Electronic Age, Fifth Edition
Resources for Multilingual Writers and ESL
Writing in the Disciplines: Advice and Models
Strategies for Online Learners
Writing about Literature

Online

Rules for Writers e-Book
CompClass for Rules for Writers

Acknowledgments

I am grateful for the expertise, enthusiasm, and classroom experience that so many individuals brought to the seventh edition.

Reviewers

Martha R. Bachman, Camden County College; Thomas P. Barrett, Ocean County College; Suzanne Biedenbach, University of Memphis; Sally Ann Boccippio, Ocean County College; Jennifer Costello Brezina, College of the Canyons; Mary Carney, Gainesville State College; Jia-Yi Cheng-Levine, College of the Canyons; Malkiel Choseed, Onondaga Community College; Amy Cruickshank, Cuyahoga Community College; Catherine P. Dice, University of Memphis; Marylynne Diggs, Clark College; Shawn M. Dowiak, Ramapo College of New Jersey; Crystal Edmonds, Robeson Community College; Don Erskine, Clark College; Rima S. Gulshan, Northern Virginia Community College; Eunice Hargett, Broward College; Anne Helms, Alamance Community College; David Hennessy, Broward College; Paula Hester,

Indian Hills Community College; Matthew Horton, Gainesville State College; Kristen Iversen, University of Memphis; Laura Jeffries, Florida State College at Jacksonville; Robert Johnson, Midwestern State University; Joseph Jones, University of Memphis; Grace Kessler, California State University–San Marcos; Monique Kluczykowski, Gainesville State College; Michael Kula, Carroll University; M. Douglas Lamborne, Lord Fairfax Community College; Lisa Lopez Levers, Duquesne University; Ben Levy, Ramapo College of New Jersey; Michael Levy, University of Wisconsin–Stout; Susan P. Livermore, Millersville University; Dolores Mac-Naughton, Umpqua Community College; Heidi Marshall, Florida State College at Jacksonville; Christopher Minnix, University of Arizona; Miriam P. Moore, Lord Fairfax Community College; Andrea Muldoon, University of Wisconsin–Stout; Meena Nayak, Northern Virginia Community College; D. Erik Nielson, Northern Virginia Community College; Wendy Perkins, Prince George's Community College; Linda Y. Peters, Onondaga Community College; Lynn M. Peterson, Carroll University; James P. Purdy, Duquesne University; Richard W. Rawnsley, College of the Desert; Stacy Rice, Northern Virginia Community College; Susan Roberts, United States Coast Guard Academy; Aline Carole Rogalski, Ocean County College; Marsha A. Rutter, Southwestern College; Tristan Saldaña, College of Marin; Jennifer P. Schaefer, Lord Fairfax Community College; Arthur L. Schuhart, Northern Virginia Community College–Annandale; Frances Shapiro-Skrobe, Ramapo College of New Jersey; Tracey Sherard, College of the Canyons; Katherine P. Simpson, Lord Fairfax Community College; Charles Smires, Florida State College at Jacksonville; Cheri Spiegel, Northern Virginia Community College; Jack R. Tapleshay, College of the Desert; Debra Thomas, Harrisburg Area Community College; Anita Turlington, Gainesville State College; and Michelle Wagner, Broward College.

Contributors

I am grateful to the following individuals, fellow teachers of writing, for their smart contributions to key content: Joe Bizup, Boston University, updated the coverage of writing about literature with fresh selections and relevant advice; and Marcy Carbajal Van Horn, ESL specialist, experienced composition instructor, and former online writing lab director, served as lead author for *Teaching with Hacker Handbooks* and improved our coverage for multilingual writers both in the handbook and on the companion Web site.

Student contributors

A number of bright and willing students helped identify which instructor comments provide the best guidance for revision. From Green River Community College: Kyle Baskin, Josué Cardona, Emily Dore, Anthony Hines, Stephanie Humphries, Joshua Kin, Jessica Llapitan, James Mitchell, Derek Pegram, Charlie Piehler, Lindsay Allison Rae Richards, Kristen Saladis, Jacob Simpson, Christina Starkey, Ariana Stone, and Joseph Vreeburg. From Northern Kentucky University: Sarah Freidhoff, Marisa Hempel, Sarah Laughlin, Sean Moran, Laren Reis, and Carissa Spencer. From Palm Beach Community College: Alexis Day, Shawn Gibbons, Zachary Jennison, Jean Lacz, Neshia Neal, Sarah Reich, Jude Rene, and Sam Smith. And from the University of Maine at Farmington: Nicole Carr, Hannah Courtright, Timothy Doyle, Janelle Gallant, Amy Hobson, Shawn Menard, Jada Molton, Jordan Nicholas, Nicole Phillips, Tessa Rockwood, Emily Rose, Nicholas Tranten, and Ashley Wyman. I also thank the students who have let us use and adapt their papers as models in the handbook and on its companion Web site: Ned Bishop, Lucy Bonilla, Jamal Hammond, Sam Jacobs, Albert Lee, Luisa Mirano, Anna Orlov, Emilia Sanchez, and Matt Watson.

Bedford/St. Martin's

A handbook is truly a collaborative writing project, and it is a pleasure to acknowledge and thank the enormously talented Bedford/St. Martin's editorial team, whose deep commitment to students informs each new feature of *Rules for Writers*. Joan Feinberg, Bedford's president and Diana Hacker's first editor, offers her superb judgment on every aspect of the book. Joan's graceful and generous leadership, both within Bedford and in the national composition community, is a never-ending source of inspiration for those who work closely with her. Michelle Clark, executive editor, is the kind of editor every author dreams of having — a treasured friend and colleague — and an endless source of creativity and joy. Michelle combines wisdom with patience, imagination with practicality, and hard work with good cheer. Mara Weible, senior editor, brings to the seventh edition her teacher's sensibility and editor's unerring eye, shaping the innovative research coverage and new synthesis section and contributing wonderful ideas to strengthen the seventh edition's new features on academic writing and research. Barbara Flanagan, senior editor, who has worked on Diana Hacker's handbooks for more than twenty-five years, brings her unrelenting insistence on clarity and precision as well as her expertise in documentation. Thanks to Kylie Paul, editorial assistant, for expertly managing the review process, preparing documents, and managing many small details related to both our Web and print projects.

The passionate commitment to *Rules for Writers* of many Bedford colleagues — Denise Wydra, editorial director; Karen Henry, editor in chief; and Marjorie Adler, marketing manager — ensures that the seventh edition remains the most innovative and practical handbook on the market. Special thanks go to Jimmy Fleming, senior English specialist, for his abundant contributions, always wise and judicious, and for his enthusiasm and support as we traveled to colleges near and far. Many thanks to Rosemary Jaffe, senior production editor, who kept us on schedule and efficiently and gracefully turned a manuscript into a handbook. And thanks to Linda McLatchie, copyeditor, for her thoroughness and attention to detail; to Claire Seng-Niemoeller, text designer, who always has clarity and ease of use in mind as she designs *Rules for Writers*; to Marine Miller, cover designer, who has given the book a strikingly beautiful cover; and to Sarah Ferguson, new media editor, who developed the book's companion Web site and e-book.

Most important, I want to thank Diana Hacker. She cared enough to study her own students at Prince George's Community College, puzzling out their challenges and their needs and observing their practices. I'm honored to acknowledge her work, her legacy, and her innovative spirit — and pleased to continue in the tradition of this brilliant teacher and writer.

Last, but never least, I offer thanks to Maxine Rodburg, Laura Saltz, and Kerry Walk, friends and colleagues, for sustaining conversations about teaching writing. And I thank my family: Joshua, an attentive reader of life and literature, for his steadfastness across the drafts; Sam and Kate, for lively conversations about writing; Louise, Walter, Ron, and Charles Mary, for their wit and wisdom; and Rachel and Alexandra, whose good-natured and humorous observations about their real lives as college writers are a constant source of instruction and inspiration.

Nancy Sommers

How to use this book and its companion Web site

Though it is small enough to hold in your hand, *Rules for Writers* will answer most of the questions you are likely to ask as you plan, draft, and revise a piece of writing:

How do I choose and narrow a topic?

How do I know when to begin a new paragraph?

Should I write *each was* or *each were*?

When should I place a comma before *and*?

What is counterargument?

What is the difference between *accept* and *except*?

How do I cite a source from the Web?

The book's companion Web site extends the book beyond its covers. See page xvii for details.

How to find information with an instructor's help

When you are revising an essay that your instructor has marked, tracking down information is simple. If your instructor indicates problems with a number such as *16* or a number and letter such as *12e*, you can turn directly to the appropriate section of the handbook. Just flip through the tabs at the top of the pages until you find the number in question.

If your instructor uses an abbreviation such as *w* or *dm* instead of a number, consult the list of abbreviations and revision symbols on the next-to-last page of the book. There you will find the name of the problem (*wordy*; *dangling modifier*) and the number of the section to consult. See the following page for an example.

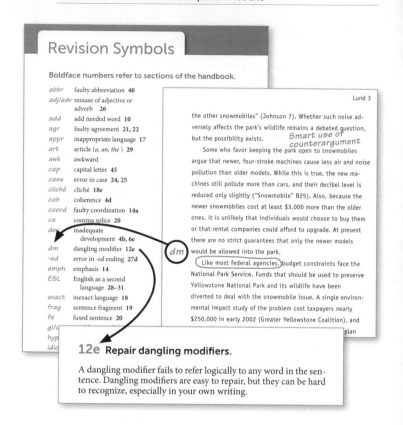

Revision Symbols

Boldface numbers refer to sections of the handbook.

abbr	faulty abbreviation **40**
adj/adv	misuse of adjective or adverb **26**
add	add needed word **10**
agr	faulty agreement **21, 22**
appr	inappropriate language **17**
art	article (*a, an, the*) **29**
awk	awkward
cap	capital letter **45**
case	error in case **24, 25**
cliché	cliché **18e**
coh	coherence **4d**
coord	faulty coordination **14a**
cs	comma splice **20**
dev	inadequate development **4b, 6e**
dm	dangling modifier **12e**
-ed	error in *-ed* ending **27d**
emph	emphasis **14**
ESL	English as a second language **28–31**
exact	inexact language **18**
frag	sentence fragment **19**
fs	fused sentence **20**
gl/u	
hyp	
idio	

Lund 3

the other snowmobiles" (Johnson 7). Whether such noise adversely affects the park's wildlife remains a debated question, but the possibility exists.   *Smart use of counterargument*

Some who favor keeping the park open to snowmobiles argue that newer, four-stroke machines cause less air and noise pollution than older models. While this is true, the new machines still pollute more than cars, and their decibel level is reduced only slightly ("Snowmobile" B25). Also, because the newer snowmobiles cost at least $3,000 more than the older ones, it is unlikely that individuals would choose to buy them or that rental companies could afford to upgrade. At present there are no strict guarantees that only the newer models would be allowed into the park.

Like most federal agencies, budget constraints face the National Park Service. Funds that should be used to preserve Yellowstone National Park and its wildlife have been diverted to deal with the snowmobile issue. A single environmental impact study of the problem cost taxpayers nearly $250,000 in early 2002 (Greater Yellowstone Coalition), and   plan

12e Repair dangling modifiers.

A dangling modifier fails to refer logically to any word in the sentence. Dangling modifiers are easy to repair, but they can be hard to recognize, especially in your own writing.

How to find information on your own

This handbook is designed to allow you to find information without an instructor's help — usually by consulting the brief menu inside the front cover. At times, you may consult the detailed menu inside the back cover, the index, the glossary of usage, the list of revision symbols, or one of the directories to documentation models.

The brief menu.   The brief menu inside the front cover displays the book's contents. Let's say that you want to find out how you can write with more active verbs. Your first step is to scan the menu for the appropriate numbered topic — in this case "8 Active Verbs." Then you can use the blue tabs at the top of the pages to find section 8.

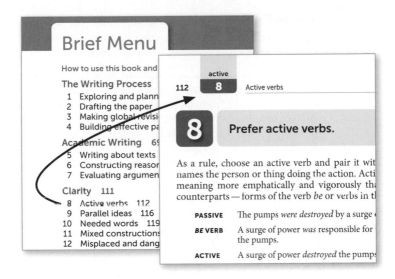

The detailed menu. The detailed menu appears inside the back cover. When the numbered section you're looking for is broken up into quite a few lettered subsections, try consulting this menu.

For instance, if you have a question about the proper use of commas after introductory elements, this menu will quickly lead you to section 32b.

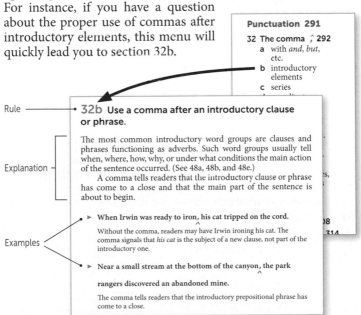

Once you find the right lettered subsection, you will see three kinds of advice to help you edit your writing — a rule, an explanation, and one or more hand-edited examples.

The index.   If you aren't sure which topic to choose from one of the menus, consult the index at the back of the book. For example, you may not realize that the issue of whether to use *have* or *has* is a matter of subject-verb agreement (section 21). In that case, simply look up "*has* vs. *have*" in the index. You will be directed to specific pages in two sections covering subject-verb agreement.

Making the most of your handbook.   You will find your way to helpful advice by using the index, the menus, or the contents. Once you get to where you need to be, you may also find references to additional related advice and models. These boxes help you pull together what you need from the handbook for each assignment.

> **Making the most of your handbook**
> Integrating visuals can strengthen your writing.
> ▸ Choosing appropriate visuals: page 407
> ▸ Placing and labeling visuals: page 407
> ▸ Using visuals responsibly: page 408

The glossary of usage.   When in doubt about the correct use of a particular word (such as *affect* and *effect*), consult the glossary of usage at the back of the book. This glossary explains the difference between commonly confused words; it also includes words that are inappropriate in formal written English.

Directories to documentation models.   When you are documenting a research paper with MLA or APA style, you can find documentation models by consulting the appropriate color-coded directories.

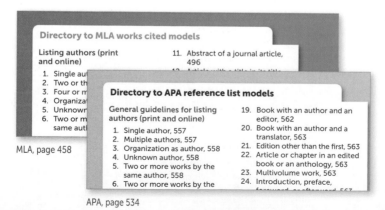

Directory to MLA works cited models

Listing authors (print and online)

1. Single au
2. Two or th
3. Four or m
4. Organiza
5. Unknowr
6. Two or m
   same auth

11. Abstract of a journal article, 496

MLA, page 458

Directory to APA reference list models

General guidelines for listing authors (print and online)

1. Single author, 557
2. Multiple authors, 557
3. Organization as author, 558
4. Unknown author, 558
5. Two or more works by the same author, 558
6. Two or more works by the

19. Book with an author and an editor, 562
20. Book with an author and a translator, 563
21. Edition other than the first, 563
22. Article or chapter in an edited book or an anthology, 563
23. Multivolume work, 563
24. Introduction, preface,

APA, page 534

Answers to exercises. *Rules for Writers* is designed to help you learn from it on your own. By providing answers to some exercise sentences, it allows you to test your understanding of the material. Most exercise sets begin with five sentences lettered *a* through *e* and conclude with five or ten numbered sentences. Answers to lettered sentences appear at the back of the book.

Using the book's companion Web site: hackerhandbooks.com/rules

Throughout *Rules for Writers*, Seventh Edition, you will see references to exercises and model papers on the book's companion Web site. Here is a complete list of resources on the site. Your instructor may use some of this material in class; each area of the site, however, has been developed for you to use on your own whenever you need it.

- *Writing exercises* Interactive exercises, including feedback for every answer, on topics such as choosing a thesis statement and conducting peer review

- *Grammar exercises* Interactive exercises on grammar, style, and punctuation, including feedback for every answer

- *Research exercises* Interactive exercises, including feedback for every answer, on topics such as integrating quotations and documenting sources in MLA and APA styles

- *Model papers* Annotated sample papers in MLA, APA, *Chicago*, CSE, and USGS styles

- *Multilingual/ESL help* Resources, strategies, model papers, and exercises to help multilingual speakers improve their college writing skills

- *Research and Documentation Online* Advice on finding sources in a variety of academic disciplines and up-to-date guidelines for documenting print and online sources in MLA, APA, *Chicago*, and CSE styles

- *Resources for writers and tutors* Revision checklists and helpsheets for common writing problems

- *Language Debates* Mini-essays exploring controversial issues of grammar and usage, such as split infinitives

- *Additional resources* Print-format versions of the book's exercises and links to additional online resources for every part of the book

- ***Re:Writing*** A free collection of resources for composition and other college classes: help with preparing presentation slides, avoiding plagiarism, evaluating online sources, and more
- ***Tutorials*** Interactive resources that teach essential college skills such as integrating sources in a research paper and revising with peer comments (This area of the Web site requires an activation code.)

Contents

Academic Writing   69

5 Writing about texts   70

6 Constructing reasonable arguments   84

7 Evaluating arguments   102

Clarity   111

8 Prefer active verbs.   112

Document Design 401

Research 419

Writing Papers in MLA Style   457

Writing Papers in APA Style   533

The Writing Process

The Writing Process

Writing is a process of figuring out what you think, not a matter of recording already developed thoughts. Since it's not possible to think about everything all at once, most experienced writers handle a piece of writing in stages. You will generally move from planning to drafting to revising, but be prepared to return to earlier stages as your ideas develop.

Explore ideas; then sketch a plan.

Before attempting a first draft, spend some time generating ideas. Mull over your subject while listening to music or driving to work, jot down inspirations, and explore your insights with a willing listener. Ask yourself questions: What do you find puzzling, striking, or interesting about your subject? What would you like to know more about? At this stage, you should be collecting information and experimenting with ways of focusing and organizing it to reach your readers.

1a   Assess the writing situation.

Begin by taking a look at your writing situation. The key elements of a writing situation include the following:

- your subject
- your purpose
- your audience
- the sources of information available to you
- any constraints (length, document design, deadlines)

It is likely that you will make final decisions about all of these matters later in the writing process — after a first draft, for example — but you can save yourself time by thinking about as many of them as possible in advance. For a quick checklist, see the chart on pages 3–4.

Academic English What counts as good writing varies from culture to culture and even among groups within cultures. In some situations, you will need to become familiar with the writing styles — such as direct or indirect, personal or impersonal, plain or embellished — that are valued by the culture or discipline for which you are writing.

Checklist for assessing the writing situation

Subject

- Has the subject (or a range of possible subjects) been given to you, or are you free to choose your own?
- What interests you about your subject? What questions would you like to explore?
- Why is your subject worth writing about? How might readers benefit from reading about it?
- Do you need to narrow your subject to a more specific topic (because of length restrictions, for instance)?

Purpose and audience

- Why are you writing: To inform readers? To persuade them? To call them to action? To entertain them? Some combination of these?
- Who are your readers? How well informed are they about the subject? What do you want them to learn?
- How interested and attentive are they likely to be? Will they resist any of your ideas?
- What is your relationship to your readers: Student to instructor? Employee to supervisor? Citizen to citizen? Expert to novice?

Sources of information

- Where will your information come from: Reading? Personal experience? Research? Direct observation? Interviews? Questionnaires?
- What documentation style is required: MLA? APA?

Checklist for assessing the writing situation (continued)

Length and document design

- Do you have any length specifications? If not, what length seems appropriate, given your subject, purpose, and audience?
- Does the assignment call for a particular kind of paper: A report? A proposal? An essay? An analysis of data? A reflection?
- Is a particular format required? If so, do you have guidelines to follow or examples to consult?
- How might visuals — charts, graphs, tables, images — help you convey information?

Reviewers and deadlines

- Who will be reviewing your draft in progress: Your instructor? A writing center tutor? Your classmates? A family member?
- What are your deadlines? How much time will you need to allow for the various stages of writing, including proofreading and printing the final draft?

Subject

Frequently your subject will be given to you. In a psychology class, for example, you might be asked to explain Bruno Bettelheim's Freudian analysis of fairy tales. In a composition course, assignments often ask you to respond to readings. In the business world, your assignment might be to draft a marketing plan.

When you are free to choose your own subject, it's a good idea to focus on something you are genuinely curious about. If you are studying television, radio, and the Internet in a communication course, for example, you might ask yourself which of these subjects interests you most. Perhaps you want to learn more about the role streaming video can play in activism and social change. Look through your readings and class notes to see if you can identify questions you'd like to explore further in an essay.

> **Making the most of your handbook**
> Effective research writers often start by asking a question.
> ▶ Posing questions for research: 53a

THE WRITING CENTER   hackerhandbooks.com/rules
> Resources for writers and tutors > Tips from writing tutors:
Invention strategies

Ways to narrow a subject to a topic

Subdividing your subject by asking questions

One way to subdivide a subject is to ask questions sparked by reading or by talking to your classmates.

SUBJECT	teen pregnancy
QUESTION	Why do Waterford and Troy, neighboring cities, have different rates of teen pregnancy?

This question would give you a manageable topic for a short paper.

Restricting your purpose

Often you can restrict your purpose. You might realize on reflection that your initial goal — your draft purpose — is more than you could hope to accomplish in a brief paper.

SUBJECT	teen pregnancy
DRAFT PURPOSE	preventing teen pregnancy
MORE LIMITED PURPOSE	showing how changing the health curriculum for sixth graders results in lower rates of teen pregnancy

Rethinking your purpose in this way would give you a manageable topic.

Restricting your audience

Consider writing for a particular audience.

SUBJECT	teen pregnancy
AUDIENCE	general public
MORE LIMITED AUDIENCE	educators; school administrators

Addressing a specific group with a special interest is a way to make your topic more manageable.

Considering the information available to you

Look at the information you have collected. If you have gathered a great deal of information on one aspect of your subject (birth control education) and less information on other aspects (counseling for expectant teen parents), you may have found your topic.

Make sure that you can reasonably investigate your subject in the space you have. If you are limited to a few pages, for example, you could not do justice to a subject as broad as "videos as agents of social change." You could, however, focus on one aspect of the subject — perhaps experts' contradictory claims about the effectiveness of "narrowcasting," or creating video content for small, specific audiences. The chart on page 5 suggests ways to narrow a subject to a manageable topic for a paper.

Whether or not you choose your own subject, it's important to be aware of the expectations of each writing situation.

Purpose

Your purpose will often be dictated by your writing situation. Perhaps you have been asked to draft a proposal requesting funding for a student organization, to report the results of a psychology experiment, or to write about the growing controversy surrounding genetically modified (GM) foods for the school newspaper. Even though your overall purpose is fairly obvious in such situations, a closer look at the assignment can help you make a variety of necessary decisions. How detailed should the proposal be? How technical does your psychology professor expect your report to be? Do you want to inform students about the GM food controversy or change their attitudes toward it?

In many writing situations, part of your challenge will be discovering a purpose. Asking yourself why readers should care about what you are saying can help you decide what your purpose might be. Perhaps your subject is magnet schools — schools that draw students from different neighborhoods because of features such as advanced science classes or a concentration on the arts. If you have discussed magnet schools in class, a description of how these schools work probably will not interest you or your readers. But maybe you have discovered that your county's magnet schools are not promoting diversity as had been planned and you want to call your readers to action. Or maybe you are interested in comparing student performance at magnet schools and traditional schools.

Although no precise guidelines will lead you to a purpose, you can begin by asking yourself which one or more of the following aims you hope to accomplish.

PURPOSES FOR WRITING

to inform	to evaluate
to persuade	to recommend
to entertain	to request
to call readers to action	to propose
to change attitudes	to provoke thought
to analyze	to express feelings
to argue	to summarize

Writers often misjudge their own purposes, summarizing when they should be analyzing, or expressing feelings about problems instead of proposing solutions. Before beginning any writing task, pause to ask, "Why am I communicating with my readers?" This question will lead you to another important question: "Just who are my readers?"

Audience

Audience analysis can often lead you to an effective strategy for reaching your readers. A writer whose purpose was to encourage college students to recycle more by broadening their ideas about recycling began by making some observations about her audience (see p. 8).

This analysis led the writer to appeal to her reader's competitive nature — inviting college students to think about trying different kinds of recycling as achieving different levels in a video game. Her audience analysis also warned against adopting a preachy tone that her readers might find offensive. Instead of lecturing, she decided to draw examples from her own journey through the "levels" of being green — recycling paper products and plastic water bottles, carrying a refillable water bottle, biking to campus, buying used clothing, taking notes on a laptop, and so on. The result was an essay that reached its readers rather than alienating them.

Of course, in some writing situations the audience will not be neatly defined for you. Nevertheless, the choices you make as you write will tell readers who you think they are (novices or experts, for example), so it is best to be consistent.

For help with audience analysis, see the chart on pages 3–4.

AUDIENCE ANALYSIS

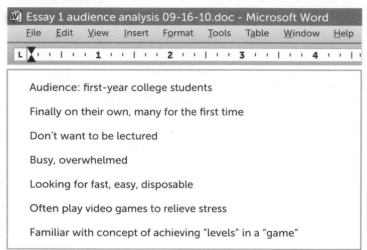

Academic audiences   In college writing, considerations of audience can be more complex than they seem at first. Your instructor will read your essay, of course, but most instructors play multiple roles while reading. Their first and most obvious roles are as coach and evaluator; but they are also intelligent and objective readers, the kind of people who might reasonably be informed, convinced, entertained, or called to action by what you have to say.

Some instructors specify an audience, such as a hypothetical supervisor, readers of a local newspaper, or peers in a particular field. Other instructors expect you to imagine an audience appropriate to your purpose and your subject. Still others prefer that you write for a general audience of educated readers — nonspecialists who can be expected to read with an intelligent, critical eye.

Business audiences   Writers in the business world often find themselves writing for multiple audiences. A letter to a client, for instance, might be distributed to sales representatives as well. Readers of a report might include persons with and without technical expertise or readers who want details and those who prefer a quick overview.

To satisfy the demands of multiple audiences, business writers have developed a variety of strategies: attaching cover letters to detailed reports, adding boldface headings, placing summaries of key ideas in the margin, and so on.

Public audiences Writers in communities often write for a specific audience — the local school superintendent, a legislative representative, fellow members of a social group, readers of a local paper. With public writing, it is more likely that you are familiar with the views your readers hold and the assumptions they make, so you may be better able to judge how to engage those readers. If you are writing to a group of other parents to share ideas for lowering school bus transportation costs, for instance, you may have a good sense of whether to lead with a logical analysis of other school-related fees or with a fiery criticism of key decision makers.

Considering audience when writing e-mail messages

In academic, business, and civic contexts, you will want to show readers that you value their time. Your e-mail message may be just one of many that your readers have to wade through. Here are some strategies for writing effective e-mails:

- Use a meaningful, concise subject line to help readers sort messages and set priorities.
- Put the most important part of your message at the beginning so that your reader sees it without scrolling.
- Write concisely; keep paragraphs short.
- For long, detailed messages, provide a summary at the beginning.
- Avoid writing in all capital letters or all lowercase letters.
- Proofread for typos and obvious errors that are likely to slow down readers.

You will also want to follow conventions of good etiquette and avoid violating standards of academic integrity. Here are some strategies for writing responsible e-mails:

- E-mail messages can easily be forwarded to others and reproduced. Do not write anything that you would not want attributed to you.
- Do not forward another person's message without asking his or her permission.
- If you write an e-mail message that includes someone else's words — opinions, statistics, song lyrics, and so forth — it's best to let your reader know the source for that material and where any borrowed material begins and ends.

Considering audience when writing e-mail messages (continued)

- Choose your words carefully because e-mail messages can easily be misread. Without your voice, facial gestures, or body language, a message can be misunderstood.
- Pay careful attention to tone; avoid writing anything that you wouldn't be comfortable saying directly to a reader.

Sources of information

Where will your facts, details, and examples come from? Can you develop your topic from personal experience alone, or will you need to search for relevant information through reading, observation, interviews, or questionnaires?

Reading Reading is an important way to deepen your understanding of a topic and expand your perspective. Reading will be your primary source of information for many college assignments, which will generally be of two kinds: (1) analytical essays that call for a close reading of one book, essay, literary work, or visual and (2) research assignments that ask you to find and consult a variety of sources on a topic.

For an analytical essay, you will select details from the work to support an interpretation. You can often assume that your readers are familiar with the work and have a copy of it on hand, but be sure to provide enough context so that someone who doesn't know the work well can still follow your interpretation. When you quote from the work, page references are usually sufficient. When in doubt about the need for documentation, ask your instructor.

For a research paper, you cannot assume that your readers are familiar with your sources. Therefore, you must document all quoted, summarized, or paraphrased material.

> **Making the most of your handbook**
> Academic writing often requires that you read critically and cite your sources.
> ▶ Guidelines for active reading: page 71
> ▶ Analyzing an essay: 5d
> ▶ Quoting, paraphrasing, and summarizing sources: 55c

Personal experience If your interest in a subject stems from your personal experience, you will want to ask what it is about your experience that would interest your audience and why. For example, if you volunteered at a homeless shelter, you might have spent some time talking to homeless children and learning about their needs. Perhaps you can use your experience to broaden your readers' understanding of the issues, to persuade an organization to fund an after-school program for homeless children, or to propose changes in legislation.

Observation Observation is an excellent means of collecting information about a wide range of subjects, such as gender relationships on a popular television program, the clichéd language of sports announcers, or the appeal of a local art museum. For such subjects, do not rely on your memory alone; your information will be fresher and more detailed if you actively collect it, with a notebook, laptop, or voice recorder in hand.

Interviews and questionnaires Interviews and questionnaires can supply detailed and interesting information on many subjects. A nursing student interested in the care of terminally ill patients might interview hospice nurses; a criminal justice major might speak with a local judge about alternative sentencing for first offenders; a future teacher might conduct a survey on the use of smart board technology in local elementary schools.

It is a good idea to record interviews to preserve any lively quotations that you might want to weave into your essay. Circulating questionnaires by e-mail or on a Web site will facilitate responses. Keep questions simple and specify a deadline to ensure that you get a reasonable number of replies. (See also 53g.)

Length and document design

Writers seldom have complete control over length. Journalists usually write within strict word limits set by their editors, businesspeople routinely aim for conciseness, and most college assignments specify an approximate length.

Your writing situation may also require a certain document design. Specific formats are used in business for letters, memos, and reports. In the academic world, you may need to learn precise conventions for lab reports, critiques, research papers, and so on. For most undergraduate essays, a standard format is acceptable (see 51).

In some writing situations, you will be free to create your own design, complete with headings, displayed lists, and perhaps visuals such as charts and graphs. For a discussion of document design, see 50.

Reviewers and deadlines

Professional and business writers rarely work alone. They work with reviewers, often called *editors*, who offer advice throughout the writing process. In college classes, too, the use of reviewers is common. Some instructors play the role of reviewer for you; others may ask you to visit the writing center. Still others schedule peer review sessions in class or online. Such sessions give you a chance to hear what other students think about your draft in progress — and to play the role of reviewer yourself.

Deadlines are a key element of any writing situation. They help you plan your time and map out what you can accomplish in that time. For complex writing projects, such as research papers, you'll need to plan your time carefully. By working backward from the final deadline, you can create a schedule of target dates for completing parts of the project. (See p. 420 for an example.)

EXERCISE 1–1   Narrow three of the following subjects into topics that would be manageable for an essay of two to five pages.

1. Treatments for mental illness
2. An experience with racism or sexism
3. Handheld electronic devices in the classroom
4. Images of women in video games
5. Mandatory drug testing in the workplace

EXERCISE 1–2   Suggest a purpose and an audience for three of the following subjects.

1. Genetic modification of cash crop foods
2. Government housing for military veterans
3. The future of online advertising
4. Working with special needs children
5. Hybrid cars

1b Experiment with ways to explore your subject.

Instead of just plunging into a first draft, experiment with one or more techniques for exploring your subject, perhaps one of these:

- talking and listening
- reading and annotating texts
- listing
- clustering
- freewriting
- asking questions
- keeping a journal
- blogging

Whatever technique you turn to, the goal is the same: to generate ideas that will lead you to a question, a problem, or a topic that you want to explore. At this early stage of the writing process, don't censor yourself. Sometimes an idea that initially seems trivial or far-fetched will turn out to be worthwhile.

Talking and listening

Because writing is a process of figuring out what you think about a subject, it can be useful to try out your ideas on other people. Conversation can deepen and refine your ideas before you even begin to set them down on paper. By talking and listening to others, you can also discover what they find interesting, what they are curious about, and where they disagree with you. If you are planning to advance an argument, you can try it out on listeners with other points of view.

Many writers begin a writing project by brainstorming ideas in a group, debating a point with friends, or chatting with an instructor. Others prefer to record themselves talking through their thoughts. Some writers exchange ideas by sending e-mail or instant messages or by posting to discussion boards or blogs. You may be encouraged to share ideas with your classmates and instructor in an online workshop where you can begin to refine your thoughts before starting a draft.

Reading and annotating texts

Reading is an important way to deepen your understanding of a topic and expand your perspective. Annotating a text, written or visual, encourages you to read actively — to highlight key concepts, to note possible contradictions in an argument, or to raise questions for further research and investigation. Here, for example, is a paragraph from an essay on medical ethics, Michael Sandel's "The Case against Perfection," as one student annotated it:

> **Making the most of your handbook**
> Read critically and take notes before you write.
> ▸ Guidelines for active reading: page 71
> ▸ Taking notes: 55c
> ▸ Analyzing texts: 5

SAMPLE ANNOTATED ARTICLE

What breakthroughs?
Do all breakthroughs have the same consequences?

Stem cell research?

Is everyone really uneasy?
Is something a breakthrough if it creates a predicament?

Breakthroughs in genetics present us with a promise and a predicament. The promise is that we may soon be able to treat and prevent a host of debilitating diseases. The predicament is that our newfound genetic knowledge may also enable us to manipulate our own nature — to enhance our muscles, memories, and moods; to choose the sex, height, and other genetic traits of our children; to make ourselves "better than well." When science moves faster than moral understanding, as it does today, men and women struggle to articulate their unease. In liberal societies they reach first for the language of autonomy, fairness, and individual rights. But this part of our moral vocabulary is ill equipped to address the hardest questions posed by genetic engineering. The genomic revolution has induced a kind of moral vertigo.

Sandel's key dilemma

What does he mean by "moral understanding"?

Which questions? He doesn't seem to be taking sides.

After reading and annotating the entire article, the student noticed that several of his annotations pointed to the question of whether a scientific breakthrough should be viewed in terms of its moral consequences. He decided to reread the article, taking detailed notes with this question in mind.

Listing

Listing ideas — a technique sometimes known as *brainstorming* — is a good way to figure out what you know and what questions you have. Here is a list one student writer jotted down for an essay about community service requirements for college students:

- Volunteered in high school.
- Teaching adults to read motivated me to study education.
- "The best way to find yourself is to lose yourself in the service of others." — Gandhi
- Volunteering helps students find interests and career paths.
- Volunteering as requirement? Contradiction?
- Many students need to work to pay college tuition.
- Enough time to study, work, and volunteer?
- Can't students volunteer for their own reasons?
- What schools have community service requirements?
- What do students say about community service requirements?

Listing questions and ideas helped the writer narrow her subject and identify her position. In other words, she treated her early list as a record of her thoughts and a springboard to new ideas, not as an outline.

Clustering

Unlike listing, clustering highlights relationships among ideas. To cluster ideas, write your subject in the center of a sheet of paper, draw a circle around it, and surround the circle with related ideas connected to it with lines. If some of the satellite ideas lead to more specific clusters, write them down as well. The writer of the diagram on page 16 was exploring ideas for an essay on obesity in children.

Freewriting

In its purest form, freewriting is simply nonstop writing. You set aside ten minutes or so and write whatever comes to mind, without pausing to think about word choice, spelling, or even meaning. If you get stuck, you can write about being stuck, but you should keep your fingers moving. If nothing much happens, you have lost only ten minutes. It's more likely, though, that something interesting will emerge — perhaps an eloquent sentence, a genuine expression of curiosity, or an idea worth further investigation.

CLUSTER DIAGRAM

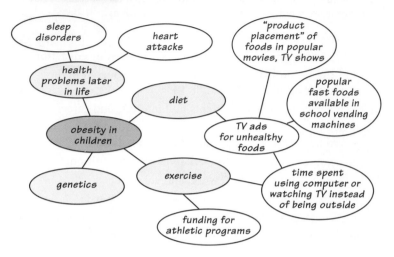

To explore ideas on a particular topic, consider using a technique known as *focused freewriting*. Again, you write quickly and freely, but this time you focus on a subject and pay attention to the connections among your ideas.

Asking questions

When gathering material for a story, journalists routinely ask themselves Who? What? When? Where? Why? and How? In addition to helping journalists get started, these questions ensure that they will not overlook an important fact.

Whenever you are writing about events, whether current or historical, asking questions is one way to get started. One student, whose topic was the negative reaction in 1915 to D. W. Griffith's silent film *The Birth of a Nation*, began exploring her topic with this set of questions:

- *Who* objected to the film?
- *What* were the objections?
- *When* were protests first voiced?
- *Where* were protests most strongly expressed?
- *Why* did protesters object to the film?
- *How* did protesters make their views known?

As often happens, the answers to these questions led to another question the writer wanted to explore. After she discovered that protesters objected to the film's racist portrayal of African Americans, she wondered whether their protests had changed attitudes. This question prompted an interesting topic for a paper: Did the film's stereotypes lead to positive, if unintended, consequences?

In academic writing, scholars often generate ideas by posing questions related to a specific discipline: one set of questions for analyzing literature, another for evaluating experiments in social psychology, still another for reporting field experiences in criminal justice. If you are writing in a particular discipline, try to find out which questions its scholars typically explore.

Keeping a journal

A journal is a collection of informal, exploratory, sometimes experimental writing. In a journal, often meant for your eyes only, you can take risks. You might freewrite, pose questions, comment on an interesting idea from one of your classes, or keep a list of questions that occur to you while reading. You might imagine a conversation between yourself and your readers or stage a debate to understand opposing positions. A journal can also serve as a sourcebook of ideas to draw on in future essays.

Blogging

Although a blog (Weblog) is a type of journal, it is a public writing space rather than a private one. In a blog, you might express opinions, make observations, recap events, have fun with language, or interpret an image. Since most blogs have a commenting feature, you can create a conversation by inviting readers to give you feedback — ask questions, pose counterarguments, or suggest other readings on a topic.

As you write

American author Annie Dillard has written: "There is something you find interesting, for a reason hard to explain. It is hard to explain because you have never read it on any page; there you begin." What subject interests you? What questions do you have about that subject? Choose a question you *don't have an answer to,* and use three different ways to explore your subject. (Eight are described in this section.) Which of these methods seems most productive for you? Why?

1c Draft a working thesis.

As you explore your topic and identify questions to investigate, you will begin to see possible ways to focus your material. At this point, try to settle on a tentative central idea. The more complex your topic, the more your focus will change as your drafts evolve. For many types of writing, you will be able to assert your central idea in a sentence or two. Such a statement, which ordinarily appears in the opening paragraph of your finished essay, is called a *thesis statement* (see also 2a).

A thesis is often one or more of the following:

- the answer to a question you have posed
- the resolution of a problem you have identified
- a statement that takes a position on a debatable topic

A tentative or working thesis will help you organize your draft. Don't worry about the exact wording because your main point may change as you refine your efforts. Here, for example, are one student's efforts to pose a question and draft a thesis statement for an essay in his film course.

QUESTION

In *Rebel without a Cause*, how does the filmmaker show that Jim Stark becomes alienated from his family and friends?

WORKING THESIS

In *Rebel without a Cause*, Jim Stark, the main character, is often seen literally on the edge of physical danger, suggesting that he is becoming more and more agitated by his family and by society.

The working thesis will need to be revised as the student thinks through and revises his paper, but it provides a useful place to start writing.

Here, another student identifies and responds to a problem to focus an argument paper.

PROBLEM

Americans who earn average incomes cannot run effective national political campaigns.

WORKING THESIS

Congress should pass legislation that would make it possible for Americans who are not wealthy to be viable candidates in national political campaigns.

The student has roughed out language for how to solve the problem—enacting federal legislation. As she reads more and learns more about her topic, she will be able to refine her thesis and suggest a specific solution, such as federal restriction of campaign spending.

Testing a working thesis

Once you have come up with a working thesis, you can use the following questions to evaluate it.

- Does your thesis answer a question, propose a solution to a problem, or take a position in a debate?
- Does the thesis require an essay's worth of development? Or will you run out of points too quickly?
- Is the thesis too obvious? If you cannot come up with interpretations that oppose your own, consider revising your thesis.
- Can you support your thesis with the evidence available?
- Can you explain why readers will want to read an essay with this thesis? Can you respond when a reader asks "So what?" or "Why does it matter?"

Keep in mind as you draft your working thesis that an effective thesis is a promise to the reader; it points both the writer and the reader in a definite direction. For a more detailed discussion of the thesis, see 2a.

1d Sketch a plan.

Once you have drafted a working thesis, listing and organizing your supporting ideas is a good next step. Creating outlines, whether formal or informal, can help you make sure your writing is credible and logical and can help you identify any gaps in your support.

When to use an informal outline

You might want to sketch an informal outline to see how you will support your thesis and to figure out a tentative structure for your ideas. Informal outlines can take many forms. Perhaps the most common is simply the thesis followed by a list of major ideas.

Working thesis: Television advertising should be regulated to help prevent childhood obesity.

- Children watch more television than ever.
- Snacks marketed to children are often unhealthy and fattening.
- Childhood obesity can cause sleep disorders and other problems.
- Addressing these health problems costs taxpayers billions of dollars.
- Therefore, these ads are actually costing the public money.
- If advertising is free speech, do we have the right to regulate it?
- We regulate alcohol and cigarette ads on television, so why not advertisements for soda and junk food?

If you began by jotting down a list of ideas (see p. 15), you can turn the list into a rough outline by crossing out some ideas, adding others, and putting the ideas in a logical order.

When to use a formal outline

Early in the writing process, rough outlines have certain advantages: They can be produced quickly, they are obviously tentative, and they can be revised easily. However, a formal outline may be useful later in the writing process, after you have written a rough draft, especially if your topic is complex. It can help you see whether the parts of your essay work together and whether your essay's structure is logical.

The following formal outline brought order to the research paper in 60c, on Internet surveillance in the workplace. The student's thesis is an important part of the outline. Everything else in the outline supports it, either directly or indirectly.

Thesis: Although companies often have legitimate concerns that lead them to monitor employees' Internet usage—from expensive security breaches to reduced productivity—the benefits of electronic surveillance are outweighed by its costs to employees' privacy and autonomy.

I.   Although employers have always monitored employees, electronic surveillance is more efficient than other methods.
   A.   Employers can gather data in large quantities.
   B.   Electronic surveillance can be continuous.

    C.   Electronic surveillance can be conducted secretly, with keystroke logging programs.

II. Some experts argue that employers have legitimate reasons to monitor employees' Internet usage.

    A.   Unmonitored employees could accidentally breach security.

    B.   Companies are legally accountable for the online actions of employees.

III. Despite valid concerns, employers should value employee morale and autonomy and avoid creating an atmosphere of distrust.

    A.   Setting the boundaries for employee autonomy is difficult in the wired workplace.

       1.   Using the Internet is the most popular way of wasting time at work.

       2.   Employers can't easily determine if employees are working or surfing the Web.

    B.   Surveillance can create resentment among employees.

       1.   Web surfing can relieve stress, and restricting it can generate tension between managers and workers.

       2.   Enforcing Internet usage can seem arbitrary.

IV. Surveillance may not increase employee productivity, and trust may benefit productivity.

    A.   A company shouldn't care how many hours salaried employees work as long as they get the job done.

    B.   Casual Internet use can actually benefit companies.

       1.   The Internet may spark business ideas.

       2.   The Internet may suggest ideas about how to operate more efficiently.

V. Employees' rights to privacy are not well defined by the law.

    A.   Few federal guidelines on electronic surveillance exist.

    B.   Employers and employees are negotiating the boundaries without legal guidance.

    C.   As technological capabilities increase, the need to define boundaries will also increase.

Guidelines for constructing an outline

1. Put the thesis at the top.
2. Make items at the same level parallel grammatically (see section 9).
3. Use sentences unless phrases are clear.
4. Use the conventional system of numbers, letters, and indents:
   I.
       A.
       B.
           1.
           2.
               a.
               b.
   II.
       A.
       B.
           1.
           2.
               a.
               b.
5. Always include at least two items at each level.
6. Limit the number of major sections in the outline; if the list of roman numerals (at the first level) gets too long, try clustering the items into fewer major categories with more subcategories.

When to consider using visuals

You may decide that some of the support for your thesis could be one or more visuals. Visuals can convey information concisely and powerfully. Charts, graphs, and tables, for example, can simplify complex numerical information. Images — including photographs and diagrams — often express an idea more vividly than words can. With access to the Internet, digital photography, and word processing or desktop publishing software, you can download or create your own visuals to enhance your document. Keep in mind that if you download a visual — or use published information to create your own visual — you must credit your source (see p. 409).

Always consider how a visual supports your purpose and how your audience might respond to it. A student writing about electronic surveillance in the workplace, for example, used a cartoon to illustrate her point about employees' personal use of the Internet at work (see 60c). Another student, writing about treatments for childhood obesity, created a table to display data she had found in two different sources and discussed in her paper (see 65b).

As you plan your essay, carefully choose visuals that will support your point, and avoid overloading a draft with too many images. Use visuals to supplement your writing, not to substitute for it. The chart on pages 24–25 describes eight types of visuals and their purposes.

2 Draft the paper.

As you rough out a first draft, focus your attention on ideas and organization. You can deal with sentence structure and word choice later.

Before you begin to write, gather any prewriting materials — lists, diagrams, outlines, and so on — as well as sources that you plan to use. Having these close by will help you get started and keep you moving because you won't need to search for ideas. Writing tends to flow better when it is drafted relatively quickly, without many stops and starts.

2a For most types of writing, draft an introduction that includes a thesis.

Drafting an introduction

Your introduction will usually be a paragraph of 50 to 150 words (in a longer paper, it may be more than one paragraph). Perhaps the most common strategy is to open the paragraph with a few sentences that engage the reader and establish your purpose for writing and then to state your main point. (See the example on p. 26.) The statement of your main point is called the *thesis*. (See also 1c.)

THE WRITING CENTER hackerhandbooks.com/rules
> Resources for writers and tutors > Tips from writing tutors: Writing
introductions and conclusions

Choosing visuals to suit your purpose

Pie chart

Pie charts compare a part or parts to the whole. Segments of the pie represent percentages of the whole (and always total 100 percent).

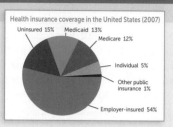

Health insurance coverage in the United States (2007)
Uninsured 15%   Medicaid 13%
Medicare 12%
Individual 5%
Other public insurance 1%
Employer-insured 54%

Line graph

Line graphs highlight trends over a period of time or compare numerical data.

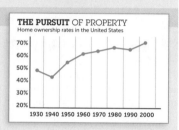

THE PURSUIT OF PROPERTY
Home ownership rates in the United States

Bar graph

Bar graphs can be used for the same purpose as line graphs. This bar graph displays the same data as in the line graph above.

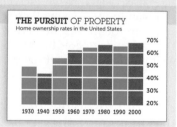

THE PURSUIT OF PROPERTY
Home ownership rates in the United States

Table

Tables organize complicated numerical information into a digestible format.

Sources [top to bottom]: Kaiser Foundation; US Census Bureau; US Census Bureau; UNAIDS.

Prices of daily doses of AIDS drugs ($US)

Drug	Brazil	Uganda	Côte d'Ivoire	US
3TC (Lamuvidine)	1.56	3.28	2.95	8.70
ddC (Zalcitabine)	0.24	4.17	3.75	8.80
Didanosine	2.04	5.26	3.48	7.25
Efavirenz	6.96	n/a	6.41	13.13
Indinavir	10.32	12.79	9.07	14.93
Nelfinavir	4.14	4.45	4.39	6.47
Nevirapine	5.04	n/a	n/a	8.48
Saquinavir	6.24	7.37	5.52	6.50
Stavudine	0.56	6.19	4.10	9.07
ZDV/3TC	1.44	7.34	n/a	18.78
Zidovudine	1.08	4.34	2.43	10.12

Source: UNAIDS, 2000

Photograph

Photographs vividly depict
people, scenes, or objects
discussed in a text.

Diagram

Diagrams, useful in scientific
and technical writing, concisely
illustrate processes, structures,
or interactions.

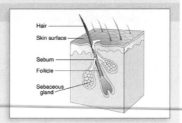

Flowchart

Flowcharts show structures or
steps in a process. (See also p. 133
for another example of a
flowchart.)

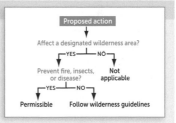

Map

Maps indicate distances,
historical information, or
demographics.

Sources [top to bottom]: Fred Zwicky;
NIAMS; Arizona Board of Regents;
Lynn Hunt et al.

In the following introduction, the thesis is highlighted.

> As the United States industrialized in the nineteenth century, using immigrant labor, social concerns took a backseat to the task of building a prosperous nation. The government did not regulate industries and did not provide an effective safety net for the poor or for those who became sick or injured on the job. Immigrants and the poor did have a few advocates, however. Settlement houses such as Hull-House in Chicago provided information, services, and a place for reform-minded individuals to gather and work to improve the conditions of the urban poor. Alice Hamilton was one of these reformers. Hamilton's efforts helped to improve the lives of immigrants and drew attention and respect to the problems and people that until then had been ignored.
>
> —Laurie McDonough, student

Ideally, the sentences leading to the thesis should hook the reader, perhaps with one of the following:

a startling statistic or an unusual fact

a vivid example

a description or an image

a paradoxical statement

a quotation or a bit of dialogue

a question

an analogy

an anecdote

Whether you are writing for a scholarly audience, a professional audience, a public audience, or a general audience, you cannot assume your readers' interest in the topic. The hook should spark curiosity and offer readers a reason to continue.

Although the thesis frequently appears at the end of the introduction, it can just as easily appear at the beginning. Much work-related writing, for example, requires a straightforward approach and commonly begins with the thesis.

> Flextime scheduling, which has proved its effectiveness at the Library of Congress, should be introduced on a trial basis at the main branch of the Montgomery County Public Library. By offering flexible work hours, the library can boost employee morale, cut down on absenteeism, and expand its hours of operation.
>
> — David Warren, student

For some types of writing, it may be difficult or impossible to express the central idea in a thesis statement; or it may be unwise or unnecessary to put a thesis statement in the essay. A personal narrative, for example, may have a focus too subtle to be distilled in a single statement. Strictly informative writing, like that found in many business memos, may be difficult to summarize in a thesis. In some academic fields, such as nursing, writers may produce reports that do not require a thesis. In such instances, do not try to force the central idea into a thesis statement. Instead, think in terms of an overriding purpose, which may or may not be stated directly.

> **Making the most of your handbook**
> The thesis statement is central to many types of writing.
> ▸ Writing about texts: 5
> ▸ Writing arguments: 6
> ▸ Writing research papers: 56 (MLA), 61 (APA)

As you write
Review the advice given on pages 23 and 26–27 for writing effective introductions. Exchange drafts with a classmate and evaluate each other's introductions. What hook have you used to focus your draft and spark readers' curiosity? Based on feedback from a classmate, what other hooks might be appropriate for your purpose and audience?

Writing effective thesis statements

An effective thesis statement is a central idea that requires supporting evidence; its scope is appropriate for the required length of the essay; and it is sharply focused. It should answer a question you have posed, resolve a problem you have identified, or take a position in a debate.

When constructing a thesis statement, ask yourself whether you can successfully develop it with the sources available to you and for the purposes you've identified. Also ask if you can explain why readers should be interested in reading an essay that explores this thesis.

> **Academic English** If you come from a culture that prefers an indirect approach in writing, you may feel that asserting a thesis early in an essay sounds unrefined or even rude. In the United States, however, readers appreciate a direct approach; when you state your point as directly as possible, you show that you understand your topic and value your readers' time.

A thesis must require proof or further development through facts and details; it cannot itself be a fact or a description.

DRAFT
THESIS   The first polygraph was developed by Dr. John A. Larson in 1921.

PROBLEM   The thesis is *too factual*. A reader could not disagree with it or debate it; no further development of this idea is required.

STRATEGY   *Enter a debate* by posing a question about your topic that has more than one possible answer. For example: Should the polygraph be used by private employers? Your thesis should be your answer to the question.

REVISED
THESIS   Because the polygraph has not been proved reliable, even under controlled conditions, its use by employers should be banned.

A thesis should be an answer to a question, not a question itself.

DRAFT
THESIS   Would John F. Kennedy have continued to escalate the war in Vietnam if he had lived?

PROBLEM   The thesis is a *question*, not an answer to a question.

STRATEGY   *Take a position* on your topic by answering the question you have posed. Your thesis should be your answer to the question.

REVISED
THESIS   Although John F. Kennedy sent the first American troops to Vietnam before he died, an analysis of his foreign policy suggests that he would not have escalated the war had he lived.

A thesis should be of sufficient scope for your assignment; it should not be too broad.

DRAFT
THESIS   Mapping the human genome has many implications for health and science.

PROBLEM   The thesis is *too broad*. Even in a very long research paper, you would not be able to discuss all the implications of mapping the human genome.

STRATEGY   *Consider subtopics of your original topic.* Once you have chosen a subtopic, take a position in an ongoing debate and pose a question that has more than one answer. For example: Should people be tested for genetic diseases? Your thesis should be your answer to the question.

REVISED THESIS   Although scientists can now detect genetic predisposition for specific diseases, policymakers should establish guidelines about whom to test and under what circumstances.

A thesis also should not be too narrow.

DRAFT THESIS   A person who carries a genetic mutation linked to a particular disease might or might not develop that disease.

PROBLEM   The thesis is *too narrow*. It does not suggest any argument or debate about the topic.

STRATEGY   *Identify challenging questions* that readers might have about your topic. Then pose a question that has more than one answer. For example: Do the risks of genetic testing outweigh its usefulness? Your thesis should be your answer to this question.

REVISED THESIS   Though positive results in a genetic test do not guarantee that the disease will develop, such results can cause psychological trauma; genetic testing should therefore be avoided in most cases.

A thesis should be sharply focused, not too vague. Avoid fuzzy, hard-to-define words such as *interesting*, *good*, or *disgusting*.

DRAFT THESIS   The Vietnam Veterans Memorial is an interesting structure.

PROBLEM   This thesis is *too fuzzy and unfocused*. It's difficult to define *interesting*, and the sentence doesn't give the reader any cues about where the essay is going.

STRATEGY   *Focus your thesis with concrete language and a clear plan.* Pose a question about the topic that has more than one answer. For example: How does the physical structure of the Vietnam Veterans Memorial shape the experience of visitors? Your thesis — your answer to the question — should use specific language that engages readers to follow your argument.

REVISED THESIS   By inviting visitors to see their own reflections in the wall, the Vietnam Veterans Memorial creates a link between the present and the past.

Revising with comments
Unclear thesis

UNDERSTANDING THE COMMENT

When readers point out that your thesis is unclear, the comment often signals that they have a hard time identifying your essay's main point.

> Fathers are more involved in the lives of their children today than they used to be. In the past, the father's primary role was as the provider; child care was most often left to the mother or other relatives. However, today's father drives to dance lessons, coaches his child's baseball team, hosts birthday parties, and provides homework help. Do more involved fathers help or hinder the development of their children?
>
> *Unclear thesis*

One student wrote this introductory paragraph in response to an assignment that asked her to analyze the changing roles of mothers or fathers.

A writer's thesis, or main point, should be phrased as a statement, not a question. To revise, the student could answer the question she has posed, or she could pose a new question and answer it. After considering her evidence, she needs to decide what position she wants to take, state this position clearly, and show readers *why* this position — her thesis — matters.

SIMILAR COMMENTS: vague thesis • state your position • your main point?

REVISING WHEN *YOUR* THESIS IS UNCLEAR

1. *Ask questions.* What is the thesis, position, or main point of the draft? Can you support it with the available evidence?

2. *Reread your entire draft.* Because ideas develop as you write, you may find that your conclusion contains a clearer statement of your main point than your current thesis does. Or you may find your thesis elsewhere in your draft.

3. *Try revising your thesis* by framing it as an answer to a question you pose, the resolution of a problem you identify, or a position you take in a debate. And put your thesis to the "So what?" test: Why would a reader be interested in this thesis?

More help with writing a clear thesis: 1c and 2a

As you write

Review the advice and examples on pages 27–29 for writing effective thesis statements. Exchange drafts with a classmate, use the problem/strategy approach to evaluate each other's thesis, and then talk through how each of you might go about revising. What do you learn about your draft thesis from this discussion? What single piece of advice might help you strengthen your thesis?

EXERCISE 2–1 In each of the following pairs, which sentence might work well as a thesis for a short paper? What is the problem with the other one? Is it too factual? Too broad? Too vague?

1a. By networking with friends, a single parent can manage to strike a balance among work, school, a social life, and family.

  b. Single parents face many challenges as they try to juggle all of their responsibilities.

2a. At the Special Olympics, athletes with disabilities show that, with hard work and support from others, they can accomplish anything—that they can indeed be winners.

  b. Working with the Special Olympics program is rewarding.

3a. History 201, taught by Professor Brown, is offered at 10:00 a.m. on Tuesdays and Thursdays.

  b. Whoever said that history is nothing but polishing tombstones must have missed History 201, because in Professor Brown's class history is very much alive.

4a. So far, research suggests that zero-emissions vehicles are not a sensible solution to the problem of steadily increasing air pollution.

  b. Because air pollution is of serious concern to many people today, several US government agencies have implemented plans to begin solving the problem.

5a. Anorexia nervosa is a dangerous and sometimes deadly eating disorder occurring mainly in young, upper-middle-class teens.

  b. The eating disorder anorexia nervosa is rarely cured by one treatment alone; only by combining drug therapy with psychotherapy and family therapy can the patient begin the long journey to wellness.

PRACTICE hackerhandbooks.com/rules
> The writing process > 2–2 to 2–4

2b Draft the body.

The body of your essay develops support for your thesis, so it's important to have at least a working thesis before you start writing. What does your thesis promise readers? Try to keep your response to that question in mind as you draft the body.

You may have already written an introduction that includes your working thesis. If not, as long as you have a draft thesis, you can begin developing the body and return later to the introduction. If your thesis suggests a plan or if you have sketched a preliminary outline, try to block out your paragraphs accordingly. Draft the body of your essay by writing at least a paragraph about each supporting point you listed in the planning stage. If you do not have a plan, pause for a few moments and sketch one (see 1d).

Keep in mind that often you might not know what you want to say until you have written a draft. It is possible to begin without a plan — assuming you are prepared to treat your first attempt as a "discovery draft" that will be radically rewritten once you discover what you really want to say. Whether or not you have a plan when you begin drafting, you can often figure out a workable order for your ideas by stopping each time you start a new paragraph to think about what your readers will need to know to follow your train of thought.

For more detailed advice about paragraphs in the body of an essay, see 4. For specific help with drafting paragraphs, see 4a. For more on developing paragraphs, see 4b.

TIP: As you draft, keep careful notes and records of any sources you read and consult. (See 55b.) If you quote, paraphrase, or summarize a source, include a citation, even in your draft. You will save time and avoid plagiarism if you follow the rules of citation and documentation while drafting.

2c Draft a conclusion.

A conclusion should remind readers of the essay's main idea without repeating it. Often the concluding paragraph can be relatively short. By the end of the essay, readers should already understand your main point; your conclusion drives it home and, perhaps, gives readers some larger idea to consider.

Revising with comments
Be specific

UNDERSTANDING THE COMMENT

When readers say that you need to "be specific," the comment often signals that you could strengthen your writing with additional details.

> There are many cultural differences between the United States and Italy. Italian citizens do not share many of the same (attitudes) or (values) as American citizens. Such (differences) make it hard for some Italian students to feel comfortable coming to the United States for extended periods of time, even for an academic year.

Be specific!

In this body paragraph, a student responds to an assignment that asked him to interview a group of international students and describe the challenges of studying in the United States.

The student presents a claim but doesn't include specific examples or evidence to support the claim. To revise, the student might focus on *one* specific example of cultural differences between the United States and Italy. The student might then ask: What vivid details illustrate this cultural difference? The answer to that question will provide specific evidence to inform and persuade readers.

SIMILAR COMMENTS: *need examples • too general • evidence?*

STRATEGIES FOR REVISING WHEN *YOUR* WRITING NEEDS TO BE MORE SPECIFIC

1. *Reread your topic sentence* to understand the focus of the paragraph.
2. *Ask questions.* Does the paragraph contain claims that need support? What does the paragraph promise? Have you provided evidence — specific examples, vivid details and illustrations, statistics and facts — to help readers understand your ideas and find them persuasive?
3. *Interpret your evidence.* Remember that details and examples don't speak for themselves. You'll need to show readers how your evidence supports your claims.

More help with using specific evidence: 6e

Revising with comments
Narrow your introduction

UNDERSTANDING THE COMMENT

When readers point out that your introduction needs to be "narrowed," the comment often signals that the beginning sentences of your essay are not specific or focused.

> Sports fans are an interesting breed. They have many ways of showing support for the team they love. Many fans perform elaborate rituals before, during, or after a sporting event. These rituals are performed both privately in homes with family or friends and at the stadiums and arenas where the games take place. Experiencing a sports competition where the fans are participating in rituals to support the team makes the game exciting. Some fans even believe that rituals are necessary and that their actions influence the outcome of a game. However, some fans go beyond cheering, and their actions, verbal harassment, and chanted slurs reveal a darker side of sports. *Narrow your introduction*

One student wrote this introductory paragraph in response to an assignment that asked her to analyze a ritual.

This opening begins with such general statements that the purpose of the essay is unclear. To revise, the student might delete her first few sentences — generalizations about sports fans and rituals — and focus on one specific sports ritual. She might describe how fans who wear lucky clothes, eat certain foods, or chant a particular expression think they can influence the outcome of a game. Using a quotation, a vivid example, or a startling statistic, the student might show how a particular ritual not only unites fans but also reveals a dark side of sports. Whatever "hook" she chooses should lead readers to her thesis.

SIMILAR COMMENTS: focus your intro • too general • engage your readers

REVISING WHEN YOU NEED TO NARROW *YOUR* INTRODUCTION

1. *Reread your introduction and ask questions.* Are the sentences leading to your thesis specific enough to engage readers and communicate your purpose? Do these sentences lead logically to your thesis? Do they spark your readers' curiosity and offer them a reason to continue reading?

2. *Try revising your introduction with a "hook" that will engage readers* — a question, quotation, paradoxical statement, or vivid example.

More advice on writing introductions: 2a

In addition to echoing your main idea, a conclusion might

- briefly summarize your essay's key points
- propose a course of action
- offer a recommendation
- discuss the topic's wider significance or implications
- pose a question for future study

To conclude an essay analyzing the shifting roles of women in the military services, one student discusses her topic's implications for society as a whole:

> As the military continues to train women in jobs formerly reserved for men, our understanding of women's roles in society will no doubt continue to change. As news reports of women training for and taking part in combat operations become commonplace, reports of women becoming CEOs, police chiefs, and even president of the United States will cease to surprise us. Or perhaps we have already reached this point.
>
> — Rosa Broderick, student

To make the conclusion memorable, you might include a detail, an example, or an image from the introduction to bring readers full circle; a quotation or a bit of dialogue; an anecdote; or a witty or ironic comment. Whatever concluding strategy you choose, keep in mind that an effective conclusion is decisive and unapologetic. Avoid introducing wholly new ideas at the end of an essay. And because the conclusion is so closely tied to the rest of the essay in both content and tone, be prepared to rework it (or even replace it) when you revise.

Make global revisions; then revise sentences.

Revising is rarely a one-step process. Global matters — focus, purpose, organization, content, and overall strategy — generally receive attention first. Improvements in sentence structure, word choice, grammar, punctuation, and mechanics come later.

PRACTICE AND MODELS   hackerhandbooks.com/rules

> The writing process > 3–1 and 3–2
> Revising > Sample global revision
> Sample sentence-level revision

3a Make global revisions: Think big.

Writers often resist global revisions because they find it difficult to view their work from their audience's perspective. What is clear to them, because they know what they mean to say after all, is not always clear to their audience. To distance yourself from a draft, put it aside for a while, preferably overnight or even longer. When you return to it, try

> **Making the most of your handbook**
> Seeking and using feedback are critical steps in revising a college paper.
> ▶ Guidelines for peer reviewers: page 38

to play the role of your audience as you read. If possible, enlist friends or family to be the audience for your draft. Or visit your school's writing center to go over your draft with a writing tutor. Ask your reviewers to focus on the larger issues of writing, such as purpose and organization, not on word- or sentence-level issues. You might begin with a basic question: *Do you see my main point?* The checklist for global revision below may help you and your reviewers get started.

Checklist for global revision

Purpose and audience

- Does the draft address a question, a problem, or an issue that readers care about?
- Is the draft appropriate for its audience? Does it account for the audience's knowledge of and possible attitudes toward the subject?

Focus

- Is the thesis clear? Is it prominently placed?
- If there is no thesis, is there a good reason for omitting one?
- Scan the supporting paragraphs: Are any ideas obviously off the point?

Organization and paragraphing

- Are there enough organizational cues for readers (such as topic sentences or headings)?
- Are ideas presented in a logical order?
- Are any paragraphs too long or too short for easy reading?

Content

- Is the supporting material relevant and persuasive?
- Which ideas need further development? Have you left your reader with any unanswered questions?
- Are the parts proportioned sensibly? Do major ideas receive enough attention?
- Where might material be deleted? Look for redundant or irrelevant information.

Point of view

- Is the dominant point of view — first person (*I* or *we*), second person (*you*), or third person (*he, she, it, one,* or *they*) — appropriate for your purpose and audience? (See 13a.)

As you write

Use the Checklist for global revision (pp. 36–37) to gain perspective on your draft. Does your draft accomplish its purpose? Does it reach its audience? Share your draft with a writing center tutor or with a peer. What did you learn from the feedback you received? Take a moment to identify three or four revision goals.

3b Revise and edit sentences.

Much of this book offers advice on revising sentences for clarity and on editing them for grammar, punctuation, and mechanics. Some writers handle sentence-level revisions directly at the computer, experimenting with a variety of possible improvements. Other writers prefer to print out a hard copy of the draft and mark it up before making changes in the file. Page 38 shows a rough-draft paragraph as one student edited it on-screen for a variety of sentence-level problems.

> **Guidelines for peer reviewers**
>
> - View yourself as a coach, not a judge. Work with the writer to identify the draft's strengths and areas for improvement.
> - Restate the writer's main ideas to check that they are clearly expressed.
> - Where possible, give specific compliments. Let the writer know which of his or her strategies are successful.
> - Ask to hear more about passages you find confusing or interesting.
> - Express interest in reading the next draft.

Although some cities have found creative ways to improve access to public transportation for passengers with physical disabilities, ~~and to fund other programs, there have been problems in~~ our city has struggled with ~~due to the need to address~~ budget constraints and competing ~~needs~~ priorities. ~~This~~ The budget crunch has led citizens to question how funds are distributed.~~?~~ For example, last year ~~when~~ city officials voted to use available funds to support ~~had to choose between allocating funds for accessible transportation or allocating funds to~~ after-school programs rather than transportation upgrades. ~~, they voted for the after-school programs.~~ It is not clear to some citizens why ~~these~~ after-school programs are more important.

The original paragraph was flawed by wordiness, a problem that can be addressed through any number of revisions. The following revision would also be acceptable:

> Some cities have funded improved access to public transportation for passengers with physical disabilities. Because of budget constraints, our city chose to fund after-school programs rather than transportation programs. As a result, citizens have begun to question how funds are distributed and why certain programs are more important than others.

Some of the paragraph's improvements do not involve choice and must be fixed in any revision. The hyphen in *after-school programs* is necessary; a noun must be substituted for the pronoun *these* in the last sentence; and the question mark in the second sentence must be changed to a period.

3c Proofread the final manuscript.

After revising and editing, you are ready to prepare your final copy. (See 51 for guidelines.) Make sure to allow yourself enough time for proofreading — the final step in manuscript preparation.

Proofreading is a special kind of reading: a slow and methodical search for misspellings, typographical mistakes, and omitted words or word endings. Such errors can be difficult to spot in your own work because you may read what you intended to write, not what is actually on the page. To fight this tendency, try proofreading out loud, articulating each word as it is actually written. You might also try proofreading your sentences in reverse order, a strategy that takes your attention away from the meanings you intended and forces you to focus on one word at a time.

Although proofreading may be slow, it is crucial. Errors strewn throughout an essay are distracting and annoying. If the writer doesn't care about this piece of writing, the reader might wonder, why should I? A carefully proofread essay, however, sends a positive message that you value your writing and respect your readers.

3d Use software tools wisely.

Grammar checkers, spell checkers, and autoformatting are software tools designed to help you avoid errors and save time. These tools can alert you to possible errors in words, sentence structures, or formatting. But they're not always right. If a program suggests or makes a change, be sure the change is one you really want to make. Familiarizing yourself with your software's settings can help you use these tools effectively.

Grammar checkers

Grammar checkers can help with some of the sentence-level problems in a typical draft. But they will often misdiagnose errors, especially because they cannot account for your intended meaning. When the grammar checker makes a suggestion for revision, you must decide whether the change is more effective than your original.

It's just as important to be aware of what your grammar checker isn't picking up on. If you count on your grammar checker to identify trouble spots, you might overlook problems with coordination and subordination (see 14), sentence variety (see 15), sexist language (see 17e), and passive verbs (see 28a), for example.

Spell checkers

Spell checkers flag words not found in their dictionaries; they will suggest a replacement for any word they don't recognize. They can help you spot many errors, but don't let them be your only proofreader. If you're writing about the health benefits of a Mediterranean diet, for example, don't let your software change *briam* (a vegetable dish) to *Brian*. Even if your spell checker identifies a real misspelling, the replacement word it suggests might carry a different connotation or even be nonsensical. After misspelling *probably*, you might end up with *portly*. Consider changes carefully before accepting them. If you're not sure what word or spelling you need, consult a dictionary.

Because spell checkers flag only unrecognized words, they won't catch misused words, such as *accept* when you mean *except*. For help with commonly confused or misused words and with avoiding informal speech and jargon, consult the glossary of usage at the back of the book.

Autoformatting

As you write, your software may attempt to save you effort with autoformatting. It might recognize that you've typed a URL and turn it into a link. Or if you're building a list, it might add numbering for you. Be aware of such changes and make sure they are appropriate for your paper and applied to the right text.

3e Manage your files.

Your instructor may ask you to complete assignments in stages, including notes, outlines, annotated bibliographies, rough drafts, and a final draft. Keeping track of all of these documents can be challenging. Be sure to give your files distinct names that reflect the appropriate stage of your writing process, and store them in a logical place.

Writing online or in a word processing program can make writing and revising easier. You can undo changes or return to an earlier draft if a revision misfires. Applying the following steps can help you explore revision possibilities with little risk.

- Create folders and subfolders for each assignment. Save notes, outlines, and drafts together.
- Label revised drafts with different file names and dates.

MANAGING FILES

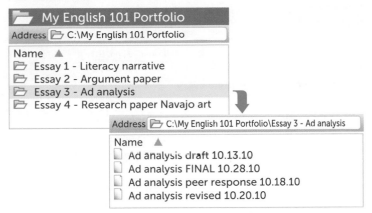

- Print hard copies, make backup copies, and press the Save button early and often (every five to ten minutes).
- Always record complete bibliographic information about sources, including images.
- Use a comment function to make notes to yourself or to respond to the drafts of peers.

3f Student essay

Matt Watson wrote the essay "Hooked on Credit Cards" (pp. 46–49) in response to the following assignment.

> In an essay of 500–1,000 words, discuss a significant problem facing today's college students. Assume that your audience consists of general readers, not simply college students.
>
> If you use any sources, document them with in-text citations and a list of works cited in MLA style (see section 59b).

When he received the assignment, Watson considered several possibilities before settling on the topic of credit cards. He already knew something about the topic because his older sister had run up large credit card bills while in college and was working hard to pay them off. Because the assignment required him to *discuss* a problem, he decided that a good strategy would be to identify a *how* or *why* question to answer.

SAMPLE NOTES

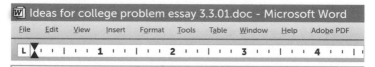

> **Ideas for college problem essay**
> Phone call with Rebecca Watson, 3.3.01
> - Easy to get hooked on credit cards and run up huge debts
> - Why do credit card companies try to sign up students? Aren't we a bad risk? But they must be profiting, or they'd stop.
> - High interest rates
> - Ads for credit cards appear on campus and on the Web
> - Using plastic doesn't seem like spending money
> - Tactics used by the companies—offering low interest rates at first, setting high credit limits, allowing a revolving balance
> - What happens to students who get in debt but don't have parents who can bail them out?

To get started on his paper, Watson talked with his sister about her experience with credit card debt and typed some ideas on his laptop (see above).

After he listed these ideas, Watson identified the question that would drive his essay:

> Why do credit card companies put so many resources into soliciting students, who often have poor credit profiles?

Watson decided that his purpose would be to answer this question for himself and his audience. He would do so by taking a position and making an argument. He wrote his first draft quickly, focusing more on ideas and evidence than on grammar, style, and mechanics. Here is the draft he submitted, together with the most helpful comments he received from classmates. The peer reviewers were asked to comment on global issues — audience appeal, focus, organization, content, and point of view — and to ignore any problems with grammar and punctuation.

ROUGH DRAFT WITH PEER COMMENTS

Hooked on Credit Cards

Credit card companies love to extend credit to college students. You see ads for these cards on campus bulletin boards and also on the Web. Why do companies market their product to a population that has no job and lacks a substantial credit history? They seem to be trying to hook us on their cards; unfortunately many of us do get hooked on a cycle of spending that leads to financial ruin.

> Good question. Is there more to the answer than you've written here? That is, why are these companies trying to hook us? (Mark)

> Some students do have jobs. (Sara)

> The assignment asks for a general audience; your thesis shouldn't be about "us." (Sara)

> Shouldn't your thesis also explain *how* the companies hook students? (Tim)

Banks require applicants for a loan to demonstrate a good credit history and some evidence of a source of income, but credit card companies don't. On campus, students are bombarded with offers of preapproved credit cards. Then there are the Web sites. Sites with lots of student traffic are plastered with banner ads like this one: "To get a credit card, you need to establish credit. To establish credit, you need a credit card. Stop the vicious cycle! Apply for our student MasterCard."

> Good point. I never thought of it that way. (Sara)

> Mention the solicitors who show up during orientation? (Mark)

> This sentence sounds less formal than the rest of your essay. (Tim)

> I like this example. (Mark)

Credit card companies often entice students with low interest rates, then they jack up the rates later. A student may not think about the cost of interest. That new stereo or back-to-school wardrobe can get pretty expensive at 17.9% interest if it's compounded over several months. Would you have bought that $600 item if you knew it would end up costing you $900?

> Why not give us some numbers here? Just how low and how high? (Sara)

> The shift to "you" seems odd. (Sara)

Most cards allow the holder to keep a revolving balance, which means that they don't have to pay the whole bill, they just pay a minimum amount.

The minimum is usually not too much, but a young person may be tempted to keep running up debt. The companies also give students an unrealistically high credit limit. I've heard of undergraduates who had a limit as high as $4,000.

Card companies make money not just from high interest rates. Often they charge fees for late payments. I've heard of penalties for going over the credit limit too.

Often students discover too late that they are thoroughly trapped. Some drop out of school, others graduate and then can't find a good job because they have a poor credit rating. There are psychological problems too. Your parents may bail you out of debt, but you'll probably feel guilty. On a Web site, I read that two students felt so bad they committed suicide.

Credit cards are a part of life these days, and everyone is probably wise to have a charge account for emergencies. But college students must take a hard look at their financial picture. The very things that make those cards so convenient and easy to use can lead to a mountain of debt that will take years to pay off.

Maybe you could search *LexisNexis* for some statistical information. (Mark)

This paragraph seems sort of skimpy. (Tim)

This would be more convincing if you provided some evidence to back up your claim. (Mark)

You shift from "you" to "I" here. (Sara)

Cite this? (Sara)

Your paper focuses on the tactics that the companies use, but your conclusion doesn't mention them. (Tim)

After rereading his draft and considering the feedback from his classmates, Watson realized that he needed to develop his thesis further. He set out some goals for revising his essay.

MATT WATSON'S REVISION GOALS

Answer Mark's question about what credit card companies gain by hooking students.

Expand explanation of both why and how credit card companies market cards to students.

Include evidence to back up claims about how credit card companies hook students. Look at reputable Web sites: student loan provider Nellie Mae and the Consumer Federation of America.

Rework introduction to explain why credit card companies profit from students who have no steady source of income.

Adjust point of view so that essay is appropriate for a general audience, not just for other students.

When he was more or less satisfied with the paper as a whole, Watson worked to polish his sentences. His final draft begins on the next page.

Watson 1

Matt Watson

Professor Mills

English 101

12 March 2001

Hooked on Credit Cards

Introduction hooks readers with interesting details.

Introduction poses a question that leads readers to the thesis.

Thesis announces Watson's main point.

Clear topic sentences guide readers through the body of the paper.

Essay is double-spaced throughout.

Credit card companies love to extend credit to college students, especially those just out of high school. Ads for credit cards line campus bulletin boards, flash across commercial Web sites for students, and get stuffed into shopping bags at college bookstores. Why do the companies market their product so vigorously to a population that lacks a substantial credit history and often has no steady source of income? The answer is that significant profits can be earned through high interest rates and assorted penalties and fees. By granting college students liberal lending arrangements, credit card companies often hook them on a cycle of spending that can ultimately lead to financial ruin.

Whereas banks require applicants for a loan to demonstrate a good credit history and some evidence of income, credit card companies make no such demands on students. On campus, students find themselves bombarded with offers of preapproved cards—and not just on flyers pinned to bulletin boards. Many campuses allow credit card vendors to solicit applications during orientation week. In addition to offering preapproved cards, these vendors often give away T-shirts or CDs to entice students to apply. Some companies even offer rewards program bonuses based on a student's GPA. Students are bombarded on the Web as well. Sites with heavy student traffic are emblazoned with banner ads like this one: "To get a credit

Marginal annotations indicate MLA-style formatting and effective writing.

Watson 2

card, you need to establish credit. To establish credit, you
need a credit card. Stop the vicious cycle! Apply for our
student MasterCard."

Credit card companies often entice students with low
"teaser" interest rates of 13% and later raise those rates
to 18% or even higher. Others charge high rates up front,
trusting that students won't read the fine print. Some young
people don't think about the cost of interest, let alone
the cost of interest compounding month after month. That
back-to-school wardrobe can get pretty expensive at 17.9%
interest compounded over several months. A $600 trip to
Fort Lauderdale is not such a bargain when in the long run
it costs $900 or more.

In addition to charging high interest rates, credit
card companies try to maximize the amount of interest
generated. One tactic is to extend an unreasonably high
credit limit to students. According to Nellie Mae statistics,
in 1998 undergraduates were granted an average credit
limit of $3,683; for graduate students, the figure jumped
to $15,721. Nearly 10% of the students in the Nellie Mae
study carried balances near or exceeding these credit limits
(Blair).

Another tactic is to allow students to maintain a
revolving balance. A revolving balance permits the debtor
to pay only part of a current bill, often an amount just a
little larger than the accumulated interest. The indebted
student is tempted to keep on charging, paying a minimum
amount every month, because there aren't any immediate
consequences to doing so.

Once a student is hooked on a cycle of debt, the
companies profit even further by assessing a variety of

Body paragraphs
are developed
with details and
examples.

Transition
serves as a
bridge between
paragraphs.

Summary of
the source is in
Watson's own
words.

Source is
documented
with an MLA
in-text citation.

Watson 3

Watson cites
a Web article
from a reputable
source.

fees and penalties. According to a press release issued by
Consumer Action and the Consumer Federation of America,
many credit card companies charge late fees and "over the
limit" penalties as high as $29 per month. In addition,
grace periods are often shortened to ensure that late fees
kick in earlier. Many companies also raise interest rates
for those who fail to pay on time or who exceed the credit
limit. Those "penalty" rates can climb as high as 25% (1-2).

Often students discover too late that they are
thoroughly hooked. The results can be catastrophic.
Some students are forced to drop out of school and take
low-paying full-time jobs. Others, once they graduate, have
difficulty landing good jobs because of their poor credit
rating. Many students suffer psychologically as well. Even
those who have parents willing to bail them out of debt
often experience a great deal of anxiety and guilt. Two
students grew so stressed by their accumulating debt that
they committed suicide (Consumer Federation of Amer. 3).

Conclusion
echoes Watson's
main idea.

Credit cards are a convenient part of life, and there
is nothing wrong with having one or two of them. Before
signing up for a particular card, however, college students
should take time to read the fine print and do some
comparison shopping. Students also need to learn to resist
the many seductive offers that credit card companies extend
to them after they have signed up. Students who can't
"just say no" to temptations such as high credit limits and
revolving balances could well become hooked on a cycle of
debt from which there is no easy escape.

Watson 4

Works Cited

Blair, Alan D. "A High Wire Act: Balancing Student Loan and
Credit Card Debt." *Credit World* 86.2 (1997): 15-17.
Business Source Premier. Web. 4 Mar. 2001.

Consumer Action and Consumer Federation of America.
"Card Issuers Hike Fees and Rates to Bolster Profits."
Consumer Federation of America. Consumer Federation
of Amer., 5 Nov. 1998. Web. 4 Mar. 2001.

Consumer Federation of America. "Credit Card Debt Imposes
Huge Costs on Many College Students." *Consumer
Federation of America.* Consumer Federation of Amer.,
8 June 1999. Web. 4 Mar. 2001.

Works cited page
follows MLA
format.

As you write
What do you learn about composing and revising from
studying Matt Watson's process (pages 41–49)? How has Matt's
revised essay benefited from the advice of his peers and from
his focused revision goals? How is your writing process similar
to or different from Matt's?

4 Build effective paragraphs.

Except for special-purpose paragraphs, such as introductions and conclusions (see 2a and 2c), paragraphs are clusters of information supporting an essay's main point (or advancing a story's action). Aim for paragraphs that are clearly focused, well developed, organized, coherent, and neither too long nor too short for easy reading.

4a Focus on a main point.

A paragraph should be unified around a main point. The point should be clear to readers, and every sentence in the paragraph should relate to it.

Stating the main point in a topic sentence

As readers move into a paragraph, they need to know where they are — in relation to the whole essay — and what to expect in the sentences to come. A good topic sentence, a one-sentence summary of the paragraph's main point, acts as a signpost pointing in two directions: backward toward the thesis of the essay and forward toward the body of the paragraph.

Like a thesis sentence (see 1c and 2a), a topic sentence is more general than the material supporting it. Usually the topic sentence (highlighted in the following example) comes first in the paragraph.

> All living creatures manage some form of communication. The dance patterns of bees in their hive help to point the way to distant flower fields or announce successful foraging. Male stickleback fish regularly swim upside-down to indicate outrage in a courtship contest. Male deer and lemurs mark territorial ownership by rubbing their own body secretions on boundary stones or trees. Everyone has seen a frightened dog put his tail between his legs and run in panic. We, too, use gestures, expressions, postures, and movement to give our words point.
>
> — Olivia Vlahos, *Human Beginnings*

Sometimes the topic sentence is introduced by a transitional sentence linking it to earlier material. In the following paragraph, the topic sentence has been delayed to allow for a transition.

But flowers are not the only source of spectacle in the wilderness. An opportunity for late color is provided by the berries of wildflowers, shrubs, and trees. Baneberry presents its tiny white flowers in spring but in late summer bursts forth with clusters of red berries. Bunchberry, a ground-cover plant, puts out red berries in the fall, and the red berries of wintergreen last from autumn well into the winter. In California, the bright red, fist-sized clusters of Christmas berries can be seen growing beside highways for up to six months of the year.

— James Crockett et al., *Wildflower Gardening*

To hook readers, writers are sometimes tempted to begin paragraphs with vivid quotations or compelling statistics from a source. A topic sentence in the writer's own words, however, can remind readers of the claim of the paper, advance the argument, and introduce the evidence from a source. In the following paragraph on the effects of the 2010 oil spill in the Gulf of Mexico, the writer uses a topic sentence to state that the extent of the threat is unknown before quoting three sources that illustrate her point.

To date, the full ramifications [of the oil spill] remain a question mark. An August report from the National Oceanic and Atmospheric Administration estimated that 75 percent of the oil had "either evaporated or been burned, skimmed, recovered from the wellhead, or dispersed." However, Woods Hole Oceanographic Institution researchers reported that a 1.2-mile-wide, 650-foot-high plume caused by the spill "will persist for some time." And University of Georgia scientists conclude that almost 80 percent of the released oil hadn't been recovered and "remains a threat to the ecosystem."

— Michele Wilson, "Volunteer Army"

Some professional writers, such as informal essayists, may not always use clear topic sentences. In college writing, however, topic sentences are often necessary for clarifying the lines of an argument or for reporting the research in a field. In business writing, topic sentences (along with headings) are essential because readers often scan for information.

Sticking to the point

Sentences that do not support the topic sentence destroy the unity of a paragraph. If the paragraph is otherwise focused, such sentences can simply be deleted or perhaps moved elsewhere. In the following paragraph describing the inadequate facilities in a high school, the information about the chemistry instructor (highlighted) is clearly off the point.

> As the result of tax cuts, the educational facilities of Lincoln High School have reached an all-time low. Some of the books date back to 1990 and have long since shed their covers. The few computers in working order must share one printer. The lack of lab equipment makes it necessary for four or five students to work at one table, with most watching rather than performing experiments. Also, the chemistry instructor left to have a baby at the beginning of the semester, and most of the students don't like the substitute. As for the furniture, many of the upright chairs have become recliners, and the desk legs are so unbalanced that they play seesaw on the floor.

Sometimes the solution for a disunified paragraph is not as simple as deleting or moving material. Writers often wander into uncharted territory because they cannot think of enough evidence to support a topic sentence. Feeling that it is too soon to break into a new paragraph, they move on to new ideas for which they have not prepared the reader. When this happens, the writer is faced with a choice: Either find more evidence to support the topic sentence or adjust the topic sentence to mesh with the evidence that is available.

EXERCISE 4–1 Underline the topic sentence in the following paragraph and cross out any material that does not clarify or develop the central idea.

> Quilt making has served as an important means of social, political, and artistic expression for women. In the nineteenth century, quilting circles provided one of the few opportunities for women to forge social bonds outside of their families. Once a week or more, they came together to sew as well as trade small talk, advice, and news. They used dyed cotton fabrics much like the fabrics quilters use today; surprisingly, quilters' basic materials haven't changed that much over the years. Sometimes the women joined their efforts in support of a political cause, making quilts that would be raffled to raise money for temperance societies, hospitals for sick and wounded soldiers, and the fight against slavery. Quilt making also afforded women a means of artistic expression at a time when they had few other creative outlets. Within their socially acceptable roles as homemakers, many quilters subtly pushed back at the restrictions placed on them by experimenting with color, design, and technique.

Revising with comments
More than one point in this paragraph

UNDERSTANDING THE COMMENT

When readers tell you that you have "more than one point in this paragraph," the comment often signals that not all sentences in your paragraph support the topic sentence.

> Bringing casino gaming to Massachusetts would benefit the state in a number of ways. First, it would provide needed property tax relief for many of the state's towns and cities. Casino gaming would also bring in revenue needed to fix the state's roads and bridges. The speaker of the House of Representatives is blocking the governor's proposal because he believes the social costs are greater than the economic benefits. Many people agree with the speaker. Most important, casino gaming would provide jobs in areas of the state that have suffered economically in recent years.

More than one point in this paragraph

One student wrote this body paragraph in response to an assignment that asked him to take a position on a current issue.

The topic sentence promises a discussion of benefits, but the detour into risks strays from the point. To revise, the student should focus on the key word in his topic sentence — *benefit* — because that signals to readers that the paragraph will examine the advantages of casino gaming. He might focus his paragraph by providing specific examples of benefits and deleting references to risks, perhaps using risks as counterpoints in a separate paragraph.

SIMILAR COMMENTS: *unfocused* • *lacks unity* • *hard to follow*

STRATEGIES FOR REVISING WHEN *YOU* HAVE MORE THAN ONE POINT IN A PARAGRAPH

1. *Reread your paragraph and ask questions.* What is the main point of the paragraph? Is there a topic sentence that signals to readers what to expect in the rest of the paragraph? Does each sentence support the topic sentence and logically follow from the one before? Have you included sentences that perhaps belong elsewhere in your paper?

2. *Remember the purpose of topic sentences;* they serve as important signposts for readers. Make sure that the wording of your topic sentence is precise and that you have enough evidence to support it in the paragraph.

More advice on unifying paragraphs: 4d

4b Develop the main point.

Though an occasional short paragraph is fine, particularly if it functions as a transition or emphasizes a point, a series of brief paragraphs suggests inadequate development. How much development is enough? That varies, depending on the writer's purpose and audience.

For example, when health columnist Jane Brody wrote a paragraph attempting to convince readers that it is impossible to lose fat quickly, she knew that she would have to present a great deal of evidence because many dieters want to believe the opposite. She did *not* write only the following:

> When you think about it, it's impossible to lose — as many diets suggest — 10 pounds of *fat* in ten days, even on a total fast. Even a moderately active person cannot lose so much weight so fast. A less active person hasn't a prayer.

This three-sentence paragraph is too skimpy to be convincing. But the paragraph that Brody did write contains enough evidence to convince even skeptical readers.

> When you think about it, it's impossible to lose — as many . . . diets suggest — 10 pounds of *fat* in ten days, even on a total fast. A pound of body fat represents 3,500 calories. To lose 1 pound of fat, you must expend 3,500 more calories than you consume. Let's say you weigh 170 pounds and, as a moderately active person, you burn 2,500 calories a day. If your diet contains only 1,500 calories, you'd have an energy deficit of 1,000 calories a day. In a week's time that would add up to a 7,000-calorie deficit, or 2 pounds of real fat. In ten days, the accumulated deficit would represent nearly 3 pounds of lost body fat. Even if you ate nothing at all for ten days and maintained your usual level of activity, your caloric deficit would add up to 25,000 calories. . . . At 3,500 calories per pound of fat, that's still only 7 pounds of lost fat.
>
> — Jane Brody, *Jane Brody's Nutrition Book*

4c Choose a suitable pattern of organization.

Although paragraphs (and indeed whole essays) may be patterned in any number of ways, certain patterns of organization occur frequently, either alone or in combination: examples and illustrations, narration, description, process, comparison and contrast, analogy, cause and effect, classification and division, and definition. These patterns (sometimes called *methods of development*) have different uses, depending on the writer's subject and purpose.

Examples and illustrations

Providing examples, perhaps the most common method of development, is appropriate whenever the reader might be tempted to ask, "For example?" Though examples are just selected instances, not a complete catalog, they are enough to suggest the truth of many topic sentences, as in the following paragraph.

> Normally my parents abided scrupulously by "The Budget," but several times a year Dad would dip into his battered black strongbox and splurge on some irrational, totally satisfying luxury. Once he bought over a hundred comic books at a flea market, doled out to us thereafter at the tantalizing rate of two a week. He always got a whole flat of pansies, Mom's favorite flower, for us to give her on Mother's Day. One day a boy stopped at our house selling fifty-cent raffle tickets on a sailboat and Dad bought every ticket the boy had left — three books' worth.
>
> — Connie Hailey, student

Illustrations are extended examples, frequently presented in story form. Because they require several sentences, they are used more sparingly than examples. When well selected, however, they can be a vivid and effective means of developing a point. The writer of the following paragraph uses illustrations to demonstrate that Harriet Tubman, the underground railroad's most famous conductor, was a genius at eluding her pursuers.

> Part of [Harriet Tubman's] strategy of conducting was, as in all battle-field operations, the knowledge of how and when to retreat. Numerous allusions have been made to her moves when she suspected that she was in danger. When she feared the party was closely pursued, she would take it for a time on a train southward bound. No one seeing Negroes going in this direction would for an instant suppose them to be fugitives. Once on her return she was at a railroad station. She saw some men reading a poster and she heard one of them reading it aloud. It was a description of her, offering a reward for her capture. She took a southbound train to avert suspicion. At another time when Harriet heard men talking about her, she pretended to read a book which

she carried. One man remarked, "This can't be the woman. The one we want can't read or write." Harriet devoutly hoped the book was right side up.

— Earl Conrad, *Harriet Tubman*

Narration

A paragraph of narration tells a story or part of a story. Narrative paragraphs are usually arranged in chronological order, but they may also contain flashbacks, interruptions that take the story back to an earlier time. The following paragraph, from Jane Goodall's *In the Shadow of Man*, recounts one of the author's experiences in the African wild.

> One evening when I was wading in the shallows of the lake to pass a rocky outcrop, I suddenly stopped dead as I saw the sinuous black body of a snake in the water. It was all of six feet long, and from the slight hood and the dark stripes at the back of the neck I knew it to be a Storm's water cobra — a deadly reptile for the bite of which there was, at that time, no serum. As I stared at it an incoming wave gently deposited part of its body on one of my feet. I remained motionless, not even breathing, until the wave rolled back into the lake, drawing the snake with it. Then I leaped out of the water as fast as I could, my heart hammering.
>
> — Jane Goodall, *In the Shadow of Man*

Description

A descriptive paragraph sketches a portrait of a person, place, or thing by using concrete and specific details that appeal to one or more of our senses — sight, sound, smell, taste, and touch. Consider, for example, the following description of the grasshopper invasions that devastated the midwestern landscape in the late 1860s.

> They came like dive bombers out of the west. They came by the millions with the rustle of their wings roaring overhead. They came in waves, like the rolls of the sea, descending with a terrifying speed, breaking now and again like a mighty surf. They came with the force of a williwaw and they formed a huge, ominous, dark brown cloud that eclipsed the sun. They dipped and touched earth, hitting objects and people like hailstones. But they were not hail. These were *live* demons. They popped, snapped, crackled, and roared. They were dark brown, an inch or longer in length, plump in the middle and

tapered at the ends. They had transparent wings, slender legs, and two black eyes that flashed with a fierce intelligence.

— Eugene Boe, "Pioneers to Eternity"

Process

A process paragraph is structured in chronological order. A writer may choose this pattern either to describe how something is made or done or to explain to readers, step by step, how to do something. The following paragraph describes what happens when water freezes.

> In school we learned that with few exceptions the solid phase of matter is more dense than the liquid phase. Water, alone among common substances, violates this rule. As water begins to cool, it contracts and becomes more dense, in a perfectly typical way. But about four degrees above the freezing point, something remarkable happens. It ceases to contract and begins expanding, becoming less dense. At the freezing point the expansion is abrupt and drastic. As water turns to ice, it adds about one-eleventh to its liquid volume.
>
> — Chet Raymo, "Curious Stuff, Water and Ice"

Here is a paragraph explaining how to perform a "roll cast," a popular fly-fishing technique.

> Begin by taking up a suitable stance, with one foot slightly in front of the other and the rod pointing down the line. Then begin a smooth, steady draw, raising your rod hand to just above shoulder height and lifting the rod to the 10:30 or 11:00 position. This steady draw allows a loop of line to form between the rod top and the water. While the line is still moving, raise the rod slightly, then punch it rapidly forward and down. The rod is now flexed and under maximum compression, and the line follows its path, bellying out slightly behind you and coming off the water close to your feet. As you power the rod down through the 3:00 position, the belly of line will roll forward. Follow through smoothly so that the line unfolds and straightens above the water.
>
> — *The Dorling Kindersley Encyclopedia of Fishing*

Comparison and contrast

To compare two subjects is to draw attention to their similarities, although the word *compare* also has a broader meaning that includes a consideration of differences. To contrast is to focus only on differences.

Whether a paragraph stresses similarities or differences, it may be patterned in one of two ways. The two subjects may be presented one at a time, as in the following paragraph of contrast.

> So Grant and Lee were in complete contrast, representing two diametrically opposed elements in American life. Grant was the modern man emerging; beyond him, ready to come on the stage, was the great age of steel and machinery, of crowded cities and a restless, burgeoning vitality. Lee might have ridden down from the old age of chivalry, lance in hand, silken banner fluttering over his head. Each man was the perfect champion of his cause, drawing both his strengths and his weaknesses from the people he led.
>
> — Bruce Catton, "Grant and Lee: A Study in Contrasts"

Or a paragraph may proceed point by point, treating the two subjects together, one aspect at a time. The following paragraph uses the point-by-point method to contrast speeches given by Abraham Lincoln in 1860 and Barack Obama in 2008.

> Two men, two speeches. The men, both lawyers, both from Illinois, were seeking the presidency, despite what seemed their crippling connection with extremists. Each was young by modern standards for a president. Abraham Lincoln had turned fifty-one just five days before delivering his speech. Barack Obama was forty-six when he gave his. Their political experience was mainly provincial, in the Illinois legislature for both of them, and they had received little exposure at the national level — two years in the House of Representatives for Lincoln, four years in the Senate for Obama. Yet each was seeking his party's nomination against a New York senator of longer standing and greater prior reputation — Lincoln against Senator William Seward, Obama against Senator Hillary Clinton. They were both known for having opposed an initially popular war — Lincoln against President Polk's Mexican War, raised on the basis of a fictitious provocation; Obama against President Bush's Iraq War, launched on false claims that Saddam Hussein possessed WMDs [weapons of mass destruction] and had made an alliance with Osama bin Laden.
>
> — Garry Wills, "Two Speeches on Race"

Analogy

Analogies draw comparisons between items that appear to have little in common. Writers turn to analogies for a variety of reasons: to make the unfamiliar seem familiar, to provide a concrete understanding of an abstract topic, to argue a point, or to provoke fresh thoughts or changed feelings about a subject. In the following paragraph, physician Lewis Thomas draws an analogy between the behavior of ants and that of humans.

> Ants are so much like human beings as to be an embarrassment. They farm fungi, raise aphids as livestock, launch armies into wars, use chemical sprays to alarm and confuse enemies, capture slaves. The families of weaver ants engage in child labor, holding their larvae like shuttles to spin out the thread that sews the leaves together for their fungus gardens. They exchange information ceaselessly. They do everything but watch television.
>
> — Lewis Thomas, "On Societies as Organisms"

Although analogies can be a powerful tool for illuminating a subject, they should be used with caution in arguments. Just because two things may be alike in one respect, we cannot conclude that they are alike in all respects. (See p. 103.)

Cause and effect

When causes and effects are a matter of argument, they are too complex to be reduced to a simple pattern (see p. 105). However, if a writer wishes merely to describe a cause-and-effect relationship that is generally accepted, then the effect may be stated in the topic sentence, with the causes listed in the body of the paragraph.

> The fantastic water clarity of the Mount Gambier sinkholes results from several factors. The holes are fed from aquifers holding rainwater that fell decades — even centuries — ago, and that has been filtered through miles of limestone. The high level of calcium that limestone adds causes the silty detritus from dead plants and animals to cling together and settle quickly to the bottom. Abundant bottom vegetation in the shallow sinkholes also helps bind the silt. And the rapid turnover of water prohibits stagnation.
>
> — Hillary Hauser, "Exploring a Sunken Realm in Australia"

Or the paragraph may move from cause to effects, as in this paragraph from a student paper on the effects of the industrial revolution on American farms.

> The rise of rail transport in the nineteenth century forever changed American farming — for better and for worse. Farmers

who once raised crops and livestock to sustain just their own families could now make a profit by selling their goods in towns and cities miles away. These new markets improved the living standard of struggling farm families and encouraged them to seek out innovations that would increase their profits. On the downside, the competition fostered by the new markets sometimes created hostility among neighboring farm families where there had once been a spirit of cooperation. Those farmers who couldn't compete with their neighbors left farming forever, facing poverty worse than they had ever known.

— Chris Mileski, student

Classification and division

Classification is the grouping of items into categories according to some consistent principle. For example, an elementary school teacher might classify children's books according to their level of difficulty, but a librarian might group them by subject matter. The principle of classification that a writer chooses ultimately depends on the purpose of the classification. The following paragraph classifies species of electric fish.

> Scientists sort electric fishes into three categories. The first comprises the strongly electric species like the marine electric rays or the freshwater African electric catfish and South American electric eel. Known since the dawn of history, these deliver a punch strong enough to stun a human. In recent years, biologists have focused on a second category: weakly electric fish in the South American and African rivers that use tiny voltages for communication and navigation. The third group contains sharks, nonelectric rays, and catfish, which do not emit a field but possess sensors that enable them to detect the minute amounts of electricity that leak out of other organisms.
>
> — Anne and Jack Rudloe, "Electric Warfare: The Fish That Kill with Thunderbolts"

Division takes one item and divides it into parts. As with classification, division should be made according to some consistent principle. The following passage describes the components that make up a baseball.

> Like the game itself, a baseball is composed of many layers. One of the delicious joys of childhood is to take apart a baseball and examine the wonders within. You begin by removing the red cotton thread and peeling off the leather cover — which comes from the hide of a Holstein cow and has been tanned, cut, printed,

and punched with holes. Beneath the cover is a thin layer of cotton string, followed by several hundred yards of woolen yarn, which makes up the bulk of the ball. Finally, in the middle is a rubber ball, or "pill," which is a little smaller than a golf ball. Slice into the rubber and you'll find the ball's heart — a cork core. The cork is from Portugal, the rubber from southeast Asia, the covers are American, and the balls are assembled in Costa Rica.

—Dan Gutman, *The Way Baseball Works*

Definition

A definition puts a word or concept into a general class and then provides enough details to distinguish it from others in the same class. In the following paragraph, the writer defines *envy* as a particular kind of desire.

> Envy is so integral and so painful a part of what animates behavior in market societies that many people have forgotten the full meaning of the word, simplifying it into one of the synonyms of desire. It is that, which may be why it flourishes in market societies: democracies of desire, they might be called, with money for ballots, stuffing permitted. But envy is more or less than desire. It begins with an almost frantic sense of emptiness inside oneself, as if the pump of one's heart were sucking on air. One has to be blind to perceive the emptiness, of course, but that's just what envy is, a selective blindness. *Invidia*, Latin for envy, translates as "non-sight," and Dante has the envious plodding along under cloaks of lead, their eyes sewn shut with leaden wire. What they are blind to is what they have, God-given and humanly nurtured, in themselves.

—Nelson W. Aldrich Jr., *Old Money*

4d Make paragraphs coherent.

When sentences and paragraphs flow from one to another without discernible bumps, gaps, or shifts, they are said to be coherent. Coherence can be improved by strengthening the ties between old information and new. A number of techniques for strengthening those ties are detailed in this section.

Linking ideas clearly

Readers expect to learn a paragraph's main point in a topic sentence early in the paragraph. Then, as they move into the body of the paragraph, they expect to encounter specific details, facts, or examples that support the topic sentence — either directly or indirectly. In the following paragraph, all of the sentences following the topic sentence directly support it.

> A passenger list of the early years [of the Orient Express] would read like a *Who's Who of the World*, from art to politics. Sarah Bernhardt and her Italian counterpart Eleonora Duse used the train to thrill the stages of Europe. For musicians there were Toscanini and Mahler. Dancers Nijinsky and Pavlova were there, while lesser performers like Harry Houdini and the girls of the Ziegfeld Follies also rode the rails. Violinists were allowed to practice on the train, and occasionally one might see trapeze artists hanging like bats from the baggage racks.
>
> — Barnaby Conrad III, "Train of Kings"

If a sentence does not support the topic sentence directly, readers expect it to support another sentence in the paragraph and therefore to support the topic sentence indirectly. The following paragraph begins with a topic sentence. The highlighted sentences are direct supports, and the rest of the sentences are indirect supports.

> Though the open-space classroom works for many children, it is not practical for my son, David. First, David is hyperactive. When he was placed in an open-space classroom, he became distracted and confused. He was tempted to watch the movement going on around him instead of concentrating on his own work. Second, David has a tendency to transpose letters and numbers, a tendency that can be overcome only by individual attention from the instructor. In the open classroom he was moved from teacher to teacher, with each one responsible for a different subject. No single teacher worked with David long enough to diagnose the problem, let alone help him with it. Finally, David is not a highly motivated learner. In the open classroom, he was graded "at his own level," not by criteria for a certain grade. He could receive a B in reading and still be a grade level behind, because he was doing satisfactory work "at his own level."
>
> — Margaret Smith, student

Repeating key words

Repetition of key words is an important technique for gaining coherence. To prevent repetitions from becoming dull, you can

use variations of a key word (*hike, hiker, hiking*), pronouns referring to the word (*gamblers . . . they*), and synonyms (*run, spring,
race, dash*). In the following paragraph describing plots among
indentured servants in the seventeenth century, historian Richard Hofstadter binds sentences together by repeating the key
word *plots* and echoing it with a variety of synonyms (which are
highlighted).

> Plots hatched by several servants to run away together
> occurred mostly in the plantation colonies, and the few recorded
> servant uprisings were entirely limited to those colonies. Virginia
> had been forced from its very earliest years to take stringent steps
> against mutinous plots, and severe punishments for such behavior
> were recorded. Most servant plots occurred in the seventeenth
> century: a contemplated uprising was nipped in the bud in York
> County in 1661; apparently led by some left-wing offshoots of the
> Great Rebellion, servants plotted an insurrection in Gloucester
> County in 1663, and four leaders were condemned and executed;
> some discontented servants apparently joined Bacon's Rebellion in
> the 1670's. In the 1680's the planters became newly apprehensive
> of discontent among the servants "owing to their great necessities
> and want of clothes," and it was feared they would rise up
> and plunder the storehouses and ships; in 1682 there were
> plant-cutting riots in which servants and laborers, as well as some
> planters, took part.
>
> — Richard Hofstadter, *America at 1750*

Using parallel structures

Parallel structures are frequently used within sentences to underscore the similarity of ideas (see 9). They may also be used
to bind together a series of sentences expressing similar information. In the following passage describing folk beliefs, anthro-
pologist Margaret Mead presents similar information in parallel
grammatical form.

> Actually, almost every day, even in the most sophisticated
> home, something is likely to happen that evokes the memory of
> some old folk belief. The salt spills. A knife falls to the floor. Your
> nose tickles. Then perhaps, with a slightly embarrassed smile, the
> person who spilled the salt tosses a pinch over his left shoulder. Or
> someone recites the old rhyme, "Knife falls, gentleman calls." Or as
> you rub your nose you think, That means a letter. I wonder who's
> writing?
>
> — Margaret Mead, "New Superstitions for Old"

Maintaining consistency

Coherence suffers whenever a draft shifts confusingly from one point of view to another or from one verb tense to another. (See 13.) In addition, coherence can suffer when new information is introduced with the subject of each sentence. For advice on avoiding shifts, see 13.

Providing transitions

Transitions are bridges between what has been read and what is about to be read. Transitions help readers move from sentence to sentence; they also alert readers to more global connections of ideas — those between paragraphs or even larger blocks of text.

Sentence-level transitions Certain words and phrases signal connections between (or within) sentences. Frequently used transitions are included in the chart below.

Skilled writers use transitional expressions with care, making sure, for example, not to use *consequently* when *also* would be more precise. They are also careful to select transitions with an appropriate tone, perhaps preferring *so* to *thus* in an informal piece, *in summary* to *in short* for a scholarly essay.

In the following paragraph, taken from an argument that dinosaurs had the "'right-sized' brains for reptiles of their body size," biologist Stephen Jay Gould uses transitions (highlighted) with skill.

> I don't wish to deny that the flattened, minuscule head of large bodied Stegosaurus houses little brain from our subjective, top-heavy perspective, but I do wish to assert that we should not expect more of the beast. First of all, large animals have relatively smaller brains than related, small animals. The correlation of brain size with body size among kindred animals (all reptiles, all mammals, for example) is remarkably regular. As we move from small to large animals, from mice to elephants or small lizards to Komodo dragons, brain size increases, but not so fast as body size. In other words, bodies grow faster than brains, and large animals have low ratios of brain weight to body weight. In fact, brains grow only about two-thirds as fast as bodies. Since we have no reason to believe that large animals are consistently stupider than their smaller relatives, we must conclude that large animals require relatively less brain to do as well as smaller animals. If we do not recognize this relationship, we are likely to underestimate the mental power of very large animals, dinosaurs in particular.
>
> — Stephen Jay Gould, "Were Dinosaurs Dumb?"

Common transitions

To show addition: and, also, besides, further, furthermore, in addition, moreover, next, too, first, second

To give examples: for example, for instance, to illustrate, in fact

To compare: also, in the same manner, similarly, likewise

To contrast: but, however, on the other hand, in contrast, nevertheless, still, even though, on the contrary, yet, although

To summarize or conclude: in short, in summary, in conclusion, to sum up, therefore

To show time: after, as, before, next, during, later, finally, meanwhile, then, when, while, immediately

To show place or direction: above, below, beyond, nearby, opposite, close, to the left

To indicate logical relationship: if, so, therefore, consequently, thus, as a result, for this reason, because, since

---

Paragraph-level transitions   Paragraph-level transitions usually link the *first* sentence of a new paragraph with the *first* sentence of the previous paragraph. In other words, the topic sentences signal global connections.

Look for opportunities to allude to the subject of a previous paragraph (as summed up in its topic sentence) in the topic sentence of the next one. In his essay "Little Green Lies," Jonathan H. Alder uses this strategy in the following topic sentences, which appear in a passage describing the benefits of plastic packaging.

> Consider aseptic packaging, the synthetic packaging for the "juice boxes" so many children bring to school with their lunch. One criticism of aseptic packaging is that it is nearly impossible to recycle, yet on almost every other count, aseptic packaging is environmentally preferable to the packaging alternatives. Not only do aseptic containers not require refrigeration to keep their contents from spoiling, but their manufacture requires less than one-10th the energy of making glass bottles.
>
> What is true for juice boxes is also true for other forms of synthetic packaging. The use of polystyrene, which is commonly (and mistakenly) referred to as "Styrofoam," can reduce food waste dramatically due to its insulating properties. (Thanks to these properties, polystyrene cups are much preferred over paper for that morning cup of coffee.) Polystyrene also requires significantly fewer resources to produce than its paper counterpart.

Transitions between blocks of text   In long essays, you will need to alert readers to connections between blocks of text that are more than one paragraph long. You can do this by inserting transitional sentences or short paragraphs at key points in the essay. Here, for example, is a transitional paragraph from a student research paper. It announces that the first part of the paper has come to a close and the second part is about to begin.

> Although the great apes have demonstrated significant language skills, one central question remains: Can they be taught to use that uniquely human language tool we call grammar, to learn the difference, for instance, between "ape bite human" and "human bite ape"? In other words, can an ape create a sentence?

Another strategy to help readers move from one block of text to another is to insert headings in your essay. Headings, which usually sit above blocks of text, allow you to announce a new topic boldly, without the need for subtle transitions. (See 50b.)

4e If necessary, adjust paragraph length.

Most readers feel comfortable reading paragraphs that range between one hundred and two hundred words. Shorter paragraphs require too much starting and stopping, and longer ones strain readers' attention span. There are exceptions to this guideline, however. Paragraphs longer than two hundred words frequently appear in scholarly writing, where scholars explore complex ideas. Paragraphs shorter than one hundred words occur in newspapers because of narrow columns; in informal essays to quicken the pace; and in business writing and Web sites, where readers routinely skim for main ideas.

In an essay, the first and last paragraphs will ordinarily be the introduction and the conclusion. These special-purpose paragraphs are likely to be shorter than the paragraphs in the body of the essay. Typically, the body paragraphs will follow the essay's outline: one paragraph per point in short essays, several paragraphs per point in longer ones. Some ideas require more development than others, however, so it is best to be flexible. If an idea stretches to a length unreasonable for a paragraph, you should

Revising with comments

Need a transition

UNDERSTANDING THE COMMENT

When readers point out that you "need a transition," the comment often signals that they need bridges — transitional words — to follow the progression from one idea to the next.

> The United States of America is one of many countries in the world that were created by immigration. This essential characteristic is perhaps America's greatest weakness and its greatest strength. Our country has the potential to be swallowed up by the diverse beliefs, values, and social practices of its immigrants so that nothing is common to anyone. America can benefit from embracing the amazing cultural diversity within itself.   *Need a transition*

In this body paragraph, a student responded to an assignment that asked him to analyze a central feature of American identity.

Transitional words or phrases help readers follow the connections between sentences and ideas. To revise, the student might begin by asking: What idea is expressed in each sentence? Does each sentence point clearly back to the previous one? If not, what words or phrases might be added to help readers see how one idea moves to the next? The answers to these questions will help the student recognize that his last two sentences contrast with each other (one about weaknesses, one about strengths) but that he needs to provide a transitional word or phrase, such as *however*, before the last sentence to make the contrast clear.

SIMILAR COMMENTS: *something missing?* • *missing connection* • *transition?*

REVISING WHEN *YOU* NEED A TRANSITION BETWEEN SENTENCES

1. *Read your paragraph aloud* to a peer or a tutor. Ask your listeners what is missing between sentences that would help them follow the progression from one idea to the next.

2. *Ask questions.* What words or phrases might be added to help readers move from sentence to sentence? For instance, do you need transitions to show addition (*furthermore*), to give examples (*specifically*), to compare (*similarly*), to contrast (*however*), or to summarize (*in summary*)?

3. *Revise with an appropriate transition* to show connections between ideas.

More help with transitions: pages 64–66

divide the paragraph, even if you have presented comparable points in the essay in single paragraphs.

Paragraph breaks are not always made for strictly logical reasons. Writers use them for the following reasons as well.

REASONS FOR BEGINNING A NEW PARAGRAPH

- to mark off the introduction and the conclusion
- to signal a shift to a new idea
- to indicate an important shift in time or place
- to emphasize a point (by placing it at the beginning or the end, not in the middle, of a paragraph)
- to highlight a contrast
- to signal a change of speakers (in dialogue)
- to provide readers with a needed pause
- to break up text that looks too dense

Beware of using too many short, choppy paragraphs, however. Readers want to see how your ideas connect, and they become irritated when you break their momentum by forcing them to pause every few sentences. Here are some reasons you might have for combining some of the paragraphs in a rough draft.

REASONS FOR COMBINING PARAGRAPHS

- to clarify the essay's organization
- to connect closely related ideas
- to bind together text that looks too choppy

Academic Writing

Academic Writing, 69

Academic Writing

5   Writing about texts

The word *texts* can refer to a variety of works, including essays, articles, government reports, books, Web sites, advertisements, and photographs. Most assignments that ask you to respond to a text call for a summary or an analysis or both.

A summary is neutral in tone and demonstrates that you have understood the author's key ideas. Assignments calling for an analysis of a text vary widely, but they usually ask you to look at how the text's parts contribute to its central argument or purpose, often with the aim of judging its evidence or overall effect.

When you write about a text, you will need to read it — or, in the case of a visual text, view it — several times to discover meaning. Two techniques will help you move beyond a superficial first reading: (1) annotating the text with your observations and questions and (2) outlining the text's key points. These techniques will help you analyze both written and visual texts.

5a   Read actively: Annotate the text.

Read actively by jotting down your questions and thoughts in a notebook or in the margins of the text or visual. Use a pencil instead of a highlighter; with a pencil you can underline key concepts, mark points, or circle elements that intrigue you. If you change your mind, you can erase your early annotations and replace them with new ones. To annotate an electronic document, take notes in a separate file or use software features to highlight, underline, or insert comments.

As you write

Using the guidelines for active reading on page 71, annotate an assigned text. Pay particular attention to what surprises or intrigues you about the text and what you notice on a second reading. How do your annotations help you understand the text? If you could talk with the author of the text, what one or two questions would you pose?

Guidelines for active reading
Identify the basic features and structure of a text.

- What kind of text are you reading: An essay? An editorial? A scholarly article? An advertisement? A photograph? A Web site?
- What is the author's purpose: To inform? To persuade? To call to action?
- Who is the audience? How does the author appeal to the audience?
- What is the author's thesis? What question does the text attempt to answer?
- What evidence does the author provide to support the thesis?
- What key terms does the author define?

Note details that surprise, puzzle, or intrigue you.

- Has the author revealed a fact or made a point that counters your assumptions? Is anything surprising?
- Has the author made a generalization you disagree with? Can you think of evidence that would challenge the generalization?
- Do you see any contradictions or inconsistencies in the text?
- Does the text contain words, statements, or phrases that you don't understand? If so, what reference materials do you need to consult?

Read and reread to discover meaning.

- What do you notice on a second or third reading that you didn't notice earlier?
- Does the text raise questions that it does not resolve?
- If you could address the author directly, what questions would you pose? Where do you agree and disagree with the author? Why?

Apply additional critical thinking strategies to visual texts.

- What first strikes you about the visual text? What elements do you notice immediately?
- Who or what is the main subject of the visual text?
- What colors and textures dominate?
- What is in the background? In the foreground?
- What role, if any, do words or numbers play in the text?
- When was the visual created or the information collected?

On this page and on page 73 are an article from *CQ Researcher*, a newsletter about social and political issues, and an advertisement, both annotated by students. The students, Emilia Sanchez and Ren Yoshida, were assigned to analyze these texts. They began by reading actively.

ANNOTATED ARTICLE

Big Box Stores Are Bad for Main Street

BETSY TAYLOR

There is plenty of reason to be concerned about the proliferation of Wal-Marts and other so-called "big box" stores. The question, however, is not whether or not these types of stores create jobs (although several studies claim they produce a net job loss in local communities) or whether they ultimately save consumers money. The real concern about having a 25-acre slab of concrete with a 100,000 square foot box of stuff land on a town is whether it's good for a community's soul.

Opening strategy — the problem is not x, it's y.

Sentimental — what is a community's soul?

The worst thing about "big boxes" is that they have a tendency to produce Ross Perot's famous "big sucking sound" — sucking the life out of cities and small towns across the country. On the other hand, small businesses are great for a community. They offer more personal service; they won't threaten to pack up and leave town if they don't get tax breaks, free roads and other blandishments; and small-business owners are much more responsive to a customer's needs. (Ever try to complain about bad service or poor quality products to the president of Home Depot?)

Lumps all big boxes together.

Assumes all small businesses are attentive.

Logic problem? Why couldn't customer complain to store manager?

Yet, if big boxes are so bad, why are they so successful? One glaring reason is that we've become a nation of hyperconsumers, and the big-box boys know this. Downtown shopping districts comprised of small businesses take some of the efficiency out of overconsumption. There's all that hassle of having to travel from store to store, and having to pull out your credit card so many times. Occasionally, we even find ourselves chatting with the shopkeeper, wandering into a coffee shop to visit with a friend or otherwise wasting precious time that could be spent on acquiring more stuff.

True?

Taylor wishes for a time that is long gone or never was.

But let's face it — bustling, thriving city centers are fun. They breathe life into a community. They allow cities and towns to stand out from each other. They provide an atmosphere for people to interact with each other that just cannot be found at Target, or Wal-Mart or Home Depot.

Community vs. economy. What about prices?

Is it anti-American to be against having a retail giant set up shop in one's community? Some people would say so. On the other hand, if you board up Main Street, what's left of America?

Ends with emotional appeal.

ANNOTATED ADVERTISEMENT

What is being exchanged?

"Empowering" — why in an elegant font? Who is empowering farmers?

"Farmers" in all capital letters — shows strength?

Straightforward design and not much text.

Outstretched hands. Is she giving a gift? Inviting a partnership?

Raw coffee is earthy, natural.

When you choose Equal Exchange fairly traded coffee, tea or chocolate, you join a network that empowers farmers in Latin America, Africa, and Asia to:

- **Stay on their land**
- **Care for the environment**
- **Farm organically**
- **Support their family**
- **Plan for the future**

www.equalexchange.coop

Photo: Jesus Choqueheranca de Quevero, Coffee farmer & CEPICAFE Cooperative member, Peru

Positive verbs: consumers choose, join, empower; farmers stay, care, farm, support, plan.

Source: Equal Exchange.

5b Sketch a brief outline of the text.

After reading, rereading, and annotating a text, try to outline it. Seeing how the author has constructed a text can help you understand it. As you sketch an outline, pay special attention to the text's thesis (central idea) and its topic sentences. The thesis of a written text usually appears in the introduction, often in the first or second paragraph. Topic sentences can be found at the beginnings of most body paragraphs, where they announce a shift to a new topic. (See 2a and 4a.)

In your outline, put the author's thesis and key points in your own words. Here, for example, is the outline that Emilia Sanchez developed as she prepared to write her summary and analysis of the text on page 72. Notice that Sanchez's informal outline does not trace the author's ideas paragraph by paragraph; instead, it sums up the article's key points.

OUTLINE OF "BIG BOX STORES ARE BAD FOR MAIN STREET"

Thesis: Whether or not they take jobs away from a community or offer low prices to consumers, we should be worried about "big-box" stores like Wal-Mart, Target, and Home Depot because they harm communities by taking the life out of downtown shopping districts.

I.   Small businesses are better for cities and towns than big-box stores are.

   A. Small businesses offer personal service, but big-box stores do not.

   B. Small businesses don't make demands on community resources as big-box stores do.

   C. Small businesses respond to customer concerns, but big-box stores do not.

II. Big-box stores are successful because they cater to consumption at the expense of benefits to the community.

   A. Buying everything in one place is convenient.

   B. Shopping at small businesses may be inefficient, but it provides opportunities for socializing.

   C. Downtown shopping districts give each city or town a special identity.

Conclusion: Although some people say that it's anti-American to oppose big-box stores, actually these stores threaten the communities that make up America by encouraging buying at the expense of the traditional interactions of Main Street.

A visual often doesn't state an explicit thesis or an explicit line of reasoning. Instead, you must sometimes infer the meaning beneath the image's surface and interpret its central point and supporting ideas from the elements of its design. One way to outline a visual text is to try to define its purpose and sketch a list of its key elements. Here, for example, are the key features that Ren Yoshida identified for the advertisement printed on page 73. Note that the student is able to draw a preliminary conclusion about the advertisement.

OUTLINE OF EQUAL EXCHANGE ADVERTISEMENT

Purpose: To persuade readers that they can improve the lives of organic farmers and their families by purchasing Equal Exchange coffee.

Key features:

- The farmer's heart-shaped hands are outstretched, offering the viewer partnership and the product of her hard work.
- The raw coffee is surprisingly fruitlike and fresh—natural and healthy looking.
- Words above and below the photograph describe the equal exchange between farmers and consumers.
- Consumer support leads to a higher quality of life for the farmers and for all people, since these farmers care for the environment and plan for the future.
- The simplicity of the design echoes the simplicity of the exchange. The consumer only has to buy a cup of coffee to make a difference.

Conclusion: Equal Exchange is selling more than a product—coffee. It is selling the idea that together farmers and consumers hold the future of land, environment, farms, and family in their hands.

5c Summarize to demonstrate your understanding.

Your goal in summarizing a text is to state the work's main ideas and key points simply, briefly, and accurately in your own words. Writing a summary does not require you to judge the author's ideas; it requires you to *understand* the author's ideas. If you have sketched a brief outline of the text (see 5b), refer to it as you draft your summary.

> **Making the most of your handbook**
> Summarizing is a key research skill.
> ► Summarizing without plagiarizing: 55c
> ► Putting summaries and paraphrases in your own words: 57c, 62c

To summarize a written text, first find the author's central idea — the thesis. Then divide the whole piece into a few major and perhaps minor ideas. Since a summary must be fairly short, you must make judgments about what is most important.

Guidelines for writing a summary

- In the first sentence, mention the title of the text, the name of the author, and the author's thesis or the visual's central point.
- Maintain a neutral tone; be objective.
- As you present the author's ideas, use the third-person point of view and the present tense: *Taylor argues.* . . . (If you are writing in APA style, see 62c.)
- Keep your focus on the text. Don't state the author's ideas as if they were your own.
- Put all or most of your summary in your own words; if you borrow a phrase or a sentence from the text, put it in quotation marks and give the page number in parentheses.
- Limit yourself to presenting the text's key points.
- Be concise; make every word count.

To summarize a visual text, begin with essential information such as who created the visual, who the intended audience is, where the visual appeared, and when it was created. Briefly explain the visual's main point or purpose and identify its key features (see p. 75).

Following is Emilia Sanchez's summary of the article that is printed on page 72.

In her essay "Big Box Stores Are Bad for Main Street," Betsy
Taylor argues that chain stores harm communities by taking the life
out of downtown shopping districts. Explaining that a community's
"soul" is more important than low prices or consumer convenience,
she argues that small businesses are better than stores like Home
Depot and Target because they emphasize personal interactions and
don't place demands on a community's resources. Taylor asserts that
big-box stores are successful because "we've become a nation of
hyper-consumers" (1011), although the convenience of shopping in
these stores comes at the expense of benefits to the community. She
concludes by suggesting that it's not "anti-American" to oppose
big-box stores because the damage they inflict on downtown
shopping districts extends to America itself.

— Emilia Sanchez, student

5d Analyze to demonstrate your critical thinking.

Whereas a summary most often answers the question of *what* a text says,
an analysis looks at *how* a text makes
its point.

Typically, an analysis takes the
form of an essay that makes its own
argument about a text. Include an introduction that briefly summarizes
the text, a thesis that states your own
judgment about the text, and body
paragraphs that support your thesis

> **Making the most of
> your handbook**
> When you analyze a text, you
> weave words and ideas from
> the source into your own
> writing.
> ► Guidelines for using
>   quotation marks: 55c
> ► Quoting or paraphrasing:
>   57, 62
> ► Using signal phrases: 58b,
>   63b

with evidence. If you are analyzing a visual, examine it as a whole
and then reflect on how the individual elements contribute to its
overall meaning. If you have written a summary of the text or
visual, you may find it useful to refer to the main points of the
summary as you write your analysis.

Using interpretation in an analysis

Student writer Emilia Sanchez begins her essay about Betsy
Taylor's article (see p. 72) by summarizing Taylor's argument. She

Revising with comments
Summarize less, analyze more

UNDERSTANDING THE COMMENT

When readers point out that you need to "summarize less, analyze more," the comment often signals that they want to hear your interpretation of a text, not a summary of the text itself.

> Growing up as a borderlander, I have always considered myself bilingual. Reading "How to Tame a Wild Tongue" by Gloria Anzaldúa made me rethink that label. In the "*El lenguaje de la frontera*" section of the essay, Anzaldúa explains the origins of Chicano Spanish, a "border tongue" (326). Then she says that most Chicanos actually speak as many as eight languages. Anzaldúa lists these languages and then tells which languages she speaks with which people in her life. For example, she speaks Tex-Mex with friends, Chicano Texas Spanish with her mother, and working-class English at school (327). Finally, she talks about her experience with speaking made-up languages.

Summarize less, analyze more

One student wrote this body paragraph in response to an assignment that asked students to analyze Gloria Anzaldúa's essay "How to Tame a Wild Tongue."

The student writer needs to go beyond summary to offer his insights about Anzaldúa's text. To revise this paragraph, the student might begin by underlining the verbs in his own sentences: *explains, says, lists, tells,* and *talks*. These sentences simply restate what Anzaldúa has written. Although the student may need to summarize briefly, he should move quickly to exploring the meaning of the text. In his analysis, the student might ask questions about Anzaldúa's strategies. For instance, why does she combine Spanish with English? Or why does she list the eight separate languages that most Chicanos speak?

SIMILAR COMMENTS: *too much summary* • *show, don't tell* • *go deeper*

REVISING WHEN *YOU* NEED TO SUMMARIZE LESS AND ANALYZE MORE

1. *Reread your paragraph* and highlight the sentences that summarize. Then, in a different color, highlight the sentences that contain your analysis. (Think about the differences between summary and analysis: Summary answers the question of *what* a text says; analysis offers a judgment or an interpretation of the text.)

2. *Reread the text* (or passages of the text) that you are analyzing, paying attention to the language and structure of the text.
3. *Ask questions.* What strategies does the author use? How do these strategies convey the meaning of the text? What insights can you convey to your readers about the text? How can you deepen your readers' understanding of the text?

More advice on analyzing a text: 5d and 66b

then states her own thesis, or claim, which offers her judgment of Taylor's article, and begins her analysis. In her first body paragraph, Sanchez interprets Taylor's use of language.

Topic sentence includes Sanchez's claim.

Quoted material shows Taylor's language and is placed in quotation marks.

Taylor's use of colorful language reveals that she has a sentimental view of American society and does not understand economic realities. In her first paragraph, Taylor refers to a big-box store as a "25-acre slab of concrete with a 100,000 square foot box of stuff" that "land[s] on a town," evoking images of a powerful monster crushing the American way of life (1011). But she oversimplifies a complex issue. Taylor does not consider. . . .

Signal phrase introduces a quotation from the text.

Quotation is followed by Sanchez's interpretation of Taylor's language.

Transition to Sanchez's next point.

5e Sample student essay: Analysis of an article

Beginning on page 80 is Emilia Sanchez's analysis of the article by Betsy Taylor (see p. 72). Sanchez used Modern Language Association (MLA) style to format her paper and cite the source.

Sanchez 1

Emilia Sanchez

Professor Goodwin

English 10

23 October 2009

Rethinking Big-Box Stores

Opening briefly summarizes the article's purpose and thesis.

In her essay "Big Box Stores Are Bad for Main Street," Betsy Taylor focuses not on the economic effects of large chain stores but on the effects these stores have on the "soul" of America. She argues that stores like Home Depot, Target, and Wal-Mart are bad for America because they draw people out of downtown shopping districts and cause them to focus on consumption. In contrast, she believes that small businesses are good for America because they provide personal attention, encourage community interaction, and make each city

Sanchez begins to analyze Taylor's argument.

and town unique. But Taylor's argument is unconvincing because it is based on sentimentality—on idealized images of a quaint Main Street—rather than on the roles that businesses play in consumers' lives and communities.

Thesis expresses Sanchez's judgment of Taylor's article.

By ignoring the complex economic relationship between large chain stores and their communities, Taylor incorrectly assumes that simply getting rid of big-box stores would have a positive effect on America's communities.

Taylor's use of colorful language reveals that she has a sentimental view of American society and does not

Signal phrase introduces quotations from the source; Sanchez uses an MLA in-text citation.

understand economic realities. In her first paragraph, Taylor refers to a big-box store as a "25-acre slab of concrete with a 100,000 square foot box of stuff" that "land[s] on a town," evoking images of a powerful monster crushing the American way of life (1011). But she oversimplifies

Marginal annotations indicate MLA-style formatting and effective writing.

Sanchez 2

a complex issue. Taylor does not consider that many downtown business districts failed long before chain stores moved in, when factories and mills closed and workers lost their jobs. In cities with struggling economies, big-box stores can actually provide much-needed jobs. Similarly, while Taylor blames big-box stores for harming local economies by asking for tax breaks, free roads, and other perks, she doesn't acknowledge that these stores also enter into economic partnerships with the surrounding communities by offering financial benefits to schools and hospitals.

> Sanchez begins to identify and challenge Taylor's assumptions.
>
> Transition to another point in Sanchez's analysis.

Taylor's assumption that shopping in small businesses is always better for the customer also seems driven by nostalgia for an old-fashioned Main Street rather than by the facts. While she may be right that many small businesses offer personal service and are responsive to customer complaints, she does not consider that many customers appreciate the service at big-box stores. Just as customer service is better at some small businesses than at others, it is impossible to generalize about service at all big-box stores. For example, customers depend on the lenient return policies and the wide variety of products at stores like Target and Home Depot.

> Clear topic sentence announces a shift to a new topic.
>
> Sanchez refutes Taylor's claim.

Taylor blames big-box stores for encouraging American "hyper-consumerism," but she oversimplifies by equating big-box stores with bad values and small businesses with good values. Like her other points, this claim ignores the economic and social realities of American society today. Big-box stores do not force Americans to buy more. By offering lower prices in a convenient setting, however,

Sanchez 3

they allow consumers to save time and purchase goods
they might not be able to afford from small businesses. The
existence of more small businesses would not change what
most Americans can afford, nor would it reduce their desire
to buy affordable merchandise.

Sanchez treats the
author fairly.

Taylor may be right that some big-box stores have a
negative impact on communities and that small businesses
offer certain advantages. But she ignores the economic
conditions that support big-box stores as well as the fact
that Main Street was in decline before the big-box store
arrived. Getting rid of big-box stores will not bring back a
simpler America populated by thriving, unique Main Streets;
in reality, Main Street will not survive if consumers cannot
afford to shop there.

Conclusion
returns to the
thesis and
shows the wider
significance of
Sanchez's analysis.

Sanchez 4

Work Cited

Work cited page is
in MLA style.

Taylor, Betsy. "Big Box Stores Are Bad for Main Street." *CQ
Researcher* 9.44 (1999): 1011. Print.

Guidelines for analyzing a text

Written texts

Instructors who ask you to analyze an essay or an article often expect you to address some of the following questions.

- What is the author's thesis or central idea? Who is the audience?
- What questions (stated or unstated) does the author address?
- How does the author structure the text? What are the key parts, and how do they relate to one another and to the thesis?
- What strategies has the author used to generate interest in the argument and to persuade readers of its merit?
- What evidence does the author use to support the thesis? How persuasive is the evidence? (See 6d and 6e.)
- Does the author anticipate objections and counter opposing views? (See 6f.)
- Does the author use any faulty reasoning? (See 7a.)

Visual texts

If you are analyzing a visual text, the following additional questions will help you evaluate an image's purpose and meaning.

- What confuses, surprises, or intrigues you about the image?
- What is the source of the visual, and who created it? What is its purpose?
- What clues suggest the visual text's intended audience? How does the image appeal to its audience?
- If the text is an advertisement, what product is it selling? Does it attempt to sell an idea or a message as well?
- If the visual text includes words, how do the words contribute to the meaning?
- How do design elements — colors, shapes, perspective, background, foreground — help convey the visual text's meaning or serve its purpose?

As you write

Using the guidelines for analyzing visual texts on this page, study a visual of your choice—for example, a photograph, a cartoon, or an advertisement. Use the guidelines to help you determine the visual's purpose and meaning. Discuss your observations with a classmate.

6   Constructing reasonable arguments

In writing an argument, you take a stand on a debatable issue. The question being debated might be a matter of public policy:

> Should companies be allowed to advertise on public school property?
>
> What is the least dangerous way to dispose of hazardous waste?
>
> Should motorists be banned from texting while driving?
>
> Should a state limit the number of charter schools?

On such questions, reasonable people may disagree.

Reasonable men and women also disagree about many scholarly issues. Psychologists debate the role of genes and environment in determining behavior; historians interpret the causes of the Civil War quite differently; biologists challenge one another's predictions about the effects of global warming.

When you construct a *reasonable* argument, your goal is not simply to win or to have the last word. Your aim is to explain your understanding of the truth about a subject or to propose the best

---

Academic English Some cultures value writers who argue with force; other cultures value writers who argue subtly or indirectly. Academic audiences in the United States will expect your writing to be assertive and confident — neither aggressive nor passive. You can create an assertive tone by acknowledging different positions and supporting your ideas with specific evidence.

TOO AGGRESSIVE	Of course only registered organ donors should be eligible for organ transplants. It's selfish and shortsighted to think otherwise.
TOO PASSIVE	I might be wrong, but I think that maybe people should have to register as organ donors if they want to be considered for a transplant.
ASSERTIVE	If only registered organ donors are eligible for transplants, more people will register as donors.

If you are uncertain about the tone of your work, ask for help at your school's writing center.

solution to a problem — without being needlessly combative. In constructing your argument, you join a conversation with other writers and readers. Your aim is to convince readers to reconsider their positions by offering new reasons to question existing viewpoints.

6a Examine your issue's social and intellectual contexts.

Arguments appear in social and intellectual contexts. Public policy debates arise in social contexts and are conducted among groups with competing values and interests. For example, the debate over offshore oil drilling has been renewed in the United States in light of skyrocketing energy costs and terrorism concerns — with environmentalists, policymakers, oil company executives, and consumers all weighing in on the argument. Most public policy debates also have intellectual dimensions that address scientific or theoretical questions. In the case of the drilling issue, geologists, oceanographers, and economists all contribute their expertise.

Scholarly debates play out in intellectual contexts, but they have a social dimension as well. For example, scholars respond to the contributions of other specialists in the field, often building on others' views and refining them, but at times challenging them.

Because many of your readers will be aware of the social and intellectual contexts in which your issue is grounded, you will be at a disadvantage if you are not informed. That's why it is a good idea to conduct some

> **Making the most of your handbook**
> Supporting your claims with evidence from sources strengthens your argument.
> ▶ Conducting research: 53

research before preparing your argument; consulting even a few sources can deepen your understanding of the debates surrounding your topic. For example, the student whose paper appears on pages 96–101 became more knowledgeable about his issue — the shift from print to online news — after reading and annotating a few sources.

As you write

Select a public policy debate and locate two documents arguing different sides of the debate. Briefly summarize the opposing positions. Which position seems more reasonable to you? Which author seems more credible? Why? Join the conversation by writing a letter to one of the authors to explain your position in the debate.

6b View your audience as a panel of jurors.

Do not assume that your audience already agrees with you; instead, envision skeptical readers who, like a panel of jurors, will make up their minds after listening to all sides of the argument. If you are arguing a public policy issue, aim your paper at readers who represent a variety of positions. In the case of the debate over offshore drilling, for example, imagine a jury that represents those who have a stake in the matter: environmentalists, policymakers, oil company executives, and consumers.

At times, you can deliberately narrow your audience. If you are working within a word limit, for example, you might not have the space in which to address all the concerns surrounding the offshore drilling debate. Or you might be primarily interested in reaching one segment of a general audience, such as consumers. In such instances, you can still view your audience as a panel of jurors; the jury will simply be a less diverse group.

In the case of scholarly debates, you will be addressing readers who share your interest in a discipline, such as literature or psychology. Such readers belong to a group with an agreed-upon way of investigating and talking about issues. Though they generally agree about disciplinary methods of asking questions and share specialized vocabulary, scholars in an academic discipline often disagree about particular issues. Once you see how they disagree about your issue, you should be able to imagine a jury that reflects the variety of positions they hold.

6c In your introduction, establish credibility and state your position.

When you are constructing an argument, make sure your introduction contains a thesis that states your position on the issue you have chosen to debate. In the sentences leading up to the thesis, establish your credibility with readers by showing that you

> **Making the most of your handbook**
> When you write an argument, you state your position in a thesis.
> ▶ Writing effective thesis statements: 1c, 2a

are knowledgeable about the issue and fair-minded. If possible, build common ground with readers who may not at first agree with your views, and show them why they should consider your thesis.

In the following introduction, student Kevin Smith presents himself as someone worth listening to. Because Smith introduces both sides of the debate, readers are likely to approach his essay with an open mind.

Smith shows that he is familiar with the legal issues surrounding school prayer.

Although the Supreme Court has ruled against prayer in public schools on First Amendment grounds, many people still feel that prayer should be allowed. Such people value prayer as a practice central to their faith and believe that prayer is a way for schools to reinforce moral principles. They also compellingly point out a paradox in the First Amendment itself: at what point does the separation of church and state restrict the freedom of those who wish to practice their religion? What proponents of school prayer fail to realize, however, is that the Supreme Court's decision, although it was made on legal grounds, makes sense on religious grounds as well. Prayer is too important to be trusted to our public schools.   — Kevin Smith, student

Smith is fair-minded, presenting the views of both sides.

Smith's thesis builds common ground.

TIP: A good way to test a thesis while drafting and revising is to imagine a counterargument to your argument (see 6f). If you can't think of an opposing point of view, rethink your thesis and ask a classmate or writing center tutor to respond to your argument.

6d Back up your thesis with persuasive lines of argument.

Arguments of any complexity contain lines of argument that, when taken together, might reasonably persuade readers that the thesis has merit. The following, for example, are the main lines of argument that Sam Jacobs used in his paper about the shift from print to online news (see pp. 96–101).

CENTRAL CLAIM   Thesis: The shift from print to online news provides unprecedented opportunities for readers to become more engaged with the news, to hold journalists accountable, and to participate as producers, not simply as consumers.

(continued)

THE WRITING CENTER   hackerhandbooks.com/rules
  > Resources for writers and tutors > Tips from writing tutors:
                                          Writing assignments;
                                          Writing essays in English

SUPPORTING
CLAIMS

- Print news has traditionally had a one-sided relationship with its readers, delivering information for passive consumption.
- Online news invites readers to participate in a collaborative process—to question and even contribute to the content.
- Links within news stories provide transparency, allowing readers to move easily from the main story to original sources, related articles, or background materials.
- Technology has made it possible for readers to become news producers—posting text, audio, images, and video of news events.
- Citizen journalists can provide valuable information, sometimes more quickly than traditional journalists can.

If you sum up your main lines of argument, as Jacobs did, you will have a rough outline of your essay. In your paper, you will provide evidence for each of your claims.

As you write
Study Sam Jacobs's line of argument above. Draft an outline of your central claim and supporting claims, as he did. Ask a classmate to comment on the effectiveness of your thesis and claims. Do you have enough support for your thesis? Are your claims persuasive?

6e Support your claims with specific evidence.

You will need to support your central claim and any subordinate claims with evidence: facts, statistics, examples and illustrations, visuals, expert opinion, and so on. Most debatable topics require that you consult some written sources. As you read through the sources, you will learn more about the arguments and counter-arguments at the center of your debate.

Making the most of your handbook
Sources, when used responsibly, can provide supporting evidence.
► Paraphrasing, summarizing, and quoting sources: 55c
► Punctuating direct quotations: 37a
► Citing sources: 57a, 62a

Remember that you must document your sources. Documentation gives credit to the authors and shows readers how to locate a source in case they want to assess its credibility or explore the issues further.

Using facts and statistics

A fact is something that is known with certainty because it has been objectively verified: The capital of Wyoming is Cheyenne. Carbon has an atomic weight of 12. John F. Kennedy was assassinated on November 22, 1963. Statistics are collections of numerical facts: Alcohol abuse is a factor in nearly 40 percent of traffic fatalities. More than four in ten businesses in the United States are owned by women.

Most arguments are supported at least to some extent by facts and statistics. For example, in the following passage the writer uses statistics to show that college students are granted unreasonably high credit limits.

> A 2009 study by Sallie Mae revealed that undergraduates are carrying record-high credit card balances and are relying on credit cards more than ever, especially in the economic downturn. The average credit card debt per college undergraduate is $3,173, and 82 percent of undergraduates carry balances and incur finance charges each month (Sallie Mae).

Writers often use statistics in selective ways to bolster their own positions. If you suspect that a writer's handling of statistics is not quite fair, track down the original sources for those statistics or read authors with opposing views, who may give you a fuller understanding of the numbers.

Using examples and illustrations

Examples and illustrations (extended examples, often in story form) rarely prove a point by themselves, but when used in combination with other forms of evidence they flesh out an argument with details and specific instances and bring it to life. Because examples are often concrete and sometimes vivid, they can reach readers in ways that statistics and abstract ideas cannot.

In a paper arguing that online news provides opportunities for readers that print news does not, Sam Jacobs describes how regular citizens armed with only cell phones and laptops helped save lives during Hurricane Katrina by relaying critical news updates.

Using visuals

Visuals — charts, graphs, diagrams, photographs — can support your argument by providing vivid and detailed evidence and by capturing your readers' attention. Bar or line graphs, for instance, describe and organize complex statistical data; photographs can immediately and evocatively convey abstract ideas. Writers in almost every academic field use visual evidence to support their arguments or to counter opposing arguments. For example, to explain a conflict among Southeast Asian countries, a historian might choose a map to illustrate the geography and highlight particular issues. Or to refute another scholar's hypothesis about the dangers of a vegetarian diet, a nutritionist might support her claims by using a table to organize and highlight detailed numerical information. (See pp. 24–25.)

As you consider using visual evidence, ask yourself the following questions:

- Is the visual accurate, credible, and relevant?
- How will the visual appeal to readers? Logically? Ethically? Emotionally?
- How will the visual evidence function? Will it provide background information? Present complex numerical information or an abstract idea? Lend authority? Anticipate or refute counterarguments?

> **Making the most of your handbook**
> Integrating visuals can strengthen your writing.
> ▸ Choosing appropriate visuals: page 407
> ▸ Placing and labeling visuals: page 407
> ▸ Using visuals responsibly: page 408

Like all forms of evidence, visuals don't speak for themselves; you'll need to analyze and interpret the evidence to show readers how the visuals inform and support your argument.

As you write

Review an argument you are drafting. Analyze the types of evidence you selected. Have you varied the type of evidence? Could you strengthen your argument with more vivid or more detailed evidence? How might visual evidence, for example, lend authority to your argument and appeal to readers? Note what changes you might make to your evidence.

Citing expert opinion

Although they are no substitute for careful reasoning of your own, the views of an expert can contribute to the force of your argument. For example, to help him make the case that print journalism has a one-sided relationship with its readers, Sam Jacobs integrates an expert's key description:

> With the rise of the Internet, however, this one-sided relationship has been criticized by journalists such as Dan Gillmor, founder of the Center for Citizen Media, who argues that traditional print journalism treats "news as a lecture," whereas online news is "more of a conversation" (xxiv).

When you rely on expert opinion, make sure that your source is an expert in the field you are writing about. In some cases, you may need to provide credentials showing why your source is worth listening to. When including expert testimony in your paper, you can summarize or paraphrase the expert's opinion or you can quote the expert's exact words. You will of course need to document the source, as Jacobs did in the example just given.

Anticipating and countering opposing arguments

To anticipate a possible objection (see 6f) to your argument, consider the following questions:

- Could a reasonable person draw a different conclusion from your facts or examples?
- Might a reader question any of your assumptions?
- Could a reader offer an alternative explanation of this issue?
- Is there any evidence that might weaken your position?

The following questions may help you respond to a reader's potential objection:

- Can you concede the point to the opposition but challenge the point's importance or usefulness?
- Can you explain why readers should consider a new perspective or question a piece of evidence?
- Should you explain how your position responds to contradictory evidence?
- Can you suggest a different interpretation of the evidence?

When you write, use phrasing to signal to readers that you're about to present an objection. Often the signal phrase can go in the lead sentence of a paragraph:

Critics of this view argue that. . . .

Some readers might point out that. . . .

Researchers challenge these claims by. . . .

Revising with comments
Develop more

UNDERSTANDING THE COMMENT

When readers suggest that you "develop more," the comment often signals that you stopped short of providing a full and detailed discussion of your idea.

> Distancing ourselves from our family is a natural part of growing up. There are many ways in which we try doing so. For essayist Richard Rodriguez, it was his drive for academic success that separated him from his parents and his past (195). In his desire to become educated, he (removed himself) from his family and (distanced himself) from his culture. In his essay "The Achievement of Desire," he admits regretting the separation from his family and acknowledges the particular challenges of growing up between two cultures.

Develop more

In this body paragraph, a student responded to an assignment that asked her to explore one theme in Richard Rodriguez's essay "The Achievement of Desire."

The student has not included enough evidence or developed a thorough analysis of that evidence. To revise, she might look for specific examples and details from Rodriguez's essay to support her claim that Rodriguez "removed . . . and distanced himself" from his family. Then she might develop the claim by analyzing *how* and *why* Rodriguez's "desire to become educated" removed him from his family.

SIMILAR COMMENTS: *undeveloped • give examples • explain*

REVISING WHEN *YOU* NEED TO DEVELOP MORE

1. *Read your paragraph to a peer or a tutor* and ask specific questions: What's missing? Do readers need more background information or examples to understand your point? Do they need more evidence to be convinced? Is it clear what point you are making with your details?

2. *Keep your purpose in mind.* You aren't being asked to restate what you've already written or what the author has written.

3. *Think about why your main point matters to your readers.* Take another look at your points and support, and answer the question "So what?"

More advice on using specific evidence: 6e

6f Anticipate objections; counter opposing arguments.

Readers who already agree with you need no convincing, but indifferent or skeptical readers may resist your arguments. To be willing to give up positions that seem reasonable to them, readers need to see that another position is even more reasonable. In addition to presenting your own case, therefore, you should consider the opposing arguments and attempt to counter them. (See the box on p. 91.)

It might seem at first that drawing attention to an opposing point of view or contradictory evidence would weaken your argument. But by anticipating and countering objections, you show yourself as a reasonable and well-informed writer. You also establish your purpose, demonstrate the significance of the issue you are debating, and ultimately strengthen your argument.

There is no best place in an essay to deal with opposing views. Often it is useful to summarize the opposing position early in your essay. After stating your thesis but before developing your own arguments, you might have a paragraph that addresses the most important counterargument. Or you can anticipate objections paragraph by paragraph as you develop your case. Wherever you decide to address opposing arguments, you will enhance your credibility if you explain the arguments of others accurately and fairly.

As you write

Exchange drafts with your classmates. Pose objections to their arguments, and invite them to pose objections to yours. Practice using the language of counterargument: "Some readers might point out . . . " or "But isn't it possible that . . . ?" What do you learn about the persuasiveness of your argument from hearing objections? Do you need to revise your thesis? Modify your position? Consider new evidence? Which counterarguments would you need to address to convince readers that you are a reasonable and informed writer?

6g Build common ground.

As you counter opposing arguments, try to seek out one or two assumptions you might share with readers who do not initially agree with your views. If you can show that you share their concerns, your readers may be more likely to acknowledge the

Revising with comments
Consider opposing viewpoints

UNDERSTANDING THE COMMENT

When readers suggest that you "consider opposing viewpoints," the comment often signals that you need to recognize and respond to possible objections to your argument.

> For many American workers, drug testing is a routine part of their working life. In her book *Nickel and Dimed*, Barbara Ehrenreich observes how random drug testing leads to a hostile work environment (128). In addition, researchers Shepard and Clifton have found that companies using drug-testing programs are likelier to have lower productivity levels than those that have not adopted such practices (1). *Consider* Drug testing in the workplace has shown *opposing* no benefits for employers or employees. *viewpoints*

In response to an assignment about changes in the workplace, one student wrote this body paragraph.

The student jumps to a conclusion too quickly without recognizing any opposing points of view. To revise, the student might begin by reading two or more sources to gain a different perspective and to learn more about the debate surrounding her topic. As she reads more sources, she might ask: What evidence do those in favor of drug testing provide to support their point of view? How would they respond to my conclusion against drug testing? By anticipating and countering opposing views, she will show herself as a fair and reasonable writer.

SIMILAR COMMENTS: *what about the other side?* • *counterargument?*

REVISING WHEN *YOU* NEED TO CONSIDER OTHER POINTS OF VIEW

1. *Read more* to learn about the debates surrounding the topic. Ask questions: Are there other sides to the issue? Would a reasonable person offer an alternative explanation for the evidence?

2. *Be open-minded.* Although it might seem counterintuitive to introduce opposing arguments, you'll show your knowledge of the topic by recognizing that not everyone draws the same conclusion.

3. *Introduce and counter objections* with phrases like these: "Some readers might point out that . . ." or "Critics of this view argue that. . . ."

4. *Revise your thesis,* if necessary, to account for multiple points of view.

More advice on considering opposing viewpoints: 6f and 7c

validity of your argument. For example, to persuade people op-posed to controlling the deer population with a regulated hunt-ing season, a state wildlife commission would have to show that it too cares about preserving deer and does not want them to die needlessly. Having established these values in common, the com-mission might be able to persuade critics that reducing the total number of deer prevents starvation caused by overpopulation.

People believe that intelligence and decency support their side of an argument. To be persuaded, they must see these qualities in your argument. Otherwise they will persist in their opposition.

6h Sample argument paper

In the paper that begins on the next page, student Sam Jacobs argues that the shift from print to online news benefits readers by providing them with new opportunities to produce news and to think more critically as consumers of news. Notice that he is careful to present opposing views fairly before providing his counterarguments.

In writing the paper, Jacobs consulted both print and online sources. When he quotes or uses information from a source, he cites the source with an MLA (Modern Language Association) in-text citation. Citations in the paper refer readers to the list of works cited at the end of the paper. (For more details about citing sources, see 59.)

MODELS hackerhandbooks.com/rules

> Model papers > MLA argument papers: Jacobs; Hammond; Lund;
            Sanghvi
        > MLA research papers: Orlov; Daly; Levi

Jacobs 1

Sam Jacobs

Professor Alperini

English 101

19 March 2010

From Lecture to Conversation: Redefining What's "Fit to Print"

"All the news that's fit to print," the motto of the
New York Times since 1896, plays with the word *fit*,
asserting that a news story must be newsworthy and must

In his opening sentences, Jacobs provides background for his thesis.

not exceed the limits of the printed page. The increase
in online news consumption, however, challenges both
meanings of the word *fit*, allowing producers and consumers
alike to rethink who decides which topics are worth covering
and how extensive that coverage should be. Any cultural
shift usually means that something is lost, but in this

Thesis states the main point.

case there are clear gains. The shift from print to online
news provides unprecedented opportunities for readers to
become more engaged with the news, to hold journalists
accountable, and to participate as producers, not simply
as consumers.

Jacobs does not need a citation for common knowledge.

Guided by journalism's code of ethics—accuracy,
objectivity, and fairness—print news reporters have
gathered and delivered stories according to what editors
decide is fit for their readers. Except for op-ed pages and
letters to the editor, print news has traditionally had a
one-sided relationship with its readers. The print news
media's reputation for objective reporting has been held up
as "a stop sign" for readers, sending a clear message that
no further inquiry is necessary (Weinberger). With the rise
of the Internet, however, this model has been criticized by
journalists such as Dan Gillmor, founder of the Center for
Citizen Media, who argues that traditional print journalism

Marginal annotations indicate MLA-style formatting and effective writing.

Jacobs 2

treats "news as a lecture," whereas online news is "more
of a conversation" (xxiv). Print news arrives on the
doorstep every morning as a fully formed lecture, a
product created without participation from its readership.
By contrast, online news invites readers to participate in a
collaborative process—to question and even help produce
the content.

One of the most important advantages online news
offers over print news is the presence of built-in hyperlinks,
which carry readers from one electronic document to
another. If readers are curious about the definition of a
term, the roots of a story, or other perspectives on a topic,
links provide a path. Links help readers become more critical
consumers of information by engaging them in a totally new
way. For instance, the link embedded in the story "Window
into Fed Debate over a Crucial Program" (Healy) allows
readers to find out more about the trends in consumer
spending and to check the journalist's handling of an
original source (see Fig. 1). This kind of link gives readers
the opportunity to conduct their own evaluation of the
evidence and verify the journalist's claims.

Links provide a kind of transparency impossible in
print because they allow readers to see through online
news to the "sources, disagreements, and the personal
assumptions and values" that may have influenced a news
story (Weinberger). The International Center for Media and
the Public Agenda underscores the importance of news
organizations letting "customers in on the often tightly held
little secrets of journalism." To do so, they suggest, will
lead to "accountability and accountability leads to
credibility" ("Openness"). These tools alone don't guarantee

Transition moves
from Jacobs's main
argument to specific
examples.

Jacobs clarifies key
terms (*transparency*
and *accountability*).

Source is cited in
MLA style.

Jacobs 3

that news producers will be responsible and trustworthy, but they encourage an open and transparent environment that benefits news consumers.

But economists greeted the news with a small cheer because sales excluding automobiles actually grew in September, suggesting that consumer spending was stabilizing.

Over all, retail sales fell 1.5 percent in September from a month earlier, the Commerce Department reported, better than an anticipated decline of 2.1 percent.

Retail sales excluding automobiles and parts grew 0.5 percent, largely because of higher sales at gas stations and grocery stores.

Auto dealers bore the brunt of the month's declines.

Consumers swamped dealerships in late July and August to take advantage of the government's $3 billion cash-for-clunkers program, which offered rebates of up to $4,500 to entice people to swap their older cars for more fuel-efficient models.

Sales at auto dealers surged in August, but fell 11 percent in September.

Sign in to Recommend

A version of this article appeared in print on October 15, 2009, on page B3 of the New York edition.

More Articles in Business »

Timothy Winters / Ian Thomas   CB09-154
Service Sector Statistics Division
(301) 763-2713

U.S. Census Bureau News
U.S. Department of Commerce - Washington, D.C. 20233

FOR IMMEDIATE RELEASE

WEDNESDAY, OCTOBER 14, 2009 AT 8:30 A.M. EDT

INSIDE NY

ADVANCE MONTHLY SALES FOR RETAIL TRADE AND FOOD SERVICES

SEPTEMBER 2009

The U.S. Census Bureau announced today that advance estimates of U.S. retail and food services sales for September, adjusted for seasonal variation and holiday and trading-day differences, but not for price changes, were $344.7 billion, a decrease of 1.5 percent (±0.5%) from the previous month and 5.7 percent (±0.7%) below September 2008. Total sales for the July through September 2009 period were down 6.6 percent (±0.3%) from the same period a year ago. The July to

Fig. 1. Links embedded in online news articles allow readers to move from the main story to original sources, related articles, or background materials. The link in this online article (Healy) points to a government report, the original source of the author's data on consumer spending.

Jacobs 4

Not only has technology allowed readers to become more critical news consumers, but it also has helped some to become news producers. The Web gives ordinary people the power to report on the day's events. Anyone with an Internet connection can publish on blogs and Web sites, engage in online discussion forums, and contribute video and audio recordings. Citizen journalists with laptops, cell phones, and digital camcorders have become news producers alongside large news organizations.

Not everyone embraces the spread of unregulated news reporting online. Critics point out that citizen journalists are not necessarily trained to be fair or ethical, for example, nor are they subject to editorial oversight. Acknowledging that citizen reporting is more immediate and experimental, critics also question its accuracy and accountability: "While it has its place . . . it really isn't journalism at all, and it opens up information flow to the strong probability of fraud and abuse. . . . Information without journalistic standards is called gossip," writes David Hazinski in the *Atlanta Journal-Constitution* (23A). In his book *Losing the News*, media specialist Alex S. Jones argues that what passes for news today is in fact "pseudo news" and is "far less reliable" than traditional print news (27). Even a supporter like Gillmor is willing to agree that citizen journalists are "nonexperts," but he argues that they are "using technology to make a profound contribution, and a real difference" (140).

Citizen reporting made a difference in the wake of Hurricane Katrina in 2005. Armed with cell phones and laptops, regular citizens relayed critical news updates in a rapidly developing crisis, often before traditional journalists were even on the scene. In 2006, the enormous

Jacobs develops the thesis.

Opposing views are presented fairly.

Jacobs counters opposing arguments.

A vivid example helps Jacobs make his point.

Jacobs 5

contributions of citizen journalists were recognized when
the New Orleans *Times-Picayune* received the Pulitzer
Prize in public service for its online coverage—largely

Jacobs uses specific
evidence for support.

citizen-generated—of Hurricane Katrina. In recognizing
the paper's "meritorious public service," the Pulitzer Prize
board credited the newspaper's blog for "heroic, multi-
faceted coverage of [the storm] and its aftermath" ("2006
Pulitzer"). Writing for the *Online Journalism Review*, Mark
Glaser emphasizes the role that blog updates played in
saving storm victims' lives. Further, he calls the *Times-
Picayune*'s partnership with citizen journalists a "watershed
for online journalism."

Conclusion echoes
the thesis without
dully repeating it.

The Internet has enabled consumers to participate
in a new way in reading, questioning, interpreting, and
reporting the news. Decisions about appropriate content
and coverage are no longer exclusively in the hands of news
editors. Ordinary citizens now have a meaningful voice in
the conversation—a hand in deciding what's "fit to print."
Some skeptics worry about the apparent free-for-all and loss
of tradition. But the expanding definition of news provides
opportunities for consumers to be more engaged with events
in their communities, their nations, and the world.

Jacobs 6

Works Cited

Gillmor, Dan. *We the Media: Grassroots Journalism by the People, for the People*. Sebastopol: O'Reilly, 2006. Print.

Glaser, Mark. "NOLA.com Blogs and Forums Help Save Lives after Katrina." *OJR: The Online Journalism Review*. Knight Digital Media Center, 13 Sept. 2005. Web. 2 Mar. 2010.

Hazinski, David. "Unfettered 'Citizen Journalism' Too Risky." *Atlanta Journal-Constitution* 13 Dec. 2007: 23A. *General OneFile*. Web. 2 Mar. 2010.

Healy, Jack. "Window into Fed Debate over a Crucial Program." *New York Times*. New York Times, 14 Oct. 2009. Web. 4 Mar. 2010.

Jones, Alex S. *Losing the News: The Future of the News That Feeds Democracy*. New York: Oxford UP, 2009. Print.

"Openness and Accountability: A Study of Transparency in Global Media Outlets." *ICMPA: International Center for Media and the Public Agenda*. Intl. Center for Media and the Public Agenda, 2006. Web. 26 Feb. 2010.

"The 2006 Pulitzer Prize Winners: Public Service." *The Pulitzer Prizes*. Columbia U, n.d. Web. 2 Mar. 2010.

Weinberger, David. "Transparency Is the New Objectivity." *Joho the Blog*. David Weinberger, 19 July 2009. Web. 26 Feb. 2010.

Works cited page uses MLA style.

List is alphabetized by authors' last names (or by title when a work has no author).

Abbreviation "n.d." indicates that the online source has no update date.

7   Evaluating arguments

In your reading and in your own writing, evaluate all arguments for logic and fairness. Many arguments can stand up to critical scrutiny. Sometimes, however, a line of argument that at first seems reasonable turns out to be illogical, unfair, or both. Recognizing flawed arguments as you read can help you avoid such problems in your own writing.

7a Distinguish between reasonable and fallacious argumentative tactics.

A number of unreasonable argumentative tactics are known as *logical fallacies*. Most of the fallacies — such as hasty generalizations and false analogies — are misguided or dishonest uses of legitimate argumentative strategies. The examples in this section suggest when such strategies are reasonable and when they are not.

Generalizing (inductive reasoning)

Writers and thinkers generalize all the time. We look at a sample of data and conclude that data we have not observed will most likely conform to what we have seen. From a spoonful of soup, we conclude just how salty the whole bowl will be. After numerous unpleasant experiences with an airline, we decide to book future flights with a competitor.

When we draw a conclusion from an array of facts, we are engaged in inductive reasoning. Such reasoning deals in probability, not certainty. For a conclusion to be highly probable, it must be based on evidence that is sufficient, representative, and relevant. (See the chart on p. 104.)

The fallacy known as *hasty generalization* is a conclusion based on insufficient or unrepresentative evidence.

HASTY GENERALIZATION

In a single year, scores on standardized tests in California's public schools rose by ten points. Therefore, more children than ever are succeeding in America's public school systems.

Data from one state do not justify a conclusion about the whole United States.

A *stereotype* is a hasty generalization about a group. Here are a few examples.

STEREOTYPES

Women are bad bosses.

All politicians are corrupt.

Athletes are never strong students.

Stereotyping is common because of our tendency to perceive selectively. We tend to see what we want to see; we notice evidence confirming our already formed opinions and fail to notice evidence to the contrary. For example, if you have concluded that all politicians are corrupt, this stereotype will be confirmed by news reports of legislators being indicted — even though every day the media describe conscientious officials serving the public honestly and well.

> **Academic English** Many hasty generalizations contain words such as *all*, *ever*, *always*, and *never*, when qualifiers such as *most*, *many*, *usually*, and *seldom* would be more accurate.

Drawing analogies

An analogy points out a similarity between two things that are otherwise different. Analogies can be an effective means of arguing a point. Our system of judicial decision making, or case law, which relies heavily on previous decisions, makes extensive use of reasoning by analogy. One lawyer may point out, for example, that specific facts or circumstances resemble those from a previous case and will thus argue for a similar result or decision. In response, the opposing lawyer may maintain that such facts or circumstances bear only a superficial resemblance to those in the previous case and that in legally relevant respects they are quite different and thus require a different result or decision.

It is not always easy to draw the line between a reasonable and an unreasonable analogy. At times, however, an analogy is clearly off base, in which case it is called a *false analogy*.

FALSE ANALOGY

If we can send a spacecraft to Pluto, we should be able to find a cure for the common cold.

The writer has falsely assumed that because two things are alike in one respect, they must be alike in others. Exploring the outer reaches of the solar system and finding a cure for the common cold are both scientific challenges, but the problems confronting medical researchers are quite different from those solved by space scientists.

Testing inductive reasoning

Though inductive reasoning leads to probable and not absolute truth, you can assess a conclusion's likely probability by asking three questions. This chart shows how to apply those questions to a sample conclusion based on a survey.

CONCLUSION The majority of students on our campus would volunteer at least five hours a week in a community organization if the school provided a placement service for volunteers.

EVIDENCE In a recent survey, 723 of 1,215 students questioned said they would volunteer at least five hours a week in a community organization if the school provided a placement service for volunteers.

1. Is the evidence sufficient?

   That depends. On a small campus (say, 3,000 students), the pool of students surveyed would be sufficient for market research, but on a large campus (say, 30,000), 1,215 students are only 4 percent of the population. If that 4 percent were known to be truly representative of the other 96 percent, however, even such a small sample would be sufficient (see question 2).

2. Is the evidence representative?

   The evidence is representative if those responding to the survey reflect the characteristics of the entire student population: age, sex, race, field of study, overall number of extracurricular commitments, and so on. If most of those surveyed are majors in a field like social work, however, the researchers would be wise to question the survey's conclusion.

3. Is the evidence relevant?

   Yes. The results of the survey are directly linked to the conclusion. Evidence based on a survey about the number of hours students work for pay, by contrast, would not be relevant because it would not be about *choosing to volunteer*.

Tracing causes and effects

Demonstrating a connection between causes and effects is rarely simple. For example, to explain why a chemistry course has a high failure rate, you would begin by listing possible causes: inadequate preparation of students, poor teaching, lack of qualified tutors, and so on. Next you would investigate each possible cause. Only after investigating the possible causes would you be able to weigh the relative impact of each cause and suggest appropriate remedies.

Because cause-and-effect reasoning is so complex, it is not surprising that writers frequently oversimplify it. In particular, writers sometimes assume that because one event follows another, the first is the cause of the second. This common fallacy is known as *post hoc*, from the Latin *post hoc, ergo propter hoc*, meaning "after this, therefore because of this."

POST HOC FALLACY

Since Governor Cho took office, unemployment of minorities in the state has decreased by 7 percent. Governor Cho should be applauded for reducing unemployment among minorities.

The writer must show that Governor Cho's policies are responsible for the decrease in unemployment; it is not enough to show that the decrease followed the governor's taking office.

Weighing options

Especially when reasoning about problems and solutions, writers must weigh options. To be fair, a writer should mention the full range of options, showing why one is superior to the others or might work well in combination with others.

It is unfair to suggest that there are only two alternatives when in fact there are more. When writers set up a false choice between their preferred option and one that is clearly unsatisfactory, they create an *either . . . or* fallacy.

EITHER . . . OR FALLACY

Our current war against drugs has not worked. Either we should legalize drugs or we should turn the drug war over to our armed forces and let them fight it.

Clearly there are other options, such as increased funding for drug abuse prevention and treatment.

Making assumptions

An assumption is a claim that is taken to be true — without the need of proof. Most arguments are based to some extent on assumptions, since writers rarely have the time and space to prove all the conceivable claims on which an argument is based. For example, someone arguing about the best means of limiting population growth in developing countries might well assume that the goal of limiting population growth is worthwhile. For most audiences, there would be no need to articulate this assumption or to defend it.

There is a danger, however, in failing to spell out and prove a claim that is clearly controversial. Consider the following short argument, in which a key claim is missing.

ARGUMENT WITH MISSING CLAIM

Violent crime is increasing. Therefore, we should vigorously enforce the death penalty.

The writer seems to be assuming that the death penalty deters violent criminals — and that most audiences will agree. The writer also assumes that the death penalty is a fair punishment for violent crimes. These are not safe assumptions; the writer will need to state and support both claims.

When a missing claim is an assertion that few would agree with, we say that a writer is guilty of a *non sequitur* (Latin for "it does not follow").

NON SEQUITUR

Christopher gets plenty of sleep; therefore he will be a successful student in the university's pre-med program.

Few people would agree with the missing claim — that people with good sleep habits always make successful students.

Deducing conclusions (deductive reasoning)

When we deduce a conclusion, we — like Sherlock Holmes — put things together. We establish that a general principle is true, that a specific case is an example of that principle, and that therefore a particular conclusion about that case is a certainty. In real life, such absolute reasoning rarely happens. Approximations of it, however, sometimes occur.

Deductive reasoning can often be structured in a three-step argument called a *syllogism*. The three steps are the major premise, the minor premise, and the conclusion.

1. Anything that increases radiation in the environment is dangerous to public health. (Major premise)
2. Nuclear reactors increase radiation in the environment. (Minor premise)
3. Therefore, nuclear reactors are dangerous to public health. (Conclusion)

The major premise is a generalization. The minor premise is a specific case. The conclusion follows from applying the generalization to the specific case.

Deductive arguments break down if one of the premises is not true or if the conclusion does not logically follow from the premises. In the following argument, the major premise is very likely untrue.

UNTRUE PREMISE

The police do not give speeding tickets to people driving less than five miles per hour over the limit. Dominic is driving fifty-nine miles per hour in a fifty-five-mile-per-hour zone. Therefore, the police will not give Dominic a speeding ticket.

The conclusion is true only if the premises are true. If the police sometimes give speeding tickets for driving less than five miles per hour over the limit, Dominic cannot safely conclude that he will avoid a ticket.

In the following argument, both premises might be true, but the conclusion does not follow logically from them.

CONCLUSION DOES NOT FOLLOW

All members of our club ran in this year's Boston Marathon. Jay ran in this year's Boston Marathon. Therefore, Jay is a member of our club.

The fact that Jay ran the marathon is no guarantee that he is a member of the club. Presumably, many marathon runners are nonmembers.

Assuming that both premises are true, the following argument holds up.

CONCLUSION FOLLOWS

All members of our club ran in this year's Boston Marathon. Jay is a member of our club. Therefore, Jay ran in this year's Boston Marathon.

7b Distinguish between legitimate and unfair emotional appeals.

There is nothing wrong with appealing to readers' emotions. After all, many issues worth arguing about have an emotional as well as a logical dimension. Even the Greek logician Aristotle lists *pathos* (emotion) as a legitimate argumentative tactic. For example, in an essay criticizing big-box stores, writer Betsy Taylor has a good reason for tugging at readers' emotions: Her subject is the decline of city and town life. In her conclusion, Taylor appeals to readers' emotions by invoking their national pride.

LEGITIMATE EMOTIONAL APPEAL

Is it anti-American to be against having a retail giant set up shop in one's community? Some people would say so. On the other hand, if you board up Main Street, what's left of America?

As we all know, however, emotional appeals are frequently misused. Many of the arguments we see in the media, for instance, strive to win our sympathy rather than our intelligent agreement. A TV commercial suggesting that you will be thin and sexy if you drink a certain diet beverage is making a pitch to emotions. So is a political speech that recommends electing a candidate because he is a devoted husband and father who serves as a volunteer firefighter. The following passage illustrates several types of unfair emotional appeals.

UNFAIR EMOTIONAL APPEALS

This progressive proposal to build a ski resort in the state park has been carefully researched by Western Trust, the largest bank in the state; furthermore, it is favored by a majority of the local merchants. The only opposition comes from narrow-minded, hippie environmentalists who care more about trees than they do about people; one of their leaders was actually arrested for disturbing the peace several years ago.

Words with strong positive or negative connotations, such as *progressive* and *hippie*, are examples of *biased language*. Attacking the people who hold a belief (environmentalists) rather than refuting their argument is called *ad hominem*, a Latin term meaning "to the man." Associating a prestigious name (Western Trust) with the writer's side is called *transfer*. Claiming that an idea should be accepted because a large number of people (the majority of merchants) are in favor is called the *bandwagon appeal*. Bringing in irrelevant issues (the arrest) is a *red herring*, named after a trick used in fox hunts to mislead the dogs by dragging a smelly fish across the trail.

7c Judge how fairly a writer handles opposing views.

The way in which a writer deals with opposing views is revealing. Some writers address the arguments of the opposition fairly, conceding points when necessary and countering others, all in a civil spirit. Other writers will do almost anything to win an argument: either ignoring opposing views altogether or misrepresenting such views and attacking their proponents.

In your own writing, you build credibility by addressing opposing arguments fairly. (See also 6f.) In your reading, you can assess the credibility of your sources by looking at how they deal with views not in agreement with their own.

Describing the views of others

Writers and politicians often deliberately misrepresent the views of others. One way they do this is by setting up a "straw man," a character so weak that he is easily knocked down. The *straw man* fallacy consists of an oversimplification or outright distortion of opposing views. For example, in a California debate over attempts to control the mountain lion population, pro-lion groups characterized their opponents as trophy hunters bent on shooting harmless lions and sticking them on the walls of their dens. In truth, such hunters were only one faction of those who saw a need to control the lion population.

During the District of Columbia's struggle for voting representation, some politicians set up a straw man, as shown in the following example.

STRAW MAN FALLACY

Washington, DC, residents are lobbying for statehood. Giving a city such as the District of Columbia the status of a state would be unfair.

The straw man wanted statehood. In fact, most District citizens lobbied for voting representation in any form, not necessarily through statehood.

Quoting opposing views

Writers often quote the words of writers who hold opposing views. In general, this is a good idea, for it assures some level of fairness and accuracy. At times, though, both the fairness and the accuracy are an illusion.

A source may be misrepresented when it is quoted out of context. All quotations are to some extent taken out of context, but a fair writer will explain the context to readers. To select a provocative sentence from a source and to ignore the more moderate sentences surrounding it is both unfair and misleading. Sometimes a writer deliberately distorts a source by using ellipsis dots. Ellipsis dots tell readers that words have been omitted from the original source. When those words are crucial to an author's meaning, omitting them is unfair. (See 39d.)

ORIGINAL SOURCE

Johnson's *History of the American West* is riddled with inaccuracies and astonishing in its blatantly racist description of the Indian wars.

— B. R., reviewer

MISLEADING QUOTATION

According to B. R., Johnson's *History of the American West* is "astonishing in its . . . description of the Indian wars."

EXERCISE 7–1   Explain what is illogical in the following brief arguments. It may be helpful to identify the logical fallacy or fallacies by name. Answers to lettered sentences appear in the back of the book.

a. My roommate, who is an engineering major, is taking a course called Structures of Tall Buildings. All engineers have to know how to design tall buildings.

b. If you're old enough to vote, you're old enough to drink. Therefore, the drinking age should be lowered to eighteen.

c. If you're not part of the solution, you're part of the problem.

d. Whenever I wash my car, it rains. I have discovered a way to end all droughts — get all the people to wash their cars.

e. Ninety percent of the students oppose a tuition increase; therefore, the board of trustees should not pass the proposed increase.

Clarity

Grammar

Multilingual Writers and ESL Challenges

Clarity

9/10

11/12

8   Prefer active verbs.

As a rule, choose an active verb and pair it with a subject that names the person or thing doing the action. Active verbs express meaning more emphatically and vigorously than their weaker counterparts — forms of the verb *be* or verbs in the passive voice.

PASSIVE   The pumps *were destroyed* by a surge of power.

***BE* VERB**   A surge of power *was* responsible for the destruction of the pumps.

ACTIVE   A surge of power *destroyed* the pumps.

Verbs in the passive voice lack strength because their subjects receive the action instead of doing it. Forms of the verb *be* (*be, am, is, are, was, were, being, been*) lack vigor because they convey no action.

Although passive verbs and the forms of *be* have legitimate uses, choose an active verb if it can carry your meaning. Even among active verbs, some are more active — and therefore more vigorous and colorful — than others. Carefully selected verbs can energize a piece of writing.

▶   The goalie crouched low, ~~reached~~ out his stick, and ~~sent~~ the
                            swept   *hooked*
                            ^   ^
rebound away from the mouth of the net.

> **Academic English**   Although you may be tempted to avoid the passive voice completely, keep in mind that some writing situations call for it, especially scientific writing. For appropriate uses of the passive voice, see page 113; for advice about forming the passive voice, see 28b and 47c.

8a   Use the active voice unless you have a good reason for choosing the passive.

In the active voice, the subject does the action; in the passive voice, the subject receives the action (see also 47c). Although both voices are grammatically correct, the active voice is usually more effective because it is clearer and more direct.

ACTIVE Hernando *caught* the fly ball.

PASSIVE The fly ball *was caught* by Hernando.

Passive sentences often identify the actor in a *by* phrase, as in the preceding example. Sometimes, however, that phrase is omitted, and who or what is responsible for the action becomes unclear: *The fly ball was caught.*
Most of the time, you will want to emphasize the actor, so you should use the active voice. To replace a passive verb with an active one, make the actor the subject of the sentence.

▶ *The settlers stripped the land of timber before realizing* ~~The land was stripped of timber before the settlers realized~~ the
  ^
  consequences of their actions.

The revision emphasizes the actors (*settlers*) by naming them in the subject.

▶ *The contractor removed the* ~~The~~ debris ~~was removed~~ from the construction site.
  ^
Sometimes the actor does not appear in a passive-voice sentence. To turn such a sentence into the active voice, the writer must determine an appropriate subject, in this case *contractor*.

Appropriate uses of the passive

The passive voice is appropriate if you wish to emphasize the receiver of the action or to minimize the importance of the actor.

APPROPRIATE PASSIVE Many Hawaiians *were forced* to leave their homes after the earthquake.

APPROPRIATE PASSIVE As the time for harvest approaches, the tobacco plants *are sprayed* with a chemical to retard the growth of suckers.

The writer of the first sentence wished to emphasize the receiver of the action, *Hawaiians*. The writer of the second sentence wished to focus on the tobacco plants, not on the people spraying them.
In much scientific writing, the passive voice properly emphasizes the experiment or process being described, not the researcher. Check with your instructor for the preference in your discipline.

APPROPRIATE PASSIVE The solution *was heated* to the boiling point, and then it was reduced in volume by 50%.

8b Replace *be* verbs that result in dull or wordy sentences.

Not every *be* verb needs replacing. The forms of *be* (*be, am, is, are, was, were, being, been*) work well when you want to link a subject to a noun that clearly renames it or to an adjective that describes it: *Orchard House was the home of Louisa May Alcott. The harvest will be bountiful after the summer rains.* And *be* verbs are essential as helping verbs before present participles (*is flying, are disappearing*) to express ongoing action: *Derrick was fighting the fire when his wife went into labor.* (See 27f.)

If using a *be* verb makes a sentence needlessly dull and wordy, however, consider replacing it. Often a phrase following the verb will contain a noun or an adjective (such as *violation, resistant*) that suggests a more vigorous, active verb (*violate, resist*).

▶ Burying nuclear waste in Antarctica would ~~be in violation of~~ *violate* an international treaty.

Violate is less wordy and more vigorous than *be in violation of.*

▶ When Rosa Parks ~~was resistant to~~ *resisted* giving up her seat on the bus, she became a civil rights hero.

Resisted is stronger than *was resistant to.*

8c As a rule, choose a subject that names the person or thing doing the action.

In weak, unemphatic prose, both the actor and the action may be buried in sentence elements other than the subject and the verb. In the following sentence, for example, both the actor and the action appear in prepositional phrases, word groups that do not receive much attention from readers.

WEAK   The institution of the New Deal had the effect of reversing some of the economic inequalities of the Great Depression.

EMPHATIC The New Deal reversed some of the economic inequalities of the Great Depression.

Consider the subjects and verbs of the two versions — *institution had* versus *New Deal reversed*. The latter expresses the writer's point more emphatically.

▶ ~~The use of~~ ᴾ pure oxygen can ~~cause~~ heal~~ing in~~ wounds that are

otherwise untreatable.

In the original sentence, the subject and verb — *use can cause* — express the point blandly. *Pure oxygen can heal* makes the point more emphatically and directly.

EXERCISE 8–1 Revise any weak, unemphatic sentences by replacing *be* verbs or passive verbs with active alternatives and, if necessary, by naming in the subject the person or thing doing the action. Some sentences are emphatic; do not change them. Revisions of lettered sentences appear in the back of the book. Example:

The ranger doused the campfire before giving us
~~The campfire was doused by the ranger before we were given~~

a ticket for unauthorized use of a campsite.

a. The Prussians were victorious over the Saxons in 1745.
b. The entire operation is managed by Ahmed, the producer.
c. The sea kayaks were expertly paddled by the tour guides.
d. At the crack of rocket and mortar blasts, I jumped from the top bunk and landed on my buddy below, who was crawling on the floor looking for his boots.
e. There were shouting protesters on the courthouse steps.

1. A strange sound was made in the willow tree by the monkey that had escaped from the zoo.
2. Her letter was in acknowledgment of the student's participation in the literacy program.
3. The bomb bay doors rumbled open, and freezing air whipped through the plane.
4. The work of Paul Oakenfold and Sandra Collins was influential in my choice of music for my audition.
5. The only responsibility I was given by my parents was putting my little brother to bed when they had to work late.

9 Balance parallel ideas.

If two or more ideas are parallel, they are easier to grasp when expressed in parallel grammatical form. Single words should be balanced with single words, phrases with phrases, clauses with clauses.

> A kiss can be a comma, a question mark, or an exclamation point.
> — Mistinguett

> This novel is not to be tossed lightly aside, but to be hurled with great force.
> — Dorothy Parker

> In matters of principle, stand like a rock; in matters of taste, swim with the current.
> — Thomas Jefferson

Writers often use parallelism to create emphasis. (See p. 151.)

9a Balance parallel ideas in a series.

Readers expect items in a series to appear in parallel grammatical form. When one or more of the items violate readers' expectations, a sentence will be needlessly awkward.

▶ Children who study music also learn confidence, discipline, ~~creativity.~~
and ~~they are creative.~~
creativity.

The revision presents all the items in the series as nouns: *confidence*, *discipline*, and *creativity*.

▶ Impressionist painters believed in focusing on ordinary subjects, capturing the effects of light on those subjects, and ~~to use~~ using short brushstrokes.

The revision uses *-ing* forms for all the items in the series: *focusing*, *capturing*, and *using*.

▶ Racing to get to work on time, Sam drove down the middle
                                          ignored
of the road, ran one red light, and two stop signs.
                                    ^
The revision adds a verb to make the three items parallel: *drove, ran,* and *ignored.*

In headings and lists, aim for as much parallelism as the content allows. (See 50b and 50c.)

9b Balance parallel ideas presented as pairs.

When pairing ideas, underscore their connection by expressing them in similar grammatical form. Paired ideas are usually connected in one of these ways:

- with a coordinating conjunction such as *and*, *but*, or *or*
- with a pair of correlative conjunctions such as *either . . . or* or *not only . . . but also*
- with a word introducing a comparison, usually *than* or *as*

Parallel ideas linked with coordinating conjunctions

Coordinating conjunctions (*and, but, or, nor, for, so,* and *yet*) link ideas of equal importance. When those ideas are closely parallel in content, they should be expressed in parallel grammatical form.

▶ Emily Dickinson's poetry features the use of dashes and
   the capitalization of
   ~~capitalizing~~ common words.
   ^
   The revision balances the nouns *use* and *capitalization.*

▶ Many states are reducing property taxes for home owners
      extending
   and ~~extend~~ financial aid in the form of tax credits to renters.
   ^
   The revision balances the verb *reducing* with the verb *extending.*

Parallel ideas linked with correlative conjunctions

Correlative conjunctions come in pairs: *either . . . or, neither . . . nor, not only . . . but also, both . . . and, whether . . . or.* Make sure that the grammatical structure following the second half of the pair is the same as that following the first half.

▶ Thomas Edison was not only a prolific inventor but also ~~was~~ a

successful entrepreneur.

The words *a prolific inventor* follow *not only*, so *a successful entrepreneur* should follow *but also*. Repeating *was* creates an unbalanced effect.

to
▶ The clerk told me either to change my flight or ^ take the train.

To change my flight, which follows *either*, should be balanced with *to take the train*, which follows *or*.

Comparisons linked with *than* or *as*

In comparisons linked with *than* or *as*, the elements being compared should be expressed in parallel grammatical structure.

to ground
▶ It is easier to speak in abstractions than ~~grounding~~ ^ one's thoughts

in reality.

To speak is balanced with *to ground*.

Comparisons should also be logical and complete. (See 10c.)

9c Repeat function words to clarify parallels.

Function words such as prepositions (*by*, *to*) and subordinating conjunctions (*that*, *because*) signal the grammatical nature of the word groups to follow. Although you can sometimes omit them, be sure to include them whenever they signal parallel structures that readers might otherwise miss.

▶ Our study revealed that left-handed students were more likely

that
to have trouble with classroom desks and ^ rearranging desks for

exam periods was useful.

A second subordinating conjunction helps readers sort out the two parallel ideas: *that* left-handed students have trouble with classroom desks and *that* rearranging desks was useful.

EXERCISE 9–1   Edit the following sentences to correct faulty parallelism. Revisions of lettered sentences appear in the back of the book. Example:

> Rowena began her workday by pouring a cup of coffee and
> *checking*
> ~~checked~~ her e-mail.
>   ^

a. Police dogs are used for finding lost children, tracking criminals, and the detection of bombs and illegal drugs.

b. Hannah told her rock-climbing partner that she bought a new harness and of her desire to climb Otter Cliffs.

c. It is more difficult to sustain an exercise program than starting one.

d. During basic training, I was not only told what to do but also what to think.

e. Jan wanted to drive to the wine country or at least Sausalito.

1. Camp activities include fishing trips, dance lessons, and computers.

2. Arriving at Lake Powell in a thunderstorm, the campers found it safer to remain in their cars than setting up their tents.

3. The streets were not only too steep but also were too narrow for anything other than pedestrian traffic.

4. More digital artists in the show are from the South Shore than the North Shore.

5. To load her toolbox, Anika the Clown gathered hats of different sizes, put in two tubes of face paint, arranged a bundle of extra-long straws, added a bag of colored balloons, and a battery-powered hair dryer.

10   Add needed words.

Sometimes writers leave out words intentionally, and the meaning of the sentence is not affected. But leaving out words can occasionally cause confusion for readers or make the sentence ungrammatical. Readers need to see at a glance how the parts of a sentence are connected.

PRACTICE hackerhandbooks.com/rules
  > Clarity > 9–2 to 9–5

MULTILINGUAL Languages sometimes differ in the need for certain words. In particular, be alert for missing articles, verbs, subjects, or expletives. See 29, 30a, and 30b.

10a Add words needed to complete compound structures.

In compound structures, words are often left out for economy: *Tom is a man who means what he says and [who] says what he means.* Such omissions are acceptable as long as the omitted words are common to both parts of the compound structure.

If a sentence defies grammar or idiom because an omitted word is not common to both parts of the compound structure, the simplest solution is to put the word back in.

▶ Successful advertisers target customers whom they identify
who
through demographic research or have purchased their product
^
in the past.

The word *who* must be included because *whom . . . have purchased* is not grammatically correct.

accepted
▶ Mayor Davis never has and never will accept a bribe.
^
Has . . . accept is not grammatically correct.

in
▶ Many South Pacific islanders still believe and live by ancient laws.
^
Believe . . . by is not idiomatic in English. (For a list of common idioms, see 18d.)

NOTE: Even when the omitted word is common to both parts of the compound structure, occasionally it must be inserted to avoid ambiguity.

My favorite *professor* and *mentor* influenced my choice of a career. [Professor and mentor are the same person.]

My favorite *professor* and *my mentor* influenced my choice of a career. [Professor and mentor are two different people; *my* must be repeated.]

10b Add the word *that* if there is any danger of misreading without it.

If there is no danger of misreading, the word *that* may be omitted when it introduces a subordinate clause. *The value of a principle is the number of things [that] it will explain.* Occasionally, however, a sentence might be misread without *that.*

▶ In his famous obedience experiments, psychologist Stanley
        that
  Milgram discovered ordinary people were willing to inflict
                    ^
  physical pain on strangers.

  Milgram didn't discover ordinary people; he discovered that ordinary people were willing to inflict pain on strangers. The word *that* tells readers to expect a clause, not just *ordinary people*, as the direct object of *discovered.*

10c Add words needed to make comparisons logical and complete.

Comparisons should be made between items that are alike. To compare unlike items is illogical and distracting.

▶ The forests of North America are much more extensive than
  those of
  Europe.
  ^
  Forests must be compared with forests, not with all of Europe.

                                            | *died*
▶ ~~The death rate of~~ *I*nfantry soldiers in the Vietnam War ~~was~~
  at a   *rate*   ^
  much higher than the other combat troops.
  ^   ^
  The death rate cannot logically be compared to troops. The writer could revise the sentence by inserting *that of* after *than*, but the preceding revision is more concise.

▶ Some say that Ella Fitzgerald's renditions of Cole Porter's
                                    singer's.
  songs are better than any other ~~singer.~~
                                  ^
  Ella Fitzgerald's renditions cannot logically be compared with a singer. The revision uses the possessive form *singer's*, with the word *renditions* being implied.

Sometimes the word *other* must be inserted to make a comparison logical.

►   *other*
Jupiter is larger than any ʌ planet in our solar system.

Jupiter is a planet, and it cannot be larger than itself.

Sometimes the word *as* must be inserted to make a comparison grammatically complete.

►   *as*
The city of Lowell is as old, if not older than, the neighboring
ʌ

city of Lawrence.

The construction *as old* is not complete without a second *as: as old as . . . the neighboring city of Lawrence.*

Comparisons should be complete enough to ensure clarity. The reader should understand what is being compared.

INCOMPLETE   Brand X is less salty.

COMPLETE   Brand X is less salty than Brand Y.

Finally, comparisons should leave no ambiguity for readers. If more than one interpretation is possible, revise the sentence to state clearly which interpretation you intend. In the following ambiguous sentence, two interpretations are possible.

AMBIGUOUS   Ken helped me more than my roommate.

CLEAR   Ken helped me more than *he helped* my roommate.

CLEAR   Ken helped me more than my roommate *did.*

10d Add the articles *a, an,* and *the* where necessary for grammatical completeness.

It is not always necessary to repeat articles with paired items: *We bought a computer and printer.* However, if one of the items requires *a* and the other requires *an,* both articles must be included.

►   *an*
We bought a computer and antivirus program.
ʌ

Articles are sometimes omitted in recipes and other instructions that are meant to be followed while they are being

read. In nearly all other forms of writing, whether formal or informal, such omissions are inappropriate.

MULTILINGUAL Choosing and using articles can be challenging for
multilingual writers. See 29.

EXERCISE 10–1 Add any words needed for grammatical or logical
completeness in the following sentences. Revisions of lettered sentences
appear in the back of the book. Example:

that

The officer feared the prisoner would escape.
                     ^

a. A grapefruit or orange is a good source of vitamin C.
b. The women entering VMI can expect haircuts as short as the
   male cadets.
c. Looking out the family room window, Sarah saw her favorite tree,
   which she had climbed as a child, was gone.
d. The graphic designers are interested and knowledgeable about
   producing posters for the balloon race.
e. The Great Barrier Reef is larger than any coral reef in the world.

1. Very few black doctors were allowed to serve in the Civil War, and
   their qualifications had to be higher than white doctors.
2. Rachel is interested and committed to working at a school in Ecuador next semester.
3. Vassily likes mathematics more than his teacher.
4. The inspection team saw many historic buildings had been damaged
   by the earthquake.
5. Lila knows seven languages, but she found English harder to learn
   than any language.

Untangle mixed constructions.

A mixed construction contains sentence parts that do not sensibly fit together. The mismatch may be a matter of grammar or
of logic.

11a Untangle the grammatical structure.

Once you begin a sentence, your choices are limited by the range of grammatical patterns in English. (See 47 and 48.) You cannot begin with one grammatical plan and switch without warning to another. Often you must rethink the purpose of the sentence and revise.

MIXED   For most drivers who have a blood alcohol content of .05 percent double their risk of causing an accident.

The writer begins the sentence with a long prepositional phrase and makes it the subject of the verb *double*. But a prepositional phrase can serve only as a modifier; it cannot be the subject of a sentence.

REVISED   For most drivers who have a blood alcohol content of .05 percent, the risk of causing an accident is doubled.

REVISED   Most drivers who have a blood alcohol content of .05 percent double their risk of causing an accident.

In the first revision, the writer begins with the prepositional phrase and finishes the sentence with a proper subject and verb (*risk . . . is doubled*). In the second revision, the writer stays with the original verb (*double*) and heads into the sentence another way, making *drivers* the subject of *double*.

> *Electing*
> ▶ ~~When the country elects~~ a president is the most important
>   ^
> responsibility in a democracy.

The adverb clause *When the country elects a president* cannot serve as the subject of the verb *is*. The revision replaces the adverb clause with a gerund phrase, a word group that can function as a subject. (See 48e and 48b.)

▶ Although the United States is one of the wealthiest nations in

the world, ~~but~~ more than twelve million of our children live

in poverty.

The coordinating conjunction *but* cannot link a subordinate clause (*Although the United States . . .*) with an independent clause (*more than twelve million of our children live in poverty*).

Occasionally a mixed construction is so tangled that it defies grammatical analysis. When this happens, back away from the sentence, rethink what you want to say, and then rewrite the sentence.

MIXED   In the whole-word method, children learn to recognize entire words rather than by the phonics method in which they learn to sound out letters and groups of letters.

REVISED   The whole-word method teaches children to recognize entire words; the phonics method teaches them to sound out letters and groups of letters.

MULTILINGUAL English does not allow double subjects, nor does it allow an object or an adverb to be repeated in an adjective clause. Unlike some other languages, English does not allow a noun and a pronoun to be repeated in a sentence if they have the same grammatical function. See 30c and 30d.

▶ My father ~~he~~ moved to Peru before he met my mother.

the final exam
▶ ~~The final exam~~ I should really study for ~~it~~ to pass the
                                              ^

course.

11b Straighten out the logical connections.

The subject and the predicate (the verb and its modifiers) should make sense together; when they don't, the error is known as *faulty predication*.

Tiffany
▶ We decided that ~~Tiffany's welfare~~ would not be safe living with
                               ^

her mother.

Tiffany, not her welfare, may not be safe.

double personal exemption for the
▶ Under the revised plan, the elderly, ~~who now receive a double~~
                                     ^

~~personal exemption,~~ will be abolished.

The exemption, not the elderly, will be abolished.

An appositive is a noun that renames a nearby noun. When an appositive and the noun it renames are not logically equivalent, the error is known as *faulty apposition*. (See 48c.)

> *Tax accounting,*
> ~~The tax accountant,~~ a very lucrative profession, requires
>   ^
>
> intelligence, patience, and attention to mathematical detail.

The tax accountant is a person, not a profession.

11c Avoid *is when, is where,* and *reason . . . is because* constructions.

In formal English, readers sometimes object to *is when, is where,* and *reason . . . is because* constructions on grammatical or logical grounds.

> The ~~reason the~~ experiment failed ~~is~~ because conditions in the lab
>
> were not sterile.

Grammatically, the verb *is* should not be followed by an adverb clause beginning with *because.* (See 62b and 62e.) The writer might have changed *because* to *that* (*The reason the experiment failed is that conditions in the lab were not sterile*), but the preceding revision is more concise.

> *a disorder suffered by people who*
> Anorexia nervosa is ~~where people~~ think they are too fat and diet
>   ^
>
> to the point of starvation.

Where refers to places. Anorexia nervosa is a disorder, not a place.

EXERCISE 11–1   Edit the following sentences to untangle mixed constructions. Revisions of lettered sentences appear in the back of the book. Example:

> *Taking*
> ~~By taking~~ the oath of allegiance made Ling a US citizen.
>   ^

a. Using surgical gloves is a precaution now worn by dentists to prevent contact with patients' blood and saliva.

b. A physician, the career my brother is pursuing, requires at least ten years of challenging work.

c. The reason the pharaohs had bad teeth was because tiny particles of sand found their way into Egyptian bread.

d. Recurring bouts of flu among team members set a record for number of games forfeited.

e. In this box contains the key to your future.

1. Early diagnosis of prostate cancer is often curable.

2. Depending on our method of travel and our destination determines how many suitcases we are allowed to pack.

3. Dyslexia is where people have a learning disorder that impairs reading ability.

4. Even though Ellen had heard French spoken all her life, yet she could not speak it.

5. In understanding artificial intelligence code is a critical skill for computer game designers.

12 Repair misplaced and dangling modifiers.

Modifiers, whether they are single words, phrases, or clauses, should point clearly to the words they modify. As a rule, related words should be kept together.

12a Put limiting modifiers in front of the words they modify.

Limiting modifiers such as *only*, *even*, *almost*, *nearly*, and *just* should appear in front of a verb only if they modify the verb: *At first, I couldn't even touch my toes, much less grasp them.* If they limit the meaning of some other word in the sentence, they should be placed in front of that word.

▶ St. Vitus Cathedral, commissioned by Charles IV in the mid-
  almost
  fourteenth century, ~~almost~~ took six centuries to complete.

Almost limits the meaning of *six centuries*, not *took*.

▶ If you ~~just~~ *just* interview chemistry majors, your picture of the
^

student body's response to the new grading policies will

be incomplete.

The adverb *just* limits the meaning of *chemistry majors*, not *interview*.

When the limiting modifier *not* is misplaced, the sentence usually suggests a meaning the writer did not intend.

▶ In the United States in 1860, all black southerners were ~~not~~ *not*
^

slaves.

The original sentence says that no black southerners were slaves. The revision makes the writer's real meaning clear: Some (but not all) black southerners were slaves.

12b Place phrases and clauses so that readers can see at a glance what they modify.

Although phrases and clauses can appear at some distance from the words they modify, you will want to make sure your meaning is clear. When phrases or clauses are oddly placed, absurd misreadings can result.

MISPLACED The soccer player returned to the clinic where he had undergone emergency surgery in 2004 in a limousine sent by Adidas.

REVISED Traveling in a limousine sent by Adidas, the soccer player returned to the clinic where he had undergone emergency surgery in 2004.

The revision corrects the false impression that the soccer player underwent emergency surgery in a limousine.

▶ *On the walls* ~~There~~ are many pictures of comedians who have performed
^

at Gavin's. ~~on the walls.~~
^

The comedians weren't performing on the walls; the pictures were on the walls.

> *170-pound,*
> The robber was described as a six-foot-tall man with a heavy
> ^
> mustache. ~~weighing 170 pounds.~~
> ^

The robber, not the mustache, weighed 170 pounds.

Occasionally the placement of a modifier leads to an ambiguity—a squinting modifier. In such a case, two revisions will be possible, depending on the writer's intended meaning.

AMBIGUOUS   The exchange students we met for coffee occasionally questioned us about our latest slang.

CLEAR   The exchange students we occasionally met for coffee questioned us about our latest slang.

CLEAR   The exchange students we met for coffee questioned us occasionally about our latest slang.

In the original version, it was not clear whether the meeting or the questioning happened occasionally. Both revisions eliminate the ambiguity.

12c Move awkwardly placed modifiers.

As a rule, a sentence should flow from subject to verb to object, without lengthy detours along the way. When a long adverbial word group separates a subject from its verb, a verb from its object, or a helping verb from its main verb, the result is often awkward.

> *A*   *Hong Kong*
> ~~Hong Kong,~~ after more than 150 years of British rule, was
> ^   ^
> transferred back to Chinese control in 1997.

There is no reason to separate the subject, *Hong Kong*, from the verb, *was transferred*, with a long phrase.

MULTILINGUAL English does not allow an adverb to appear between a verb and its object. See 30f.

> *easily*
> Yolanda lifted ~~easily~~ the fifty-pound weight.
> ^

12d Avoid split infinitives when they are awkward.

An infinitive consists of *to* plus the base form of a verb: *to think, to breathe, to dance.* When a modifier appears between *to* and the verb, an infinitive is said to be "split": *to carefully balance, to completely understand.* When a long word or a phrase appears between the parts of the infinitive, the result is usually awkward.

> *If possible, the*
> ~~The~~ patient should try to ~~if possible~~ avoid going up and
> ^
> down stairs.

Attempts to avoid split infinitives can result in equally awkward sentences. When alternative phrasing sounds unnatural, most experts allow — and even encourage — splitting the infinitive.

AWKWARD　We decided actually to enforce the law.

BETTER　We decided to actually enforce the law.

At times, neither the split infinitive nor its alternative sounds particularly awkward. In such situations, it is usually better not to split the infinitive, especially in formal writing.

> Nursing students learn to ~~accurately~~ record a patient's vital
>   *accurately.*
> signs/
>   ^

EXERCISE 12–1　Edit the following sentences to correct misplaced or awkwardly placed modifiers. Revisions of lettered sentences appear in the back of the book. Example:

> *in a telephone survey*
> Answering questions can be annoying. ~~in a telephone survey.~~
>   ^   ^

a. More research is needed to effectively evaluate the risks posed by volcanoes in the Pacific Northwest.

b. Many students graduate with debt from college totaling more than fifty thousand dollars.

c. It is a myth that humans only use 10 percent of their brains.

d. A coolhunter is a person who can find in the unnoticed corners of modern society the next wave of fashion.

e. All geese do not fly beyond Narragansett for the winter.

1. The flood nearly displaced half of the city's residents, who packed into several overcrowded shelters.

2. Most lions at night hunt for medium-size prey, such as zebra.

3. Several recent studies have encouraged heart patients to more carefully watch their cholesterol levels.

4. The garden's centerpiece is a huge sculpture that was carved by three women called *Walking in Place*.

5. The old Marlboro ads depicted a man on a horse smoking a cigarette.

12e Repair dangling modifiers.

A dangling modifier fails to refer logically to any word in the sentence. Dangling modifiers are easy to repair, but they can be hard to recognize, especially in your own writing.

Recognizing dangling modifiers

Dangling modifiers are usually word groups (such as verbal phrases) that suggest but do not name an actor. When a sentence opens with such a modifier, readers expect the subject of the next clause to name the actor. If it doesn't, the modifier dangles.

▶ Understanding the need to create checks and balances on power,
the framers of
the Constitution divided the government into three branches.
^

The framers of the Constitution (not the document itself) understood the need for checks and balances.

▶ After completing seminary training, *women have often been denied* ~~women's~~ access to the
^
priesthood. ~~has often been denied.~~
^
Women (not their access to the priesthood) complete the training.

The following sentences illustrate four common kinds of dangling modifiers.

DANGLING *Deciding to join the navy*, the recruiter enthusiastically pumped Joe's hand. [Participial phrase]

DANGLING *Upon entering the doctor's office*, a skeleton caught my attention. [Preposition followed by a gerund phrase]

DANGLING *To satisfy her mother*, the piano had to be practiced every day. [Infinitive phrase]

DANGLING *Though not eligible for the clinical trial*, the doctor was willing to prescribe the drug for Ethan on compassionate grounds. [Elliptical clause with an understood subject and verb]

These dangling modifiers falsely suggest that the recruiter decided to join the navy, that the skeleton entered the doctor's office, that the piano intended to satisfy the mother, and that the doctor was not eligible for the clinical trial.

Although most readers will understand the writer's intended meaning in such sentences, the inadvertent humor can be distracting.

Repairing dangling modifiers

To repair a dangling modifier, you can revise the sentence in one of two ways:

- Name the actor in the subject of the sentence.
- Name the actor in the modifier.

Depending on your sentence, one of these revision strategies may be more appropriate than the other.

ACTOR NAMED IN SUBJECT

▶ Upon entering the doctor's office, a skeleton. ~~caught my~~
     I noticed
     ^   ^
~~attention.~~

▶ To satisfy her mother, the piano ~~had to be practiced~~ every day.
     Jing-mei had to practice
     ^

Checking for dangling modifiers

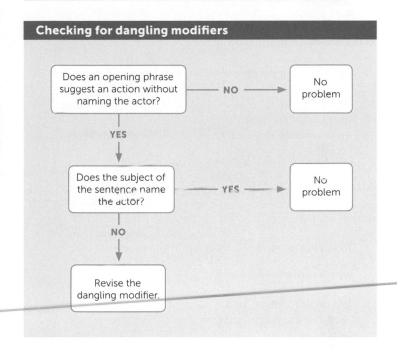

Does an opening phrase suggest an action without naming the actor? — NO → No problem

YES
↓

Does the subject of the sentence name the actor? — YES → No problem

NO
↓

Revise the dangling modifier.

ACTOR NAMED IN MODIFIER

When Joe decided
► ~~Deciding~~ to join the navy, the recruiter enthusiastically
        ^   *his*
pumped ~~Joe's~~ hand.
        ^

        Ethan was
► Though not eligible for the clinical trial, the doctor was
        ^   *him*
willing to prescribe the drug for ~~Ethan~~ on compassionate
                                   ^
grounds.

NOTE: You cannot repair a dangling modifier just by moving it. Consider, for example, the sentence about the skeleton. If you put the modifier at the end of the sentence (*A skeleton caught my attention upon entering the doctor's office*), you are still suggesting — absurdly, of course — that the skeleton entered the office. The only way to avoid the problem is to put the word *I* in the sentence, either as the subject or in the modifier.

► Upon entering the doctor's office, a skeleton. *I noticed* ~~caught my~~
   ^   ^
~~attention.~~

As I entered
► ~~Upon entering~~ the doctor's office, a skeleton caught my
   ^
attention.

EXERCISE 12–2 Edit the following sentences to correct dangling modifiers. Most sentences can be revised in more than one way. Revisions of lettered sentences appear in the back of the book. Example:

a student must complete
To acquire a degree in almost any field, two science courses.
                                         ^   ^
~~must be completed.~~

a. Though only sixteen, UCLA accepted Martha's application.
b. To replace the gear mechanism, attached is a form to order the part by mail.
c. Settled in the cockpit, the pounding of the engine was muffled only slightly by my helmet.
d. After studying polymer chemistry, computer games seemed less complex to Phuong.
e. When a young man, my mother enrolled me in tap dance classes.

1. While working as a ranger in Everglades National Park, a Florida panther crossed the road in front of my truck one night.
2. By following the new recycling procedure, the city's landfill costs will be reduced significantly.
3. Serving as president of the missionary circle, one of Sophia's duties is to raise money for the church.
4. After buying an album by Ali Farka Toure, the rich and rolling rhythms of Malian music made more sense to Silas.
5. Opening the window to let out a huge bumblebee, the car swerved into an oncoming truck.

13 Eliminate distracting shifts.

The following sections can help you avoid unnecessary shifts that might distract or confuse your readers: shifts in point of view, in verb tense, in mood or voice, or from indirect to direct questions or quotations.

13a Make the point of view consistent in person and number.

The point of view of a piece of writing is the perspective from which it is written: first person (*I* or *we*), second person (*you*), or third person (*he, she, it, one, they*, or any noun).

The *I* (or *we*) point of view, which emphasizes the writer, is a good choice for informal letters and writing based primarily on personal experience. The *you* point of view, which emphasizes the reader, works well for giving advice or explaining how to do something. The third-person point of view, which emphasizes the subject, is appropriate in formal academic and professional writing.

Writers who are having difficulty settling on an appropriate point of view sometimes shift confusingly from one to another. The solution is to choose a suitable perspective and then stay with it.

> Our class practiced rescuing a victim trapped in a wrecked car.
> We learned to dismantle the car with the essential tools. ~~You~~
>   We
> were graded on ~~your~~ speed and ~~your~~ skill in freeing the victim.
>   our   our

The writer should have stayed with the *we* point of view. *You* is inappropriate because the writer is not addressing readers directly. *You* should not be used in a vague sense meaning "anyone." (See 23d.)

> You need
> ~~One needs~~ a password and a credit card number to access the
> database. You will be billed at an hourly rate.

You is an appropriate choice because the writer is giving advice directly to readers.

EXERCISE 13–1   Edit the following paragraph to eliminate distracting shifts in point of view (person and number).

When online dating first became available, many people thought that it would simplify romance. We believed that you could type in a list of criteria — sense of humor, college education, green eyes, good job — and a database would select the perfect mate. Thousands of people signed up for services and filled out their profiles, confident that true love was only a few mouse clicks away. As it turns out, however, virtual dating is no easier than traditional dating. I still have to contact the people I find, exchange e-mails and phone calls, and meet him in the real world. Although a database might produce a list of possibilities and screen out obviously undesirable people, you can't predict chemistry. More often than not, people who seem perfect online just don't click in person. Electronic services do help a single person expand their pool of potential dates, but it's no substitute for the hard work of romance.

13b Maintain consistent verb tenses.

Consistent verb tenses clearly establish the time of the actions being described. When a passage begins in one tense and then shifts without warning and for no reason to another, readers are distracted and confused.

► There was no way I could fight the current and win. Just as I

was losing hope, a stranger ~~jumps~~ *jumped* off a passing boat and

~~swims~~ *swam* toward me.

The writer thought that the present tense (*jumps, swims*) would convey immediacy and drama. But having begun in the past tense (*could fight, was losing*), the writer should follow through in the past tense.

Writers often encounter difficulty with verb tenses when writing about literature. Because fictional events occur outside the time frames of real life, the past tense and the present tense may seem equally appropriate. The literary convention, however,

is to describe fictional events consistently in the present tense.
(See 69b.)

> The scarlet letter is a punishment sternly placed on Hester's
>
> breast by the community, and yet it ~~was~~ *is* a fanciful and
>
> imaginative product of Hester's own needlework.

EXERCISE 13–2   Edit the following paragraphs to eliminate distracting shifts in tense.

The English colonists who settled in Massachusetts received assistance at first from the local Indian tribes, but by 1675 there had been friction between the English and the Indians for many years. On June 20 of that year, Metacomet, whom the colonists called Philip, leads the Wampanoag tribe in the first of a series of attacks on the colonial settlements. The war, known today as King Philip's War, rages on for more than a year and leaves three thousand Indians and six hundred colonists dead. Metacomet's attempt to retain power in his native land failed. Finally he too is killed, and the victorious colonists sell his wife and children into slavery.

The Indians did not leave records of their encounters with the English settlers, but the settlers recorded some of their experiences at the hands of the Indians. One of the few accounts to survive was written by a captured colonist, Mrs. Mary Rowlandson. She is a minister's wife who is kidnapped by an Indian war party and held captive for eleven weeks in 1676. Her history, *A Narrative of the Captivity and Restoration of Mrs. Mary Rowlandson*, tells the story of her experiences with the Wampanoags. Although it did not paint a completely balanced picture of the Indians, Rowlandson's narrative, which is considered a classic early American text, showed its author to be a keen observer of life in an Indian camp.

13c Make verbs consistent in mood and voice.

Unnecessary shifts in the mood of a verb can be distracting and confusing to readers. There are three moods in English: the *indicative,* used for facts, opinions, and questions; the *imperative,* used for orders or advice; and the *subjunctive,* used in certain contexts to express wishes or conditions contrary to fact (see 27g).

The following passage shifts confusingly from the indicative to the imperative mood.

> The counselor advised us to spread out our core requirements
>
>   *She also suggested that we*
> over two or three semesters. ~~Also,~~ pay attention to pre-
>   ^
> requisites for elective courses.

The writer began by reporting the counselor's advice in the indicative mood (*counselor advised*) and switched to the imperative mood (*pay attention*); the revision puts both sentences in the indicative.

A verb may be in either the active voice (with the subject doing the action) or the passive voice (with the subject receiving the action). (See 8a.) If a writer shifts without warning from one to the other, readers may be left wondering why.

>   *gives it*
> Each student completes a self-assessment /, ~~The self-assessment~~
>   ^
>   *exchanges*
> ~~is then given~~ to the teacher, and a copy ~~is exchanged~~ with
>   ^   ^
> a classmate.

Because the passage began in the active voice (*student completes*) and then switched to the passive (*self-assessment is given, copy is exchanged*), readers are left wondering who gives the self-assessment to the teacher and the classmate. The active voice, which is clearer and more direct, leaves no ambiguity.

13d   Avoid sudden shifts from indirect to direct questions or quotations.

An indirect question reports a question without asking it: *We asked whether we could visit Miriam.* A direct question asks directly: *Can we visit Miriam?* Sudden shifts from indirect to direct questions are awkward. In addition, sentences containing such shifts are impossible to punctuate because indirect questions must end with a period and direct questions must end with a question mark. (See 38b.)

▶ I wonder whether Karla knew of the theft and, if so, ~~did~~

whether she reported
~~she report~~ it to the police~~?~~.
    ^   ^

The revision poses both questions indirectly. The writer could also ask both questions directly: *Did Karla know of the theft, and, if so, did she report it to the police?*

An indirect quotation reports someone's words without quoting word for word: *Annabelle said that she is a Virgo.* A direct quotation presents the exact words of a speaker or writer, set off with quotation marks: *Annabelle said, "I am a Virgo."* Unannounced shifts from indirect to direct quotations are distracting and confusing, especially when the writer fails to insert the necessary quotation marks, as in the following example.

▶ The patient said she had been experiencing heart palpitations

       asked me to   *was*
and ~~please~~ run as many tests as possible to find out what'~~s~~
   ^   ^

~~wrong.~~

The revision reports the patient's words indirectly. The writer also could quote the words directly: *The patient said, "I have been experiencing heart palpitations. Please run as many tests as possible to find out what's wrong."*

EXERCISE 13–3 Edit the following sentences to make the verbs consistent in mood and voice and to eliminate distracting shifts from indirect to direct questions or quotations. Revisions of lettered sentences appear in the back of the book. Example:

As a public relations intern, I wrote press releases, managed
                      fielded all phone calls.
the Web site, and ~~all phone calls were fielded by me.~~
                    ^

a. An incredibly talented musician, Ray Charles mastered R&B, soul, and gospel styles. Even country music was performed well by him.

b. Environmentalists point out that shrimp farming in Southeast Asia is polluting water and making farmlands useless. They warn that action must be taken by governments before it is too late.

c. The samples were observed for five days before we detected any growth.

d. In his famous soliloquy, Hamlet contemplates whether death would be preferable to his difficult life and, if so, is he capable of committing suicide?

e. The lawyer told the judge that Miranda Hale was innocent and allow her to prove the allegations false.

1. When the photographs were taken on the beach at sunset, I intentionally left the foreground out of focus.

2. If the warning sirens sound, evacuate at once. It is not advised that you return to the building until the alarm has stopped.

3. Most baby products warn parents to follow all directions carefully. Also, supervise children closely during use.

4. The advertisement promised that results would be seen in five days or consumers could return the product for a full refund.

5. Investigators need to determine first whether there was a forcible entry and then what was the motive?

EXERCISE 13–4 Edit the following sentences to eliminate distracting shifts. Revisions of lettered sentences appear in the back of the book. Example:

> For many first-year engineering students, adjusting to a
>
> rigorous course load can be so challenging that ~~you~~ *they*
>
> sometimes feel overwhelmed.

a. A courtroom lawyer has more than a touch of theater in their blood.

b. The interviewer asked if we had brought our proof of citizenship and did we bring our passports?

c. The reconnaissance scout often has to make fast decisions and use sophisticated equipment to keep their team from being detected.

d. After the animators finish their scenes, the production designer arranges the clips according to the storyboard. Synchronization notes must also be made for the sound editor and the composer.

e. Madame Defarge is a sinister figure in Dickens's *A Tale of Two Cities*. On a symbolic level, she represents fate; like the Greek Fates, she knitted the fabric of individual destiny.

1. Everyone should protect yourself from the sun, especially on the first day of extensive exposure.

2. Our neighbors told us that the island was being evacuated because of the coming storm. Also, take the northern route to the mainland.
3. Rescue workers put water on her face and lifted her head gently onto a pillow. Finally, she opens her eyes.
4. In my first tai chi class, the instructor asked if I had ever done yoga stretches and did I have good balance?
5. The artist has often been seen as a threat to society, especially when they refuse to conform to conventional standards of taste.

14   Emphasize key ideas.

Within each sentence, emphasize your point by expressing it in the subject and verb of an independent clause, the words that receive the most attention from readers (see 14a–14e).

Within longer stretches of prose, you can draw attention to ideas deserving special emphasis by using a variety of techniques, often involving an unusual twist or some element of surprise (see 14f).

14a Coordinate equal ideas; subordinate minor ideas.

When combining two or more ideas in one sentence, you have two choices: coordination or subordination. Choose coordination to indicate that the ideas are equal or nearly equal in importance. Choose subordination to indicate that one idea is less important than another.

Coordination

Coordination draws attention equally to two or more ideas. To coordinate single words or phrases, join them with a coordinating conjunction or with a pair of correlative conjunctions: *bananas and strawberries; not only a lackluster plot but also inferior acting* (see 46g).

To coordinate independent clauses — word groups that express a complete thought and that can stand alone as a sentence — join them with a comma and a coordinating conjunction or with a semicolon:

, and   , but   , or   , nor

, for   , so   , yet   ;

The semicolon is often accompanied by a conjunctive adverb such as *moreover, furthermore, therefore,* or *however* or by a transitional phrase such as *for example, in other words,* or *as a matter of fact.* (For a longer list, see p. 143.)

Assume, for example, that your intention is to draw equal attention to the following two ideas.

> Social networking Web sites offer ways for people to connect in the virtual world. They do not replace face-to-face forms of social interaction.

To coordinate these ideas, you can join them with a comma and the coordinating conjunction *but* or with a semicolon and the conjunctive adverb *however.*

> Social networking Web sites offer ways for people to connect in the virtual world, but they do not replace face-to-face forms of social interaction.

> Social networking Web sites offer ways for people to connect in the virtual world; however, they do not replace face-to-face forms of social interaction.

It is important to choose a coordinating conjunction or conjunctive adverb appropriate to your meaning. In the preceding example, the two ideas contrast with each other, calling for *but* or *however.* (For specific coordination strategies, see the chart on p. 143.)

Subordination

To give unequal emphasis to two or more ideas, express the major idea in an independent clause and place any minor ideas in subordinate clauses or phrases. (For specific subordination strategies, see the chart on p. 144.)

Let your intended meaning determine which idea you emphasize. Consider the two ideas about social networking Web sites.

> Social networking Web sites offer ways for people to connect in the virtual world. They do not replace face-to-face forms of social interaction.

If your purpose is to stress the ways that people can connect in the virtual world rather than the limitations of these connections, subordinate the idea about the limitations.

> Although they do not replace face-to-face forms of social interaction, social networking Web sites offer ways for people to connect in the virtual world.

To focus on the limitations of the virtual world, subordinate the idea about the Web sites.

> Although social networking Web sites offer ways for people to connect in the virtual world, they do not replace face-to-face forms of social interaction.

Using coordination to combine sentences of equal importance

1. Consider using a comma and a coordinating conjunction. (See 32a.)

, and	, but	, or	, nor
, for	, so	, yet	

▶ In Orthodox Jewish funeral ceremonies, the shroud is a simple linen
  and the
  vestment /. ~~The~~ coffin is plain wood.
                    ^

2. Consider using a semicolon with a conjunctive adverb or transitional phrase. (See 34b.)

also	however	next
as a result	in addition	now
besides	in fact	of course
consequently	in other words	otherwise
finally	in the first place	still
for example	meanwhile	then
for instance	moreover	therefore
furthermore	nevertheless	thus

                          moreover, she
▶ Alicia scored well on the SAT /. ~~She also~~ had excellent grades and a
                               ^
  record of community service.

3. Consider using a semicolon alone. (See 34a.)

                        in
▶ In youth we learn /. ~~In~~ age we understand.
                    ^

emph

Using subordination to combine sentences of unequal importance

1. Consider putting the less important idea in a subordinate clause beginning with one of the following words. (See 48e.)

after	before	that	which
although	even though	unless	while
as	if	until	who
as if	since	when	whom
because	so that	where	whose

When
► Elizabeth Cady Stanton proposed a convention to discuss the
   ^

   status of women in America/, Lucretia Mott agreed.
                           ^

2. Consider putting the less important idea in an appositive phrase. (See 48c.)

► Karate, ~~is~~ a discipline based on the philosophy of nonviolence/,
         ^   ^

   ~~It~~ teaches the art of self-defense.

3. Consider putting the less important idea in a participial phrase. (See 48b.)

   Noticing
► ~~I noticed~~ the EpiPen in her tote bag/, I asked her if she has
   ^   ^

   food allergies.

EXERCISE 14–1 Use the coordination or subordination technique in brackets to combine each pair of independent clauses. Revisions of lettered sentences appear in the back of the book. Example:

Ted Williams was one of the best hitters in the history of
baseball, but he
~~baseball. He~~ never won a World Series ring. [*Use a comma*
^

and a coordinating conjunction.]

a. Williams played for the Boston Red Sox from 1939 to 1960. He managed the Washington Senators and the Texas Rangers for several years after retiring as a player. [*Use a comma and a coordinating conjunction.*]

b. In 1941, Williams finished the season with a batting average of .406. No player has hit over .400 for a season since then. [*Use a semicolon.*]

c. Williams acknowledged that Joe DiMaggio was a better all-around player. Williams felt that he was a better hitter than DiMaggio. [*Use the subordinating conjunction* although.]

d. Williams was a stubborn man. He always refused to tip his cap to the crowd after a home run because he claimed that fans were fickle. [*Use a semicolon and the transitional phrase* for example.]

e. Williams's relationship with the media was unfriendly at best. He sarcastically called baseball writers the "knights of the keyboard" in his memoir. [*Use a semicolon.*]

1. Williams took time out from his baseball career to serve in the Marines during World War II. He went on active duty a second time during the Korean War. [*Use a semicolon and the transitional phrase* in addition.]

2. Williams was named most valuable player twice in his career. He was listed as the eighth-best baseball player of all time by the *Sporting News* in 1999. [*Use the relative pronoun* who.]

3. Williams hit a home run in his final at bat in September 1960. Then he retired as a player. [*Use a comma and a coordinating conjunction.*]

4. Williams surprised many people with his 1966 Hall of Fame induction speech. It called for recognition of Negro League players and their inclusion in the Hall of Fame. [*Use the relative pronoun* which.]

5. At the 1999 All-Star game, Ted Williams returned to Fenway Park in Boston to throw out the ceremonial first pitch. For the first time he waved his hat to the cheering fans. [*Use a comma and a coordinating conjunction.*]

14b Combine choppy sentences.

Short sentences demand attention, so you should use them primarily for emphasis. Too many short sentences, one after the other, make for a choppy style.

If an idea is not important enough to deserve its own sentence, try combining it with a sentence close by. Put any minor ideas in subordinate structures such as phrases or subordinate clauses. (See 48.)

▶ The Parks Department keeps the use of insecticides to a

        because the
minimum/ ~~The~~ city is concerned about the environment.

The writer wanted to emphasize that the Parks Department minimizes
its use of chemicals, so she put the reason in a subordinate clause
beginning with *because.*

▶ The Chesapeake and Ohio Canal , ~~is~~ a 184-mile waterway
                                       ^

constructed in the 1800s/. ~~It~~ was a major source of
                    ^

transportation for goods during the Civil War.

A minor idea is now expressed in an appositive phrase (*a 184-mile
waterway constructed in the 1800s*).

                 E
▶ ~~Sister Consilio was~~ ḙnveloped in a black robe with only her
              ^   *Sister Consilio*
face and hands visible/. ~~She~~ was an imposing figure.
                ^

Because Sister Consilio's overall impression was more important to
the writer's purpose, the writer put the description of the clothing in a
participial phrase beginning with *Enveloped.*

Although subordination is ordinarily the most effective
technique for combining short, choppy sentences, coordination
is appropriate when the ideas are equal in importance.

                                     and
▶ At 3:30 p.m., Forrest displayed a flag of truce/~~Forrest~~ sent
                                       ^

in a demand for unconditional surrender.

Combining two short sentences by joining their predicates (*displayed . . .
sent*) is an effective coordination technique.

MULTILINGUAL Unlike some other languages, English does not
repeat objects or adverbs in adjective clauses. The relative pronoun
(*that, which, whom*) or relative adverb (*where*) in the adjective clause
represents the object or adverb. See 30d.

▶ The apartment that we rented ~~it~~ needed repairs.

The pronoun *it* cannot repeat the relative pronoun *that.*

▶ The small town where my grandfather was born ~~there~~ is
now a big city.

The adverb *there* cannot repeat the relative adverb *where.*

EXERCISE 14–2 Combine the following sentences by subordinating minor ideas or by coordinating ideas of equal importance. You must decide which ideas are minor because the sentences are given out of context. Revisions of lettered sentences appear in the back of the book. Example:

> Agnes, ~~was~~ another girl I worked with~~.~~/, ~~She~~ was a hyperactive child.

a. The X-Men comic books and Japanese woodcuts of kabuki dancers were part of Marlena's research project on popular culture. They covered the tabletop and the chairs.

b. Our waitress was costumed in a kimono. She had painted her face white. She had arranged her hair in a lacquered beehive.

c. Students can apply for a spot in the leadership program. The program teaches thinking and communication skills.

d. Shore houses were flooded up to the first floor. Beaches were washed away. Brant's Lighthouse was swallowed by the sea.

e. Laura Thackray is an engineer at Volvo Car Corporation. She addressed women's safety needs. She designed a pregnant crash-test dummy.

1. I noticed that the sky was glowing orange and red. I bent down to crawl into the bunker.

2. The Market Inn is located on North Wharf. It doesn't look very impressive from the outside. The food, however, is excellent.

3. He walked up to the pitcher's mound. He dug his toe into the ground. He swung his arm around backward and forward. Then he threw the ball and struck the batter out.

4. Eryn and Maeve have decided to start a business. They have known each other since kindergarten. They will renovate homes for people with disabilities.

5. The first football card set was released by the Goudey Gum Company in 1933. The set featured only three football players. They were Red Grange, Bronko Nagurski, and Knute Rockne.

14c Avoid ineffective or excessive coordination.

Coordinate structures are appropriate only when you intend to draw readers' attention equally to two or more ideas: *Professor Sakellarios praises loudly, and she criticizes softly.* If one idea is more important than another — or if a coordinating conjunction does not clearly signal the relationship between the ideas — you should subordinate the less important idea.

> **INEFFECTIVE**   Closets were taxed as rooms, and most colonists
> **COORDINATION**   stored their clothes in chests or clothespresses.

> **IMPROVED WITH**   Because closets were taxed as rooms, most colonists
> **SUBORDINATION**   stored their clothes in chests or clothespresses.

Because it is so easy to string ideas together with *and*, writers often rely too heavily on coordination in their rough drafts. The cure for excessive coordination is simple: Look for opportunities to tuck minor ideas into subordinate clauses or phrases.

> *After four hours,*
> ▶ ~~Four hours went by, and~~ a rescue truck finally arrived, but
>   ^
>
> by that time we had been evacuated in a helicopter.

Three independent clauses were excessive. The least important idea has become a prepositional phrase.

EXERCISE 14–3   The following sentences show coordinated ideas (ideas joined with a coordinating conjunction or a semicolon). Restructure the sentences by subordinating minor ideas. You must decide which ideas are minor because the sentences are given out of context. Revisions of lettered sentences appear in the back of the book. Example:

> *where they*
> The rowers returned to shore, ~~and~~ had a party on the beach
>   ^
> *to celebrate*
> ~~and celebrated~~ the start of the season.
> ^

a. These particles are known as "stealth liposomes," and they can hide in the body for a long time without detection.

b. Jan is a competitive gymnast and majors in biology; her goal is to apply her athletic experience and her science degree to a career in sports medicine.

c. Students, textile workers, and labor unions have loudly protested sweatshop abuses, so apparel makers have been forced to examine their labor practices.

d. IRC (Internet relay chat) was developed in a European university; it was created as a way for a group of graduate students to talk about projects from their dorm rooms.

e. The cafeteria's new menu has an international flavor, and it includes everything from enchiladas and pizza to pad thai and sauerbraten.

1. Victor switched on his remote-control lawn mower, and it began to shudder and emit clouds of smoke.

2. Iguanas are dependent on ultraviolet rays from the sun, so in the winter months they must be put under ultraviolet-coated lights that can be purchased at most pet stores.

3. The Civil War Trust was founded in 1991; it spearheads a nation-wide campaign to protect America's Civil War battlefields.

4. We did not expect to receive so many large orders so quickly, and we are short on inventory.

5. Mother spread her love equally among us all, but she made each of us feel special in our own way.

14d Do not subordinate major ideas.

If a sentence buries its major idea in a subordinate construction, readers may not give the idea enough attention. Make sure to express your major idea in an independent clause and to subordinate any minor ideas.

▶ Harry S. Truman, who was the unexpected winner of the 1948 presidential election/. *defeated Thomas E. Dewey.* (revision: *defeated Thomas E. Dewey,*)

The writer wanted to focus on Truman's unexpected victory, but the original sentence buried this information in an adjective clause. The revision puts the more important idea in an independent clause and tucks the less important idea into an adjective clause (*who defeated Thomas E. Dewey*).

▶ *As* I was driving home from my new job, heading down Ranchitos Road, ~~when~~ my car suddenly overheated.

The writer wanted to emphasize that the car overheated, not the fact of driving home. The revision expresses the major idea in an independent clause and places the less important idea in an adverb clause (*As I was driving home from my new job*).

14e Do not subordinate excessively.

In attempting to avoid short, choppy sentences, writers sometimes go to the opposite extreme, putting more subordinate ideas
into a sentence than its structure can bear. If a sentence collapses
of its own weight, occasionally it can be restructured. More often,
however, such sentences must be divided.

> In *Animal Liberation*, Peter Singer argues that animals possess
>
> nervous systems and can feel pain. ~~and that~~ ʜ̂e therefore
>
> believes that "the ethical principle on which human equality
>
> rests requires us to extend equal consideration to animals" (1).

Excessive subordination makes it difficult for the reader to focus on
the quoted passage. By splitting the original sentence into two separate
sentences, the writer draws attention to Peter Singer's main claim, that
humans should give "equal consideration to animals."

EXERCISE 14–4   In each of the following sentences, the idea that the
writer wished to emphasize is buried in a subordinate construction.
Restructure each sentence so that the independent clause expresses the
major idea, as indicated in brackets, and lesser ideas are subordinated.
Revisions of lettered sentences appear in the back of the book. Example:

> *Although*
> Catherine has weathered many hardships, ~~although~~ she has
>
> rarely become discouraged. [*Emphasize that Catherine has*
>
> *rarely become discouraged.*]

a. Gina worked as an aide for the relief agency, distributing food
   and medical supplies. [*Emphasize distributing food and medical
   supplies.*]
b. Janbir spent every Saturday learning tabla drumming, noticing
   with each hour of practice that his memory for complex patterns
   was improving. [*Emphasize Janbir's memory.*]
c. The rotor hit, gouging a hole about an eighth of an inch deep in
   my helmet. [*Emphasize that the rotor gouged a hole in the helmet.*]

   d. My grandfather, who raised his daughters the old-fashioned way, was born eighty years ago in Puerto Rico. [*Emphasize how the grandfather raised his daughters.*]

   e. The Narcan reversed the depressive effect of the drug, saving the patient's life. [*Emphasize that the patient's life was saved.*]

  1. Fatima, who studied Persian miniature painting after college, majored in early childhood education. [*Emphasize Fatima's studies after college.*]

  2. I was losing consciousness when my will to live kicked in. [*Emphasize the will to live.*]

  3. Using a sliding compound miter saw, the carpenter made intricate edges on the cabinets. [*Emphasize the carpenter's use of the saw.*]

  4. Ernie was using origami to solve some tricky manufacturing problems when he decided to leave engineering and become an artist. [*Emphasize Ernie's decision.*]

  5. As the undulating waves glinted in the sun, the paddlers synchronized their strokes. [*Emphasize the brightness of the waves.*]

14f Experiment with techniques for gaining special emphasis.

By experimenting with certain techniques, usually involving some element of surprise, you can draw attention to ideas that deserve special emphasis. Use such techniques sparingly, however, or they will lose their punch. The writer who tries to emphasize everything ends up emphasizing nothing.

Using sentence endings for emphasis

You can highlight an idea simply by withholding it until the end of a sentence. The technique works something like a punch line. In the following example, the sentence's meaning is not revealed until its very last word.

> The only completely consistent people are the dead.
>
>   — Aldous Huxley

Using parallel structure for emphasis

Parallel grammatical structure draws special attention to paired ideas or to items in a series. (See 9.) When parallel ideas are paired, the emphasis falls on words that underscore comparisons or contrasts, especially when they occur at the end of a phrase or clause.

> We must *stop talking* about the *American dream* and *start listening* to the *dreams of Americans.*
> — Reubin Askew

In a parallel series, the emphasis falls at the end, so it is generally best to end with the most dramatic or climactic item in the series.

> Sister Charity enjoyed passing out writing punishments: translate the Ten Commandments into Latin, type a thousand-word essay on good manners, copy the New Testament with a quill pen.
> — Marie Visosky, student

Using an occasional short sentence for emphasis

Too many short sentences in a row will fast become monotonous (see 14b), but an occasional short sentence, when played off against longer sentences in the same passage, will draw attention to an idea.

> The great secret, known to internists and learned early in marriage by internists' wives [or husbands], but still hidden from the general public, is that most things get better by themselves. Most things, in fact, are better by morning.
> — Lewis Thomas

15 Provide some variety.

When a rough draft is filled with too many sentences that begin the same way or have the same structure, try injecting some variety — as long as you can do so without sacrificing clarity or ease of reading.

15a Vary your sentence openings.

Most sentences in English begin with the subject, move to the verb, and continue to the object, with modifiers tucked in along the way or put at the end. For the most part, such sentences are fine. Put too many of them in a row, however, and they become monotonous.

Adverbial modifiers are easily movable when they modify verbs; they can often be inserted ahead of the subject. Such modifiers might be single words, phrases, or clauses.

▶ *Eventually a*
   A few drops of sap ~~eventually~~ began to trickle into the
    ^

   bucket.

Like most adverbs, *eventually* does not need to appear close to the verb it modifies (*began*).

▶ *Just as the sun was coming up, a*
   A pair of black ducks flew over the pond. ~~just as the sun was~~
   ^   ^

   ~~coming up.~~

The adverb clause, which modifies the verb *flew*, is as clear at the beginning of the sentence as it is at the end.

Adjectives and participial phrases can frequently be moved to the beginning of a sentence without loss of clarity.

▶ *Dejected and withdrawn,*
   Edward , ~~dejected and withdrawn,~~ nearly gave up his search
      ^

   for a job.

▶   *A*   *John and I*
   ~~John and I,~~ anticipating a peaceful evening, sat down at the
           ^   ^

   campfire to brew a cup of coffee.

TIP: When beginning a sentence with an adjective or a participial phrase, make sure that the subject of the sentence names the person or thing described in the introductory phrase. If it doesn't, the phrase will dangle. (See 12e.)

15b   Use a variety of sentence structures.

A writer should not rely too heavily on simple sentences and compound sentences, for the effect tends to be both monotonous and choppy. (See 14b and 14c.) Too many complex or compound-complex sentences, however, can be equally monotonous. If your style tends to one or the other extreme, try to achieve a better mix of sentence types.

The major sentence types are illustrated in the following sentences, all taken from Flannery O'Connor's "The King of the Birds," an essay describing the author's pet peafowl.

SIMPLE	Frequently the cock combines the lifting of his tail with the raising of his voice.
COMPOUND	Any chicken's dusting hole is out of place in a flower bed, but the peafowl's hole, being the size of a small crater, is more so.
COMPLEX	The peacock does most of his serious strutting in the spring and summer when he has a full tail to do it with.
COMPOUND-COMPLEX	The cock's plumage requires two years to attain its pattern, and for the rest of his life, this chicken will act as though he designed it himself.

For a fuller discussion of sentence types, see 49a.

15c Try inverting sentences occasionally.

A sentence is inverted if it does not follow the normal subject-verb-object pattern (see 47c). Many inversions sound artificial and should be avoided except in the most formal contexts. But if an inversion sounds natural, it can provide a welcome touch of variety.

> *Opposite the produce section is a*
> ► A refrigerated case of mouthwatering cheeses, is opposite
>
> the produce section; a friendly attendant will cut off just
>
> the amount you want.

The revision inverts the normal subject-verb order by moving the verb, *is*, ahead of its subject, *case*.

> *Set at the top two corners of the stage were huge*
> ► Huge lavender hearts outlined in bright white lights. were
>
> set at the top two corners of the stage.

In the revision, the subject, *hearts*, appears after the verb, *were set*. Notice that the two parts of the verb are also inverted—and separated from each other (*Set . . . were*)—without any awkwardness or loss of meaning.

Inverted sentences are used for emphasis as well as for variety (see 14f).

EXERCISE 15–1 Improve sentence variety in each of the following sentences by using the technique suggested in brackets. Revisions of lettered sentences appear in the back of the book. Example:

> *To protect endangered marine turtles, fishing*
> ~~Fishing~~ crews place turtle excluder devices in fishing nets.
> ^   ^
> ~~to protect endangered marine turtles.~~ [*Begin the sentence*
> *with the adverbial infinitive phrase.*]

a. The exhibits for insects and spiders are across the hall from the fossils exhibit. [*Invert the sentence.*]

b. Sayuri becomes a successful geisha after growing up desperately poor in Japan. [*Move the adverb clause to the beginning of the sentence.*]

c. The 1980 eruption of Mount St. Helens was the deadliest, most destructive volcanic eruption in US history. Researchers believe that a series of nearby earthquakes contributed to the eruption. [*Combine the two sentences into a complex sentence.*]

d. Ice cream typically contains 10 percent milk fat. Premium ice cream may contain up to 16 percent milk fat and has considerably less air in the product. [*Combine the two sentences as a compound sentence.*]

e. The economy may recover more quickly than expected if home values climb. [*Move the adverb clause to the beginning of the sentence.*]

1. The Dust Bowl farmers, looking wearily into the cameras of US government photographers, represented the harshest effects of the Great Depression. [*Move the participial phrase to the beginning of the sentence.*]

2. The Trans Alaska Pipeline was completed in 1977. It has moved more than fifteen billion barrels of oil since 1977. [*Combine the two sentences into a complex sentence.*]

3. Mr. Guo habitually dresses in loose clothing and canvas shoes for his wushu workout. [*Move the adverb to the beginning of the sentence.*]

4. A number of obstacles are strategically placed throughout a firefighter training maze. [*Invert the sentence.*]

5. Ian McKellen is a British actor who made his debut in 1961 and was knighted in 1991, and he played Gandalf in the movie trilogy *The Lord of the Rings*. [*Make a simple sentence. See also 49a.*]

w

EXERCISE 15–2　Edit the following paragraph to increase sentence variety.

Making architectural models is a skill that requires patience and precision. It is an art that illuminates a design. Architects come up with a grand and intricate vision. Draftspersons convert that vision into blueprints. The model maker follows the blueprints. The model maker builds a miniature version of the structure. Modelers can work in traditional materials like wood and clay and paint. Modelers can work in newer materials like Styrofoam and liquid polymers. Some modelers still use cardboard, paper, and glue. Other modelers prefer glue guns, deformable plastic, and thin aluminum and brass wire. The modeler may seem to be making a small mess in the early stages of model building. In the end the modeler has completed a small-scale structure. Architect Rem Koolhaas has insisted that plans reveal the logic of a design. He has argued that models expose the architect's vision. The model maker's art makes this vision real.

16 Tighten wordy sentences.

Long sentences are not necessarily wordy, nor are short sentences always concise. A sentence is wordy if it can be tightened without loss of meaning.

16a Eliminate redundancies.

Writers often repeat themselves unnecessarily, thinking that expressions such as *cooperate together*, *yellow in color*, or *basic essentials* add emphasis to their writing. In reality, such redundancies do just the opposite. There is no need to say the same thing twice.

>   *works*
> Daniel ~~is now employed~~ at a private rehabilitation center
>   ^
> ~~working~~ as a registered physical therapist.

Though modifiers ordinarily add meaning to the words they modify, occasionally they are redundant.

> Sylvia ~~very hurriedly~~ scribbled her name, address, and phone
> number on a greasy napkin.

The word *scribbled* already suggests that Sylvia wrote *very hurriedly*.

▶ Gabriele Muccino's film *The Pursuit of Happyness* tells the

story of a single father determined ~~in his mind~~ to pull

himself and his son out of homelessness.

The word *determined* contains the idea that his resolution formed
in his mind.

16b Avoid unnecessary repetition of words.

Though words may be repeated deliberately for effect, repetitions
will seem awkward if they are clearly unnecessary. When a more
concise version is possible, choose it.

▶ Our fifth patient, in room six, is a̷ mentally ill. ~~patient.~~

▶ The best teachers help each student _{grow} ~~become a better student~~

both academically and emotionally.

16c Cut empty or inflated phrases.

An empty phrase can be cut with little or no loss of meaning.
Common examples are introductory word groups that weaken
the writer's authority by apologizing or hedging: *in my opinion, I
think that, it seems that, one must admit that,* and so on.

▶ ~~In my opinion,~~ O̷ur current immigration policy is misguided.

Readers understand without being told that they are hearing the
writer's opinion.

Inflated phrases can be reduced to a word or two without
loss of meaning.

INFLATED	CONCISE
along the lines of	like
as a matter of fact	in fact
at all times	always
at the present time	now, currently
at this point in time	now, currently
because of the fact that	because

INFLATED	CONCISE
by means of	by
by virtue of the fact that	because
due to the fact that	because
for the purpose of	for
for the reason that	because
have the ability to	be able to, can
in light of the fact that	because
in order to	to
in spite of the fact that	although, though
in the event that	if
in the final analysis	finally
in the nature of	like
in the neighborhood of	about
until such time as	until

M
► ~~At this point in time~~ my skills and experience are a perfect

match for the position of assistant manager.

16d Simplify the structure.

If the structure of a sentence is needlessly indirect, try simplifying it. Look for opportunities to strengthen the verb.

► The financial analyst claimed that because of volatile market

conditions she could not ~~make an~~ estimate ~~of~~ the company's

future profits.

The verb *estimate* is more vigorous and concise than *make an estimate of.*

The colorless verbs *is, are, was,* and *were* frequently generate
excess words.

studied
► Investigators ~~were involved in studying~~ the effect of classical

music on unborn babies.

The revision is more direct and concise. The action (*studying*), originally appearing in a subordinate structure, has become a strong verb, *studied*.

The expletive constructions *there is* and *there are* (or *there was* and *there were*) can also generate excess words. The same is true of expletive constructions beginning with *it*. (See 47c.)

▶ ~~There is~~ ₐnother module ~~that~~ tells the story of Charles Darwin

and introduces the theory of evolution.

▶ ~~It is imperative that~~ ᴀll night managers *must* follow strict procedures

when locking the safe.

Finally, verbs in the passive voice may be needlessly indirect. When the active voice expresses your meaning as effectively, use it. (See 8a.)

▶ All too often, athletes with marginal academic skills. ~~have~~   *our coaches have recruited*

~~been recruited by our coaches.~~

16e Reduce clauses to phrases, phrases to single words.

Word groups functioning as modifiers can often be made more compact. Look for any opportunities to reduce clauses to phrases or phrases to single words.

▶ We took a side trip to Monticello, ~~which was~~ the home of

Thomas Jefferson.

▶ In ~~the~~ essay, ~~that follows,~~ I argue against Immanuel Kant's   *this*

claim that we should not lie under any circumstances ~~,~~/.   *problematic*

~~which is a problematic claim.~~

EXERCISE 16−1   Edit the following sentences to reduce wordiness. Revisions of lettered sentences appear in the back of the book. Example:

even though
The Wilsons moved into the house ~~in spite of the fact that~~
 ^

the back door was only ten yards from the train tracks.

a. Martin Luther King Jr. was a man who set a high standard for future leaders to meet.
b. Alice has been deeply in love with cooking since she was little and could first peek over the edge of a big kitchen tabletop.
c. In my opinion, Bloom's race for the governorship is a futile exercise.
d. It is pretty important in being a successful graphic designer to have technical knowledge and at the same time an eye for color and balance.
e. Your task will be the delivery of correspondence to all employees in the company.

1. Seeing the barrels, the driver immediately slammed on his brakes.
2. A really well-stocked bookshelf should have classical literature on it as well as important modern works of the current day.
3. China's enormously huge workforce has an effect on the global world of high-tech manufacturing of things.
4. A typical autocross course consists of at least two straightaways, and the rest of the course is made up of numerous slaloms and several sharp turns.
5. At breakfast time, Mehrdad always started his day with cantaloupe, lemon yogurt, and black coffee.

EXERCISE 16−2   Edit the following business memo to reduce wordiness.

To: District managers
From: Margaret Davenport, Vice President
Subject: Customer database

It has recently been brought to my attention that a percentage of our sales representatives have been failing to log reports of their client calls in our customer database each and every day. I have also learned that some representatives are not checking the database on a routine basis.

ır clients sometimes receive a multiple number of sales calls
ɔm us when a sales representative is not cognizant of the fact
ıt the client has been contacted at a previous time. Repeated
telephone calls from our representatives annoy our customers.
These repeated telephone calls also portray our company as one
that is lacking in organization.

Effective as of immediately, direct your representatives to do the
following:

- Record each and every customer contact in the customer
  database at the end of each day, without fail.

- Check the database at the very beginning of each day to ensure
  that telephone communications will not be initiated with
  clients who have already been called.

Let me extend my appreciation to you for cooperating in this
important matter.

17 Choose appropriate language.

Language is appropriate when it suits your subject, engages your
audience, and blends naturally with your own voice.

To some extent, your choice of language will be governed by
the conventions of the genre in which you are writing. When in
doubt about the conventions of a particular genre — lab reports,
informal essays, business memos, and so on — consult your
instructor or look at models written by experts in the field.

17a Stay away from jargon.

Jargon is specialized language used among members of a trade,
profession, or group. Use jargon only when readers will be familiar
with it; even then, use it only when plain English will not do as well.

JARGON	We outsourced the work to an outfit in Ohio because we didn't have the bandwidth to tackle it in-house.
REVISED	We hired a company in Ohio because we had too few employees to do the work.

Broadly defined, jargon includes puffed-up language designed more to impress readers than to inform them. The following are common examples from business, government, higher education, and the military, with plain English alternatives in parentheses.

ameliorate (improve)	indicator (sign)
commence (begin)	optimal (best, most favorable)
components (parts)	parameters (boundaries, limits)
endeavor (try)	peruse (read, look over)
facilitate (help)	prior to (before)
impact (v.) (affect)	utilize (use)

Sentences filled with jargon are hard to read, and they are often wordy as well.

► All ~~employees functioning in the capacity of~~ work-study
        must prove that they are currently enrolled.
students ~~are required to give evidence of current enrollment.~~

      talk   *working*
► The CEO should ~~dialogue~~ with investors about ~~partnering~~
      buy   *poor neighborhoods.*
with clients to ~~purchase~~ land in ~~economically deprived zones.~~

17b Avoid pretentious language, most euphemisms, and "doublespeak."

Hoping to sound profound or poetic, some writers embroider their thoughts with large words and flowery phrases. Such pretentious language is so ornate and wordy that it obscures the writer's meaning.

      use of colorful language reveals that she has a
► Taylor's ~~employment of multihued means of expression draws~~

               view of
~~back the curtains and lets slip the~~ nostalgic ~~vantage point~~

             and does not
~~from which she observes~~ American society ~~as well as her lack~~
understand
~~of comprehension of~~ economic realities.

Euphemisms — nice-sounding words or phrases substituted for words thought to sound harsh or ugly — are sometimes appropriate.

Many cultures, for example, accept euphemisms when speaking or writing about excretion (*I have to go to the bathroom*), sexual intercourse (*They did not sleep together*), and the like. Most euphemisms, however, are needlessly evasive or even deceitful. Like pretentious language, they obscure the intended meaning.

EUPHEMISM	PLAIN ENGLISH
adult entertainment	pornography
preowned automobile	used car
economically deprived	poor
negative savings	debts
strategic withdrawal	retreat or defeat
revenue enhancers	taxes
chemical dependency	drug addiction
downsize	lay off, fire
correctional facility	prison

The term *doublespeak* applies to any deliberately evasive or deceptive language, including euphemisms. Doublespeak is especially common in politics and business. A military retreat is described as *tactical redeployment*; *enhanced interrogation* is a euphemism for "torture"; and *downsizing* really means "firing employees."

EXERCISE 17–1 Edit the following sentences to eliminate jargon, pretentious or flowery language, euphemisms, and doublespeak. You may need to make substantial changes in some sentences. Revisions of lettered sentences appear in the back of the book. Example:

After two weeks in the legal department, Sue has ~~worked~~ mastered

into the routine, ~~of the office,~~ and her ~~functional and self-management skills have~~ performance has exceeded all expectations.

a. In my youth, my family was under the constraints of difficult financial circumstances.
b. In order that I may increase my expertise in the area of delivery of services to clients, I feel that participation in this conference will be beneficial.

    c. The prophetic meteorologist cautioned the general populace regarding the possible deleterious effects of the impending tempest.

    d. Government-sanctioned investigations into the continued value of after-school programs indicate a perceived need in the public realm at large.

    e. Passengers should endeavor to finalize the customs declaration form prior to exiting the aircraft.

1. We learned that the mayor had been engaging in a creative transfer of city employees' pension funds.

2. After a cursory examination of brand-new research findings on textiles, Patricia and the members of her team made the decision to engage in a series of visits to fashion manufacturers in the local vicinity.

3. The nurse announced that there had been a negative patient-care outcome due to a therapeutic misadventure on the part of the surgeon.

4. A generally leisurely pace at the onset of tai chi exercises can yield a variety of beneficial points within a short period of time.

5. The bottom line is that the company is experiencing a negative cash flow.

EXERCISE 17–2   Edit the following e-mail message to eliminate jargon.

Dear Ms. Jackson:

We members of the Nakamura Reyes team value our external partnering arrangements with Creative Software, and I look forward to seeing you next week at the trade show in Fresno. Per Mr. Reyes, please let me know when you'll have some downtime there so that he and I can conduct a strategizing session with you concerning our production schedule. It's crucial that we all be on the same page re our 2011–2012 product release dates.

Before we have some face time, however, I have some findings to share. Our customer-centric approach to the new products will necessitate that user testing periods trend upward. The enclosed data should help you effectuate any adjustments to your timeline; let me know ASAP if you require any additional information to facilitate the above.

Before we convene in Fresno, Mr. Reyes and I will agendize any further talking points. Thanks for your help.

Sincerely,

Sylvia Nakamura

17c In most contexts, avoid slang, regional expressions, and nonstandard English.

Slang is an informal and sometimes private vocabulary that expresses the solidarity of a group such as teenagers, rock musicians, or football fans; it is subject to more rapid change than standard English. For example, the slang teenagers use to express approval changes every few years; *cool*, *groovy*, *neat*, *awesome*, *phat*, and *sick* have replaced one another within the last three decades. Sometimes slang becomes so widespread that it is accepted as standard vocabulary. *Jazz*, for example, started out as slang but is now a standard term for a style of music.

Although slang has a certain vitality, it is a code that not everyone understands, and it is very informal. Therefore, it is inappropriate in most written work.

▶ When the server crashed unexpectedly, *we lost* three hours of

unsaved data. ~~went down the tubes.~~

▶ The government's "filth" guidelines for food will ~~make you~~ *disgust you.*

~~yack.~~

Regional expressions are common to a group in a geographic area. *Let's talk with the bark off* (for *Let's speak frankly*) is an expression in the southern United States, for example. Regional expressions have the same limitations as slang and are therefore inappropriate in most writing.

▶ John was four blocks from the house before he remembered
to ~~cut~~ *turn on* the headlights. ~~on.~~

▶ Seamus wasn't ~~for~~ sure, but he thought the whales might

be migrating during his visit to Oregon.

Standard English is the language used in all academic, business, and professional fields. Nonstandard English is spoken by people with a common regional or social heritage. Although nonstandard

English may be appropriate when spoken within a close group, it is out of place in most formal and informal writing.

> *doesn't*
> ▶ The governor said he ~~don't~~ know if he will approve the budget
>   ^
> without the clean air provision.

If you speak a nonstandard dialect, try to identify the ways in which your dialect differs from standard English. Look especially for the following features of nonstandard English, which commonly cause problems in writing.

Misusing verb forms such as *began* and *begun* (See 27a.)

Leaving *-s* endings off verbs (See 27c.)

Leaving *-ed* endings off verbs (See 27d.)

Leaving out necessary verbs (See 27e.)

Using double negatives (See 26e.)

17d Choose an appropriate level of formality.

In deciding on a level of formality, consider both your subject and your audience. Does the subject demand a dignified treatment, or is a relaxed tone more suitable? Will readers be put off if you assume too close a relationship with them, or might you alienate them by seeming too distant?

For most college and professional writing, some degree of formality is appropriate. In a job application letter, for example, it is a mistake to sound too breezy and informal.

TOO INFORMAL   I'd like to get that sales job you've got in the
               paper.

MORE FORMAL   I would like to apply for the position of sales
               associate advertised in the *Peoria Journal Star.*

Informal writing is appropriate for private letters, personal e-mail and text messages, and business correspondence between close associates. Like spoken conversation, informal writing allows contractions (*don't, I'll*) and colloquial words (*kids, kinda*). Vocabulary and sentence structure are rarely complex.

In choosing a level of formality, above all be consistent. When a writer's voice shifts from one level of formality to another, readers receive mixed messages.

► Once a pitcher for the Blue Jays, Jorge shared with me
                                                began
the secrets of his trade. His lesson ~~commenced~~ with his
                        thrown
                         ^
famous curveball, ~~implemented~~ by tucking the little finger
                 ^
                            revealed
behind the ball. Next he ~~elucidated~~ the mysteries of the
                         ^
sucker pitch, a slow ball coming behind a fast windup.

Words such as *commenced* and *elucidated* are inappropriate for the
subject matter, and they clash with informal terms such as *sucker pitch*
and *fast windup*.

EXERCISE 17–3   Revise the following passage so that the level of formality is appropriate for a letter to the editor of a major newspaper.

In pop culture, college grads who return home to live with
the folks are seen as good-for-nothing losers who mooch off their
families. And many older adults seem to feel that the trend of
moving back home after school, which was rare in their day, is
becoming too commonplace today. But society must realize that
times have changed. Most young adults want to live on their own
ASAP, but they graduate with heaps of debt and need some time to
get back on their feet. College tuition and the cost of housing have
increased way more than salary increases in the past fifty years. Also,
the job market is tighter and more jobs require advanced degrees
than in the past. So before people go off on college graduates who
move back into their parents' house for a spell, they'd better consider
all the facts.

17e Avoid sexist language.

Sexist language is language that stereotypes or demeans women
or men. Using nonsexist language is a matter of courtesy — of
respect for and sensitivity to the feelings of others.

Recognizing sexist language

Some sexist language is easy to recognize because it reflects genuine contempt for women: referring to a woman as a "chick," for
example, or calling a lawyer a "lady lawyer."
    Other forms of sexist language are less blatant. The following
practices, while they may not result from conscious sexism, reflect

stereotypical thinking: referring to members of one profession as exclusively male or exclusively female (teachers as women or computer engineers as men, for instance), using different conventions when naming or identifying women and men, or assuming that all of one's readers are men.

STEREOTYPICAL LANGUAGE

After a nursing student graduates, *she* must face a difficult state board examination. [Not all nursing students are women.]

Running for city council are Boris Stotsky, an attorney, and *Mrs.* Cynthia Jones, a professor of English and *mother of three.* [The title *Mrs.* and the phrase *mother of three* are irrelevant.]

Still other forms of sexist language result from outdated traditions. The pronouns *he, him,* and *his,* for instance, were traditionally used to refer generically to persons of either sex. Nowadays, to avoid that sexist usage, some writers use *she, her,* and *hers* generically or substitute the female pronouns alternately with the male pronouns.

GENERIC PRONOUNS

A journalist is motivated by *his* deadline.

A good interior designer treats *her* clients' ideas respectfully.

But both forms are sexist — for excluding one sex entirely and for making assumptions about the members of particular professions.

Similarly, the nouns *man* and *men* were once used to refer generically to persons of either sex. Current usage demands gender-neutral terms for references to both men and women.

INAPPROPRIATE	APPROPRIATE
chairman	chairperson, moderator, chair, head
congressman	member of Congress, representative, legislator
fireman	firefighter
foreman	supervisor
mailman	mail carrier, postal worker, letter carrier
to man	to operate, to staff
mankind	people, humans
manpower	personnel, staff
policeman	police officer
weatherman	forecaster, meteorologist

Revising sexist language

When revising sexist language, you may be tempted to substitute *he or she* and *his or her*. These terms are inclusive but wordy; fine in small doses, they can become awkward when repeated throughout an essay. A better revision strategy is to write in the plural; yet another strategy is to recast the sentence so that the problem does not arise.

SEXIST

A journalist is motivated by *his* deadline.

A good interior designer treats *her* clients' ideas respectfully.

ACCEPTABLE BUT WORDY

A journalist is motivated by *his or her* deadline.

A good interior designer treats *his or her* clients' ideas respectfully.

BETTER: USING THE PLURAL

Journalists are motivated by *their* deadlines.

Good interior designers treat *their* clients' ideas respectfully.

BETTER: RECASTING THE SENTENCE

A journalist is motivated by *a* deadline.

A good interior designer treats clients' ideas respectfully.

For more examples of these revision strategies, see 22.

EXERCISE 17–4 Edit the following sentences to eliminate sexist language or sexist assumptions. Revisions of lettered sentences appear in the back of the book. Example:

> *Scholarship athletes*   *their*
> ~~A scholarship athlete~~ must be as concerned about ~~his~~
>   *they are*   *their*
> academic performance as ~~he is~~ about ~~his~~ athletic performance.

a. Mrs. Geralyn Farmer, who is the mayor's wife, is the chief surgeon at University Hospital. Dr. Paul Green is her assistant.

b. Every applicant wants to know how much he will earn.

c. An elementary school teacher should understand the concept of nurturing if she intends to be effective.

d. An obstetrician needs to be available to his patients at all hours.

e. If man does not stop polluting his environment, mankind will perish.

1. A fireman must always be on call even when he is off duty.

2. The chairman for the new program in digital art is Ariana Tamlin, an accomplished portrait painter, computer programmer, and cookie baker.

3. In the governor's race, Lena Weiss, a defense lawyer and mother of two, easily defeated Harvey Tower, an architect.

4. Recent military history has shown that lady combat helicopter pilots are as skilled, reliable, and resourceful as men.

5. An emergency room head nurse must know how to use sophisticated digital equipment if she is to keep track of all her patients' data and guide her medical team.

EXERCISE 17–5   Eliminate sexist language or sexist assumptions in the following job posting for an elementary school teacher.

We are looking for qualified women for the position of elementary school teacher. The ideal candidate should have a bachelor's degree, a state teaching certificate, and one year of student teaching. She should be knowledgeable in all elementary subject areas, including science and math. While we want our new teacher to have a commanding presence in the classroom, we are also looking for motherly characteristics such as patience and trustworthiness. She must be able to both motivate an entire classroom and work with each student one-on-one to assess his individual needs. She must also be comfortable communicating with the parents of her students. For salary and benefits information, including maternity leave policy, please contact the Martin County School Board. Any qualified applicant should submit her résumé by March 15.

17f Revise language that may offend groups of people.

Obviously it is impolite to use offensive terms such as *Polack* and *redneck*, but biased language can take more subtle forms. Because language evolves over time, names once thought acceptable may become offensive. When describing groups of people, choose names that the groups currently use to describe themselves.

▶ North Dakota takes its name from the ~~Indian~~ *Lakota* word meaning

"friend" or "ally."

▶ Many ~~Oriental~~ *Asian* immigrants have recently settled in our town.

Negative stereotypes (such as "drives like a teenager" or "sour as a spinster") are of course offensive. But you should avoid stereotyping a person or a group even if you believe your generalization to be positive.

▶ It was no surprise that Greer, ~~a Chinese American,~~ *an excellent math and science student,* was

selected for the honors chemistry program.

---

18 Find the exact words.

Two reference works (or their online equivalents) will help you find words to express your meaning exactly: a good dictionary, such as *The American Heritage Dictionary* or *Merriam-Webster's Online Dictionary*, and a collection of synonyms and antonyms, such as *Roget's International Thesaurus*.

TIP: Do not turn to a thesaurus in search of flowery or impressive words. Look instead for words that exactly express your meaning.

18a Select words with appropriate connotations.

In addition to their strict dictionary meanings (or *denotations*), words have *connotations*, emotional colorings that affect how readers respond to them. The word *steel* denotes "commercial iron that contains carbon," but it also calls up a cluster of images associated with steel. These associations give the word its connotations — cold, hard, smooth, unbending.

If the connotation of a word does not seem appropriate for your purpose, your audience, or your subject matter, you should change the word. When a more appropriate synonym does not come quickly to mind, consult a dictionary or a thesaurus.

▶ When American soldiers returned home after World War II,
    left
    many women a̶b̶a̶n̶d̶o̶n̶e̶d̶ their jobs in favor of marriage.
                  ^
    The word *abandoned* is too negative for the context.

EXERCISE 18–1 Use a dictionary and a thesaurus to find at least four synonyms for each of the following words. Be prepared to explain any slight differences in meaning.

1. decay (verb)   3. hurry (verb)   5. secret (adjective)
2. difficult (adjective) 4. pleasure (noun)   6. talent (noun)

18b Prefer specific, concrete nouns.

Unlike general nouns, which refer to broad classes of things, specific nouns point to particular items. *Film*, for example, names a general class, *fantasy film* names a narrower class, and *The Golden Compass* is more specific still. Other examples: *team, football team, Denver Broncos; music, symphony, Beethoven's Ninth.*

Unlike abstract nouns, which refer to qualities and ideas (*justice, beauty, realism, dignity*), concrete nouns point to immediate, often sensory experience and to physical objects (*steeple, asphalt, lilac, stone, garlic*).

Specific, concrete nouns express meaning more vividly than general or abstract ones. Although general and abstract language is sometimes necessary to convey your meaning, use specific, concrete words whenever possible.

▶ The senator spoke about the challenges of the future:
    pollution, dwindling resources, and terrorism.
    t̶h̶e̶ ̶e̶n̶v̶i̶r̶o̶n̶m̶e̶n̶t̶ ̶a̶n̶d̶ ̶w̶o̶r̶l̶d̶ ̶p̶e̶a̶c̶e̶.̶
    ^

Nouns such as *thing, area, aspect, factor,* and *individual* are especially dull and imprecise.

                              motherhood, and memory.
▶ Toni Morrison's *Beloved* is about slavery, a̶m̶o̶n̶g̶ ̶o̶t̶h̶e̶r̶ ̶t̶h̶i̶n̶g̶s̶.̶
                                         ^

                      experienced technician.
▶ Try pairing a trainee with an i̶n̶d̶i̶v̶i̶d̶u̶a̶l̶ ̶w̶i̶t̶h̶ ̶t̶e̶c̶h̶n̶i̶c̶a̶l̶ ̶e̶x̶p̶e̶r̶i̶e̶n̶c̶e̶.̶
                                ^

18c Do not misuse words.

If a word is not in your active vocabulary, you may find yourself misusing it, sometimes with embarrassing consequences. When in doubt, check the dictionary.

▶ The fans were ~~migrating~~ _climbing_ up the bleachers in search of seats.

▶ The Internet has so ~~diffused~~ _permeated_ our culture that it touches all

segments of society.

Be especially alert for misused word forms — using a noun such as _absence, significance,_ or _persistence,_ for example, when your meaning requires the adjective _absent, significant,_ or _persistent._

▶ Most dieters are not ~~persistence~~ _persistent_ enough to make a permanent

change in their eating habits.

EXERCISE 18-2 Edit the following sentences to correct misused words. Revisions of lettered sentences appear in the back of the book. Example:

These days the training required for a ballet dancer

is ~~all-absorbent.~~ _all-absorbing._

a. We regret this delay; thank you for your patients.

b. Ada's plan is to require education and experience to prepare herself for a position as property manager.

c. Peyton Manning, the penultimate competitor, has earned millions of dollars just in endorsements.

d. Many people take for granite that public libraries have up-to-date computer systems.

e. The affect of Gao Xinjian's novels on Chinese exiles is hard to gauge.

1. Because Anne Tyler often writes about family loyalties, her illusions to _King Lear_ are not surprising.

2. Designers of handheld devices understand that changes in ambience temperatures can damage the tiny circuit boards.

3. The Keweenaw Peninsula is surrounded on three sides by Lake Superior.
4. At the cooking school in Tuscany, I learned that rosemary is a perfect compliment to lamb.
5. The person who complained to the human resources manager wishes to remain unanimous.

18d Use standard idioms.

Idioms are speech forms that follow no easily specified rules. The English say "Bernice went *to hospital*," an idiom strange to American ears, which are accustomed to hearing *the* in front of *hospital*. Native speakers of a language seldom have problems with idioms, but prepositions (such as *with*, *to*, *at*, and *of*) sometimes cause trouble, especially when they follow certain verbs and adjectives. When in doubt, consult a dictionary.

UNIDIOMATIC	IDIOMATIC
abide with (a decision)	abide by (a decision)
according with	according to
agree to (an idea)	agree with (an idea)
angry at (a person)	angry with (a person)
capable to	capable of
comply to	comply with
desirous to	desirous of
different than (a person or thing)	different from (a person or thing)
intend on doing	intend to do
off of	off
plan on doing	plan to do
preferable than	preferable to
prior than	prior to
similar than	similar to
superior than	superior to
sure and	sure to
think on	think of, about
try and	try to
type of a	type of

MULTILINGUAL Because idioms follow no particular rules, you must learn them individually. You may find it helpful to keep a list of idioms that you frequently encounter in conversation and in reading.

EXERCISE 18–3 Edit the following sentences to eliminate errors in the use of idiomatic expressions. If a sentence is correct, write "correct" after it. Answers to lettered sentences appear in the back of the book. Example:

We agreed to abide ~~with~~ *by* the decision of the judge.

a. Queen Anne was so angry at Sarah Churchill that she refused to see her again.

b. Jean-Pierre's ambitious travel plans made it impossible for him to comply with the residency requirement for in-state tuition.

c. The parade moved off of the street and onto the beach.

d. The frightened refugees intend on making the dangerous trek across the mountains.

e. What type of a wedding are you planning?

1. Be sure and report on the danger of releasing genetically engineered bacteria into the atmosphere.

2. Why do you assume that embezzling bank assets is so different than robbing the bank?

3. The wilderness guide seemed capable to show us where the trail of petroglyphs was located.

4. In Evan's cautious mind, packing his own parachute seemed preferable to letting an indifferent teenager fold all that silk and cord into a small pack.

5. Andrea plans on joining the Peace Corps after graduation.

18e Do not rely heavily on clichés.

The pioneer who first announced that he had "slept like a log" no doubt amused his companions with a fresh and unlikely comparison. Today, however, that comparison is a cliché, a saying that has lost its dazzle from overuse. No longer can it surprise.

PRACTICE hackerhandbooks.com/rules
> Clarity > 18–6

To see just how dully predictable clichés are, put your hand over the right-hand column in the following list and then finish the phrases on the left.

cool as a	cucumber
beat around	the bush
blind as a	bat
busy as a	bee, beaver
crystal	clear
dead as a	doornail
out of the frying pan and	into the fire
light as a	feather
like a bull	in a china shop
playing with	fire
nutty as a	fruitcake
selling like	hotcakes
starting out at the bottom	of the ladder
water under the	bridge
white as a	sheet, ghost
avoid clichés like the	plague

The solution for clichés is simple: Just delete them or rewrite them.

▶ When I received a full scholarship from my second-choice
                    felt squeezed to settle for second best.
school, I ~~found myself between a rock and a hard place.~~
                    ^

Sometimes you can write around a cliché by adding an element of surprise. One student, for example, who had written that she had butterflies in her stomach, revised her cliché like this:

If all of the action in my stomach is caused by butterflies, there must be a horde of them, with horseshoes on.

The image of butterflies wearing horseshoes is fresh and unlikely, not predictable like the original cliché.

18f Use figures of speech with care.

A figure of speech is an expression that uses words imaginatively (rather than literally) to make abstract ideas concrete. Most often, figures of speech compare two seemingly unlike things to reveal surprising similarities.

In a *simile*, the writer makes the comparison explicitly, usually by introducing it with *like* or *as*: *By the time cotton had to be picked, Grandfather's neck was as red as the clay he plowed.* In a *metaphor*, the *like* or *as* is omitted, and the comparison is implied. For example, in the Old Testament Song of Solomon, a young woman compares the man she loves to a fruit tree: *With great delight I sat in his shadow, and his fruit was sweet to my taste.*

Although figures of speech are useful devices, writers sometimes use them without thinking through the images they evoke. The result is sometimes a *mixed metaphor*, the combination of two or more images that don't make sense together.

► Our manager decided to put all controversial issues

~~in a holding pattern~~ on a back burner until after the

annual meeting.

Here the writer is mixing airplanes and stoves. Simply deleting one of the images corrects the problem.

EXERCISE 18–4 Edit the following sentences to replace worn-out expressions and clarify mixed figures of speech. Revisions of lettered sentences appear in the back of the book. Example:

the color drained from his face.
When he heard about the accident, ~~he turned white as a sheet.~~
                                       ∧

a. John stormed into the room like a bull in a china shop.

b. Some people insist that they'll always be there for you, even when they haven't been before.

c. The Cubs easily beat the Mets, who were in the soup early in the game today at Wrigley Field.

PRACTICE hackerhandbooks.com/rules
   > Clarity > 18–7

d. We ironed out the sticky spots in our relationship.

e. My mother accused me of beating around the bush when in fact I was just talking off the top of my head.

1. Priscilla was used to burning the candle at both ends to get her assignments done.

2. No matter how many books he reads, André can never seem to quench his thirst for knowledge.

3. In an era of cutbacks and outsourcing, the best tech-savvy workers discover that being a jack of all trades is a solid gold key to continued success.

4. Too many cooks are spoiling the broth at corporate headquarters.

5. Juanita told Kyle that keeping skeletons in the closet would be playing with fire.

Grammar

19   Repair sentence fragments.

A sentence fragment is a word group that pretends to be a sentence. Sentence fragments are easy to recognize when they appear out of context, like these:

> When the cat leaped onto the table.

> Running for the bus.

> And immediately popped their flares and life vests.

When fragments appear next to related sentences, however, they are harder to spot.

> We had just sat down to dinner. When the cat leaped onto the table.

> I tripped and twisted my ankle. Running for the bus.

> The pilots ejected from the burning plane, landing in the water not far from the ship. And immediately popped their flares and life vests.

Recognizing sentence fragments

To be a sentence, a word group must consist of at least one full independent clause. An independent clause includes a subject and a verb, and it either stands alone or could stand alone.

To test whether a word group is a complete sentence or a fragment, use the flowchart on page 181. By using the flowchart, you can see exactly why *When the cat leaped onto the table* is a fragment: It has a subject (*cat*) and a verb (*leaped*), but it begins with a subordinating word (*When*), which makes the word group a dependent clause. *Running for the bus* is a fragment because it lacks a subject and a verb (*Running* is a verbal, not a verb). *And immediately popped their flares and life vests* is a fragment because it lacks a subject. (See also 48b and 48e.)

Test for fragments

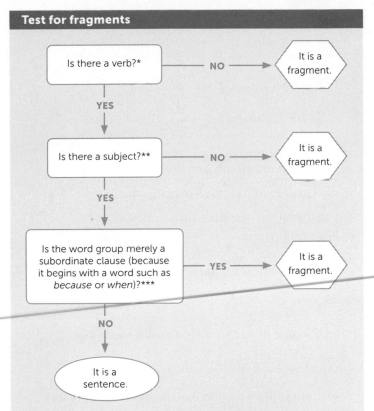

*Do not mistake verbals for verbs. A verbal is a verb form (such as *walking, to act*) that does not function as a verb of a clause. (See 48b.)

**The subject of a sentence may be *you*, understood but not present in the sentence. (See 47a.)

***A sentence may open with a subordinate clause, but the sentence must also include an independent clause. (See 19a and 49a.)

If you find any fragments, try one of these methods of revision (see 19a–19c):

1. Attach the fragment to a nearby sentence.
2. Rewrite the fragment as a complete sentence.

MULTILINGUAL Unlike some other languages, English requires a subject and a verb in every sentence (except in commands, where the subject *you* is understood but not present: *Sit down*). See 30a and 30b.

It is
► ~~Is~~ often hot and humid during the summer.
   ^

         are
► Students usually very busy at the end of the semester.
                ^

Repairing sentence fragments

You can repair most fragments in one of two ways:

- Pull the fragment into a nearby sentence.
- Rewrite the fragment as a complete sentence.

                                  when
► We had just sat down to dinner./ ~~When~~ the cat leaped onto
                                  ^
   the table.

Running for the bus,
► I tripped and twisted my ankle. ~~Running for the bus.~~
   ^

► The pilots ejected from the burning plane, landing in the
                           They
   water not far from the ship. ~~And~~ immediately popped their
                                ^
   flares and life vests.

19a Attach fragmented subordinate clauses or turn them into sentences.

A subordinate clause is patterned like a sentence, with both a subject and a verb, but it begins with a word that marks it as subordinate. The following words commonly introduce subordinate clauses.

after	before	so that	until	while
although	even though	than	when	who
as	how	that	where	whom
as if	if	though	whether	whose
because	since	unless	which	why

Subordinate clauses function within sentences as adjectives, as
adverbs, or as nouns. They cannot stand alone. (See 48e.)
   Most fragmented clauses beg to be pulled into a sentence
nearby.

▶ Americans have come to fear the West Nile virus,/Because *because*

   it is transmitted by the common mosquito.

Because introduces a subordinate clause, so it cannot stand alone. (For
punctuation of subordinate clauses appearing at the end of a sentence,
see 33f.)

▶ Although psychiatrist Peter Kramer expresses concerns

   about Prozac,/, Many *many* other doctors believe that the

   benefits of antidepressants outweigh the risks.

Although introduces a subordinate clause, so it cannot stand alone.
(For punctuation of subordinate clauses at the beginning of a sentence,
see 32b.)

   If a fragmented clause cannot be attached to a nearby sentence or if you feel that attaching it would be awkward, try
turning the clause into a sentence. The simplest way to do
this is to delete the opening word or words that mark it as
subordinate.

▶ Population increases and uncontrolled development are

   taking a deadly toll on the environment. So that across *Across* the

   globe, fragile ecosystems are collapsing.

19b Attach fragmented phrases or turn them into sentences.

Like subordinate clauses, phrases function within sentences as
adjectives, as adverbs, or as nouns. They cannot stand alone.
Fragmented phrases are often prepositional or verbal phrases;
sometimes they are appositives, words or word groups that rename nouns or pronouns. (See 48a, 48b, and 48c.)

Often a fragmented phrase may simply be pulled into a nearby sentence.

▶ The archaeologists worked slowly, ~~Examining~~ *examining* and labeling

every pottery shard they uncovered.

The word group beginning with *Examining* is a verbal phrase.

▶ The patient displayed symptoms of ALS, ~~A~~ *a* neuro-

degenerative disease.

A neurodegenerative disease is an appositive renaming the noun *ALS*. (For punctuation of appositives, see 32e.)

If a fragmented phrase cannot be pulled into a nearby sentence effectively, turn the phrase into a sentence. You may need to add a subject, a verb, or both.

▶ In the training session, Jamie explained how to access our new

database. ~~Also~~ *She also taught us* how to submit expense reports and request

vendor payments.

The revision turns the fragmented phrase into a sentence by adding a subject and a verb.

19c Attach other fragmented word groups or turn them into sentences.

Other word groups that are commonly fragmented include parts of compound predicates, lists, and examples introduced by *for example*, *in addition*, or similar expressions.

Parts of compound predicates

A predicate consists of a verb and its objects, complements, and modifiers (see 47b). A compound predicate includes two or more predicates joined with a coordinating conjunction such as *and*, *but*,

incomplete sentences • implied vs. dictionary meaning •
lists as fragments • fragments with *for example, such as*, etc.

frag

19c

185

or *or*. Because the parts of a compound predicate have the same subject, they should appear in the same sentence.

▶ The woodpecker finch of the Galápagos Islands carefully
    and
    selects a twig of a certain size and shape./~~And~~ then uses this
                                              ^

    tool to pry out grubs from trees.

    The subject is *finch*, and the compound predicate is *selects . . . and . . . uses*.
    (For punctuation of compound predicates, see 33a.)

Lists

To correct a fragmented list, often you can attach it to a nearby sentence with a colon or a dash. (See 35a and 39a.)

▶ It has been said that there are only three indigenous American
    musical
    art forms./: ~~Musical~~ comedy, jazz, and soap opera.
             ^

Sometimes terms like *especially*, *namely*, *like*, and *such as* introduce fragmented lists. Such fragments can usually be attached to the preceding sentence.

▶ In the twentieth century, the South produced some great
    such
    American writers,/ ~~Such~~ as Flannery O'Connor, William
                   ^

    Faulkner, Alice Walker, and Tennessee Williams.

Examples introduced by *for example, in addition*, or similar expressions

Other expressions that introduce examples or explanations can lead to unintentional fragments. Although you may begin a sentence with some of the following words or phrases, make sure that what follows has a subject and a verb.

also	for example	mainly
and	for instance	or
but	in addition	that is

Often the easiest solution is to turn the fragment into a sentence.

> In his memoir, Primo Levi describes the horrors of living
> *he worked*
> in a concentration camp. For example, ~~working~~ without
> ^
> *suffered*
> food and ~~suffering~~ emotional abuse.
> ^

The writer corrected this fragment by adding a subject — *he* — and substituting verbs for the verbals *working* and *suffering*.

> Deborah Tannen's research reveals that men and women
>
> have different ideas about communication. For example,
> *Tannen explains*
> that a woman "expects her husband to be a new and
> ^
> improved version of her best friend" (441).

A quotation must be part of a complete sentence. *That a woman "expects her husband to be a new and improved version of her best friend"* is a fragment — a subordinate clause. In this case, adding a signal phrase that includes a subject and a verb (*Tannen explains*) corrects the fragment and clarifies that the quotation is from Tannen.

19d Exception: A fragment may be used for effect.

Writers occasionally use sentence fragments for special purposes.

FOR EMPHASIS	Following the dramatic Americanization of their children, even my parents grew more publicly confident. *Especially my mother.* — Richard Rodriguez
TO ANSWER A QUESTION	Are these new drug tests 100 percent reliable? *Not in the opinion of most experts.*
TRANSITIONS	*And now the opposing arguments.*
EXCLAMATIONS	*Not again!*
IN ADVERTISING	*Fewer carbs. Improved taste.*

Although fragments are sometimes appropriate, writers and readers do not always agree on when they are appropriate. That's why you will find it safer to write in complete sentences.

EXERCISE 19–1 Repair any fragment by attaching it to a nearby sentence or by rewriting it as a complete sentence. If a word group is correct, write "correct" after it. Revisions of lettered sentences appear in the back of the book. Example:

> One Greek island that should not be missed is Mykonos. A̬
>
> vacation spot for Europeans and a playground for the rich
>
> and famous.

a. Listening to the CD her sister had sent, Mia was overcome with a mix of emotions. Happiness, homesickness, and nostalgia.

b. Cortés and his soldiers were astonished when they looked down from the mountains and saw Tenochtitlán. The magnificent capital of the Aztecs.

c. Although my spoken Spanish is not very good. I can read the language with ease.

d. There are several reasons for not eating meat. One reason being that dangerous chemicals are used throughout the various stages of meat production.

e. To learn how to sculpt beauty from everyday life. This is my intention in studying art and archaeology.

1. The panther lay motionless behind the rock. Waiting for its prey.

2. Aunt Mina loved to play all my favorite games. Cat's cradle, Uno, mancala, and even hopscotch.

3. With machetes, the explorers cut their way through the tall grasses to the edge of the canyon. Then they began to lay out the tapes for the survey.

4. The owners of the online grocery store rented a warehouse in the Market district. An area catering to small businesses.

5. If a woman from the desert tribe showed anger toward her husband, she was whipped in front of the whole village. And shunned by the rest of the women.

EXERCISE 19–2 Repair each fragment in the following passage by attaching it to a sentence nearby or by rewriting it as a complete sentence.

> Digital technology has revolutionized information delivery. Forever blurring the lines between information and entertainment. Yesterday's readers of books and newspapers are today's readers of e-books and news blogs. Countless readers have moved on from print information entirely. Choosing instead to point, click,

and scroll their way through a text on their Amazon Kindle or in an online forum. Once a nation of people spoon-fed television commercials and the six o'clock evening news. We are now seemingly addicted to *YouTube*. Remember the family trip when Dad or Mom wrestled with a road map? On the way to St. Louis or Seattle? No wrestling is required with a slick GPS navigator by the driver's side. Unless it's Mom and Dad wrestling over who gets to program the address. Accessing information now seems to be America's favorite pastime. John Horrigan, associate director for research at the Pew Internet and American Life Project, reports that 31 percent of American adults are "elite" users of technology. Who are "highly engaged" with digital content. As a country, we embrace information and communication technologies. Which include iPods, cell phones, laptops, and handheld devices. Among children and adolescents, Internet and other personal technology use is on the rise. For activities like socializing, gaming, and information gathering.

20   Revise run-on sentences.

Run-on sentences are independent clauses that have not been joined correctly. An independent clause is a word group that can stand alone as a sentence. (See 49a.) When two independent clauses appear in one sentence, they must be joined in one of these ways:

- with a comma and a coordinating conjunction (*and*, *but*, *or*, *nor*, *for*, *so*, *yet*)
- with a semicolon (or occasionally with a colon or a dash)

Recognizing run-on sentences

There are two types of run-on sentences. When a writer puts no mark of punctuation and no coordinating conjunction between independent clauses, the result is called a *fused sentence*.

┌────── INDEPENDENT CLAUSE ──────┐ ┌──────
FUSED   Air pollution poses risks to all humans it can be
── INDEPENDENT CLAUSE ──┐
deadly for asthma sufferers.

A far more common type of run-on sentence is the *comma splice* — two or more independent clauses joined with a comma but without a coordinating conjunction. In some comma splices, the comma appears alone.

COMMA SPLICE	Air pollution poses risks to all humans, it can be deadly for asthma sufferers.

In other comma splices, the comma is accompanied by a joining word that is *not* a coordinating conjunction. There are only seven coordinating conjunctions in English: *and, but, or, nor, for, so,* and *yet.*

COMMA SPLICE	Air pollution poses risks to all humans, however, it can be deadly for asthma sufferers.

However is a transitional expression and cannot be used with only a comma to join two independent clauses (see 20b).

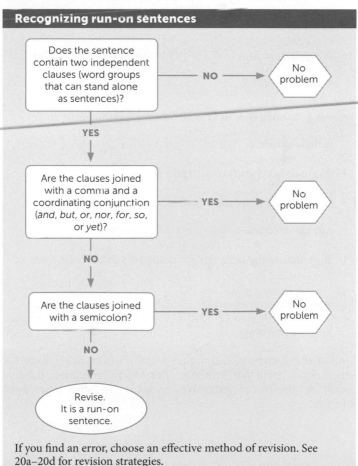

Recognizing run-on sentences

Does the sentence contain two independent clauses (word groups that can stand alone as sentences)? — **NO** → No problem

YES

Are the clauses joined with a comma and a coordinating conjunction (*and, but, or, nor, for, so,* or *yet*)? — **YES** → No problem

NO

Are the clauses joined with a semicolon? — **YES** → No problem

NO

Revise. It is a run-on sentence.

If you find an error, choose an effective method of revision. See 20a–20d for revision strategies.

Revising run-on sentences

To revise a run-on sentence, you have four choices.

1. Use a comma and a coordinating conjunction (*and, but, or, nor, for, so, yet*).

   ► Air pollution poses risks to all humans, *but* it can be deadly for

   asthma sufferers.

2. Use a semicolon (or, if appropriate, a colon or a dash). A semicolon may be used alone or with a transitional expression.

   ► Air pollution poses risks to all humans; it can be deadly

   for asthma sufferers.

   ► Air pollution poses risks to all humans; *however,* it can be deadly for

   asthma sufferers.

3. Make the clauses into separate sentences.

   ► Air pollution poses risks to all humans. *It* can be deadly for

   asthma sufferers.

4. Restructure the sentence, perhaps by subordinating one of the clauses.

   ► *Although air* Air pollution poses risks to all humans, it can be deadly for

   asthma sufferers.

One of these revision techniques usually works better than the others for a particular sentence. The fourth technique, the one requiring the most extensive revision, is often the most effective.

20a Consider separating the clauses with a comma and a coordinating conjunction.

There are seven coordinating conjunctions in English: *and, but, or, nor, for, so,* and *yet.* When a coordinating conjunction joins independent clauses, it is usually preceded by a comma. (See 32a.)

▶ Some lesson plans include exercises, *but* completing them should

not be the focus of all class periods.

20b Consider separating the clauses with a semicolon (or, if appropriate, with a colon or a dash).

When the independent clauses are closely related and their relation is clear without a coordinating conjunction, a semicolon is an acceptable method of revision. (See 34a.)

▶ Tragedy depicts the individual confronted with the fact of

death*;* comedy depicts the adaptability of human society.

A semicolon is required between independent clauses that have been linked with a transitional expression (such as *however, therefore, moreover, in fact,* or *for example*). For a longer list, see 34b.

▶ In his film adaptation of the short story "Killings," director

Todd Field changed key details of the plot*;* in fact, he added

whole scenes that do not appear in the story.

A colon or a dash may be more appropriate if the first independent clause introduces the second or if the second clause summarizes or explains the first. (See 35b and 39a.) In formal writing, the colon is usually preferred to the dash.

► Nuclear waste is hazardous; *This* this is an indisputable fact.

► The female black widow spider is often a widow of her own making, she has been known to eat her partner after mating.

A colon is an appropriate method of revision if the first independent clause introduces a quoted sentence.

► Nobel Peace Prize winner Al Gore had this to say about climate change,: "The truth is that our circumstances are not only new; they are completely different than they have ever been in all of human history."

20c Consider making the clauses into separate sentences.

► Why should we spend money on expensive space exploration,? *We* we have enough underfunded programs here on Earth.

Since one independent clause is a question and the other is a statement, they should be separate sentences.

► Some studies have suggested that the sexual relationships of bonobos set them apart from common chimpanzees,. *According* according to Stanford (1998), these differences have been exaggerated.

Using a comma to join two independent clauses creates a comma splice. In this example, an effective revision is to separate the first independent clause (*Some studies . . .*) from the second independent clause (*these differences . . .*) and to keep the signal phrase with the second clause. (See also 63.)

NOTE: When two quoted independent clauses are divided by explanatory words, make each clause its own sentence.

> "It's always smart to learn from your mistakes," quipped my
>
> supervisor*./* "it's even smarter to learn from the mistakes of   *"It's*
>
> others."

20d Consider restructuring the sentence, perhaps by subordinating one of the clauses.

If one of the independent clauses is less important than the other, turn it into a subordinate clause or phrase. (For more about subordination, see 14, especially the chart on p. 144.)

> One of the most famous advertising slogans is Wheaties
>
> cereal's "Breakfast of Champions," it was penned in 1933.   *which*

> Mary McLeod Bethune, was the seventeenth child of former
>
> slaves, she founded the National Council of Negro Women
>
> in 1935.

Minor ideas in these sentences are now expressed in subordinate clauses or phrases.

EXERCISE 20–1 Revise the following run-on sentences using the method of revision suggested in brackets. Revisions of lettered sentences appear in the back of the book. Example:

> *Because*
> Daniel had been obsessed with his weight as a teenager, he
>
> rarely ate anything sweet. [*Restructure the sentence.*]

  a. The city had one public swimming pool, it stayed packed with children all summer long. [*Restructure the sentence.*]

  b. The building is being renovated, therefore at times we have no heat, water, or electricity. [*Use a comma and a coordinating conjunction.*]

c. The view was not what the travel agent had described, where were the rolling hills and the shimmering rivers? [*Make two sentences.*]

d. All those gnarled equations looked like toxic insects, maybe I was going to have to rethink my major. [*Use a semicolon.*]

e. City officials had good reason to fear a major earthquake, most of the business district was built on landfill. [*Use a colon.*]

1. The car was hardly worth trading, the frame was twisted and the block was warped. [*Restructure the sentence.*]

2. The next time an event is canceled because of bad weather, don't blame the meteorologist, blame nature. [*Make two sentences.*]

3. Ray was fluent in American Sign Language he could sign as easily as he could speak. [*Restructure the sentence.*]

4. Susanna arrived with a stack of her latest hats she hoped the gift shop would place a big winter order. [*Restructure the sentence.*]

5. There was one major reason for John's wealth, his grandfather had been a multimillionaire. [*Use a colon.*]

EXERCISE 20–2   Revise any run-on sentences using a technique that you find effective. If a sentence is correct, write "correct" after it. Revisions of lettered sentences appear in the back of the book. Example:

> Crossing so many time zones on an eight-hour flight, I knew
>
>   but
> I would be tired when I arrived, ~~however,~~ I was too excited
>   ^
> to sleep on the plane.

a. Wind power for the home is a supplementary source of energy, it can be combined with electricity, gas, or solar energy.

b. Aidan viewed Sofia Coppola's *Lost in Translation* three times and then wrote a paper describing the film as the work of a mysterious modern painter.

c. In the Middle Ages, the streets of London were dangerous places, it was safer to travel by boat along the Thames.

d. "He's not drunk," I said, "he's in a state of diabetic shock."

e. Are you able to endure extreme angle turns, high speeds, frequent jumps, and occasional crashes, then supermoto racing may be a sport for you.

1. Death Valley National Monument, located in southern California and Nevada, is one of the hottest places on Earth, temperatures there have soared as high as 134° Fahrenheit.

2. Anamaria opened the boxes crammed with toys, out sprang griffins, dragons, and phoenixes.

3. Subatomic physics is filled with strange and marvelous particles, tiny bodies of matter that shiver, wobble, pulse, and flatten to no thickness at all.

4. As his first major project, Frederick Law Olmsted designed New York City's Central Park, one of the most beautiful urban spaces in the United States.

5. The neurosurgeon explained that the medication could have one side effect, it might cause me to experience temporary memory loss.

EXERCISE 20-3 In the rough draft that follows, revise any run-on sentences.

Some parents and educators argue that requiring uniforms in public schools would improve student behavior and performance. They think that uniforms give students a more professional attitude toward school, moreover, they believe that uniforms help create a sense of community among students from diverse backgrounds. But parents and educators should consider the drawbacks to requiring uniforms in public schools.

Uniforms do create a sense of community, they do this, however, by stamping out individuality. Youth is a time to express originality, it is a time to develop a sense of self. One important way young people express their identities is through the clothes they wear. The self-patrolled dress code of high school students may be stricter than any school-imposed code, nevertheless, trying to control dress habits from above will only lead to resentment or to mindless conformity.

If children are going to act like adults, they need to be treated like adults, they need to be allowed to make their own choices. Telling young people what to wear to school merely prolongs their childhood. Requiring uniforms undermines the educational purpose of public schools, which is not just to teach facts and figures but to help young people grow into adults who are responsible for making their own choices.

Make subjects and verbs agree.

In the present tense, verbs agree with their subjects in number (singular or plural) and in person (first, second, third): *I sing, you sing, he sings, she sings, we sing, they sing*. Even if your ear recognizes the standard subject-verb combinations presented in 21a, you will no doubt encounter tricky situations such as those described in 21b–21k.

21a Consult this section for standard subject-verb combinations.

This section describes the basic guidelines for making present-tense verbs agree with their subjects. The present-tense ending -*s* (or -*es*) is used on a verb if its subject is third-person singular (*he, she, it*, and singular nouns); otherwise, the verb takes no ending. Consider, for example, the present-tense forms of the verbs *love* and *try*, given at the beginning of the chart on the following page.

The verb *be* varies from this pattern; unlike any other verb, it has special forms in *both* the present and the past tense. These forms appear at the end of the chart.

If you aren't confident that you know the standard forms, use the charts on pages 198 and 199 as you proofread for subject-verb agreement. You may also want to look at 27c on -*s* endings of regular and irregular verbs.

21b Make the verb agree with its subject, not with a word that comes between.

Word groups often come between the subject and the verb. Such word groups, usually modifying the subject, may contain a noun that at first appears to be the subject. By mentally stripping away such modifiers, you can isolate the noun that is in fact the subject.

The *samples* on the tray in the lab *need* testing.

► High levels of air pollution causes damage to the respiratory

tract.

The subject is *levels*, not *pollution*. Strip away the phrase *of air pollution* to hear the correct verb: *levels cause.*

has
► The slaughter of pandas for their pelts ~~have~~ caused the
        ^

panda population to decline drastically.

The subject is *slaughter*, not *pandas* or *pelts.*

NOTE: Phrases beginning with the prepositions *as well as, in addition to, accompanied by, together with,* and *along with* do not make a singular subject plural.

was
► The governor as well as his press secretary ~~were~~ on the plane.

To emphasize that two people were on the plane, the writer could use *and* instead: *The governor and his press secretary were on the plane.*

21c Treat most subjects joined with *and* as plural.

A subject with two or more parts is said to be compound. If the parts are connected with *and*, the subject is almost always plural.

Leon and Jan often *jog* together.

► The Supreme Court's willingness to hear the case and its
                                    have
affirmation of the original decision ~~has~~ set a new precedent.
                                    ^

EXCEPTIONS: When the parts of the subject form a single unit or when they refer to the same person or thing, treat the subject as singular.

Fish and chips was a last-minute addition to the menu.

Sue's friend and adviser was surprised by her decision.

Subject-verb agreement at a glance

Present-tense forms of *love* and *try* (typical verbs)

	SINGULAR		**PLURAL**	
FIRST PERSON	I	love	we	love
SECOND PERSON	you	love	you	love
THIRD PERSON	he/she/it*	loves	they**	love

	SINGULAR		**PLURAL**	
FIRST PERSON	I	try	we	try
SECOND PERSON	you	try	you	try
THIRD PERSON	he/she/it*	tries	they**	try

Present-tense forms of *have*

	SINGULAR		**PLURAL**	
FIRST PERSON	I	have	we	have
SECOND PERSON	you	have	you	have
THIRD PERSON	he/she/it*	has	they**	have

Present-tense forms of *do* (including negative forms)

	SINGULAR		**PLURAL**	
FIRST PERSON	I	do/don't	we	do/don't
SECOND PERSON	you	do/don't	you	do/don't
THIRD PERSON	he/she/it*	does/doesn't	they**	do/don't

Present-tense and past-tense forms of *be*

	SINGULAR		**PLURAL**	
FIRST PERSON	I	am/was	we	are/were
SECOND PERSON	you	are/were	you	are/were
THIRD PERSON	he/she/it*	is/was	they**	are/were

*And singular nouns (*child, Roger*)
**And plural nouns (*children, the Mannings*)

When to use the -s (or -es) form of a present-tense verb

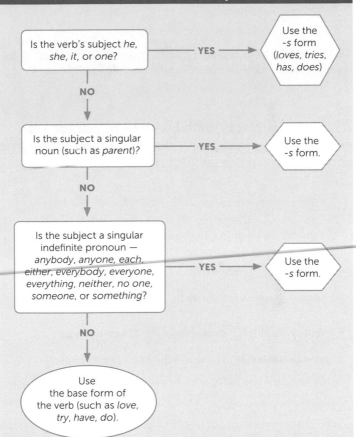

Is the verb's subject *he, she, it,* or *one*? — **YES** → Use the -s form (*loves, tries, has, does*)

NO ↓

Is the subject a singular noun (such as *parent*)? — **YES** → Use the -s form.

NO ↓

Is the subject a singular indefinite pronoun — *anybody, anyone, each, either, everybody, everyone, everything, neither, no one, someone,* or *something*? — **YES** → Use the -s form.

NO ↓

Use the base form of the verb (such as *love, try, have, do*).

EXCEPTION: Choosing the correct present-tense form of *be* (*am, is,* or *are*) is not quite so simple. See the chart on the previous page for both present- and past-tense forms of *be*.

TIP: Do not use the -s form of a verb if it follows a modal verb such as *can, must,* or *should* or another helping verb. (See 28c.)

When a compound subject is preceded by *each* or *every*, treat it as singular.

Every car, truck, and van is required to pass inspection.

This exception does not apply when a compound subject is followed by *each*: *Alan and Marcia each have different ideas.*

21d With subjects joined with *or* or *nor* (or with *either . . . or* or *neither . . . nor*), make the verb agree with the part of the subject nearer to the verb.

A driver's *license* or credit *card is* required.

A driver's *license* or two credit *cards are* required.

▸ If an infant or a child ~~are~~ *is* having difficulty breathing, seek

    medical attention immediately.

▸ Neither the chief financial officer nor the marketing

    managers ~~was~~ *were* able to convince the client to reconsider.

The verb must be matched with the part of the subject closer to it: *child is* in the first sentence, *managers were* in the second.

NOTE: If one part of the subject is singular and the other is plural, put the plural one last to avoid awkwardness.

21e Treat most indefinite pronouns as singular.

Indefinite pronouns are pronouns that do not refer to specific persons or things. The following commonly used indefinite pronouns are singular.

anybody	each	everyone	nobody	somebody
anyone	either	everything	no one	someone
anything	everybody	neither	nothing	something

Many of these words appear to have plural meanings, and they
are often treated as such in casual speech. In formal written English, however, they are nearly always treated as singular.

Everyone on the team *supports* the coach.

has
► Each of the essays ~~have~~ been graded.
        ^

was
► Nobody who participated in the clinical trials ~~were~~ given a
                                                     ^

placebo.

The subjects of these sentences are *Each* and *Nobody*. These indefinite pronouns are third-person singular, so the verbs must
be *has* and *was*.

A few indefinite pronouns (*all, any, none, some*) may be
singular or plural depending on the noun or pronoun they
refer to.

SINGULAR   *Some* of our *luggage was* lost.

None of his *advice makes* sense.

PLURAL   *Some* of the *rocks are* slippery.

None of the *eggs were* broken.

NOTE: When the meaning of *none* is emphatically "not one," *none*
may be treated as singular: *None* [meaning "Not one"] *of the eggs
was broken.* Using *not one* instead is sometimes clearer: *Not one
of the eggs was broken.*

21f Treat collective nouns as singular unless the meaning is clearly plural.

Collective nouns such as *jury, committee, audience, crowd, troop,
family,* and *couple* name a class or a group. In American English,
collective nouns are nearly always treated as singular: They emphasize the group as a unit. Occasionally, when there is some reason to

draw attention to the individual members of the group, a collective noun may be treated as plural. (See also 22b.)

SINGULAR   The *class respects* the teacher.

PLURAL   The *class are* debating among themselves.

To underscore the notion of individuality in the second sentence, many writers would add a clearly plural noun.

PLURAL   The class *members are* debating among themselves.

> The board of trustees ~~meet~~ *meets* in Denver twice a year.

The board as a whole meets; there is no reason to draw attention to its individual members.

> A young couple ~~was~~ *were* arguing about politics while holding hands.

The meaning is clearly plural. Only separate individuals can argue and hold hands.

NOTE: The phrase *the number* is treated as singular, *a number* as plural.

SINGULAR   *The number* of school-age children *is* declining.

PLURAL   *A number* of children *are* attending the wedding.

NOTE: In general, when fractions or units of measurement are used with a singular noun, treat them as singular; when they are used with a plural noun, treat them as plural.

SINGULAR   *Three-fourths* of the salad *has* been eaten.

                 Twenty *inches* of wallboard *was* covered with mud.

PLURAL   *One-fourth* of the drivers *were* texting.

                 Two *pounds* of blueberries *were* used to make the pie.

21g Make the verb agree with its subject even when the subject follows the verb.

Verbs ordinarily follow subjects. When this normal order is reversed, it is easy to become confused. Sentences beginning with *there is* or *there are* (or *there was* or *there were*) are inverted; the subject follows the verb.

There *are* surprisingly few *honeybees* left in southern China.

► There ~~was~~ *were* a social worker and a neighbor at the meeting.

The subject, *worker and neighbor*, is plural, so the verb must be *were*.

Occasionally you may decide to invert a sentence for variety or effect. When you do so, check to make sure that your subject and verb agree.

► Of particular concern ~~is~~ *are* penicillin and tetracycline, antibiotics used to make animals more resistant to disease.

The subject, *penicillin and tetracycline*, is plural, so the verb must be *are*.

21h Make the verb agree with its subject, not with a subject complement.

One basic sentence pattern in English consists of a subject, a linking verb, and a subject complement: *Jack is a lawyer.* Because the subject complement (*lawyer*) names or describes the subject (*Jack*), it is sometimes mistaken for the subject. (See 47b on subject complements.)

These *exercises are* a way to test your ability to perform under pressure.

► A major force in today's economy ~~are~~ *is* children — as consumers, decision makers, and trend spotters.

Force is the subject, not *children*. If the corrected version seems too awkward, make *children* the subject: *Children are a major force in today's economy — as consumers, decision makers, and trend spotters.*

▶ A tent and a sleeping bag ~~is~~ *are* the required equipment for all

campers.

Tent and bag is the subject, not *equipment*.

21i *Who, which,* and *that* take verbs that agree with their antecedents.

Like most pronouns, the relative pronouns *who, which,* and *that* have antecedents, nouns or pronouns to which they refer. Relative pronouns used as subjects of subordinate clauses take verbs that agree with their antecedents.

ANT   PN   V

Take a *course that prepares* you for classroom management.

One of the

Constructions such as *one of the students who* [or *one of the things that*] cause problems for writers. Do not assume that the antecedent must be *one.* Instead, consider the logic of the sentence.

▶ Our ability to use language is one of the things that sets us

apart from animals.

The antecedent of *that* is *things,* not *one.* Several things set us apart from animals.

Only one of the

When the phrase *the only* comes before *one,* you are safe in assuming that *one* is the antecedent of the relative pronoun.

▶ Veronica was the only one of the first-year Spanish students

who ~~were~~ *was* fluent enough to apply for the exchange program.

The antecedent of *who* is *one,* not *students.* Only one student was fluent enough.

21j Words such as *athletics, economics, mathematics, physics, politics, statistics, measles,* and *news* are usually singular, despite their plural form.

> *is*
> Politics ~~are~~ among my mother's favorite pastimes.
> ^

EXCEPTION: Occasionally some of these words, especially *economics, mathematics, politics,* and *statistics,* have plural meanings.

> Office politics often sway decisions about hiring and
>
> promotion.

> The economics of the building plan are prohibitive.

21k Titles of works, company names, words mentioned as words, and gerund phrases are singular.

> *describes*
> *Lost Cities* ~~describe~~ the discoveries of fifty ancient civilizations.
> ^

> *specializes*
> Delmonico Brothers ~~specialize~~ in organic produce and
> ^
>
> additive-free meats.

> *is*
> *Controlled substances* ~~are~~ a euphemism for illegal drugs.
> ^

A gerund phrase consists of an *-ing* verb form followed by any objects, complements, or modifiers (see 48b). Treat gerund phrases as singular.

> *makes*
> Encountering long hold times ~~make~~ customers impatient with
> ^
>
> telephone tech support.

EXERCISE 21–1 For each sentence in the following passage, underline the subject (or compound subject) and then select the verb that agrees with it. (If you have trouble identifying the subject, consult 47a.)

Loggerhead sea turtles (migrate / migrates) thousands of miles before returning to their nesting location every two to three years. The nesting season for loggerhead turtles (span / spans) the hottest months of the summer. Although the habitat of Atlantic loggerheads (range / ranges) from Newfoundland to Argentina, nesting for these turtles (take / takes) place primarily along the southeastern coast of the United States. Female turtles that have reached sexual maturity (crawl / crawls) ashore at night to lay their eggs. The cavity that serves as a nest for the eggs (is / are) dug out with the female's strong flippers. Deposited into each nest (is / are) anywhere from fifty to two hundred spherical eggs, also known as a *clutch*. After a two-month incubation period, all eggs in the clutch (begin / begins) to hatch, and within a few days the young turtles attempt to make their way into the ocean. A major cause of the loggerhead's decreasing numbers (is / are) natural predators such as raccoons, birds, and crabs. Beach erosion and coastal development also (threaten / threatens) the turtles' survival. For example, a crowd of curious humans or lights from beachfront residences (is / are) enough to make the female abandon her nesting plans and return to the ocean. Since only one in one thousand loggerheads survives to adulthood, special care should be taken to protect this threatened species.

EXERCISE 21–2 Edit the following sentences to eliminate problems with subject-verb agreement. If a sentence is correct, write "correct" after it. Answers to lettered sentences appear in the back of the book. Example:

> *were*
> Jack's first days in the infantry ~~was~~ grueling.
>   ^

a. One of the main reasons for elephant poaching are the profits received from selling the ivory tusks.

b. Not until my interview with Dr. Hwang were other possibilities opened to me.

c. A number of students in the seminar was aware of the importance of joining the discussion.

   d. Batik cloth from Bali, blue and white ceramics from Delft, and a bocce ball from Turin has made Angelie's room the talk of the dorm.

   e. The board of directors, ignoring the wishes of the neighborhood, has voted to allow further development.

1. Measles is a contagious childhood disease.

2. Adorning a shelf in the lab is a Vietnamese figurine, a set of Korean clay gods, and an American plastic village.

3. The presence of certain bacteria in our bodies is one of the factors that determines our overall health.

4. Sheila is the only one of the many applicants who has the ability to step into this job.

5. Neither the explorer nor his companions was ever seen again.

22 Make pronouns and antecedents agree.

A pronoun is a word that substitutes for a noun. (See 46b.) Many pronouns have antecedents, nouns or pronouns to which they refer. A pronoun and its antecedent agree when they are both singular or both plural.

SINGULAR   *Dr. Ava Berto* finished *her* rounds.

PLURAL   The hospital *interns* finished *their* rounds.

 MULTILINGUAL The pronouns *he, his, she, her, it,* and *its* must agree in gender (masculine, feminine, or neuter) with their antecedents, not with the words they modify.

   Steve visited *his* [not *her*] sister in Seattle.

22a Do not use plural pronouns to refer to singular antecedents.

Writers are frequently tempted to use plural pronouns to refer to two kinds of singular antecedents: indefinite pronouns and generic nouns.

Indefinite pronouns

Indefinite pronouns refer to nonspecific persons or things. Even though some of the following indefinite pronouns may seem to have plural meanings, treat them as singular in formal English.

anybody	each	everyone	nobody	somebody
anyone	either	everything	no one	someone
anything	everybody	neither	nothing	something

Everyone performs at *his or her* [not *their*] own fitness level.

When a plural pronoun refers mistakenly to a singular indefinite pronoun, you can usually choose one of three options for revision:

1. Replace the plural pronoun with *he or she* (or *his or her*).
2. Make the antecedent plural.
3. Rewrite the sentence so that no problem of agreement exists.

▶ When someone travels outside the United States for the
  he or she needs
  first time, ~~they need~~ to apply for a passport.

▶ *people travel*
  When ~~someone travels~~ outside the United States for the
  first time, they need to apply for a passport.

  Anyone who
▶ ~~When someone~~ travels outside the United States for the
  first time, / ~~they need~~ to apply for a passport.
                 needs

Because the *he or she* construction is wordy, often the second or third revision strategy is more effective. Using *he* (or *his*) to refer to persons of either sex, while less wordy, is considered sexist, as is using *she* (or *her*) for all persons. Some writers alternate male and female pronouns throughout a text, but the result is often awkward. See 17e and the chart on page 210 for strategies that avoid sexist usage.

NOTE: If you change a pronoun from singular to plural (or vice versa), check to be sure that the verb agrees with the new pronoun (see 21e).

Generic nouns

A generic noun represents a typical member of a group, such as a typical student, or any member of a group, such as any lawyer. Although generic nouns may seem to have plural meanings, they are singular.

Every *runner* must train rigorously if *he or she wants* [not *they want*] to excel.

When a plural pronoun refers mistakenly to a generic noun, you will usually have the same three revision options as mentioned on page 208 for indefinite pronouns.

> *he or she wants*
> A medical student must study hard if ~~they want~~ to succeed.

> *Medical students*
> ~~A medical student~~ must study hard if they want to succeed.
> ^

> A medical student must study hard ~~if they want~~ to succeed.

22b Treat collective nouns as singular unless the meaning is clearly plural.

Collective nouns such as *jury, committee, audience, crowd, class, troop, family, team,* and *couple* name a group. Ordinarily the group functions as a unit, so the noun should be treated as singular; if the members of the group function as individuals, however, the noun should be treated as plural. (See also 21f.)

AS A UNIT   The *committee* granted *its* permission to build.

AS INDIVIDUALS   The *committee* put *their* signatures on the document.

When treating a collective noun as plural, many writers prefer to add a clearly plural antecedent such as *members* to the

Choosing a revision strategy that avoids sexist language

Because many readers object to sexist language, avoid using *he, him,* and *his* (or *she, her,* and *hers*) to refer to both men and women. Also try to avoid the wordy expressions *he or she* and *his or her.* More graceful alternatives are usually possible.

Use an occasional *he or she* (or *his or her*).

▶ In our office, everyone works at ~~their~~ *his or her* own pace.

Make the antecedent plural.

▶ ~~An employee~~ *Employees* on extended disability leave may continue their

life insurance.

Recast the sentence.

▶ The amount of vacation time a federal worker may accrue depends

on ~~their~~ length of service.

▶ ~~If a~~ *A* child ~~is~~ born to parents who are both bipolar, ~~they have~~ *has* a high

chance of being bipolar.

▶ In his autobiography, Benjamin Franklin suggests that anyone can

achieve success ~~as long as they live~~ *by living* a virtuous life and ~~work~~ *working* hard.

---

sentence: *The members of the committee put their signatures on the document.*

▶ Defense attorney Clarence Darrow surprisingly urged the

jury to find his client, John Scopes, guilty so that he could

appeal the case to a higher court. The jury complied,

returning ~~their~~ *its* verdict in only nine minutes.

There is no reason to draw attention to the individual members of the jury, so *jury* should be treated as singular.

22c Treat most compound antecedents joined with *and* as plural.

In 1987, *Reagan and Gorbachev* held a summit where *they* signed the Intermediate-Range Nuclear Forces Treaty.

22d With compound antecedents joined with *or* or *nor* (or with *either . . . or* or *neither . . . nor*), make the pronoun agree with the nearer antecedent.

Either *Bruce* or *Tom* should receive first prize for *his* poem.

Neither the *mouse* nor the *rats* could find *their* way through the maze.

NOTE: If one of the antecedents is singular and the other plural, as in the second example, put the plural one last to avoid awkwardness.

EXCEPTION: If one antecedent is male and the other female, do not follow the traditional rule. The sentence *Either Bruce or Elizabeth should receive first prize for her short story* makes no sense. The best solution is to recast the sentence: *The prize for best short story should go to either Bruce or Elizabeth.*

EXERCISE 22–1 Edit the following sentences to eliminate problems with pronoun-antecedent agreement. Most of the sentences can be revised in more than one way, so experiment before choosing a solution. If a sentence is correct, write "correct" after it. Revisions of lettered sentences appear in the back of the book. Example:

Recruiters
~~The recruiter~~ may tell the truth, but there is much that they
^
choose not to tell.

a. Every presidential candidate must appeal to a wide variety of ethnic and social groups if they want to win the election.
b. David lent his motorcycle to someone who allowed their friend to use it.

c. The aerobics teacher motioned for everyone to move their arms in wide, slow circles.

d. The parade committee was unanimous in its decision to allow all groups and organizations to join the festivities.

e. The applicant should be bilingual if they want to qualify for this position.

1. If a driver refuses to take a blood or breath test, he or she will have their licenses suspended for six months.

2. Why should anyone learn a second language? One reason is to sharpen their minds.

3. The Department of Education issued guidelines for school security. They were trying to anticipate problems and avert disaster.

4. The logger in the Northwest relies on the old forest growth for their living.

5. If anyone notices any suspicious activity, they should report it to the police.

EXERCISE 22–2 Edit the following paragraph to eliminate problems with pronoun-antecedent agreement or sexist language.

A common practice in businesses is to put each employee in their own cubicle. A typical cubicle resembles an office, but their walls don't reach the ceiling. Many office managers feel that a cubicle floor plan has its advantages. Cubicles make a large area feel spacious. In addition, they can be moved around so that each new employee can be accommodated in his own work area. Of course, the cubicle model also has problems. The typical employee is not as happy with a cubicle as they would be with a traditional office. Also, productivity can suffer. Neither a manager nor a frontline worker can ordinarily do their best work in a cubicle because of noise and lack of privacy. Each worker can hear his neighbors tapping on computer keyboards, making telephone calls, and muttering under their breath.

23 Make pronoun references clear.

Pronouns substitute for nouns; they are a kind of shorthand. In a sentence like *After Andrew intercepted the ball, he kicked it as hard as he could*, the pronouns *he* and *it* substitute for the nouns *Andrew* and *ball*. The word a pronoun refers to is called its *antecedent*.

23a Avoid ambiguous or remote pronoun reference.

Ambiguous pronoun reference occurs when a pronoun could refer to two possible antecedents.

> *The pitcher broke when Gloria set it*
> ► ~~When Gloria set the pitcher~~ on the glass-topped table./
>   ^   ^
>
> ~~it broke.~~

> *"You have*
> ► Tom told James, ~~that he had~~ won the lottery.*"*
>   ^   ^

What broke — the pitcher or the table? Who won the lottery — Tom or James? The revisions eliminate the ambiguity.

Remote pronoun reference occurs when a pronoun is too far away from its antecedent for easy reading.

> ► After the court ordered my ex-husband to pay child support,
>
> he refused. Approximately eight months later, we were back
>
> in court. This time the judge ordered him to make payments
>
> directly to the Support and Collections Unit, which would in
>
> turn pay me. For the first six months, I received regular pay-
>   *my ex-husband*
> ments, but then they stopped. Again ~~he~~ was summoned to
>   ^
> appear in court; he did not respond.

The pronoun *he* was too distant from its antecedent, *ex-husband*, which appeared several sentences earlier.

23b Generally, avoid broad reference of *this, that, which,* and *it*.

For clarity, the pronouns *this, that, which,* and *it* should ordinarily refer to specific antecedents rather than to whole ideas or sentences. When a pronoun's reference is needlessly broad, either replace the pronoun with a noun or supply an antecedent to which the pronoun clearly refers.

▶ By advertising on television, pharmaceutical companies gain

exposure for their prescription drugs. Patients respond to
   the ads
~~this~~ by requesting drugs they might not need.
   ^

For clarity, the writer substituted the noun *ads* for the pronoun *this*,
which referred broadly to the idea expressed in the preceding sentence.

▶ Romeo and Juliet were both too young to have acquired
                       a fact
much wisdom, ~~and~~ that accounts for their rash actions.
             ^

The writer added an antecedent (*fact*) that the pronoun *that* clearly
refers to.

23c Do not use a pronoun to refer to an implied antecedent.

A pronoun should refer to a specific antecedent, not to a word
that is implied but not present in the sentence.

                                   the braids
▶ After braiding Ann's hair, Sue decorated ~~them~~ with ribbons.
                                            ^

The pronoun *them* referred to Ann's braids (implied by the term
braiding), but the word *braids* did not appear in the sentence.

Modifiers, such as possessives, cannot serve as antecedents.
A modifier may strongly imply the noun that a pronoun might
logically refer to, but it is not itself that noun.

                        Jamaica Kincaid
▶ In ~~Jamaica Kincaid's~~ "Girl," ~~she~~ describes the advice a
                                   ^

mother gives her daughter, including the mysterious

warning not to be "the kind of woman who the baker won't

let near the bread" (454).

Using the possessive form of an author's name to introduce a source
leads to a problem later in this sentence: The pronoun *she* cannot refer
logically to a possessive modifier (*Jamaica Kincaid's*). The revision
substitutes the noun *Jamaica Kincaid* for the pronoun *she*, thereby
eliminating the problem.

23d Avoid the indefinite use of *they, it,* and *you.*

Do not use the pronoun *they* to refer indefinitely to persons who have not been specifically mentioned. *They* should always refer to a specific antecedent.

> *the board*
> ► In June, ~~they~~ announced that parents would have to pay a fee
>   ^
>
> for their children to participate in sports and music programs
>
> starting in September.

The word *it* should not be used indefinitely in constructions such as *It is said on television . . .* or *In the article, it says that. . . .*

> *The*
> ► ~~In the~~ encyclopedia ~~it~~ states that male moths can smell
>   ^
>
> female moths from several miles away.

The pronoun *you* is appropriate only when the writer is addressing the reader directly: *Once you have kneaded the dough, let it rise in a warm place.* Except in informal contexts, however, *you* should not be used to mean "anyone in general." Use a noun instead.

> *a guest*
> ► Ms. Pickersgill's *Guide to Etiquette* stipulates that ~~you~~ should
>   ^
>
> not arrive at a party too early or leave too late.

23e To refer to persons, use *who, whom,* or *whose,* not *which* or *that.*

In most contexts, use *who, whom,* or *whose* to refer to persons, *which* or *that* to refer to animals or things. *Which* is reserved only for animals or things, so it is impolite to use it to refer to persons.

> *whom*
> ► All thirty-two women in the study, half of ~~which~~ were
>   ^
>
> unemployed for more than six months, reported higher
>
> self-esteem after job training.

Although *that* is sometimes used to refer to persons, many readers will find such references dehumanizing. It is more polite to use a form of *who* — a word reserved only for people.

► During the two-day festival El Día de los Muertos (Day of the

　Dead), Mexican families celebrate loved ones ~~that~~ who have died.

EXERCISE 23–1　Edit the following sentences to correct errors in pronoun reference. In some cases, you will need to decide on an antecedent that the pronoun might logically refer to. Revisions of lettered sentences appear in the back of the book. Example:

Although Apple makes the most widely recognized MP3

player, other companies have gained a share of the market.

The competition
~~This~~ has kept prices from skyrocketing.

a. They say that engineering students should have hands-on experience with dismantling and reassembling machines.

b. She had decorated her living room with posters from chamber music festivals. This led her date to believe that she was interested in classical music. Actually she preferred rock.

c. In my high school, you didn't need to get all A's to be considered a success; you just needed to work to your ability.

d. Marianne told Jenny that she was worried about her mother's illness.

e. Though Lewis cried for several minutes after scraping his knee, eventually it subsided.

1. Our German conversation group is made up of six people, three of which I had never met before.

2. Many people believe that the polygraph test is highly reliable if you employ a licensed examiner.

3. Parent involvement is high at Mission San Jose High School. They participate in many committees and activities that affect all aspects of school life.

4. Because of Paul Robeson's outspoken attitude toward fascism, he was labeled a Communist.

5. In the report, it points out that the bald eagle, after several decades of protection, was removed from the endangered species list in 1997.

EXERCISE 23–2   Edit the following passage to correct errors in pronoun reference. In some cases, you will need to decide on an antecedent that the pronoun might logically refer to.

Since the Internet's inception in the 1980s, it has grown to be one of the largest communications forums in the world. The Internet was created by a team of academics who were building on a platform that government scientists had started developing in the 1950s. They initially viewed it as a noncommercial enterprise that would serve only the needs of the academic and technical communities. But with the introduction of user-friendly browser technology in the 1990s, it expanded tremendously. By the late 1990s, many businesses were connecting to the Internet with high-speed broadband and fiber-optic connections, which is also true of many home users today. Accessing information, shopping, and communicating are easier than ever before. This, however, can lead to some possible drawbacks. You can be bombarded with spam and pop-up ads or attacked by harmful viruses and worms. They say that the best way to protect home computers from harm is to keep antivirus protection programs up-to-date and to shut them down when not in use.

24   Distinguish between pronouns such as *I* and *me*.

The personal pronouns in the following chart change what is known as *case form* according to their grammatical function in a sentence. Pronouns functioning as subjects or subject complements appear in the *subjective* case; those functioning as objects appear in the *objective* case; and those showing ownership appear in the *possessive* case.

	SUBJECTIVE CASE	OBJECTIVE CASE	POSSESSIVE CASE
SINGULAR	I	me	my
	you	you	your
	he/she/it	him/her/it	his/her/its
PLURAL	we	us	our
	you	you	your
	they	them	their

Pronouns in the subjective and objective cases are frequently confused. Most of the rules in this section specify when to use one or the other of these cases (*I* or *me*, *he* or *him*, and so on). Section 24g explains a special use of pronouns and nouns in the possessive case.

24a Use the subjective case (*I, you, he, she, it, we, they*) for subjects and subject complements.

When personal pronouns are used as subjects, ordinarily your ear will tell you the correct pronoun. Problems sometimes arise, however, with compound word groups containing a pronoun, so it is not always safe to trust your ear.

> Joel ran away from home because his stepfather and ~~him~~ had
> *he*
>   ^
> quarreled.

His stepfather and he is the subject of the verb *had quarreled*. If we strip away the words *his stepfather and*, the correct pronoun becomes clear: *he had quarreled* (not *him had quarreled*).

When a pronoun is used as a subject complement (a word following a linking verb), your ear may mislead you, since the incorrect form is frequently heard in casual speech. (See "subject complement," 47b.)

> During the Lindbergh trial, Bruno Hauptmann repeatedly
> *he.*
> denied that the kidnapper was ~~him.~~
>   ^

If *kidnapper was he* seems too stilted, rewrite the sentence: *During the Lindbergh trial, Bruno Hauptmann repeatedly denied that he was the kidnapper.*

24b Use the objective case (*me, you, him, her, it, us, them*) for all objects.

When a personal pronoun is used as a direct object, an indirect object, or the object of a preposition, ordinarily your ear will lead you to the correct pronoun. When an object is compound, however, you may occasionally become confused.

▶ Janice was indignant when she realized that the salesclerk

                                                  her.
   was insulting her mother and ~~she.~~
                                          ^

Her mother and her is the direct object of the verb *was insulting.* Strip away the words *her mother and* to hear the correct pronoun: *was insulting her* (not *was insulting she*).

                                                    me
▶ The most traumatic experience for her father and ~~I~~ occurred
                                                     ^

   long after her operation.

Her father and me is the object of the preposition *for.* Strip away the words *her father and* to test for the correct pronoun: *for me* (not *for I*).

When in doubt about the correct pronoun, some writers try to avoid making the choice by using a reflexive pronoun such as *myself.* Using a reflexive pronoun in such situations is nonstandard.

                                        me
▶ The Indian cab driver gave my cousin and ~~myself~~ some good
                                                ^

   tips on traveling in New Delhi.

My cousin and me is the indirect object of the verb *gave.* For correct uses of *myself,* see the glossary of usage.

24c   Put an appositive and the word to which it refers in the same case.

Appositives are noun phrases that rename nouns or pronouns. A pronoun used as an appositive has the same function (usually subject or object) as the word(s) it renames.

                                    I,
▶ The chief strategists, Dr. Bell and ~~me,~~ could not agree on a plan.
                                           ^

The appositive *Dr. Bell and I* renames the subject, *strategists.* Test: *I could not agree* (not *me could not agree*).

▶ The reporter interviewed only two witnesses, the bicyclist

       me.
   and ~~I.~~
      ^

The appositive *the bicyclist and me* renames the direct object, *witnesses.* Test: *interviewed me* (not *interviewed I*).

24d Following *than* or *as*, choose the pronoun that expresses your meaning.

When a comparison begins with *than* or *as*, your choice of a pronoun will depend on your meaning. To test for the correct pronoun, mentally complete the sentence: *My roommate likes football more than I [do]*.

► In our position paper supporting nationalized health care

in the United States, we argued that Canadians are much

               we.
  better off than ~~us.~~
             ^

We is the subject of the verb *are*, which is understood: *Canadians are much better off than we [are]*. If the correct English seems too formal, you can always add the verb.

► We respected no other candidate for the city council as much

     her.
  as ~~she.~~
     ^

This sentence means that we respected no other candidate as much as *we respected her*. *Her* is the direct object of the understood verb *respected*.

24e For *we* or *us* before a noun, choose the pronoun that would be appropriate if the noun were omitted.

    We
► ~~Us~~ tenants would rather fight than move.
  ^

                      us
► Management is shortchanging ~~we~~ tenants.
                       ^

No one would say *Us would rather fight than move* or *Management is shortchanging we*.

24f Use the objective case for subjects and objects of infinitives.

An infinitive is the word *to* followed by the base form of a verb. (See 48b.) Subjects of infinitives are an exception to the rule that subjects must be in the subjective case. Whenever an infinitive has

pronouns following *than* or *as* • *we* vs. *us* • object pronouns
with infinitives (*to see*) • pronouns with *-ing* noun form

case
24g 221

a subject, it must be in the objective case. Objects of infinitives also are in the objective case.

> *me* *her*
> Sue asked John and ~~I~~ to drive the senator and ~~she~~ to the airport.
> ^   ^

John and me is the subject of the infinitive *to drive; senator and her* is the direct object of the infinitive.

24g Use the possessive case to modify a gerund.

A pronoun that modifies a gerund or a gerund phrase should be in the possessive case (*my, our, your, his, her, its, their*). A gerund is a verb form ending in *-ing* that functions as a noun. Gerunds frequently appear in phrases; when they do, the whole gerund phrase functions as a noun. (See 48b.)

> *your*
> The chances of ~~you~~ being hit by lightning are about two million
> ^
>
> to one.

Your modifies the gerund phrase *being hit by lightning.*

Nouns as well as pronouns may modify gerunds. To form the possessive case of a noun, use an apostrophe and an *-s* (*victim's*) or just an apostrophe (*victims'*). (See 36a.)

> *aristocracy's*
> The old order in France paid a high price for the ~~aristocracy~~
> ^
>
> exploiting the lower classes.

The possessive noun *aristocracy's* modifies the gerund phrase *exploiting the lower classes.*

EXERCISE 24–1 Edit the following sentences to eliminate errors in pronoun case. If a sentence is correct, write "correct" after it. Answers to lettered sentences appear in the back of the book. Example:

> *he.*
> Papa chops wood for neighbors much younger than ~~him.~~
> ^

a. Rick applied for the job even though he heard that other candidates were more experienced than he.

PRACTICE hackerhandbooks.com/rules
> Grammar > 24–3 and 24–4
> 25–3 and 25–4 (pronoun review)

b. The volleyball team could not believe that the coach was she.

c. She appreciated him telling the truth in such a difficult situation.

d. The director has asked you and I to draft a proposal for a new recycling plan.

e. Five close friends and myself rented a station wagon, packed it with food, and drove two hundred miles to Mardi Gras.

1. The squawk of the brass horns nearly overwhelmed us oboe and bassoon players.

2. Ushio, the last rock climber up the wall, tossed Teri and she the remaining pitons and carabiners.

3. The programmer realized that her and the interface designers were creating an entirely new Web application.

4. My desire to understand classical music was aided by me working as an usher at Symphony Hall.

5. The shower of sinking bricks caused he and his diving partner to race away from the collapsing seawall.

EXERCISE 24-2   In the following paragraph, choose the correct pronoun in each set of parentheses.

We may blame television for the number of products based on characters in children's TV shows — from Big Bird to SpongeBob — but in fact merchandising that capitalizes on a character's popularity started long before television. Raggedy Ann began as a child's rag doll, and a few years later books about (she / her) and her brother, Raggedy Andy, were published. A cartoonist named Johnny Gruelle painted a cloth face on a family doll and applied for a patent in 1915. Later Gruelle began writing and illustrating stories about Raggedy Ann, and in 1918 (he / him) and a publisher teamed up to publish the books and sell the dolls. He was not the only one to try to sell products linked to children's stories. Beatrix Potter published the first of many Peter Rabbit picture books in 1902, and no one was better than (she / her) at making a living from spin-offs. After Peter Rabbit and Benjamin Bunny became popular, Potter began putting pictures of (they / them) and their little animal friends on merchandise. Potter had fans all over the world, and she understood (them / their) wanting to see Peter Rabbit not only in books but also on teapots and plates and lamps and other furnishings for the nursery. Potter and Gruelle, like countless others before and since, knew that entertaining children could be a profitable business.

25 Distinguish between *who* and *whom*.

The choice between *who* and *whom* (or *whoever* and *whomever*) occurs primarily in subordinate clauses and in questions. *Who* and *whoever*, subjective-case pronouns, are used for subjects and subject complements. *Whom* and *whomever*, objective-case pronouns, are used for objects. (See 25a and 25b.)

An exception to this general rule occurs when the pronoun functions as the subject of an infinitive (see 25c). See also 24f.

25a In subordinate clauses, use *who* and *whoever* for subjects and subject complements, *whom* and *whomever* for all objects.

When *who* and *whom* (or *whoever* and *whomever*) introduce subordinate clauses, their case is determined by their function *within the clause they introduce.*

In the following two examples, the pronouns *who* and *whoever* function as the subjects of the clauses they introduce.

>   *who*
> First prize goes to the runner ~~whom~~ earns the most points.

The subordinate clause is *who earns the most points.* The verb of the clause is *earns*, and its subject is *who.*

> Maya Angelou's *I Know Why the Caged Bird Sings* should be
>   *whoever*
> read by ~~whomever~~ is interested in the effects of racial prejudice
> on children.

The writer selected the pronoun *whomever*, thinking that it was the object of the preposition *by*. However, the object of the preposition is the entire subordinate clause *whoever is interested in the effects of racial prejudice on children.* The verb of the clause is *is*, and the subject of the verb is *whoever.*

When functioning as an object in a subordinate clause, *whom* (or *whomever*) also appears out of order, before the subject and verb. To choose the correct pronoun, you can mentally restructure the clause.

▸ You will work with our senior traders, ~~who~~ *whom* you will meet later.

> The subordinate clause is *whom you will meet later*. The subject of the clause is *you*, and the verb is *will meet*. *Whom* is the direct object of the verb. The correct choice becomes clear if you mentally restructure the clause: *you will meet whom*.

When functioning as the object of a preposition in a subordinate clause, *whom* is often separated from its preposition.

▸ The tutor ~~who~~ *whom* I was assigned to was very supportive.

> *Whom* is the object of the preposition *to*. In this sentence, the writer might choose to drop *whom*: *The tutor I was assigned to was very supportive*.

NOTE: Inserted expressions such as *they know*, *I think*, and *she says* should be ignored in determining whether to use *who* or *whom*.

▸ The speech pathologist reported a particularly difficult session with a stroke patient ~~whom~~ *who* she knew was suffering from aphasia.

> *Who* is the subject of *was suffering*, not the object of *knew*.

25b In questions, use *who* and *whoever* for subjects, *whom* and *whomever* for all objects.

When *who* and *whom* (or *whoever* and *whomever*) are used to open questions, their case is determined by their function within the question. In the following example, *who* functions as the subject of the question.

▸ ~~Whom~~ *Who* was responsible for creating that computer virus?

> *Who* is the subject of the verb *was*.

When *whom* functions as the object of a verb or the object of a preposition in a question, it appears out of normal order. To choose the correct pronoun, you can mentally restructure the question.

> *Whom*
> ~~Who~~ did the Democratic Party nominate in 2008?
>   ^

> *Whom* is the direct object of the verb *did nominate*. This becomes clear if you restructure the question: *The Democratic Party did nominate whom in 2008?*

25c Use *whom* for subjects or objects of infinitives.

An infinitive is the word *to* followed by the base form of a verb. (See 48b.) Subjects of infinitives are an exception to the rule that subjects must be in the subjective case. The subject of an infinitive must be in the objective case. Objects of infinitives also are in the objective case.

> *whom*
> ▶ When it comes to money, I know ~~who~~ to believe.
>   ^

> The infinitive phrase *whom to believe* is the direct object of the verb *know*, and *whom* is the subject of the infinitive *to believe*.

NOTE: In spoken English, *who* is frequently used when the correct *whom* sounds too stuffy. Even educated speakers are likely to say *Who* [not *Whom*] *did Senator Boxer replace?* Although some readers will accept such constructions in informal written English, it is safer to use *whom* in formal English.

EXERCISE 25–1 Edit the following sentences to eliminate errors in the use of *who* and *whom* (or *whoever* and *whomever*). If a sentence is correct, write "correct" after it. Answers to lettered sentences appear in the back of the book. Example:

> *whom*
> What is the address of the artist ~~who~~ Antonio hired?
>   ^

a. The roundtable featured scholars who I had never heard of.
b. Arriving late for rehearsal, we had no idea who was supposed to dance with whom.
c. Whom did you support for student government president?
d. Daniel always gives a holiday donation to whomever needs it.
e. So many singers came to the audition that Natalia had trouble deciding who to select for the choir.

PRACTICE hackerhandbooks.com/rules
> Grammar > 25–2
> 25–3 and 25–4 (pronoun review)

1. My cousin Sylvie, who I am teaching to fly a kite, watches us every time we compete.
2. Who decided to research the history of Hungarians in New Brunswick?
3. According to Greek myth, the Sphinx devoured those who could not answer her riddles.
4. The people who ordered their medications from Canada were retirees whom don't have health insurance.
5. Who did the committee select?

26 Choose adjectives and adverbs with care.

Adjectives modify nouns or pronouns. They usually come before the word they modify; occasionally they function as complements following the word they modify. Adverbs modify verbs, adjectives, or other adverbs. (See 46d and 46e.)

Many adverbs are formed by adding *-ly* to adjectives (*normal, normally; smooth, smoothly*). But don't assume that all words ending in *-ly* are adverbs or that all adverbs end in *-ly*. Some adjectives end in *-ly* (*lovely, friendly*), and some adverbs don't (*always, here, there*). When in doubt, consult a dictionary.

MULTILINGUAL Placement of adjectives and adverbs can be a tricky matter for multilingual writers. See 30f and 30h.

26a Use adjectives to modify nouns.

Adjectives ordinarily precede the nouns they modify. But they can also function as subject complements or object complements, following the nouns they modify.

MULTILINGUAL In English, adjectives are not pluralized to agree with the words they modify: *The red* [not *reds*] *roses were a surprise.*

Subject complements

A subject complement follows a linking verb and completes the meaning of the subject. (See 47b.) When an adjective functions as a subject complement, it describes the subject.

Justice is *blind.*

Problems can arise with verbs such as *smell, taste, look,* and *feel,* which sometimes, but not always, function as linking verbs. If the word following one of these verbs describes the subject, use an adjective; if the word following the verb modifies the verb, use an adverb.

ADJECTIVE   The detective looked *cautious.*

ADVERB   The detective looked *cautiously* for fingerprints.

The adjective *cautious* describes the detective; the adverb *cautiously* modifies the verb *looked.*

Linking verbs suggest states of being, not actions. Notice, for example, the different meanings of *looked* in the preceding examples. To look cautious suggests the state of being cautious; to look cautiously is to perform an action in a cautious way.

▶ The lilacs in our backyard smell especially ~~sweetly~~ *sweet* this year.

The verb *smell* suggests a state of being, not an action. Therefore, it should be followed by an adjective, not an adverb.

▶ The drawings looked ~~well~~ *good* after the architect made a few changes.

The verb *looked* is a linking verb suggesting a state of being, not an action. The adjective *good* is appropriate following the linking verb to describe *drawings.* (See also 26c.)

Object complements

An object complement follows a direct object and completes its meaning. (See 47b.) When an adjective functions as an object complement, it describes the direct object.

Sorrow makes *us wise.*

Object complements occur with verbs such as *call, consider, create, find, keep,* and *make.* When a modifier follows the direct object of one of these verbs, use an adjective to describe the direct object; use an adverb to modify the verb.

ADJECTIVE The referee called the plays *perfect.*

ADVERB The referee called the plays *perfectly.*

The first sentence means that the referee considered the plays to be perfect; the second means that the referee did an excellent job of calling the plays.

26b Use adverbs to modify verbs, adjectives, and other adverbs.

When adverbs modify verbs (or verbals), they nearly always answer the question When? Where? How? Why? Under what conditions? How often? or To what degree? When adverbs modify adjectives or other adverbs, they usually qualify or intensify the meaning of the word they modify. (See 46e.)

Adjectives are often used incorrectly in place of adverbs in casual or nonstandard speech.

▶ The travel arrangement worked out ~~perfect~~ *perfectly* for everyone.

▶ The manager must see that the office runs ~~smooth~~ *smoothly* and ~~efficient.~~ *efficiently.*

The adverb *perfectly* modifies the verb *worked out*; the adverbs *smoothly* and *efficiently* modify the verb *runs.*

▶ The chance of recovering any property lost in the fire looks ~~real~~ *really* slim.

Only adverbs can modify adjectives or other adverbs. *Really* intensifies the meaning of the adjective *slim.*

26c Distinguish between *good* and *well, bad* and *badly.*

Good is an adjective (*good performance*). *Well* is an adverb when it modifies a verb (*speak well*). The use of the adjective *good* in place of the adverb *well* to modify a verb is nonstandard and especially common in casual speech.

adverbs with verb, adjective, adverb • *good* vs. *well* •
bad vs. *badly* • *more* vs. *most* • *-er* vs. *-est* forms

adj/adv
26d
229

▶ We were glad that Sanya had done ~~good~~ *well* on the CPA exam.
^

The adverb *well* modifies the verb *had done*.

Confusion can arise because *well* is an adjective when it modifies a noun or pronoun and means "healthy" or "satisfactory" (*The babies were well and warm*).

▶ Adrienne did not feel ~~good~~ *well,* but she made her presentation
^

anyway.

As an adjective following the linking verb *did feel*, *well* describes Adrienne's health.

Bad is always an adjective and should be used to describe a noun; *badly* is always an adverb and should be used to modify a verb. The adverb *badly* is often used inappropriately to describe a noun, especially following a linking verb.

▶ The sisters felt ~~badly~~ *bad* when they realized they had left their
^

brother out of the planning.

The adjective *bad* is used after the linking verb *felt* to describe the noun *sisters*.

26d Use comparatives and superlatives with care.

Most adjectives and adverbs have three forms: the positive, the comparative, and the superlative.

POSITIVE	COMPARATIVE	SUPERLATIVE
soft	softer	softest
fast	faster	fastest
careful	more careful	most careful
bad	worse	worst
good	better	best

Comparative versus superlative

Use the comparative to compare two things, the superlative to compare three or more.

▶ Which of these two low-carb drinks is ~~best?~~ *better?*

▶ Though Shaw and Jackson are impressive, Zhao is the ~~more~~ *most*
qualified of the three candidates running for mayor.

Forming comparatives and superlatives

To form comparatives and superlatives of most one- and two-syllable adjectives, use the endings *-er* and *-est*: *smooth, smoother, smoothest; easy, easier, easiest.* With longer adjectives, use *more* and *most* (or *less* and *least* for downward comparisons): *exciting, more exciting, most exciting; helpful, less helpful, least helpful.*

Some one-syllable adverbs take the endings *-er* and *-est* (*fast, faster, fastest*), but longer adverbs and all of those ending in *-ly* form the comparative and superlative with *more* and *most* (or *less* and *least*).

The comparative and superlative forms of some adjectives and adverbs are irregular: *good, better, best; well, better, best; bad, worse, worst; badly, worse, worst.*

▶ The Kirov is the ~~talentedest~~ *most talented* ballet company we have seen.

▶ According to our projections, sales at local businesses will
be ~~worser~~ *worse* than those at the chain stores this winter.

Double comparatives or superlatives

Do not use double comparatives or superlatives. When you have added *-er* or *-est* to an adjective or adverb, do not also use *more* or *most* (or *less* or *least*).

▶ Of all her family, Julia is the ~~most~~ happiest about the move.

▶ All the polls indicated that Gore was more ~~likelier~~ *likely* to win
than Bush.

Absolute concepts

Avoid expressions such as *more straight, less perfect, very round,* and *most unique.* Either something is unique or it isn't. It is illogical to suggest that absolute concepts come in degrees.

> *unusual*
> That is the most ~~unique~~ wedding gown I have ever seen.
> ^

> *valuable*
> The painting would have been even more ~~priceless~~ had it
> ^
> been signed.

26e Avoid double negatives.

Standard English allows two negatives only if a positive meaning
is intended: *The orchestra was not unhappy with its performance*
(meaning that the orchestra was happy). Using a double negative
to emphasize a negative meaning is nonstandard.

Negative modifiers such as *never, no*, and *not* should not be
paired with other negative modifiers or with negative words such
as *neither, none, no one, nobody*, and *nothing*.

> *anything*
> The county is not doing ~~nothing to see that the trash is~~
> ^
> picked up.

The double negative *not . . . nothing* is nonstandard.

The modifiers *hardly, barely*, and *scarcely* are considered
negatives in standard English, so they should not be used with
negatives such as *not, no one*, or *never*.

> *can*
> Maxine is so weak that she ~~can't~~ hardly climb stairs.
> ^

EXERCISE 26–1 Edit the following sentences to eliminate errors in the
use of adjectives and adverbs. If a sentence is correct, write "correct" after
it. Answers to lettered sentences appear in the back of the book. Example:

> *well*
> We weren't surprised by how ~~good~~ the sidecar racing team
> ^
> flowed through the tricky course.

a. Did you do good on last week's chemistry exam?
b. With the budget deadline approaching, our office hasn't hardly
   had time to handle routine correspondence.
c. Some flowers smell surprisingly bad.

d. The customer complained that he hadn't been treated nice.

e. Of all my relatives, Uncle Roberto is the most cleverest.

1. When you answer the phone, speak clear and courteous.

2. Who was more upset about the loss? Was it the coach or the quarterback or the owner of the team?

3. To a novice skateboarder, even the basic ollie seems real challenging.

4. After checking how bad I had been hurt, my sister dialed 911.

5. If the college's Web page had been updated more regular, students would have learned about the new course offerings.

EXERCISE 26–2   Edit the following passage to eliminate errors in the use of adjectives and adverbs.

Doctors recommend that to give skin the most fullest protection from ultraviolet rays, people should use plenty of sunscreen, limit sun exposure, and wear protective clothing. The commonest sunscreens today are known as "broad spectrum" because they block out both UVA and UVB rays. These lotions don't feel any differently on the skin from the old UVA-only types, but they work best at preventing premature aging and skin cancer. Many sunscreens claim to be waterproof, but they won't hardly provide adequate coverage after extended periods of swimming or perspiring. To protect good, even waterproof sunscreens should be reapplied liberal and often. All areas of exposed skin, including ears, backs of hands, and tops of feet, need to be coated good to avoid burning or damage. Some people's skin reacts bad to PABA, or para-aminobenzoic acid, so PABA-free (hypoallergenic) sunscreens are widely available. In addition to recommending sunscreen, doctors almost unanimously agree that people should stay out of the sun when rays are the most strongest — between 10:00 a.m. and 3:00 p.m. — and should limit time in the sun. They also suggest that people wear long-sleeved shirts, broad-brimmed hats, and long pants whenever possible.

27   Choose appropriate verb forms, tenses, and moods in standard English.

In speech, some people use verb forms and tenses that match a home dialect or variety of English. In writing, use standard English verb forms unless you are quoting nonstandard speech or using alternative forms for literary effect. (See 17c.)

standard verb forms • verbs with irregular
endings (*go, went, gone; see, saw, seen*, etc.)

vb

27a   233

Except for the verb *be*, all verbs in English have five forms. The following list shows the five forms and provides a sample sentence in which each might appear.

BASE FORM	Usually I (*walk, ride*).
PAST TENSE	Yesterday I (*walked, rode*).
PAST PARTICIPLE	I have (*walked, ridden*) many times before.
PRESENT PARTICIPLE	I am (*walking, riding*) right now.
-*S* FORM	He/she/it (*walks, rides*) regularly.

The verb *be* has eight forms instead of the usual five: *be, am, is, are, was, were, being, been.*

27a Choose standard English forms of irregular verbs.

For all regular verbs, the past-tense and past-participle forms are the same (ending in *-ed* or *-d*), so there is no danger of confusion. This is not true, however, for irregular verbs, such as the following.

BASE FORM	PAST TENSE	PAST PARTICIPLE
go	went	gone
break	broke	broken
fly	flew	flown
sing	sang	sung

The past-tense form always occurs alone, without a helping verb. It expresses action that occurred entirely in the past: *I rode to work yesterday. I walked to work last Tuesday.* The past participle is used with a helping verb. It forms the perfect tenses with *has, have,* or *had*; it forms the passive voice with *be, am, is, are, was, were, being,* or *been.* (See 46c for a complete list of helping verbs and 27f for a survey of tenses.)

PAST TENSE	Last July, we *went* to Paris.
HELPING VERB + PAST PARTICIPLE	We *have gone* to Paris twice.

The list of common irregular verbs beginning on the next page will help you distinguish between the past tense and the past participle. Choose the past-participle form if the verb in your sentence requires a helping verb; choose the past-tense form if the verb does not require a helping verb. (See verb tenses in 27f.)

▶ Yesterday we ~~seen~~ *saw* a documentary about Isabel Allende.

The past-tense *saw* is required because there is no helping verb.

▶ The truck was apparently ~~stole~~ *stolen* while the driver ate lunch.

▶ By Friday, the stock market had ~~fell~~ *fallen* two hundred points.

Because of the helping verbs *was* and *had*, the past-participle forms are required: *was stolen, had fallen.*

Common irregular verbs

BASE FORM	PAST TENSE	PAST PARTICIPLE
arise	arose	arisen
awake	awoke, awaked	awaked, awoke, awoken
be	was, were	been
beat	beat	beaten, beat
become	became	become
begin	began	begun
bend	bent	bent
bite	bit	bitten, bit
blow	blew	blown
break	broke	broken
bring	brought	brought
build	built	built
burst	burst	burst
buy	bought	bought
catch	caught	caught
choose	chose	chosen
cling	clung	clung
come	came	come
cost	cost	cost
deal	dealt	dealt
dig	dug	dug
dive	dived, dove	dived
do	did	done

BASE FORM	PAST TENSE	PAST PARTICIPLE
drag	dragged	dragged
draw	drew	drawn
dream	dreamed, dreamt	dreamed, dreamt
drink	drank	drunk
drive	drove	driven
eat	ate	eaten
fall	fell	fallen
fight	fought	fought
find	found	found
fly	flew	flown
forget	forgot	forgotten, forgot
freeze	froze	frozen
get	got	gotten, got
give	gave	given
go	went	gone
grow	grew	grown
hang (execute)	hanged	hanged
hang (suspend)	hung	hung
have	had	had
hear	heard	heard
hide	hid	hidden
hurt	hurt	hurt
keep	kept	kept
know	knew	known
lay (put)	laid	laid
lead	led	led
lend	lent	lent
let (allow)	let	let
lie (recline)	lay	lain
lose	lost	lost
make	made	made
prove	proved	proved, proven
read	read	read
ride	rode	ridden
ring	rang	rung
rise (get up)	rose	risen

(continued)

BASE FORM	PAST TENSE	PAST PARTICIPLE
run	ran	run
say	said	said
see	saw	seen
send	sent	sent
set (place)	set	set
shake	shook	shaken
shoot	shot	shot
shrink	shrank	shrunk
sing	sang	sung
sink	sank	sunk
sit (be seated)	sat	sat
slay	slew	slain
sleep	slept	slept
speak	spoke	spoken
spin	spun	spun
spring	sprang	sprung
stand	stood	stood
steal	stole	stolen
sting	stung	stung
strike	struck	struck, stricken
swear	swore	sworn
swim	swam	swum
swing	swung	swung
take	took	taken
teach	taught	taught
throw	threw	thrown
wake	woke, waked	waked, woken
wear	wore	worn
wring	wrung	wrung
write	wrote	written

27b Distinguish among the forms of *lie* and *lay*.

Writers and speakers frequently confuse the various forms of *lie* (meaning "to recline or rest on a surface") and *lay* (meaning "to put or place something"). *Lie* is an intransitive verb; it does not take a direct object: *The tax forms lie on the table.* The verb *lay* is transitive; it takes a direct object: *Please lay the tax forms on the table.* (See 47b.)

In addition to confusing the meaning of *lie* and *lay*, writers and speakers are often unfamiliar with the standard English forms of these verbs.

BASE FORM	PAST TENSE	PAST PARTICIPLE	PRESENT PARTICIPLE
lie ("recline")	lay	lain	lying
lay ("put")	laid	laid	laying

▶ Sue was so exhausted that she ~~laid~~ *lay* down for a nap.

The past-tense form of *lie* ("to recline") is *lay.*

▶ The patient had ~~laid~~ *lain* in an uncomfortable position all night.

The past-participle form of *lie* ("to recline") is *lain.* If the correct English seems too stilted, recast the sentence: *The patient had been lying in an uncomfortable position all night.*

▶ The prosecutor ~~lay~~ *laid* the pistol on a table close to the jurors.

The past-tense form of *lay* ("to place") is *laid.*

▶ Letters dating from the Civil War were ~~laying~~ *lying* in the corner of the chest.

The present participle of *lie* ("to rest on a surface") is *lying.*

EXERCISE 27–1 Edit the following sentences to eliminate problems with irregular verbs. If a sentence is correct, write "correct" after it. Answers to lettered sentences appear in the back of the book. Example:

The ranger ~~seen~~ *saw* the forest fire ten miles away.

a. When I get the urge to exercise, I lay down until it passes.
b. Grandmother had drove our new hybrid to the sunrise church service on Savage Mountain, so we were left with the station wagon.
c. A pile of dirty rags was laying at the bottom of the stairs.

d. How did the game know that the player had went from the room with the blue ogre to the hall where the gold was heaped?

e. Abraham Lincoln took good care of his legal clients; the contracts he drew for the Illinois Central Railroad could never be broke.

1. The burglar must have gone immediately upstairs, grabbed what looked good, and took off.

2. Have you ever dreamed that you were falling from a cliff or flying through the air?

3. Tomás reached for the pen, signed the title page of his novel, and then laid the book on the table for the first customer in line.

4. In her junior year, Cindy run the 400-meter dash in 58.1 seconds.

5. Larry claimed that he had drank too much soda, but Esther suspected the truth.

27c Use -*s* (or -*es*) endings on present-tense verbs that have third-person singular subjects.

All singular nouns (*child, tree*) and the pronouns *he, she,* and *it* are third-person singular; indefinite pronouns such as *everyone* and *neither* are also third-person singular. When the subject of a sentence is third-person singular, its verb takes an -*s* or -*es* ending in the present tense. (See also 21.)

	SINGULAR		PLURAL	
FIRST PERSON	I	know	we	know
SECOND PERSON	you	know	you	know
THIRD PERSON	he/she/it	knows	they	know
	child	knows	parents	know
	everyone	knows		

>   *drives*
> ▶ My neighbor ~~drive~~ to Marco Island every weekend.
>   ^

>   *turns*   *dissolves*   *eats*
> ▶ Sulfur dioxide ~~turn~~ leaves yellow, ~~dissolve~~ marble, and ~~eat~~
>   ^   ^   ^
>
> away iron and steel.

The subjects *neighbor* and *sulfur dioxide* are third-person singular, so the verbs must end in -*s*.

TIP: Do not add the -s ending to the verb if the subject is not third-person singular. The writers of the following sentences, knowing they sometimes dropped -s endings from verbs, over-corrected by adding the endings where they don't belong.

► I prepare~~s~~ program specifications and logic diagrams for

every installation.

The writer mistakenly concluded that the -s ending belongs on present-tense verbs used with *all* singular subjects, not just *third-person* singular subjects. The pronoun *I* is first-person singular, so its verb does not require the -s.

► The dirt floors require~~s~~ continual sweeping.

The writer mistakenly thought that the verb needed an -s ending because of the plural subject. But the -s ending is used only on present-tense verbs with third-person *singular* subjects.

Has versus *have*

In the present tense, use *has* with third-person singular subjects; all other subjects require *have*.

	SINGULAR		**PLURAL**	
FIRST PERSON	I	have	we	have
SECOND PERSON	you	have	you	have
THIRD PERSON	he/she/it	has	they	have

► This respected musician almost always ~~have~~ *has* a message to

convey in his work.

The subject *musician* is third-person singular, so the verb should be *has*.

► My law classes ~~has~~ *have* helped me understand contracts.

The subject of this sentence — *classes* — is third-person plural, so standard English requires *have*. *Has* is used only with third-person singular subjects.

Does versus *do* and *doesn't* versus *don't*

In the present tense, use *does* and *doesn't* with third-person singular subjects; all other subjects require *do* and *don't*.

	SINGULAR		PLURAL	
FIRST PERSON	I	do/don't	we	do/don't
SECOND PERSON	you	do/don't	you	do/don't
THIRD PERSON	he/she/it	does/doesn't	they	do/don't

                   doesn't
▶ Grandfather really ~~don't~~ have a place to call home.
               ^

Grandfather is third-person singular, so the verb should be *doesn't*.

Am, is, and *are; was* and *were*

The verb *be* has three forms in the present tense (*am, is, are*) and two in the past tense (*was, were*).

	SINGULAR		PLURAL	
FIRST PERSON	I	am/was	we	are/were
SECOND PERSON	you	are/were	you	are/were
THIRD PERSON	he/she/it	is/was	they	are/were

          were
▶ Did you think you ~~was~~ going to drown?
            ^

The subject *you* is second-person singular, so the verb should be *were*.

27d Do not omit -*ed* endings on verbs.

Speakers who do not fully pronounce -*ed* endings sometimes omit them unintentionally in writing. Leaving off -*ed* endings is common in many dialects and in informal speech even in standard English. In the following frequently used words and phrases, for example, the -*ed* ending is not always fully pronounced.

advised	developed	prejudiced	supposed to
asked	fixed	pronounced	used to
concerned	frightened	stereotyped	

When a verb is regular, both the past tense and the past participle are formed by adding -ed (or -d) to the base form of the verb.

Past tense

Use the ending -ed or -d to express the past tense of regular verbs. The past tense is used when the action occurred entirely in the past.

> Over the weekend, Ed ~~fix~~ ^*fixed*^ his brother's skateboard and tuned
>
> up his mother's 1991 Fiat.

> Last summer, my counselor ~~advise~~ ^*advised*^ me to ask my chemistry
>
> instructor for help.

Past participles

Past participles are used in three ways: (1) following *have*, *has*, or *had* to form one of the perfect tenses; (2) following *be*, *am*, *is*, *are*, *was*, *were*, *being*, or *been* to form the passive voice; and (3) as adjectives modifying nouns or pronouns. The perfect tenses are listed on page 244, and the passive voice is discussed in 8a. For a discussion of participles as adjectives, see 48b.

> Robin has ~~ask~~ ^*asked*^ for more housing staff for next year.
>
> *Has asked* is present perfect tense (*have* or *has* followed by a past participle).

> Though it is not a new phenomenon, domestic violence is
> now ~~publicize~~ ^*publicized*^ more than ever.
>
> *Is publicized* is a verb in the passive voice (a form of *be* followed by a past participle).

> All kickboxing classes end in a cool-down period to stretch
> ~~tighten~~ ^*tightened*^ muscles.
>
> The past participle *tightened* functions as an adjective modifying the noun *muscles*.

27e Do not omit needed verbs.

Although standard English allows some linking verbs and helping verbs to be contracted in informal contexts, it does not allow
them to be omitted.

Linking verbs, used to link subjects to subject complements,
are frequently a form of *be*: *be, am, is, are, was, were, being, been*.
(See 47b.) Some of these forms may be contracted (*I'm, she's, we're,
you're, they're*), but they should not be omitted altogether.

> *are*
> When we quiet in the evening, we can hear crickets in the woods.
>   ^

Helping verbs, used with main verbs, include forms of *be,
do,* and *have* and the modal verbs *can, will, shall, could, would,
should, may, might,* and *must*. (See 46c.) Some helping verbs may
be contracted (*he's leaving, we'll celebrate, they've been told*), but
they should not be omitted altogether.

> *have*
> We been in Chicago since last Thursday.
>   ^

> *would*
> Do you know someone who be good for the job?
>   ^

MULTILINGUAL Some languages do not require a linking verb
between a subject and its complement. English, however, requires a
verb in every sentence. See 30a.

> *am*
> Every night, I read a short book to my daughter. When I too busy,
>   ^
>
> my husband reads to her.

EXERCISE 27–2 Edit the following sentences to eliminate problems
with -*s* and -*ed* verb forms and with omitted verbs. If a sentence is correct, write "correct" after it. Answers to lettered sentences appear in the
back of the book. Example:

> *covers*
> The Pell Grant sometimes ~~cover~~ the student's full tuition.
>   ^

missing verbs • linking verbs (*is, were*) • tenses •
simple (*walk*) • perfect (*had walked*) • progressive (*am walking*)

vb
27f   243

a. The glass sculptures of the Swan Boats was prominent in the brightly lit lobby.

b. Visitors to the glass museum were not suppose to touch the exhibits.

c. Our church has all the latest technology, even a close-circuit television.

d. Christos didn't know about Marlo's promotion because he never listens. He always talking.

e. Most psychologists agree that no one performs well under stress.

1. Have there ever been a time in your life when you were too depressed to get out of bed?

2. My days in this department have taught me to do what I'm told without asking questions.

3. We have change our plan and are waiting out the storm before leaving.

4. Winter training for search-and-rescue divers consist of building up a tolerance to icy water temperatures.

5. How would you feel if a love one had been a victim of a crime like this?

27f Choose the appropriate verb tense.

Tenses indicate the time of an action in relation to the time of the speaking or writing about that action.

The most common problem with tenses — shifting confusingly from one tense to another — is discussed in section 13. Other problems with tenses are detailed in this section, after the following survey of tenses.

Survey of tenses

Tenses are classified as present, past, and future, with simple, perfect, and progressive forms for each.

Simple tenses   The simple tenses indicate relatively simple time relations. The *simple present* tense is used primarily for actions occurring at the same time they are being discussed or for actions occurring regularly. The *simple past* tense is used for actions completed in the past. The *simple future* tense is used for actions that will occur in the future. In the following table, the simple tenses are given for the regular verb *walk*, the irregular verb *ride*, and the highly irregular verb *be*.

SIMPLE PRESENT

SINGULAR		PLURAL	
I	walk, ride, am	we	walk, ride, are
you	walk, ride, are	you	walk, ride, are
he/she/it	walks, rides, is	they	walk, ride, are

SIMPLE PAST

SINGULAR		PLURAL	
I	walked, rode, was	we	walked, rode, were
you	walked, rode, were	you	walked, rode, were
he/she/it	walked, rode, was	they	walked, rode, were

SIMPLE FUTURE

I, you, he/she/it, we, they	will walk, ride, be

Perfect tenses More complex time relations are indicated by the perfect tenses. A verb in one of the perfect tenses (a form of *have* plus the past participle) expresses an action that was or will be completed at the time of another action.

PRESENT PERFECT

I, you, we, they	have walked, ridden, been
he/she/it	has walked, ridden, been

PAST PERFECT

I, you, he/she/it, we, they	had walked, ridden, been

FUTURE PERFECT

I, you, he/she/it, we, they	will have walked, ridden, been

Progressive forms The simple and perfect tenses have progressive forms that describe actions in progress. A progressive verb consists of a form of *be* followed by a present participle. The progressive forms are not normally used with certain verbs, such as *believe, know, hear, seem,* and *think.*

PRESENT PROGRESSIVE

I	am walking, riding, being
he/she/it	is walking, riding, being
you, we, they	are walking, riding, being

PAST PROGRESSIVE

| I, he/she/it | was walking, riding, being |
| you, we, they | were walking, riding, being |

FUTURE PROGRESSIVE

| I, you, he/she/it, we, they | will be walking, riding, being |

PRESENT PERFECT PROGRESSIVE

| I, you, we, they | have been walking, riding, being |
| he/she/it | has been walking, riding, being |

PAST PERFECT PROGRESSIVE

| I, you, he/she/it, we, they | had been walking, riding, being |

FUTURE PERFECT PROGRESSIVE

| I, you, he/she/it, we, they | will have been walking, riding, being |

MULTILINGUAL See 28a for more specific examples of verb tenses that can be challenging for multilingual writers.

Special uses of the present tense

Use the present tense when expressing general truths, when writing about literature, and when quoting, summarizing, or paraphrasing an author's views.

General truths or scientific principles should appear in the present tense unless such principles have been disproved.

> *revolves*
> ► Galileo taught that the earth ~~revolved~~ around the sun.
> ^

Because Galileo's teaching has not been discredited, the verb should be in the present tense. The following sentence, however, is acceptable: *Ptolemy taught that the sun revolved around the earth.*

When writing about a work of literature, you may be tempted to use the past tense. The convention, however, is to describe fictional events in the present tense.

>   In Masuji Ibuse's *Black Rain*, a child ~~reached~~ *reaches* for a

    pomegranate in his mother's garden, and a moment later

    he ~~was~~ *is* dead, killed by the blast of the atomic bomb.

When you are quoting, summarizing, or paraphrasing the author of a nonliterary work, use present-tense verbs such as *writes, reports, asserts,* and so on to introduce the source. This convention is usually followed even when the author is dead (unless a date or the context specifies the time of writing).

>   Dr. Jerome Groopman ~~argued~~ *argues* that doctors are "susceptible
>
>   to the subtle and not so subtle efforts of the pharmaceutical
>
>   industry to sculpt our thinking" (9).

In MLA style, signal phrases are written in the present tense, not the past tense. (See also 59a.)

APA NOTE: When you are documenting a paper with the APA (American Psychological Association) style of in-text citations, use past tense verbs such as *reported* or *demonstrated* or present perfect verbs such as *has reported* or *has demonstrated* to introduce the source.

> E. Wilson (1994) reported that positive reinforcement alone was a less effective teaching technique than a mixture of positive reinforcement and constructive criticism.

The past perfect tense

The past perfect tense consists of a past participle preceded by *had* (*had worked, had gone*). This tense is used for an action already completed by the time of another past action or for an action already completed at some specific past time.

> Everyone *had spoken* by the time I arrived.

> I pleaded my case, but Paula *had made up* her mind.

Writers sometimes use the simple past tense when they should use the past perfect.

> We built our cabin high on a pine knoll, forty feet above an

had been

abandoned quarry that ~~was~~ flooded in 1920 to create a lake.
^

The building of the cabin and the flooding of the quarry both occurred in the past, but the flooding was completed before the time of building.

had

> By the time dinner was served, the guest of honor left.
^

The past perfect tense is needed because the action of leaving was already completed at a specific past time (when dinner was served).

Some writers tend to overuse the past perfect tense. Do not use the past perfect if two past actions occurred at the same time.

wrote

> When Ernest Hemingway lived in Cuba, he ~~had written~~
^

~~*For Whom the Bell Tolls.*~~

Sequence of tenses with infinitives and participles

An infinitive is the base form of a verb preceded by *to*. (See 48b.) Use the present infinitive to show action at the same time as or later than the action of the verb in the sentence.

raise

> The club had hoped to ~~have raised~~ a thousand dollars by
^

April 1.

The action expressed in the infinitive (*to raise*) occurred later than the action of the sentence's verb (*had hoped*).

Use the perfect form of an infinitive (*to have* followed by the past participle) for an action occurring earlier than that of the verb in the sentence.

have joined

> Dan would like to ~~join~~ the navy, but he did not pass the
^

physical.

The liking occurs in the present; the joining would have occurred in the past.

Like the tense of an infinitive, the tense of a participle is governed by the tense of the sentence's verb. Use the present participle (ending in *-ing*) for an action occurring at the same time as that of the sentence's verb.

> *Hiking* the Appalachian Trail in early spring, we spotted many wildflowers.

Use the past participle (such as *given* or *helped*) or the present perfect participle (*having* plus the past participle) for an action occurring before that of the verb.

> *Discovered* off the coast of Florida, the Spanish galleon yielded many treasures.

> *Having worked* her way through college, Lee graduated debt-free.

27g Use the subjunctive mood in the few contexts that require it.

There are three moods in English: the *indicative*, used for facts, opinions, and questions; the *imperative*, used for orders or advice; and the *subjunctive*, used in certain contexts to express wishes, requests, or conditions contrary to fact. For many writers, the subjunctive causes the most problems.

Forms of the subjunctive

In the subjunctive mood, present-tense verbs do not change form to indicate the number and person of the subject (see 21). Instead, the subjunctive uses the base form of the verb (*be, drive, employ*) with all subjects.

> It is important that you *be* [not *are*] prepared for the interview.

> We asked that she *drive* [not *drives*] more slowly.

Also, in the subjunctive mood, there is only one past-tense form of *be: were* (never *was*).

> If I *were* [not *was*] you, I'd try a new strategy.

Uses of the subjunctive

The subjunctive mood appears only in a few contexts: in contrary-to-fact clauses beginning with *if* or expressing a wish; in *that* clauses following verbs such as *ask, insist, recommend, request,* and *suggest*; and in certain set expressions.

In contrary-to-fact clauses beginning with *if*   When a subordinate clause beginning with *if* expresses a condition contrary to fact, use the subjunctive *were* in place of *was.*

> ► If I ~~was~~ a member of Congress, I would vote for the new
>   ^*were*^
> health care bill.

> ► The astronomers would be able to see the moons of Jupiter
> tonight if the weather ~~was~~ clearer.
>   ^*were*^
>
> The verbs in these sentences express conditions that do not exist: The writer is not a member of Congress, and the weather is not clear.

Do not use the subjunctive mood in *if* clauses expressing conditions that exist or may exist.

If Dana *wins* the contest, she will leave for Barcelona in June.

In contrary-to-fact clauses expressing a wish   In formal English, use the subjunctive *were* in clauses expressing a wish or desire. While use of the indicative is common in informal speech, it is not appropriate in academic writing.

INFORMAL   I wish that Dr. Vaughn *was* my professor.

FORMAL   I wish that Dr. Vaughn *were* my professor.

In *that* clauses following verbs such as *ask, insist, request,* and *suggest*   Because requests have not yet become reality, they are expressed in the subjunctive mood.

> ► Professor Moore insists that her students ~~are~~ on time.
>   ^*be*^

> ► We recommend that Lambert ~~files~~ form 1050 soon.
>   ^*file*^

In certain set expressions   The subjunctive mood, once more widely used, remains in certain set expressions: *Be that as it may, as it were, far be it from me,* and so on.

EXERCISE 27–3 Edit the following sentences to eliminate errors in verb tense or mood. If a sentence is correct, write "correct" after it. Answers to lettered sentences appear in the back of the book. Example:

had been
After the path ~~was~~ plowed, we were able to walk through
          ^

the park.

a. The palace of Knossos in Crete is believed to have been destroyed by fire around 1375 BCE.

b. Watson and Crick discovered the mechanism that controlled inheritance in all life: the workings of the DNA molecule.

c. When city planners proposed rezoning the waterfront, did they know that the mayor promised to curb development in that neighborhood?

d. Tonight's concert begins at 9:30. If it were earlier, I'd consider going.

e. As soon as my aunt applied for the position of pastor, the post was filled by an inexperienced seminary graduate who had been so hastily snatched that his mortarboard was still in midair.

1. Don Quixote, in Cervantes's novel, was an idealist ill suited for life in the real world.

2. Visiting the technology museum inspired the high school seniors and had reminded them that science could be fun.

3. I would like to have been on the *Mayflower* but not to have experienced the first winter.

4. When the director yelled "Action!" I forgot my lines, even though I practiced my part every waking hour for three days.

5. If midday naps were a regular practice in American workplaces, employees would be far more productive.

Multilingual Writers and ESL Challenges

This section of *Rules for Writers* is primarily for multilingual writers. You may find this section helpful if you learned English as a second language (ESL) or if you speak a language other than English with your friends and family.

28   Verbs

Both native and nonnative speakers of English encounter challenges with verbs. Section 28 focuses on specific challenges that multilingual writers sometimes face. You can find more help with verbs in other sections in the book:

> making subjects and verbs agree (21)
>
> using irregular verb forms (27a, 27b)
>
> leaving off verb endings (27c, 27d)
>
> choosing the correct verb tense (27f)
>
> avoiding inappropriate uses of the passive voice (8a)

28a   Use the appropriate verb form and tense.

This section offers a brief review of English verb forms and tenses. For additional help, see 27 and 46c.

Basic verb forms

Every main verb in English has five forms, which are used to create all of the verb tenses in standard English. The chart at the top of page 253 shows these forms for the regular verb *help* and the irregular verbs *give* and *be*. See 27a for the forms of other common irregular verbs.

PRACTICE AND MODELS   hackerhandbooks.com/rules

> Multilingual/ESL > Charts and study help

> Sample student paper (draft and final)

> Exercises

> Links to online resources

Basic verb forms

	REGULAR VERB *HELP*	IRREGULAR VERB *GIVE*	IRREGULAR VERB *BE**
BASE FORM	help	give	be
PAST TENSE	helped	gave	was, were
PAST PARTICIPLE	helped	given	been
PRESENT PARTICIPLE	helping	giving	being
-S FORM	helps	gives	is

*Be also has the forms *am* and *are*, which are used in the present tense

Verb tenses

Section 27f describes all the verb tenses in English, showing the forms of a regular verb, an irregular verb, and the verb *be* in each tense. The chart on this page provides more details about the tenses commonly used in the active voice in writing; the chart on page 256 gives details about tenses commonly used in the passive voice.

Verb tenses commonly used in the active voice

For descriptions and examples of all verb tenses, see 27f. For verb tenses commonly used in the passive voice, see the chart on page 256.

Simple tenses
For general facts, states of being, habitual actions

Simple present   **Base form or -s form**

- general facts   College students often *study* late at night.
- states of being   Water *becomes* steam at 100° centigrade.
- habitual, repetitive actions   We *donate* to a different charity each year.
- scheduled future events   The train *arrives* tomorrow at 6:30 p.m.

NOTE: For uses of the present tense in writing about literature, see page 245.

Verb tenses commonly used in the active voice (continued)

Simple past | **Base form + -ed or -d or irregular form**

- completed actions at a specific time in the past

  The storm *destroyed* their property.
  She *drove* to Montana three years ago.

- facts or states of being in the past

  When I *was* young, I usually *walked* to school with my sister.

Simple future | **will + base form**

- future actions, promises, or predictions

  I *will exercise* tomorrow. The snowfall *will begin* around midnight.

Simple progressive forms
For continuing actions

Present progressive | **am, is, are + present participle**

- actions in progress at the present time, not continuing indefinitely

  The students *are taking* an exam in Room 105.
  The valet *is parking* the car.

- future actions (with *leave, go, come, move*, etc.)

  I *am leaving* tomorrow morning.

Past progressive | **was, were + present participle**

- actions in progress at a specific time in the past

  They *were swimming* when the storm struck.

- *was going to, were going to* for past plans that did not happen

  We *were going to* drive to Florida for spring break, but the car broke down.

NOTE: Some verbs are not normally used in the progressive: *appear, believe, belong, contain, have, hear, know, like, need, see, seem, taste, understand,* and *want.*

> want
> ▶ I ~~am wanting~~ to see August Wilson's *Radio Golf.*
>   ^

Perfect tenses
For actions that happened or will happen before another time

Present perfect | **has, have + past participle**

- repetitive or constant actions that began in the past and continue to the present

  I *have loved* cats since I was a child.
  Alicia *has worked* in Kenya for ten years.

Present perfect	**has, have + past participle**
• actions that happened at an unknown or unspecific past time	Stephen *has visited* Wales three times.

Past perfect	**had + past participle**
• actions that began or occurred before another time in the past	She *had* just *crossed* the street when the runaway car crashed into the building.

NOTE: For more discussion of uses of the past perfect, see 27f. For uses of the past perfect in conditional sentences, see 28e.

Perfect progressive forms
For continuous past actions before another time

Present perfect progressive	**has, have + been + present participle**
• continuous actions that began in the past and continue to the present	Yolanda *has been trying* to get a job in Boston for five years.

Past perfect progressive	**had + been + present participle**
• actions that began and continued in the past until another past action	By the time I moved to Georgia, I *had been supporting* myself for five years.

28b To write a verb in the passive voice, use a form of *be* with the past participle.

When a sentence is written in the passive voice, the subject receives the action instead of doing it. (See 47c.)

> The solution *was measured* by the lab assistant.

To form the passive voice, use a form of *be* — *am, is, are, was, were, being, be,* or *been* — followed by the past participle of the main verb: *was sent, are served.* (Sometimes a form of *be* follows another helping verb: *will be cut, could have been done.*)

> ► *Dreaming in Cuban* was ~~writing~~ by Cristina García.
>   written

In the passive voice, the past participle *written*, not the present participle *writing*, must follow *was* (the past tense of *be*).

Verb tenses commonly used in the passive voice

For details about verb tenses in the active voice, see pages 253–55.

Simple tenses (passive voice)

Simple present — *am, is, are* **+ past participle**
- general facts — Breakfast *is served* daily.
- habitual, repetitive actions — The receipts *are counted* every night.

Simple past — *was, were* **+ past participle**
- completed past actions — He *was punished* for being late.

Simple future — *will be* **+ past participle**
- future actions, promises, or predictions — The decision *will be made* by the committee next week.

Simple progressive forms (passive voice)

Present progressive — *am, is, are* **+** *being* **+ past participle**
- actions in progress at the present time — The new stadium *is being built* with private money.
- future actions (with *leave, go, come, move,* etc.) — Jo *is being moved* to a new class next month.

Past progressive — *was, were* **+** *being* **+ past participle**
- actions in progress at a specific time in the past — We thought we *were being followed*.

Perfect tenses (passive voice)

Present perfect — *has, have* **+** *been* **+ past participle**
- actions that began in the past and continue to the present — The flight *has been delayed* because of storms in the Midwest.
- actions that happened at an unknown or unspecific time in the past — Wars *have been fought* throughout history.

Past perfect — *had* **+** *been* **+ past participle**
- actions that began or occurred before another time in the past — He *had been given* all the hints he needed to complete the puzzle.

NOTE: Future progressive, future perfect, and perfect progressive forms are not used in the passive voice.

                                be
▶ Senator Dixon will defeated.
                              ^

The passive voice requires a form of *be* before the past participle.

                          teased.
▶ The child was being ~~tease.~~
                            ^

The past participle *teased*, not the base form *tease*, must be used with *was being* to form the passive voice.

For details on forming the passive in various tenses, consult the chart on page 256. (For appropriate uses of the passive voice, see 8a.)

NOTE: Only transitive verbs, those that take direct objects, may be used in the passive voice. Intransitive verbs such as *occur, happen, sleep, die, become,* and *fall* are not used in the passive. (See 47b.)

▶ The accident ~~was~~ happened suddenly.

EXERCISE 28–1   Revise the following sentences to correct errors in verb forms and tenses in the active and the passive voice. You may need to look at 27a for the correct form of some irregular verbs and at 27f for help with tenses. Answers to lettered sentences appear in the back of the book. Example:

               begins
The meeting ~~begin~~ tonight at 7:30.
              ^

a. In the past, tobacco companies deny any connection between smoking and health problems.

b. There is nothing in the world that TV has not touch on.

c. I am wanting to register for a summer tutoring session.

d. By the end of the year, the state will have test 139 birds for avian flu.

e. The benefits of eating fruits and vegetables have been promoting by health care providers.

1. By the time he was twelve years old, Mozart had compose an entire opera.

2. The sound was occurred whenever someone stepped on the loose board.

3. My family has been gone to Sam's restaurant ever since we moved to this neighborhood.

4. I have ate Thai food only once before.
5. The bear is appearing to be sedated.

28c Use the base form of the verb after a modal.

The modal verbs are *can, could, may, might, must, shall, should, will,* and *would.* (*Ought to* is also considered a modal verb.) The modals are used with the base form of a verb to show certainty, necessity, or possibility.

Modals and the verbs that follow them do not change form to indicate tense. For a summary of modals and their meanings, see the chart on pages 259–60. (See also 27e.)

> *launch*
> ▶ The art museum will ~~launches~~ its fundraising campaign
> ^
> next month.

> The modal *will* must be followed by the base form *launch,* not the present tense *launches.*

> *speak*
> ▶ The translator could ~~spoke~~ many languages, so the ambas-
> ^
> sador hired her for the European tour.

> The modal *could* must be followed by the base form *speak,* not the past tense *spoke.*

TIP: Do not use *to* in front of a main verb that follows a modal.

> ▶ Gina can ~~to~~ drive us home if we miss the last train.

For the use of modals in conditional sentences, see 28e.

EXERCISE 28–2 Edit the following sentences to correct errors in the use of verb forms with modals. You may find it helpful to consult the chart on pages 259–60. If a sentence is correct, write "correct" after it. Answers to lettered sentences appear in the back of the book. Example:

> We should ~~to~~ order pizza for dinner.

a. A major league pitcher can to throw a baseball more than ninety-five miles per hour.

b. The writing center tutor will helps you revise your essay.

c. A reptile must adjusted its body temperature to its environment.

d. In some states, individuals may renew a driver's license online or in person.

e. My uncle, a cartoonist, could sketched a face in less than two minutes.

1. Working more than twelve hours a day might to contribute to insomnia, according to researchers.

2. A wasp will carry its immobilized prey back to the nest.

3. Hikers should not wandered too far from the trail.

4. Should we continued to submit hard copies of our essays?

5. Physical therapy may to help people after heart surgery.

Modals and their meanings

can

• general ability (present)	Ants *can survive* anywhere, even in space. Jorge *can run* a marathon faster than his brother.
• informal requests or permission	*Can* you *tell* me where the light is? Sandy *can borrow* my calculator.

could

• general ability (past)	Lea *could read* when she was only three years old.
• polite, informal requests or permission	*Could* you *give* me that pen?

may

• formal requests or permission	*May* I *see* the report? Students *may park* only in the yellow zone.
• possibility	I *may try* to finish my homework tonight, or I *may wake up* early and *finish* it tomorrow.

Modals and their meanings (continued)

might

- possibility   Funding for the language lab *might double* by 2017.

NOTE: *Might* usually expresses a stronger possibility than *may*.

must

- necessity (present or future)   To be effective, welfare-to-work programs *must provide* access to job training.

- strong probability   Amy *must be* nervous. [She is probably nervous.]

- near certainty (present or past)   I *must have left* my wallet at home. [I almost certainly left my wallet at home.]

should

- suggestions or advice   Diabetics *should drink* plenty of water every day.

- obligations or duties   The government *should protect* citizens' rights.

- expectations   The books *should arrive* soon. [We expect the books to arrive soon.]

will

- certainty   If you don't leave now, you *will be* late for your rehearsal.

- requests   *Will* you *help* me study for my psychology exam?

- promises and offers   Jonah *will arrange* the carpool.

would

- polite requests   *Would* you *help* me carry these books? I *would like* some coffee. [*Would like* is more polite than *want*.]

- habitual or repeated actions (past)   Whenever Elena needed help with sewing, she *would call* her aunt.

28d To make negative verb forms, add *not* in the appropriate place.

If the verb is the simple present or past tense of *be* (*am, is, are, was, were*), add *not* after the verb.

Gianna *is not* a member of the club.

For simple present-tense verbs other than *be*, use *do* or *does* plus *not* before the base form of the verb. (For the correct forms of *do* and *does*, see the chart on p. 198.)

>   *does not*
> ► Mariko ~~no~~ want more dessert.
>   ^

> ► Mariko does not want~~s~~ more dessert.

For simple past-tense verbs other than *be*, use *did* plus *not* before the base form of the verb.

>   *plant*
> ► They did not ~~planted~~ corn this year.
>   ^

In a verb phrase consisting of one or more helping verbs and a present or past participle (*is watching, were living, has played, could have been driven*), use the word *not* after the first helping verb.

>   *not*
> ► Inna should have ~~not~~ gone dancing last night.
>   ^

>   *not*
> ► Bonnie is ~~no~~ singing this weekend.
>   ^

NOTE: English allows only one negative in an independent clause to express a negative idea; using more than one is an error known as a *double negative* (see 26e).

>   *any*
> ► We could not find ~~no~~ books about the history of our school.
>   ^

28e In a conditional sentence, choose verb tenses according to the type of condition expressed in the sentence.

Conditional sentences contain two clauses: a subordinate clause (usually starting with *if, when,* or *unless*) and an independent clause. The subordinate clause (sometimes called the *if* or *unless* clause) states the condition or cause; the independent clause states the result or effect. In each example in this section, the subordinate clause (*if* clause) is marked SUB, and the independent clause is marked IND. (See 48e on clauses.)

Factual

Factual conditional sentences express factual relationships. If the relationship is a scientific truth, use the present tense in both clauses.

$$\underbrace{\text{If water } cools \text{ to 32° Fahrenheit,}}_{\text{SUB}} \underbrace{\text{it } freezes.}_{\text{IND}}$$

If the sentence describes a condition that is (or was) habitually true, use the same tense in both clauses.

$$\underbrace{\text{When Sue } jogs \text{ along the canal,}}_{\text{SUB}} \underbrace{\text{her dog } runs \text{ ahead of her.}}_{\text{IND}}$$

$$\underbrace{\text{Whenever the coach } asked \text{ for help,}}_{\text{SUB}} \underbrace{\text{I } volunteered.}_{\text{IND}}$$

Predictive

Predictive conditional sentences are used to predict the future or to express future plans or possibilities. To form a predictive sentence, use a present-tense verb in the subordinate clause; in the independent clause, use the modal *will, can, may, should,* or *might* plus the base form of the verb.

$$\underbrace{\text{If you } practice \text{ regularly,}}_{\text{SUB}} \underbrace{\text{your tennis game } should\ improve.}_{\text{IND}}$$

$$\underbrace{\text{We } will\ lose \text{ our remaining wetlands}}_{\text{IND}} \underbrace{\text{unless we } act \text{ now.}}_{\text{SUB}}$$

TIP: In all types of conditional sentences (factual, predictive, and speculative), *if* or *unless* clauses do not use the modal verb *will.*

>   *passes*
> ▶ If Jenna ~~will pass~~ her history test, she will graduate this year.
>   ^

Speculative

Speculative conditional sentences express unlikely, contrary-to-fact, or impossible conditions. English uses the past or past perfect tense in the *if* clause, even for conditions in the present or the future.

Unlikely possibilities   If the condition is possible but unlikely in the present or the future, use the past tense in the subordinate clause; in the independent clause, use *would, could,* or *might* plus the base form of the verb.

```
        ┌──────SUB──────┐ ┌────────IND────────┐
```
If I *won* the lottery, I *would travel* to Egypt.

The writer does not expect to win the lottery. Because this is a possible but unlikely present or future situation, the subordinate clause uses the past tense.

Conditions contrary to fact   In conditions that are currently unreal or contrary to fact, use the past-tense verb *were* (not *was*) in the *if* clause for all subjects. (See also 27g, on the subjunctive mood.)

>   *were*
> ► If I ~~was~~ president, I would make children's issues a priority.
>   ^

The writer is not president, so *were* is correct in the *if* clause.

Events that did not happen   In a conditional sentence that speculates about an event that did not happen or was impossible in the past, use the past perfect tense in the *if* clause; in the independent clause, use *would have, could have,* or *might have* with the past participle. (See also past perfect tense, p. 255.)

```
        ┌───────SUB───────┐ ┌─────────IND─────────┐
```
If I *had saved* more money, I *would have visited* Laos last year.

The writer did not save more money and did not travel to Laos. This sentence shows a possibility that did not happen.

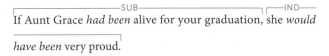
```
     ┌────────────────SUB────────────────┐ ┌──IND──┐
```
If Aunt Grace *had been* alive for your graduation, she *would*
```
  ┌──────────────────────┐
```
have been very proud.

Aunt Grace was not alive at the time of the graduation. This sentence shows an impossible situation in the past.

EXERCISE 28–3   Edit the following sentences to correct problems with verbs. In some cases, more than one revision is possible. Suggested revisions of lettered sentences appear in the back of the book. Example:

>   *had*
> If I ~~have~~ time, I would study both French and Russian next
>   ^
> semester.

a. The electrician might have discovered the broken circuit if she went through the modules one at a time.
b. If Verena wins a scholarship, she would go to graduate school.
c. Whenever there is a fire in our neighborhood, everybody came out to watch.
d. Sarah did not understood the terms of her internship.
e. If I live in Budapest with my cousin Szusza, she would teach me Hungarian cooking.

1. If the science fiction festival starts Monday, we wouldn't need to plan entertainment for our visitors.
2. If everyone has voted in the last election, the results would have been very different.
3. The tenants will not pay the rent unless the landlord fixed the furnace.
4. When dark gray clouds appeared on a hot summer afternoon, a thunderstorm often follows.
5. Rosalie should no offer to volunteer at the shelter on school nights.

28f   Become familiar with verbs that may be followed by gerunds or infinitives.

A gerund is a verb form that ends in *-ing* and is used as a noun: *sleeping, dreaming.* (See 48b.) An infinitive is the word *to* plus the base form of the verb: *to sleep, to dream.* (The word *to* is an infinitive marker, not a preposition, in this use.)

A few verbs may be followed by either a gerund or an infinitive; others may be followed by a gerund but not by an infinitive; still others may be followed by an infinitive but not by a gerund.

Verb + gerund or infinitive (no change in meaning)

The following commonly used verbs may be followed by a gerund or an infinitive, with little or no difference in meaning:

begin	hate	love
continue	like	start

I love *skiing*. I love *to ski*.

Verb + gerund or infinitive (change in meaning)

With a few verbs, the choice of a gerund or an infinitive changes the meaning dramatically:

forget	remember	stop	try

She stopped *speaking* to Lucia. [She no longer spoke to Lucia.]

She stopped *to speak* to Lucia. [She paused so that she could speak to Lucia.]

Verb + gerund

These verbs may be followed by a gerund but not by an infinitive:

admit	discuss	imagine	put off	risk
appreciate	enjoy	miss	quit	suggest
avoid	escape	postpone	recall	tolerate
deny	finish	practice	resist	

Bill enjoys *playing* [not *to play*] the piano.

Jamie quit *smoking*.

Verb + infinitive

These verbs may be followed by an infinitive but not by a gerund:

agree	decide	manage	plan	wait
ask	expect	mean	pretend	want
beg	help	need	promise	wish
claim	hope	offer	refuse	would like

Jill has offered *to water* [not *watering*] the plants while we are away.

Joe finally managed *to find* a parking space.

The man refused *to join* the rebellion.

A few of these verbs may be followed either by an infinitive directly or by a noun or pronoun plus an infinitive:

ask	help	promise	would like
expect	need	want	

We asked *to speak* to the congregation.

We asked *Rabbi Abrams to speak* to our congregation.

Alex expected *to get* the lead in the play.

Ira expected *Alex to get* the lead in the play.

Verb + noun or pronoun + infinitive

With certain verbs in the active voice, a noun or pronoun must come between the verb and the infinitive that follows it. The noun or pronoun usually names a person who is affected by the action of the verb.

advise	convince	order	tell
allow	encourage	persuade	urge
cause	have ("own")	remind	warn
command	instruct	require	

The class encouraged Luis to tell the story of his escape.

The counselor *advised Haley to take* four courses instead of five.

Professor Howlett *instructed us to write* our names on the left side of the paper.

Verb + noun or pronoun + unmarked infinitive

An unmarked infinitive is an infinitive without *to*. A few verbs (often called *causative verbs*) may be followed by a noun or pronoun and an unmarked infinitive.

have ("cause")	let ("allow")
help	make ("force")

Jorge *had the valet park* his car.

► Please let me ~~to~~ pay for the tickets.

► Frank made me ~~to~~ carry his book for him.

verb + gerund (*running*) • verb + infinitive (*to run*) • articles
(*a, an, the*) • other noun markers (*my, their, this, any, most*)

ESL

29a

267

NOTE: *Help* can be followed by a noun or pronoun and either an unmarked or a marked infinitive.

> Emma *helped Brian wash* the dishes.

> Emma *helped Brian to wash* the dishes.

EXERCISE 28–4 Form sentences by adding gerund or infinitive constructions to the following sentence openings. In some cases, more than one kind of construction is possible. Possible answers to lettered items appear in the back of the book. Example:

> **Please remind** *your sister to call me.*
>   ^

a. I enjoy
b. The tutor told Samantha
c. The team hopes
d. Ricardo and his brothers miss
e. The babysitter let

1. Pollen makes
2. The club president asked
3. Next summer we plan
4. My supervisor intends
5. Please stop

29   Articles

Articles (*a, an, the*) are part of a category of words known as *noun markers* or *determiners*.

29a Be familiar with articles and other noun markers.

Standard English uses noun markers to help identify the nouns that follow. In addition to articles (*a, an,* and *the*), noun markers include

- possessive nouns, such as *Elena's* (See 36a.)

- possessive pronoun/adjectives: *my, your, his, her, its, our, their* (See 46b.)
- demonstrative pronoun/adjectives: *this, that, these, those* (See 46b.)
- quantifiers: *all, any, each, either, every, few, many, more, most, much, neither, several, some,* and so on (See 29d.)
- numbers: *one, twenty-three,* and so on

Using articles and other noun markers

Articles and other noun markers always appear before nouns; sometimes other modifiers, such as adjectives, come between a noun marker and a noun.

> ART N
> Felix is reading a book about mythology.

> ART ADJ N
> We took an exciting trip to Alaska last summer.

> NOUN
> MARKER ADV ADJ N
> That very delicious meal was expensive.

In most cases, do not use an article with another noun marker.

▶ ~~The~~ Natalie's older brother lives in Wisconsin.

Expressions like *a few, the most,* and *all the* are exceptions: *a few potatoes, all the rain.* See also 29d.

Types of articles and types of nouns

To choose an appropriate article for a noun, you must first determine whether the noun is *common* or *proper, count* or *noncount, singular* or *plural,* and *specific* or *general.* The chart on pages 270–71 describes the types of nouns.

Articles are classified as *indefinite* and *definite.* The indefinite articles, *a* and *an,* are used with general nouns. The definite article, *the,* is used with specific nouns. (The last section of the chart on p. 271 explains general and specific nouns.)

A and *an* both mean "one" or "one among many." Use *a* before a consonant sound: *a banana, a tree, a picture, a happy child, a united family.* Use *an* before a vowel sound: *an eggplant, an occasion, an uncle, an honorable person.* (See also *a, an* in the glossary of usage.)

other noun markers (*this, any,* etc.) • indefinite article (*a, an*) • definite article (*the*) • *the* with specific nouns

ESL
29b   269

The shows that a noun is specific; use *the* with one or more than one specific thing: *the newspaper, the soldiers.*

29b   Use *the* with most specific common nouns.

The definite article, *the*, is used with most nouns — both count and noncount — that the reader can identify specifically. Usually the identity will be clear to the reader for one of the following reasons. (See also the chart on pages 272–73.)

1. The noun has been previously mentioned.

▶ A truck cut in front of our van. When ^{the} truck skidded a few

   seconds later, we almost crashed into it.

> The article *A* is used before *truck* when the noun is first mentioned.
> When the noun is mentioned again, it needs the article *the* because
> readers can now identify which truck skidded — the one that cut in front
> of the van.

2. A phrase or clause following the noun restricts its identity.

▶ Bryce warned me that ^{the} GPS in his car was not working.

> The phrase *in his car* identifies the specific GPS.

NOTE: Descriptive adjectives do not necessarily make a noun specific. A specific noun is one that readers can identify within a group of nouns of the same type.

▶ If I win the lottery, I will buy ^a ~~the~~ brand-new bright red

   sports car.

> The reader cannot identify which specific brand-new bright red sports
> car the writer will buy. Even though *car* has many adjectives in front of
> it, it is a general noun in this sentence.

3. A superlative adjective such as *best* or *most intelligent* makes the noun's identity specific. (See also 26d on comparatives and superlatives.)

▶ Our petite daughter dated ^{the} tallest boy in her class.

> The superlative *tallest* makes the noun *boy* specific. Although there
> might be several tall boys, only one boy can be the tallest.

ESL

Types of nouns

Common or proper

Common nouns

- name general persons, places, things, or ideas
- begin with lowercase

Examples

religion   beauty
knowledge   student
rain   country

Proper nouns

- name specific persons, places, things, or ideas
- begin with capital letter

Examples

Hinduism   President Adams
Philip   Washington Monument
Vietnam   Renaissance

Count or noncount (common nouns only)

Count nouns

- name persons, places, things, or ideas that can be counted
- have plural forms

Examples

girl, girls
city, cities
goose, geese
philosophy, philosophies

Noncount nouns

- name things or abstract ideas that cannot be counted
- cannot be made plural

Examples

water   patience
silver   knowledge
furniture   air

NOTE: See the chart on page 273 for commonly used noncount nouns.

Singular or plural (both common and proper)

**Singular nouns
(count and noncount)**

- represent one person, place, thing, or idea

Examples

backpack   rain
country   beauty
woman   Nile River
achievement   Block Island

Plural nouns (count only)

- represent more than one person, place, thing, or idea
- must be count nouns

Examples

backpacks   Ural Mountains
countries   Falkland Islands
women   achievements

Specific (definite) or general (indefinite) (count and noncount)	
Specific nouns	**Examples**
• name persons, places, things, or ideas that can be identified within a group of the same type	*The students* in Professor Martin's *class* should study.
	The airplane carrying *the senator* was late.
	The furniture in *the truck* was damaged.
General nouns	**Examples**
• name categories of persons, places, things, or ideas (often plural)	*Students* should study.
	Books bridge *gaps* between *cultures*.
	The airplane has made commuting between *cities* easy.

4. The noun describes a unique person, place, or thing.

                                        the

► **During an eclipse, one should not look directly at sun.**

There is only one sun in our solar system, so its identity is clear.

5. The context or situation makes the noun's identity clear.

         the

► **Please don't slam door when you leave.**

Both the speaker and the listener know which door is meant.

6. The noun is singular and refers to a scientific class or category of items (most often animals, musical instruments, and inventions).

     The tin

► ~~Tin~~ **whistle is common in traditional Irish music.**

The writer is referring to the tin whistle as a class of musical instruments.

29c Use *a* (or *an*) with common singular count nouns that refer to "one" or "any."

If a count noun refers to one unspecific item (not a whole category), use the indefinite article, *a* or *an*. *A* and *an* usually mean "one among many" but can also mean "any one." (See the chart below.)

▶ My English professor asked me to bring *a* dictionary to class.

The noun *dictionary* refers to "one unspecific dictionary" or "any dictionary."

▶ We want to rent *an* apartment close to the lake.

The noun *apartment* refers to "any apartment close to the lake," not a specific apartment.

Choosing articles for common nouns

Use *the*

- if the reader has enough information to identify the noun specifically

  COUNT: Please turn on *the lights*. We're going to *the lake* tomorrow.

  NONCOUNT: *The food* throughout Italy is excellent.

Use *a* or *an*

- if the noun refers to one item

  and

- if the item is singular but not specific

  COUNT: Bring *a pencil* to class. Charles wrote *an essay* about his first job.

NOTE: Do not use *a* or *an* with plural or noncount nouns.

Use a quantifier (*enough, many, some,* etc.)

- if the noun represents an unspecified amount of something

- if the amount is more than one but not all items in a category

  COUNT (plural): Amir showed us *some photos* of India. *Many turtles* return to the same nesting site each year.

  NONCOUNT: We didn't get *enough rain* this summer.

NOTE: Sometimes no article conveys an unspecified amount: *Amir showed us photos of India.*

Use no article

- if the noun represents all items in a category

  COUNT (plural): *Students* can attend the show for free.

● if the noun represents a   **NONCOUNT:** *Coal* is a natural resource.
  category in general

NOTE: *The* is occasionally used when a singular count noun refers to
all items in a class or a specific category: *The bald eagle is no longer
endangered in the United States.*

Commonly used noncount nouns

Food and drink

beef, bread, butter, candy, cereal, cheese, cream, meat, milk, pasta,
rice, salt, sugar, water, wine

Nonfood substances

air, cement, coal, dirt, gasoline, gold, paper, petroleum, plastic, rain,
silver, snow, soap, steel, wood, wool

Abstract nouns

advice, anger, beauty, confidence, courage, employment, fun,
happiness, health, honesty, information, intelligence, knowledge,
love, poverty, satisfaction, wealth

Other

biology (and other areas of study), clothing, equipment, furniture, homework, jewelry, luggage, machinery, mail, money, news,
poetry, pollution, research, scenery, traffic, transportation, violence,
weather, work

NOTE: A few noncount nouns (such as *love*) can also be used as
count nouns: *He had two loves: music and archery.*

29d Use a quantifier such as *some* or *more*, not *a* or *an*, with a noncount noun to express an approximate amount.

Do not use *a* or *an* with noncount nouns. Also do not use numbers or words such as *several* or *many* because they must be

used with plural nouns, and noncount nouns do not have plural forms. (See the chart on p. 273 for a list of commonly used noncount nouns.)

▶ Dr. Snyder gave us ~~an~~ information about the Peace Corps.

▶ Do you have ~~many~~ money with you?

You can use quantifiers such as *enough, less,* and *some* to suggest approximate amounts or nonspecific quantities of noncount nouns: *a little salt, any homework, enough wood, less information, much pollution.*

▶ Vincent's mother told him that she had a *some* news that would
surprise him.

29e Do not use articles with nouns that refer to all of something or something in general.

When a noncount noun refers to all of its type or to a concept in general, it is not marked with an article.

▶ *Kindness*
~~The kindness~~ is a virtue.
The noun represents kindness in general; it does not represent a specific type of kindness.

▶ In some parts of the world, ~~the~~ rice is preferred to all other
grains.
The noun *rice* represents rice in general, not a specific type or serving of rice.

In most cases, when you use a count noun to represent a general category, make the noun plural. Do not use unmarked singular count nouns to represent whole categories.

▶ *Fountains are*
~~Fountain is~~ an expensive element of landscape design.
Fountains is a count noun that represents fountains in general.

EXCEPTION: In some cases, *the* can be used with singular count nouns to represent a class or specific category: *The Chinese alligator is smaller than the American alligator.* See also number 6 in 29b.

29f Do not use articles with most singular proper nouns. Use *the* with most plural proper nouns.

Since singular proper nouns are already specific, they typically do not need an article: *Prime Minister Cameron, Jamaica, Lake Huron, Mount Etna.*

There are, however, many exceptions. In most cases, if the proper noun consists of a common noun with modifiers (adjectives or an *of* phrase), use *the* with the proper noun.

▶ We visited *the* Great Wall of China last year.

▶ Rob wants to be a translator for *the* Central Intelligence Agency.

The is used with most plural proper nouns: *the McGregors, the Bahamas, the Finger Lakes, the United States.*

Geographic names create problems because there are so many exceptions to the rules. When in doubt, consult the chart on page 276, check a dictionary, or ask a native speaker.

EXERCISE 29–1   Edit the following sentences for proper use of articles and nouns. If a sentence is correct, write "correct" after it. Answers to lettered sentences appear in the back of the book. Example:

~~The~~ Josefina's dance routine was flawless.

a. Doing volunteer work often brings a satisfaction.
b. As I looked out the window of the plane, I could see the Cape Cod.
c. Melina likes to drink her coffees with lots of cream.
d. Recovering from abdominal surgery requires patience.
e. I completed the my homework assignment quickly.

1. The attorney argued that her client should receive a money for emotional suffering.
2. Please check to see if there is a mail in the mailbox.
3. The Times Square in New York City is known for its billboards and theaters.
4. A cement is one of the components of concrete.
5. I took all the boys on the roller coaster after lunch.

Using *the* with geographic nouns

When to omit *the*

streets, squares, parks	Ivy Street, Union Square, Denali National Park
cities, states, counties	Miami, New Mexico, Bee County
most countries, continents	Italy, Nigeria, China, South America, Africa
bays, single lakes	Tampa Bay, Lake Geneva
single mountains, islands	Mount Everest, Crete

When to use *the*

country names with *of* phrase	the United States (of America), the People's Republic of China
large regions, deserts	the East Coast, the Sahara
peninsulas	the Baja Peninsula, the Sinai Peninsula
oceans, seas, gulfs	the Pacific Ocean, the Dead Sea, the Persian Gulf
canals and rivers	the Panama Canal, the Amazon
mountain ranges	the Rocky Mountains, the Alps
groups of islands	the Solomon Islands

EXERCISE 29–2 Articles have been omitted from the following description of winter weather. Insert the articles *a, an,* and *the* where English requires them and be prepared to explain the reasons for your choices.

Many people confuse terms *hail, sleet,* and *freezing rain.* Hail normally occurs in thunderstorm and is caused by strong updrafts that lift growing chunks of ice into clouds. When chunks of ice, called hailstones, become too heavy to be carried by updrafts, they fall to ground. Hailstones can cause damage to crops, windshields, and people. Sleet occurs during winter storms and is caused by snowflakes falling from layer of cold air into warm layer, where they become raindrops, and then into another cold layer. As they fall through last layer of cold air, raindrops freeze and become small ice pellets, forming sleet. When it hits car windshield or windows of house, sleet can make annoying racket. Driving and walking can be hazardous when sleet accumulates on roads and sidewalks. Freezing rain is basically rain that falls onto ground and then freezes after it hits ground. It causes icy glaze on trees and any surface that is below freezing.

Sentence structure

Although their structure can vary widely, sentences in English generally flow from subject to verb to object or complement: *Bears eat fish.* This section focuses on the major challenges that multilingual students face when writing sentences in English. For more details on the parts of speech and the elements of sentences, consult sections 46–49.

30a Use a linking verb between a subject and its complement.

Some languages, such as Russian and Turkish, do not use linking verbs (*is, are, was, were*) between subjects and complements (nouns or adjectives that rename or describe the subject). Every English sentence, however, must include a verb. For more on linking verbs, see 27e.

▶ Jim <u>is</u> intelligent.

▶ Many streets in San Francisco <u>are</u> very steep.

30b Include a subject in every sentence.

Some languages, such as Spanish and Japanese, do not require a subject in every sentence. Every English sentence, however, needs a subject. Commands are an exception: The subject *you* is understood but not present in the sentence ([*You*] *Give me the book*).

▶ Your aunt is very energetic. <u>She seems</u> ~~Seems~~ young for her age.

The word *it* is used as the subject of a sentence describing the weather or temperature, stating the time, indicating distance, or suggesting an environmental fact.

▶ <u>It is</u> ~~Is~~ raining in the valley and snowing in the mountains.

► In July, *it* is very hot in Arizona.

► ~~Is~~ *It is* 9:15 a.m.

In most English sentences, the subject appears before the verb. Some sentences, however, are inverted: The subject comes after the verb. In these sentences, a placeholder called an *expletive* (*there* or *it*) often comes before the verb.

EXP V ┌——— S ———┐   ┌——— S ———┐ V
There are many people here today. (Many people are here today.)

► ~~Is~~ *There is* an apple pie in the refrigerator.

► As you know, *there are* many religious sects in India.

Notice that the verb agrees with the subject that follows it: *apple pie is, sects are.* (See 21g.)

Sometimes an inverted sentence has an infinitive (*to work*) or a noun clause (*that she is intelligent*) as the subject. In such sentences, the placeholder *it* is needed before the verb. (Also see 48b and 48e.)

EXP V   ┌—S—┐   ┌—S—┐   V
It is important to study daily. (To study daily is important.)

► Because the road is flooded, *it* is necessary to change our route.

TIP: The words *here* and *there* are not used as subjects. When they mean "in this place" (*here*) or "in that place" (*there*), they are adverbs, not nouns.

► I just returned from a vacation in Japan. ~~There~~ *It* is very beautiful*/ there.*

► ~~Here~~ *This school* offers a master's degree in physical therapy; ~~there~~ *that school* has

only a bachelor's program.

30c Do not use both a noun and a pronoun to perform the same grammatical function in a sentence.

English does not allow a subject to be repeated in its own clause.

▶ The doctor ~~she~~ advised me to cut down on salt.

The pronoun *she* cannot repeat the subject, *doctor.*

Do not add a pronoun even when a word group comes between the subject and the verb.

▶ The watch that I lost on vacation ~~it~~ was in my backpack.

The pronoun *it* cannot repeat the subject, *watch.*

Some languages allow "topic fronting," placing a word or phrase (a "topic") at the beginning of a sentence and following it with an independent clause that explains something about the topic. This form is not allowed in English because the sentence seems to start with one subject but then introduces a new subject in an independent clause.

<pre>
            ┌─TOPIC─┐ ┌──────IND CLAUSE──────┐
INCORRECT   The seeds I planted them last fall.
</pre>

The sentence can be corrected by bringing the topic (*seeds*) into the independent clause.

▶ ~~The seeds~~ I planted ~~them~~ last fall.
    the seeds ^

30d Do not repeat an object or an adverb in an adjective clause.

Adjective clauses begin with relative pronouns (*who, whom, whose, which, that*) or relative adverbs (*when, where*). Relative pronouns usually serve as subjects or objects in the clauses they introduce; another word in the clause cannot serve the same function. Relative adverbs should not be repeated by other adverbs later in the clause.

┌─────────ADJ CLAUSE─────────┐
The cat ran under the car that was parked on the street.

▶ The cat ran under the car that ~~it~~ was parked on the street.

The relative pronoun *that* is the subject of the adjective clause, so the pronoun *it* cannot be added as a subject.

▶ Myrna enjoyed the investment seminars that she attended

~~them~~ last week.

The relative pronoun *that* is the object of the verb *attended*. The pronoun *them* cannot also serve as an object.

Sometimes the relative pronoun is understood but not present in the sentence. In such cases, do not add another word with the same function as the omitted pronoun.

▶ Myrna enjoyed the investment seminars she attended ~~them~~

last week.

The relative pronoun *that* is understood after *seminars* even though it is not present in the sentence.

If the clause begins with a relative adverb, do not use another adverb with the same meaning later in the clause.

▶ The office where I work ~~there~~ is one hour from the city.

The adverb *there* cannot repeat the relative adverb *where*.

EXERCISE 30–1 In the following sentences, add needed subjects or expletives and delete any repeated subjects, objects, or adverbs. Answers to lettered sentences appear in the back of the book. Example:

The new geology professor is the one whom we saw ~~him~~ on TV

this morning.

a. Are some cartons of ice cream in the freezer.
b. I don't use the subway because am afraid.
c. The prime minister she is the most popular leader in my country.
d. We tried to get in touch with the same manager whom we spoke to him earlier.
e. Recently have been a number of earthquakes in Turkey.
1. We visited an island where several ancient ruins are being excavated there.
2. In this city is difficult to find a high-paying job.
3. Beginning knitters they are often surprised that their fingers are sore at first.
4. Is a banyan tree in our backyard.
5. The CD that teaches Italian for opera lovers it was stolen from my backpack.

30e Avoid mixed constructions beginning with *although* or *because*.

A word group that begins with *although* cannot be linked to a word group that begins with *but* or *however*. The result is an error called a *mixed construction* (see also 11a). Similarly, a word group that begins with *because* cannot be linked to a word group that begins with *so* or *therefore*.

If you want to keep *although* or *because*, drop the other linking word.

▶ Although Nikki Giovanni is best known for her poetry for

adults, ~~but~~ she has written several books for children.

▶ Because German and Dutch are related languages, ~~therefore~~

tourists from Berlin can usually read a few signs in Amsterdam.

If you want to keep the other linking word, omit *although* or *because*.

▶ ~~Although~~ Nikki Giovanni is best known for her poetry for

adults, but she has written several books for children.

▶ ~~Because~~ German and Dutch are related languages/; therefore,

tourists from Berlin can usually read a few signs in

Amsterdam.

For advice about using commas and semicolons with linking words, see 32a and 34b.

30f Do not place an adverb between a verb and its direct object.

Adverbs modifying verbs can appear in various positions: at the beginning or end of a sentence, before or after a verb, or between a helping verb and its main verb.

> *Slowly*, we drove along the rain-slick road.

> Mia handled the teapot *very carefully*.

> Martin *always* wins our tennis matches.

> Christina is *rarely* late for our lunch dates.

> My daughter has *often* spoken of you.

> The election results were being *closely* followed by analysts.

However, an adverb cannot appear between a verb and its direct object.

> ▶ Mother wrapped ~~carefully~~ the gift.
>
> carefully

The adverb *carefully* cannot appear between the verb, *wrapped*, and its direct object, *the gift*.

EXERCISE 30–2 Edit the following sentences for proper sentence structure. If a sentence is correct, write "correct" after it. Answers to lettered sentences appear in the back of the book. Example:

> slowly.
>
> She peeled ~~slowly~~ the banana/

a. Although freshwater freezes at 32° Fahrenheit, however ocean water freezes at 28° Fahrenheit.

b. Because we switched cable packages, so our channel lineup has changed.

c. The competitor mounted confidently his skateboard.

d. My sister performs well the *legong*, a Balinese dance.

e. Because product development is behind schedule, we will have to launch the product next spring.

1. The bank teller counted methodically the stack of twenty-dollar bills.

2. I gasped when I saw lightning strike repeatedly the barn.

3. Although hockey is traditionally a winter sport, but many towns offer skills programs all year long.

4. Because salmon can survive in both freshwater and salt water, so they are classified as anadromous fish.

5. A surveyor determines precisely the boundaries of a piece of property.

30g Distinguish between present participles and past participles used as adjectives.

Both present and past participles may be used as adjectives. The present participle always ends in *-ing*. Past participles usually end in *-ed, -d, -en, -n,* or *-t.* (See 27a.)

| PRESENT PARTICIPLES | confusing, speaking, boring |
| PAST PARTICIPLES | confused, spoken, bored |

Like all other adjectives, participles can come before nouns; they also can follow linking verbs, in which case they describe the subject of the sentence. (See 47b.)

Use a present participle to describe a person or thing *causing or stimulating an experience.*

The *boring lecture* put us to sleep. [The lecture caused boredom.]

Use a past participle to describe a person or thing *undergoing an experience.*

The *audience* was *bored* by the lecture. [The audience experienced boredom.]

Participles that describe emotions or mental states often cause the most confusion.

annoying/annoyed	exhausting/exhausted
boring/bored	fascinating/fascinated
confusing/confused	frightening/frightened
depressing/depressed	satisfying/satisfied
exciting/excited	surprising/surprised

          exhausting.
► **Our hike was ~~exhausted.~~**
        ^

Exhausting suggests that the hike caused exhaustion.

    exhausted
► **The ~~exhausting~~ hikers reached the campground at sunset.**
  ^

Exhausted describes how the hikers felt.

EXERCISE 30–3 Edit the following sentences for proper use of present and past participles. If a sentence is correct, write "correct" after it. Answers to lettered sentences appear in the back of the book. Example:

                     excited
Danielle and Monica were very ~~exciting~~ to be going to a
                    ^

Broadway show for the first time.

  a. Listening to everyone's complaints all day was irritated.
  b. The long flight to Singapore was exhausted.
  c. His skill at chess is amazing.
  d. After a great deal of research, the scientist made a fascinated discovery.
  e. Surviving that tornado was one of the most frightened experiences I've ever had.
  1. I couldn't concentrate on my homework because I was distracted.
  2. The directions to the new board game seem extremely complicating.
  3. How interested are you in visiting Civil War battlefields?
  4. The aerial view of the devastated villages was depressing.
  5. Even after the lecturer went over the main points again, the students were still confusing.

30h Place cumulative adjectives in an appropriate order.

Adjectives usually come before the nouns they modify and may also come after linking verbs. (See 46d and 47b.)

ADJ   N   V   ADJ
Janine wore a new necklace. Janine's necklace was new.

Cumulative adjectives, which cannot be joined by the word *and* or separated by commas, must come in a particular order. If you use cumulative adjectives before a noun, see the chart on page 286. The chart is only a guide; don't be surprised if you encounter exceptions. (See also 33d.)

▶ My dorm room has only a desk and a ~~plastic red stained~~ chair.
                                   stained red plastic
                                  ^

▶ Nice weather, ~~blue clear~~ water, and ancient monuments
                clear blue
                ^

   attract many people to Italy.

EXERCISE 30–4 Using the chart on page 286 as necessary, arrange the following modifiers and nouns in their proper order. Answers to lettered items appear in the back of the book. Example:

   two new French racing bicycles
   new, French, two, bicycles, racing

a. sculptor, young, an, Vietnamese, intelligent

b. dedicated, a, priest, Catholic

c. old, her, sweater, blue, wool

d. delicious, Joe's, Scandinavian, bread

e. many, boxes, jewelry, antique, beautiful

1. oval, nine, brass, lamps, miniature

2. several, yellow, tulips, tiny

3. the, tree, gingko, yellow, ancient, Mongolian

4. courtyard, a, square, small, brick

5. charming, restaurants, Latvian, several

Order of cumulative adjectives

FIRST	**ARTICLE OR OTHER NOUN MARKER**	a, an, the, her, Joe's, two, many, some
	EVALUATIVE WORD	attractive, dedicated, delicious, ugly, disgusting
	SIZE	large, enormous, small, little
	LENGTH OR SHAPE	long, short, round, square
	AGE	new, old, young, antique
	COLOR	yellow, blue, crimson
	NATIONALITY	French, Peruvian, Vietnamese
	RELIGION	Catholic, Protestant, Jewish, Muslim
	MATERIAL	silver, walnut, wool, marble
LAST	**NOUN/ADJECTIVE**	tree (as in *tree* house), kitchen (as in *kitchen* table)
THE NOUN MODIFIED		house, coat, bicycle, bread, woman, coin

My large blue wool coat is in the attic.

Joe's collection includes *two small antique silver* coins.

31 Prepositions and idiomatic expressions

31a Become familiar with prepositions that show time and place.

The most frequently used prepositions in English are *at*, *by*, *for*, *from*, *in*, *of*, *on*, *to*, and *with*. Prepositions can be difficult to master because the differences among them are subtle and idiomatic. The chart on page 288 is limited to three troublesome prepositions that show time and place: *at*, *on*, and *in*.

Not every possible use is listed in the chart, so don't be surprised when you encounter exceptions and idiomatic uses that you must learn one at a time. For example, in English a person rides *in* a car but *on* a bus, plane, train, or subway.

▶ My first class starts ~~on~~ *at* 8:00 a.m.

▶ The farmers go to market ~~in~~ *on* Wednesday.

▶ I want to work at one of the biggest companies ~~on~~ *in* the world.

EXERCISE 31–1 In the following sentences, replace prepositions that are not used correctly. You may need to refer to the chart on page 288. If a sentence is correct, write "correct" after it. Answers to lettered sentences appear in the back of the book. Example:

The play begins ~~on~~ *at* 7:20 p.m.

a. Whenever we eat at the Centerville Café, we sit at a small table on the corner of the room.

b. In the 1990s, entrepreneurs created new online businesses in record numbers.

c. In Thursday, Nancy will attend her first home repair class at the community center.

d. Alex began looking for her lost mitten in another location.

e. We decided to go to a restaurant because there was no fresh food on the refrigerator.

1. I like walking at my neighborhood in night.

2. If the train is on time, it will arrive on six o'clock at the morning.

3. In the corner of the room is a large bookcase with a pair of small Russian dolls standing at the top shelf.

4. She licked the stamp, stuck it in the envelope, put the envelope on her pocket, and walked to the nearest mailbox.

5. The mailbox was in the intersection of Laidlaw Avenue and Williams Street.

31b Use nouns (including *-ing* forms) after prepositions.

In a prepositional phrase, use a noun (not a verb) after the preposition. Sometimes the noun will be a gerund, the *-ing* verb form that functions as a noun (see 48b).

▶ Our student government is good at ~~save~~ *saving* money.

At, on, and in to show time and place

Showing time

AT   *at* a specific time: *at* 7:20, *at* dawn, *at* dinner

ON   *on* a specific day or date: *on* Tuesday, *on* June 4

IN   *in* a part of a 24-hour period: *in* the afternoon, *in* the daytime

   [but *at* night]

   in a year or month: *in* 2008, *in* July

   in a period of time: finished *in* three hours

Showing place

AT   *at* a meeting place or location: *at* home, *at* the club

   at the edge of something: sitting *at* the desk

   at the corner of something: turning *at* the intersection

   at a target: throwing the snowball *at* Lucy

ON   *on* a surface: placed *on* the table, hanging *on* the wall

   on a street: the house *on* Spring Street

   on an electronic medium: *on* television, *on* the Internet

IN   *in* an enclosed space: *in* the garage, *in* an envelope

   in a geographic location: *in* San Diego, *in* Texas

   in a print medium: *in* a book, *in* a magazine

Distinguish between the preposition *to* and the infinitive marker *to*. If *to* is a preposition, it should be followed by a noun or a gerund.

> ► We are dedicated to ~~help~~ ^{helping} the poor.

If *to* is an infinitive marker, it should be followed by the base form of the verb.

> ► We want to ~~helping~~ ^{help} the poor.

To test whether *to* is a preposition or an infinitive marker, insert a word that you know is a noun after the word *to*. If the noun makes sense in that position, *to* is a preposition. If the noun does not make sense after *to*, then *to* is an infinitive marker.

> Zoe is addicted *to* _____.

> They are planning *to* _____.

In the first sentence, a noun (such as *magazines*) makes sense after *to*, so *to* is a preposition and should be followed by a noun or a gerund: Zoe is addicted *to* *magazines*. Zoe is addicted *to* *running*.

In the second sentence, a noun (such as *magazines*) does not make sense after *to*, so *to* is an infinitive marker and must be followed by the base form of the verb: They are planning *to build* a new school.

31c Become familiar with common adjective + preposition combinations.

Some adjectives appear only with certain prepositions. These expressions are idiomatic and may be different from the combinations used in your native language.

>   *to*
> ► Paula is married ~~with~~ Jon.
>   ^

Check an ESL dictionary for combinations that are not listed in the chart on page 290.

31d Become familiar with common verb + preposition combinations.

Many verbs and prepositions appear together in idiomatic phrases. Pay special attention to the combinations that are different from the combinations used in your native language.

>   *on*
> ► Your success depends ~~of~~ your effort.
>   ^

Check an ESL dictionary for combinations that are not listed in the chart on page 290.

Adjective + preposition combinations

accustomed to
addicted to
afraid of
angry with
ashamed of
aware of
committed to
concerned
   about
concerned with

connected to
covered with
dedicated to
devoted to
different from
engaged in
engaged to
excited about
familiar with
full of

guilty of
interested in
involved in
involved with
known as
known for
made of (*or*
   made from)
married to
opposed to

preferable to
proud of
responsible
   for
satisfied with
scared of
similar to
tired of
worried
   about

Verb + preposition combinations

agree with
apply to
approve of
arrive at
arrive in
ask for
believe in
belong to
care about
care for
compare to

compare with
concentrate on
consist of
count on
decide on
depend on
differ from
disagree with
dream about
dream of
feel like

forget about
happen to
hope for
insist on
listen to
participate in
rely on
reply to
respond to
result in
search for

speak to (*or*
   speak with)
stare at
succeed at
succeed in
take advantage of
take care of
think about
think of
wait for
wait on

Punctuation
Mechanics
Grammar Basics
Document Design

9(b)

Punctuation, 291

9(b)

Mechanics, 341

9(a)

Grammar Basics, 367

Document Design 401

Punctuation

9/10

32 The comma

The comma was invented to help readers. Without it, sentence parts can collide into one another unexpectedly, causing misreadings.

CONFUSING   If you cook Elmer will do the dishes.

CONFUSING   While we were eating a rattlesnake approached our campsite.

Add commas in the logical places (after *cook* and *eating*), and suddenly all is clear. No longer is Elmer being cooked, the rattlesnake being eaten.

Various rules have evolved to prevent such misreadings and to speed readers along through complex grammatical structures. Those rules are detailed in this section. (Section 33 explains when not to use commas.)

32a Use a comma before a coordinating conjunction joining independent clauses.

When a coordinating conjunction connects two or more in-dependent clauses — word groups that could stand alone as separate sentences — a comma must precede it. There are seven coordinating conjunctions in English: *and, but, or, nor, for, so,* and *yet.*

A comma tells readers that one independent clause has come to a close and that another is about to begin.

▶ The department sponsored a seminar on college survival

skills, and it also hosted a barbecue for new students.
  ^

EXCEPTION: If the two independent clauses are short and there is no danger of misreading, the comma may be omitted.

The plane took off and we were on our way.

TIP: As a rule, do *not* use a comma to separate coordinate word groups that are not independent clauses. (See 33a.)

▶ A good money manager controls expenses,/and invests surplus

dollars to meet future needs.

The word group following *and* is not an independent clause; it is the second half of a compound predicate (*controls . . . and invests*).

32b Use a comma after an introductory clause or phrase.

The most common introductory word groups are clauses and phrases functioning as adverbs. Such word groups usually tell when, where, how, why, or under what conditions the main action of the sentence occurred. (See 48a, 48b, and 48e.)

A comma tells readers that the introductory clause or phrase has come to a close and that the main part of the sentence is about to begin.

▶ When Irwin was ready to iron, his cat tripped on the cord.

Without the comma, readers may have Irwin ironing his cat. The comma signals that *his cat* is the subject of a new clause, not part of the introductory one.

▶ Near a small stream at the bottom of the canyon, the park

rangers discovered an abandoned mine.

The comma tells readers that the introductory prepositional phrase has come to a close.

EXCEPTION: The comma may be omitted after a short adverb clause or phrase if there is no danger of misreading.

In no time we were at 2,800 feet.

Sentences also frequently begin with participial phrases describing the noun or pronoun immediately following them. The comma tells readers that they are about to learn the identity of the person or thing described; therefore, the comma is usually required even when the phrase is short. (See 48b.)

▶ Thinking his motorcade drive through Dallas was routine,

President Kennedy smiled and waved at the crowds.

▶ **Buried under layers of younger rocks, the earth's oldest rocks**
⌃
contain no fossils.

NOTE: Other introductory word groups include transitional expressions and absolute phrases (see 32f).

EXERCISE 32–1   Add or delete commas where necessary in the following sentences. If a sentence is correct, write "correct" after it. Answers to lettered sentences appear in the back of the book. Example:

Because we had been saving molding for a few weeks, we had
⌃
enough wood to frame all thirty paintings.

a. Alisa brought the injured bird home, and fashioned a splint out of Popsicle sticks for its wing.
b. Considered a classic of early animation *The Adventures of Prince Achmed* used hand-cut silhouettes against colored backgrounds.
c. If you complete the evaluation form and return it within two weeks you will receive a free breakfast during your next stay.
d. After retiring from the New York City Ballet in 1965, legendary dancer Maria Tallchief went on to found the Chicago City Ballet.
e. Roger had always wanted a handmade violin but he couldn't afford one.
1. While I was driving a huge delivery truck ran through a red light.
2. He pushed the car beyond the tollgate, and poured a bucket of water on the smoking hood.
3. Lit by bright halogen lamps hundreds of origami birds sparkled like diamonds in sunlight.
4. As the first chord sounded, Aileen knew that her spirits were about to rise.
5. Many musicians of Bach's time played several instruments but few mastered them as early or played with as much expression as Bach.

EXERCISE 32–2   Add or delete commas where necessary in the following sentences. If a sentence is correct, write "correct" after it. Answers to lettered sentences appear in the back of the book. Example:

The car had been sitting idle for a month, so the battery was
⌃
completely dead.

a. J. R. R. Tolkien finished writing his draft of *The Lord of the Rings* trilogy in 1949 but the first book in the series wasn't published until 1954.

b. In the first two minutes of its ascent the space shuttle had broken the sound barrier and reached a height of over twenty-five miles.

c. German shepherds can be gentle guide dogs or they can be fierce attack dogs.

d. Some former professional cyclists claim that the use of performance-enhancing drugs is widespread in cycling and they argue that no rider can be competitive without doping.

e. As an intern, I learned most aspects of the broadcasting industry but I never learned about fundraising,

1. To be considered for the position candidates must demonstrate initiative and strong communication skills.

2. The cinematic lighting effect known as *chiaroscuro* was first used in German Expressionist filmmaking, and was later seen in American film noir.

3. Reptiles are cold-blooded and they are covered with scales.

4. Using a variety of techniques, advertisers grab the audience's attention and imprint their messages onto consumers' minds.

5. By the end of the first quarter the operating budget will be available online.

32c Use a comma between all items in a series.

When three or more items are presented in a series, those items should be separated from one another with commas. Items in a series may be single words, phrases, or clauses.

▶ Langston Hughes's poetry is concerned with racial pride,

social justice, and the diversity of the African American
         ^

experience.

▶ Bubbles of air, leaves, ferns, bits of wood, and insects are
                                            ^

often found trapped in amber.

Although some writers view the comma between the last two items as optional, most experts advise using the comma because its omission can result in ambiguity or misreading.

► My uncle willed me all of his property, houses, and boats.

Did the uncle will his property *and* houses *and* boats — or simply his property, consisting of houses and boats? If the former meaning is intended, a comma is necessary to prevent ambiguity.

► The activities include touring the White House, visiting

the Air and Space Museum, attending a lecture about the

Founding Fathers, and kayaking on the Potomac River.

Without the comma, the activities might seem to include a lecture about kayaking, not participating in kayaking. The comma makes it clear that *kayaking on the Potomac River* is a separate item in the series.

32d Use a comma between coordinate adjectives not joined with *and*. Do not use a comma between cumulative adjectives.

When two or more adjectives each modify a noun separately, they are coordinate.

Roberto is a *warm, gentle, affectionate* father.

If the adjectives can be joined with *and*, the adjectives are coordinate, so you should use commas: *warm* and *gentle* and *affectionate* (*warm, gentle, affectionate*).

Adjectives that do not modify the noun separately are cumulative.

Three large gray shapes moved slowly toward us.

Beginning with the adjective closest to the noun *shapes*, these modifiers lean on one another, piggyback style, with each modifying a larger word group. *Gray* modifies *shapes*, *large* modifies *gray shapes*, and *three* modifies *large gray shapes*. Cumulative adjectives cannot be joined with *and* (not *three* and *large* and *gray shapes*).

COORDINATE ADJECTIVES

► Should patients with severe, irreversible brain damage be put

on life support systems?

Adjectives are coordinate if they can be connected with *and*: *severe and irreversible*.

CUMULATIVE ADJECTIVES

▶ Ira ordered a rich/chocolate/layer cake.

Ira didn't order a cake that was rich and chocolate and layer: He ordered a *layer cake* that was *chocolate*, a *chocolate layer cake* that was *rich*.

EXERCISE 32–3 Add or delete commas where necessary in the following sentences. If a sentence is correct, write "correct" after it. Answers to lettered sentences appear in the back of the book. Example:

We gathered our essentials, took off for the great outdoors,

and ignored the fact that it was Friday the 13th.

a. The cold impersonal atmosphere of the university was unbearable.
b. An ambulance threaded its way through police cars, fire trucks and irate citizens.
c. The *1812 Overture* is a stirring, magnificent piece of music.
d. After two broken arms, three cracked ribs and one concussion, Ken quit the varsity football team.
e. My cat's pupils had constricted to small black shining slits.
1. We prefer our staff to be orderly, prompt and efficient.
2. For breakfast the children ordered cornflakes, English muffins with peanut butter and cherry Cokes.
3. It was a small, unimportant part, but I was happy to have it.
4. Cyril was clad in a luminous orange rain suit and a brilliant white helmet.
5. Animation master Hironobu Sakaguchi makes computer-generated scenes look realistic, vivid and seductive.

EXERCISE 32–4 Add or delete commas where necessary in the following sentences. If a sentence is correct, write "correct" after it. Answers to lettered sentences appear in the back of the book. Example:

Good social workers excel in patience, diplomacy, and

positive thinking.

a. NASA's rovers on Mars are equipped with special cameras that can take close-up high-resolution pictures of the terrain.

b. A baseball player achieves the triple crown by having the highest batting average, the most home runs, and the most runs batted in during the regular season.

c. If it does not get enough sunlight, a healthy green lawn can turn into a shriveled brown mess within a matter of days.

d. Love, vengeance, greed and betrayal are common themes in Western literature.

e. Many experts believe that shark attacks on surfers are a result of the sharks' mistaking surfboards for small, injured seals.

1. In Sherman's march to the sea, the Union army set fire to all crops, killed all livestock and destroyed all roads and bridges in its path.

2. Milk that comes from grass-fed steroid-free cows has been gaining market share.

3. The film makes three main points about global warming: It is real, it is the result of human activity, and it should not be ignored.

4. The three, handmade, turquoise bracelets brought in the most money at the charity auction.

5. Matisse is well known for vibrant colorful prints that have been reproduced extensively on greeting cards and posters.

32e Use commas to set off nonrestrictive (nonessential) elements. Do not use commas to set off restrictive (essential) elements.

Certain word groups that modify nouns or pronouns can be restrictive or nonrestrictive — that is, essential or not essential to the meaning of a sentence. These word groups are usually adjective clauses, adjective phrases, or appositives.

Restrictive elements

A restrictive element defines or limits the meaning of the word it modifies; it is therefore essential to the meaning of the sentence and is not set off with commas. If you remove a restrictive modifier from a sentence, the meaning changes significantly, becoming more general than you intended.

RESTRICTIVE (NO COMMAS)

The campers need clothes *that are durable.*

Scientists *who study the earth's structure* are called geologists.

The first sentence does not mean that the campers need clothes in general. The intended meaning is more limited: The campers need durable clothes. The second sentence does not mean that scientists in general are called geologists; only those scientists who specifically study the earth's structure are called geologists. The italicized word groups are essential and are therefore not set off with commas.

Nonrestrictive elements

A nonrestrictive modifier describes a noun or pronoun whose meaning has already been clearly defined or limited. Because the modifier contains nonessential or parenthetical information, it is set off with commas. If you remove a nonrestrictive element from a sentence, the meaning does not change dramatically. Some meaning may be lost, but the defining characteristics of the person or thing described remain the same.

NONRESTRICTIVE (WITH COMMAS)

The campers need sturdy shoes, *which are expensive.*

The scientists, *who represented eight different universities*, met to review applications for the prestigious O'Hara Award.

In the first sentence, the campers need sturdy shoes, and the shoes happen to be expensive. In the second sentence, the scientists met to review applications for the O'Hara Award; that they represented eight different universities is informative but not critical to the meaning of the sentence. The nonessential information in both sentences is set off with commas.

NOTE: Often it is difficult to tell whether a word group is restrictive or nonrestrictive without seeing it in context and considering the writer's meaning. Both of the following sentences are grammatically correct, but their meaning is slightly different.

The dessert made with fresh raspberries was delicious.

The dessert, made with fresh raspberries, was delicious.

In the first example, the phrase *made with fresh raspberries* tells readers which of two or more desserts the writer is referring to. In the example with commas, the phrase merely adds information about the dessert.

Adjective clauses

Adjective clauses are patterned like sentences, containing subjects and verbs, but they function within sentences as modifiers of nouns or pronouns. They always follow the word they modify, usually immediately. Adjective clauses begin with a relative pronoun (*who, whom, whose, which, that*) or with a relative adverb (*where, when*). Nonrestrictive adjective clauses are set off with commas; restrictive adjective clauses are not.

NONRESTRICTIVE CLAUSE (WITH COMMAS)

▶ Ed's house, which is located on thirteen acres, was completely
  furnished with bats in the rafters and mice in the kitchen.

The adjective clause *which is located on thirteen acres* does not restrict the meaning of *Ed's house*; the information is nonessential and is therefore enclosed in commas.

RESTRICTIVE CLAUSE (NO COMMAS)

▶ The giant panda/that was born at the San Diego Zoo in
  2003/was sent to China in 2007.

Because the adjective clause *that was born at the San Diego Zoo in 2003* identifies one particular panda out of many, the information is essential and is therefore not enclosed in commas.

NOTE: Use *that* only with restrictive (essential) clauses. Many writers prefer to use *which* only with nonrestrictive (nonessential) clauses, but usage varies.

Adjective phrases

Prepositional or verbal phrases functioning as adjectives may be restrictive or nonrestrictive. Nonrestrictive phrases are set off with commas; restrictive phrases are not.

NONRESTRICTIVE PHRASE (WITH COMMAS)

▶ The helicopter, with its million-candlepower spotlight
  illuminating the area, circled above.

The *with* phrase is nonessential because its purpose is not to specify which of two or more helicopters is being discussed. The phrase is not required for readers to understand the meaning of the sentence.

RESTRICTIVE PHRASE (NO COMMAS)

▶ One corner of the attic was filled with newspapers/dating

from the early 1900s.

Dating from the early 1900s restricts the meaning of *newspapers*, so the comma should be omitted.

▶ The bill/proposed by the Illinois representative/would

lower taxes and provide services for middle-income

families.

Proposed by the Illinois representative identifies exactly which bill is meant.

Appositives

An appositive is a noun or noun phrase that renames a nearby noun. Nonrestrictive appositives are set off with commas; restrictive appositives are not.

NONRESTRICTIVE APPOSITIVE (WITH COMMAS)

▶ Darwin's most important book, *On the Origin of Species*,

was the result of many years of research.

Most important restricts the meaning to one book, so the appositive *On the Origin of Species* is nonrestrictive and should be set off with commas.

RESTRICTIVE APPOSITIVE (NO COMMAS)

▶ The song/ "Viva la Vida/" was blasted out of huge amplifiers

at the concert.

Once they've read *song*, readers still don't know precisely which song the writer means. The appositive following *song* restricts its meaning, so the appositive should not be enclosed in commas.

EXERCISE 32–5 Add or delete commas where necessary in the following sentences. If a sentence is correct, write "correct" after it. Answers to lettered sentences appear in the back of the book. Example:

> My sister, who plays center on the Sparks, now lives at
>
> The Sands, a beach house near Los Angeles.

a. Choreographer Alvin Ailey's best-known work *Revelations* is more than just a crowd-pleaser.

b. Twyla Tharp's contemporary ballet *Push Comes to Shove* was made famous by the Russian dancer Baryshnikov. [*Tharp has written more than one contemporary ballet.*]

c. The glass sculptor sifting through hot red sand explained her technique to the other glassmakers. [*There is more than one glass sculptor.*]

d. A member of an organization, that provides job training for teens, was also appointed to the education commission.

e. Brian Eno who began his career as a rock musician turned to meditative compositions in the late 1970s.

1. I had the pleasure of talking to a woman who had just returned from India where she had lived for ten years.

2. Patrick's oldest sister Fiona graduated from MIT with a degree in aerospace engineering.

3. The artist painting a portrait of Aung San Suu Kyi, the Burmese civil rights leader, was once a political prisoner himself.

4. *Jumanji*, the 1982 Caldecott Medal winner, is my nephew's favorite book.

5. The flame crawled up a few blades of grass to reach a low-hanging palmetto branch which quickly ignited.

32f Use commas to set off transitional and parenthetical expressions, absolute phrases, and word groups expressing contrast.

Transitional expressions

Transitional expressions serve as bridges between sentences or parts of sentences. They include conjunctive adverbs such as *however*, *therefore*, and *moreover* and transitional phrases such as *for example, as a matter of fact,* and *in other words.* (For complete lists of these expressions, see 34b.)

When a transitional expression appears between independent clauses in a compound sentence, it is preceded by a semicolon and is usually followed by a comma. (See 34b.)

> Minh did not understand our language; moreover, he was
>
> unfamiliar with our customs.

When a transitional expression appears at the beginning of a sentence or in the middle of an independent clause, it is usually set off with commas.

> As a matter of fact, American football was established in the
>
> mid-nineteenth century by fans who wanted to play a more
>
> organized game of rugby.

> Natural foods are not always salt free; celery, for example,
>
> contains more sodium than most people would imagine.

EXCEPTION: If a transitional expression blends smoothly with the rest of the sentence, calling for little or no pause in reading, it does not need to be set off with a comma. Expressions such as *also, at least, certainly, consequently, indeed, of course, moreover, no doubt, perhaps, then,* and *therefore* do not always call for a pause.

Alice's bicycle is broken; *therefore* you will need to borrow Sue's.

Parenthetical expressions

Expressions that are distinctly parenthetical, providing only supplemental information, should be set off with commas. They interrupt the flow of a sentence or appear at the end as afterthoughts.

> Evolution, as far as we know, doesn't work this way.

> The bass weighed about twelve pounds, give or take a few
>
> ounces.

Absolute phrases

An absolute phrase, which modifies the whole sentence, usually consists of a noun followed by a participle or participial phrase. (See 48d.) Absolute phrases may appear at the beginning or at the end of a sentence. Wherever they appear, they should be set off with commas.

```
┌──────────── ABSOLUTE PHRASE ────────────┐
│   N    PARTICIPLE                        │
```
The sun appearing for the first time in a week, we were at last able to begin the archaeological dig.

▶ Elvis Presley made music industry history in the 1950s, his

records having sold more than ten million copies.

NOTE: Do not insert a comma between the noun and the participle in an absolute construction.

▶ The next contestant／being five years old, the host adjusted

the height of the microphone.

Word groups expressing contrast

Sharp contrasts beginning with words such as *not, never,* and *unlike* are set off with commas.

▶ The Epicurean philosophers sought mental, not bodily,

pleasures.

▶ Unlike Robert, Celia loved dance contests.

32g Use commas to set off nouns of direct address, the words *yes* and *no*, interrogative tags, and mild interjections.

▶ Forgive me, Angela, for forgetting your birthday.

▶ Yes, the loan will probably be approved.

▶ The film was faithful to the book, wasn't it?

▶ Well, cases like these are difficult to decide.

32h Use commas with expressions such as *he said* to set off direct quotations. (See also 37e.)

▶ In his "Letter from Birmingham Jail," Martin Luther King

Jr. wrote, "We know through painful experience that freedom

is never voluntarily given by the oppressor; it must be

demanded by the oppressed" (225).

▶ "Happiness in marriage is entirely a matter of chance," says

Charlotte Lucas in *Pride and Prejudice,* a novel that ends with

two happy marriages (ch. 6; 69).

See 37 on the use of quotation marks and pages 489–90 on citing literary sources in MLA style.

32i Use commas with dates, addresses, titles, and numbers.

Dates

In dates, the year is set off from the rest of the sentence with a pair of commas.

▶ On December 12, 1890, orders were sent out for the arrest of

Sitting Bull.

EXCEPTIONS: Commas are not needed if the date is inverted or if only the month and year are given.

The security alert system went into effect on 15 April 2009.

January 2008 was an extremely cold month.

Addresses

The elements of an address or a place name are separated with commas. A zip code, however, is not preceded by a comma.

▶ John Lennon was born in Liverpool, England, in 1940.

▶ Please send the package to Greg Tarvin at 708 Spring Street,

Washington, IL 61571.

Titles

If a title follows a name, separate the title from the rest of the sentence with a pair of commas.

▶ Ann Hall, MD, has been appointed to the board of trustees.

Numbers

In numbers more than four digits long, use commas to separate the numbers into groups of three, starting from the right. In numbers four digits long, a comma is optional.

    3,500 [*or* 3500]

    100,000

    5,000,000

EXCEPTIONS: Do not use commas in street numbers, zip codes, telephone numbers, or years with four or fewer digits.

32j Use a comma to prevent confusion.

In certain situations, a comma is necessary to prevent confusion. If the writer has intentionally left out a word or phrase, for example, a comma may be needed to signal the omission.

▶ To err is human; to forgive, divine.

If two words in a row echo each other, a comma may be needed for ease of reading.

▶ The catastrophe that we had feared might happen, happened.

Sometimes a comma is needed to prevent readers from grouping words in ways that do not match the writer's intention.

▶ Patients who can, walk up and down the halls every day.

EXERCISE 32–6 This exercise covers the major uses of the comma described in 32a–32e. Add or delete commas where necessary. If a sentence is correct, write "correct" after it. Answers to lettered sentences appear in the back of the book. Example:

> Even though our brains actually can't focus on two tasks
>
> at a time, many people believe they can multitask.

a. Cricket which originated in England is also popular in Australia, South Africa and India.

b. At the sound of the starting pistol the horses surged forward toward the first obstacle, a sharp incline three feet high.

c. After seeing an exhibition of Western art Gerhard Richter escaped from East Berlin, and smuggled out many of his notebooks.

d. Corrie's new wet suit has an intricate, blue pattern.

e. The cookies will keep for two weeks in sturdy airtight containers.

1. Research on Andean condors has shown that high levels of the pesticide chlorinated hydrocarbon can cause the thinning of eggshells.

2. Founded in 1868 Hampton University was one of the first colleges for African Americans.

3. Aunt Emilia was an impossible demanding guest.

4. The Mirage, a high-tech fighter, is an astonishing machine to fly.

5. At the bottom of the ship's rusty hold sat several, well-preserved trunks, reminders of a bygone era of sea travel.

EXERCISE 32–7 This exercise covers all uses of the comma. Add or delete commas where necessary in the following sentences. If a sentence is correct, write "correct" after it. Answers to lettered sentences appear in the back of the book. Example:

> "Yes, dear, you can have dessert," my mother said.

a. On January 15, 2008 our office moved to 29 Commonwealth Avenue, Mechanicsville VA 23111.

b. The coach having bawled us out thoroughly, we left the locker room with his harsh words ringing in our ears.

c. Ms. Carlson you are a valued customer whose satisfaction is very important to us.

d. Mr. Mundy was born on July 22, 1939 in Arkansas, where his family had lived for four generations.

e. Her board poised at the edge of the half-pipe, Nina waited her turn to drop in.

1. President Lincoln's original intention was to save the Union, not to destroy slavery.

2. For centuries people believed that Greek culture had developed in isolation from the world. Today however scholars are acknowledging the contributions made by Egypt and the Middle East.

3. Putting together a successful fundraiser, Patricia discovered, requires creativity and good timing.

4. Fortunately science is creating many alternatives to research performed on animals.

5. While the machine was printing the oversize paper jammed the input tray.

33 Unnecessary commas

Many common misuses of the comma result from a misunderstanding of the major comma rules presented in 32.

33a Do not use a comma between compound elements that are not independent clauses.

Though a comma should be used before a coordinating conjunction joining independent clauses (see 32a), this rule should not be extended to other compound word groups.

► Marie Curie discovered radium/and later applied her work on

radioactivity to medicine.

And links two verbs in a compound predicate: *discovered* and *applied*.

▶ Jake told us that his illness is serious/ but that changes in

his lifestyle can improve his chances for survival.

The coordinating conjunction *but* links two subordinate clauses, each
beginning with *that*: *that his illness is serious* and *that changes in his
lifestyle.* . . .

33b Do not use a comma to separate a verb from its subject or object.

A sentence should flow from subject to verb to object without
unnecessary pauses. Commas may appear between these major
sentence elements only when a specific rule calls for them.

▶ Zoos large enough to give the animals freedom to roam/ are

becoming more popular.

The comma should not separate the subject, *Zoos*, from the verb, *are
becoming*.

▶ Maxine Hong Kingston writes/ that many Chinese American

families struggle "to figure out how the invisible world the

emigrants built around our childhoods fits in solid America" (107).

The comma should not separate the verb, *writes*, from its object, the
subordinate clause beginning with *that*. A signal phrase ending in a
word like *writes* or *says* is followed by a comma only when a direct
quotation immediately follows: *Kingston writes, "Those of us in the first
American generations have had to figure out how the invisible world . . ."
(107).* (See also 37e.)

33c Do not use a comma before the first or after the last item in a series.

Though commas are required between items in a series (32c), do
not place them either before or after the whole series.

▶ Other causes of asthmatic attacks are/ stress, change in

temperature, and cold air.

▶ Ironically, even novels that focus on horror, evil, and alienation⁄

often have themes of spiritual renewal and redemption as well.

33d Do not use a comma between cumulative adjectives, between an adjective and a noun, or between an adverb and an adjective.

Commas are required between coordinate adjectives (those that can be joined with *and*), but they do not belong between cumulative adjectives (those that cannot be joined with *and*). (For a full discussion, see 32d.)

▶ In the corner of the closet, we found an old⁄maroon hatbox.

A comma should never be used between an adjective and the noun that follows it.

▶ It was a senseless, dangerous⁄mission.

Nor should a comma be used between an adverb and an adjective that follows it.

▶ The Hillside is a good home for severely⁄disturbed youths.

33e Do not use commas to set off restrictive or mildly parenthetical elements.

Restrictive elements are modifiers or appositives that restrict the meaning of the nouns they follow. Because they are essential to the meaning of the sentence, they are not set off with commas. (For a full discussion of restrictive and nonrestrictive elements, see 32e.)

▶ Drivers⁄who think they own the road⁄make cycling a

dangerous sport.

The modifier *who think they own the road* restricts the meaning of *Drivers* and is essential to the meaning of the sentence. Putting commas around the *who* clause falsely suggests that all drivers think they own the road.

▶ Margaret Mead's book/*Coming of Age in Samoa*/stirred up

considerable controversy when it was published in 1928.

Since Mead wrote more than one book, the appositive contains information essential to the meaning of the sentence.

Although commas should be used with distinctly parenthetical expressions (see 32f), do not use them to set off elements that are only mildly parenthetical.

▶ Texting has/essentially/replaced e-mail for casual

communication.

33f Do not use a comma to set off a concluding adverb clause that is essential to the meaning of the sentence.

When adverb clauses introduce a sentence, they are nearly always followed by a comma (see 32b). When they conclude a sentence, however, they are not set off by commas if their content is essential to the meaning of the earlier part of the sentence. Adverb clauses beginning with *after*, *as soon as*, *because*, *before*, *if*, *since*, *unless*, *until*, and *when* are usually essential.

▶ Don't visit Paris at the height of the tourist season/unless

you have booked hotel reservations.

Without the *unless* clause, the meaning of the sentence might at first seem broader than the writer intended.

When a concluding adverb clause is nonessential, it should be preceded by a comma. Clauses beginning with *although*, *even though*, *though*, and *whereas* are usually nonessential.

▶ The lecture seemed to last only a short time‚ although the
                                                   ^
clock said it had gone on for more than an hour.

33g Do not use a comma after a phrase that begins an inverted sentence.

Though a comma belongs after most introductory phrases (see 32b), it does not belong after phrases that begin an inverted sentence. In an inverted sentence, the subject follows the verb, and a phrase that ordinarily would follow the verb is moved to the beginning (see 47c).

▶ At the bottom of the hill,/sat the stubborn mule.

33h Avoid other common misuses of the comma.

Do not use a comma in the following situations.

AFTER A COORDINATING CONJUNCTION (*AND, BUT, OR, NOR, FOR, SO, YET*)

▶ Occasionally TV talk shows are performed live, but,/more

often they are taped.

AFTER *SUCH AS* OR *LIKE*

▶ Shade-loving plants such as,/begonias, impatiens, and coleus

can add color to a shady garden.

BEFORE *THAN*

▶ Touring Crete was more thrilling for us,/than visiting the

Greek islands frequented by the rich.

AFTER *ALTHOUGH*

▶ Although,/the air was balmy, the water was too cold for

swimming.

BEFORE A PARENTHESIS

▶ At InterComm, Sylvia began at the bottom,/(with only three

and a half walls and a swivel chair), but within three years she

had been promoted to supervisor.

TO SET OFF AN INDIRECT (REPORTED) QUOTATION

▶ Samuel Goldwyn once said/that a verbal contract isn't worth the paper it's written on.

WITH A QUESTION MARK OR AN EXCLAMATION POINT

▶ "Why don't you try it?/" she coaxed. "You can't do any worse than the rest of us."

EXERCISE 33–1 Delete any unnecessary commas in the following sentences. If a sentence is correct, write "correct" after it. Answers to lettered sentences appear in the back of the book. Example:

In his Silk Road Project, Yo-Yo Ma incorporates work by

musicians such as/ Kayhan Kahlor and Richard Danielpour.

a. After the morning rains cease, the swimmers emerge from their cottages.
b. Tricia's first artwork was a bright, blue, clay dolphin.
c. Some modern musicians, (trumpeter John Hassell is an example) blend several cultural traditions into a unique sound.
d. Myra liked hot, spicy foods such as, chili, kung pao chicken, and buffalo wings.
e. On the display screen, was a soothing pattern of light and shadow.
1. Mesquite, the hardest of the softwoods, grows primarily in the Southwest.
2. Jolie's parents encouraged independent thinking, but required respect for others' opinions.
3. The border guards told their sergeant, that their heat-sensing equipment was malfunctioning.
4. The streets that three hours later would be bumper to bumper with commuters, were quiet and empty except for a few prowling cats.
5. Some first-year architecture students, expect to design intricate structures immediately.

EXERCISE 33–2   Delete unnecessary commas in the following passage.

Each spring since 1970, New Orleans has hosted the Jazz and Heritage Festival, an event that celebrates the music, food, and culture, of the region. Although, it is often referred to as "Jazz Fest," the festival typically includes a wide variety of musical styles such as, gospel, Cajun, blues, zydeco, and, rock and roll. Famous musicians who have appeared regularly at Jazz Fest, include Dr. John, B. B. King, and Aretha Franklin. Large stages are set up throughout the fairgrounds in a way, that allows up to ten bands to play simultaneously without any sound overlap. Food tents are located throughout the festival, and offer popular, local dishes like crawfish Monica, jambalaya, and fried, green tomatoes. In 2009, New Orleans held its fortieth annual Jazz Fest. Fans, who could not attend the festival, still enjoyed the music by downloading MP3 files, and watching performances online.

34   The semicolon

The semicolon is used to connect major sentence elements of equal grammatical rank.

34a Use a semicolon between closely related independent clauses not joined with a coordinating conjunction.

When two independent clauses appear in one sentence, they are usually linked with a comma and a coordinating conjunction (*and, but, or, nor, for, so, yet*). The coordinating conjunction signals the relation between the clauses. If the clauses are closely related and the relation is clear without a conjunction, they may be linked with a semicolon instead.

> In film, a low-angle shot makes the subject look powerful; a high-angle shot does just the opposite.

A semicolon must be used whenever a coordinating conjunction has been omitted between independent clauses. To use merely a comma creates a type of run-on sentence known as a *comma splice*. (See 20.)

▶ In 1800, a traveler needed six weeks to get from New York City

to Chicago/; in 1860, the trip by railroad took only two days.
    ^

34b Use a semicolon between independent clauses linked with a transitional expression.

Transitional expressions include conjunctive adverbs and transitional phrases.

CONJUNCTIVE ADVERBS

accordingly	furthermore	moreover	still
also	hence	nevertheless	subsequently
anyway	however	next	then
besides	incidentally	nonetheless	therefore
certainly	indeed	now	thus
consequently	instead	otherwise	
conversely	likewise	similarly	
finally	meanwhile	specifically	

TRANSITIONAL PHRASES

after all	even so	in fact
as a matter of fact	for example	in other words
as a result	for instance	in the first place
at any rate	in addition	on the contrary
at the same time	in conclusion	on the other hand

When a transitional expression appears between independent clauses, it is preceded by a semicolon and usually followed by a comma.

► Many corals grow very gradually; in fact, the creation of a

coral reef can take centuries.

When a transitional expression appears in the middle or at the end of the second independent clause, the semicolon goes *between the clauses.*

► Biologists have observed laughter in primates other than

humans; chimpanzees, however, sound more like they are

panting than laughing.

Transitional expressions should not be confused with the coordinating conjunctions *and, but, or, nor, for, so,* and *yet,* which are preceded by a comma when they link independent clauses. (See 32a.)

34c Use a semicolon between items in a series containing internal punctuation.

▶ Classic science fiction sagas are *Star Trek*, with Mr. Spock/;
                                                            ^

Battlestar Galactica, with its Cylons/; and Star Wars, with
                                    ^

Han Solo, Luke Skywalker, and Darth Vader.

Without the semicolons, the reader would have to sort out the major groupings, distinguishing between important and less important pauses according to the logic of the sentence. By inserting semicolons at the major breaks, the writer does this work for the reader.

34d Avoid common misuses of the semicolon.

Do not use a semicolon in the following situations.

BETWEEN A SUBORDINATE CLAUSE AND THE REST OF THE SENTENCE

▶ Although children's literature was added to the National

Book Awards in 1969/, it has had its own award, the Newbery
                    ^

Medal, since 1922.

BETWEEN AN APPOSITIVE AND THE WORD IT REFERS TO

▶ The scientists were fascinated by the species *Argyroneta*

aquatica/, a spider that lives underwater.
        ^

TO INTRODUCE A LIST

▶ Some of my favorite celebrities have their own blogs/:
                                                      ^

Ashton Kutcher, Rosie O'Donnell, and Zach Braff.

BETWEEN INDEPENDENT CLAUSES JOINED BY *AND, BUT, OR*, NOR, FOR, SO, OR *YET*

▶ Five of the applicants had worked with spreadsheets, but
‸
only one was familiar with database management.

EXCEPTIONS: If at least one of the independent clauses contains internal punctuation, you may use a semicolon even though the clauses are joined with a coordinating conjunction.

> As a vehicle [the model T] was hard-working, commonplace, and heroic; and it often seemed to transmit those qualities to the person who rode in it. —E. B. White

Although a comma would also be correct in this sentence, the semicolon is more effective, for it indicates the relative weights of the pauses.

Occasionally, a semicolon may be used to emphasize a sharp contrast or a firm distinction between clauses joined with a coordinating conjunction.

> We hate some persons because we do not know them; and we will not know them because we hate them. —Charles Caleb Colton

EXERCISE 34–1 Add commas or semicolons where needed in the following well-known quotations. If a sentence is correct, write "correct" after it. Answers to lettered sentences appear in the back of the book. Example:

> If an animal does something, we call it instinct; if we do
>   ‸   ‸
> the same thing, we call it intelligence. —Will Cuppy
>   ‸

a. Do not ask me to be kind just ask me to act as though I were.
   —Jules Renard

b. When men talk about defense they always claim to be protecting women and children but they never ask the women and children what they think. —Pat Schroeder

c. When I get a little money I buy books if any is left I buy food and clothes. —Desiderius Erasmus

d. America is a country that doesn't know where it is going but is determined to set a speed record getting there.
   —Lawrence J. Peter

e. Wit has truth in it wisecracking is simply calisthenics with words.

      —Dorothy Parker

   1. Standing in the middle of the road is very dangerous you get
      knocked down by the traffic from both sides.

      —Margaret Thatcher

   2. I do not believe in an afterlife, although I am bringing a change of
      underwear.   —Woody Allen

   3. Once the children were in the house the air became more vivid
      and more heated every object in the house grew more alive.

      —Mary Gordon

   4. We don't know what we want but we are ready to bite someone to
      get it.   —Will Rogers

   5. I've been rich and I've been poor rich is better.   —Sophie Tucker

EXERCISE 34–2   Edit the following sentences to correct errors in the
use of the comma and the semicolon. If a sentence is correct, write
"correct" after it. Answers to lettered sentences appear in the back of
the book. Example:

Love is blind ; envy has its eyes wide open.
              ^

   a. Strong black coffee will not sober you up, the truth is that time is
      the only way to get alcohol out of your system.

   b. Margaret was not surprised to see hail and vivid lightning, condi-
      tions had been right for violent weather all day.

   c. There is often a fine line between right and wrong; good and bad;
      truth and deception.

   d. My mother always says that you can't learn common sense; either
      you're born with it or you're not.

   e. Severe, unremitting pain is a ravaging force; especially when the
      patient tries to hide it from others.

   1. Another delicious dish is the chef's special; a roasted duck rubbed
      with spices and stuffed with wild rice.

   2. Martin Luther King Jr. had not always intended to be a preacher,
      initially, he had planned to become a lawyer.

   3. We all assumed that the thief had been Jean's boyfriend; even
      though we had seen him only from the back.

   4. The Victorians avoided the subject of sex but were obsessed with
      death, a hundred years later, people were obsessed with sex but
      avoided thinking about death.

   5. Some educators believe that African American history should be
      taught in separate courses, others prefer to see it integrated into
      survey courses.

35   The colon

The colon is used primarily to call attention to the words that follow it. In addition, the colon has some conventional uses.

35a Use a colon after an independent clause to direct attention to a list, an appositive, a quotation, or a summary or an explanation.

A LIST

The daily routine should include at least the following: twenty knee bends, fifty sit-ups, and five minutes of running in place.

AN APPOSITIVE

My roommate is guilty of two of the seven deadly sins: gluttony and sloth.

A QUOTATION

Consider the words of Benjamin Franklin: "There never was a good war or a bad peace."

A SUMMARY OR AN EXPLANATION

Faith is like love: It cannot be forced.

The novel is clearly autobiographical: The author even gives his own name to the main character.

NOTE: For other ways of introducing quotations, see "Introducing quoted material" on pages 329–31. When an independent clause follows a colon, begin with a capital letter. Some disciplines use a lowercase letter instead. See 45f for variations.

35b Use a colon according to convention.

SALUTATION IN A LETTER   Dear Sir or Madam:

HOURS AND MINUTES   5:30 p.m.

PROPORTIONS   The ratio of women to men was 2:1.

TITLE AND SUBTITLE   *The Glory of Hera*: *Greek Mythology and the Greek Family*

BIBLIOGRAPHIC ENTRIES   Boston: Bedford, 2009

NOTE: In biblical references, a colon is ordinarily used between chapter and verse (Luke 2:14). The Modern Language Association (MLA) recommends a period instead (Luke 2.14).

35c Avoid common misuses of the colon.

A colon must be preceded by a full independent clause. Therefore, avoid using it in the following situations.

BETWEEN A VERB AND ITS OBJECT OR COMPLEMENT

▶ Some important vitamins found in vegetables are:/vitamin A, thiamine, niacin, and vitamin C.

BETWEEN A PREPOSITION AND ITS OBJECT

▶ The heart's two pumps each consist of:/an upper chamber, or atrium, and a lower chamber, or ventricle.

AFTER *SUCH AS, INCLUDING,* OR *FOR EXAMPLE*

▶ The NCAA regulates college athletic teams, including:/ basketball, baseball, softball, and football.

EXERCISE 35–1 Edit the following sentences to correct errors in the use of the comma, the semicolon, or the colon. If a sentence is correct, write "correct" after it. Answers to lettered sentences appear in the back of the book. Example:

Lifting the cover gently, Luca found the source of the odd

sound;/: a marble in the gears.
　　　　^

a. We always looked forward to Thanksgiving in Vermont: It was our only chance to see our Grady cousins.

b. If we have come to fight, we are far too few, if we have come to die, we are far too many.

c. The travel package includes: a round-trip ticket to Athens, a cruise through the Cyclades, and all hotel accommodations.

d. The news article portrays the land use proposal as reckless; although 62 percent of the town's residents support it.

e. Psychologists Kindlon and Thompson (2000) offer parents a simple starting point for raising male children, "Teach boys that there are many ways to be a man" (p. 256).

1. Harry Potter prevails against pain and evil for one reason, his heart is pure.

2. While traveling through France, Rose visited: the Loire Valley, Chartres, the Louvre, and the McDonald's stand at the foot of the Eiffel Tower.

3. There are three types of leave; annual leave, used for vacations, sick leave, used for medical appointments and illness, and personal leave, used for a variety of personal reasons.

4. American poet Carl Sandburg once asked these three questions, "Who paid for my freedom? What was the price? And am I somehow beholden?"

5. Amelie had four goals: to be encouraging, to be effective, to be efficient, and to be elegant.

36   The apostrophe

36a Use an apostrophe to indicate that a noun is possessive.

Possessive nouns usually indicate ownership, as in *Tim's hat*, *the lawyer's desk*, or *someone's glove*. Frequently, however, ownership is only loosely implied: *the tree's roots*, *a day's work*. If you are not sure whether a noun is possessive, try turning it into an *of* phrase: *the roots of the tree*, *the work of a day*.

When to add -'s

1. If the noun does not end in -s, add -'s.

   Luck often propels a rock musician's career.

   The Children's Defense Fund is a nonprofit organization that supports programs for poor and minority children.

2. If the noun is singular and ends in -*s* or an *s* sound, add -*'s* to indicate possession.

> Lois's sister spent last year in India.

> Her article presents an overview of Marx's teachings.

NOTE: To avoid potentially awkward pronunciation, some writers use only the apostrophe with a singular noun ending in -*s*: *Sophocles'*.

When to add only an apostrophe

If the noun is plural and ends in -*s*, add only an apostrophe.

> Both diplomats' briefcases were searched by guards.

Joint possession

To show joint possession, use -*'s* or (-*s'*) with the last noun only; to show individual possession, make all nouns possessive.

> Have you seen Joyce and Greg's new camper?

> John's and Marie's expectations of marriage couldn't have been more different.

Joyce and Greg jointly own one camper. John and Marie individually have different expectations.

Compound nouns

If a noun is compound, use -*'s* (or -*s'*) with the last element.

> My father-in-law's memoir about his childhood in Sri Lanka was published in October.

36b Use an apostrophe and -*s* to indicate that an indefinite pronoun is possessive.

Indefinite pronouns refer to no specific person or thing: *everyone, someone, no one, something.* (See 46b.)

> Someone's raincoat has been left behind.

36c Use an apostrophe to mark omissions in contractions and numbers.

In a contraction, the apostrophe takes the place of one or more missing letters.

> It's a shame that Frank can't go on the tour.

It's stands for *it is*, *can't* for *cannot*.

The apostrophe is also used to mark the omission of the first two digits of a year (*the class of '08*) or years (*the '60s generation*).

36d Do not use an apostrophe to form the plural of numbers, letters, abbreviations, and words mentioned as words.

An apostrophe typically is not used to pluralize numbers, letters, abbreviations, and words mentioned as words. Note the few exceptions and be consistent throughout your paper.

Plural of numbers

Do not use an apostrophe in the plural of any numbers, including decades.

> Oksana skated nearly perfect figure 8s.

> The 1920s are known as the Jazz Age.

Plural of letters

Italicize the letter and use roman (regular) font style for the *-s* ending. Do not italicize academic grades.

> Two large *J*s were painted on the door.

> He received two Ds for the first time in his life.

EXCEPTIONS: To avoid misreading, use an apostrophe to form the plural of lowercase letters and the capital letters *A* and *I*.

> Beginning readers often confuse *b*'s and *d*'s.

> Students with straight A's earn high honors.

MLA NOTE: The Modern Language Association recommends using an apostrophe for the plural of both capital and lowercase letters: *J*'s, *p*'s.

Plural of abbreviations

Do not use an apostrophe to pluralize an abbreviation.

> Harriet has thirty DVDs on her desk.

> Marco earned two PhDs before his thirtieth birthday.

Plural of words mentioned as words

Generally, omit the apostrophe to form the plural of words mentioned as words. If the word is italicized, the *-s* ending appears in roman (regular) type.

> We've heard enough *maybes*.

Words mentioned as words may also appear in quotation marks. When you choose this option, use the apostrophe.

> We've heard enough "maybe's."

36e Avoid common misuses of the apostrophe.

Do not use an apostrophe in the following situations.

WITH NOUNS THAT ARE NOT POSSESSIVE

> ▶ Some ~~outpatient's~~ *outpatients* have special parking permits.

IN THE POSSESSIVE PRONOUNS *ITS, WHOSE, HIS, HERS, OURS, YOURS,* AND *THEIRS*

> ▶ Each area has ~~it's~~ *its* own conference room.

> *It's* means "it is." The possessive pronoun *its* contains no apostrophe despite the fact that it is possessive.

> ▶ *The House on Mango Street* was written by Sandra Cisneros, ~~who's~~ *whose* work focuses on the Latino community in the United States.

> *Who's* means "who is." The possessive pronoun is *whose*.

EXERCISE 36–1 Edit the following sentences to correct errors in the use of the apostrophe. If a sentence is correct, write "correct" after it. Answers to lettered sentences appear in the back of the book. Example:

Our favorite barbecue restaurant is Poor ~~Richards~~ Richard's Ribs.

a. This diet will improve almost anyone's health.

b. The innovative shoe fastener was inspired by the designers young son.

c. Each days menu features a different European country's dish.

d. Sue worked overtime to increase her families earnings.

e. Ms. Jacobs is unwilling to listen to students complaints about computer failures.

1. Siddhartha sat by the river and listened to its many voices.

2. Three teenage son's can devour about as much food as four full-grown field hands. The only difference is that they dont do half as much work.

3. The small biotech company has contracts with NASA and other government agency's.

4. Patience and humor are key tools in a travelers survival kit.

5. My sister-in-law's quilts are being shown at the Fendrick Gallery.

EXERCISE 36–2 Edit the following passage to correct errors in the use of the apostrophe.

Its never too soon to start holiday shopping. In fact, some people choose to start shopping as early as January, when last seasons leftover's are priced at their lowest. Many stores try to lure customers in with promise's of savings up to 90 percent. Their main objective, of course, is to make way for next years inventory. The big problem with postholiday shopping, though, is that there isn't much left to choose from. Store's shelves have been picked over by last-minute shoppers desperately searching for gifts. The other problem is that its hard to know what to buy so far in advance. Next year's hot items are anyones guess. But proper timing, mixed with lot's of luck and determination, can lead to good purchases at great price's.

37 Quotation marks

Writers use quotation marks primarily to enclose direct quotations of another person's spoken or written words. You will also find these other uses and exceptions:

- for quotations within quotations (single quotation marks: 37b)
- for titles of short works (37c)
- for words used as words (37d)
- with other marks of punctuation (37e)
- with brackets and ellipsis marks (39c–39d)
- no quotation marks for long quotations (p. 327)
- no quotation marks for indirect quotations, summaries, and paraphrases (p. 327)

37a Use quotation marks to enclose direct quotations.

Direct quotations of a person's words, whether spoken or written, must be in quotation marks.

> "The contract negotiations are stalled," the airline executive told reporters, "but I am prepared to work night and day to bring both sides together."

In dialogue, begin a new paragraph to mark a change in speaker.

> "Mom, his name is Willie, not William. A thousand times I've told you, it's *Willie.*"
> "Willie is a derivative of William, Lester. Surely his birth certificate doesn't have Willie on it, and I like calling people by their proper names."
> "Yes, it does, ma'am. My mother named me Willie K. Mason."
> — Gloria Naylor

If a single speaker utters more than one paragraph, introduce each paragraph with a quotation mark, but do not use a closing quotation mark until the end of the speech.

Exception: indirect quotations

Do not use quotation marks around indirect quotations. An indirect quotation reports someone's ideas without using that person's exact words. In academic writing, indirect quotation is called *paraphrase* or *summary*. (See p. 452.)

> The airline executive told reporters that although contract negotiations were at a standstill, she was prepared to work hard with both labor and management to bring about a settlement.

Exception: long quotations

Long quotations of prose or poetry are generally set off from the text by indenting. Quotation marks are not used because the indented format tells readers that the quotation is taken word-for word from the source.

> After making an exhaustive study of the historical record, James Horan evaluates Billy the Kid like this:
>
> > The portrait that emerges of [the Kid] from the thousands of pages of affidavits, reports, trial transcripts, his letters, and his testimony is neither the mythical Robin Hood nor the stereotyped adenoidal moron and pathological killer. Rather Billy appears as a disturbed, lonely young man, honest, loyal to his friends, dedicated to his beliefs, and betrayed by our institutions and the corrupt, ambitious, and compromising politicians in his time. (158)

The number in parentheses is a citation handled according to MLA style. (See p. 465.)

MLA and APA have specific guidelines for what constitutes a long quotation and how it should be indented (see pp. 471 and 545, respectively).

37b Use single quotation marks to enclose a quotation within a quotation.

> Megan Marshall notes that what Elizabeth Peabody "hoped to accomplish in her school was not merely 'teaching' but 'educating children morally and spiritually as well as intellectually from the first'" (107).

37c Use quotation marks around the titles of short works.

Short works include newspaper and magazine articles, poems, short stories, songs, episodes of television and radio programs, and chapters or subdivisions of books.

> James Baldwin's story "Sonny's Blues" tells the story of two brothers who come to understand each other's suffering.

NOTE: Titles of books, plays, Web sites, television and radio programs, films, magazines, and newspapers are put in italics. (See 42a.)

37d Quotation marks may be used to set off words used as words.

Although words used as words are ordinarily italicized (see 42d), quotation marks are also acceptable. Be consistent throughout your paper.

> The words "accept" and "except" are frequently confused.

> The words *accept* and *except* are frequently confused.

37e Use punctuation with quotation marks according to convention.

This section describes the conventions American publishers use in placing various marks of punctuation inside or outside quotation marks. It also explains how to punctuate when introducing quoted material.

Periods and commas

Place periods and commas inside quotation marks.

> "I'm here as part of my service-learning project," I told the classroom teacher. "I'm hoping to become a reading specialist."

This rule applies to single quotation marks as well as double quotation marks. (See 37b.) It also applies to all uses of quotation marks: for quoted material, for titles of works, and for words used as words.

EXCEPTION: In the Modern Language Association's style of parenthetical in-text citations (see p. 465), the period follows the citation in parentheses.

> James M. McPherson comments, approvingly, that the Whigs "were not averse to extending the blessings of American liberty, even to Mexicans and Indians" (48).

Colons and semicolons

Put colons and semicolons outside quotation marks.

> Harold wrote, "I regret that I am unable to attend the fundraiser for AIDS research"; his letter, however, came with a substantial contribution.

Question marks and exclamation points

Put question marks and exclamation points inside quotation marks unless they apply to the whole sentence.

> Contrary to tradition, bedtime at my house is marked by "Mommy, can I tell you a story now?"

> Have you heard the old proverb "Do not climb the hill until you reach it"?

In the first sentence, the question mark applies only to the quoted question. In the second sentence, the question mark applies to the whole sentence.

NOTE: In MLA style for a quotation that ends with a question mark or an exclamation point, the parenthetical citation and a period should follow the entire quotation.

> Rosie Thomas asks, "Is nothing in life ever straight and clear, the way children see it?" (77).

Introducing quoted material

After a word group introducing a quotation, choose a colon, a comma, or no punctuation at all, whichever is appropriate in context. See page 330.

Formal introduction   If a quotation is formally introduced, a colon is appropriate. A formal introduction is a full independent clause, not just an expression such as *he said* or *she remarked*.

> Thomas Friedman provides a challenging yet optimistic view of the future: "We need to get back to work on our country and on our planet. The hour is late, the stakes couldn't be higher, the project couldn't be harder, the payoff couldn't be greater" (25).

Expression such as *he said*   If a quotation is introduced with an expression such as *he said* or *she remarked* — or if it is followed by such an expression — a comma is needed.

> About New England's weather, Mark Twain once declared, "In the spring I have counted one hundred and thirty-six different kinds of weather within four and twenty hours" (55).

> "Unless another war is prevented it is likely to bring destruction on a scale never before held possible and even now hardly conceived," Albert Einstein wrote in the aftermath of the atomic bomb (29).

Blended quotation   When a quotation is blended into the writer's own sentence, either a comma or no punctuation is appropriate, depending on the way in which the quotation fits into the sentence structure.

> The future champion could, as he put it, "float like a butterfly and sting like a bee."

> Virginia Woolf wrote in 1928 that "a woman must have money and a room of her own if she is to write fiction; and that, as you will see, leaves the great problem of the true nature of woman and the true nature of fiction unsolved" (4).

Beginning of sentence   If a quotation appears at the beginning of a sentence, use a comma after it unless the quotation ends with a question mark or an exclamation point.

> "I've always thought of myself as a reporter," claimed American poet Gwendolyn Brooks (162).

> "What is it?" she asked, bracing herself.

Interrupted quotation   If a quoted sentence is interrupted by explanatory words, use commas to set off the explanatory words.

> "With regard to air travel," Stephen Ambrose notes, "Jefferson was a full century ahead of the curve" (53).

If two successive quoted sentences from the same source are interrupted by explanatory words, use a comma before the explanatory
words and a period after them.

> "Everyone agrees journalists must tell the truth," Bill Kovach and
> Tom Rosenstiel write. "Yet people are befuddled about what 'the
> truth' means" (37).

37f Avoid common misuses of quotation marks.

Do not use quotation marks to draw attention to familiar slang,
to disown trite expressions, or to justify an attempt at humor.

► The economist estimated that single-family home prices would

decline another 5 percent by the end of the year, emphasizing

that this was only a ~~"~~ballpark figure.~~"~~

Do not use quotation marks around the title of your own essay.

EXERCISE 37–1   Add or delete quotation marks as needed and make
any other necessary changes in punctuation in the following sentences.
If a sentence is correct, write "correct" after it. Answers to lettered sentences appear in the back of the book. Example:

Gandhi once said, "An eye for an eye only ends up making
                  ^
the whole world blind."
                     ^

a. As for the advertisement "Sailors have more fun", if you consider
   chipping paint and swabbing decks fun, then you will have plenty
   of it.
b. Even after forty minutes of discussion, our class could not agree
   on an interpretation of Robert Frost's poem "The Road Not
   Taken."
c. After winning the lottery, Juanita said that "she would give half the
   money to charity."
d. After the movie, Vicki said, "The reviewer called this flick "trash of
   the first order." I guess you can't believe everything you read."

e. "Cleaning your house while your kids are still growing," said Phyllis Diller, "is like shoveling the walk before it stops snowing."

1. "That's the most beautiful seashell I've ever seen!", shouted Alexa.

2. "Get your head in the game, and the rest will come" advised the coach just before the whistle.

3. Gloria Steinem once twisted an old proverb like this, "A woman without a man is like a fish without a bicycle."

4. "Even when freshly washed and relieved of all obvious confections," says Fran Lebowitz, "children tend to be sticky."

5. Have you heard the Cowboy Junkies' cover of Hank Williams's "I'm So Lonesome I Could Cry?"

EXERCISE 37–2   Add or delete quotation marks as needed and make any other necessary changes in punctuation in the following passage. Citations should conform to MLA style (see 57a).

In his article The Moment of Truth, former vice president Al Gore argues that global warming is a genuine threat to life on Earth and that we must act now to avoid catastrophe. Gore calls our situation a "true *planetary emergency*" and cites scientific evidence of the greenhouse effect and its consequences (170-71). "What is at stake, Gore insists, is the survival of our civilization and the habitability of the Earth (197)." With such a grim predicament at hand, Gore questions why so many political and economic leaders are reluctant to act. "Is it simply more convenient to ignore the warnings," he asks (171)?

The crisis, of course, will not go away if we just pretend it isn't there. Gore points out that in Chinese two symbols form the character for the word crisis. The first of those symbols means "danger", and the second means "opportunity." The danger we face, he claims, is accompanied by "unprecedented opportunity." (172) Gore contends that throughout history we have won battles against seemingly unbeatable evils such as slavery and fascism and that we did so by facing the truth and choosing the moral high ground. Gore's final appeal is to our humanity:

> "Ultimately, [the fight to end global warming] is not about any scientific discussion or political dialogue; it is about who we are as human beings. It is about our capacity to transcend our limitations, to rise to this new occasion. To see with our hearts, as well as our heads, the response that is now called for." (244)

Gore feels that the fate of our world rests in our own hands, and his hope is that we will make the choice to save the planet.
Source of quotations: Al Gore; "The Moment of Truth"; *Vanity Fair* May 2006: 170+; print.

38 End punctuation

38a The period

Use a period to end all sentences except direct questions or genuine exclamations. Also use periods in abbreviations according to convention.

To end sentences

Most sentences should end with a period. Problems sometimes arise when a writer must choose between a period and a question mark or between a period and an exclamation point.

If a sentence reports a question instead of asking it directly, it should end with a period, not a question mark.

▶ The professor asked whether talk therapy was more beneficial

than antidepressants~~?~~.
            ^

If a sentence is not a genuine exclamation, it should end with a period, not an exclamation point. (See also 38c.)

▶ After years of working her way through school, Geeta finally

graduated with high honors~~!~~.
                          ^

In abbreviations

A period is conventionally used in abbreviations of titles and Latin words or phrases, including the time designations for morning and afternoon.

Mr.	i.e.	a.m. (or AM)
Ms.	e.g.	p.m. (or PM)
Dr.	etc.	

NOTE: If a sentence ends with a period marking an abbreviation, do not add a second period.

Do not use a period with US Postal Service abbreviations for states: MD, TX, CA.

Current usage is to omit the period in abbreviations of organization names, academic degrees, and designations for eras.

NATO	UNESCO	UCLA	BS	BC
IRS	AFL-CIO	NIH	PhD	BCE

38b The question mark

A direct question should be followed by a question mark.

What is the horsepower of a 777 engine?

If a polite request is written in the form of a question, it may be followed by a period.

Would you please send me your catalog of lilies.

TIP: Do not use a question mark after an indirect question, one that is reported rather than asked directly. Use a period instead.

▶ He asked me who was teaching the mythology course this year⸮.
                                                               ^

NOTE: Questions in a series may be followed by question marks even when they are not complete sentences.

We wondered where Calamity had hidden this time. Under the sink? Behind the furnace? On top of the bookcase?

38c The exclamation point

Use an exclamation point after a word group or sentence to express exceptional feeling or to provide special emphasis. The exclamation point is rarely appropriate in academic writing.

When Gloria entered the room, I switched on the lights, and we all yelled, "Surprise!"

TIP: Do not overuse the exclamation point.

▶ In the fisherman's memory, the fish lives on, increasing in

length and weight with each passing year, until at last it is

big enough to shade a fishing boat!.
                                    ^

This sentence doesn't need to be pumped up with an exclamation point. It is emphatic enough without it.

► Whenever I see my favorite hitter, Derek Lee, up at bat,

I dream of making it to the big leagues! My team would
  ^

win every time!

The first exclamation point should be deleted so that the second one will have more force.

EXERCISE 38–1 Add appropriate end punctuation in the following paragraph.

Although I am generally rational, I am superstitious I never walk under ladders or put shoes on the table If I spill the salt, I go into frenzied calisthenics picking up the grains and tossing them over my left shoulder As a result of these curious activities, I've always wondered whether knowing the roots of superstitions would quell my irrational responses Superstition has it, for example, that one should never place a hat on the bed This superstition arises from a time when head lice were common and placing a guest's hat on the bed stood a good chance of spreading lice through the host's bed Doesn't this make good sense And doesn't it stand to reason that, if I know that my guests don't have lice, I shouldn't care where their hats go Of course it does It is fair to ask, then, whether I have changed my ways and place hats on beds Are you kidding I wouldn't put a hat on a bed if my life depended on it

Other punctuation marks: the dash, parentheses, brackets, the ellipsis mark, the slash

39a The dash

When typing, use two hyphens to form a dash (--). Do not put spaces before or after the dash. If your word processing program has what is known as an "em-dash" (—), you may use it instead, with no space before or after it. Dashes are used for the following purposes.

To set off parenthetical material that deserves emphasis

Everything that went wrong — from the peeping Tom at her window last night to my head-on collision today — we blamed on our move.

To set off appositives that contain commas

An appositive is a noun or noun phrase that renames a nearby noun. Ordinarily most appositives are set off with commas (32e), but when the appositive itself contains commas, a pair of dashes helps readers see the relative importance of all the pauses.

> In my hometown, people's basic needs — food, clothing, and shelter — are less costly than in a big city like Los Angeles.

To introduce a list, a restatement, an amplification, or a dramatic shift in tone or thought

> Along the wall are the bulk liquids — sesame seed oil, honey, safflower oil, and that half-liquid "peanuts only" peanut butter.

> In his last semester, Peter tried to pay more attention to his priorities — applying to graduate school and getting financial aid.

> Everywhere we looked there were little kids — a bag of Skittles in one hand and their mommy or daddy's sleeve in the other.

> Kiere took a few steps back, came running full speed, kicked a mighty kick — and missed the ball.

In the first two examples, the writer could also use a colon. (See 35a.) The colon is more formal than the dash and not quite as dramatic.

TIP: Unless there is a specific reason for using the dash, avoid it. Unnecessary dashes create a choppy effect.

> ► Insisting that students use computers as instructional
>
> tools ⧸ for information retrieval ⧸ makes good sense. Herding
>
> them ⧸ sheeplike ⧸ into computer technology does not.

39b Parentheses

Use parentheses to enclose supplemental material, minor digressions, and afterthoughts.

> Nurses record patients' vital signs (temperature, pulse, and blood pressure) several times a day.

for word groups containing commas • parentheses •
brackets • for inserted material • with [sic]   **[ ]**
39c   337

Use parentheses to enclose letters or numbers labeling items
in a series.

Regulations stipulated that only the following equipment could
be used on the survival mission: (1) a knife, (2) thirty feet of
parachute line, (3) a book of matches, (4) two ponchos, (5) an E
tool, and (6) a signal flare.

TIP: Do not overuse parentheses. Rough drafts are likely to contain more afterthoughts than necessary. As writers head into a
sentence, they often think of additional details, occasionally
working them in as best they can with parentheses. Usually such
sentences should be revised so that the additional details no longer seem to be afterthoughts.

> Researchers have said that seventeen million *from* ~~(estimates run~~
>
> ~~as high as~~ twenty-three million) *to* Americans have diabetes.

39c Brackets

Use brackets to enclose any words or phrases that you have inserted into an otherwise word-for-word quotation.

> *Audubon* reports that "if there are not enough young to balance
> deaths, the end of the species [California condor] is inevitable" (4).

The sentence quoted from the *Audubon* article did not contain
the words *California condor* (since the context of the full article
made clear what species was meant), so the writer needed to add
the name in brackets.

The Latin word "sic" in brackets indicates that an error in a
quoted sentence appears in the original source.

> According to the review, Nelly Furtado's performance was brilliant,
> "exceding [sic] the expectations of even her most loyal fans."

Do not overuse "sic," however, since calling attention to others' mistakes can appear snobbish. The preceding quotation, for
example, might have been paraphrased instead: *According to the
review, even Nelly Furtado's most loyal fans were surprised by the
brilliance of her performance.*

39d The ellipsis mark

The ellipsis mark consists of three spaced periods. Use an ellipsis mark to indicate that you have deleted words from an otherwise word-for-word quotation.

> Shute (2010) acknowledges that treatment for autism can be expensive: "Sensory integration therapy . . . can cost up to $200 an hour" (82).

If you delete a full sentence or more in the middle of a quoted passage, use a period before the three ellipsis dots.

> "If we don't properly train, teach, or treat our growing prison population," says long-time reform advocate Luis Rodríguez, "somebody else will. . . . This may well be the safety issue of the new century" (16).

TIP: Ordinarily, do not use the ellipsis mark at the beginning or at the end of a quotation. Readers will understand that the quoted material is taken from a longer passage. If you have cut some words from the end of the final quoted sentence, however, MLA requires an ellipsis mark.

In quoted poetry, use a full line of ellipsis dots to indicate that you have dropped a line or more from the poem, as in this example from "To His Coy Mistress" by Andrew Marvell:

> Had we but world enough, and time,
> This coyness, lady, were no crime.
> . . . .
> But at my back I always hear
> Time's wingèd chariot hurrying near; (1-2, 21-22)

The ellipsis mark may also be used for other purposes — to indicate a hesitation or an interruption in speech or to suggest unfinished thoughts.

> "The apartment building next door . . . it's going up in flames!" yelled Marcia.

> Before falling into a coma, the victim whispered, "It was a man with a tattoo on his . . . "

39e The slash

Use the slash to separate two or three lines of poetry that have been run into your text. Add a space both before and after the slash.

> In the opening lines of "Jordan," George Herbert pokes gentle fun at popular poems of his time: "Who says that fictions only and false hair / Become a verse? Is there in truth no beauty?" (1-2).

More than three lines of poetry should be handled as an indented quotation. (See p. 327.)

The slash may occasionally be used to separate paired terms such as *pass/fail* and *producer/director*. Do not use a space before or after the slash. Be sparing in this use of the slash. In particular, avoid the use of *and/or*, *he/she*, and *his/her*. Instead of using *he/she* and *his/her* to solve sexist language problems, you can usually find more graceful alternatives. (See 17e and 22a.)

EXERCISE 39–1   Edit the following sentences to correct errors in punctuation, focusing especially on appropriate use of the dash, parentheses, brackets, the ellipsis mark, and the slash. If a sentence is correct, write "correct" after it. Answers to lettered sentences appear in the back of the book. Example:

> Social insects/——bees, for example/——are able to
>   ^   ^
> communicate complicated messages to one another.

a. A client left his/her cell phone in our conference room after the meeting.

b. The films we made of Kilauea — on our trip to Hawaii Volcanoes National Park — illustrate a typical spatter cone eruption.

c. Although he was confident in his course selections, Greg chose the pass/fail option for Chemistry 101.

d. Masahiro poked through his backpack — laptop, digital camera, guidebook — to make sure he was ready for a day's study at the Ryoanji Temple garden.

e. Of three engineering fields, chemical, mechanical, and materials, Keegan chose materials engineering for its application to toy manufacturing.

1. The old Valentine verse we used to chant says it all: "Sugar is sweet, / And so are you."

2. In studies in which mothers gazed down at their infants in their cribs but remained facially unresponsive, for example, not smiling, laughing, or showing any change of expression, the infants responded with intense weariness and eventual withdrawal.

3. There are three points of etiquette in poker: 1. always allow someone else to cut the cards, 2. don't forget to ante up, and 3. never stack your chips.

4. In *Lifeboat*, Alfred Hitchcock appears [some say without his knowledge] in a newspaper advertisement for weight loss.

5. The writer Chitra Divakaruni explained her work with other Indian American immigrants: "Many women who came to Maitri [a women's support group in San Francisco] needed to know simple things like opening a bank account or getting citizenship. . . . Many women in Maitri spoke English, but their English was functional rather than emotional. They needed someone who understands their problems and speaks their language."

Mechanics

40 Abbreviations

40a Use standard abbreviations for titles immediately before and after proper names.

TITLES BEFORE PROPER NAMES	TITLES AFTER PROPER NAMES
Mr. Rafael Zabala	William Albert Sr.
Ms. Nancy Linehan	Thomas Hines Jr.
Mrs. Edward Horn	Anita Lor, PhD
Dr. Margaret Simmons	Robert Simkowski, MD
Rev. John Stone	Margaret Chin, LLD
Prof. James Russo	Polly Stein, DDS

Do not abbreviate a title if it is not used with a proper name.

>   *professor*
> My history ~~prof.~~ is an expert on race relations in South Africa.
>   ^

Avoid redundant titles such as *Dr. Amy Day, MD.* Choose one title or the other: *Dr. Amy Day* or *Amy Day, MD.*

40b Use abbreviations only when you are sure your readers will understand them.

Familiar abbreviations, written without periods, are acceptable.

CIA	FBI	MD	NAACP
NBA	CEO	PhD	CD-ROM
YMCA	CBS	USA	ESL

Talk show host Conan O'Brien is a Harvard graduate with a BA in history.

The YMCA has opened a new gym close to my office.

NOTE: When using an unfamiliar abbreviation (such as NASW for National Association of Social Workers) throughout a paper, write the full name followed by the abbreviation in parentheses at the first mention of the name. Then use just the abbreviation throughout the rest of the paper.

for titles with names (*Dr., Prof.*) • for familiar terms (*YMCA, FBI*) • dates • times of day • money • Latin (*e.g., et al.*)

abbr

40d

343

40c Use *BC, AD, a.m., p.m., No.,* and *$* only with specific dates, times, numbers, and amounts.

The abbreviation *BC* ("before Christ") follows a date, and *AD* ("*anno Domini*") precedes a date. Acceptable alternatives are *BCE* ("before the common era") and *CE* ("common era"), both of which follow a date.

40 BC (or 40 BCE)	4:00 a.m. (or AM)	No. 12 (or no. 12)
AD 44 (or 44 CE)	6:00 p.m. (or PM)	$150

Avoid using *a.m., p.m., No.,* or *$* when not accompanied by a specific figure.

► The governor argued that the new sales tax would raise

  money
  much-needed $ for the state.
            ^

40d Be sparing in your use of Latin abbreviations.

Latin abbreviations are acceptable in footnotes and bibliographies and in informal writing for comments in parentheses.

cf. (Latin *confer*, "compare")

e.g. (Latin *exempli gratia*, "for example")

et al. (Latin *et alia*, "and others")

etc. (Latin *et cetera*, "and so forth")

i.e. (Latin *id est*, "that is")

N.B. (Latin *nota bene*, "note well")

Harold Simms et al., *The Race for Space*

Alfred Hitchcock directed many classic thrillers (e.g., *Psycho, Rear Window,* and *Vertigo*).

In formal writing, use the appropriate English phrases.

► Many obsolete laws remain on the books. A law in

  for example,
  Vermont, e.g., forbids an unmarried man and woman to
           ^

  sit closer than six inches apart on a park bench.

40e Avoid inappropriate abbreviations.

In formal writing, abbreviations for the following are not commonly accepted: personal names, units of measurement, days of the week, holidays, months, courses of study, divisions of written works, states, and countries (except in complete addresses and except Washington, DC). Do not abbreviate *Company* and *Incorporated* unless their abbreviated forms are part of an official name.

PERSONAL NAMES   Charles (not Chas.)

UNITS OF MEASUREMENT   feet (not ft.)

DAYS OF THE WEEK   Monday (not Mon.)

HOLIDAYS   Christmas (not Xmas)

MONTHS   January, February, March (not Jan., Feb., Mar.)

COURSES OF STUDY   political science (not poli. sci.)

DIVISIONS OF WRITTEN WORKS   chapter, page (not ch., p.)

STATES AND COUNTRIES   Massachusetts (not MA or Mass.)

PARTS OF A BUSINESS NAME   Adams Lighting Company (not Adams Lighting Co.); Kim and Brothers (not Kim and Bros.)

▶ The American Red Cross requires that blood donors be at
                    years   *pounds,*
least seventeen ~~yrs.~~ old, weigh at least 110 ~~lb.,~~ and not
                 ^   ^
                                weeks. ^
have given blood in the past eight ~~wks.~~
                                    ^

EXCEPTION: Abbreviate states and provinces in complete addresses, and always abbreviate *DC* when used with *Washington.*

EXERCISE 40–1   Edit the following sentences to correct errors in abbreviations. If a sentence is correct, write "correct" after it. Answers to lettered sentences appear in the back of the book. Example:

                Christmas   *Tuesday.*
This year ~~Xmas~~ will fall on a ~~Tues.~~
          ^   ^

a. Since its inception, the BBC has maintained a consistently high standard of radio and television broadcasting.
b. Some combat soldiers are trained by govt. diplomats to be sensitive to issues of culture, history, and religion.

c. Mahatma Gandhi has inspired many modern leaders, including Martin Luther King Jr.

d. How many lb. have you lost since you began running four miles a day?

e. Denzil spent all night studying for his psych. exam.

1. My favorite prof., Dr. Barker, is on sabbatical this semester.

2. When we visited NYU in early September, we were charmed by the lull of summer crickets in Washington Square Park.

3. Some historians think that the New Testament was completed by AD 100.

4. My mother's birthday was on Fri. the 13th this year.

5. Some first-time Flash users panic before the complex menus — i.e., they develop a blank stare and the tingling of a migraine.

Numbers

41a Follow the conventions in your discipline for spelling out or using numerals to express numbers.

In the humanities, which generally follow Modern Language Association (MLA) style, use numerals only for specific numbers above one hundred: *353, 1,020*. Spell out numbers one hundred and below and large round numbers: *eleven, thirty-five, sixty, fifteen million*.

The social sciences, which follow American Psychological Association (APA) style, use numerals for all but the numbers one through nine.

In all fields, treat related numbers in a passage consistently: *The survey found that 89 of 157 respondents had not taken any courses related to alcohol use.*

When one number immediately follows another, spelling out one number and using numerals for the other is usually effective: *three 100-meter events, 25 four-poster beds*.

▶   *eight*
   It's been 8̸ years since I visited Peru.
         ^

▶   Enrollment in the charter school in its first year will be
      340
   limited to ~~three hundred forty~~ students.
      ^

If a sentence begins with a number, spell out the number or rewrite the sentence.

> *One hundred fifty*
> ~~150~~ children in our program need expensive dental treatment.
  ^

Rewriting the sentence will also correct the error and may be less
awkward if the number is long: *In our program, 150 children need
expensive dental treatment.*

41b Use numerals according to convention in dates, addresses, and so on.

DATES   July 4, 1776; 56 BC; AD 30

ADDRESSES   77 Latches Lane, 519 West 42nd Street

PERCENTAGES   55 percent (or 55%)

FRACTIONS, DECIMALS $^1/_2$, 0.047

SCORES   7 to 3, 21–18

STATISTICS   average age 37, average weight 180

SURVEYS   4 out of 5

EXACT AMOUNTS OF MONEY $105.37, $106,000

DIVISIONS OF BOOKS   volume 3, chapter 4, page 189

DIVISIONS OF PLAYS   act 3, scene 3 (or act III, scene iii)

IDENTIFICATION NUMBERS   serial number 10988675

TIME OF DAY   4:00 p.m., 1:30 a.m.

> *$430,000*
> The foundation raised ~~four hundred thirty thousand dollars~~
>   ^
> for cancer research.

NOTE: When not using *a.m.* or *p.m.*, write out the time in words
(*two o'clock in the afternoon, twelve noon, seven in the morning*).

EXERCISE 41–1   Edit the following sentences to correct errors in the
use of numbers. If a sentence is correct, write "correct" after it. Answers
to lettered sentences appear in the back of the book. Example:

> *$3.06*
> By the end of the evening, Ashanti had only ~~three dollars~~
>   ^
> ~~and six cents~~ left.

a. The carpenters located 3 maple timbers, 21 sheets of cherry, and 10 oblongs of polished ebony for the theater set.

b. The program's cost is well over one billion dollars.

c. The score was tied at 5–5 when the momentum shifted and carried the Standards to a decisive 12–5 win.

d. 8 students in the class had been labeled "learning disabled."

e. The Vietnam Veterans Memorial in Washington, DC, had fifty-eight thousand one hundred thirty-two names inscribed on it when it was dedicated in 1982.

1. One of my favorite scenes in Shakespeare is the property division scene in act 1 of *King Lear*.

2. The botany lecture will begin at precisely 3:30 p.m.

3. 40 percent of all gamers in the United States are women.

4. In two thousand twelve, the world population may reach 7 billion.

5. On a normal day, I spend at least 4 to 5 hours surfing the Internet.

42   Italics

This section describes conventional uses for italics. While italics is accepted by both style guides covered in this handbook (MLA and APA), some instructors may prefer underlining in student papers. If that is the case in your course, simply substitute underlining for italics in the examples in this section.

Some computer and online applications do not allow for italics. To indicate words that should be italicized, you can use underscore marks or asterisks before and after the italic words.

I am planning to write my senior thesis on _The Kite Runner_.

NOTE: Excessive use of italics to emphasize words or ideas, especially in academic writing, is distracting and should be avoided.

42a Italicize the titles of works according to convention.

Titles of the following types of works, including electronic works, should be italicized.

TITLES OF BOOKS   *The Color Purple, Middlesex, Encarta*

MAGAZINES   *Time, Scientific American, Salon.com*

NEWSPAPERS   the *Baltimore Sun,* the *Orlando Sentinel Online*

PAMPHLETS   *Common Sense, Facts about Marijuana*

LONG POEMS   *The Waste Land, Paradise Lost*

PLAYS   *'Night Mother, Wicked*

FILMS   *Casablanca, Do the Right Thing*

TELEVISION PROGRAMS   *American Idol, Frontline*

RADIO PROGRAMS   *All Things Considered*

MUSICAL COMPOSITIONS   *Porgy and Bess*

CHOREOGRAPHIC WORKS   *Brief Fling*

WORKS OF VISUAL ART   *American Gothic*

ELECTRONIC DATABASES   *ProQuest*

WEB SITES   *ZDNet, Google*

ELECTRONIC GAMES   *Everquest, Call of Duty*

The titles of other works, such as short stories, essays, episodes of radio and television programs, songs, and short poems, are enclosed in quotation marks. (See 37c.)

NOTE: Do not use italics when referring to the Bible, titles of books in the Bible (Genesis, not *Genesis*), or titles of legal documents (the Constitution, not the *Constitution*). Do not italicize the titles of computer software (Keynote, Photoshop). Do not italicize the title of your own paper.

42b Italicize the names of specific ships, spacecraft, and aircraft.

Queen Mary 2, Challenger, Spirit of St. Louis

The success of the Soviets' *Sputnik* energized the US space program.

42c Italicize foreign words used in an English sentence.

Shakespeare's Falstaff is a comic character known for both his excessive drinking and his general *joie de vivre*.

EXCEPTION: Do not italicize foreign words that have become a standard part of the English language—"laissez-faire," "fait accompli," "modus operandi," and "per diem," for example.

42d Italicize words mentioned as words, letters mentioned as letters, and numbers mentioned as numbers.

Tomás assured us that the chemicals could probably be safely mixed, but his *probably* stuck in our minds.

Some toddlers have trouble pronouncing the letters *f* and *s*.

A big *3* was painted on the stage door.

NOTE: Quotation marks may be used instead of italics to set off words mentioned as words. (See 37d.)

EXERCISE 42–1 Edit the following sentences to correct errors in the use of italics. If a sentence is correct, write "correct" after it. Answers to lettered sentences appear in the back of the book. Example:

We had a lively discussion about Gini Alhadeff's memoir

The Sun at Midday. Correct

a. Howard Hughes commissioned the Spruce Goose, a beautifully built but thoroughly impractical wooden aircraft.

b. The old man *screamed* his anger, *shouting* to all of us, "I will not leave my money to you worthless layabouts!"

c. I learned the Latin term ad infinitum from an old nursery rhyme about fleas: "Great fleas have little fleas upon their back to bite 'em, / Little fleas have lesser fleas and so on ad infinitum."

d. Cinema audiences once gasped at hearing the word *damn* in *Gone with the Wind.*

e. Neve Campbell's lifelong interest in ballet inspired her involvement in the film "The Company," which portrays a season with the Joffrey Ballet.

1. Yasmina spent a year painting white flowers in imitation of Georgia O'Keeffe's Calla Lilies.

2. On the monastery walls are murals depicting scenes from the book of Kings and the book of Proverbs.

3. My per diem allowance was $200.
4. Cecily watched in amazement as the tattoo artist made angles and swooping loops into the Gothic letter G.
5. The blend of poetic lyrics and progressive instruments on Seal's "Human Being" makes it one of my favorite CDs.

43   Spelling

You learned to spell from repeated experience with words in both reading and writing, but especially writing. Words have a look, a sound, and even a feel to them as the hand moves across the page or keyboard. As you proofread, you can probably tell if a word doesn't look quite right. In such cases, the solution is simple: Look up the word in the dictionary. (See 43b.)

43a Become familiar with the major spelling rules.

i before *e* except after *c*

In general, use *i* before *e* except after *c* and except when sounded like *ay*, as in *neighbor* and *weigh*.

I BEFORE *E*	relieve, believe, sieve, niece, fierce, frieze
E BEFORE *I*	receive, deceive, sleigh, freight, eight
EXCEPTIONS	seize, either, weird, height, foreign, leisure

Suffixes

Final silent -e   Generally, drop a final silent -*e* when adding a suffix that begins with a vowel. Keep the final -*e* if the suffix begins with a consonant.

combine, combination	achieve, achievement
desire, desiring	care, careful
prude, prudish	entire, entirety
remove, removable	gentle, gentleness

Words such as *changeable*, *judgment*, *argument*, and *truly* are exceptions.

Final -y   When adding -*s* or -*d* to words ending in -*y*, ordinarily change -*y* to -*ie* when the -*y* is preceded by a consonant but not when it is preceded by a vowel.

comedy, comedies   monkey, monkeys
dry, dried   play, played

With proper names ending in -*y*, however, do not change the -*y* to -*ie* even if it is preceded by a consonant: *the Dougherty family, the Doughertys.*

Final consonants   If a final consonant is preceded by a single vowel *and* the consonant ends a one-syllable word or a stressed syllable, double the consonant when adding a suffix beginning with a vowel.

bet, betting   occur, occurrence
commit, committed

Plurals

-s or -es   Add -*s* to form the plural of most nouns; add -*es* to singular nouns ending in -*s*, -*sh*, -*ch*, and -*x*.

table, tables   church, churches
paper, papers   dish, dishes

Ordinarily add -*s* to nouns ending in -*o* when the -*o* is preceded by a vowel. Add -*es* when it is preceded by a consonant.

radio, radios   hero, heroes
video, videos   tomato, tomatoes

Other plurals   To form the plural of a hyphenated compound word, add -*s* to the chief word even if it does not appear at the end.

mother-in-law, mothers-in-law

English words derived from other languages such as Latin, Greek, or French sometimes form the plural as they would in their original language.

medium, media   chateau, chateaux
criterion, criteria

MULTILINGUAL Spelling varies slightly among English-speaking countries. This can be particularly confusing for multilingual students in the United States, who may have learned British English. Following is a list of some common words spelled differently in American and British English. Consult a dictionary for others.

AMERICAN	BRITISH
canceled, traveled	cancelled, travelled
color, humor	colour, humour
judgment	judgement
check	cheque
realize, apologize	realise, apologise
defense	defence
anemia, anesthetic	anaemia, anaesthetic
theater, center	theatre, centre
fetus	foetus
mold, smolder	mould, smoulder
civilization	civilisation
connection, inflection	connexion, inflexion
licorice	liquorice

43b Become familiar with your dictionary.

A good dictionary, whether print or online—such as *The American Heritage Dictionary of the English Language, The Random House College Dictionary,* or *Merriam-Webster's Collegiate Dictionary*— is an indispensable writer's aid.

A sample print dictionary entry, taken from *The American Heritage Dictionary,* appears on page 353. Labels show where various kinds of information about a word can be found in that dictionary.

A sample online dictionary entry, taken from *Merriam-Webster Online,* appears on page 354.

Spelling, word division, pronunciation

The main entry (*re·gard* in the sample entries) shows the correct spelling of the word. When there are two correct spellings of a word (as in *collectible, collectable,* for example), both are given, with the preferred spelling usually appearing first.

The main entry also shows how the word is divided into syllables. The dot between *re* and *gard* separates the two syllables and indicates where the word should be divided if it can't fit at the end of a line of type (see 44f). When a word is compound, the main entry shows how to write it: as one word (*crossroad*), as a hyphenated word (*cross-stitch*), or as two words (*cross section*).

The word's pronunciation is given just after the main entry. The accents indicate which syllables are stressed; the other marks are explained in the dictionary's pronunciation key. In print dictionaries, this key usually appears at the bottom of every page or every other page. Many online entries include an audio link to a person's voice pronouncing the word. And most online dictionaries have an audio pronunciation guide.

PRINT DICTIONARY ENTRY

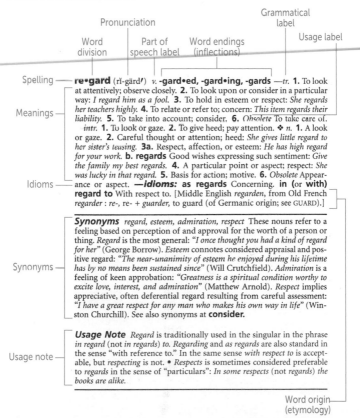

Pronunciation

Grammatical label

Word division

Part of speech label

Word endings (inflections)

Usage label

Spelling

Meanings

Idioms

re•gard (rĭ-gärd′) *v.* **-gard•ed, -gard•ing, -gards** —*tr.* **1.** To look at attentively; observe closely. **2.** To look upon or consider in a particular way: *I regard him as a fool.* **3.** To hold in esteem or respect: *She regards her teachers highly.* **4.** To relate or refer to; concern: *This item regards their liability.* **5.** To take into account; consider. **6.** *Obsolete* To take care of. —*intr.* **1.** To look or gaze. **2.** To give heed; pay attention. ❖ *n.* **1.** A look or gaze. **2.** Careful thought or attention; heed: *She gives little regard to her sister's teasing.* **3a.** Respect, affection, or esteem: *He has high regard for your work.* **b. regards** Good wishes expressing such sentiment: *Give the family my best regards.* **4.** A particular point or aspect; respect: *She was lucky in that regard.* **5.** Basis for action; motive. **6.** *Obsolete* Appearance or aspect. **—*idioms:* as regards** Concerning. **in (or with) regard to** With respect to. [Middle English *regarden*, from Old French *regarder : re-*, re- + *guarder*, to guard (of Germanic origin; see GUARD).]

Synonyms

Synonyms *regard, esteem, admiration, respect* These nouns refer to a feeling based on perception of and approval for the worth of a person or thing. *Regard* is the most general: *"I once thought you had a kind of regard for her"* (George Borrow). *Esteem* connotes considered appraisal and positive regard: *"The near-unanimity of esteem he enjoyed during his lifetime has by no means been sustained since"* (Will Crutchfield). *Admiration* is a feeling of keen approbation: *"Greatness is a spiritual condition worthy to excite love, interest, and admiration"* (Matthew Arnold). *Respect* implies appreciative, often deferential regard resulting from careful assessment: *"I have a great respect for any man who makes his own way in life"* (Winston Churchill). See also synonyms at **consider.**

Usage note

Usage Note *Regard* is traditionally used in the singular in the phrase *in regard* (not *in regards*) *to*. *Regarding* and *as regards* are also standard in the sense "with reference to." In the same sense *with respect to* is acceptable, but *respecting* is not. ● *Respects* is sometimes considered preferable to *regards* in the sense of "particulars": *In some respects* (not *regards*) *the books are alike.*

Word origin (etymology)

ONLINE DICTIONARY ENTRY

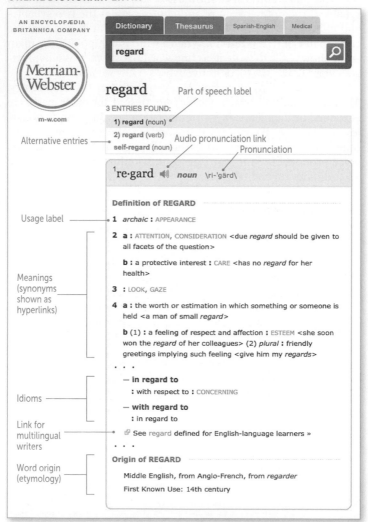

AN ENCYCLOPÆDIA
BRITANNICA COMPANY

Merriam-Webster

m-w.com

Dictionary | Thesaurus | Spanish-English | Medical

regard

regard — Part of speech label

3 ENTRIES FOUND:

Alternative entries —
1) regard (noun)
2) regard (verb) — Audio pronunciation link
self-regard (noun) — Pronunciation

¹re·gard 🔊 *noun* \ri-ˈgärd\

Definition of REGARD

Usage label — 1 *archaic* : APPEARANCE

2 **a** : ATTENTION, CONSIDERATION <due *regard* should be given to
all facets of the question>

b : a protective interest : CARE <has no *regard* for her
health>

Meanings
(synonyms
shown as
hyperlinks)

3 : LOOK, GAZE

4 **a** : the worth or estimation in which something or someone is
held <a man of small *regard*>

b (1) : a feeling of respect and affection : ESTEEM <she soon
won the *regard* of her colleagues> (2) *plural* : friendly
greetings implying such feeling <give him my *regards*>

. . .

Idioms —
— **in regard to**
: with respect to : CONCERNING

— **with regard to**
: in regard to

Link for
multilingual
writers

📖 See regard defined for English-language learners »

. . .

Word origin
(etymology)

Origin of REGARD

Middle English, from Anglo-French, from *regarder*

First Known Use: 14th century

Source: Merriam-Webster, www.Merriam-Webster.com (2010).

Word endings and grammatical labels

When a word takes endings to indicate grammatical functions (called *inflections*), the endings are listed in boldface, as with *-garded*, *-garding*, and *-gards* in the sample print entry (p. 353).

Labels for the parts of speech and for other grammatical terms are sometimes abbreviated, as they are in the print entry. The most commonly used abbreviations are these:

n.	noun	adj.	adjective
pl.	plural	adv.	adverb
sing.	singular	pron.	pronoun
v.	verb	prep.	preposition
tr.	transitive verb	conj.	conjunction
intr.	intransitive verb	interj.	interjection

Meanings, word origin, synonyms, and antonyms

Each meaning for the word is given a number. Occasionally a word's use is illustrated in a quoted sentence.

Sometimes a word can be used as more than one part of speech (*regard*, for instance, can be used as either a verb or a noun). In such a case, all the meanings for one part of speech are given before all the meanings for another, as in the sample entries. The entries also give idiomatic uses of the word.

The origin of the word, called its *etymology*, appears in brackets after all the meanings in the print and online versions.

Synonyms, words similar in meaning to the main entry, are frequently listed. In the sample print entry, the dictionary draws distinctions in meaning among the various synonyms. In the online entry, synonyms appear as hyperlinks. Antonyms, which do not appear in the sample entries, are words having a meaning opposite from that of the main entry.

Usage

Usage labels indicate when, where, or under what conditions a particular meaning for a word is appropriately used. Common labels are *informal* (or *colloquial*), *slang*, *archaic*, *poetic*, *nonstandard*, *dialect*, *obsolete*, and *British*. In the sample print entry (p. 353), two meanings of *regard* are labeled *obsolete* because they are no longer in use. The sample online entry (p. 354) has one meaning labeled *archaic*.

Dictionaries sometimes include usage notes as well. In the sample print entry, the dictionary offers advice on several uses of *regard* not specifically covered by the meanings. Such advice is based on the opinions of many experts and on actual usage in current magazines, newspapers, and books.

43c Discriminate between words that sound alike but have different meanings.

Words that sound alike or nearly alike but have different meanings and spellings are called *homophones*. The following sets of words are so commonly confused that a careful writer will double-check their every use.

> affect (verb: to exert an influence)
> effect (verb: to accomplish; noun: result)
>
> its (possessive pronoun: of or belonging to it)
> it's (contraction of *it is* or *it has*)
>
> loose (adjective: free, not securely attached)
> lose (verb: to fail to keep, to be deprived of)
>
> principal (adjective: most important; noun: head of a school)
> principle (noun: a fundamental guideline or truth)
>
> their (possessive pronoun: belonging to them)
> they're (contraction of *they are*)
> there (adverb: that place or position)
>
> who's (contraction of *who is* or *who has*)
> whose (possessive form of *who*)
>
> your (possessive pronoun: belonging to you)
> you're (contraction of *you are*)

To check for the correct use of these and other commonly confused words, see the glossary of usage at the back of the book.

43d Be alert to commonly misspelled words.

absence	accommodate	acquaintance	all right
academic	achievement	acquire	amateur
accidentally	acknowledge	address	analyze

answer	desperate	irresistible	publicly
apparently	dictionary	knowledge	quiet
appearance	different	library	quite
arctic	disastrous	license	quizzes
argument	eighth	lightning	receive
arithmetic	eligible	loneliness	recognize
arrangement	embarrass	maintenance	referred
ascend	emphasize	maneuver	restaurant
athlete	entirely	marriage	rhythm
athletics	environment	mathematics	roommate
attendance	especially	mischievous	sandwich
basically	exaggerated	necessary	schedule
beautiful	exercise	noticeable	seize
beginning	exhaust	occasion	separate
believe	existence	occurred	sergeant
benefited	extraordinary	occurrence	siege
bureau	extremely	pamphlet	similar
business	familiar	parallel	sincerely
calendar	fascinate	particularly	sophomore
candidate	February	pastime	strictly
cemetery	foreign	permanent	subtly
changeable	forty	permissible	succeed
column	fourth	perseverance	surprise
commitment	friend	phenomenon	thorough
committed	government	physically	tomorrow
committee	grammar	playwright	tragedy
competitive	guard	practically	transferred
completely	harass	precede	tries
conceivable	height	preference	truly
conscience	humorous	preferred	unnecessarily
conscientious	incidentally	prejudice	usually
conscious	incredible	presence	vacuum
criticism	independence	prevalent	vengeance
criticize	indispensable	privilege	villain
decision	inevitable	proceed	weird
definitely	intelligence	professor	whether
descendant	irrelevant	pronunciation	writing

EXERCISE 43–1   The following memo has been run through a spell checker. Proofread it carefully, editing the spelling and typographical errors that remain.

November 3, 2010

To: Patricia Wise
From: Constance Mayhew
Subject: Express Tours annual report

Thank you for agreeing to draft the annual report for Express Tours. Before you begin you're work, let me outline the initial steps.

First, its essential for you to include brief profiles of top management. Early next week, I'll provide profiles for all manages accept Samuel Heath, who's biographical information is being revised. You should edit these profiles carefully and than format them according to the enclosed instructions. We may ask you to include other employee's profiles at some point.

Second, you should arrange to get complete financial information for fiscal year 2010 from our comptroller, Richard Chang. (Helen Boyes, to, can provide the necessary figures.) When you get this information, precede according tot he plans we discuss in yesterday's meeting. By the way, you will notice from the figures that the sale of our Charterhouse division did not significantly effect net profits.

Third, you should submit first draft of the report by December 15. I assume that you won a laser printer, but if you don't, you can e-mail a file and we'll print out a draft here. Of coarse, you should proofread you writing.

I am quiet pleased that you can take on this project. If I can answers questions, don't hesitate to call.

44   The hyphen

44a Consult the dictionary to determine how to treat a compound word.

The dictionary will tell you whether to treat a compound word as a hyphenated compound (*water-repellent*), one word (*waterproof*), or two words (*water table*). If the compound word is not in the dictionary, treat it as two words.

► The prosecutor chose not to cross-examine any witnesses.

► All students are expected to record their data in a small

note⁀book.

► Alice walked through the looking⁄glass into a backward world.

44b Hyphenate two or more words used together as an adjective before a noun.

► Mrs. Douglas gave Toshiko a seashell and some newspaper-

wrapped fish to take home to her mother.

► Richa Gupta is not yet a well-known candidate.

Newspaper-wrapped and *well-known* are adjectives used before the
nouns *fish* and *candidate*.

Generally, do not use a hyphen when such compounds follow
the noun.

► After our television campaign, Richa Gupta will be well⁄known.

Do not use a hyphen to connect *-ly* adverbs to the words
they modify.

► A slowly⁄moving truck tied up traffic.

NOTE: When two or more hyphenated adjectives in a row modify
the same noun, you can suspend the hyphens.

Do you prefer first-, second-, or third-class tickets?

44c Hyphenate fractions and certain numbers when they are spelled out.

► One-fourth of my income goes to pay my child care

expenses.

44d Use a hyphen with the prefixes *all-*, *ex-* (meaning "former"), and *self-* and with the suffix *-elect*.

▶ The private foundation is funneling more money into

   self-help projects.
   ^

▶ The Student Senate bylaws require the president-elect to
                                                      ^
   attend all senate meetings between the election and the

   official transfer of office.

44e Use a hyphen in certain words to avoid ambiguity or to separate awkward double or triple letters.

Without the hyphen, there would be no way to distinguish between words such as *re-creation* and *recreation*.

Bicycling in the city is my favorite form of recreation.

The film was praised for its astonishing re-creation of nineteenth-century London.

Hyphens are sometimes used to separate awkward double or triple letters in compound words (*anti-intellectual*, *cross-stitch*). Always check a dictionary for the standard form of the word.

44f Check for correct word breaks when words must be divided at the end of a line.

Some word processing programs and other computer applications automatically generate word breaks at the ends of lines. When you're writing an academic paper, it's best to set your computer application not to hyphenate automatically. This setting will ensure that only words already containing a hyphen (such as *long-distance*, *pre-Roman*) will be hyphenated at the ends of lines.

E-mail addresses and URLs need special attention when they occur at the end of a line of text or in bibliographic citations. You can't rely on your word processor to divide these terms correctly, so you must make a decision in each case. Do not insert a hyphen to divide electronic addresses. Instead, break an e-mail address after the @ symbol or before a period. Break a URL after a slash or a double slash or before any other punctuation mark.

> I repeatedly e-mailed Janine at janine.r.rose@dunbaracademy.org before I gave up and called her cell phone.

> To find a zip code quickly, I always use the United States Postal Service Web site at http://zip4.usps.com/zip4/welcome.jsp.

For breaks in URLs in MLA and APA documentation styles, see pages 506 and 566.

EXERCISE 44–1 Edit the following sentences to correct errors in hyphenation. If a sentence is correct, write "correct" after it. Answers to lettered sentences appear in the back of the book. Example:

Zola's first readers were scandalized by his slice-of-life novels.

a. Gold is the seventy-ninth element in the periodic table.
b. The swiftly-moving tugboat pulled alongside the barge and directed it away from the oil spill in the harbor.
c. The Moche were a pre-Columbian people who established a sophisticated culture in ancient Peru.
d. Your dog is well-known in our neighborhood.
e. Road-blocks were set up along all the major highways leading out of the city.

1. We knew we were driving too fast when our tires skidded on the rain slick surface.
2. The Black Death reduced the population of some medieval villages by two thirds.
3. Sewing forty-eight sequined tutus for the ballet recital nearly made Karyn cross-eyed.
4. Olivia had hoped to find a pay as you go plan to finance the construction of her observatory.
5. Gail Sheehy writes that at age twenty five many people assume that the choices they make are irrevocable.

Capitalization

In addition to the rules in this section, a good dictionary can tell you when to use capital letters.

45a Capitalize proper nouns and words derived from them; do not capitalize common nouns.

Proper nouns are the names of specific persons, places, and things. All other nouns are common nouns. The following types of words are usually capitalized: names of deities, religions, religious followers, sacred books; words of family relationship used as names; particular places; nationalities and their languages, races, tribes; educational institutions, departments, degrees, particular courses; government departments, organizations, political parties; historical movements, periods, events, documents; specific electronic sources; and trade names.

PROPER NOUNS	COMMON NOUNS
God (used as a name)	a god
Book of Common Prayer	a sacred book
Uncle Pedro	my uncle
Father (used as a name)	my father
Lake Superior	a picturesque lake
the Capital Center	a center for advanced studies
the South	a southern state
Wrigley Field	a baseball stadium
University of Wisconsin	a state university
Geology 101	geology
Environmental Protection Agency	a federal agency
Phi Kappa Psi	a fraternity
the Democratic Party	a political party
the Enlightenment	the eighteenth century
the Treaty of Versailles	a treaty
the World Wide Web, the Web	a home page
the Internet, the Net	a computer network
Advil	a painkiller

Months, holidays, and days of the week are treated as proper nouns; the seasons and numbers of the days of the month are not.

Our academic year begins on a Tuesday in early September, right after Labor Day.

Graduation is in late spring, on the second of June.

EXCEPTION: Capitalize Fourth of July (or July Fourth) when referring to the holiday.

Names of school subjects are capitalized only if they are names of languages. Names of particular courses are capitalized.

This semester Austin is taking math, geography, geology, French, and English.

Professor Obembe offers Modern American Fiction 501 to graduate students.

CAUTION: Do not capitalize common nouns to make them seem important: *Our company is currently hiring computer programmers* [not *Company, Computer Programmers*].

45b Capitalize titles of persons when used as part of a proper name but usually not when used alone.

Professor Margaret Barnes; Dr. Sinyee Sein; John Scott Williams Jr.

District Attorney Marshall was reprimanded for badgering the witness.

The district attorney was elected for a two-year term.

Usage varies when the title of an important public figure is used alone: *The president* [or *President*] *vetoed the bill.*

45c Capitalize the first, last, and all major words in titles and subtitles of works such as books, articles, songs, and online documents.

In both titles and subtitles, major words such as nouns, pronouns, verbs, adjectives, and adverbs should be capitalized. Minor words such as articles, prepositions, and coordinating conjunctions are not capitalized unless they are the first or last word of a title or subtitle. Capitalize the second part of a hyphenated term in a title if it is a major word but not if it is a minor word. Capitalize chapter titles and the titles of other major divisions of a work following the same guidelines used for titles of complete works.

Seizing the Enigma: The Race to Break the German U-Boat Codes
A River Runs through It
"I Want to Hold Your Hand"
The Canadian Green Page

To see why some of the titles in the list are italicized and some are put in quotation marks, see 42a and 37c.

45d Capitalize the first word of a sentence.

The first word of a sentence should be capitalized. When a sentence appears within parentheses, capitalize its first word unless the parentheses appear within another sentence.

Early detection of breast cancer significantly increases survival rates. (See table 2.)

Early detection of breast cancer significantly increases survival rates (see table 2).

45e Capitalize the first word of a quoted sentence but not a quoted phrase.

Robert Hughes writes, "There are only about sixty Watteau paintings on whose authenticity all experts agree" (102).

Russell Baker has written that in this country, sports are "the opiate of the masses" (46).

If a quoted sentence is interrupted by explanatory words, do not capitalize the first word after the interruption. (See 37e.)

"If you want to go out," he said, "tell me now."

When quoting poetry, copy the poet's capitalization exactly. Many poets capitalize the first word of every line of poetry; a few contemporary poets dismiss capitalization altogether.

it was the week   that
i felt the city's narrow breezes rush about
me   —Don L. Lee

45f Capitalize the first word after a colon if it begins an independent clause.

If a group of words following a colon could stand on its own as a complete sentence, capitalize the first word.

> Clinical trials called into question the safety profile of the drug: A high percentage of participants reported hypertension and kidney problems.

> Preferences vary among academic disciplines. See 60c and 65b.

Always use lowercase for a list or an appositive that follows a colon (see 35a).

> Students were divided into two groups: residents and commuters.

45g Capitalize abbreviations according to convention.

Abbreviations for government agencies, companies, and other organizations as well as call numbers for radio and television stations are capitalized.

> EPA, FBI, DKNY, IBM, WCRB, KNBC-TV

EXERCISE 45–1 Edit the following sentences to correct errors in capitalization. If a sentence is correct, write "correct" after it. Answers to lettered sentences appear in the back of the book. Example:

> On our trip to the West, we visited the ~~g~~rand ~~c~~anyon and the
> <small>G   C</small>
> ~~g~~reat ~~s~~alt ~~d~~esert.
> <small>G   S   D</small>

a. Assistant dean Shirin Ahmadi recommended offering more world language courses.

b. We went to the Mark Taper Forum to see a production of *Angels in America*.

c. Kalindi has an ambitious semester, studying differential calculus, classical hebrew, brochure design, and greek literature.

d. Lydia's Aunt and Uncle make modular houses as beautiful as modernist works of art.

e. We amused ourselves on the long flight by discussing how Spring in Kyoto stacks up against Summer in London.

1. When the truck will not start, I try a few tricks with the ignition key: Jiggling it to the left, pulling it out a quarter of an inch, and gently pulling down on it.

2. When you slowly bake a clove of garlic, the most amazing thing happens: It loses its bitter tang and becomes sweet and buttery.

3. After World War II, aunt Helena left Poland to study in Italy.

4. When we drove through the south last year, we enjoyed stopping at the peanut stands along the road.

5. Following in his sister's footsteps, Leonid is pursuing a degree in Marketing Research.

Grammar Basics

46 Parts of speech

Traditional grammar recognizes eight parts of speech: noun, pronoun, verb, adjective, adverb, preposition, conjunction, and interjection. Many words can function as more than one part of speech. For example, depending on its use in a sentence, the word *paint* can be a noun (*The paint is wet*) or a verb (*Please paint the ceiling next*).

46a Nouns

A noun is the name of a person, place, thing, or concept.

> N   N   N
> The *lion* in the *cage* growled at the *zookeeper*.

Nouns sometimes function as adjectives modifying other nouns. Because of their dual roles, nouns used in this manner may be called *noun/adjectives*.

> N/ADJ   N/ADJ
> The *leather* notebook was tucked in the *student's* backpack.

Nouns are classified in a variety of ways. *Proper* nouns are capitalized, but *common* nouns are not (see 45a). For clarity, writers choose between *concrete* and *abstract* nouns (see 18b). The distinction between *count* nouns and *noncount* nouns can be especially helpful to multilingual writers (see 29a). Most nouns have singular and plural forms; *collective* nouns may be either singular or plural, depending on how they are used (see 21f and 22b). *Possessive* nouns require an apostrophe (see 36a).

EXERCISE 46–1 Underline the nouns (and noun/adjectives) in the following sentences. Answers to lettered sentences appear in the back of the book. Example:

> The best <u>part</u> of <u>dinner</u> was the <u>chef</u>'s newest <u>dessert</u>.

a. The stage was set for a confrontation of biblical proportions.
b. The courage of the mountain climber was an inspiration to the rescuers.

PRACTICE hackerhandbooks.com/rules
> Grammar basics > 46–5 and 46–6
> 46–15 and 46–16 (all parts of speech)

nouns • persons, places, things, ideas • pronouns •
substitutes for nouns (*we, their, yourself, who, anyone,* etc.)

basic
46b

369

   c. The need to arrive before the guest of honor motivated us to navigate the thick fog.

   d. The defense attorney made a final appeal to the jury.

   e. A national museum dedicated to women artists opened in 1987.

   1. Truthfulness is a virtue lacking in some public officials.

   2. The Wright Brothers used a wind tunnel to test their airplane designs.

   3. The miners' work clothes were clogged with fine black dust.

   4. Virginia Woolf wrote that women needed their own income and their own space.

   5. The child's language was a charming combination of her father's English and her mother's French.

46b Pronouns

A pronoun is a word used in place of a noun. Usually the pronoun substitutes for a specific noun, known as its *antecedent.*

When the *battery* wears down, we recharge *it.*

Although most pronouns function as substitutes for nouns, some can function as adjectives modifying nouns. Because they have the form of a pronoun and the function of an adjective, such pronouns may be called *pronoun/adjectives.*

   PN/ADJ
This bird was at the same window yesterday morning.

Pronouns are classified as personal, possessive, intensive and reflexive, relative, interrogative, demonstrative, indefinite, and reciprocal.

Personal pronouns   Personal pronouns refer to specific persons or things. They always function as noun equivalents.

   Singular: I, me, you, she, her, he, him, it

   Plural: we, us, you, they, them

Possessive pronouns   Possessive pronouns indicate ownership.

   Singular: my, mine, your, yours, her, hers, his, its

   Plural: our, ours, your, yours, their, theirs

Some of these possessive pronouns function as adjectives modifying nouns: *my, your, his, her, its, our, their.*

Intensive and reflexive pronouns Intensive pronouns emphasize a noun or another pronoun (The senator *herself* met us at the door). Reflexive pronouns, which have the same form as intensive pronouns, name a receiver of an action identical with the doer of the action (Paula cut *herself*).

> *Singular:* myself, yourself, himself, herself, itself
>
> *Plural:* ourselves, yourselves, themselves

Relative pronouns Relative pronouns introduce subordinate clauses functioning as adjectives (The writer *who won the award* refused to accept it). In addition to introducing the clause, the relative pronoun, in this case *who*, points back to a noun or pronoun that the clause modifies (*writer*). (See 48e.)

> who, whom, whose, which, that

Some textbooks also treat *whichever, whoever, whomever, what,* and *whatever* as relative pronouns. These words introduce noun clauses; they do not point back to a noun or pronoun. (See "Noun clauses" in 48e.)

Interrogative pronouns Interrogative pronouns introduce questions (*Who* is expected to win the election?).

> who, whom, whose, which, what

Demonstrative pronouns Demonstrative pronouns identify or point to nouns. Frequently they function as adjectives (*This* chair is my favorite), but they may also function as noun equivalents (*This* is my favorite chair).

> this, that, these, those

Indefinite pronouns Indefinite pronouns refer to nonspecific persons or things. Most are always singular (*everyone, each*); some are always plural (*both, many*); a few may be singular or plural (see 21e). Most indefinite pronouns function as noun equivalents (*Something* is burning), but some can also function as adjectives (*All* campers must check in at the lodge).

pronouns • substitutes for nouns (we, their,
yourself, who, anyone, etc.)

basic
46b   371

all	anything	everyone	nobody	several
another	both	everything	none	some
any	each	few	no one	somebody
anybody	either	many	nothing	someone
anyone	everybody	neither	one	something

Reciprocal pronouns   Reciprocal pronouns refer to individual parts of a plural antecedent (By turns, the penguins fed *one another*).

each other, one another

NOTE: Using pronouns correctly can be challenging. See pronoun-antecedent agreement (22), pronoun reference (23), distinguishing between pronouns such as *I* and *me* (24), and distinguishing between *who* and *whom* (25).

EXERCISE 46-2   Underline the pronouns (and pronoun/adjectives) in the following sentences. Answers to lettered sentences appear in the back of the book. Example:

We were intrigued by the video that the fifth graders

produced as their final project.

a. The governor's loyalty was his most appealing trait.
b. In the fall, the geese that fly south for the winter pass through our town in huge numbers.
c. Carl Sandburg once said that even he himself did not understand some of his poetry.
d. I appealed my parking ticket, but you did not get one.
e. Angela did not mind gossip as long as no one gossiped about her.

1. The Tigers stood unhappily in front of their dugout while the victorious Jaguars tossed their hats in the air.
2. Nothing fascinated the toddler like something that was not his.
3. We understood that we were expected to submit our dissertations in triplicate.
4. The trick-or-treaters helped themselves to their neighbors' candy.
5. She found herself peering into the mouth of a creepy cave.

PRACTICE hackerhandbooks.com/rules
> Grammar basics > 46-7 and 46-8
> 46-15 and 46-16 (all parts of speech)

46c Verbs

The verb of a sentence usually expresses action (*jump*, *think*) or being (*is*, *become*). It is composed of a main verb possibly preceded by one or more helping verbs.

MV
The horses exercise every day.

HV   MV
The task force report was not completed on schedule.

HV HV   MV
No one has been defended with more passion than our pastor.

Notice that words, usually adverbs, can intervene between the helping verb and the main verb (was *not* completed). (See 46e.)

Helping verbs

There are twenty-three helping verbs in English: forms of *have*, *do*, and *be*, which may also function as main verbs; and nine modals, which function only as helping verbs. *Have, do,* and *be* change form to indicate tense; the nine modals do not.

FORMS OF *HAVE, DO,* AND *BE*

have, has, had

do, does, did

be, am, is, are, was, were, being, been

MODALS

can, could, may, might, must, shall, should, will, would

The verb phrase *ought to* is often classified as a modal as well.

Main verbs

The main verb of a sentence is always the kind of word that would change form if put into these test sentences:

BASE FORM	Usually I (*walk, ride*).
PAST TENSE	Yesterday I (*walked, rode*).
PAST PARTICIPLE	I have (*walked, ridden*) many times before.
PRESENT PARTICIPLE	I am (*walking, riding*) right now.
-S FORM	Usually he/she/it (*walks, rides*).

actions • states of being (*be, seem, become*, etc.) •
helping verbs (*have, do, be*) • modals (*can, may, must*, etc.)

basic

46c

373

If a word doesn't change form when slipped into the test sentences, you can be certain that it is not a main verb. For example, the noun *revolution*, though it may seem to suggest an action, can never function as a main verb. Just try to make it behave like one (*Today I revolution . . . Yesterday I revolutioned . . .*) and you'll see why.

When both the past-tense and the past-participle forms of a verb end in *-ed*, the verb is regular (*walked, walked*). Otherwise, the verb is irregular (*rode, ridden*). (See 27a.)

The verb *be* is highly irregular, having eight forms instead of the usual five: the base form *be*; the present-tense forms *am, is,* and *are*; the past-tense forms *was* and *were*; the present participle *being*; and the past participle *been*.

Helping verbs combine with the various forms of main verbs to create tenses. For a survey of tenses, see 28a.

NOTE: Some verbs are followed by words that look like prepositions but are so closely associated with the verb that they are a part of its meaning. These words are known as *particles*. Common verb-particle combinations include *bring up, call off, drop off, give in, look up, run into,* and *take off.*

> Sharon *packed up* her broken laptop and *sent* it *off* to the repair shop.

TIP: You can find more information about using verbs in other sections of the handbook: active verbs (8), subject-verb agreement (21), standard English verb forms (27), verb tense and mood (27f and 27g), and Multilingual/ESL challenges with verbs (28).

EXERCISE 46–3 Underline the verbs in the following sentences, including helping verbs and particles. If a verb is part of a contraction (such as *is* in *isn't* or *would* in *I'd*), underline only the letters that represent the verb. Answers to lettered sentences appear in the back of the book. Example:

> The ground under the pine trees wasn't wet from the rain.

a. My grandmother always told me a soothing story before bed.
b. There were fifty apples on the tree before the frost killed them.
c. Morton brought down the box of letters from the attic.

PRACTICE **hackerhandbooks.com/rules**
> Grammar basics > 46–9 and 46–10
> 46–15 and 46–16 (all parts of speech)

d. Stay on the main road and you'll arrive at the base camp before us.

e. The fish struggled vigorously but was trapped in the net.

1. Do not bring up that issue again.

2. Galileo lived the last years of his life under house arrest because of his revolutionary theories about the universe.

3. Cynthia asked for a raise, but she didn't expect one immediately.

4. We should plant the roses early this year.

5. The documentary was engrossing. It humanized World War II.

46d Adjectives

An adjective is a word used to modify, or describe, a noun or pronoun. An adjective usually answers one of these questions: Which one? What kind of? How many?

ADJ
the *frisky* horse [Which horse?]

ADJ   ADJ
cracked old plates [What kind of plates?]

ADJ
nine months [How many months?]

Adjectives usually precede the words they modify. They may also follow linking verbs, in which case they describe the subject. (See 47b.)

ADJ
The decision was *unpopular.*

The definite article *the* and the indefinite articles *a* and *an* are also classified as adjectives.

ART   ART   ART
A defendant should be judged on *the* evidence provided to *the* jury, not on hearsay.

Some possessive, demonstrative, and indefinite pronouns can function as adjectives: *their, its, this, all* (see 46b). And nouns can function as adjectives when they modify other nouns: *apple pie* (the noun *apple* modifies the noun *pie*; see 46a).

TIP: You can find more details about using adjectives in 26. If you are a multilingual writer, you may also find help with articles and specific uses of adjectives in 29, 30g, and 30h.

46e Adverbs

An adverb is a word used to modify, or qualify, a verb (or verbal), an adjective, or another adverb. It usually answers one of these questions: When? Where? How? Why? Under what conditions? To what degree?

> Pull *firmly* on the emergency handle. [Pull how?]

> Read the text *first* and *then* work the exercises. [Read when? Work when?]

Adverbs modifying adjectives or other adverbs usually intensify or limit the intensity of the word they modify.

>   ADV   ADV
> Be *extremely* kind, and you will *probably* have many friends.

The words *not* and *never* are classified as adverbs.

EXERCISE 46–4   Underline the adjectives and circle the adverbs in the following sentences. If a word is a noun or pronoun functioning as an adjective, underline it and mark it as a noun/adjective or pronoun/adjective. Also treat the articles *a*, *an*, and *the* as adjectives. Answers to lettered sentences appear in the back of the book. Example:

> Finding <u>an</u> <u>available</u> room during <u>the</u> convention
>
> was (not) easy.

a. Generalizations lead to weak, unfocused essays.
b. The Spanish language is wonderfully flexible.
c. The wildflowers smelled especially fragrant after the steady rain.
d. I'd rather be slightly hot than bitterly cold.
e. The cat slept soundly in its wicker basket.

1. Success can be elusive to those who object to working hard.
2. After three hours, the discussion had dwindled from a lively sprint to a tedious crawl.
3. She made a fairly earnest attempt at solving the most difficult calculus problems.
4. The black bear sniffed eagerly at the broken honeycomb.
5. The bacteria in the dish grew steadily over twenty-four hours.

PRACTICE hackerhandbooks.com/rules
> Grammar basics > 46–11 to 46–14
> 46–15 and 46–16 (all parts of speech)

46f Prepositions

A preposition is a word placed before a noun or pronoun to form a phrase modifying another word in the sentence. The prepositional phrase nearly always functions as an adjective or as an adverb.

P   P   P

The road *to* the summit travels *past* craters *from* an extinct volcano.

To the summit functions as an adjective modifying the noun *road*; *past craters* functions as an adverb modifying the verb *travels*; *from an extinct volcano* functions as an adjective modifying the noun *craters*. (For more on prepositional phrases, see 48a.)

English has a limited number of prepositions. The most common are included in the following list.

about	beside	from	outside	toward
above	besides	in	over	under
across	between	inside	past	underneath
after	beyond	into	plus	unlike
against	but	like	regarding	until
along	by	near	respecting	unto
among	concerning	next	round	up
around	considering	of	since	upon
as	despite	off	than	with
at	down	on	through	within
before	during	onto	throughout	without
behind	except	opposite	till	
below	for	out	to	

Some prepositions are more than one word long. *Along with, as well as, in addition to, next to,* and *rather than* are common examples.

TIP: Prepositions are used in idioms such as *capable of* and *dig up* (see 18d). For a discussion of specific issues for multilingual writers, see 31.

46g Conjunctions

Conjunctions join words, phrases, or clauses, and they indicate the relation between the elements joined.

prepositions (*in, at, between*, etc.) • conjunctions (*and, but, or, either . . . or, after, however*, etc.) • exclamations

basic
46h

377

Coordinating conjunctions   A coordinating conjunction is used to connect grammatically equal elements. (See 9b and 14a.) The coordinating conjunctions are *and, but, or, nor, for, so,* and *yet.*

Correlative conjunctions   Correlative conjunctions come in pairs. Like coordinating conjunctions, they connect grammatically equal elements.

either . . . or	whether . . . or
neither . . . nor	both . . . and
not only . . . but also	

Subordinating conjunctions   A subordinating conjunction introduces a subordinate clause and indicates the relation of the clause to the rest of the sentence. (See 48e.) The most common subordinating conjunctions are *after, although, as, as if, because, before, if, in order that, once, since, so that, than, that, though, unless, until, when, where, whether,* and *while.* (For a complete list, see p. 396.)

Conjunctive adverbs   Conjunctive adverbs connect independent clauses and indicate the relation between the clauses. They can be used with a semicolon to join two independent clauses in one sentence, or they can be used alone with an independent clause. The most common conjunctive adverbs are *finally, furthermore, however, moreover, nevertheless, similarly, then, therefore,* and *thus.* (For a complete list, see p. 380.)

TIP: The ability to distinguish between conjunctive adverbs and coordinating conjunctions will help you avoid run-on sentences and make punctuation decisions (see 20, 32a, and 32f). The ability to recognize subordinating conjunctions will help you avoid sentence fragments (see 19).

46h   Interjections

An interjection is a word used to express surprise or emotion (*Oh! Hey! Wow!*).

Parts of speech

- A **noun** names a person, place, thing, or concept.

  N   N   N
  Repetition does not transform a *lie* into *truth.*

- A **pronoun** substitutes for a noun.

                              PN   PN   PN
  Before the attendant let *us* board the small plane, *he* weighed *us*
      PN
  and *our* baggage.

  Personal pronouns: I, me, you, he, him, she, her, it, we, us, they,
  them

  Possessive pronouns: my, mine, your, yours, her, hers, his, its,
  our, ours, their, theirs

  Intensive and reflexive pronouns: myself, yourself, himself,
  herself, itself, ourselves, yourselves, themselves

  Relative pronouns: that, which, who, whom, whose

  Interrogative pronouns: who, whom, whose, which, what

  Demonstrative pronouns: this, that, these, those

  Indefinite pronouns

all	each	many	one
another	either	neither	several
any	everybody	nobody	some
anybody	everyone	none	somebody
anyone	everything	no one	someone
anything	few	nothing	something
both			

  Reciprocal pronouns: each other, one another

- A **helping verb** comes before a main verb.

  Modals: can, could, may, might, must, shall, should, will, would
  (*also* ought to)

  Forms of *be*: be, am, is, are, was, were, being, been

  Forms of *have*: have, has, had

  Forms of *do*: do, does, did

(The forms of *be*, *have*, and *do* may also function as main verbs.)

* A **main verb** shows action or a state of being.

MV
The novel *opens* with a tense description of a grim murder, but

HV   MV
the author *does* not *maintain* the initial level of suspense.

A main verb will always change form when put into these positions in sentences:

Usually I _____ .   (*walk, ride*)
Yesterday I _____ .   (*walked, rode*)
I have _____ many times before. (*walked, ridden*)
I am _____ right now.   (*walking, riding*)
Usually he _____ .   (*walks, rides*)

The highly irregular verb *be* has eight forms: *be, am, is, are, was, were, being, been.*

* An **adjective** modifies a noun or pronoun, usually answering one of these questions: Which one? What kind of? How many? The articles *a*, *an*, and *the* are also adjectives.

PN/ADJ N/ADJ ADJ   ADJ   PN/ADJ
Our family's strong ties gave us *welcome* comfort in *our*

grief.

* An **adverb** modifies a verb, an adjective, or an adverb, usually answering one of these questions: When? Where? Why? How? Under what conditions? To what degree?

ADV   ADV
Young people *often* approach history *skeptically.*

* A **preposition** indicates the relationship between the noun or pronoun that follows it and another word in the sentence.

P   P
A journey *of* a thousand miles begins *with* a single step.

Parts of speech (continued)

Common prepositions

about	besides	like	since
above	between	near	than
across	beyond	next	through
after	but	next to	throughout
against	by	of	till
along	concerning	off	to
along with	considering	on	toward
among	despite	onto	under
around	down	opposite	underneath
as	during	out	unlike
as well as	except	outside	until
at	for	over	unto
because of	from	past	up
before	in	plus	upon
behind	in addition to	rather than	with
below	inside	regarding	within
beside	into	respecting	without

- A **conjunction** connects words or word groups.

  Coordinating conjunctions: and, but, or, nor, for, so, yet

  Subordinating conjunctions: after, although, as, as if, because, before, even though, if, in order that, once, since, so that, than, that, though, unless, until, when, where, whether, while

  Correlative conjunctions: either . . . or; neither . . . nor; not only . . . but also; both . . . and; whether . . . or

  Conjunctive adverbs: accordingly, also, anyway, besides, certainly, consequently, conversely, finally, furthermore, hence, however, incidentally, indeed, instead, likewise, meanwhile, moreover, nevertheless, next, nonetheless, now, otherwise, similarly, specifically, still, subsequently, then, therefore, thus

- An **interjection** expresses surprise or emotion (*Oh! Wow! Hooray!*).

Sentence patterns

Most English sentences flow from subject to verb to any objects or complements. The vast majority of sentences conform to one of these five patterns:

> subject/verb/subject complement
> subject/verb/direct object
> subject/verb/indirect object/direct object
> subject/verb/direct object/object complement
> subject/verb

Adverbial modifiers (single words, phrases, or clauses) may be added to any of these patterns, and they may appear nearly anywhere — at the beginning, in the middle, or at the end.

Predicate is the grammatical term given to the verb plus its objects, complements, and adverbial modifiers.

For a quick-reference chart of sentence patterns, see page 386.

47a Subjects

The subject of a sentence names who or what the sentence is about. The simple subject is always a noun or pronoun; the complete subject consists of the simple subject and any words or word groups modifying the simple subject.

The complete subject

To find the complete subject, ask Who? or What?, insert the verb, and finish the question. The answer is the complete subject.

> ┌──── COMPLETE SUBJECT ────┐
> The devastating effects of famine can last for many years.

Who or what can last for many years? *The devastating effects of famine.*

> ┌──────── COMPLETE SUBJECT ────────┐
> Adventure novels that contain multiple subplots are often made
> into successful movies.

Who or what are often made into movies? *Adventure novels that contain multiple subplots.*

COMPLETE
┌── SUBJECT ──┐
In our program, student teachers work full-time for ten months.

Who or what works full-time for ten months? *Student teachers.*
Notice that *In our program, student teachers* is not a sensible answer to the question. (It is not safe to assume that the subject
must always appear first in a sentence.)

The simple subject

To find the simple subject, strip away all modifiers in the complete subject. This includes single-word modifiers such as *the* and
devastating, phrases such as *of famine*, and subordinate clauses
such as *that contain multiple subplots.*

┌─SS─┐
The devastating effects of famine can last for many years.

┌─SS─┐
Adventure novels that contain multiple subplots are often made into
successful movies.

A sentence may have a compound subject containing two
or more simple subjects joined with a coordinating conjunction
such as *and, but,* or *or.*

┌────SS────┐   ┌─SS─┐
Great commitment and a little luck make a successful actor.

Understood subjects

In imperative sentences, which give advice or issue commands,
the subject is understood but not actually present in the sentence.
The subject of an imperative sentence is understood to be *you.*

[*You*] Put your hands on the steering wheel.

Subject after the verb

Although the subject ordinarily comes before the verb (*The planes
took off*), occasionally it does not. When a sentence begins with
There is or *There are* (or *There was* or *There were*), the subject follows the verb. In such inverted constructions, the word *There* is an
expletive, an empty word serving merely to get the sentence started.

┌─SS─┐
There are *eight planes waiting to take off.*

Occasionally a writer will invert a sentence for effect.

```
        ┌SS┐
```
Joyful is *the child whose school closes for snow.*

Joyful is an adjective, so it cannot be the subject. Turn this sentence around and its structure becomes obvious.

The *child* whose school closes for snow is joyful.

In questions, the subject frequently appears between the helping verb and the main verb.

```
HV              ┌───SS───┐  MV
```
Do *Kenyan marathoners* train year-round?

TIP: The ability to recognize the subject of a sentence will help you edit for a variety of problems: sentence fragments (19), subject-verb agreement (21), choice of pronouns such as *I* and *me* (24), missing subjects (30b), and repeated subjects (30c).

EXERCISE 47–1 In the following sentences, underline the complete subject and write *SS* above the simple subject(s). If the subject is an understood *you*, insert *you* in parentheses. Answers to lettered sentences appear in the back of the book. Example:

```
┌─SS─┐              ┌─SS─┐
```
<u>Parents and their children</u> often look alike.

a. The hills and mountains seemed endless, and the snow atop them glistened.

b. In foil fencing, points are scored by hitting an electronic target.

c. Do not stand in the aisles or sit on the stairs.

d. There were hundreds of fireflies in the open field.

e. The evidence against the defendant was staggering.

1. The size of the new building caused an uproar in the town.

2. Eat heartily. You need your strength.

3. In the opinion of the court, siblings must be kept together.

4. All of the books in the old library smelled like mothballs.

5. There were no tour buses at the customs booth.

47b Verbs, objects, and complements

Section 46c explains how to find the verb of a sentence. A sentence's verb is classified as linking, transitive, or intransitive, depending on the kinds of objects or complements the verb can (or cannot) take.

Linking verbs and subject complements

Linking verbs connect the subject to a subject complement, a word or word group that completes the meaning of the subject by renaming or describing it.

If the subject complement renames the subject, it is a noun or noun equivalent (sometimes called a *predicate noun*).

```
         ┌─────────────────── S ───────────────────┐ ┌─ V ─┐ ┌─ SC ─┐
         An e-mail requesting personal information may be a scam.
```

If the subject complement describes the subject, it is an adjective or adjective equivalent (sometimes called a *predicate adjective*).

```
         ┌────────── S ──────────┐  V    SC
         Last month's temperatures were mild.
```

Whenever they appear as main verbs (rather than helping verbs), the forms of *be* — *be, am, is, are, was, were, being, been* — usually function as linking verbs. In the preceding examples, for instance, the main verbs are *be* and *were*.

Verbs such as *appear, become, feel, grow, look, make, seem, smell, sound,* and *taste* are linking when they are followed by a word group that renames or describes the subject.

```
                      ┌─ S ─┐┌─ V ─┐    SC
         As it thickens, the sauce will look unappealing.
```

Transitive verbs and direct objects

A transitive verb takes a direct object, a word or word group that names a receiver of the action.

```
         ┌──── S ────┐  V   ┌──────── DO ────────┐
         The hungry cat clawed the bag of dry food.
```

The simple direct object is always a noun or pronoun, in this case *bag*. To find it, simply strip away all modifiers.

Transitive verbs usually appear in the active voice, with the subject doing the action and a direct object receiving the action. Active-voice sentences can be transformed into the passive voice, with the subject receiving the action instead. (See 47c.)

Transitive verbs, indirect objects, and direct objects

The direct object of a transitive verb is sometimes preceded by an indirect object, a noun or pronoun telling to whom or for whom the action of the sentence is done.

$$
\begin{array}{cccc}
\text{S} & \text{V} & \text{IO} & \text{┌─DO─┐} & & \text{S} & \text{┌─V─┐} & \text{IO} & \text{┌─DO─┐}
\end{array}
$$

You give her some yarn, and she will knit you a scarf.

Transitive verbs, direct objects, and object complements

The direct object of a transitive verb is sometimes followed by an object complement, a word or word group that renames or describes the object.

$$
\begin{array}{cccc}
\text{S} & \text{V} & \text{DO} & \text{┌───OC───┐}
\end{array}
$$

People often consider chivalry a thing of the past.

$$
\begin{array}{cccc}
\text{┌─S─┐} & \text{V} & \text{DO} & \text{┌───OC───┐}
\end{array}
$$

The kiln makes clay firm and strong.

When the object complement renames the direct object, it is a noun or pronoun (such as *thing*). When it describes the direct object, it is an adjective (such as *firm* and *strong*).

Intransitive verbs

Intransitive verbs take no objects or complements.

$$
\begin{array}{cc}
\text{┌───S───┐} & \text{V}
\end{array}
$$

The audience laughed.

$$
\begin{array}{cc}
\text{┌───S───┐} & \text{V}
\end{array}
$$

The driver accelerated in the straightaway.

Nothing receives the actions of laughing and accelerating in these sentences, so the verbs are intransitive. Notice that such verbs may or may not be followed by adverbial modifiers. In the second sentence, *in the straightaway* is an adverbial prepositional phrase modifying *accelerated*.

Sentence patterns

Subject / linking verb / subject complement

S   V SC
Acting is art. [*Art* renames *Acting*.]

————— S ————— V   SC
Good researchers are curious. [*Curious* describes *researchers*.]

Subject / transitive verb / direct object

————— S ————— ——V—— ———— DO ————
An antihistamine may prevent an allergic reaction.

Subject / transitive verb / indirect object / direct object

————————— S ————————— V IO ———— DO ————
The elevator's rapid ascent gave Irina an attack of vertigo.

Subject / transitive verb / direct object / object complement

———— S ———— V —DO— ——OC——
The reviewer called the film a masterpiece. [*Masterpiece* renames *film*.]

————————— S ————————— V —DO— OC
The new double-glazed windows made the house warmer.
[*Warmer* describes *house*.]

Subject / intransitive verb

——S—— V
The kettle whistles.

NOTE: The dictionary will tell you whether a verb is transitive or intransitive. Some verbs have both transitive and intransitive functions.

TRANSITIVE   Sandra *flew* her small plane over the canyon.

INTRANSITIVE   A flock of migrating geese *flew* overhead.

In the first example, *flew* has a direct object that receives the action: *her small plane*. In the second example, the verb is followed by an adverb (*overhead*), not by a direct object.

EXERCISE 47–2 Label the subject complements and direct objects in the following sentences, using the labels *SC* and *DO*. If a subject complement or direct object consists of more than one word, bracket and label all of it. Example:

┌─── *DO* ───┐
The sharp right turn confused most drivers.

a. Textbooks are expensive.
b. Samurai warriors never fear death.
c. Successful coaches always praise their players' efforts.
d. St. Petersburg was the capital of the Russian Empire for two centuries.
e. The medicine tasted bitter.
1. Solar flares emit UV radiation.
2. The friends' quarrel was damaging their relationship.
3. Feng shui is the practice of achieving harmony between the physical and the spiritual in one's environment.
4. A well-made advertisement captures viewers' attention.
5. The island's climate was neither too hot nor too rainy.

EXERCISE 47–3 Each of the following sentences has either an indirect object followed by a direct object or a direct object followed by an object complement. Label the objects and complements, using the labels *IO*, *DO*, and *OC*. If an object or a complement consists of more than one word, bracket and label all of it. Example:

┌─────── *DO* ───────┐ ┌─ *OC* ─┐
Most people consider their own experience normal.

a. Stress can make adults and children weary.
b. Zita has made community service her priority this year.
c. Consider the work finished.
d. We showed the agent our tickets, and she gave us boarding passes.
e. The dining hall offered students healthy meal choices.
1. Send the registrar your scholarship form today.
2. The independent research institute gives its scholars the freedom to work without government or military interference.
3. Computer viruses make networks vulnerable.
4. Give me a book's title, and I can tell you the author.
5. The dire forecast made us extremely cautious about riding out the storm at home.

47c Pattern variations

Although most sentences follow one of the five patterns in the chart on page 386, variations of these patterns commonly occur in questions, commands, sentences with delayed subjects, and passive transformations.

Questions and commands

Questions are sometimes patterned in normal word order, with the subject preceding the verb.

      S   — V —
Who will have the most hits this season?

Just as frequently, however, the pattern of a question is inverted, with the subject appearing between the helping verb and the main verb or after the verb.

      HV S MV
Will he have the most hits this season?

      V   ——— S ———
Why is the number of hits an important statistic?

In commands, the subject of the sentence is an understood *you.*

      S   V
[You] Pay attention to the road.

Sentences with delayed subjects

Writers sometimes choose to delay the subject of a sentence to achieve a special effect such as suspense or humor.

               V ——— S ———
Behind the phony tinsel of Hollywood lies the real tinsel.

The subject of the sentence is also delayed in sentences opening with the expletive *There* or *It.* When used as expletives, the words *There* and *It* have no strict grammatical function; they serve merely to get the sentence started.

      V ——————— S ———————
There are thirty thousand spectators in the stadium.

      V   ——— S ———
It is best to avoid trans fats.

The subject in the second example is an infinitive phrase. (See 48b.)

Passive transformations

Transitive verbs, those that can take direct objects, usually appear in the active voice. In the active voice, the subject does the action, and a direct object receives the action.

               ┌─────── S ───────┐ V ┌───────DO───────
ACTIVE   The fireworks display dazzled the viewers on the

               ┌──────┐
               Esplanade.

Sentences in the active voice may be transformed into the passive voice, with the subject receiving the action instead.

               ┌────────── S ──────────┐ HV   MV
PASSIVE   The viewers on the Esplanade were dazzled by the
               fireworks display.

What was once the direct object (*the viewers on the Esplanade*) has become the subject in the passive-voice transformation, and the original subject appears in a prepositional phrase beginning with *by*. The *by* phrase is frequently omitted in passive-voice constructions.

PASSIVE   The viewers on the Esplanade were dazzled.

Verbs in the passive voice can be identified by their form alone. The main verb is always a past participle, such as *dazzled* (see 46c), preceded by a form of *be* (*be, am, is, are, was, were, being, been*): *were dazzled*. Sometimes adverbs intervene (*were usually dazzled*).

TIP: Avoid using the passive voice when the active voice would be more appropriate (see 8a).

48   Subordinate word groups

Subordinate word groups include phrases and clauses. Phrases are subordinate because they lack a subject and a verb; they are classified as prepositional, verbal, appositive, and absolute (see 48a–48d). Subordinate clauses have a subject and a verb, but they begin with a word (such as *although*, *that*, or *when*) that marks them as subordinate (see 48e).

48a Prepositional phrases

A prepositional phrase begins with a preposition such as *at, by, for, from, in, of, on, to,* or *with* (see 46f) and usually ends with a noun or noun equivalent: *on the table, for him, by sleeping late.* The noun or noun equivalent is known as the *object of the preposition.*

Prepositional phrases function either as adjectives or as adverbs. When functioning as an adjective, a prepositional phrase nearly always appears immediately following the noun or pronoun it modifies.

The hut had *walls of mud.*

Adjective phrases usually answer one or both of the questions Which one? and What kind of? If we ask Which walls? or What kind of walls? we get a sensible answer: *walls of mud.*

Adverbial prepositional phrases usually modify the verb, but they can also modify adjectives or other adverbs. When a prepositional phrase modifies the verb, it can appear nearly anywhere in a sentence.

James *walked* his dog *on a leash.*

Sabrina *will in time adjust* to life in Ecuador.

During a mudslide, the terrain *can change* drastically.

Adverbial word groups usually answer one of these questions: When? Where? How? Why? Under what conditions? To what degree?

James walked his dog *how? On a leash.*

Sabrina will adjust to life in Ecuador *when? In time.*

The terrain can change drastically *under what conditions? During a mudslide.*

EXERCISE 48–1   Underline the prepositional phrases in the following sentences. Tell whether each one is an adjective phrase or an adverb phrase and what it modifies in the sentence. Answers to lettered sentences appear in the back of the book. Example:

> **Flecks <u>of mica</u> glittered <u>in the new granite floor</u>.** (Adjective phrase modifying "Flecks"; adverb phrase modifying "glittered")

a. In northern Italy, some people speak German as their first language.
b. William completed the hike through the thick forest with ease.
c. To my boss's dismay, I was late for work again.
d. The traveling exhibit of Mayan artifacts gave viewers new insight into pre-Columbian culture.
e. In 2002, the euro became the official currency in twelve European countries.

1. The Silk Road was an old trade route between China and other parts of the world.
2. Dough with too much flour yields heavy baked goods.
3. On one side of the barricades were revolutionary students; on the other was a government militia.
4. You can tell with just one whiff whether the milk is fresh.
5. At first, we couldn't decide whether to take the car or the train, but in the end we decided to take the train.

48b Verbal phrases

A verbal is a verb form that does not function as the verb of a clause. Verbals include infinitives (the word *to* plus the base form of the verb), present participles (the *-ing* form of the verb), and past participles (the verb form usually ending in *-d*, *-ed*, *-n*, *-en*, or *-t*). (See 27a and 46c.)

INFINITIVE	PRESENT PARTICIPLE	PAST PARTICIPLE
to dream	dreaming	dreamed
to choose	choosing	chosen
to build	building	built
to grow	growing	grown

Instead of functioning as the verb of a clause, a verbal functions as an adjective, a noun, or an adverb.

ADJECTIVE   *Broken* promises cannot be fixed.

NOUN   Constant *complaining* becomes wearisome.

ADVERB   Can you wait *to celebrate*?

Verbals with objects, complements, or modifiers form verbal phrases. Like verbals, verbal phrases function as adjectives, nouns, or adverbs. Verbal phrases are ordinarily classified as participial, gerund, and infinitive.

Participial phrases

Participial phrases always function as adjectives. Their verbals are either present participles (such as *dreaming, asking*) or past participles (such as *stolen, reached*).

Participial phrases frequently appear immediately following the noun or pronoun they modify.

Congress shall make no *law abridging the freedom of speech or of the press.*

Unlike other word groups that function as adjectives (prepositional phrases, infinitive phrases, adjective clauses), which must always follow the noun or pronoun they modify, participial phrases are often movable. They can precede the word they modify.

Being a weight-bearing joint, the *knee* is among the most frequently injured.

They may also appear at some distance from the word they modify.

Last night we saw a *play* that affected us deeply, *written with profound insight into the lives of immigrants.*

participle (*stolen from the bank, waking early*) • gerund
(*following the crowd*) • -*ing* verb forms • infinitive (*to ask*)

basic

48b

393

Gerund phrases

Gerund phrases are built around present participles (verb forms that end in -*ing*), and they always function as nouns: usually as subjects, subject complements, direct objects, or objects of a preposition.

┌────── S ──────┐
Rationalizing a fear can eliminate it.

┌────────── DO ──────────┐
Lizards usually enjoy sunning themselves.

Infinitive phrases

Infinitive phrases, usually constructed around *to* plus the base form of the verb (*to call, to drink*), can function as nouns, as adjectives, or as adverbs. When functioning as a noun, an infinitive phrase may appear in almost any noun slot in a sentence, usually as a subject, subject complement, or direct object.

┌────────────── S ──────────────┐
To live without health insurance is risky.

Infinitive phrases functioning as adjectives usually appear immediately following the noun or pronoun they modify.

The Twentieth Amendment gave women the *right to vote.*

Adverbial infinitive phrases usually qualify the meaning of the verb, telling when, where, how, why, under what conditions, or to what degree an action occurred.

Volunteers *rolled up* their pants *to wade through the flood waters.*

Why did they roll up their pants? *To wade through the flood waters.*

NOTE: In some constructions, the infinitive is unmarked; in other words, the *to* does not appear. (See 28f.)

Graphs and charts can help researchers [*to*] *present complex data.*

EXERCISE 48–2   Underline the verbal phrases in the following sentences. Tell whether each phrase is participial, gerund, or infinitive and how each is used in the sentence. Answers to lettered sentences appear in the back of the book. Example:

> **Do you want <u>to watch that documentary</u>?** *(Infinitive phrase used as direct object of "Do want")*

a. Updating your software will fix the computer glitch.

b. The challenge in decreasing the town budget is identifying nonessential services.

c. Cathleen tried to help her mother by raking the lawn.

d. Understanding little, I had no hope of passing my biology final.

e. Working with animals gave Steve a sense of satisfaction.

1. Driving through South Carolina, we saw kudzu growing out of control along the roadside.

2. Some people now use a patch to repel mosquitoes.

3. We helped the schoolchildren find their way to the station.

4. Painting requires the ability to keep a steady hand.

5. My father could not see a weed without pulling it out of the ground.

48c Appositive phrases

Appositive phrases describe nouns or pronouns. Instead of modifying nouns or pronouns, however, appositive phrases rename them. In form they are nouns or noun equivalents.

> Bloggers, *conversationalists at heart*, are the online equivalent of radio talk show hosts.

48d Absolute phrases

An absolute phrase modifies a whole clause or sentence, not just one word. It consists of a noun or noun equivalent usually followed by a participial phrase.

> *Her words reverberating in the hushed arena*, the senator urged the crowd to support her former opponent.

appositive • phrase that renames a noun • absolute phrase •
adjective clause • begin with *who, that, where,* etc.

basic
48e   395

48e Subordinate clauses

Subordinate clauses are patterned like sentences, having subjects and verbs and sometimes objects or complements. But they function within sentences as adjectives, adverbs, or nouns. They cannot stand alone as complete sentences.

Adjective clauses

Adjective clauses modify nouns or pronouns, usually answering the question Which one? or What kind of? They begin with a relative pronoun (*who, whom, whose, which,* or *that*) or occasionally with a relative adverb (usually *when, where,* or *why*). (See the box on p. 396.)

The coach chose *players who would benefit from intense drills.*

In addition to introducing the clause, the relative pronoun points back to the noun that the clause modifies.

A *book that goes unread* is a writer's worst nightmare.

Relative pronouns are sometimes "understood."

The things [*that*] *we cherish most* are the things [*that*] *we might lose.*

The parts of an adjective clause are often arranged as in sentences (subject/verb/object or complement).

                          S   V   DO
Sometimes it is our closest friends who disappoint us.

Frequently, however, the object or complement appears first, violating the normal order of subject/verb/object.

                         DO S   V
They can be the very friends whom we disappoint.

TIP: For punctuation of adjective clauses, see 32e and 33e. For advice about avoiding repeated words in adjective clauses, see 30d.

Words that introduce subordinate clauses

Words introducing adjective clauses

Relative pronouns: that, which, who, whom, whose
Relative adverbs: when, where, why

Words introducing adverb clauses

Subordinating conjunctions: after, although, as, as if, because, before, even though, if, in order that, since, so that, than, that, though, unless, until, when, where, whether, while

Words introducing noun clauses

Relative pronouns: that, which, who, whom, whose
Other pronouns: what, whatever, whichever, whoever, whomever
Other subordinating words: how, if, when, whenever, where, wherever, whether, why

Adverb clauses

Adverb clauses modify verbs, adjectives, or other adverbs, usually answering one of these questions: When? Where? Why? How? Under what conditions? To what degree? They always begin with a subordinating conjunction (such as *after, although, because, that, though, unless,* or *when*). (For a complete list, see the box on this page.)

When the sun went down, the hikers *prepared* their camp.

Kate *would have made* the team *if she hadn't broken her ankle.*

Noun clauses

A noun clause functions just like a single-word noun, usually as a subject, a subject complement, a direct object, or an object of a preposition. It usually begins with one of the following words: *how, if, that, what, whatever, when, where, whether, which, who,*

adverb clauses (begin with *because, if,* etc.) •
noun clauses (begin with *that, what, who,* etc.)

basic

48e

397

whoever, whom, whomever, whose, why. (For a complete list, see the box on p. 396.)

$$\overline{\quad\quad\text{S}\quad\quad}$$
Whoever leaves the house last must double-lock the door.

$$\overline{\quad\quad\quad\quad\text{DO}\quad\quad\quad\quad}$$
Copernicus argued that the sun is the center of the universe.

The subordinating word introducing the clause may or may not play a significant role in the clause. In the preceding example sentences, *Whoever* is the subject of its clause, but *that* does not perform a function in its clause.

As with adjective clauses, the parts of a noun clause may appear in normal order (subject/verb/object or complement) or out of their normal order.

$$\text{S}\quad\text{V}\quad\overline{\text{DO}}$$
Loyalty is what keeps a friendship strong.

$$\overline{\text{DO}}\quad\text{S}\quad\text{V}$$
New Mexico is where we live.

EXERCISE 48-3 Underline the subordinate clauses in the following sentences. Tell whether each clause is an adjective, adverb, or noun clause and how it is used in the sentence. Answers to lettered sentences appear in the back of the book. Example:

> Show the committee the latest draft before you print the
>
> final report. *(Adverb clause modifying "Show")*

a. The city's electoral commission adjusted the voting process so that every vote would count.

b. A marketing campaign that targets baby boomers may not appeal to young professionals.

c. After the Tambora volcano erupted in the southern Pacific in 1815, no one realized that it would contribute to the "year without a summer" in Europe and North America.

d. The concept of peak oil implies that at a certain point there will be no more oil to extract from the earth.

e. Details are easily overlooked when you are rushing.

1. What her internship taught her was that she worked well with children with special needs.

2. Whether you like it or not, you cannot choose your family.
3. The meteorologist who underestimated the total snowfall of the first winter storm was right on target about the second storm.
4. If Ramon didn't have to work every afternoon, he would be willing to sign up for the yoga class with Andrea.
5. The book that we saw in the shop in Dublin was not available when we returned home.

Sentence types

Sentences are classified in two ways: according to their structure (simple, compound, complex, and compound-complex) and according to their purpose (declarative, imperative, interrogative, and exclamatory).

49a Sentence structures

Depending on the number and the types of clauses they contain, sentences are classified as simple, compound, complex, or compound-complex.

Clauses come in two varieties: independent and subordinate. An independent clause contains a subject and a predicate, and it either stands alone or could stand alone as a sentence. A subordinate clause also contains a subject and a predicate, but it functions within a sentence as an adjective, an adverb, or a noun; it cannot stand alone. (See 48e.)

Simple sentences

A simple sentence is one independent clause with no subordinate clauses.

———————————— INDEPENDENT CLAUSE ————————————
Without a passport, Eva could not visit her grandparents in

Hungary.

A simple sentence may contain compound elements—a compound subject, verb, or object, for example—but it does not contain more than one full sentence pattern. The following sentence is simple because its two verbs (*comes in* and *goes out*) share a subject (*Spring*).

┌──────────── INDEPENDENT CLAUSE ────────────┐
Spring comes in like a lion and goes out like a lamb.

Compound sentences

A compound sentence is composed of two or more independent clauses with no subordinate clauses. The independent clauses are usually joined with a comma and a coordinating conjunction (*and, but, or, nor, for, so, yet*) or with a semicolon. (See 14a.)

INDEPENDENT   INDEPENDENT
┌──── CLAUSE ────┐   ┌──────── CLAUSE ────────┐
The car broke down, but a rescue van arrived within minutes.

┌──── INDEPENDENT CLAUSE ────┐ ┌─ INDEPENDENT CLAUSE ─┐
A shark was spotted near shore; people left immediately.

Complex sentences

A complex sentence is composed of one independent clause with one or more subordinate clauses. (See 48e.)

SUBORDINATE
┌──── CLAUSE ────┐
ADJECTIVE   The pitcher who won the game is a rookie.

SUBORDINATE
┌──── CLAUSE ────┐
ADVERB   If you leave late, take a cab home.

SUBORDINATE
┌──────── CLAUSE ────────┐
NOUN   What matters most to us is a quick commute.

Compound-complex sentences

A compound-complex sentence contains at least two independent clauses and at least one subordinate clause. The following sentence contains two independent clauses, each of which contains a subordinate clause.

┌──── INDEPENDENT CLAUSE ────┐   ┌──── INDEPENDENT CLAUSE
┌──── SUB CL ────┐
Tell the doctor how you feel, and she will decide whether

┌──── SUB CL ────┐
you can go home.

49b Sentence purposes

Writers use declarative sentences to make statements, imperative sentences to issue requests or commands, interrogative sentences to ask questions, and exclamatory sentences to make exclamations.

DECLARATIVE	The echo sounded in our ears.
IMPERATIVE	Love your neighbor.
INTERROGATIVE	Did the better team win tonight?
EXCLAMATORY	We're here to save you!

EXERCISE 49–1 Identify the following sentences as simple, compound, complex, or compound-complex. Identify the subordinate clauses and classify them according to their function: adjective, adverb, or noun. (See 48e.) Answers to lettered sentences appear in the back of the book. Example:

The deli in Courthouse Square was crowded with lawyers

at lunchtime. (Simple)

a. Fires that are ignited in dry areas spread especially quickly.
b. The early Incas were advanced; they used a calendar and developed a decimal system.
c. Elaine's jacket was too thin to block the wintry air.
d. Before we leave for the station, we always check the Amtrak Web site.
e. Decide when you want to leave, and I will be there to pick you up.

1. The fact is that the network outage could have been avoided.
2. Those who lose a loved one in a tragic accident may find group therapy comforting.
3. The outlets in the garment district are the best places to find Halloween costumes.
4. There were six lunar Apollo missions, but people usually remember Apollo 13 best.
5. Our generator kicks in whenever we lose power.

Document Design

The term *document* is broad enough to describe anything you might write in a college class, in the business world, and in everyday life. How you design a document (format it for the printed page or for a computer screen) will affect how readers respond to it.

50 Become familiar with the principles of document design.

Good document design promotes readability, but what *readability* means depends on your purpose and audience and perhaps on other elements of your writing situation, such as your subject, length restrictions, or any other specific requirements. All of your design choices — formatting options, headings, and lists — should be made with your writing situation in mind. Likewise, different types of visuals — tables, charts, and images — can support your writing if they are used appropriately.

50a Select appropriate format options.

Similar documents share common design features. Together, these features — layout, margins and line spacing, alignment, fonts, and font styles — can help guide readers through a document.

Layout

Most readers have set ideas about how different kinds of documents should look. Advertisements, for example, have a distinctive appearance, as do newsletters and brochures. Instructors have expectations about how a college paper should look (see 51). Employers, too, expect documents such as letters, résumés, memos, and e-mail messages to be presented in standard ways (see 52).

Unless you have a compelling reason to stray from convention, it's best to choose a document layout that conforms to your readers' expectations. If you're not sure what readers expect, look at examples of the kind of document you are producing.

Margins and line spacing

Margins help control the look of a page. For most academic and business documents, leave a margin of one to one and a half inches on all sides. These margins create a visual frame for the text and provide room for annotations, such as an instructor's comments or a peer's suggestions. Tight margins generally make a page crowded and difficult to read.

Most manuscripts in progress are double-spaced to allow room for editing. Final copy is often double-spaced as well, since single-spaced text is less inviting to read. If you are unsure about margin and spacing requirements for your document, check with your instructor or consult documents similar to the one you are writing.

At times, the advantages of wide margins and double-spaced lines are offset by other considerations. For example, most business and technical documents are single-spaced, with double-spacing between paragraphs, to save paper and promote quick scanning. Keep your purpose and audience in mind as you determine appropriate margins and line spacing for your document.

SINGLE-SPACED, UNFORMATTED   **DOUBLE-SPACED, FORMATTED**

Planning a document: Design checklist for purpose and audience

- What is the purpose of your document? How can your document design help you achieve this purpose?
- Who are your readers? What are their expectations?
- What format is required? What format options — layout, margins, line spacing, and font styles — will readers expect?
- How can you use visuals — charts, graphs, tables, images — to help you convey information and achieve your purpose?

As you write

Using the checklist on page 403, evaluate the design of a paper you're working on. Exchange drafts with a classmate, and ask for specific feedback. How can your document design help you better achieve your purpose and reach your audience?

Fonts

If you have a choice, select a font that fits your writing situation in an easy-to-read size (usually 10 to 12 points). Although offbeat fonts may seem attractive, they slow readers down and can distract them from your ideas. For example, using *Comic Sans*, a font with a handwritten, childish feel, can make an essay seem too informal or unpolished, regardless of how well it's written. Fonts that are easy to read and appropriate for college and workplace documents include the following: Arial, Courier, Georgia, Times New Roman, and Verdana. Check with your instructor; he or she may expect or prefer a particular font.

Font styles

Font styles — such as **boldface**, *italics*, and <u>underlining</u> — can be useful for calling attention to parts of a document. On the whole, it is best to use restraint when selecting styles. Applying too many different styles within a document can result in busy-looking pages and may confuse readers.

TIP: Never write a document in all capital or all lowercase letters. Although some readers have become accustomed to instant messages and e-mails that omit capital letters entirely, their absence makes a piece of writing difficult to read and too informal.

50b Use headings to guide readers.

In short essays, you will have little need for headings, especially if you use paragraphing and clear topic sentences to guide readers. In more complex documents, however, such as longer essays, research papers, business reports, and Web sites, headings can be a useful visual cue for readers.

Headings help readers see at a glance the organization of a document. If more than one level of heading is used, the headings also indicate the hierarchy of ideas — as they do throughout this book.

Headings can serve a number of functions in a document, depending on the needs of different readers. When readers are looking for specific information and don't want to read the entire document, headings can guide them to the appropriate place quickly. When

> **Making the most of your handbook**
> Headings can help writers plan and readers understand a document.
> ▸ Paper organized with headings: page 580

readers are scanning, hoping to pick up a document's meaning or message, headings can provide an overview. Even when readers are committed enough to read every word, headings can help them preview a document before they begin reading or can help them easily revisit a specific section after they've read through the document once.

TIP: While headings can be useful, they cannot substitute for transitions between paragraphs (see 4d).

Phrasing headings

Headings should be as brief and as informative as possible. Certain styles of headings — the most common being -*ing* phrases, noun phrases, questions, and imperative sentences — work better for some purposes, audiences, and subjects than for others.

Whatever style you choose, use it consistently. Headings on the same level of organization should be written in parallel structure (see 9), as in the following examples from a report, a history textbook, a financial brochure, and a nursing manual, respectively.

-*ING* PHRASES AS HEADINGS
Safeguarding the earth's atmosphere
Charting the path to sustainable energy
Conserving global forests

NOUN PHRASES AS HEADINGS
The civil rights movement
The antiwar movement
The feminist movement

QUESTIONS AS HEADINGS
How do I buy shares?
How do I redeem shares?
How has the fund performed in the past three years?

IMPERATIVE SENTENCES AS HEADINGS

Ask the patient to describe current symptoms.

Take a detailed medical history.

Record the patient's vital signs.

Placing and formatting headings

Headings on the same level of organization should be placed and formatted in a consistent way. If you have more than one level of heading, you might center your first-level headings and make them boldface; then you might make the second-level headings left-aligned and italicized.

First-level heading

Second-level heading

A college paper with headings typically has only one level, and the headings are often centered, as in the sample paper on pages 583–94. In a report or a brochure, important headings can be highlighted by using white space above and below them. Less important headings can be downplayed by using less white space or by running them into the text.

50c Use lists to guide readers.

Lists are easy to read or scan when they are displayed, item by item, rather than run into your text. You might choose to display the following kinds of lists:

- steps in a process
- advice or recommendations
- items to be discussed
- criteria for evaluation (as in checklists)
- parts of an object

Lists are usually introduced with an independent clause followed by a colon (*All mammals share the following five characteristics:*). Periods are not used after items in a list unless the items are complete sentences. Lists are most readable when they are presented in parallel grammatical form (see 9).

Use bullets (circles or squares) or dashes to draw readers' eyes to a list and to emphasize individual items. If you are describing a sequence or a set of steps, number your list with arabic numerals (1, 2, 3) followed by periods.

Although lists can be useful visual cues, don't overdo them. Too many will clutter a document.

50d Add visuals that support your purpose.

In many business and professional contexts, readers expect visuals in a text. Visuals — charts, graphs, tables, and photos, for example — are often used to display data, show trends, illustrate ideas, or humanize a problem or issue. You may be encouraged or required to use visuals in your college assignments. Be sure to think through how visuals support your purpose and satisfy the expectations of your readers. See pages 24–25 for a chart that describes different types of visuals and their purposes. See also the research sections in this book; one student uses a cartoon to illustrate a point in her paper (p. 531), and another uses a table to display key data (p. 589).

Choosing appropriate visuals

In many cases, the same information can be presented visually in different formats. When you're deciding whether to display data in a table or a graph, for example, think about the message you want to convey and the information your readers need. Take a look at the examples on page 408.

If your discussion refers to specific numbers, a table will be more useful to readers. If, however, you want readers to grasp at a glance that sales of hybrid electric vehicles increased from 2001 to 2008 and then declined, a line graph will be more effective.

As you draft and revise a document, carefully choose or design only those visuals that support your main point.

Placing and labeling visuals

A visual may be placed in the text of a document, near a discussion to which it relates, or it can be put in an appendix, labeled, and referred to in the text.

INFORMATION DISPLAYED IN TWO TYPES OF VISUALS These visuals present the same information in two different ways. The table provides exact numbers for comparison. The line graph allows readers to see the trend in sales.

Hybrid electric vehicle sales by year in the United States

Year	Number of vehicles sold
2001	20,282
2002	36,035
2003	47,600
2004	84,199
2005	209,711
2006	252,636
2007	352,274
2008	312,386

Source: US Dept. of Energy (2009).

Hybrid electric vehicle sales by year in the United States

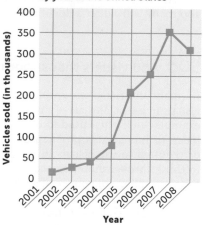

Placing visuals in the text of a document can be tricky. Usually you will want the visual to appear close to the sentences that relate to it, but page breaks won't always allow this placement. At times you may need to insert the visual at a later point and tell readers where it can be found; sometimes you can make the text flow, or wrap, around the visual. No matter where you place a visual, refer to it in your text. Don't expect visuals to speak for themselves.

> **Making the most of your handbook**
> Guidelines for using visuals vary by academic discipline.
> ► English and other humanities: 60a
> ► Social sciences: 65a

Most of the visuals you include in a document will require some sort of label. A label, which is typically placed above or below the visual, should be brief but descriptive. Most commonly, a visual is labeled with the word "Figure" or the abbreviation "Fig.," followed by a number: *Fig. 4.* Sometimes a title might be included to explain how the visual relates to the text: *Fig. 4. Voter turnout by age.*

Using visuals responsibly

Most word processing and spreadsheet software will allow you to produce your own visuals. If you create a chart, a table, or a graph using information from your research, you must cite the source of the information even though the visual is your own. The visual at the right credits the source of its data.

If you download a photograph from the Web or scan an image from a magazine or book, you must credit the person or organization that created it, just as you would cite any other source you use in a college paper (see 55). Make sure any cropping or other changes you make to the visual do not distort the meaning of the original. If your document is written for publication outside the classroom, you will need to request permission to use any visual you borrow.

VISUAL WITH A SOURCE CREDITED

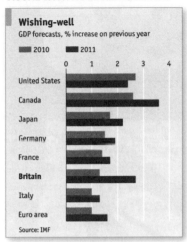

Source: International Monetary Fund (2010).

---

51   Use standard academic formatting.

Instructors have certain expectations about how a college paper should look. If your instructor provides guidelines for formatting an essay, a report, a research paper, or another document, you should follow them. Otherwise, use the manuscript format that is recommended for your academic discipline.

In most English and other humanities classes, you will be asked to use the MLA (Modern Language Association) format (see 60a). In most social science classes, such as psychology and sociology, and in most business and health-related classes, you will be asked to use APA (American Psychological Association) format (see 65a).

Most composition instructors require MLA format, which is illustrated in the sample on pages 410–11. For more detailed MLA manuscript guidelines and a sample MLA-style research paper, see 60.

MLA ESSAY FORMAT

1″

1/2″

Orlov 1

1″

Anna Orlov

Professor Willis

English 101

17 March 2009

Title is centered.

Online Monitoring:

A Threat to Employee Privacy in the Wired Workplace

1/2″ As the Internet has become an integral tool of businesses,

company policies on Internet usage have become as common as

1″

policies regarding vacation days or sexual harassment. A 2005

study by the American Management Association and ePolicy

Institute found that 76% of companies monitor employees' use

of the Web, and the number of companies that block employees'

access to certain Web sites has increased 27% since 2001 (1).

Double-spacing is used throughout.

Unlike other company rules, however, Internet usage policies

often include language authorizing companies to secretly monitor

their employees, a practice that raises questions about rights

in the workplace. Although companies often have legitimate

concerns that lead them to monitor employees' Internet usage—

from expensive security breaches to reduced productivity—the

benefits of electronic surveillance are outweighed by its costs to

employees' privacy and autonomy.

While surveillance of employees is not a new phenomenon,

electronic surveillance allows employers to monitor workers

with unprecedented efficiency. In his book *The Naked*

Employee, Frederick Lane describes offline ways in which

employers have been permitted to intrude on employees'

privacy for decades, such as drug testing, background checks,

psychological exams, lie detector tests, and in-store video

surveillance. The difference, Lane argues, between these old

methods of data gathering and electronic surveillance involves

quantity:

1″

Marginal annotations indicate MLA-style formatting.

½"

1"

Orlov 6

Works Cited

Heading is centered.

Adams, Scott. *Dilbert and the Way of the Weasel*. New York: Harper, 2002. Print.

American Management Association and ePolicy Institute. "2005 Electronic Monitoring and Surveillance Survey." *American Management Association*. Amer. Management Assn., 2005. Web. 15 Feb. 2009.

"Automatically Record Everything They Do Online! Spector Pro 5.0 FAQ's." *Netbus.org*. Netbus.Org, n.d. Web. 17 Feb. 2009.

Flynn, Nancy. "Internet Policies." *ePolicy Institute*. ePolicy Inst., n.d. Web. 15 Feb. 2009.

Frauenheim, Ed. "Stop Reading This Headline and Get Back to Work." *CNET News.com*. CNET Networks, 11 July 2005. Web. 17 Feb. 2009.

Gonsalves, Chris. "Wasting Away on the Web." *eWeek.com*. Ziff Davis Enterprise Holdings, 8 Aug. 2005. Web. 16 Feb. 2009.

Kesan, Jay P. "Cyber-Working or Cyber-Shirking? A First Principles Examination of Electronic Privacy in the Workplace." *Florida Law Review* 54.2 (2002): 289-332. Print.

Lane, Frederick S., III. *The Naked Employee: How Technology Is Compromising Workplace Privacy*. New York: Amer. Management Assn., 2003. Print.

Tam, Pui-Wing, et al. "Snooping E-mail by Software Is Now a Workplace Norm." *Wall Street Journal* 9 Mar. 2005: B1+. Print.

Tynan, Daniel. "Your Boss Is Watching." *PC World*. PC World Communications, 6 Oct. 2004. Web. 17 Feb. 2009.

Verespej, Michael A. "Inappropriate Internet Surfing." *Industry Week*. Penton Media, 7 Feb. 2000. Web. 16 Feb. 2009.

Double-spacing is used throughout; no extra space between entries.

52 Use standard business formatting.

This section provides guidelines for preparing business letters, résumés, and memos.

52a Use established conventions for business letters.

In writing a business letter, be direct, clear, and courteous, but do not hesitate to be firm if necessary. State your purpose or request at the beginning of the letter and include only relevant information in the body. By being as direct and concise as possible, you show that you value your reader's time.

For the format of the letter, use established business conventions. The sample business letter on page 413 is typed in what is known as *full block* style. Paragraphs are not indented and are typed single-spaced, with double-spacing between them. This style is usually preferred when the letter is typed on letterhead stationery, as in the example.

Below the signature, aligned at the left, you may include the abbreviation *Enc.* to indicate that something is enclosed with the letter or the abbreviation *cc* followed by a colon and the name of someone who is receiving a copy of the letter.

52b Write effective résumés and cover letters.

An effective résumé gives relevant information in a clear and concise form. You may be asked to produce a traditional résumé, a scannable résumé, or a Web résumé. The cover letter gives a prospective employer a reason to look at your résumé. The goal is to present yourself in a favorable light without including unnecessary details.

Cover letters Always include a cover letter to introduce yourself, state the position you seek, and tell where you learned about it. The letter also should highlight past experiences that qualify you for the position and should emphasize what you can

BUSINESS LETTER IN FULL BLOCK STYLE

Latino Voice

March 16, 2011 ——————— Date

Jonathan Ross
Managing Editor
Latino World Today ——————— Inside
2971 East Oak Avenue   address
Baltimore, MD 21201

Dear Mr. Ross: ——————— Salutation

Thank you very much for taking the time yesterday to speak to the University of Maryland's Latino Club. A number of students have told me that they enjoyed your presentation and found your job search suggestions to be extremely helpful.

As I mentioned to you when we first scheduled your appearance, the club publishes a monthly newsletter, *Latino Voice.* Our purpose is to share up-to-date information and expert advice with members of the university's Latino population. Considering how much students benefited from your talk, I would like to publish excerpts from it in our newsletter.

I have taken the liberty of transcribing parts of your presentation and organizing them into a question-and-answer format for our readers. When you have a moment, would you mind looking through the enclosed article and letting me know if I may have your permission to print it? I would be happy, of course, to make any changes or corrections that you request. I'm hoping to include this article in our next newsletter, so I would need your response by April 4.

Once again, Mr. Ross, thank you for sharing your experiences with us. You gave an informative and entertaining speech, and I would love to be able to share it with the students who couldn't hear it in person.

Sincerely, ——————— Close

Jeffrey Richardson

Jeffrey Richardson
Associate Editor ——————— Signature

Enc.

210 Student Center University of Maryland College Park MD 20742

Body ——— (label for body section)

---

do for the employer (not what the job will do for you). End the letter with a suggestion for a meeting, and tell your prospective employer when you will be available.

Traditional résumés   Traditional résumés are produced on paper, and they are screened by people, not by computers. Because screeners often face stacks of applications, they may spend very

TRADITIONAL RÉSUMÉ

Jeffrey Richardson
121 Knox Road, #6
College Park, MD 20740
301-555-2651
jrichardson@example.net

OBJECTIVE To obtain an editorial internship with a magazine

EDUCATION
Fall 2007– present

University of Maryland
- BA expected in June 2011
- Double major: English and Latin American studies
- GPA: 3.7 (on a 4-point scale)

EXPERIENCE
Fall 2009– present

Associate editor, *Latino Voice*, newsletter of Latino Club
- Assign and edit feature articles
- Coordinate community outreach

Fall 2008– present

Photo editor, *The Diamondback*, college paper
- Shoot and organize photos for print and online publication
- Oversee photo staff assignments; evaluate photos

Summer 2009

Intern, *The Globe,* Fairfax, Virginia
- Wrote stories about local issues and personalities
- Interviewed political candidates
- Edited and proofread copy
- Coedited "The Landscapes of Northern Virginia: A Photoessay"

Summers 2008, 2009

Tutor, Fairfax County ESL Program
- Tutored Latino students in English as a Second Language
- Trained new tutors

ACTIVITIES Photographers' Workshop, Latino Club

PORTFOLIO Available at http://jrichardson.example.net/jrportfolio.htm

REFERENCES Available on request

little time looking at each résumé. Therefore, you will need to make your résumé as reader-friendly as possible. Here are a few guidelines:

- Limit your résumé to one page if possible, two pages at the most. (If your résumé is longer than a page, repeat your name at the top of the second page.)

- Organize your information into clear categories—Education, Experience, and so on.
- Present the information in each category in reverse chronological order to highlight your most recent accomplishments.
- Use bulleted lists or some other simple, clear visual device to organize information.
- Use strong, active verbs to state your accomplishments. For current activities, use present-tense verbs (*manage*); for past activities, use past-tense verbs (*managed*).

Scannable résumés Scannable résumés might be submitted on paper, by e-mail, or through an online employment service. The résumés are scanned and searched electronically, and a database matches keywords in the job description with keywords in the résumés. A human screener reads the résumés selected by the database.

A scannable résumé must be formatted simply so that the scanner can accurately pick up its content. In general, follow these guidelines when preparing a scannable résumé:

- Include a Keywords section that lists words likely to be searched by a scanner. Use nouns (*manager*), not verbs (*manage* or *managed*).
- Use standard résumé headings (for example, Education, Experience, References).
- Avoid special characters, graphics, or font styles.
- Avoid formatting such as tabs, indents, columns, or tables.

Web résumés Posting your résumé on a Web site is an easy way to provide recent information about your goals and accomplishments and examples of your work. Most guidelines for traditional résumés apply to Web résumés. You may want to include a downloadable version of your résumé and link to an electronic portfolio. Always list the date that you last updated your résumé.

52c Write clear and concise memos.

Usually brief and to the point, a memo reports information, makes a request, or recommends an action. The format of a memo, which varies from company to company, is designed for easy distribution, quick reading, and efficient filing.

BUSINESS MEMO

COMMONWEALTH PRESS

MEMORANDUM

February 24, 2011

To: Editorial assistants, Advertising Department
cc: Stephen Chapman
From: Helen Brown
Subject: New database software

The new database software will be installed on your computers next week. I have scheduled a training program to help you become familiar with the software and with our new procedures for data entry and retrieval.

Training program
A member of our IT staff will teach in-house workshops on how to use the new software. If you try the software before the workshop, please be prepared to discuss any problems you encounter.

We will keep the training groups small to encourage hands-on participation and to provide individual attention. The workshops will take place in the training room on the third floor from 10:00 a.m. to 2:00 p.m.

Lunch will be provided in the cafeteria.

Sign-up
Please sign up by March 1 for one of the following dates by adding your name in the department's online calendar:

- Wednesday, March 2
- Friday, March 4
- Monday, March 7

If you will not be in the office on any of those dates, please let me know by March 1.

Most memos display the date, the name of the recipient, the name of the sender, and the subject on separate lines at the top. Many companies have preprinted forms for memos, and most word processing programs have memo templates.

The subject line of a memo should describe the topic as clearly and concisely as possible, and the introductory paragraph should get right to the point. In addition, the body of the memo should be well organized and easy to skim. To promote skimming, use headings where possible and set off any items that deserve special attention (in a list, for example, or in boldface). A sample memo appears on page 416.

52d Write effective e-mail messages.

E-mail is one of the primary means of communicating in business settings. As in all business communications, you should keep your purpose and audience in mind as you write. Effective e-mail messages are straightforward and clear and are formatted in a way that makes them easy to read. See the chart on pages 9–10 for more advice about writing e-mail.

Research

Research, 419

Research

53 Conducting research

College research assignments ask you to pose a question worth exploring, to read widely in search of possible answers, to interpret what you read, to draw reasoned conclusions, and to support those conclusions with valid and well-documented evidence.

The process takes time: time for researching and time for drafting, revising, and documenting the paper in the style recommended by your instructor. Before beginning a research project,

SAMPLE CALENDAR FOR A RESEARCH ASSIGNMENT

2	3	4	5	6	7	8
	Receive and analyze the assignment.	Pose questions you might explore.	Talk with a reference librarian; plan a search strategy.		Settle on a topic; narrow the focus.	Revise research questions. Locate sources.
9	**10**	**11**	**12**	**13**	**14**	**15**
Read, take notes, and compile a working bibliography.				Draft a working thesis and an outline.	Draft the paper.	
16	**17**	**18**	**19**	**20**	**21**	**22**
Draft the paper.			Visit the writing center for feedback.	Do additional research if needed.		
23	**24**	**25**	**26**	**27**	**28**	**29**
Ask peers for feedback. Revise the paper; if necessary, revise the thesis.				Prepare a list of works cited.		Proofread the final draft.
30	**31**					
Proofread the final draft.	**Submit the final draft.**					

set a realistic schedule of deadlines. Think about how much time you might need for each step on the way to your final draft.

One student created a calendar to map out her tasks for a research paper assigned on October 3 and due October 31, keeping in mind that some tasks might overlap or need to be repeated. Notice that she has budgeted more than a week for drafting and revising the paper.

RESEARCH TIP: Think of research as a process. As your topic evolves, you may find new questions arising that require you to create a new search strategy, find additional sources, and challenge your initial assumptions. Keep an open mind throughout the process, be curious, and enjoy the detective work.

Throughout this section, you will encounter examples related to three sample student research papers:

- A paper on Internet surveillance in the workplace, written by a student in an English composition class (see pp. 527–32). The student, Anna Orlov, uses the MLA (Modern Language Association) style of documentation.

- A paper on the limitations of medications to treat childhood obesity, written by a student in a psychology class (see pp. 583–94). The student, Luisa Mirano, uses the APA (American Psychological Association) style of documentation.

- A paper on the extent to which Civil War general Nathan Bedford Forrest can be held responsible for the Fort Pillow massacre, written by a student in a history class. The student, Ned Bishop, uses the *Chicago Manual of Style* documentation system. Bishop's paper and guidelines for *Chicago*-style documentation appear on the *Rules for Writers* Web site (hackerhandbooks.com/rules).

53a Pose questions worth exploring.

Working within the guidelines of your assignment, pose a few questions that seem worth researching — questions that you are interested in exploring, that you feel would engage your audience, and about which there is a substantial debate. On the next page, for example, are some preliminary research questions jotted down by students enrolled in a variety of courses in different disciplines.

- Should the FCC broaden its definition of indecency to include violence?
- Which geological formations are the safest repositories for nuclear waste?
- What was Marcus Garvey's contribution to the fight for racial equality?
- How can governments and zoos help preserve Asia's endangered snow leopard?

As you think about possible questions, make sure that they are appropriate lines of inquiry for a research paper. Choose questions that are narrow (not too broad), challenging (not too bland), and grounded (not too speculative).

Choosing a narrow question

If your initial question is too broad, given the length of the paper you plan to write, look for ways to restrict your focus (see the chart on p. 5). Here, for example, is how two students narrowed their initial questions.

TOO BROAD	NARROWER
What are the hazards of fad diets?	Why are low-carbohydrate diets hazardous?
What are the benefits of stricter auto emissions standards?	How will stricter auto emissions standards create new, more competitive auto industry jobs?

Choosing a challenging question

Your research paper will be more interesting to both you and your audience if you base it on an intellectually challenging line of inquiry. Draft questions that provoke thought or engage readers in a debate.

TOO BLAND	CHALLENGING
What is obsessive-compulsive disorder?	Why is obsessive-compulsive disorder so difficult to treat?
How does DNA testing work?	How reliable is DNA testing?

You may need to address a bland question in the course of answering a more challenging one. For example, if you were writing about promising treatments for obsessive-compulsive disorder, you would no doubt answer the question "What is obsessive-compulsive disorder?" at some point in your paper. It would be a mistake, however, to use the bland question as the focus for the whole paper.

Choosing a grounded question

Finally, you will want to make sure that your research question is grounded, not too speculative. Although speculative questions — such as those that address morality or beliefs — are worth asking and may receive some attention in a research paper, they are inappropriate central questions. For most college courses, the central argument of a research paper should be grounded in facts.

TOO SPECULATIVE	GROUNDED
Is it wrong to share pornographic personal photos by cell phone?	What role should the US government play in regulating mobile content?
Do medical scientists have the right to experiment on animals?	How have technical breakthroughs made medical experiments on animals increasingly unnecessary?

As you write

Take a few minutes to talk through your tentative research question with a classmate or two. Explain what question you plan to research and why this question is worth exploring. Ask your classmates to suggest revisions to your research question to make it narrower, more challenging, or grounded. See the examples on pages 422 and 423.

53b Map out a search strategy.

A search strategy is a systematic plan for tracking down sources. To create a search strategy appropriate for your research question, consult a reference librarian and take a look at your library's Web site, which will give you an overview of available resources.

Including the library in your plan

Reference librarians are information specialists who can save you time by steering you toward relevant and reliable sources. With the help of an expert, you can make the best use of electronic databases, Web search engines, your library's catalog, and other reference tools.

Before you ask a reference librarian for help, be sure you have thought through the following questions:

- What is your assignment?
- In which academic discipline are you writing?
- What is your tentative research question?
- How long will the paper be?
- How much time can you spend on the project?

It's a good idea to bring a copy of the assignment with you.

In addition to speaking with a reference librarian, take some time to explore your library's Web site. You will typically find links to the library's catalog and to a variety of databases and electronic sources. You may also find resources listed by subject, research guides, information about interlibrary loans, and links to Web sites selected by librarians for their quality. Many libraries offer online reference assistance to help you locate information and refine your search strategy.

NOTE FOR ONLINE STUDENTS: Even if you are unable to visit the library, as an enrolled student you can still use its resources. Most libraries offer chat reference services and access to online databases, though you may have to follow special procedures to use them. Check your library's Web site for information for online students.

Starting with your library's databases

You may be tempted to go straight to the Web and ignore your library's resources, but using them early and often in the research process can save you time in the end. Libraries make a wide range of quality materials readily available, and they weed out questionable sources.

While a general Internet search might seem quick and convenient, it is often more time-consuming and can be less reliable than a search in a library's databases. Initial Internet searches may generate thousands of results. Figuring out which of these are credible, relevant, and worth further investigation can require many additional steps:

- Refining search terms (See the chart on refining keyword searches on p. 429.)
- Narrowing the domain to include only .org, .gov, or .edu sites
- Weeding out any advertisements associated with results
- Scanning titles and sometimes content for relevant results
- Combing through sites to determine their currency and relevance as well as the credibility of their authors

Starting with your library's collection of databases can save you time and effort. Because you can limit library database searches to only academic databases, you can count on finding reliable sources. Not all of the results will be worth examining in detail, but many library searches automatically sort them into subject categories that allow you to view narrowed results with just one click.

Choosing an appropriate search strategy

No single search strategy works for every topic. For some topics, it may be appropriate to search for information in popular newspapers, magazines, and Web sites. For others, the best sources might be found in scholarly journals and books and specialized reference works. Still other topics might be enhanced by field research — interviews, surveys, or direct observation.

With the help of a reference librarian, each of the students mentioned on page 421 constructed a search strategy appropriate for his or her research question.

Anna Orlov   Anna Orlov's topic, Internet surveillance in the workplace, was current and influenced by technological changes, so she relied heavily on recent sources, especially those online. To find information on her topic, Orlov decided to

- search her library's general database for articles in magazines, newspapers, and journals
- check the library's catalog for recently published books
- use Web search engines, such as *Google*, to locate articles and government publications that might not show up in a database search

Luisa Mirano Luisa Mirano's topic, the limitations of medications for childhood obesity, is the subject of psychological studies as well as articles in newspapers and magazines aimed at the general public. Thinking that both scholarly and popular works would be appropriate, Mirano decided to

- locate books through the library's online catalog
- check a specialized encyclopedia, *Encyclopedia of Psychology*
- search a specialized database, *PsycINFO*, for scholarly articles
- search the library's general database for popular articles

Ned Bishop Ned Bishop's topic, Nathan Bedford Forrest's role in the Fort Pillow massacre, has been investigated and debated by professional historians. Given the nature of his historical topic, Bishop decided to

- locate books through the library's online catalog
- locate scholarly articles by searching a specialized database, *America: History and Life*
- locate newspaper articles from 1864 by searching the historical archive at the *New York Times* Web site
- search the Web for other historical primary sources

As you write

Before you begin looking for sources, write some notes about your search strategy. Write down your tentative research question. Then answer the following questions: What is the current debate about this topic? In which online or print publications is the debate taking place? Who has written about your research topic? Show your notes to a reference librarian and ask for feedback. Based on the comments you receive, revise your search strategy and clarify your search terms.

53c To locate articles, search a database or consult a print index.

Libraries subscribe to a variety of electronic databases (sometimes called *periodical* or *article databases*) that give students access to articles and other materials without charge. Because many databases are limited to relatively recent works, you may need to consult a print index as well.

What databases offer

Your library has access to databases that can lead you to articles in periodicals such as newspapers, magazines, and scholarly or technical journals. General databases cover several subject areas; subject-specific databases cover one subject area in depth.

Many databases, especially general databases, include the full text of at least some articles; others list only citations or citations with short summaries called *abstracts* (see also p. 442). In the case of full-text articles, you may have the option to print an article, save it, or e-mail it to yourself.

When the full text is not available, a citation usually will give you enough information to track down an article. Your library's Web site will help you determine which articles are available in your library, either in print or in electronic form.

> **Making the most of your handbook**
> Freewriting, listing, and clustering can help you come up with additional search terms.
> ▶ Exploring your subject: 1h

Your library might subscribe to some of the databases listed below and on page 428.

General databases   The information in general databases is not restricted to a specific discipline or subject area. You may find searching a general database helpful in the early stages of your research process.

Academic Search Premier. An interdisciplinary database that indexes thousands of popular and scholarly journals on all subjects.

Expanded Academic ASAP. An interdisciplinary database that indexes the contents of magazines, newspapers, and scholarly journals in all subject areas.

JSTOR. A full-text archive of scholarly journals from many disciplines; unlike most databases, it includes articles published decades ago but does not include articles from the most recent issues of publications.

LexisNexis. A database that is particularly strong in coverage of news, business, legal, and political topics.

ProQuest. A database of periodical articles, many in full text. Through *ProQuest*, your library may subscribe to databases in subjects such as nursing, biology, and psychology.

Subject-specific databases Libraries have access to dozens of specialized databases, each of which covers a specific area of research. To find out what's available, consult your library's Web site or ask your reference librarian. The following are examples of subject-specific databases.

> *ERIC.* A database offering education-related documents and abstracts of articles published in education journals.

> *MLA Bibliography.* A database of literary criticism, with citations to help researchers find articles, books, and dissertations.

> *PsycINFO.* A comprehensive database of psychology research, including abstracts of articles in journals and books.

> *Public Affairs Information Service (PAIS).* A database that indexes books, journals, government documents, statistical directories, and research reports in the social sciences.

> *PubMed.* A database offering millions of abstracts of medical research studies.

How to search a database

To find articles on your topic in a database, start by searching with keywords, terms that describe the information you need. If the first keyword you try results in too few or no matches, experiment with synonyms or ask a librarian for suggestions. For example, if you're searching for sources on a topic related to education, you might also try the terms *teaching, learning,* and *curriculum.* If your keyword search generates too many matches, narrow it by using one of the strategies in the chart on the next page.

For her paper on Internet surveillance in the workplace, Anna Orlov conducted a keyword search in a general database. She typed *"internet use"* and *employee* and *surveillance* (see the database screen on p. 430). This search brought up twenty possible articles, some of which looked promising. Orlov e-mailed several full-text articles to herself and printed citations to other sources so that she could locate them in the library.

Refining keyword searches in databases and search engines

Although command terms and characters vary in electronic databases and Web search engines, some common functions are listed here.

- Use quotation marks around words that are part of a phrase: "gateway drug".

- Use AND to connect any words that must appear in a document: hyperactivity AND children. In some search engines — *Google*, for example — AND is assumed, so typing it is unnecessary. Other search engines require a plus sign instead: hyperactivity + children.

- Use NOT in front of words that must not appear in a document: Persian Gulf NOT war. Some search engines require a minus sign (hyphen) instead: Persian Gulf-war.

- Use OR if only one of the terms must appear in a document: "mountain lion" OR cougar.

- Use an asterisk as a substitute for letters that might vary: "marine biolog*" (to find *marine biology* or *marine biologist*, for example).

- Use parentheses to group a search expression and combine it with another: (standard OR student OR test*) AND reform.

NOTE: Many search engines and databases offer an advanced search option for refining your search with filters for exact phrases that must appear, specific words that should not appear, date restrictions, and so on.

When to use a print index

A print index to periodical articles is a useful tool when you are researching a historical topic, especially from the early to mid-twentieth century. The *Readers' Guide to Periodical Literature* and *Poole's Index to Periodical Literature* index magazine articles beginning around 1900, many of which are too old to appear in electronic databases. You can usually access the print articles themselves in your library's shelves or on microfilm.

DATABASE SCREEN: KEYWORD SEARCH

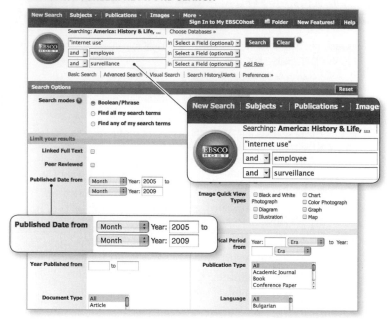

53d To locate books, consult the library's catalog.

The books your library owns, along with other resources, are listed in its catalog. You can search the catalog by author, title, or subject.

If your first search calls up too few results, try different keywords or search for books on broader topics. If your search gives you too many results, use the strategies in the chart on page 429 or try an advanced search tool to combine concepts and limit your results. If those strategies don't work, ask a librarian for suggestions.

When Luisa Mirano, whose topic was childhood obesity, entered the term *obesity* into the library's catalog, she was faced with an unmanageable number of hits. She narrowed her search by adding two more specific terms to *obesity*: *child** (to include the terms *child*, *children*, and *childhood*) and *treatment*. When she still got too many results, she limited the first two terms to subject searches

LIBRARY CATALOG SCREEN 1: ADVANCED SEARCH

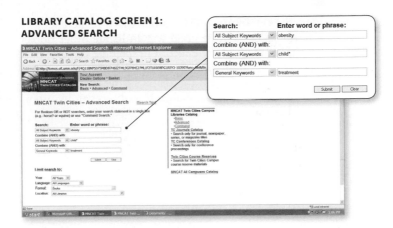

LIBRARY CATALOG SCREEN 2: COMPLETE RECORD FOR A BOOK

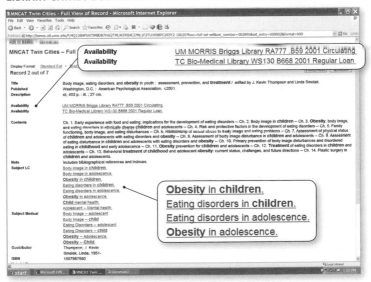

to find books that had obesity in children as their primary subject (see screen 1).

Screen 2 shows the complete record for one of the books she found. The call number, listed beside *Availability*, is the book's address on the library shelf. When you're retrieving a book from the shelf, take the time to scan other books in the area since they are likely to be on the same topic.

res

RESEARCH TIP: The catalog record for a book lists related subject headings. These headings are a good way to locate other books on your subject. For example, the record in screen 2 (p. 431) lists the terms *obesity in children* and *obesity in adolescence* as related subject headings. By clicking on these new terms, Mirano found a few more books on her subject. Subject headings can be useful terms for a database search as well.

53e To locate other sources, use a variety of online tools.

You can find a variety of reliable sources using online tools beyond those offered by your library. For example, most government agencies post information on their Web sites, and federal and state governments use Web sites to communicate with citizens. The sites of many private organizations, such as Doctors without Borders and the Sierra Club, contain useful information about current issues. Museums and libraries often post digital versions of primary sources, such as photographs, political speeches, and classic literary texts.

Although the Web at large can be a rich source of information, some of which can't be found anywhere else, it lacks quality control. The material on many sites has not necessarily been reviewed by experts. So when you're not working with your library's tools to locate online sources, carefully evaluate what you find (see 54e).

This section describes the following Web resources: search engines, directories, digital archives, government and news sites, blogs, and wikis.

Search engines

When using a search engine, such as *Google* or *Yahoo!*, focus your search as narrowly as possible. You can refine your search by using many of the tips in the chart on page 429 or by using the search engine's advanced search form. For her paper on Internet surveillance in the workplace, Anna Orlov had difficulty restricting the number of hits. When she typed the words *internet, surveillance, workplace,* and *privacy* into a search engine, she got more than 80,000 matches. After examining the first page of

SEARCH ENGINE SCREEN: RESULTS OF AN ADVANCED SEARCH

Web Results 1 - 5 of about 9 over the past 3 months for "Internet surveillance" employee "workplace privacy" site:.org (0.44 seconds)

Web Results 1 - 5 of about 9 over the past 3 months for "Internet surveillance" employee "workplace privacy" site:.org (0.44 seconds)

Tip: Try removing quotes from your search to get more results.

EPIC/PI - Privacy & Human Rights 2000
Now the supervision of **employee's** performance, behavior and ... [89] Information and
Privacy Commissioner/Ontario, **Workplace Privacy**: The Need for a..
www.privacyinternational.org/survey/phr2000/threats.html - 131k Cached - Similar pages

Privacy and Human Rights 2003: Threats to Privacy
Other issues that raise **workplace privacy** concerns are employer requirements that
employees complete medical tests, questionnaires, and polygraph tests..
www.privacyinternational.org/survey/phr2003/threats.htm - 279k Cached - Similar pages
[More results from www.privacyinternational.org]

[PDF] Monitoring **Employee** E-Mail And Internet Usage: Avoiding The..
File Format: PDF/Adobe Acrobat -View as HTML
Internet surveillance by employers in the American workplace. At present, US **employees**
in the private workplace have no constitutional, common law or statu
lsr.nellco.org/cgi/viewcontent.cgi?article=1006&context=suffolk/ip -Similar pages

Previous EPIC Top News
The agencies plan to use RFID to track **employees'** movements and in ID cards... For more
information on **workplace privacy**, see the EPIC **Workplace Privacy**
www.epic.org/news/2005.html - 163k Cached - Similar pages

results and viewing some that looked promising, Orlov grouped
her search terms into the phrases "*internet surveillance*" and
"*workplace privacy*" and added the term *employee* to narrow the
focus. The result was 422 matches. To refine her search further,
Orlov clicked on Advanced Search and restricted her search to
sites with URLs ending in *.org* and to those updated in the last
three months. (See the results screen above.)

Directories

If you want to find good resources on topics too broad for a search
engine, try a directory. Unlike search engines, directories are put
together by information specialists who choose reputable sites and
arrange them by topic: education, health, politics, and so on.
    Try the following directories for scholarly research:

Internet Scout Project: http://scout.wisc.edu/Archives
Librarian's Internet Index: http://www.lii.org
Open Directory Project: http://dmoz.org
WWW Virtual Library: http://www.vlib.org

Digital archives

Archives are a good place to find primary sources: the texts of poems, books, speeches, and historically significant documents; photographs; and political cartoons (see p. 443). The materials in these sites are usually limited to official documents and older works because of copyright laws.

American Memory: http://memory.loc.gov

Avalon Project: http://www.yale.edu/lawweb/avalon/ avalon.htm

Eurodocs: http:// eudocs.lib.byu.edu

Google Books: http:// books.google.com

Google Scholar: http://scholar.google.com

The Making of America: http://quod.lib.umich.edu/m/ moagrp

The New York Public Library Digital Collections: http://www .nypl.org/digital

Online Books Page: http://digital.library.upenn.edu/books

Government and news sites

For current topics, both government and news sites can prove useful. Many government agencies at every level provide online information. Government-maintained sites include resources such as legal texts, facts and statistics, government reports, and searchable reference databases. Here are just a few government sites:

Fedstats: http://www.fedstats.gov

GPO Access: http://www.gpoaccess.gov

United Nations: http://www.un.org

University of Michigan Documents Center: http://www .lib.umich.edu/m/moagrp

US Census Bureau: http://www.census.gov

NOTE: You can access a state's Web site by putting the two-letter state abbreviation into a standard URL: http://www.state.ga.us. Substitute any state's two-letter abbreviation for the letters *ga*, which in this case stand for Georgia.

Many news organizations offer up-to-date information on the Web. Some require registration and may charge fees for some articles. (Find out if your library subscribes to news sites so that you can access them at no charge.) The following news sites offer many free resources:

BBC: http://www.bbc.co.uk

Google News: http://news.google.com

Kidon Media-Link: http://www.kidon.com/media-link

New York Times: http://nytimes.com

Reuters: http://www.reuters.com

Blogs

A blog (short for *Weblog*) is a site that contains dated text or multimedia entries usually written and maintained by one person, with comments contributed by readers. Though some blogs are personal diaries and others are devoted to partisan politics, many journalists and academics maintain blogs that cover topics of interest to researchers. Some blogs feature short essays that provide useful insights or analysis; others point to new developments in a particular area of interest. The following Web sites can lead you to a wide range of blogs:

Academic Blog Portal: http://academicblogs.org

Google Blog Search: http://www.google.com/blogsearch

Science Blogs: http://scienceblogs.com

Technorati: http://technorati.com

Wikis

A wiki is a collaborative Web site with many contributors and with content that may change frequently. *Wikipedia*, the collaborative online encyclopedia, is one of the most frequently consulted wikis.

In general, *Wikipedia* may be helpful if you're checking for something that is common knowledge (facts available in multiple sources, such as dates and well-known historical events) or if you're looking for current information about a topic in contemporary culture that isn't covered elsewhere. However, many scholars do not consider *Wikipedia* and wikis in general to be appropriate sources for college research. Authorship is open to anyone, not limited to experts; articles may be written by enthusiastic amateurs who are not well informed. And because the articles can be changed by anyone, controversial texts are often altered to reflect a particular perspective and are especially susceptible to bias. When possible, locate and cite another, more reliable source for any useful information you find in a wiki.

53f Use other search tools.

In addition to articles, books, and online sources, you may want to consult references such as encyclopedias and almanacs. Citations in scholarly works can also lead you to additional sources.

Reference works

The reference section of the library holds both general and specialized encyclopedias, dictionaries, almanacs, atlases, and biographical references, some available in electronic form through the library's Web site. Such works often provide a good overview of your subject and include references to the most significant works on a topic. Check with a reference librarian to see which works are most appropriate for your project.

General reference works General reference works are good places to check facts and get basic information. Here are a few frequently used general references:

American National Biography
National Geographic Atlas of the World
The New Encyclopaedia Britannica
The Oxford English Dictionary
Statistical Abstract of the United States

Although general encyclopedias are often a good place to find background for your topic, you should rarely use them in your final paper. Most instructors expect you to rely on more specialized sources.

Specialized reference works Specialized reference works often explore a topic in depth, usually in the form of articles written by leading authorities. They offer a quick way to gain an expert's overview of a complex topic. Many specialized works are available, including these:

Contemporary Authors
Encyclopedia of Bioethics
Encyclopedia of Crime and Justice

Encyclopedia of Psychology
Encyclopedia of World Environmental History
International Encyclopedia of Communication
New Encyclopedia of Africa

Bibliographies and scholarly citations as shortcuts

Scholarly books and articles list the works the author has cited, usually at the end. These lists are useful shortcuts to additional reliable sources on your topic. For example, most of the scholarly articles Luisa Mirano consulted contained citations to related research studies; through these citations, she quickly located other sources related to her topic, treatments for childhood obesity.

53g Conduct field research, if appropriate.

Your own field research can enhance or be the focus of a writing project. For a composition class, for example, you might want to interview a local politician about a current issue, such as the use of alternative energy sources. For a sociology class, you might decide to conduct a survey regarding campus trends in community service. At work, you might need to learn how food industry executives have responded to reports that their products are contributing to health problems.

NOTE: Colleges and universities often require researchers to submit projects to an institutional review board (IRB) if the research involves human subjects outside of a classroom setting. Before administering a survey or conducting other fieldwork, check with your instructor to see if IRB approval is required.

54   Evaluating sources

You can often locate dozens or even hundreds of potential sources for your topic — far more than you will have time to read. Your challenge will be to determine what kinds of sources you need and to zero in on a reasonable number of quality sources, those truly worth your time and attention.

Later, once you have decided on some sources worth consulting, your challenge will be to read them with an open mind and a critical eye (see 54d).

54a Think about how sources might contribute to your writing.

How you plan to use sources will affect how you evaluate them. Not every source must directly support your thesis; sources can have other functions in a paper. They can

- provide background information or context for your topic
- explain terms or concepts that your readers might not understand
- provide evidence for your argument
- lend authority to your argument
- offer alternative interpretations and counterevidence to your argument

For examples of how student writers use sources for a variety of purposes, see 56c and 61c.

As you write

Read and reread three sources you've selected for a research project. Ask yourself: How will each source function in my research paper? Consult page 438 to understand the various ways to use sources to develop your points. For each of your sources, write a brief note about what role that source will play in your essay. Will it offer background information, an explanation of a key term, a counterpoint, expert testimony, or something else?

54b Select sources worth your time and attention.

Section 53 shows how to refine your searches in databases, in the library's book catalog, and in search engines. This section explains how to scan through the results for the most promising sources and how to preview them to see whether they are likely to live up to your expectations and meet your needs.

Scanning search results

As you scan through a list of search results, watch for clues indicating whether a source might be useful for your purposes or is not worth pursuing. You will need to use somewhat different strategies when scanning search results from a database, a library catalog, and a Web search engine.

Databases Most databases list at least the following information, which can help you decide if a source is relevant, current, scholarly enough (see the chart on p. 441), and a suitable length for your purposes.

> Title and brief description (How relevant?)
>
> Date (How current?)
>
> Name of periodical (How scholarly?)
>
> Length (How extensive in coverage?)

On this page are just a few of the hits Ned Bishop came up with when he consulted a general database for articles on the Fort Pillow massacre, using the search term *Fort Pillow*.

Many databases allow you to sort your list of results by relevance or date; sorting may help you scan the information more efficiently. By scanning the titles in his search results, Bishop saw that only one contained the words *Fort Pillow*. The name of the periodical in which it appeared, *Journal of American History*, suggested that the source was scholarly. The 1989 publication date was not a problem, since currency is not necessarily a criterion for sources in the field of history. The article's

EVALUATING SEARCH RESULTS: LIBRARY DATABASE

☐ Black, blue and gray: the other Civil War; African-American soldiers, sailors and spies were the unsung heroes. *Ebony* Feb 1991 v46 n4 p96(6) Mark View text and retrieval choices	Popular magazine. Not relevant.
☐ The Civil War. (movie reviews) Lewis Cole. *The Nation* Dec 3, 1990 v251 n19 p694(5) Mark View text and retrieval choices	Movie review. Not relevant.
☐ The hard fight was getting into the fight at all. (black soldiers in the Civil War) Jack Fincher. *Smithsonian* Oct 1990 v21 n7 p46(13) Mark View text and retrieval choices	Subject too broad.
☑ The Fort Pillow massacre: a statistical note. John Cimprich, Robert C. Mainfort Jr.. *Journal of American History* Dec 1989 v76 n3 p830(8) Mark View extended citation and retrieval choices	Brief scholarly article. Matches the topic. Promising.

length (eight pages) is given in parentheses at the end of the citation. While the article may seem short, the topic — a statistical note — is narrow enough to ensure adequate depth of coverage. Bishop decided that the article was worth consulting. Because the other sources were irrelevant or too broad, he decided not to consult them.

Library catalogs   A library's catalog usually lists enough basic information about books, periodicals, DVDs, and other material to give you a first impression. A book's title and date of publication, for example, will often be your first clues as to whether the book is worth consulting. If a title looks interesting, you can click on it for further information about the book's subject matter and its length. The table of contents may also be available, offering a glimpse of what's inside. (See also p. 431.)

Web search engines   Because anyone can publish a Web site, legitimate sources and unreliable sources live side-by-side online. As you scan through search results, look for the following clues about the probable relevance, currency, and reliability of a site — but be aware that the clues are by no means foolproof.

The title, keywords, and lead-in text (How relevant?)

A date (How current?)

An indication of the site's sponsor or purpose (How reliable?)

The URL, especially the domain name extension: for example, .com, .edu, .gov, or .org (How relevant? How reliable?)

On the next page are a few of the results that Luisa Mirano retrieved after typing the keywords *childhood obesity* into a search engine; she limited her search to works with those words in the title.

Mirano found the first site, sponsored by a research-based organization, promising enough to explore for her paper. The second and fourth sites held less promise because they seemed to offer popular rather than scholarly information. In addition, the second site was full of distracting commercial advertisements. Mirano rejected the third source not because she doubted its reliability — in fact, research from the National Institutes of Health was what she hoped to find — but because a skim of its contents revealed that the information was too general for her purposes.

EVALUATING SEARCH RESULTS: INTERNET SEARCH ENGINE

American **Obesity** Association - **Childhood Obesity**
Childhood Obesity. **Obesity** in **children** ... Note: The term "**childhood obesity**" may refer
to both **children** and adolescents. In general, we ...
www.**obesity**.org/subs/**childhood**/ - 17k - Jan 8, 2005 - Cached - Similar pages

Content from a research-based organization. Promising.

Childhood Obesity
KS Logo, **Childhood Obesity**. advertisement. Source. ERIC Clearinghouse on Teaching and
Teacher Education. Contents. ... Back to the Top Causes of **Childhood Obesity**. ...
www.kidsource.com/kidsource/content2/**obesity**.html - 18k - Cached - Similar pages

Popular rather than scholarly source. Not relevant.

Childhood Obesity, June 2002 Word on Health - National Institutes ...
Childhood Obesity on the Rise, an article in the June 2002 edition of The NIH Word on
Health - Consumer Information Based on Research from the National ...
www.nih.gov/news/WordonHealth/ jun2002/childhoodobesity.htm - 22k -
Cached - Similar pages

Content too general. Not relevant.

MayoClinic.com - **Childhood obesity**: Parenting advice
... **Childhood obesity**: Parenting advice By Mayo Clinic staff. ... Here are some other tips to
help your **obese child** — and yourself: Be a positive role model. ...
www.mayoclinic.com/invoke.cfm?id=FL00058 - 42k - Jan 8, 2005 - Cached - Similar pages

Popular and too general. Not relevant.

Determining if a source is scholarly

For many college assignments, you will be asked to use scholarly sources. These are written by experts for a knowledgeable audience and usually go into more depth than books and articles written for a general audience. (Scholarly sources are sometimes called *refereed* or *peer-reviewed* because the work is evaluated by experts in the field before publication.) To determine if a source is scholarly, you should look for the following:

- Formal language and presentation
- Authors with academic or scientific credentials
- Footnotes or a bibliography documenting the works cited by the author in the source
- Original research and interpretation rather than a summary of other people's work
- Quotations from and analysis of primary sources (in humanities disciplines such as literature, history, and philosophy)
- A description of research methods or a review of related research (in the sciences and social sciences)

NOTE: In some databases, searches can be limited to refereed or peer-reviewed journals.

54c Select appropriate versions of online sources.

An online source may appear as an abstract, an excerpt, or a full-text article or book. It is important to distinguish among these versions of sources and to use a complete version of a source for your research.

Abstracts and excerpts are shortened versions of complete works. An abstract — a summary of a work's contents — might appear in a database record for a periodical article. An excerpt is the first few sentences or paragraphs of a newspaper or magazine article; it sometimes appears in a list of hits in an online search. Abstracts and excerpts often provide enough information for you to determine whether the complete article would be useful for your paper but generally do not contain enough information to function alone as sources in a research paper. Reading the complete article is the best way to understand the author's argument before referring to it in your own writing. A full-text work may appear online as a PDF (portable document format) file or as an HTML file (sometimes called a *text file*). If your source is available in both formats, choose the PDF file for your research because it will include page numbers for your citations.

54d Read with an open mind and a critical eye.

As you begin reading the sources you have chosen, keep an open mind. Do not let your personal beliefs prevent you from listening to new ideas and opposing viewpoints. Your research question — not a snap judgment about the question — should guide your reading.

When you read critically, you are not necessarily judging an author's work harshly; you are simply examining its assumptions, assessing its evidence, and weighing its conclusions.

NOTE: When you research on the Web, it is easy to ignore views different from your own. Web pages that appeal to you will often link to other pages that support the same viewpoint. If your sources all seem to agree with you — and with one another — try to find sources with opposing views and evaluate them with an open mind.

Distinguishing between primary and secondary sources

As you begin assessing evidence in a source, determine whether you are reading a primary or a secondary source. Primary sources are original documents such as letters, diaries, legislative bills, laboratory studies, field research reports, and eyewitness accounts. Secondary sources are commentaries on primary sources — another writer's opinions about or interpretation of a primary source. A primary source for Ned Bishop was Nathan Bedford Forrest's official report on the battle at Fort Pillow. Bishop also consulted a number of secondary sources, some of which relied heavily on primary sources such as letters.

Although a primary source is not necessarily more reliable than a secondary source, it has the advantage of being a

---

Evaluating all sources

Checking for signs of bias

- Does the author or publisher endorse political or religious views that could affect objectivity?
- Is the author or publisher associated with a special-interest group, such as Greenpeace or the National Rifle Association, that might present only one side of an issue?
- Are alternative views presented and addressed? How fairly does the author treat opposing views? (See 7c.)
- Does the author's language show signs of bias? (See 7b.)

Assessing an argument

- What is the author's central claim or thesis?
- How does the author support this claim — with relevant and sufficient evidence or with just a few anecdotes or emotional examples?
- Are statistics consistent with those you encounter in other sources? Have they been used fairly? (It is possible to "lie" with statistics by using them selectively or by omitting mathematical details.) Does the author explain where the statistics come from?
- Are any of the author's assumptions questionable?
- Does the author consider opposing arguments and refute them persuasively? (See 7c.)
- Does the author fall prey to any logical fallacies? (See 7a.)

firsthand account. Naturally, you can better evaluate what a secondary source says if you have first read any primary sources it discusses.

Being alert for signs of bias

Some sources are more objective than others. Even publications that are considered reputable can be editorially biased. For example, *USA Today*, *National Review*, and *The Economist* are all credible sources, but they are also likely to interpret events quite differently from one another. If you are uncertain about a periodical's special interests, consult *Magazines for Libraries*. To check for bias in a book, see what book reviewers have written about it. A reference librarian can help you locate reviews and assess the credibility of both the book and the reviewers.

Like publishers, some authors are more objective than others. If you have reason to believe that a writer is particularly biased, you will want to assess his or her arguments with special care. For questions to ask about a source's possible bias, see the chart on page 443.

Assessing the author's argument

In nearly all academic writing, there is some element of argument, so don't be surprised to encounter experts who argue opposing sides of the same issue. When you find areas of disagreement, read the arguments of each source with special care, testing them with your own critical intelligence. The questions in the chart on page 443 can help you weigh the strengths and weaknesses of each author's arguments.

> **Making the most of your handbook**
> Good college writers read critically.
> ▸ Judging whether a source is reasonable: 7a
> ▸ Judging whether a source is fair: 7c

54e Assess Web sources with special care.

Web sources can provide valuable information, but verifying their credibility may take time. Before using a Web source in your paper, make sure you know who created the material and for what purpose.

Evaluating Web sources

Authorship

- Does the Web site or document have an author? You may need to do some clicking and scrolling to find the author's name. If you have landed directly on an internal page of a site, for example, you may need to navigate to the home page or find an "about this site" link to learn the name of the author.

- If there is an author, can you tell whether he or she is knowledgeable and credible? When the author's qualifications aren't listed on the site itself, look for links to the author's home page, which may provide evidence of his or her interests and expertise.

Sponsorship

- Who, if anyone, sponsors the site? The sponsor of a site is often named and described on the home page and is sometimes listed alongside the copyright date: © 2010 Plymouth State College.

- What does the URL tell you? The domain name extension often indicates the type of group hosting the site: commercial (.com or .co), educational (.edu), nonprofit (.org), governmental (.gov), military (.mil), or network (.net). URLs may also indicate a country of origin: .uk (United Kingdom) or .jp (Japan), for instance.

Purpose and audience

- Why was the site created: To argue a position? To sell a product? To inform readers?

- Who is the site's intended audience?

Currency

- How current is the site? Check for the date of publication or the latest update, often located at the bottom of the home page or at the beginning or end of an internal page.

- How current are the site's links? If many of the links no longer work, the site may be too dated for your purposes.

EVALUATING A WEB SITE: CHECKING RELIABILITY

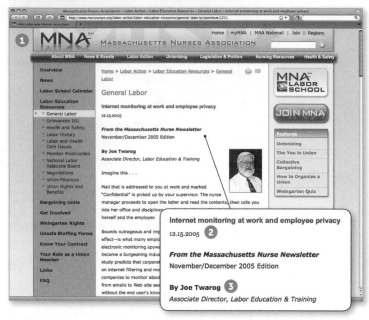

1   This article on Internet monitoring is on a site sponsored by the Massachusetts Nurses Association, a professional health care association and union whose staff and members advocate for nurses in the workplace. The URL ending .org marks this sponsor as a nonprofit organization.
2   Clear dates of publication show currency.
3   The author is a credible expert whose credentials can be verified.

Many sophisticated-looking sites contain questionable information. Even a well-designed hate site may at first appear unbiased and informative. Sites with reliable information, however, can stand up to careful scrutiny. For a checklist on evaluating Web sources, see the chart on page 445.

As you write

Using the guidelines for evaluating Web sources on page 445, evaluate two Web sources that you've selected for your research project. Evaluate the authorship, sponsorship, purpose, audience, and currency for each site. Based on your analysis, are these sources credible? Reliable? Right for your project?

EVALUATING A WEB SITE: CHECKING PURPOSE

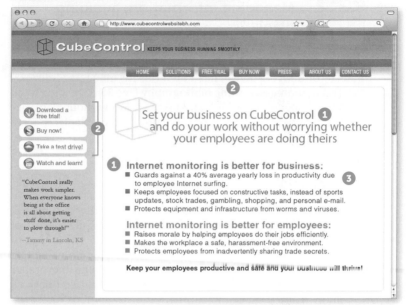

1 The site is sponsored by a company that specializes in software for monitoring employee Internet use.

2 Repeated links for trial downloads and purchase suggest the site's intended audience: consumers seeking to purchase software (probably not researchers seeking detailed information about employees' use of the Internet in the workplace).

3 The site appears to provide information and even shows statistics from studies, but ultimately the purpose of the site is to sell a product.

In researching Internet surveillance and workplace privacy, Anna Orlov encountered sites that raised her suspicions. In particular, some sites were authored by surveillance software companies, which have an obvious interest in focusing on the benefits of such software to company management.

When you know something about the creator of a site and have a sense of a site's purpose, you will be in a good position to evaluate the likely worth of its information. Consider, for example, the two sites pictured on this page and on page 446. Anna Orlov decided that the first Web site would be more useful for her project than sites like the second.

55   Managing information; avoiding plagiarism

Whether you decide to keep records on paper or on your computer — or both — you will need methods for managing information: maintaining a working bibliography (see 55a), keeping track of source materials (see 55b), and taking notes without plagiarizing your sources (see 55c). (For more on avoiding plagiarism, see 56 for MLA style and 62 for APA style.)

55a Maintain a working bibliography.

Keep a record of any sources you decide to consult. This record, called a *working bibliography*, will help you compile the list of sources that will appear at the end of your paper. The format of this list depends on the documentation style you are using (for MLA style, see 59b; for APA style, see 64b). Using the proper style in your working bibliography will ensure that you have all the information you need to correctly cite any sources you use.

Most researchers save bibliographic information from the library's online catalog, its periodical databases, and the Web. The information you need to collect is given in the chart on pages 450–51. If you download a visual, you must gather the same information as for a print source.

For Web sources, some bibliographic information may not be available, but spend time looking for it before assuming that it doesn't exist. When information isn't available on the home page, you may have to drill into the site, following links to interior pages.

Once you have created a working bibliography, you can annotate it. Writing several brief sentences summarizing key points of a source will help you identify how it relates to your argument and to your other sources. You should evaluate the source in your own words and use quotations sparingly. Clarifying the source's ideas at this stage will help you separate them from your own and avoid plagiarizing them later.

MODELS   hackerhandbooks.com/rules
>   Model papers
>>   MLA annotated bibliography: Orlov
>>   APA annotated bibliography: Haddad

SAMPLE ANNOTATED BIBLIOGRAPHY ENTRY (MLA STYLE)

Gonsalves, Chris. "Wasting Away on the Web." *eWeek.com*. Ziff Davis
Enterprise Holdings, 8 Aug. 2005. Web. 16 Feb. 2009.

Summarize
the source.

Annotations
should
be three
to seven
sentences
long.

→ In this editorial, Gonsalves considers the
implications of several surveys, including one
in which 61% of respondents said that their
companies have the right to spy on them. The
author agrees with this majority, claiming that
it's fine if his company chooses to monitor him
as long as the company discloses its monitoring
practices. He argues that "the days of Internet •——
freedom at work are justifiably finished," adding
that he would prefer not to know the extent of
the surveillance. Gonsalves writes for *eWeek.com*,•——
a publication focused on technology products.
He presents himself as an employee who is
comfortable with being monitored, but his job
may be a source of bias. This editorial contradicts •——
some of my other sources, which claim that
employees want to know and should know all the
details of their company's monitoring procedures.

Use quotations
sparingly. Keep
quotation marks
around any
words from the
source.

Evaluate the
source for bias
and relevance.

Interpret the
relationship
between this
source and
others in the
bibliography.

As you write
Develop an annotated bibliography for your research project.
In each annotation, summarize the key points of the source,
evaluate the source for bias and relevance, and comment
briefly about how each source relates to others in your
bibliography.

55b Keep track of source materials.

The best way to keep track of source materials is to save a copy of
each one. Many database subscription services will allow you to
e-mail, save, or print citations or full texts of articles, and you can
easily download, copy, or take screen shots of information from
the Web.

Information for a working bibliography

For an entire book

- All authors; any editors or translators
- Title and subtitle
- Edition (if not the first)
- Publication information: city, publisher, and date

For a periodical article

- All authors of the article
- Title and subtitle of the article
- Title of the magazine, journal, or newspaper
- Date; volume, issue, and page numbers

For a periodical article retrieved from a database (in addition to preceding information)

- Name of the database and an item number, if available
- Name of the subscription service
- URL of the subscription service (for an online database)
- Accession number or other number assigned by the database
- Digital object identifier (DOI), if there is one
- Date you retrieved the source

NOTE: Use care when printing or saving articles in PDF format. These files may not include some of the elements you need to cite the electronic source. You may need to record additional information from the database or Web site where you found the file.

For a Web source (text, visual, or audio)

- All authors, editors, or creators of the source
- Editor or compiler of the Web site, if there is one
- Title and subtitle of the source
- Title of the site
- Publication information for the source, if available
- Page or paragraph numbers, if any
- Date of online publication (or latest update)
- Sponsor of the site
- Date you accessed the source
- The site's URL

NOTE: For the exact bibliographic format to use in your working bibliography and in the final paper, see 59b (MLA) or 64b (APA).

Working with saved files or printouts — as opposed to rely-ing on memory or hastily written notes — lets you highlight key passages and make notes in the margins of the source as you read. You also reduce the chances of unintentional plagiarism, since you will be able to compare your use of a source in your paper with the actual source, not just with your notes (see 55c).

NOTE: It's especially important to keep print or electronic copies of Web sources, which may change or even become inaccessible over time. Make sure that your copy includes the site's URL and your date of access.

TIP: Your school may provide citation software, which allows re-searchers to download references directly from databases, import saved searches, or type in citations. Similarly, many databases format citations with a mouse click, and Web sites offer fill-in-the-blank forms for generating formatted citations. You must proofread these results carefully, however, because the programs sometimes provide incorrect results.

55c As you take notes, avoid unintentional plagiarism.

When you take notes and jot down ideas, be very careful not to use language from your sources unless you clearly identify bor-rowed words and phrases as quotations. Even if you half-copy the author's sentences — either by mixing the author's phrases with your own without using quotation marks or by plugging your synonyms into the author's sentence structure — you are com-mitting plagiarism, a serious academic offense. (For examples of this kind of plagiarism, see 57b and 62b.)

To prevent unintentional borrowing, resist the temptation to look at the source as you take notes — except when you are quot-ing. Keep the source close by so you can check for accuracy, but don't try to put ideas in your own words with the source's sen-tences in front of you. When you need to quote the exact words of a source, make sure you copy the words precisely and put quo-tation marks around them.

TIP: Be especially careful when using copy and paste functions in electronic files. Some researchers have unintentionally plagia-rized their sources because they lost track of which words came from sources and which were their own. To prevent unintentional plagiarism, put quotation marks around any exact language you save from your sources.

Academic English Even in the early stages of note taking, it is important to keep in mind that in the United States written texts are considered an author's property. (This "property" isn't a physical object, so it is often referred to as *intellectual property*.) The author (or publisher) owns the language as well as any original ideas contained in the writing, whether the source is published in print or electronic form. When you use another author's property in your own writing, you are required to follow certain conventions for citing the material, or you risk committing *plagiarism*.

Summarizing, paraphrasing, and quoting are three ways of taking notes. Be sure to include exact page references for all three types of notes since you will need the page numbers later if you use the information in your paper.

Summarizing without plagiarizing

A summary condenses information, perhaps reducing a chapter to a short paragraph or a paragraph to a single sentence. A summary should be written in your own words; if you use phrases from the source, put them in quotation marks.

Here is a passage from a source about mountain lions. Following the passage is the student's summary. (The bibliographic information is recorded in MLA style.)

ORIGINAL SOURCE

In some respects, the increasing frequency of mountain lion encounters in California has as much to do with a growing *human* population as it does with rising mountain lion numbers. The scenic solitude of the western ranges is prime cougar habitat, and it is falling swiftly to the developer's spade. Meanwhile, with their ideal habitat already at its carrying capacity, mountain lions are forcing younger cats into less suitable terrain, including residential areas. Add that cougars have generally grown bolder under a lengthy ban on their being hunted, and an unsettling scenario begins to emerge.

— Rychnovsky, Ray. "Clawing into Controversy."
Outdoor Life Jan. 1995: 38-42. Print. [p. 40]

SUMMARY

Source: Rychnovsky, Ray. "Clawing into Controversy." *Outdoor Life*
    Jan. 1995: 38-42. Print. [p. 40]

Encounters between mountain lions and humans are on the rise in
California because increasing numbers of lions are competing for a
shrinking habitat. As the lions' wild habitat shrinks, older lions force
younger lions into residential areas. These lions have lost some of
their fear of humans because of a ban on hunting (Rychnovsky 40).

Paraphrasing without plagiarizing

Like a summary, a paraphrase is written in your own words; but
whereas a summary reports significant information in fewer
words than the source, a paraphrase retells the information
in roughly the same number of words. If you retain occasional
choice phrases from the source, use quotation marks so that later
you will know which phrases are not your own.

As you read the following paraphrase of the original source
(see p. 452), notice that the language is significantly different
from that in the original.

PARAPHRASE

Source: Rychnovsky, Ray. "Clawing into Controversy." *Outdoor Life*
    Jan. 1995: 38-42. Print. [p. 40]

Californians are encountering mountain lions more frequently
because increasing numbers of humans and a rising population of
lions are competing for the same territory. Humans have moved into
mountainous regions once dominated by the lions, and the wild
habitat that is left cannot sustain the current lion population.
Therefore, the older lions are forcing younger lions into residential
areas. And because of a ban on hunting, these younger lions have
become bolder—less fearful of encounters with humans
(Rychnovsky 40).

Using quotation marks to avoid plagiarizing

A quotation consists of the exact words from a source. In your notes, put all quoted material in quotation marks; do not assume that you will remember later which words, phrases, and passages you have quoted and which are your own. When you quote, be sure to copy the words of your source exactly, including punctuation and capitalization.

QUOTATION

Source: Rychnovsky, Ray. "Clawing into Controversy." *Outdoor Life*
     Jan. 1995: 38-42. Print. [p. 40]

Rychnovsky explains that as humans expand residential areas into
mountain ranges, the cougar's natural habitat "is falling swiftly to
the developer's spade" (40).

Avoiding Internet plagiarism

Understand what plagiarism is. When you use another author's intellectual property — language, visuals, or ideas — in your own writing without giving proper credit, you commit a kind of academic theft called *plagiarism*.

Treat Web sources the same way you treat print sources. Any language that you find on the Internet must be carefully cited, even if the material is in the public domain or is publicly accessible on free sites. When you use material from Web sites sponsored by federal, state, or municipal governments (.gov sites) or by nonprofit organizations (.org sites), you must acknowledge that material, too, as intellectual property owned by those agencies.

Keep track of which words come from sources and which are your own. To prevent unintentional plagiarism when you copy and paste passages from Web sources to an electronic file, put quotation marks around any text that you have inserted into your own work. In addition, during note taking and drafting, you might use highlighting or a different color font to draw attention to text taken from sources — so that material from articles, Web sites, and other sources stands out unmistakably as someone else's words.

Avoid Web sites that bill themselves as "research services" and sell essays. When you use Web search engines to research a topic, you will often see links to sites that appear to offer legitimate writing support but that actually sell college essays. Of course, submitting a paper that you have purchased is cheating, but even using material from such a paper is considered plagiarism.

For details on avoiding plagiarism while working with sources, see 57 (MLA style) and 62 (APA style).

Integrating and citing sources to avoid plagiarism

Source text

> Our language is constantly changing. Like the Mississippi, it keeps forging new channels and abandoning old ones, picking up debris, depositing unwanted silt, and frequently bursting its banks. In every generation, there are people who deplore changes in the language and many who wish to stop the flow. But if our language stopped changing it would mean that American society had ceased to be dynamic, innovative, pulsing with life — that the river had frozen up.
>
> — Robert MacNeil and William Cran,
> *Do You Speak American?*, p. 1

NOTE: The examples in this chart follow MLA style (see 58). For APA style, see 63.

Avoiding plagiarism

If you are using an exact sentence from a source, with no changes . . .	→	. . . put quotation marks around the sentence. Use a signal phrase and include a page number in parentheses.
		MacNeil and Cran write, "Our language is constantly changing" (1).
If you are using a few exact words from the source but not an entire sentence . . .	→	. . . put quotation marks around the exact words that you have used from the source. Use a signal phrase and include a page number in parentheses.
		Some people, according to MacNeil and Cran, "deplore changes in the language" (1).

Integrating and citing sources to avoid plagiarism (continued)

If you are using near-exact words from the source but changing some word forms (*I* to *she*, *walk* to *walked*) or adding words to clarify and make the quotation flow with your own text . . .

→ . . . put quotation marks around the quoted words and put brackets around the changes you have introduced. Use a signal phrase and include a page number in parentheses.

MacNeil and Cran compare the English language to the Mississippi River, which "forg[es] new channels and abandon[s] old ones" (1).

MacNeil and Cran write, "In every generation, there are people who deplore changes in the [English] language and many who wish to stop the flow" (1).

If you are paraphrasing or summarizing the source, using the author's ideas but not any of the author's exact words . . .

→ . . . introduce the ideas with a signal phrase and put the page number at the end of your sentence. Do not use quotation marks. (See 57 and 62.)

MacNeil and Cran argue that changes in the English language are natural and that they represent cultural progress (1).

If you have used the source's sentence structure but substituted a few synonyms for the author's words . . .

→ STOP! This is a form of plagiarism even if you use a signal phrase and a page number. Change your sentence by using one of the techniques given in this chart or in 58 or 63.

PLAGIARIZED

MacNeil and Cran claim that, like a river, English creates new waterways and discards old ones.

INTEGRATED AND CITED CORRECTLY

MacNeil and Cran claim, "Like the Mississippi, [English] keeps forging new channels and abandoning old ones" (1).

Writing Papers in MLA Style

Writing Papers in MLA Style, 457

Writing Papers in MLA Style

Directory to MLA in-text citation models

Directory to MLA works cited models

Directory to MLA works cited models (continued)

Most English instructors and some humanities instructors will ask you to document your sources with the Modern Language Association (MLA) system of citations described in section 59.

When writing an MLA paper that is based on sources, you face three main challenges: (1) supporting a thesis, (2) citing your sources and avoiding plagiarism, and (3) integrating quotations and other source material.

Examples in sections 56–58 are drawn from a student's research related to online monitoring of employees' computer use. Anna Orlov's research paper, which argues that electronic surveillance in the workplace threatens employees' privacy, appears on pages 527–32.

NOTE: For advice on finding and evaluating sources and on managing information in all your college courses, see sections 53–55.

56 Supporting a thesis

Most college research assignments ask you to form a thesis, or main idea, and to support that thesis with well-organized evidence.

56a Form a working thesis.

Once you have read a variety of sources and considered your issue from different perspectives, you are ready to form a working thesis: a one-sentence (or occasionally a two-sentence) statement of your central idea. (See also 1c.) Because it is a working, or tentative, thesis, you can remain flexible and revise it as your ideas develop.

In a research paper, your thesis will answer the central research question that you posed earlier (see 53a). Here, for example, are Anna Orlov's research question and working thesis.

RESEARCH QUESTION

Should employers monitor their employees' online activities in the workplace?

PRACTICE hackerhandbooks.com/rules
> MLA > 56–1 and 56–2

WORKING THESIS

Employers should not monitor their employees' online activities because electronic surveillance can compromise workers' privacy.

After you have written a rough draft and perhaps done more reading, you may decide to revise your thesis, as Orlov did.

REVISED THESIS

Although companies often have legitimate concerns that lead them to monitor employees' Internet usage—from expensive security breaches to reduced productivity—the benefits of electronic surveillance are outweighed by its costs to employees' privacy and autonomy.

The thesis usually appears at the end of the introductory paragraph. To read Anna Orlov's thesis in the context of her introduction, see page 527.

56b Organize ideas with a rough outline.

The body of your paper will consist of evidence in support of your thesis. Instead of getting tangled up in a formal outline early in the process, sketch an informal plan that organizes your ideas in bold strokes. Anna Orlov, for example, used this simple plan to outline the structure of her argument:

- Compared with older types of surveillance, electronic surveillance allows employers to monitor workers more efficiently.

- Some experts argue that companies have important financial and legal reasons to monitor employees' Internet usage.

- But monitoring employees' Internet usage may lower worker productivity when the threat to privacy creates distrust.

- Current laws do little to protect employees' privacy rights, so employees and employers have to negotiate the potential risks and benefits of electronic surveillance.

> **Making the most of your handbook**
> It's helpful to start off with a working thesis and a rough outline—especially when writing from sources.
> ► Draft a working thesis: 1c
> ► Sketch a plan: 1d

After you have written a rough draft, a more formal outline can be a useful way to shape the complexities of your argument. See pages 20–21 for an example.

56c Use sources to inform and support your argument.

Used thoughtfully, the source materials you have gathered will make your argument more complex and convincing for readers. Sources can play several different roles as you develop your points.

Providing background information or context

You can use facts and statistics to support generalizations or to establish the importance of your topic, as student writer Anna Orlov does in her introduction.

> As the Internet has become an integral tool of businesses, company policies on Internet usage have become as common as policies regarding vacation days or sexual harassment. A 2005 study by the American Management Association and ePolicy Institute found that 76% of companies monitor employees' use of the Web, and the number of companies that block employees' access to certain Web sites has increased 27% since 2001 (1).

Explaining terms or concepts

If readers are unlikely to be familiar with a word or an idea important to your topic, you must explain it for them. Quoting or paraphrasing a source can help you define terms and concepts in accessible language.

> One popular monitoring method is keystroke logging, which is done by means of an undetectable program on employees' computers. . . . As Lane explains, these programs record every key entered into the computer in hidden directories that can later be accessed or uploaded by supervisors; the programs can even scan for keywords tailored to individual companies (128-29).

Supporting your claims

As you draft your argument, make sure to back up your assertions with facts, examples, and other evidence from your research. (See also 6e.) Orlov, for example, uses an anecdote from one of her sources to support her claim that limiting computer access causes resentment among a company's staff.

> Monitoring online activities can have the unintended effect of making employees resentful. . . . Kesan warns that "prohibiting personal use can seem extremely arbitrary and can seriously harm morale. . . . Imagine a concerned parent who is prohibited from checking on a sick child by a draconian company policy" (315-16). As this analysis indicates, employees can become disgruntled when Internet usage policies are enforced to their full extent.

Lending authority to your argument

Expert opinion can give weight to your argument. (See also 6e.) But don't rely on experts to make your arguments for you. Construct your argument in your own words and, when appropriate, cite the judgment of an authority in the field to support your position.

> Additionally, many experts disagree with employers' assumption that online monitoring can increase productivity. Employment law attorney Joseph Schmitt argues that, particularly for employees who are paid a salary rather than an hourly wage, "a company shouldn't care whether employees spend one or 10 hours on the Internet as long as they are getting their jobs done—and provided that they are not accessing inappropriate sites" (qtd. in Verespej).

Anticipating and countering objections

Do not ignore sources that seem contrary to your position or that offer arguments different from your own. Instead, use them to give voice to opposing points of view and to state potential objections to your argument before you counter them (see 6f). Readers often have opposing points of view in mind already, whether or not they agree with you. Anna Orlov, for example, cites conflicting evidence to acknowledge that some readers may feel that unlimited Internet access in the workplace hinders productivity. In doing so, she creates an opportunity to counter that objection and persuade those readers.

> On the one hand, computers and Internet access give employees powerful tools to carry out their jobs; on the other hand, the same technology offers constant temptations to avoid work. As a 2005 study by *Salary.com* and *America Online* indicates, the Internet ranked as the top choice among employees for ways of wasting time on the job; it beat talking with co-workers—the second most popular method—by a margin of nearly two to one (Frauenheim).

 Citing sources; avoiding plagiarism

Your research paper is a collaboration between you and your sources. To be fair and ethical, you must acknowledge your debt to the writers of those sources. When you acknowledge your sources, you avoid plagiarism, a serious academic offense.

In general, these three acts are considered plagiarism: (1) failing to cite quotations and borrowed ideas, (2) failing to enclose borrowed language in quotation marks, and (3) failing to put summaries and paraphrases in your own words. Definitions of plagiarism may vary; it's a good idea to find out how your school defines this kind of academic dishonesty.

57a Cite quotations and borrowed ideas.

Sources are cited for two reasons:

1. to tell readers where your information comes from — so that they can assess its reliability and, if interested, find and read the original source
2. to give credit to the writers from whom you have borrowed words and ideas

You must cite anything you borrow from a source, including direct quotations; statistics and other specific facts; visuals such as cartoons, graphs, and diagrams; and any ideas you present in a summary or paraphrase.

The only exception is common knowledge—information your readers could easily find in any number of general sources. For example, most encyclopedias

**Making the most of
your handbook**
When you use exact
language from a source,
you need to show that it
is a quotation.
▶ Quotation marks for
direct quotations: 37a

will tell readers that Alfred Hitchcock directed *Notorious* in 1946 and that Emily Dickinson published only a handful of her many poems during her lifetime.

As a rule, when you have seen information repeatedly in your reading, you don't need to cite it. However, when information has appeared in only one or two sources, when it is highly specific (as with statistics), or when it is controversial, you should cite the source. If a topic is new to you and you are not sure what is considered common knowledge or what is controversial, ask your instructor or someone else with expertise. When in doubt, cite the source.

The Modern Language Association recommends a system of in-text citations. Here, briefly, is how the MLA citation system usually works:

1. The source is introduced by a signal phrase that names its author.

2. The material being cited is followed by a page number in parentheses.

3. At the end of the paper, a list of works cited (arranged alphabetically by authors' last names) gives complete publication information about the source.

IN-TEXT CITATION

Legal scholar Jay Kesan points out that the law holds employers liable for employees' actions such as violations of copyright laws, the distribution of offensive or graphic sexual material, and illegal disclosure of confidential information (312).

ENTRY IN THE LIST OF WORKS CITED

Kesan, Jay P. "Cyber-Working or Cyber-Shirking? A First Principles Examination of Electronic Privacy in the Workplace." *Florida Law Review* 54.2 (2002): 289-332. Print.

This basic MLA format varies for different types of sources. For a detailed discussion of other models, see 59.

57b Enclose borrowed language in quotation marks.

To indicate that you are using a source's exact phrases or sentences, you must enclose them in quotation marks unless they have been set off from the text by indenting (see p. 471). To omit the quotation marks is to claim — falsely — that the language is your own. Such an omission is plagiarism even if you have cited the source.

ORIGINAL SOURCE

Without adequate discipline, the World Wide Web can be a tremendous time sink; no other medium comes close to matching the Internet's depth of materials, interactivity, and sheer distractive potential.   — Frederick Lane, *The Naked Employee*, p. 142

PLAGIARISM

Frederick Lane points out that if people do not have adequate discipline, the World Wide Web can be a tremendous time sink; no other medium comes close to matching the Internet's depth of materials, interactivity, and sheer distractive potential (142).

BORROWED LANGUAGE IN QUOTATION MARKS

Frederick Lane points out that for those not exercising self-control, "the World Wide Web can be a tremendous time sink; no other medium comes close to matching the Internet's depth of materials, interactivity, and sheer distractive potential" (142).

57c Put summaries and paraphrases in your own words.

A summary condenses information from a source; a paraphrase conveys the information using roughly the same number of words as the original source. When you summarize or paraphrase, it is not enough to name the source; you must restate the source's meaning using your own language. (See also 55c.) You commit plagiarism if you half-copy the author's sentences — either by mixing the author's phrases with your own without using quotation marks or by plugging your synonyms into the author's sentence structure.

The first paraphrase of the following source is plagiarized — even though the source is cited — because too much of its language is borrowed from the original. The highlighted strings of words have been copied exactly (without quotation marks). In addition, the writer has closely echoed the sentence structure of the source, merely substituting some synonyms (*restricted* for *limited*, *modern era* for *computer age*, *monitoring* for *surveillance*, and *inexpensive* for *cheap*).

ORIGINAL SOURCE

In earlier times, surveillance was limited to the information that a supervisor could observe and record firsthand and to primitive counting devices. In the computer age surveillance can be instantaneous, unblinking, cheap, and, maybe most importantly, easy.

> — Carl Botan and Mihaela Vorvoreanu, "What Do Employees Think about Electronic Surveillance at Work?," p. 126

PLAGIARISM: UNACCEPTABLE BORROWING

Scholars Carl Botan and Mihaela Vorvoreanu argue that in earlier times monitoring of employees was restricted to the information that a supervisor could observe and record firsthand. In the modern era, monitoring can be instantaneous, inexpensive, and, most importantly, easy (126).

To avoid plagiarizing an author's language, resist the temptation to look at the source while you are summarizing or paraphrasing. After you have read the original passage, set the source aside. Ask yourself, "What is the author's meaning?" In your own words, state the author's basic point. Return to the source and check that you haven't used the author's language or sentence structure or misrepresented the author's ideas. When you fully understand another writer's meaning, you can more easily and accurately present those ideas in your own words.

ACCEPTABLE PARAPHRASE

Scholars Carl Botan and Mihaela Vorvoreanu claim that the nature of workplace surveillance has changed over time. Before the arrival of computers, managers could collect only small amounts of information about their employees based on what they saw or heard. Now, because computers are standard workplace technology, employers can monitor employees efficiently (126).

Revising with comments

Your words?

UNDERSTANDING THE COMMENT

When a teacher or tutor asks "Your words?" the comment often signals that it's unclear whether certain words you've used are your own or those of your sources.

> Internet technology has made it possible for extremist groups to recruit and train members and carry out terrorist activity. The membership of these groups reaches beyond local geographic areas because of the Web. The world has become a cacophony of parochialisms where individuals seek association with coreligionists in a mystique of participation. Combating the influences of these groups is now harder than ever.

Your words?

One student wrote this body paragraph in a research paper on the Internet's role in facilitating terrorism.

Part of this paragraph doesn't sound like the student's voice. To revise, the student must determine which words are his own and which come from sources he consulted. If he chooses to include words or ideas from a source, he'll need to decide if he wants to quote, summarize, or paraphrase the source. He'll also need to properly cite the source in his paper.

SIMILAR COMMENTS: source? • quotation? • who's talking here?

REVISING WHEN _YOUR_ READERS WONDER WHOSE WORDS THEY'RE READING

1. *Reread your sentences* to see if you have clearly marked the boundaries between your source material and your own words. Is every word your own? Or have you borrowed words from sources without properly acknowledging them?

2. *Use signal phrases* to introduce each source and provide context. Doing so prepares readers for a source's words.

3. *Use quotation marks* to enclose language that you borrow word-for-word from a source, and follow each quotation with a parenthetical citation.

4. *Put summaries and paraphrases in your own words* and always cite your sources.

More advice on citing quotations, paraphrases, and summaries:
57, 58 (MLA) and 62, 63 (APA)

58   Integrating sources

Quotations, summaries, paraphrases, and facts will help you develop your argument, but they cannot speak for you. You can use several strategies to integrate information from research sources into your paper while maintaining your own voice.

58a   Use quotations appropriately.

In your academic writing, keep the emphasis on your ideas and your language; use your own words to summarize and to paraphrase your sources and to explain your points. Sometimes, however, quotations can be the most effective way to integrate a source's ideas.

Limiting your use of quotations

Although it is tempting to insert many quotations in your paper and to use your own words only for connecting passages, do not quote excessively. It is almost impossible to integrate numerous quotations smoothly into your own text.

WHEN TO USE QUOTATIONS

- When language is especially vivid or expressive
- When exact wording is needed for technical accuracy
- When it is important to let the debaters of an issue explain their positions in their own words
- When the words of an authority lend weight to an argument
- When the language of a source is the topic of your discussion (as in an analysis or interpretation)

It is not always necessary to quote full sentences from a source. To reduce your reliance on the words of others, you can often integrate language from a source into your own sentence structure.

> Kizza and Ssanyu observe that technology in the workplace has been accompanied by "an array of problems that needed quick answers," such as electronic monitoring to prevent security breaches (4).

Using the ellipsis mark and brackets

Two useful marks of punctuation, the ellipsis mark and brackets, allow you to keep quoted material to a minimum and to integrate it smoothly into your text.

The ellipsis mark To condense a quoted passage, you can use the ellipsis mark (three periods, with spaces between) to indicate that you have left words out. What remains must be grammatically complete.

> Lane acknowledges the legitimate reasons that many companies have for monitoring their employees' online activities, particularly management's concern about preventing "the theft of information that can be downloaded to a . . . disk, e-mailed to oneself . . . , or even posted to a Web page for the entire world to see" (12).

The writer has omitted from the source the words *floppy or Zip* before *disk* and *or a confederate* after *oneself.*

On the rare occasions when you want to leave out one or more full sentences, use a period before the three ellipsis dots.

> Charles Lewis, director of the Center for Public Integrity, points out that "by 1987, employers were administering nearly 2,000,000 polygraph tests a year to job applicants and employees. . . . Millions of workers were required to produce urine samples under observation for drug testing . . ." (22).

Ordinarily, do not use an ellipsis mark at the beginning or at the end of a quotation. Your readers will understand that the quoted material is taken from a longer passage, so such marks are not necessary. The only exception occurs when you have dropped words at the end of the final quoted sentence. In such cases, put three ellipsis dots before the closing quotation mark and parenthetical reference, as in the previous example.

Make sure omissions and ellipsis marks do not distort the meaning of your source.

Brackets Brackets allow you to insert your own words into quoted material. You can insert words in brackets to clarify a confusing reference or to keep a sentence grammatical in your context. You also use brackets to indicate that you are changing a letter from capital to lowercase (or vice versa) to fit into your sentence.

Legal scholar Jay Kesan notes that "[a] decade ago, losses [from employees' computer crimes] were already mounting to five billion dollars annually" (311).

This quotation began *A decade ago* . . . in the source, so the writer indicated the change to lowercase with brackets and inserted words in brackets to clarify the meaning of *losses*.

To indicate an error such as a misspelling in a quotation, insert the word "sic" in brackets right after the error.

Johnson argues that "while online monitoring is often imagined as harmles [sic], the practice may well threaten employees' rights to privacy" (14).

Setting off long quotations

When you quote more than four typed lines of prose or more than three lines of poetry, set off the quotation by indenting it one inch from the left margin.

Long quotations should be introduced by an informative sentence, usually followed by a colon. Quotation marks are unnecessary because the indented format tells readers that the passage is taken word-for-word from the source.

Botan and Vorvoreanu examine the role of gender in company practices of electronic surveillance:

There has never been accurate documentation of the extent of gender differences in surveillance, but by the middle 1990s, estimates of the proportion of surveilled employees that were women ranged from 75% to 85%. . . . Ironically, this gender imbalance in workplace surveillance may be evening out today because advances in surveillance technology are making surveillance of traditionally male dominated fields, such as long-distance truck driving, cheap, easy, and frequently unobtrusive. (127)

Notice that at the end of an indented quotation the parenthetical citation goes outside the final mark of punctuation. (When a quotation is run into your text, the opposite is true. See the sample citations on p. 470.)

Revising with comments

Cite your sources

UNDERSTANDING THE COMMENT

When a teacher or tutor responds "Cite your sources," the comment often signals that you need to acknowledge and properly credit the contributions of others.

> At the story's end, Edna Pontellier is described as a "naked . . . new-born creature" who, in the act of ending her own life, is experiencing a kind of re-birth.
>
> *Cite your sources*

One student wrote this sentence in an essay interpreting Kate Chopin's novel *The Awakening*.

The student has borrowed language from both a primary source and a secondary source without proper citation. To revise, she needs to consult her notes or return to the novel to locate the exact page number for the quotation she uses. In addition, she needs to include quotation marks around the words "a kind of re-birth," which come from a secondary source, and to provide a parenthetical citation.

SIMILAR COMMENTS: *cite this* • *documentation* • *source?*

REVISING WHEN *YOU* NEED TO CITE YOUR SOURCES

1. *Reread your sentence and ask questions.* Have you properly acknowledged all the contributions — words, ideas, or facts — that you use as evidence? Have you given credit to the sources you quote, summarize, or paraphrase? Have you made it clear to readers how to locate the source if they want to consult it?

2. *Ask your instructor* which documentation style you are required to use — MLA, APA, or *Chicago*.

3. *Read your notes* or check the source itself to find the exact words. Make sure you have the author's name, the title, the date of publication, and the page number for each source you cite.

4. *Revise* by including an in-text citation for any words, ideas, or facts that you used as evidence — and by including quotation marks around any language borrowed word-for-word from a source.

More on citing sources: 59 (MLA) and 64 (APA)

58b Use signal phrases to integrate sources.

Whenever you include a paraphrase, summary, or direct quotation of another writer in your paper, prepare your readers for it with introductory words called a *signal phrase*. A signal phrase usually names the author of the source and often provides some context. It commonly appears before the source material. To vary your sentence structure, you may decide to interrupt source material with a signal phrase or place the signal phrase after your paraphrase, summary, or quotation.

When you write a signal phrase, choose a verb that is appropriate for the way you are using the source (see 56c). Are you providing background, explaining a concept, supporting a claim, lending authority, or refuting a belief? See the chart on this page for a list of verbs commonly used in signal phrases.

Using signal phrases in MLA papers

To avoid monotony, try to vary both the language and the placement of your signal phrases.

Model signal phrases

In the words of researchers Greenfield and Davis, ". . ."

As legal scholar Jay Kesan has noted, ". . ."

The ePolicy Institute, an organization that advises companies about reducing risks from technology, reports that ". . ."

". . . ," writes Daniel Tynan, ". . ."

". . . ," attorney Schmitt claims.

Kizza and Ssanyu offer a persuasive counterargument: ". . ."

Verbs in signal phrases

acknowledges	comments	endorses	reasons
adds	compares	grants	refutes
admits	confirms	illustrates	rejects
agrees	contends	implies	reports
argues	declares	insists	responds
asserts	denies	notes	suggests
believes	disputes	observes	thinks
claims	emphasizes	points out	writes

NOTE: MLA style calls for verbs in the present or present perfect tense (*argues, has argued*) to introduce source material unless you include a date that specifies the time of the original author's writing.

Marking boundaries

Readers need to move from your words to the words of a source without feeling a jolt. Avoid dropping quotations into the text without warning. Instead, provide clear signal phrases, including at least the author's name, to indicate the boundary between your words and the source's words. (The signal phrase is highlighted in the second example.)

DROPPED QUOTATION

Some experts have argued that a range of legitimate concerns justifies employer monitoring of employee Internet usage. "Employees could accidentally (or deliberately) spill confidential corporate information . . . or allow worms to spread throughout a corporate network" (Tynan).

QUOTATION WITH SIGNAL PHRASE

Some experts have argued that a range of legitimate concerns justifies employer monitoring of employee Internet usage. As *PC World* columnist Daniel Tynan points out, "Employees could accidentally (or deliberately) spill confidential corporate information . . . or allow worms to spread throughout a corporate network."

NOTE: Because this quotation is from an unpaginated Web source, no page number appears in parentheses after the quotation. See item 4 on page 482.

Establishing authority

Good research writing uses evidence from reliable sources. The first time you mention a source, include in the signal phrase the author's title, credentials, or experience — anything that would help your readers recognize the source's authority. (Signal phrases are highlighted in the next two examples.)

SOURCE WITH NO CREDENTIALS

Jay Kesan points out that the law holds employers liable for employees' actions such as violations of copyright laws, the distribution of offensive or graphic sexual material, and illegal disclosure of confidential information (312).

SOURCE WITH CREDENTIALS

Legal scholar Jay Kesan points out that the law holds employers liable for employees' actions such as violations of copyright laws, the distribution of offensive or graphic sexual material, and illegal disclosure of confidential information (312).

When you establish your source's authority, as with the phrase *Legal scholar* in the previous example, you also signal to readers your own credibility as a responsible researcher who has located reliable sources.

Introducing summaries and paraphrases

Introduce most summaries and paraphrases with a signal phrase that names the author and places the material in the context of your argument. (See also 58c and 60b.) Readers will then understand that everything between the signal phrase and the parenthetical citation summarizes or paraphrases the cited source.

Without the signal phrase (highlighted) in the following example, readers might think that only the quotation at the end is being cited, when in fact the whole paragraph is based on the source.

Frederick Lane believes that the personal computer has posed new challenges for employers worried about workplace productivity. Whereas early desktop computers were primitive enough to prevent employees from using them to waste time, the machines have become so sophisticated that they now make non-work-related computer activities easy and inviting. Many employees spend considerable company time customizing features and playing games on their computers. But perhaps most problematic from the employer's point of view, Lane asserts, is giving employees access to the Internet, "roughly the equivalent of installing a gazillion-channel television set for each employee" (15-16).

There are times when a summary or a paraphrase does not require a signal phrase. When the context makes clear where the cited material begins, you may omit the signal phrase and include the author's last name in parentheses.

Using signal phrases with statistics and other facts

When you are citing a statistic or another specific fact, a signal phrase is often not necessary. In most cases, readers will understand that the citation refers to the statistic or fact (not the whole paragraph).

Roughly 60% of responding companies reported disciplining employees who had used the Internet in ways the companies deemed inappropriate; 30% had fired their employees for those transgressions (Greenfield and Davis 347).

There is nothing wrong, however, with using a signal phrase to introduce a statistic or fact.

Putting source material in context

Readers should not have to guess why source material appears in your paper. A signal phrase can help you make the connection between your own ideas and those of another writer by clarifying how the source will contribute to your paper (see 54a).

If you use another writer's words, you must explain how they relate to your point. It's a good idea to embed a quotation between sentences of your own. In addition to introducing it with a signal phrase, follow it with interpretive comments that link the quotation to your paper's argument (see also 58c).

QUOTATION WITH EFFECTIVE CONTEXT

The difference, Lane argues, between old methods of data gathering and electronic surveillance involves quantity:

> Technology makes it possible for employers to gather enormous amounts of data about employees, often far beyond what is necessary to satisfy safety or productivity

concerns. And the trends that drive technology—faster, smaller, cheaper—make it possible for larger and larger numbers of employers to gather ever-greater amounts of personal data. (3-4)

In an age when employers can collect data whenever employees use their computers—when they send e-mail, surf the Web, or even arrive at or depart from their workstations—the challenge for both employers and employees is to determine how much is too much.

58c Synthesize sources.

When you synthesize multiple sources in a research paper, you create a conversation about your research topic. You show readers how the ideas of one source relate to those of another by connecting and analyzing the ideas in the context of your argument. Keep the emphasis on your own writing. The thread of your argument should be easy to identify and to understand, with or without your sources.

SAMPLE SYNTHESIS (DRAFT)

Student writer Anna Orlov begins with a claim that needs support. ⟶

Productivity is not easily measured in the wired workplace. As a result, employers find it difficult to determine how much freedom to allow their employees. On the one hand, computers and Internet access give employees powerful tools to carry out their jobs; on the other hand, the same technology offers constant temptations to avoid work. As a 2005 study by *Salary.com* and *America*

Student writer

Signal phrases indicate how sources contribute to Orlov's paper and show that the ideas that follow ⟶ are not her own.

Online indicates, the Internet ranked as the top choice among employees for ways of wasting time on the job (Frauenheim). Chris Gonsalves, an editor for *eWeek.com*, argues that technology has changed the terms between employers and

Source 1

Source 2

employees: "While bosses can easily detect

and interrupt water-cooler chatter," he writes,

"the employee who is shopping at Lands' End or

IMing with fellow fantasy baseball managers may

actually appear to be working." The gap between

observable behaviors and actual online activities

has motivated some employers to invest in

surveillance programs.

| Source 2

| Student
| writer

Orlov presents a counterposition to extend her argument. → Many experts, however, disagree with

employers' assumption that online monitoring can

increase productivity. Employment law attorney

Joseph Schmitt argues that, particularly for

salaried employees, "a company shouldn't care

whether employees spend one or 10 hours on the

Internet as long as they are getting their jobs

done—and provided that they are not accessing

inappropriate sites" (qtd. in Verespej). Other

experts even argue that time spent on personal

Internet browsing can actually be productive

for companies. According to Bill Coleman, an

executive at *Salary.com,* "Personal Internet use

and casual office conversations often turn into

new business ideas or suggestions for gaining

operating efficiencies" (qtd. in Frauenheim).

Employers, in other words, may benefit from

showing more faith in their employees' ability to

exercise their autonomy.

| Source 3

| Student
| writer

| Source 4

| Student
| writer

Orlov builds her case—each quoted passage offers a more detailed claim — or example in support of her larger claim.

In this draft, Orlov uses her own analyses to shape the conversation among her sources. She does not simply string quotations together or allow her sources to overwhelm her writing. The final sentence, written in her own voice, gives her an opportunity to explain to readers how the various sources support her argument.

When synthesizing sources, ask yourself the following questions:

- Which sources inform, support, or extend your argument?
- Have you varied the function of sources — to provide background, to explain concepts, to lend authority, and to anticipate counterarguments? Do you use signal phrases to indicate these functions?
- Do you explain how your sources support your argument?
- Do you connect and analyze sources in your own voice?
- Is your own argument easy to identify and to understand, with or without your sources?

59 Documenting sources in MLA style

In English and other humanities classes, you may be asked to use the MLA (Modern Language Association) system for documenting sources, which is set forth in the *MLA Handbook for Writers of Research Papers*, 7th ed. (New York: MLA, 2009).

MLA recommends in-text citations that refer readers to a list of works cited. A typical in-text citation names the author of the source, often in a signal phrase, and gives a page number in parentheses. At the end of the paper, a list of works cited provides publication information about the source; the list is alphabetized by authors' last names (or by titles for works without authors). There is a direct connection between the in-text citation and the alphabetized listing. In the following example, that connection is highlighted in blue.

IN-TEXT CITATION

Jay Kesan notes that even though many companies now routinely monitor employees through electronic means, "there may exist less intrusive safeguards for employers" (293).

ENTRY IN THE LIST OF WORKS CITED

Kesan, Jay P. "Cyber-Working or Cyber-Shirking? A First Principles Examination of Electronic Privacy in the Workplace." *Florida Law Review* 54.2 (2002): 289-332. Print.

For a list of works cited that includes this entry, see page 532.

59a MLA in-text citations

MLA in-text citations are made with a combination of signal phrases and parenthetical references. A signal phrase introduces information taken from a source (a quotation, summary, paraphrase, or fact); usually the signal phrase includes the author's name. The parenthetical reference comes after the cited material, often at the end of the sentence. It includes at least a page number (except for unpaginated sources, such as those found online). In the models in 59a, the elements of the in-text citation are highlighted in blue.

IN-TEXT CITATION

Kwon points out that the Fourth Amendment does not give employees any protections from employers' "unreasonable searches and seizures" (6).

Readers can look up the author's last name in the alphabetized list of works cited, where they will learn the work's title and other publication information. If readers decide to consult the source, the page number will take them straight to the passage that has been cited.

Basic rules for print and online sources

The MLA system of in-text citations, which depends heavily on authors' names and page numbers, was created with print sources in mind. Although many online sources have unclear authorship and lack page numbers, the basic rules are the same for both print and online sources.

The models in this section (items 1–5) show how the MLA system usually works and explain what to do if your source has no author or page numbers.

■ **1. Author named in a signal phrase** Ordinarily, introduce the material being cited with a signal phrase that includes the author's name. In addition to preparing readers for the source, the signal phrase allows you to keep the parenthetical citation brief.

Frederick Lane reports that employers do not necessarily have
to use software to monitor how their employees use the Web:
employers can "use a hidden video camera pointed at an employee's
monitor" and even position a camera "so that a number of monitors
[can] be viewed at the same time" (147).

The signal phrase — *Frederick Lane reports* — names the author;
the parenthetical citation gives the page number of the book in
which the quoted words may be found.

Notice that the period follows the parenthetical citation.
When a quotation ends with a question mark or an exclamation
point, leave the end punctuation inside the quotation mark and
add a period at the end of your sentence. (See also the note on
p. 329.)

O'Connor asks a critical question: "When does Internet surveillance
cross the line between corporate responsibility and invasion of
privacy?" (16).

2. Author named in parentheses If a signal phrase does not
name the author, put the author's last name in parentheses along with
the page number. Use no punctuation between the name and the
page number.

Companies can monitor employees' every keystroke without legal
penalty, but they may have to combat low morale as a result
(Lane 129).

3. Author unknown Either use the complete title in a signal
phrase or use a short form of the title in parentheses. Titles of
books are italicized; titles of articles are put in quotation marks.

A popular keystroke logging program operates invisibly on workers'
computers yet provides supervisors with details of the workers'
online activities ("Automatically").

TIP: Before assuming that a Web source has no author, do some
detective work. Often the author's name is available but is not
easy to find. For example, it may appear at the end of the page, in
tiny print. Or it may appear on another page of the site, such as
the home page.

NOTE: If a source has no author and is sponsored by a corporation or government agency, name the corporation or agency as the author (see items 8 and 17 on pp. 483 and 486, respectively).

■ **4. Page number unknown** Do not include the page number if a work lacks page numbers, as is the case with many Web sources. Even if a printout from a Web site shows page numbers, treat the source as unpaginated in the in-text citation because not all printouts give the same page numbers. (When the pages of a Web source are stable, as in PDF files, supply a page number in your in-text citation.)

> As a 2005 study by *Salary.com* and *America Online* indicates, the
> Internet ranked as the top choice among employees for ways of
> wasting time on the job; it beat talking with co-workers—the
> second most popular method—by a margin of nearly two to one
> (Frauenheim).

If a source has numbered paragraphs or sections, use "par." (or "pars.") or "sec." (or "secs.") in the parentheses: (Smith, par. 4). Notice that a comma follows the author's name.

■ **5. One-page source** If the source is one page long, MLA allows (but does not require) you to omit the page number. Even so, it's a good idea to supply the page number because without it readers may not know where your citation ends or, worse, may not realize that you have provided a citation at all.

NO PAGE NUMBER IN CITATION

> Anush Yegyazarian reports that in 2000 the National Labor
> Relations Board's Office of the General Counsel helped win
> restitution for two workers who had been dismissed because
> their employers were displeased by the employees' e-mails
> about work-related issues. The case points to the ongoing
> struggle to define what constitutes protected speech in the
> workplace.

PAGE NUMBER IN CITATION

> Anush Yegyazarian reports that in 2000 the National Labor
> Relations Board's Office of the General Counsel helped win

restitution for two workers who had been dismissed because their employers were displeased by the employees' e-mails about work-related issues (62). The case points to the ongoing struggle to define what constitutes protected speech in the workplace.

Variations on the basic rules

This section describes the MLA guidelines for handling a variety of situations not covered by the basic rules in items 1–5. These rules for in-text citations are the same for both print and online sources.

■ **6. Two or three authors** Name the authors in a signal phrase, as in the following example, or include their last names in the parenthetical reference: (Kizza and Ssanyu 2).

> Kizza and Ssanyu note that "employee monitoring is a dependable, capable, and very affordable process of electronically or otherwise recording all employee activities at work" and elsewhere (2).

When three authors are named in the parentheses, separate the names with commas: (Alton, Davies, and Rice 56).

■ **7. Four or more authors** Name all of the authors or include only the first author's name followed by "et al." (Latin for "and others"). The format you use should match the format in your works cited entry (see item 3 on p. 492).

> The study was extended for two years, and only after results were reviewed by an independent panel did the researchers publish their findings (Blaine et al. 35).

■ **8. Organization as author** When the author is a corporation or an organization, name that author either in the signal phrase or in the parentheses. (For a government agency as author, see item 17 on p. 486.)

> According to a 2001 survey of human resources managers by the American Management Association, more than three-quarters of the responding companies reported disciplining employees for "misuse or personal use of office telecommunications equipment" (2).

In the list of works cited, the American Management Association is treated as the author and alphabetized under *A*. When you give the organization name in parentheses, abbreviate common words in the name: "Assn.," "Dept.," "Natl.," "Soc.," and so on.

> In a 2001 survey of human resources managers, more than three-quarters of the responding companies reported disciplining employees for "misuse or personal use of office telecommunications equipment" (Amer. Management Assn. 2).

● **9. Authors with the same last name** If your list of works cited includes works by two or more authors with the same last name, include the author's first name in the signal phrase or first initial in the parentheses.

> Estimates of the frequency with which employers monitor employees' use of the Internet each day vary widely (A. Jones 15).

● **10. Two or more works by the same author** Mention the title of the work in the signal phrase or include a short version of the title in the parentheses.

> The American Management Association and ePolicy Institute have tracked employers' practices in monitoring employees' e-mail use. The groups' 2003 survey found that one-third of companies had a policy of keeping and reviewing employees' e-mail messages ("2003 E-mail" 2); in 2005, more than 55% of companies engaged in e-mail monitoring ("2005 Electronic" 1).

Titles of articles and other short works are placed in quotation marks; titles of books are italicized.

In the rare case when both the author's name and a short title must be given in parentheses, separate them with a comma.

> A 2004 survey found that 20% of employers responding had employees' e-mail "subpoenaed in the course of a lawsuit or regulatory investigation," up 7% from the previous year (Amer. Management Assn. and ePolicy Inst., "2004 Workplace" 1).

■ **11. Two or more works in one citation** To cite more than one source in the parentheses, give the citations in alphabetical order and separate them with a semicolon.

> Several researchers have analyzed the reasons that companies
> monitor employees' use of the Internet at work (Botan and
> Vorvoreanu 128-29; Kesan 317-19; Kizza and Ssanyu 3-7).

Multiple citations can be distracting, so you should not overuse the technique. If you want to point to several sources that discuss a particular topic, consider using an information note instead (see 59c).

■ **12. Repeated citations from the same source** When your paper is about a single work of fiction or nonfiction (such as an essay), you do not need to include the author's name each time you quote from or paraphrase the work. After you mention the author's name at the beginning of your paper, you may include just the page numbers in your parenthetical citations.

> In Susan Glaspell's short story "A Jury of Her Peers," two
> women accompany their husbands and a county attorney to an
> isolated house where a farmer named John Wright has been choked
> to death in his bed with a rope. The chief suspect is Wright's wife,
> Minnie, who is in jail awaiting trial. The sheriff's wife, Mrs. Peters,
> has come along to gather some personal items for Minnie, and
> Mrs. Hale has joined her. Early in the story, Mrs. Hale sympathizes
> with Minnie and objects to the way the male investigators are
> "snoopin' round and criticizin'" her kitchen (191). In contrast, Mrs.
> Peters shows respect for the law, saying that the men are doing "no
> more than their duty" (191).

In a paper with multiple sources, if you are citing a source more than once in a paragraph, you may omit the author's name after the first mention in the paragraph as long as it is clear that you are still referring to the same source.

■ **13. Encyclopedia or dictionary entry** Unless an entry in an encyclopedia or a dictionary has an author, the source will be alphabetized in the list of works cited under the word or entry that you consulted (see item 27 on p. 501). Either in your text or in your parenthetical citation, mention the word or entry. No page number is required, since readers can easily look up the word or entry.

> The word *crocodile* has a surprisingly complex etymology ("Crocodile").

■ **14. Multivolume work**   If your paper cites more than one volume of a multivolume work, indicate in the parentheses the volume you are referring to, followed by a colon and the page number.

> In his studies of gifted children, Terman describes a pattern of accelerated language acquisition (2: 279).

If you cite only one volume of a multivolume work throughout your paper, you will include the volume number in the list of works cited and will not need to include it in the parentheses. (See the second example in item 26, on p. 501.)

■ **15. Entire work**   Use the author's name in a signal phrase or a parenthetical citation. There is no need to use a page number.

> Lane explores the evolution of surveillance in the workplace.

■ **16. Selection in an anthology**   Put the name of the author of the selection (not the editor of the anthology) in the signal phrase or the parentheses.

> In "Love Is a Fallacy," the narrator's logical teachings disintegrate when Polly declares that she should date Petey because "[h]e's got a raccoon coat" (Shulman 379).

In the list of works cited, the work is alphabetized by the author's last name, not by the name of the editor of the anthology. (See item 24 on p. 500.)

> Shulman, Max. "Love Is a Fallacy." *Current Issues and Enduring Questions.* Ed. Sylvan Barnet and Hugo Bedau. 8th ed. Boston: Bedford, 2008. 371-79. Print.

■ **17. Government document**   When a government agency is the author, you will alphabetize it in the list of works cited under the name of the government, such as *United States* or *Great Britain* (see item 73 on p. 519). For this reason, you must name the government as well as the agency in your in-text citation.

> Online monitoring by the United States Department of the Interior over a one-week period found that employees' use of "sexually explicit and gambling websites . . . accounted for over 24 hours of Internet use" and that "computer users spent over 2,004 hours accessing game and auction sites" during the same period (3).

◼ **18. Historical document**   For a historical document, such as the United States Constitution or the Canadian Charter of Rights and Freedoms, provide the document title, neither italicized nor in quotation marks, along with relevant article and section numbers. In parenthetical citations, use common abbreviations such as "art." and "sec." and abbreviations of well-known titles: (US Const., art. 1, sec. 2).

> While the United States Constitution provides for the formation of new states (art. 4, sec. 3), it does not explicitly allow or prohibit the secession of states.

For other historical documents, cite as you would any other work, by the first element in the works cited entry (see item 74 on pp. 519–20).

◼ **19. Legal source**   For legislative acts (laws) and court cases, name the act or case either in a signal phrase or in parentheses. Italicize the names of cases but not the names of acts.

> The Jones Act of 1917 granted US citizenship to Puerto Ricans.

> In 1857, Chief Justice Roger B. Taney declared in *Dred Scott v. Sandford* that blacks, whether enslaved or free, could not be citizens of the United States.

◼ **20. Visual such as a photograph, map, or chart**   To cite a visual that has a figure number in the source, use the abbreviation "fig." and the number in place of a page number in your parenthetical citation: (Manning, fig. 4). Spell out the word "figure" if you refer to it in your text.

To cite a visual that does not have a figure number in a print source, use the visual's title or a general description in your text and cite the author and page number as for any other source.

For a visual that is not contained in a source such as a book or periodical, identify the visual in your text and then cite it using the first element in the works cited entry: the photographer's or artist's name or the title of the work. (See items 69 and 72 on pp. 518–19.)

> Photographs such as *Woman Aircraft Worker* (Bransby) and *Women Welders* (Parks) demonstrate the US government's attempt to document the contributions of women on the home front during World War II.

■ **21. E-mail, letter, or personal interview** Cite e-mail messages, personal letters, and personal interviews by the name listed in the works cited entry, as you would for any other source. Identify the type of source in your text if you feel it is necessary. (See item 53 on p. 513 and items 83 and 84 on p. 522.)

■ **22. Web site or other electronic source** Your in-text citation for an electronic source should follow the same guidelines as for other sources. If the source lacks page numbers but has numbered paragraphs, sections, or divisions, use those numbers with the appropriate abbreviation in your in-text citation: "par.," "sec.," "ch.," "pt.," and so on. Do not add such numbers if the source itself does not use them; simply give the author or title in your in-text citation.

> Julian Hawthorne points out profound differences between his father and Ralph Waldo Emerson but concludes that, in their lives and their writing, "together they met the needs of nearly all that is worthy in human nature" (ch. 4).

■ **23. Indirect source (source quoted in another source)** When a writer's or a speaker's quoted words appear in a source written by someone else, begin the parenthetical citation with the abbreviation "qtd. in."

> According to Bill Coleman, an executive at *Salary.com,* "Personal Internet use and casual office conversations often turn into new business ideas or suggestions for gaining operating efficiencies" (qtd. in Frauenheim).

Literary works and sacred texts

Literary works and sacred texts are usually available in a variety of editions. Your list of works cited will specify which edition you are using, and your in-text citation will usually consist of a page number from the edition you consulted (see item 24). When possible, give enough information — such as book parts, play divisions, or line numbers — so that readers can locate the cited passage in any edition of the work (see items 25–27).

■ **24. Literary work without parts or line numbers** Many literary works, such as most short stories and many novels and plays, do not have parts or line numbers. In such cases, simply cite the page number.

> At the end of Kate Chopin's "The Story of an Hour," Mrs. Mallard
> drops dead upon learning that her husband is alive. In the final
> lines of the story, doctors report that she has died of a "joy that
> kills" (25).

■ **25. Verse play or poem** For verse plays, give act, scene, and line numbers that can be located in any edition of the work. Use arabic numerals and separate the numbers with periods.

> In Shakespeare's *King Lear,* Gloucester, blinded for suspected
> treason, learns a profound lesson from his tragic experience: "A
> man may see how this world goes / with no eyes" (4.2.148-49).

For a poem, cite the part, stanza, and line numbers, if it has them, separated by periods.

> The Green Knight claims to approach King Arthur's court "because
> the praise of you, prince, is puffed so high, / And your manor and
> your men are considered so magnificent" (1.12.258-59).

For poems that are not divided into numbered parts or stanzas, use line numbers. For a first reference, use the word "lines": (lines 5-8). Thereafter use just the numbers: (12-13).

■ **26. Novel with numbered divisions** When a novel has numbered divisions, put the page number first, followed by a semicolon and the book, part, or chapter in which the passage may be found. Use abbreviations such as "bk.," "pt.," and "ch."

> One of Kingsolver's narrators, teenager Rachel, pushes her
> vocabulary beyond its limits. For example, Rachel complains that
> being forced to live in the Congo with her missionary family is "a
> sheer tapestry of justice" because her chances of finding a boyfriend
> are "dull and void" (117; bk. 2, ch. 10).

■ **27. Sacred text**   When citing a sacred text such as the Bible or the Qur'an, name the edition in your works cited entry (see item 28 on p. 503). In your parenthetical citation, give the book, chapter, and verse (or the equivalent), separated with periods. Abbreviations for books of the Bible are acceptable.

> Consider the words of Solomon: "If your enemy is hungry, give him
> bread to eat; and if he is thirsty, give him water to drink" (*Oxford*
> *Annotated Bible*, Prov. 25.21).

The title of a sacred work is italicized when it refers to a specific edition of the work, as in the preceding example. If you refer to the book in a general sense in your text, neither italicize it nor put it in quotation marks. (See also the note in 42a, p. 348.)

> The Bible and the Qur'an provide allegories that help readers
> understand how to lead a moral life.

59b   MLA list of works cited

An alphabetized list of works cited, at the end of your paper, gives publication information for each source you have cited in the paper. Include only sources that you have quoted, summarized, or paraphrased. (For information about preparing the list, see p. 526; for a sample list of works cited, see p. 532.)

General guidelines for works cited in MLA style

In an MLA works cited entry, invert the first author's name (last name first, followed by a comma and the first name); put all other names in normal order. In titles of works, capitalize all words except articles (*a, an, the*), prepositions (*into, between*, and so on),

sacred text (Bible, Qur'an) •
works cited • one author • two or more authors **MLA**
59b 491

coordinating conjunctions (*and*, *but*, *or*, *nor*, *for*, *so*, *yet*), and the *to* in infinitives — unless they are the first or last word of the title or subtitle. Use quotation marks for titles of articles and other short works, such as brief documents from Web sites; italicize titles of books and other long works, such as entire Web sites.

Give the city of publication without a state name. Shorten publishers' names, usually to the first principal word ("Wiley" for "John Wiley and Sons," for instance); abbreviate "University" and "Press" in the names of university publishers: UP of Florida. For the date of publication, use the date on the title page or the most recent date on the copyright page.

For all works cited entries, include the medium in which a work was published, produced, or delivered. Usually put the medium at the end of the entry, capitalized but neither italicized nor in quotation marks. Typical designations for the medium are "Print," "Web," "Radio," "Television," "CD," "Film," "Videocassette," "DVD," "Photograph," "Performance," "Lecture," "MP3 file," and "PDF file." (See specific items throughout 59b.)

Listing authors (print and online)

Alphabetize entries in the list of works cited by authors' last names (or by title if a work has no author). The author's name is important because citations in the text of the paper refer to it and readers will look for it at the beginning of an entry in the alphabetized list.

NAME CITED IN TEXT

According to Nancy Flynn, . . .

BEGINNING OF WORKS CITED ENTRY

Flynn, Nancy.

1. Single author

author: last
name first · · · title (book) · · · city of
publication · publisher · date · medium

Wood, James. *How Fiction Works*. New York: Farrar, 2008. Print.

2. Two or three authors

first author:
last name first · · · second author:
in normal order · · · title (book)

Gourevitch, Philip, and Errol Morris. *Standard Operating Procedure.*

city of
publication · publisher · date · medium

New York: Penguin, 2008. Print.

first author: other authors:
last name first   in normal order   title (newspaper article)

Farmer, John, John Azzarello, and Miles Kara. "Real Heroes, Fake Stories."

         date of
newspaper title   publication   page(s) medium

New York Times 14 Sept. 2008: WK10. Print.

3. Four or more authors

first author: other authors:
last name first   in normal order

Harris, Shon, Allen Harper, Chris Eagle, and Jonathan Ness.

          edition   city of
title (book)   number   publication   publisher   date   medium

Gray Hat Hacking. 2nd ed. New York: McGraw, 2007. Print.

Name all the authors or name the first author followed by "et al."
(Latin for "and others"). In an in-text citation, use the same form
for the authors' names as you use in the works cited entry. See
item 7 on page 483.

4. Organization as author

author: organization name,
not abbreviated   title (book)

National Wildlife Federation. *Rain Check: Conservation Groups Monitor*

                    city of   publisher,
                    publication   with abbreviations

Mercury Levels in Milwaukee's Rain. Ann Arbor: Natl. Wildlife

             date   medium

Federation, 2001. Print.

For a publication by a government agency, see item 73. Your in-
text citation should also treat the organization as the author (see
item 8 on p. 483).

5. Unknown author

Article or other short work

                           newspaper   date of
title (newspaper article)   label   title   publication

"Poverty, by Outdated Numbers." Editorial. *Boston Globe* 20 Sept. 2008:

page(s) medium

A16. Print.

title (TV episode)   title (TV program)   producer   network   station   city of broadcast   date of broadcast

"Heat." *Frontline*. Prod. Martin Smith. PBS. KTWU, Topeka, 21 Oct. 2008.

medium

Television.

For other examples of an article with no author and of a television program, see items 13 and 65, respectively.

Book, entire Web site, or other long work

title (book)   city of publication   publisher   date   medium

New Concise World Atlas. New York: Oxford UP, 2007. Print.

title (Web site)

Women of Protest: Photographs from the Records of the National Woman's

sponsor of site   no date   medium   access date

Party. Lib. of Cong., n.d. Web. 29 Sept. 2008.

Before concluding that the author of an online source is unknown, check carefully (see the tip at the bottom of p. 481). Also remember that an organization or a government may be the author (see items 4 and 73).

■ **6. Two or more works by the same author** If your list of works cited includes two or more works by the same author, first alphabetize the works by title (ignoring the article *A*, *An*, or *The* at the beginning of a title). Use the author's name for the first entry only; for subsequent entries, use three hyphens followed by a period. The three hyphens must stand for exactly the same name or names as in the first entry.

Knopp, Lisa. *Field of Vision*. Iowa City: U of Iowa P, 1996. Print.

---. *The Nature of Home: A Lexicon and Essays*. Lincoln: U of Nebraska P, 2002. Print.

Articles in periodicals (print)

This section shows how to prepare works cited entries for articles in print magazines, journals, and newspapers. See "General guidelines" and "Listing authors" on pages 490 and 491 for how to handle basic parts of the entries. See also "Online sources" beginning on page 504 for articles from Web sites and articles accessed through a library's database.

For articles appearing on consecutive pages, provide the range of pages (see items 7 and 8). When an article does not appear on consecutive pages, give the first page number followed by a plus sign: 32+. For dates requiring a month, abbreviate all but May, June, and July. For an illustrated citation of an article in a periodical, see page 495.

■ **7. Article in a journal (paginated by volume or by issue)**

author: last
name first   article title

Blackburn, Robin. "Economic Democracy: Meaningful, Desirable, Feasible?"

      journal   volume,
      title   issue   year   page(s) medium

    Daedalus 136.3 (2007): 36-45. Print.

■ **8. Article in a monthly magazine**

author: last
name first   article title   magazine
                                    title   date: month + year

Lanting, Frans. "Life: A Journey through Time." *Audubon* Nov.-Dec. 2006:

    page(s) medium
    48-52. Print.

■ **9. Article in a weekly magazine**

                                   magazine date: day +
author: last name first   article title   title month + year page(s)

von Drehle, David. "The Ghosts of Memphis." *Time* 7 Apr. 2008: 34-37.

    medium
    Print.

■ **10. Article in a daily newspaper**   Give the page range of the article. If the article does not appear on consecutive pages, use a plus sign (+) after the first page number. If the city of publication is not obvious from the title of the newspaper, include the city in brackets after the name of the newspaper.

If sections are identified by letter, include the section letter as part of the page number. If sections are numbered, include the section number between the date and the page number, using the abbreviation "sec." (See the top of p. 496 for examples.)

Citation at a glance: Article in a periodical (MLA)

To cite an article in a print periodical in MLA style, include the following elements:

1 Author of article
2 Title and subtitle of article
3 Title of periodical
4 Volume and issue numbers (for journal)
5 Date or year of publication
6 Page number(s) of article
7 Medium

TITLE PAGE

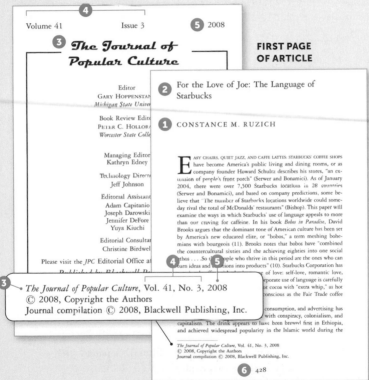

FIRST PAGE OF ARTICLE

Volume 41   Issue 3   5 2008

3 *The Journal of Popular Culture*

For the Love of Joe: The Language of Starbucks

CONSTANCE M. RUZICH

The Journal of Popular Culture, Vol. 41, No. 3, 2008
© 2008, Copyright the Authors
Journal compilation © 2008, Blackwell Publishing, Inc.

6 428

WORKS CITED ENTRY FOR AN ARTICLE IN A PRINT PERIODICAL

Ruzich, Constance M. "For the Love of Joe: The Language of Starbucks."

Journal of Popular Culture 41.3 (2008): 428-42. Print.

For more on citing print periodical articles in MLA style, see pages 493–97.

Page number with section letter

author: last
name first   article title   newspaper title

date: day +
month + year

McKenna, Phil. "It Takes Just One Village." *New York Times* 23 Sept. 2008,

name of
edition   page medium

New England ed.: D1. Print.

Page number with section number

author: last
name first   article title   newspaper title

city of
publication

Knox, David Blake. "Lord Archer, Storyteller." *Sunday Independent* [Dublin]

date: day +
month + year   section page medium

14 Sept. 2008, sec. 2: 9. Print.

■ 11. Abstract of a journal article Include the word "Abstract" after the title of the article.

Walker, Joyce. "Narratives in the Database: Memorializing September 11th

Online." Abstract. *Computers and Composition* 24.2 (2007): 121. Print.

■ 12. Article with a title in its title Use single quotation marks around a title of a short work or a quoted term that appears in an article title. Italicize a title or term normally italicized. (See also 37c.)

Shen, Min. "'Quite a Moon!' The Archetypal Feminine in *Our Town*."

American Drama 16.2 (2007): 1-14. Print.

■ 13. Editorial or other unsigned article Begin with the article title and alphabetize the entry by the title in the list of works cited.

"Getting the Message: Communicating Electronically with Doctors Can

Spur Honesty from Young Patients." Editorial. *Columbus* [OH]

Dispatch 19 June 2008: 10A. Print.

■ 14. Letter to the editor

Morris, David. "Fiercely Proud." Letter. *Progressive* Feb. 2008: 6. Print.

■ 15. Review For a review of a book, a film, or another type of work, begin with the name of the reviewer and the title of the review, if it has one. Add the words "Rev. of " and the title of the work reviewed, followed by the author, director, or other significant contributor. Give the publication information for the periodical in which the review appears. If the review has no author and no title, begin with "Rev. of " and alphabetize the entry by the first principal word in the title of the work reviewed.

Dodge, Chris. Rev. of *The Radical Jack London: Writings on War and*

  Revolution, ed. Jonah Raskni. *Utne Reader* Sept.-Oct. 2008: 35. Print.

Lane, Anthony. "Dream On." Rev. of *The Science of Sleep* and *Renaissance,*

  dir. Michel Gondry. *New Yorker* 25 Sept. 2006: 155-57. Print.

Books (print)

Items 16–33 apply to print books. For online books, see items 41 and 42. For an illustrated citation of a print book, see page 499.

■ 16. Basic format for a book

author: last
name first   book title   city of
publication

Sacks, Oliver. *Musicophilia: Tales of Music and the Brain.* New York:

publisher   date   medium

Knopf, 2007. Print.

Take the information about the book from its title page and copyright page. Use a short form of the publisher's name; omit terms such as "Press," "Inc.," and "Co." except when naming university presses ("Howard UP," for example). If the copyright page lists more than one date, use the most recent one.

■ 17. Book with an author and an editor

author: last
name first   book title   editor:
in normal order

Plath, Sylvia. *The Unabridged Journals of Sylvia Plath.* Ed. Karen V. Kukil.

city of
publication   imprint-publisher   date   medium

New York: Anchor-Doubleday, 2000. Print.

The abbreviation "Ed." means "Edited by," so it is the same for one or multiple editors.

■ **18. Book with an author and a translator** "Trans." means "Translated by," so it is the same for one or multiple translators.

Scirocco, Alfonso. *Garibaldi: Citizen of the World*. Trans. Allan Cameron.

Princeton: Princeton UP, 2007. Print.

■ **19. Book with an editor** Begin with the editor's name. For one editor, use "ed." (for "editor") after the name; for multiple editors, use "eds." (for "editors").

Lago, Mary, Linda K. Hughes, and Elizabeth MacLeod Walls, eds. *The BBC Talks*

of E. M. Forster, 1929-1960. Columbia: U of Missouri P, 2008. Print.

■ **20. Graphic narrative or illustrated book** For a book that combines text and illustrations, begin your citation with the person you wish to emphasize (writer, illustrator, artist) and list any other contributors after the title of the book. Use the abbreviation "illus." and other common labels to identify contributors. If the writer and illustrator are the same person, cite the work as you would a book, with no labels.

Weaver, Dustin, illus. *The Tenth Circle*. By Jodi Picoult. New York:

Washington Square, 2006. Print.

Moore, Alan. *V for Vendetta*. Illus. David Lloyd. New York: Vertigo-DC

Comics, 2008. Print.

Thompson, Craig. *Blankets*. Marietta: Top Shelf, 2005.

■ **21. Book with an author using a pseudonym** Give the author's name as it appears on the title page (the pseudonym), and follow it with the author's real name in brackets.

Dinesen, Isak [Karen Blixen]. *Winter's Tales*. 1942. New York: Vintage,

1993. Print.

■ **22. Book in a language other than English** If your readers are not familiar with the language of the book, include a translation of the title, italicized and in brackets. Capitalize the title according to the conventions of the book's language, and give the original publication information.

Nemtsov, Boris, and Vladimir Milov. *Putin. Itogi. Nezavisimyi Ekspertnyi*

Doklad [*Putin. The Results: An Independent Expert Report*]. Moscow:

Novaya Gazeta, 2008. Print.

Citation at a glance: Book (MLA)

To cite a print book in MLA style, include the following elements:

1 Author
2 Title and subtitle
3 City of publication
4 Publisher
5 Date of publication
6 Medium

TITLE PAGE

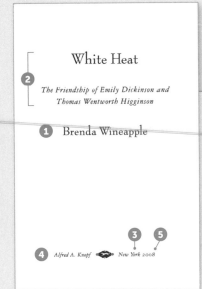

White Heat

The Friendship of Emily Dickinson and
Thomas Wentworth Higginson

Brenda Wineapple

Alfred A. Knopf · New York 2008

This Is a Borzoi Book Published by Alfred A. Knopf
Copyright © 2008 by Brenda Wineapple

COPYRIGHT PAGE

WORKS CITED ENTRY FOR A PRINT BOOK

Wineapple, Brenda. *White Heat: The Friendship of Emily Dickinson and Thomas Wentworth Higginson*. New York: Knopf, 2008. Print.

For more on citing print books in MLA style, see pages 497–504.

■ **23. Entire anthology**   An anthology is a collection of works on a common theme, often with different authors for the selections and usually with an editor for the entire volume. (For an anthology with one editor, use the abbreviation "ed." after the editor's name. For more than one editor, use "eds.")

Dumanis, Michael, and Cate Marvin, eds. *Legitimate Dangers: American*

   Poets of the New Century. Louisville: Sarabande, 2006. Print.

■ **24. One or more selections from an anthology**

One selection from anthology

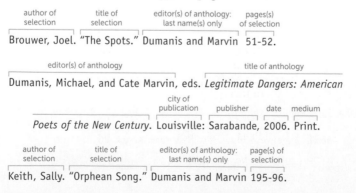

author of selection: title of
last name first   selection   title of anthology
Brouwer, Joel. "The Spots." *Legitimate Dangers: American Poets of the*

                    editor(s) of anthology: city of
                    name(s) in normal order   publication
   New Century. Ed. Michael Dumanis and Cate Marvin. Louisville:

            publisher   date   page(s) of
                                 selection   medium
   Sarabande, 2006. 51-52. Print.

The abbreviation "Ed." means "Edited by," so it is the same for one or multiple editors. For an illustrated citation of a selection from an anthology, see pages 502–03.

Two or more selections, with separate anthology entry

If you use two or more works from the same anthology in your paper, provide an entry for the entire anthology (see item 23) and give a shortened entry for each selection. Use the medium only in the entry for the complete anthology. For an illustrated citation of a selection from an anthology, see pages 502–03.

author of   title of   editor(s) of anthology: pages(s)
selection   selection   last name(s) only   of selection
Brouwer, Joel. "The Spots." Dumanis and Marvin 51-52.

            editor(s) of anthology   title of anthology
Dumanis, Michael, and Cate Marvin, eds. *Legitimate Dangers: American*

                            city of
                            publication   publisher   date   medium
   Poets of the New Century. Louisville: Sarabande, 2006. Print.

author of   title of   editor(s) of anthology: page(s) of
selection   selection   last name(s) only   selection
Keith, Sally. "Orphean Song." Dumanis and Marvin 195-96.

◼ **25. Edition other than the first** Include the number of the edition (1st, 2nd, 3rd, and so on). If the book has a translator or an editor in addition to the author, give the name of the translator or editor before the edition number, using the abbreviation "Trans." for "Translated by" (see item 18) or "Ed." for "Edited by" (see item 17).

Auletta, Ken. *The Underclass.* 2nd ed. Woodstock: Overlook, 2000. Print.

◼ **26. Multivolume work** Include the total number of volumes before the city and publisher, using the abbreviation "vols." If the volumes were published over several years, give the inclusive dates of publication. The abbreviation "Ed." means "Edited by," so it is the same for one or multiple editors.

author: last name first	title	editor: in normal order	total volumes	city of publication	publisher

Stark, Freya. *Letters.* Ed. Lucy Moorehead. 8 vols. Salisbury: Compton,

inclusive dates	medium

1974-82. Print.

If you cite only one of the volumes in your paper, include the volume number before the city and publisher and give the date of publication for that volume. After the date, give the medium of publication followed by the total number of volumes.

author: last name first	title	editor: in normal order	volume cited	city of publication	publisher

Stark, Freya. *Letters.* Ed. Lucy Moorehead. Vol. 5. Salisbury: Compton,

date of volume	medium	total volumes

1978. Print. 8 vols.

◼ **27. Encyclopedia or dictionary entry** List the author of the entry (if there is one), the title of the entry, the title of the reference work, the edition number (if any), the date of the edition, and the medium. Volume and page numbers are not necessary because the entries in the source are arranged alphabetically and are therefore easy to locate.

Posner, Rebecca. "Romance Languages." *The Encyclopaedia Britannica: Macropaedia.* 15th ed. 1987. Print.

"Sonata." *The American Heritage Dictionary of the English Language.* 4th ed. 2000. Print.

Citation at a glance: Selection from an anthology (MLA)

To cite a selection from a print anthology in MLA style, include the following elements:

1 Author of selection
2 Title of selection
3 Title and subtitle of anthology
4 Editor(s) of anthology
5 City of publication
6 Publisher
7 Date of publication
8 Page number(s) of selection
9 Medium

TITLE PAGE

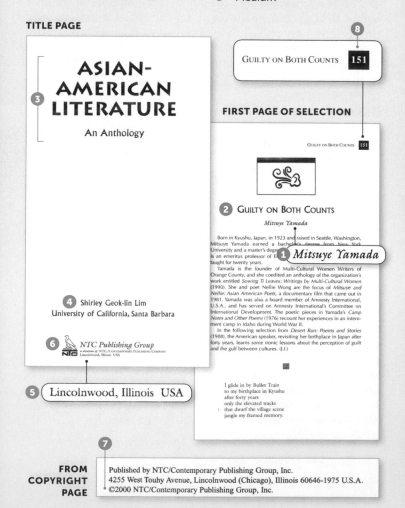

8 GUILTY ON BOTH COUNTS 151

3 ASIAN-AMERICAN LITERATURE

An Anthology

4 Shirley Geok-lin Lim
University of California, Santa Barbara

6 NTC Publishing Group
a division of NTC/Contemporary Publishing Company
Lincolnwood, Illinois USA

5 Lincolnwood, Illinois USA

FIRST PAGE OF SELECTION

GUILTY ON BOTH COUNTS 151

2 GUILTY ON BOTH COUNTS
Mitsuye Yamada

Born in Kyushu, Japan, in 1923 and raised in Seattle, Washington, Mitsuye Yamada earned a bachelor's degree from New York University and a master's degree is an emeritus professor of E taught for twenty years.

1 *Mitsuye Yamada*

Yamada is the founder of Multi-Cultural Women Writers of Orange County, and she coedited an anthology of the organization's work entitled *Sowing Ti Leaves: Writings by Multi-Cultural Women* (1990). She and poet Nellie Wong are the focus of *Mitsuye and Nellie: Asian American Poets*, a documentary film that came out in 1981. Yamada was also a board member of Amnesty International, U.S.A., and has served on Amnesty International's Committee on International Development. The poetic pieces in Yamada's *Camp Notes and Other Poems* (1976) recount her experiences in an internment camp in Idaho during World War II.

In the following selection from *Desert Run: Poems and Stories* (1988), the American speaker, revisiting her birthplace in Japan after forty years, learns some ironic lessons about the perception of guilt and the gulf between cultures. (J.I.)

I glide in by Bullet Train
to my birthplace in Kyushu
after forty years
only the elevated tracks
that dwarf the village scene
jangle my framed memory.

7

FROM COPYRIGHT PAGE

Published by NTC/Contemporary Publishing Group, Inc.
4255 West Touhy Avenue, Lincolnwood (Chicago), Illinois 60646-1975 U.S.A.
©2000 NTC/Contemporary Publishing Group, Inc.

WORKS CITED ENTRY FOR A SELECTION FROM A PRINT ANTHOLOGY

┌──── 1 ────┐ ┌──────── 2 ────────┐ ┌─────────── 3 ───────────
Yamada, Mitsuye. "Guilty on Both Counts." *Asian-American Literature:*

┌──────────┐   ┌──────── 4 ────────┐ ┌─── 5 ───┐ ┌6┐ ┌7┐
An Anthology. Ed. Shirley Geok-lin Lim. Lincolnwood: NTC, 2000.

┌─8─┐ ┌─9─┐
151-54. Print.

For more on citing selections from print anthologies in MLA style, see page 500.

◼ **28. Sacred text**   Give the title of the sacred text (taken from the title page), italicized; the editor's or translator's name (if any); publication information; and the medium. Add the name of the version, if there is one.

The Oxford Annotated Bible with the Apocrypha. Ed. Herbert G. May and

Bruce M. Metzger. New York: Oxford UP, 1965. Print. Rev. Standard Vers.

The Qur'an: Translation. Trans. Abdullah Yusuf Ali. Elmhurst: Tahrike,

2000. Print.

◼ **29. Foreword, introduction, preface, or afterword**

author of foreword:
  last name first   book part   book title
┌──────────┐ ┌────────┐ ┌────────────────────────────────┐
Bennett, Hal Zina. Foreword. *Shimmering Images: A Handy Little Guide to*

                author of book: city of
                in normal order publication imprint-publisher
                ┌──────────────┐ ┌──────────┐ ┌───────────┐
Writing Memoir. By Lisa Dale Norton. New York: Griffin-St. Martin's,

      page(s) of
date foreword medium
┌──┐ ┌────────┐ ┌────┐
2008. xiii-xvi. Print.

If the book part has a title, include it in quotation marks immediately after the author's name and before the label for the book part. If the author of the book part is also the author or editor of the complete work, give only the last name of the author the second time it is used.

Ozick, Cynthia. "Portrait of the Essay as a Warm Body." Introduction.

The Best American Essays 1998. Ed. Ozick. Boston: Houghton, 1998.

xv-xxi. Print.

⬛ **30. Book with a title in its title** If the book title contains a title normally italicized, neither italicize the internal title nor place it in quotation marks.

Woodson, Jon. *A Study of Joseph Heller's* Catch-22: *Going Around Twice*.

New York: Lang, 2001. Print.

If the title within the title is normally put in quotation marks, retain the quotation marks and italicize the entire book title.

Millás, Juan José. *"Personality Disorders" and Other Stories*. Trans. Gregory

B. Kaplan. New York: MLA, 2007. Print. MLA Texts and Trans.

⬛ **31. Book in a series** After the publication information, give the medium of publication and then the series name as it appears on the title page, followed by the series number, if any.

Douglas, Dan. *Assessing Languages for Specific Purposes*. Cambridge:

Cambridge UP, 2000. Print. Cambridge Applied Linguistics Ser.

⬛ **32. Republished book** After the title of the book, give the original publication date, followed by the current publication information. If the republished book contains new material, such as an introduction or afterword, include information about the new material after the original date.

Trilling, Lionel. *The Liberal Imagination*. 1950. Introd. Louis Menand. New

York: New York Review of Books, 2008. Print.

⬛ **33. Publisher's imprint** If a book was published by a division (an imprint) of a publishing company, give the name of the imprint, a hyphen, and the name of the publisher.

Ackroyd, Peter. *The Fall of Troy*. New York: Talese-Doubleday, 2007. Print.

Online sources

MLA guidelines assume that readers can locate most online sources by entering the author, title, or other identifying information in a search engine or a database. Consequently, the *MLA Handbook* does not require a Web address (URL) in citations for online sources. If your instructor requires one, see the note at the end of item 34.

MLA style calls for a sponsor or a publisher in works cited entries for most online sources. If a source has no sponsor or publisher, use the abbreviation "N.p." (for "No publisher") in the sponsor position. If there is no date of publication or update, use "n.d." (for "no date") after the sponsor. For an article in an online journal or an article from a database, give page numbers if they are available; if they are not, use the abbreviation "n. pag." (See item 37.)

■ 34. Entire Web site

Web site with author

author: last name first   title of Web site   sponsor of site (personal page)   update   medium

Peterson, Susan Lynn. *The Life of Martin Luther.* Susan Lynn Peterson, 2005. Web.

date of access: day + month + year

24 Jan. 2009.

Web site with organization (group) as author

organization name: not abbreviated   title of Web site   sponsor: abbreviated   update   medium

American Library Association. *American Library Association.* ALA, 2008. Web.

date of access: day + month + year

14 Jan. 2009.

Web site with no author

title of Web site   sponsor of site   update   medium

Margaret Sanger Papers Project. History Dept., New York U, 18 Oct. 2000. Web.

date of access: day + month + year

6 Jan. 2009.

Web site with editor

See item 19 (p. 498) for listing the name(s) of editor(s).

Halsall, Paul, ed. *Internet Modern History Sourcebook.* Fordham U, 22 Sept. 2001. Web. 19 Jan. 2009.

Web site with no title

Use the label "Home page" or another appropriate description in place of a title.

Yoon, Mina. Home page. Oak Ridge Natl. Laboratory, 28 Dec. 2006. Web. 12 Jan. 2009.

NOTE: If your instructor requires a URL for Web sources, include the URL, enclosed in angle brackets, at the end of the entry. When a URL in a works cited entry must be divided at the end of a line, break it after a double slash or a slash. Do not insert a hyphen.

Peterson, Susan Lynn. *The Life of Martin Luther.* Susan Lynn Peterson, 2005.

  Web. 24 Jan. 2009. <http://www.susanlynnpeterson.com/index_files/

  luther.htm>.

■ **35. Short work from a Web site** Short works include articles, poems, podcasts, songs, fact sheets, and other documents that are not book length or that appear as internal pages on a Web site. For an illustrated citation of a short work from a Web site, see pages 508–09.

Short work with author

```
   author: last                                  title of          no update
   name first         title of short work        Web site   sponsor   date
Shiva, Vandana. "Bioethics: A Third World Issue."  NativeWeb. NativeWeb, n.d.
              date of access:
     medium  day + month + year
      Web. 22 Jan. 2010.
```

Short work with no author

```
   title of          title of          sponsor
  short work        Web site           of site      update    medium
"Sister Aimee." American Experience. PBS Online, 2 Apr. 2007. Web.
     date of access:
     day + month + year
     30 Oct. 2010.
```

■ **36. Web site with an author using a pseudonym** Begin the entry with the pseudonym and add the author's or creator's real name, if known, in brackets. Follow with the information required for a Web site or a short work from a Web site (see item 34 or 35).

Grammar Girl [Mignon Fogarty]. "What Is the Plural of 'Mouse'?" *Grammar*

  Girl: Quick and Dirty Tips for Better Writing. Holtzbrinck, 16 Sept.

  2008. Web. 10 Nov. 2010.

■ **37. Article in an online journal**

author: last name first   article title

Mason, John Edwin. "'Mannenberg': Notes on the Making of an Icon and

                              volume,   not
               journal title   issue   year   paginated medium

   Anthem." *African Studies Quarterly* 9.4 (2007): n. pag. Web.

date of access:
day + month + year

   23 Feb. 2010.

■ **38. Article in an online magazine**   Give the author; the title of
the article, in quotation marks; the title of the magazine, italicized;
the sponsor or publisher of the site (use "N.p." if there is none); the
date of publication; the medium; and your date of access.

Burton, Robert. "The Certainty Epidemic." *Salon.com.* Salon Media Group,

   29 Feb. 2008. Web. 18 Jan. 2010.

■ **39. Article in an online newspaper**   Give the author; the title of
the article, in quotation marks; the title of the newspaper, italicized;
the sponsor or publisher of the site (use "N.p." if there is none); the
date of publication; the medium; and your date of access.

Smith, Andrew D. "Poll: More than 70% of US Workers Use Internet on the

   Job." *Dallasnews.com.* Dallas Morning News, 25 Sept. 2008. Web.

   29 Sept. 2008.

■ **40. Article from a database**   For an article retrieved from a
library's subscription database, first list the publication information for the article (see items 7–15) and then provide information
about the database. For an illustrated citation of an article from a
database, see page 510.

author of source: title of   volume,
    last name first   article   journal title   issue   year   page(s)

Heyen, William. "Sunlight." *American Poetry Review* 36.2 (2007): 55-56.

                                 date of access:
          database name   medium   day + month + year

   Expanded Academic ASAP. Web. 24 Mar. 2010.

Williams, Jeffrey J. "Why Today's Publishing World Is Reprising the Past."

   Chronicle of Higher Education 13 June 2008: n. pag. *LexisNexis*

   Academic. Web. 29 Sept. 2009.

Citation at a glance: Short work from a Web site (MLA)

To cite a short work from a Web site in MLA style, include the following elements:

1   Author of short work (if any)
2   Title of short work
3   Title of Web site
4   Sponsor of Web site ("N.p." if none)
5   Update date ("n.d." if none)
6   Medium
7   Date you accessed the source

INTERNAL PAGE OF WEB SITE

FOOTER ON HOME PAGE

the local area. It houses the most extensive collection of art, artifacts, and manuscripts pertaining to American whaling in the age of sail - late eighteenth century to the early twentieth, when sailing ships dominated merchant trade and whaling.

18 Johnny Cake Hill | New Bedford, MA | 02740-6398 | Tel. (508) 997-0046
Fax: (508) 997-0018 | Library Fax: (508) 207-1064

©Copyright 2009 Old Dartmouth Historical Society / New Bedford Whaling Museum

WORKS CITED ENTRY FOR A SHORT WORK FROM A WEB SITE

┌─────────2─────────┐ ┌─────────3─────────┐
"Overview of American Whaling." *New Bedford Whaling Museum.*

┌──────────────────4──────────────────┐ ┌─5─┐
Old Dartmouth Hist. Soc./New Bedford Whaling Museum, 2009.

┌─6─┐ ┌───7───┐
Web. 27 Oct. 2010.

For more on citing sources from Web sites in MLA style, see pages 505–06.

■ **41. Online book-length work** Cite an online book or an online book-length work, such as a play or a long poem, as you would a short work from a Web site (see item 35), but italicize the title of the work.

author: last
name first   title of long poem   title of Web site   sponsor of site

Milton, John. *Paradise Lost: Book I. Poetryfoundation.org.* Poetry Foundation,

date of access:
update medium day + month + year

2008. Web. 14 Dec. 2009.

Give the print publication information for the work, if available (see items 16–33), followed by the title of the Web site, the medium, and your date of access.

author: last
name first   book title

Jacobs, Harriet A. *Incidents in the Life of a Slave Girl: Written by Herself.*

editor of   city of
original book publication year   title of Web site

Ed. L. Maria Child. Boston, 1861. *Documenting the American South.*

date of access:
medium day + month + year

Web. 3 Feb. 2010.

■ **42. Part of an online book** Begin as for a part of a print book (see item 29). If the online book part has no page numbers, use "N. pag." following the publication information. End with the Web site on which the work is found, the medium, and your date of access.

Adams, Henry. "Diplomacy." *The Education of Henry Adams.* Boston: Houghton,

1918. N. pag. *Bartleby.com: Great Books Online.* Web. 8 Jan. 2010.

Citation at a glance: Article from a database (MLA)

To cite an article from a database in MLA style, include the following elements:

1 Author of article
2 Title of article
3 Title of periodical
4 Volume and issue numbers (for journal)
5 Date or year of publication

6 Page number(s) of article ("n. pag." if none)
7 Name of database
8 Medium
9 Date you accessed the source

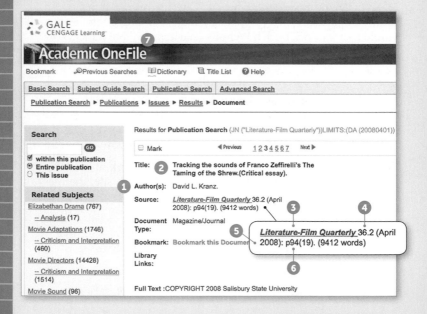

WORKS CITED ENTRY FOR AN ARTICLE FROM A DATABASE

```
      ┌───── 1 ─────┐ ┌──────────────── 2 ────────────────
Kranz, David L. "Tracking the Sounds of Franco Zeffirelli's The Taming of
         ┌────────────── 3 ──────────────┐ ┌ 4 ┐ ┌─5─┐  ┌─ 6 ─┐  ┌──── 7 ──
         the Shrew." Literature-Film Quarterly 36.2 (2008): 94-112. Academic
         ┌─────┐ ┌ 8 ┐ ┌──── 9 ────┐
         OneFile. Web. 28 Oct. 2010.
```

For more on citing articles from a database in MLA style, see item 40.

■ **43. Digital archives** Digital archives are online collections of documents or records — books, letters, photographs, data — that have been converted to digital form. Cite publication information for the original document, if it is available, using the models throughout section 59b. Then give the location of the document, if any, neither italicized nor in quotation marks; the name of the archive, italicized; the medium ("Web"); and your date of access.

Fiore, Mark. *Shockwaves.* 18 Oct. 2001. *September 11 Digital Archive.* Web.

3 Apr. 2009.

Oblinger, Maggie. Letter to Charlie Thomas. 31 Mar. 1895. Nebraska State

Hist. Soc. *Prairie Settlement: Nebraska Photographs and Family*

Letters, 1862-1912. Web. 3 Nov. 2009.

WPA Household Census for 1047 W. 50th Street, Los Angeles County. 1939. USC

Lib. Spec. Collections. *USC Libraries Digital Archive.* Web. 12 Mar. 2010.

■ **44. Entry in an online reference work** Give the author of the entry, if there is one. Otherwise begin with the title of the entry, in quotation marks. Then give the title of the site; the sponsor and the update date (use "n.d." if there is none); the medium; and your date of access.

"Native American Church." *Britannica.* Encyclopaedia Britannica, 2008.

Web. 29 Jan. 2010.

■ **45. Online poem** Cite as you would a short work from a Web site (item 35) or part of an online book (item 42).

Bell, Acton [Anne Brontë]. "Mementos." *Poems by Currer, Ellis, and Acton*

Bell. London, 1846. N. pag. *A Celebration of Women Writers.* Web.

18 Sept. 2009.

■ **46. Entire blog (Weblog)** Cite a blog as you would an entire Web site (see item 34).

Gristmill. Grist Magazine, 2008. Web. 19 Jan. 2009.

■ **47. Entry or comment in a blog (Weblog)** Cite an entry or a comment (a response to an entry) in a blog as you would a short work from a Web site (see item 35). If the comment or entry has no title, use the label "Weblog entry" or "Weblog comment."

Follow with the remaining information as for an entire blog in item 46.

"Social Media: Facebook and MySpace as University Curricula." *Open*

Education. Open Education.net, n.d. Web. 19 Sept. 2008.

Cynthia. Weblog comment. *Open Education*. Open Education.net, 8 Jan.

2010. Web. 14 Feb. 2010.

■ **48. Academic course or department home page** Cite as a short work from a Web site (see item 35). For a course home page, begin with the name of the instructor and the title of the course or title of the page (use "Course home page" if there is no other title). For a department home page, begin with the name of the department and the label "Dept. home page."

Marrone, Carole. "355:301: College Writing and Research." *Rutgers School*

of Arts and Sciences. Writing Program, Rutgers U, 2010. Web. 19 Mar.

2010.

Comparative Media Studies. Dept. home page. *Massachusetts Institute of*

Technology. MIT, 2010. Web. 6 Feb. 2010.

■ **49. *YouTube* clip or other short online video** Cite as you would a short work from a Web site (see item 35).

author: last
name first   title of
                  video title   Web site   sponsor   update
Murphy, Beth. "Tips for a Good Profile Piece." *YouTube*. YouTube, 7 Sept. 2008.

           date of access:
medium day + month + year
Web. 19 Apr. 2010.

■ **50. Online abstract** Cite as you would an abstract of a journal article (see item 11), giving whatever print information is available, followed by the medium and your date of access. If you found the abstract in an online periodical database, include the name of the database after the print publication information (see item 40).

Turner, Fred. "Romantic Automatism: Art, Technology, and Collaborative

Labor in Cold War America." Abstract. *Journal of Visual Culture* 7.1

(2008): 5. Web. 25 Oct. 2009.

■ **51. Online editorial or letter to the editor** Cite as you would an editorial or a letter to the editor in a print publication (see item 13 or 14), followed by information for a short work from a Web site (see item 35).

"Compromise Is Key with Religion at Work." Editorial. *StarTribune.com*.

Star Tribune, 18 June 2008. Web. 25 June 2008.

■ **52. Online review** Begin the entry as you would for a review in a magazine or newspaper (see item 15). If the review is published in print as well as online, first give publication information as for an article in a periodical (see items 7–10). Then add the Web site on which the review appears, the medium ("Web"), and your date of access. If the review is published only on the Web, give the information required for a short work from a Web site (see item 35). If you found the review in a database, cite as in item 40.

Greer, W. R. "Who's the Fairest One of All?" Rev. of *Mirror, Mirror*, by

Gregory Maguire. *Reviewsofbooks.com*. Reviewsofbooks.com, 2003.

Web. 26 Oct. 2009.

■ **53. E-mail message** Begin with the writer's name and the subject line. Then write "Message to" followed by the name of the recipient. End with the date of the message and the medium ("E-mail").

Lowe, Walter. "Review Questions." Message to the author. 15 Mar. 2010. E-mail.

■ **54. Posting to an online discussion list** When possible, cite archived versions of postings. If you cannot locate an archived version, keep a copy of the posting for your records. Begin with the author's name, followed by the title or subject line, in quotation marks (use the label "Online posting" if the posting has no title). Then proceed as for a short work from a Web site (see item 35).

Fainton, Peter. "Re: Backlash against New Labour." *Media Lens Message*

Board. Media Lens, 7 May 2008. Web. 2 June 2008.

■ **55. Entry in a wiki** A wiki is an online reference that is openly edited by its users. Treat an entry in a wiki as you would a short work from a Web site (see item 35). Because wiki content is, by definition, collectively edited and can be updated frequently, do not include an author. Give the title of the entry; the name of the wiki, italicized; the sponsor or publisher of the wiki (use "N.p." if there is none); the date of the last update; the medium; and your date of access.

"Hip Hop Music." *Wikipedia*. Wikimedia Foundation, 2 Mar. 2010. Web.

18 Mar. 2010.

"Negation in Languages." *UniLang Wiki*. UniLang, 12 Jan. 2009. Web.

9 Mar. 2010.

Audio and visual sources (including online versions)

⬛ **56. Digital file** A digital file is any document or image that exists in digital form, independent of a Web site. To cite a digital file, begin with information required for the source (such as a photograph, a report, a sound recording, or a radio program), following the guidelines throughout 59b. Then for the medium, indicate the type of file: "JPEG file," "PDF file," "MP3 file," and so on.

photographer	photograph title	date of composition	location of photograph

Hine, Lewis W. *Girl in Cherryville Mill*. 1908. Prints and Photographs Div.,

         medium:
         file type

Lib. of Cong. JPEG file.

"Scenes from a Recession." *This American Life*. Narr. Ira Glass. Natl. Public

Radio, 30 Mar. 2009. MP3 file.

National Institute of Mental Health. *What Rescue Workers Can Do*.

Washington: US Dept. of Health and Human Services, 2006. PDF file.

⬛ **57. Podcast** If you view or listen to a podcast online, cite it as you would a short work from a Web site (see item 35). If you download the podcast and view or listen to it on a computer or portable player, cite it as a digital file (see item 56).

Podcast online

"Calculating the Demand for Charter Schools." Narr. David Guenthner.

Texas PolicyCast. Texas Public Policy Foundation, 28 Aug. 2008. Web.

10 Jan. 2009.

Podcast downloaded as digital file

"Calculating the Demand for Charter Schools." Narr. David Guenthner. *Texas*

PolicyCast. Texas Public Policy Foundation, 28 Aug. 2008. MP3 file.

■ **58. Musical score**   For both print and online versions, begin with the composer's name; the title of the work, italicized (unless it is named by form, number, and key); and the date of composition. For a print source, give the place of publication; the name of the publisher and date of publication; and the medium. For an online source, give the title of the Web site; the publisher or sponsor of the site; the date of Web publication; the medium; and your date of access.

Handel, G. F. *Messiah: An Oratorio*. N.d. *CCARH Publications: Scores and Parts*. Center for Computer Assisted Research in the Humanities, 2003. Web. 5 Jan. 2009.

■ **59. Sound recording**   Begin with the name of the person you want to emphasize: the composer, conductor ("Cond."), or performer ("Perf."). For a long work, give the title, italicized (unless it is named by form, number, and key); the names of pertinent artists (such as performers, readers, or musicians); and the orchestra and conductor, if relevant. End with the manufacturer, the date, and the medium.

Bizet, Georges. *Carmen*. Perf. Jennifer Laramore, Thomas Moser, Angela Gheorghiu, and Samuel Ramey. Bavarian State Orch. and Chorus. Cond. Giuseppe Sinopoli. Warner, 1996. CD.

For a song, put the title in quotation marks. If you include the name of the album or CD, italicize it.

Blige, Mary J. "Be without You." *The Breakthrough*. Geffen, 2005. CD.

■ **60. Film**   Begin with the title, italicized. Then give the director ("Dir.") and the lead actors ("Perf.") or narrator ("Narr."); the distributor; the year of the film's release; and the medium ("Film," "Videocassette"). If your paper emphasizes a person or category of people involved with the film, you may begin with those names and titles (see item 61).

movie title   director   major performers
Frozen River. Dir. Courtney Hunt. Perf. Melissa Leo, Charlie McDermott, and

                            release
              distributor date medium
Misty Upham. Sony, 2008. Film.

● **61. DVD** For a film on DVD or a similar medium, such as Blu-ray Disc (BD), cite as you would a film (see item 60), giving "DVD" (or "BD") as the medium.

Forster, Marc, dir. *Finding Neverland*. Perf. Johnny Depp, Kate Winslet,

Julie Christie, Radha Mitchell, and Dustin Hoffman. Miramax,

2004. DVD.

For any other work on DVD, such as an educational work or a game, cite as you would a film, giving whatever information is available about the author, director, distributor, and so on.

Across the Drafts: Students and Teachers Talk about Feedback. Harvard

Expository Writing Program, 2005. DVD.

● **62. Special feature on a DVD** Begin with the title of the feature, in quotation marks, and the names of any important contributors, as for films or DVDs (item 60 or 61). End with information about the DVD, as in item 61, including the disc number, if any.

"Sweeney's London." Prod. Eric Young. *Sweeney Todd: The Demon Barber of*

Fleet Street. Dir. Tim Burton. DreamWorks, 2007. DVD. Disc 2.

● **63. CD-ROM** Treat a CD-ROM as you would any other source, but add the medium ("CD-ROM").

"Pimpernel." *The American Heritage Dictionary of the English Language*.

4th ed. Boston: Houghton, 2000. CD-ROM.

● **64. Computer software or video game** List the developer or author of the software (if any); the title, italicized; the distributor and date of publication; and the platform or medium.

Firaxis Games. *Sid Meier's Civilization Revolution*. Take-Two Interactive,

2008. Xbox 360.

● **65. Radio or television program** Begin with the title of the radio segment or television episode (if there is one), in quotation marks. Then give the title of the program or series, italicized; relevant information about the program, such as the writer ("By"), director ("Dir."), performers ("Perf."), or narrator ("Narr."); the network; the local station (if any) and location; the date of broadcast; and the medium ("Television," "Radio"). For a program you accessed online, after the information about the program give the network, the original broadcast date, the title of the Web site, the medium ("Web"), and your date of access.

"Machines of the Gods." *Ancient Discoveries*. History Channel. 14 Oct.

2008. Television.

"Elif Shafak: Writing under a Watchful Eye." *Fresh Air*. Narr. Terry Gross.

Natl. Public Radio, 6 Feb. 2007. *NPR.org*. Web. 22 Feb. 2009.

■ **66. Radio or television interview** Begin with the name of the person who was interviewed, followed by the word "Interview" and the interviewer's name, if relevant. End with information about the program as in item 65.

De Niro, Robert, Barry Levinson, and Art Linson. Interview by Charlie

Rose. *Charlie Rose*. PBS. WGBH, Boston, 13 Oct. 2008. Television.

■ **67. Live performance** For a live performance of a concert, a play, a ballet, or an opera, begin with the title of the work performed, italicized. Then give the author or composer of the work ("By"); relevant information such as the director ("Dir."), the choreographer ("Chor."), the conductor ("Cond."), or the major performers ("Perf."); the orchestra or the theater, ballet, or opera company, if any; the theater and location; the date of the performance; and the label "Performance."

The Brothers Size. By Tarell Alvin McCraney. Dir. Bijan Sheibani. Young Vic

Theatre, London. 15 Oct. 2008. Performance.

Symphony no. 4 in G. By Gustav Mahler. Cond. Mark Wigglesworth. Perf.

Juliane Banse and Boston Symphony Orch. Symphony Hall, Boston.

17 Apr. 2009. Performance.

■ **68. Lecture or public address** Begin with the speaker's name, followed by the title of the lecture (if any), in quotation marks; the organization sponsoring the lecture; the location; the date; and a label such as "Lecture" or "Address."

Wellbery, David E. "On a Sentence of Franz Kafka." Franke Inst. for the

Humanities. Gleacher Center, Chicago. 1 Feb. 2006. Lecture.

■ **69. Work of art** Cite the artist's name; the title of the artwork, italicized; the date of composition; the medium of composition (for instance, "Lithograph on paper," "Photograph," "Charcoal on paper"); and the institution and city in which the artwork is located. For artworks found online, omit the medium of composition and include the title of the Web site, the medium ("Web"), and your date of access.

Constable, John. *Dedham Vale*. 1802. Oil on canvas. Victoria and Albert

Museum, London.

Hessing, Valjean. *Caddo Myth*. 1976. Joslyn Art Museum, Omaha. *Joslyn*

Art Museum. Web. 19 Apr. 2009.

■ **70. Cartoon** Give the cartoonist's name; the title of the cartoon, if it has one, in quotation marks; the label "Cartoon" or "Comic strip"; publication information; and the medium. To cite an online cartoon, instead of publication information give the title of the Web site, the sponsor or publisher, the date of publication, the medium, and your date of access.

Keefe, Mike. "Veterans Affairs Overruns." Cartoon. *Denverpost.com*. Denver

Post, 11 Oct. 2009. Web. 12 Dec. 2009.

■ **71. Advertisement** Name the product or company being advertised, followed by the word "Advertisement." Give publication information for the source in which the advertisement appears.

Truth by Calvin Klein. Advertisement. *Vogue* Dec. 2000: 95-98. Print.

Arbella Insurance. Advertisement. *Boston.com*. NY Times, n.d. Web.

3 Sept. 2009.

■ **72. Map or chart** Cite a map or a chart as you would a book or a short work within a longer work. Use the word "Map" or "Chart" following the title. Add the medium and, for an online source, the sponsor or publisher and the date of access.

Joseph, Lori, and Bob Laird. "Driving While Phoning Is Dangerous." Chart.

USA Today 16 Feb. 2001: 1A. Print.

"Serbia." Map. *Syrena Maps*. Syrena, 2 Feb. 2001. Web. 17 Mar. 2009.

Other sources (including online versions)

This section includes a variety of sources not covered elsewhere. For online sources, consult the appropriate model in this section and also see items 34–55.

■ **73. Government document**   Treat the government agency as the author, giving the name of the government followed by the name of the department and the agency, if any. For print sources, add the medium at the end of the entry. For online sources, follow the model for an entire Web site (item 34) or a short work from a Web site (item 35).

government   department   agency
United States. Dept. of the Interior. Office of Inspector General. "Excessive

document title
Indulgences: Personal Use of the Internet at the Department of the

Web site title   publisher/sponsor
Interior." *Office of Inspector General*. Dept. of the Interior,

publication   date of access:
date   medium   day + month + year
Sept. 1999. Web. 20 May 2010.

Canada. Minister of Indian Affairs and Northern Dev. *Gathering Strength:*
Canada's Aboriginal Action Plan. Ottawa: Minister of Public Works
and Govt. Services Can., 2000. Print.

■ **74. Historical document**   To cite a historical document, such as the US Constitution or the Canadian Charter of Rights and Freedoms, begin with the document author, if it has one, and then give the document title, neither italicized nor in quotation marks, and the document date. For a print version, continue as for a selection in an anthology (see item 24) or for a book (with the title not italicized). For an online version, cite as a short work from a Web site (see item 35).

Jefferson, Thomas. First Inaugural Address. 1801. *The American Reader*.
Ed. Diane Ravitch. New York: Harper, 1990. 42-44. Print.

The Virginia Declaration of Rights. 1776. *A Chronology of US Historical*
Documents. U of Oklahoma Coll. of Law, 2008. Web. 23 Feb. 2009.

■ **75. Legal source**

Legislative act (law)

Begin with the name of the act, neither italicized nor in quotation marks. Then provide the act's Public Law number; its Statutes at Large volume and page numbers; its date of enactment; and the medium of publication.

Electronic Freedom of Information Act Amendments of 1996. Pub. L.

104-231. 110 Stat. 3048. 2 Oct. 1996. Print.

Court case

Name the first plaintiff and the first defendant. Then give the volume, name, and page numbers of the law report; the court name; the year of the decision; and publication information. Do not italicize the name of the case. (In the text of the paper, the name of the case is italicized; see item 19 on p. 487.)

Utah v. Evans. 536 US 452. Supreme Court of the US. 2002. *Supreme Court*

Collection. Legal Information Inst., Cornell U Law School, n.d. Web.

30 Apr. 2008.

■ **76. Pamphlet or brochure** Cite as you would a book (see items 16–33).

Commonwealth of Massachusetts. Dept. of Jury Commissioner. *A Few Facts*

about Jury Duty. Boston: Commonwealth of Massachusetts, 2004.

Print.

■ **77. Unpublished dissertation** Begin with the author's name, followed by the dissertation title in quotation marks; the abbreviation "Diss."; the name of the institution; the year the dissertation was accepted; and the medium of the dissertation.

Jackson, Shelley. "Writing Whiteness: Contemporary Southern Literature

in Black and White." Diss. U of Maryland, 2000. Print.

■ **78. Published dissertation** For dissertations that have been published in book form, italicize the title. After the title and before the book's publication information, give the abbreviation

"Diss.," the name of the institution, and the year the dissertation was accepted. Add the medium of publication at the end.

Damberg, Cheryl L. *Healthcare Reform: Distributional Consequences of an Employer Mandate for Workers in Small Firms*. Diss. Rand Graduate School, 1995. Santa Monica: Rand, 1996. Print.

■ **79. Abstract of a dissertation**   Cite an abstract as you would an unpublished dissertation. After the dissertation date, give the abbreviation *DA* or *DAI* (for *Dissertation Abstracts* or *Dissertation Abstracts International*), followed by the volume and issue numbers; the year of publication; inclusive page numbers or, if the abstract is not numbered, the item number; and the medium of publication. For an abstract accessed in an online database, give the item number in place of the page number, followed by the name of the database, the medium, and your date of access.

Chen, Shu Ling. "Mothers and Daughters in Morrison, Tan, Marshall, and Kincaid." Diss. U of Washington, 2000. *DAI* 61.6 (2000): AAT9975963. *ProQuest Dissertations and Theses*. Web. 22 Feb. 2009.

■ **80. Published proceedings of a conference**   Cite as you would a book, adding the name, date, and location of the conference after the title.

Urgo, Joseph R., and Ann J. Abadie, eds. *Faulkner and Material Culture*. Proc. of Faulkner and Yoknapatawpha Conf., 25-29 July 2004, U of Mississippi. Jackson: UP of Mississippi, 2007. Print.

■ **81. Paper in conference proceedings**   Cite as you would a selection in an anthology (see item 24), giving information about the conference after the title and editors of the conference proceedings (see item 80).

Henninger, Katherine R. "Faulkner, Photography, and a Regional Ethics of Form." *Faulkner and Material Culture*. Ed. Joseph R. Urgo and Ann J. Abadie. Proc. of Faulkner and Yoknapatawpha Conf., 25-29 July 2004, U of Mississippi. Jackson: UP of Mississippi, 2007. 121-38. Print.

■ **82. Published interview** Name the person interviewed, followed by the title of the interview (if there is one). If the interview does not have a title, include the word "Interview" after the interviewee's name. Give publication information for the work in which the interview was published.

Simon, David. "Beyond the Choir: An Interview with David Simon." *Film*

Quarterly 62.2 (2008/2009): 44-49. Print.

If you wish to include the name of the interviewer, put it after the title of the interview (or after the name of the interviewee if there is no title).

Florida, Richard. "The Great Reset." Interview by Conor Clarke. *Atlantic.*

Atlantic Monthly Group, Feb. 2009. Web. 28 Feb. 2010.

■ **83. Personal interview** To cite an interview that you conducted, begin with the name of the person interviewed. Then write "Personal interview" or "Telephone interview," followed by the date of the interview.

Akufo, Dautey. Personal interview. 11 Apr. 2010.

■ **84. Personal letter** To cite a letter that you received, begin with the writer's name and add the phrase "Letter to the author," followed by the date. Add the medium ("MS" for "manuscript," or a handwritten letter; "TS" for "typescript," or a typed letter).

Primak, Shoshana. Letter to the author. 6 May 2010. TS.

■ **85. Published letter** Begin with the writer of the letter, the words "Letter to" and the recipient, and the date of the letter (use "N.d." if the letter is undated). Then add the title of the collection and proceed as for a selection in an anthology (see item 24).

Wharton, Edith. Letter to Henry James. 28 Feb. 1915. *Henry James and*

Edith Wharton: Letters, 1900-1915. Ed. Lyall H. Powers. New York:

Scribner's, 1990. 323-26. Print.

■ **86. Manuscript** Give the author, a title or a description of the manuscript, and the date of composition, followed by the abbreviation "MS" for "manuscript" (handwritten) or "TS" for "typescript." Add the name and location of the institution housing the material. For a manuscript found online, give the preceding information but omit "MS" or "TS." Then list the title of the Web site, the medium ("Web"), and your date of access.

Arendt, Hannah. *Between Past and Present*. N.d. 1st draft. Hannah

Arendt Papers. MS Div., Lib. of Cong. *Manuscript Division, Library of*

Congress. Web. 24 Apr. 2009.

59c MLA information notes (optional)

Researchers who use the MLA system of parenthetical documentation may also use information notes for one of two purposes:

1. to provide additional material that is important but might interrupt the flow of the paper
2. to refer to several sources that support a single point or to provide comments on sources

Information notes may be either footnotes or endnotes. Footnotes appear at the foot of the page; endnotes appear on a separate page at the end of the paper, just before the list of works cited. For either style, the notes are numbered consecutively throughout the paper. The text of the paper contains a raised arabic numeral that corresponds to the number of the note.

TEXT

In the past several years, employees have filed a number of lawsuits against employers because of online monitoring practices.[1]

NOTE

1. For a discussion of federal law applicable to electronic surveillance in the workplace, see Kesan 293.

60 MLA manuscript format; sample paper

The following guidelines are consistent with advice given in the *MLA Handbook for Writers of Research Papers*, 7th ed. (New York: MLA, 2009), and with typical requirements for student papers. For a sample MLA paper, see pages 527–32.

60a MLA manuscript format

Formatting the paper

Papers written in MLA style should be formatted as follows.

Materials and font   Use good-quality 8½" × 11" white paper. If your instructor does not require a specific font, choose one that is standard and easy to read (such as Times New Roman).

Title and identification   MLA does not require a title page. On the first page of your paper, place your name, your instructor's name, the course title, and the date on separate lines against the left margin. Then center your title. (See p. 527 for a sample first page.)

If your instructor requires a title page, ask for formatting guidelines.

Pagination   Put the page number preceded by your last name in the upper right corner of each page, one-half inch below the top edge. Use arabic numerals (1, 2, 3, and so on).

Margins, line spacing, and paragraph indents   Leave margins of one inch on all sides of the page. Left-align the text.

Double-space throughout the paper. Do not add extra space above or below the title of the paper or between paragraphs.

Indent the first line of each paragraph one-half inch from the left margin.

Capitalization and italics   In titles of works, capitalize all words except articles (*a, an, the*), prepositions (*to, from, between,* and so on), coordinating conjunctions (*and, but, or, nor, for, so, yet*), and the *to* in infinitives — unless they are the first or last word of the title or subtitle. Follow these guidelines in your paper even if the title appears in all capital or all lowercase letters in the source.

In the text of an MLA paper, when a complete sentence follows a colon, lowercase the first word following the colon unless the sentence is a direct quotation or a well-known expression or principle. (See the examples in item 1 on p. 481.)

Italicize the titles of books, periodicals, and other long works, such as Web sites. Use quotation marks around the titles of periodical articles, short stories, poems, and other short works. (If your instructor prefers underlining, use it consistently in place of italics.)

Long quotations   When a quotation is longer than four typed lines of prose or three lines of verse, set it off from the text by indenting the entire quotation one inch from the left margin. Double-space the indented quotation, and do not add extra space above or below it.

Do not use quotation marks when a quotation has been set off from the text by indenting. See page 528 for an example.

URLs (Web addresses)   When you need to break a URL at the end of a line in the text of your paper, break it only after a double slash or a slash and do not insert a hyphen. For MLA rules on dividing URLs in your list of works cited, see page 526.

Headings   MLA neither encourages nor discourages the use of headings and provides no guidelines for their use. If you would like to insert headings in a long essay or research paper, check first with your instructor.

Visuals   MLA classifies visuals as tables and figures (figures include graphs, charts, maps, photographs, and drawings). Label each table with an arabic numeral ("Table 1," "Table 2," and so on) and provide a clear caption that identifies the subject. Capitalize the caption as you would a title (see 45c); do not italicize the label and caption or place them in quotation marks. The label and caption should appear on separate lines above the table, flush with the left margin.

For a table that you have borrowed or adapted, give the source below the table in a note like the following:

Source: David N. Greenfield and Richard A. Davis; "Lost in Cyberspace: The Web @ Work"; *CyberPsychology and Behavior* 5.4 (2002): 349; print.

For each figure, place the figure number (using the abbreviation "Fig.") and a caption below the figure, flush left. Capitalize the caption as you would a sentence; include source information following the caption. (When referring to the figure in your paper, use the abbreviation "fig." in parenthetical citations; otherwise spell out the word.) See page 531 for an example of a figure in a paper.

Place visuals in the text, as close as possible to the sentences that relate to them, unless your instructor prefers that visuals appear in an appendix.

Preparing the list of works cited

Begin the list of works cited on a new page at the end of the paper. Center the title "Works Cited" about one inch from the top of the page. Double-space throughout. See page 532 for a sample list of works cited.

Alphabetizing the list   Alphabetize the list by the last names of the authors (or editors); if a work has no author or editor, alphabetize by the first word of the title other than *A*, *An*, or *The*.

If your list includes two or more works by the same author, use the author's name for the first entry only. For subsequent entries, use three hyphens followed by a period. List the titles in alphabetical order. (See item 6 on p. 493.)

Indenting   Do not indent the first line of each works cited entry, but indent any additional lines one-half inch. This technique highlights the beginning of each entry, making it easy for readers to scan the alphabetized list. See page 532.

URLs (Web addresses)   If you need to include a URL in a works cited entry and it must be divided across lines, break the URL only after a double slash or a slash. Do not insert a hyphen at the end of the line. Insert angle brackets around the URL. (See the note following item 34 on p. 506.) If your word processing program automatically turns URLs into links (by underlining them and changing the color), turn off this feature.

60b Sample research paper: MLA style

On the following pages is a research paper on the topic of electronic surveillance in the workplace, written by Anna Orlov, a student in a composition class. Orlov's paper is documented with in-text citations and a list of works cited in MLA style. Annotations in the margins of the paper draw your attention to Orlov's use of MLA style and her effective writing.

MODELS   hackerhandbooks.com/rules
> Model papers > MLA research papers: Orlov; Daly; Levi
> MLA annotated bibliography: Orlov

Orlov 1

Anna Orlov

Professor Willis

English 101

17 March 2009

Online Monitoring:

A Threat to Employee Privacy in the Wired Workplace

As the Internet has become an integral tool of businesses,
company policies on Internet usage have become as common as
policies regarding vacation days or sexual harassment. A 2005
study by the American Management Association and ePolicy
Institute found that 76% of companies monitor employees' use
of the Web, and the number of companies that block employees'
access to certain Web sites has increased 27% since 2001 (1).
Unlike other company rules, however, Internet usage policies
often include language authorizing companies to secretly monitor
their employees, a practice that raises questions about rights
in the workplace. Although companies often have legitimate
concerns that lead them to monitor employees' Internet usage—
from expensive security breaches to reduced productivity—the
benefits of electronic surveillance are outweighed by its costs to
employees' privacy and autonomy.

While surveillance of employees is not a new phenomenon,
electronic surveillance allows employers to monitor workers
with unprecedented efficiency. In his book *The Naked
Employee*, Frederick Lane describes offline ways in which
employers have been permitted to intrude on employees'
privacy for decades, such as drug testing, background checks,
psychological exams, lie detector tests, and in-store video
surveillance. The difference, Lane argues, between these old
methods of data gathering and electronic surveillance involves
quantity:

Title is centered.

Opening sentences
provide background
for the thesis.

Thesis asserts Orlov's
main point.

Summary and long
quotation are each
introduced with a
signal phrase
naming the author.

Marginal annotations indicate MLA-style formatting and effective writing.

Orlov 2

Long quotation is set off from the text; quotation marks are omitted.

> Technology makes it possible for employers to gather enormous amounts of data about employees, often far beyond what is necessary to satisfy safety or productivity concerns. And the trends that drive technology—faster, smaller, cheaper—make it possible for larger and larger numbers of employers to gather ever-greater amounts of personal data. (3-4)

Page number is given in parentheses after the final period.

In an age when employers can collect data whenever employees use their computers—when they send e-mail, surf the Web, or even arrive at or depart from their workstations—the challenge for both employers and employees is to determine how much is too much.

Clear topic sentences, like this one, are used throughout the paper.

Another key difference between traditional surveillance and electronic surveillance is that employers can monitor workers' computer use secretly. One popular monitoring method is keystroke logging, which is done by means of an undetectable program on employees' computers. The Web site of a vendor for Spector Pro, a popular keystroke logging program, explains that the software can be installed to operate in "Stealth" mode so that it "does not show up as an icon, does not appear in the Windows system tray, . . . [and] cannot be uninstalled without

Source with an unknown author is cited by a shortened title.

the Spector Pro password which YOU specify" ("Automatically"). As Lane explains, these programs record every key entered into the computer in hidden directories that can later be accessed or uploaded by supervisors; the programs can even scan for keywords tailored to individual companies (128-29).

Orlov anticipates objections and provides sources for opposing views.

Some experts have argued that a range of legitimate concerns justifies employer monitoring of employee Internet usage. As *PC World* columnist Daniel Tynan points out, companies that don't monitor network traffic can be penalized for their ignorance: "Employees could accidentally (or deliberately) spill

Orlov 3

confidential information . . . or allow worms to spread throughout
a corporate network." The ePolicy Institute, an organization
that advises companies about reducing risks from technology,
reported that breaches in computer security cost institutions
$100 million in 1999 alone (Flynn). Companies also are held
legally accountable for many of the transactions conducted on
their networks and with their technology. Legal scholar Jay Kesan
points out that the law holds employers liable for employees'
actions such as violations of copyright laws, the distribution of
offensive or graphic sexual material, and illegal disclosure of
confidential information (312).

These kinds of concerns should give employers, in certain
instances, the right to monitor employee behavior. But employers
rushing to adopt surveillance programs might not be adequately
weighing the effect such programs can have on employee morale.
Employers must consider the possibility that employees will
perceive surveillance as a breach of trust that can make them
feel like disobedient children, not responsible adults who wish
to perform their jobs professionally and autonomously.

Yet determining how much autonomy workers should be
given is complicated by the ambiguous nature of productivity
in the wired workplace. On the one hand, computers and
Internet access give employees powerful tools to carry out their
jobs; on the other hand, the same technology offers constant
temptations to avoid work. As a 2005 study by *Salary.com* and
America Online indicates, the Internet ranked as the top choice
among employees for ways of wasting time on the job; it beat
talking with co-workers—the second most popular method—by
a margin of nearly two to one (Frauenheim). Chris Gonsalves, an
editor for *eWeek.com*, argues that the technology has changed
the terms between employers and employees: "While bosses can

Transition helps
readers move from
one paragraph to
the next.

Orlov treats both
sides fairly; she
provides a transition
to her own argument.

Orlov 4

easily detect and interrupt water-cooler chatter," he writes, "the
employee who is shopping at Lands' End or IMing with fellow
fantasy baseball managers may actually appear to be working."
The gap between behaviors that are observable to managers and
the employee's actual activities when sitting behind a computer
has created additional motivations for employers to invest in
surveillance programs. "Dilbert," a popular cartoon that spoofs
office culture, aptly captures how rampant recreational Internet
use has become in the workplace (see fig. 1).

But monitoring online activities can have the unintended
effect of making employees resentful. As many workers would be
quick to point out, Web surfing and other personal uses of the
Internet can provide needed outlets in the stressful work
environment; many scholars have argued that limiting and
policing these outlets can exacerbate tensions between employees
and managers. Kesan warns that "prohibiting personal use can
seem extremely arbitrary and can seriously harm morale. . . .
Imagine a concerned parent who is prohibited from checking on
a sick child by a draconian company policy" (315-16). As this
analysis indicates, employees can become disgruntled when
Internet usage policies are enforced to their full extent.

Additionally, many experts disagree with employers'
assumption that online monitoring can increase productivity.
Employment law attorney Joseph Schmitt argues that, particularly
for employees who are paid a salary rather than an hourly wage,
"a company shouldn't care whether employees spend one or
10 hours on the Internet as long as they are getting their jobs
done—and provided that they are not accessing inappropriate
sites" (qtd. in Verespej). Other experts even argue that time
spent on personal Internet browsing can actually be productive
for companies. According to Bill Coleman, an executive at

No page number is available for this Web source.

Orlov counters opposing views and provides support for her argument.

Orlov uses a brief signal phrase to move from her argument to the words of a source.

Orlov cites an indirect source: words quoted in another source.

Orlov 5

Fig. 1. This "Dilbert" comic strip suggests that personal Internet usage is widespread in the workplace (Adams 106).

Illustration has figure number, caption, and source information.

Salary.com, "Personal Internet use and casual office conversations often turn into new business ideas or suggestions for gaining operating efficiencies" (qtd. in Frauenheim). Employers, in other words, may benefit from showing more faith in their employees' ability to exercise their autonomy.

Employees' right to privacy and autonomy in the workplace, however, remains a murky area of the law. Although evaluating where to draw the line between employee rights and employer powers is often a duty that falls to the judicial system, the courts have shown little willingness to intrude on employers' exercise of control over their computer networks. Federal law provides few guidelines related to online monitoring of employees, and only Connecticut and Delaware require companies to disclose this type of surveillance to employees (Tam et al.). "It is unlikely that we will see a legally guaranteed zone of privacy in the American workplace," predicts Kesan (293). This reality leaves employees and employers to sort the potential risks and benefits of technology in contract agreements and terms of employment. With continuing advances in technology, protecting both employers and employees will require greater awareness of these programs, better disclosure to employees, and a more public discussion about what types of protections are necessary to guard individual freedoms in the wired workplace.

Orlov sums up her argument and suggests a course of action.

Orlov 6

Heading is centered.

Works Cited

Adams, Scott. *Dilbert and the Way of the Weasel*. New York:

Harper, 2002. Print.

American Management Association and ePolicy Institute.

"2005 Electronic Monitoring and Surveillance Survey."

American Management Association. Amer. Management

Assn., 2005. Web. 15 Feb. 2009.

"Automatically Record Everything They Do Online! Spector Pro 5.0

FAQ's." *Netbus.org*. Netbus.Org, n.d. Web. 17 Feb. 2009.

Flynn, Nancy. "Internet Policies." *ePolicy Institute*. ePolicy

Inst., n.d. Web. 15 Feb. 2009.

Frauenheim, Ed. "Stop Reading This Headline and Get Back

to Work." *CNET News.com*. CNET Networks, 11 July

2005. Web. 17 Feb. 2009.

Gonsalves, Chris. "Wasting Away on the Web." *eWeek.com*.

Ziff Davis Enterprise Holdings, 8 Aug. 2005. Web.

16 Feb. 2009.

Kesan, Jay P. "Cyber-Working or Cyber-Shirking? A First Principles

Examination of Electronic Privacy in the Workplace."

Florida Law Review 54.2 (2002): 289-332. Print.

Lane, Frederick S., III. *The Naked Employee: How Technology

Is Compromising Workplace Privacy*. New York: Amer.

Management Assn., 2003. Print.

Tam, Pui-Wing, et al. "Snooping E-Mail by Software Is Now

a Workplace Norm." *Wall Street Journal* 9 Mar. 2005:

B1+. Print.

Tynan, Daniel. "Your Boss Is Watching." *PC World*. PC World

Communications, 6 Oct. 2004. Web. 17 Sept. 2009.

Verespej, Michael A. "Inappropriate Internet Surfing."

Industry Week. Penton Media, 7 Feb. 2000. Web.

16 Feb. 2009.

Margin notes:
List is alphabetized by authors' last names (or by title when a work has no author).

Abbreviation "n.d." indicates that the online source has no update date.

First line of each entry is at the left margin; extra lines are indented ½".

Double-spacing is used throughout.

A work with four authors is listed by the first author's name and the abbreviation "et al." (for "and others").

Writing Papers
in APA Style

Writing Papers in APA Style, 533

Directory to APA in-text citation models, 534
Directory to APA reference list models, 534

Writing Papers in APA Style

Directory to APA in-text citation models

Directory to APA reference list models

Most social science instructors will ask you to document your sources with the American Psychological Association (APA) system of in-text citations and references described in 64. You face three main challenges when writing a social science paper that draws on sources: (1) supporting a thesis, (2) citing your sources and avoiding plagiarism, and (3) integrating quotations and other source material.

Examples in this section are drawn from one student's research for a review of the literature on treatments for childhood obesity. Luisa Mirano's paper appears on pages 583–94.

61 Supporting a thesis

Most assignments ask you to form a thesis, or main idea, and to support that thesis with well-organized evidence. (See also 1c.) In a paper reviewing the literature on a topic, the thesis analyzes the often competing conclusions drawn by a variety of researchers.

61a Form a working thesis.

Once you have read a variety of sources and considered your issue from different perspectives, you are ready to form a working thesis: a one-sentence (or occasionally a two-sentence) statement of your central idea. (See also 1c.) Because it is a working, or tentative, thesis, you can remain flexible and revise it as your ideas develop. Ultimately, your thesis will express not just your opinion but your informed, reasoned answer to your research question (see 53a). Here, for example, is a research question posed by Luisa Mirano, a student in a psychology class, followed by her thesis in answer to that question.

RESEARCH QUESTION

Is medication the right treatment for the escalating problem of childhood obesity?

WORKING THESIS

Treating cases of childhood obesity with medication alone is too narrow an approach for this growing problem.

Notice that the thesis expresses a view on a debatable issue — an issue about which intelligent, well-meaning people might disagree. The writer's job is to persuade such readers that this view is worth taking seriously.

61b Organize your ideas.

The American Psychological Association encourages the use of headings to help readers follow the organization of a paper. For an original research report, the major headings often follow a standard model: Method, Results, Discussion. The introduction is not given a heading; it consists of the material between the title of the paper and the first heading.

For a literature review, headings will vary. The student who wrote about treatments for childhood obesity used four questions to focus her research; the questions then became headings in her paper (see pp. 583–94).

> **Making the most of your handbook**
> A working thesis and rough outline can help writers get started.
> ▶ Drafting a working thesis: 1c
> ▶ Sketching a plan: 1d

61c Use sources to inform and support your argument.

Used thoughtfully, your source materials will make your argument more complex and convincing for readers. Sources can play several different roles as you develop your points.

Providing background information or context

You can use facts and statistics to support generalizations or to establish the importance of your topic, as student writer Luisa Mirano does in her introduction.

In March 2004, U.S. Surgeon General Richard Carmona called attention to a health problem in the United States that, until recently, has been overlooked: childhood obesity. Carmona said that

the "astounding" 15% child obesity rate constitutes an "epidemic."
Since the early 1980s, that rate has "doubled in children and tripled
in adolescents." Now more than 9 million children are classified
as obese.

Explaining terms or concepts

If readers are unlikely to be familiar with a word, a phrase, or an
idea important to your topic, you must explain it for them. Quoting or paraphrasing a source can help you define terms and concepts in accessible language. Luisa Mirano uses a scholarly source
to explain how one of the major obesity drugs functions.

> Sibutramine suppresses appetite by blocking the reuptake of the
> neurotransmitters serotonin and norepinephrine in the brain
> (Yanovski & Yanovski, 2002, p. 594).

Supporting your claims

As you draft your argument, make sure to back up your assertions
with facts, examples, and other evidence from your research (see
also 6e). Luisa Mirano, for example, uses one source's findings to
support her central idea that the medical treatment of childhood
obesity has limitations.

> As journalist Greg Critser (2003) noted in his book *Fat Land*, use of
> weight-loss drugs is unlikely to have an effect without the proper
> "support system"—one that includes doctors, facilities, time, and
> money (p. 3).

Lending authority to your argument

Expert opinion can add credibility to your argument (see also 6e).
But don't rely on experts to make your argument for you. Construct
your argument in your own words and, when appropriate, cite the
judgment of an authority in the field for support.

> Both medical experts and policymakers recognize that solutions
> might come not only from a laboratory but also from policy,
> education, and advocacy. A handbook designed to educate

doctors on obesity called for "major changes in some aspects of western culture" (Hoppin & Taveras, 2004, Conclusion section, para. 1).

Anticipating and countering alternative interpretations

Do not ignore sources that seem contrary to your position or that offer interpretations different from your own. Instead, use them to give voice to opposing points of view and alternative interpretations before you counter them (see 6f). Readers often have objections in mind already, whether or not they agree with you. Mirano uses a source to acknowledge value in her opponents' position that medication alone can successfully treat childhood obesity.

> As researchers Yanovski and Yanovski (2002) have explained, obesity was once considered "either a moral failing or evidence of underlying psychopathology" (p. 592). But this view has shifted: Many medical professionals now consider obesity a biomedical rather than a moral condition, influenced by both genetic and environmental factors. Yanovski and Yanovski have further noted that the development of weight-loss medications in the early 1990s showed that "obesity should be treated in the same manner as any other chronic disease . . . through the long-term use of medication" (p. 592).

62 Citing sources; avoiding plagiarism

Your research paper is a collaboration between you and your sources. To be fair and ethical, you must acknowledge your debt to the writers of those sources. When you acknowledge your sources, you avoid plagiarism, a form of academic dishonesty.

Three different acts are considered plagiarism: (1) failing to cite quotations and borrowed ideas, (2) failing to enclose borrowed language in quotation marks, and (3) failing to put summaries and paraphrases in your own words. It's a good idea to find out how your school defines and addresses academic dishonesty. (See also 55c.)

62a Cite quotations and borrowed ideas.

Sources are cited for two reasons:

- to tell readers where your information comes from — so that they can assess its reliability and, if interested, find and read the original source
- to give credit to the writers from whom you have borrowed words and ideas

You must cite anything you borrow from a source, including direct quotations; statistics and other specific facts; visuals such as tables, graphs, and diagrams; and any ideas you present in a summary or paraphrase.

The only exception is common knowledge — information that your readers may know or could easily locate in any number of reference sources. For example, most general encyclopedias will tell readers that Sigmund Freud wrote *The Interpretation of Dreams* and that chimpanzees can learn American Sign Language.

As a rule, when you have seen certain information repeatedly in your reading, you don't need to cite it. However, when information has appeared in only a few sources, when it is highly specific (as with statistics), or when it is controversial, you should cite the source.

The American Psychological Association recommends an author-date system of citations. The following is a brief description of how the author-date system often works.

1. The source is introduced by a signal phrase that includes the last name of the author followed by the date of publication in parentheses.
2. The material being cited is followed by a page number in parentheses.
3. At the end of the paper, an alphabetized list of references gives complete publication information for the source.

IN-TEXT CITATION

As researchers Yanovski and Yanovski (2002) have explained, obesity was once considered "either a moral failing or evidence of underlying psychopathology" (p. 592).

ENTRY IN THE LIST OF REFERENCES

Yanovski, S. Z., & Yanovski, J. A. (2002). Drug therapy: Obesity. *The New England Journal of Medicine, 346,* 591-602.

This basic APA format varies for different types of sources. For a detailed discussion and other models, see 64.

62b Enclose borrowed language in quotation marks.

To indicate that you are using a source's exact phrases or sentences, you must enclose them in quotation marks unless they have been set off from the text by indenting (see p. 545). To omit the quotation marks is to claim — falsely — that the language is your own. Such an omission is plagiarism even if you have cited the source.

ORIGINAL SOURCE

In an effort to seek the causes of this disturbing trend, experts have pointed to a range of important potential contributors to the rise in childhood obesity that are unrelated to media: a reduction in physical education classes and after-school athletic programs, an increase in the availability of sodas and snacks in public schools, the growth in the number of fast-food outlets across the country, the trend toward "super-sizing" food portions in restaurants, and the increasing number of highly processed high-calorie and high-fat grocery products.

— Henry J. Kaiser Family Foundation, "The Role of Media in Childhood Obesity" (2004), p. 1

PLAGIARISM

According to the Henry J. Kaiser Family Foundation (2004), experts have pointed to a range of important potential contributors to the rise in childhood obesity that are unrelated to media (p. 1).

BORROWED LANGUAGE IN QUOTATION MARKS

According to the Henry J. Kaiser Family Foundation (2004), "experts have pointed to a range of important potential contributors to the rise in childhood obesity that are unrelated to media" (p. 1).

NOTE: Quotation marks are not used when quoted sentences are set off from the text by indenting (see p. 545).

62c Put summaries and paraphrases in your own words.

Summaries and paraphrases are written in your own words. A summary condenses information; a paraphrase conveys the information using roughly the same number of words as in the original source. When you summarize or paraphrase, it is not enough to name the source; you must restate the source's meaning using your own language. (See also 55c.) You commit plagiarism if you half-copy the author's sentences — either by mixing the author's phrases with your own without using quotation marks or by plugging your own synonyms into the author's sentence structure. The following paraphrases are plagiarized — even though the source is cited — because their language and sentence structure are too close to those of the source.

ORIGINAL SOURCE

In an effort to seek the causes of this disturbing trend, experts have pointed to a range of important potential contributors to the rise in childhood obesity that are unrelated to media.

> — Henry J. Kaiser Family Foundation, "The Role of Media in Childhood Obesity" (2004), p. 1

UNACCEPTABLE BORROWING OF PHRASES

According to the Henry J. Kaiser Family Foundation (2004), experts have indicated a range of significant potential contributors to the rise in childhood obesity that are not linked to media (p. 1).

UNACCEPTABLE BORROWING OF STRUCTURE

According to the Henry J. Kaiser Family Foundation (2004), experts have identified a variety of key factors causing a rise in childhood obesity, factors that are not tied to media (p. 1).

To avoid plagiarizing an author's language, resist the temptation to look at the source while you are summarizing or paraphrasing. After you have read the passage you want to paraphrase, set the source aside. Ask yourself, "What is the author's meaning?" In your own words, state your understanding of the author's basic point. Return to the source and check that you haven't used the author's language or sentence structure or misrepresented the author's ideas. When you fully understand another writer's meaning, you can more easily and accurately present those ideas in your own words.

ACCEPTABLE PARAPHRASE

A report by the Henry J. Kaiser Family Foundation (2004) described causes other than media for the childhood obesity crisis.

 63 Integrating sources

Quotations, summaries, paraphrases, and facts will help you develop your argument, but they cannot speak for you. You can use several strategies to integrate information from sources into your paper while maintaining your own voice.

63a Use quotations appropriately.

In your academic writing, keep the emphasis on your ideas; use your own words to summarize and to paraphrase your sources and to explain your points. Sometimes, however, quotations can be the most effective way to integrate a source.

Limiting your use of quotations

Although it is tempting to insert many quotations in your paper and to use your own words only for connecting passages, do not quote excessively. It is almost impossible to integrate numerous long quotations smoothly into your own text.

WHEN TO USE QUOTATIONS

- When language is especially vivid or expressive
- When exact wording is needed for technical accuracy
- When it is important to let the debaters of an issue explain their positions in their own words
- When the words of an authority lend weight to an argument
- When the language of a source is the topic of your discussion

It is not always necessary to quote full sentences from a source. To reduce your reliance on the words of others, you can often integrate language from a source into your own sentence structure.

> Carmona (2004) advised the subcommittee that the situation constitutes an "epidemic" and that the skyrocketing statistics are "astounding."

> As researchers continue to face a number of unknowns about obesity, it may be helpful to envision treating the disorder, as Yanovski and Yanovski (2002) suggested, "in the same manner as any other chronic disease" (p. 592).

Using the ellipsis mark

To condense a quoted passage, you can use the ellipsis mark (three periods, with spaces between) to indicate that you have omitted words. What remains must be grammatically complete.

> Roman (2003) reported that "social factors are nearly as significant as individual metabolism in the formation of . . . dietary habits of adolescents" (p. 345).

The writer has omitted the words *both healthy and unhealthy* from the source.

When you want to leave out one or more full sentences, use a period before the three ellipsis dots.

> According to Sothern and Gordon (2003), "Environmental factors may contribute as much as 80% to the causes of childhood obesity. . . . Research suggests that obese children demonstrate decreased levels of physical activity and increased psychosocial problems" (p. 104).

Ordinarily, do not use an ellipsis mark at the beginning or at the end of a quotation. Readers will understand that you have taken the quoted material from a longer passage, so such marks are not necessary. The only exception occurs when you have dropped words at the end of the final quoted sentence. In such cases, put three ellipsis dots before the closing quotation mark. Make sure that omissions and ellipsis marks do not distort the meaning of your source.

Using brackets

Brackets allow you to insert your own words into quoted material. You can insert words in brackets to clarify a confusing reference or to keep a sentence grammatical in your context.

> The cost of treating obesity currently totals $117 billion per year—a
> price, according to the surgeon general, "second only to the cost of
> [treating] tobacco use" (Carmona, 2004).

To indicate an error such as a misspelling in a quotation, insert [*sic*], italicized and with brackets around it, right after the error. (See 39c.)

Setting off long quotations

When you quote forty or more words from a source, set off the quotation by indenting it one-half inch from the left margin. Use the normal right margin and do not single-space the quotation.

Long quotations should be introduced by an informative sentence, usually followed by a colon. Quotation marks are unnecessary because the indented format tells readers that the passage is taken word-for-word from the source.

> Yanovski and Yanovski (2002) have described earlier treatments of
> obesity that focused on behavior modification:
>
>> With the advent of behavioral treatments for obesity in the
>> 1960s, hope arose that modification of maladaptive eating and
>> exercise habits would lead to sustained weight loss, and that
>> time-limited programs would produce permanent changes in
>> weight. Medications for the treatment of obesity were proposed
>> as short-term adjuncts for patients, who would presumably then
>> acquire the skills necessary to continue to lose weight, reach
>> "ideal body weight," and maintain a reduced weight indefinitely.
>> (p. 592)

Notice that at the end of an indented quotation the parenthetical citation goes outside the final mark of punctuation. (When a quotation is run into your text, the opposite is true. See the sample citations on p. 544.)

63b Use signal phrases to integrate sources.

Whenever you include a paraphrase, summary, or direct quotation of another writer's work in your paper, prepare your readers for it with a signal phrase. A signal phrase usually names the author of the source, gives the publication year in parentheses, and often provides some context. It commonly appears before the source material. To vary your sentence structure, you may decide to interrupt source material with a signal phrase or place the signal phrase after your paraphrase, summary, or direct quotation. It is generally acceptable in the social sciences to call authors by their last name only, even on a first mention. If your paper refers to two authors with the same last name, use initials as well.

Using signal phrases in APA papers

To avoid monotony, try to vary both the language and the placement of your signal phrases.

Model signal phrases

In the words of Carmona (2004), ". . ."

As Yanovski and Yanovski (2002) have noted, ". . ."

Hoppin and Taveras (2004), medical researchers, pointed out that ". . ."

". . . ," claimed Critser (2003).

". . . ," wrote Duenwald (2004), ". . ."

Researchers McDuffie et al. (2003) have offered a compelling argument for this view: ". . ."

Hilts (2002) answered objections with the following analysis: ". . ."

Verbs in signal phrases

admitted	contended	reasoned
agreed	declared	refuted
argued	denied	rejected
asserted	emphasized	reported
believed	insisted	responded
claimed	noted	suggested
compared	observed	thought
confirmed	pointed out	wrote

When you write a signal phrase, choose a verb that is appropriate for the way you are using the source (see 61c). Are you providing background, explaining a concept, supporting a claim, lending authority, or refuting an argument? See the chart on page 546 for a list of verbs commonly used in signal phrases. Note that APA requires using verbs in the past tense or present perfect tense (*explained* or *has explained*) to introduce source material. Use the present tense only for discussing the results of an experiment (*the results show*) or knowledge that has been clearly established (*researchers agree*).

Marking boundaries

Readers need to move from your words to the words of a source without feeling a jolt. Avoid dropping direct quotations into your text without warning. Instead, provide clear signal phrases, including at least the author's name and the year of publication. Signal phrases mark the boundaries between source material and your own words; they can also tell readers why a source is worth quoting. (The signal phrase is highlighted in the second example.)

DROPPED QUOTATION

Obesity was once considered in a very different light. "For many years, obesity was approached as it if were either a moral failing or evidence of underlying psychopathology" (Yanovski & Yanovski, 2002, p. 592).

QUOTATION WITH SIGNAL PHRASE

Obesity was once considered in a very different light. As researchers Yanovski and Yanovski (2002) have explained, obesity was widely thought of as "either a moral failing or evidence of underlying psychopathology" (p. 592).

Using signal phrases with summaries and paraphrases

As with quotations, you should introduce most summaries and paraphrases with a signal phrase that mentions the author and the year and places the material in the context of your argument. Readers will then understand where the summary or paraphrase begins.

Without the signal phrase (highlighted) in the example on page 548, readers might think that only the last sentence is being cited, when in fact the whole paragraph is based on the source.

> Carmona (2004) advised a Senate subcommittee that the problem
> of childhood obesity is dire and that the skyrocketing statistics—
> which put the child obesity rate at 15%—are cause for alarm. More
> than 9 million children, double the number in the early 1980s, are
> classified as obese. Carmona warned that obesity can cause myriad
> physical problems that only worsen as children grow older.

There are times, however, when a summary or a paraphrase does not require a signal phrase naming the author. When the context makes clear where the cited material begins, you may omit the signal phrase and include the author's name and the year in parentheses. Unless the work is short, also include the page number in the parentheses.

Integrating statistics and other facts

When you are citing a statistic or another specific fact, a signal phrase is often not necessary. In most cases, readers will understand that the citation refers to the statistic or fact (not the whole paragraph).

> In purely financial terms, the drugs cost more than $3 a day on
> average (Duenwald, 2004).

There is nothing wrong, however, with using a signal phrase to introduce a statistic or another fact.

> Duenwald (2004) reported that the drugs cost more than $3 a day
> on average.

Putting source material in context

Readers should not have to guess why source material appears in your paper. If you use another writer's words, you must explain how they relate to your point. In other words, you must put the source in context. It's a good idea to embed a quotation between sentences of your own, introducing it with a signal phrase and following it up with interpretive comments that link the quotation to your paper's argument. (See also 63c.)

QUOTATION WITH EFFECTIVE CONTEXT

> A report by the Henry J. Kaiser Family Foundation (2004) outlined
> trends that may have contributed to the childhood obesity crisis,
> including food advertising for children as well as

a reduction in physical education classes . . . , an increase
in the availability of sodas and snacks in public schools, the
growth in the number of fast-food outlets . . . , and the
increasing number of highly processed high-calorie and
high-fat grocery products. (p. 1)

Addressing each of these areas requires more than a doctor armed with
a prescription pad; it requires a broad mobilization not just of doctors
and concerned parents but of educators, food industry executives,
advertisers, and media representatives.

63c Synthesize sources.

When you synthesize multiple sources in a research paper, you
create a conversation about your research topic. You show readers how the ideas of one source relate to those of another by connecting and analyzing the ideas in the context of your argument.
Keep the emphasis on your own writing. The thread of your argument should be easy to identify and to understand, with or
without your sources.

SAMPLE SYNTHESIS (DRAFT)

Student writer Luisa Mirano begins with a claim that needs support.

Signal phrases indicate how sources contribute to Mirano's paper and show that the ideas that follow are not her own.

Mirano interprets and connects sources. Each paragraph ends with her own thoughts.

Medical treatments have clear costs for
individual patients, including unpleasant side
effects, little information about long-term use,
and uncertainty that they will yield significant
weight loss. The financial burden is heavy as well;
the drugs cost more than $3 a day on average
(Duenwald, 2004). In each of the clinical trials,
use of medication was accompanied by expensive
behavioral therapies, including counseling,
nutrition education, fitness advising, and
monitoring. As Critser (2003) noted in his book
Fat Land, use of weight-loss drugs is unlikely
to have an effect without the proper "support
system"—one that includes doctors, facilities,
time, and money (p. 3). For many families, this
level of care is prohibitively expensive.

Student writer

Source 1

Student writer

Source 2

Student writer

> Both medical experts and policymakers | Student writer
> recognize that solutions might come not only from
> a laboratory but also from policy, education, and
> advocacy. A handbook designed to educate doctors
> on obesity called for "major changes in some | Source 3
> aspects of western culture" (Hoppin & Taveras,
> 2004, Conclusion section, para. 1). Solving the | Student writer
> childhood obesity problem will require broad
> mobilization of doctors and concerned parents
> and also of educators, food industry executives,
> advertisers, and media representatives.

In this draft, Mirano uses her own analyses to shape the conversation among her sources. She does not simply string quotations and statistics together or allow her sources to overwhelm her writing. The final sentence, written in her own voice, gives her an opportunity to explain to readers how her sources support and extend her argument.

When synthesizing sources, ask yourself these questions:

- Which sources inform, support, or extend your argument?
- Have you varied the functions of sources — to provide background, explain concepts, lend authority, and anticipate counterarguments? Do your signal phrases indicate these functions?
- Do you explain how your sources support your argument?
- Do you connect and analyze sources in your own voice?
- Is your own argument easy to identify and to understand, with or without your sources?

64 Documenting sources in APA style

In most social science classes, you will be asked to use the APA system for documenting sources, which is set forth in the *Publication Manual of the American Psychological Association*, 6th ed. (Washington: APA, 2010). APA recommends in-text citations that refer readers to a list of references.

An in-text citation usually gives the author of the source (often in a signal phrase), the year of publication, and at times a page number in parentheses. At the end of the paper, a list of references provides publication information about the source (see pp. 593–94 for a sample list). The direct link between the in-text citation and the entry in the reference list is highlighted in the following example.

IN-TEXT CITATION

Yanovski and Yanovski (2002) reported that "the current state of the treatment for obesity is similar to the state of the treatment of hypertension several decades ago" (p. 600).

ENTRY IN THE LIST OF REFERENCES

Yanovski, S. Z., & Yanovski, J. A. (2002). Drug therapy: Obesity. *The New England Journal of Medicine, 346,* 591-602.

For a reference list that includes this entry, see pages 593–94.

64a APA in-text citations

APA's in-text citations provide at least the author's last name and the year of publication. For direct quotations and some paraphrases, a page number is given as well.

NOTE: APA style requires the use of the past tense or the present perfect tense in signal phrases introducing cited material: *Smith (2005) reported . . . , Smith (2005) has argued. . . .*

■ **1. Basic format for a quotation** Ordinarily, introduce the quotation with a signal phrase that includes the author's last name followed by the year of publication in parentheses. Put the page number (preceded by "p.") in parentheses after the quotation.

Critser (2003) noted that despite growing numbers of overweight Americans, many health care providers still "remain either in ignorance or outright denial about the health danger to the poor and the young" (p. 5).

If the author is not named in the signal phrase, place the author's name, the year, and the page number in parentheses after the quotation: (Critser, 2003, p. 5).

NOTE: APA style requires the year of publication in an in-text citation. Do not include a month, even if the entry in the reference list includes the month.

■ **2. Basic format for a summary or a paraphrase** Include the author's last name and the year either in a signal phrase introducing the material or in parentheses following it. A page number is not required for a summary or a paraphrase, but include one if it would help readers find the passage in a long work. (For the use of other locators, such as paragraph numbers or section names in online sources, see p. 555.)

> Yanovski and Yanovski (2002) explained that sibutramine suppresses appetite by blocking the reuptake of the neurotransmitters serotonin and norepinephrine in the brain (p. 594).

> Sibutramine suppresses appetite by blocking the reuptake of the neurotransmitters serotonin and norepinephrine in the brain (Yanovski & Yanovski, 2002, p. 594).

■ **3. Work with two authors** Give the names of both authors in the signal phrase or the parentheses each time you cite the work. In the parentheses, use "&" between the authors' names; in the signal phrase, use "and."

> According to Sothern and Gordon (2003), "Environmental factors may contribute as much as 80% to the causes of childhood obesity" (p. 104).

> Obese children often engage in limited physical activity (Sothern & Gordon, 2003, p. 104).

■ **4. Work with three to five authors** Identify all authors in the signal phrase or the parentheses the first time you cite the source.

> In 2003, Berkowitz, Wadden, Tershakovec, and Cronquist concluded, "Sibutramine . . . must be carefully monitored in adolescents, as in adults, to control increases in [blood pressure] and pulse rate" (p. 1811).

In subsequent citations, use the first author's name followed by "et al." in either the signal phrase or the parentheses.

> As Berkowitz et al. (2003) advised, "Until more extensive safety and efficacy data are available, . . . weight-loss medications should be used only on an experimental basis for adolescents" (p. 1811).

5. Work with six or more authors Use the first author's name followed by "et al." in the signal phrase or the parentheses.

> McDuffie et al. (2002) tested 20 adolescents, aged 12-16, over a three-month period and found that orlistat, combined with behavioral therapy, produced an average weight loss of 4.4 kg, or 9.7 pounds (p. 646).

6. Work with unknown author If the author is unknown, mention the work's title in the signal phrase or give the first word or two of the title in the parenthetical citation. Titles of short works such as articles and chapters are put in quotation marks; titles of long works such as books and reports are italicized. (For online sources with no author, see item 12 on pp. 554–55.)

> Children struggling to control their weight must also struggle with the pressures of television advertising that, on the one hand, encourages the consumption of junk food and, on the other, celebrates thin celebrities ("Television," 2002).

NOTE: In the rare case when "Anonymous" is specified as the author, treat it as if it were a real name: (Anonymous, 2001). In the list of references, also use the name Anonymous as author.

7. Organization as author If the author is a government agency or another organization, name the organization in the signal phrase or in the parenthetical citation the first time you cite the source.

> Obesity puts children at risk for a number of medical complications, including Type 2 diabetes, hypertension, sleep apnea, and orthopedic problems (Henry J. Kaiser Family Foundation, 2004, p. 1).

If the organization has a familiar abbreviation, you may include it in brackets the first time you cite the source and use the abbreviation alone in later citations (see p. 554).

FIRST CITATION	(Centers for Disease Control and Prevention [CDC], 2009)
LATER CITATIONS	(CDC, 2009)

8. Authors with the same last name To avoid confusion, use initials with the last names if your reference list includes two or more authors with the same last name.

> Research by E. Smith (1989) revealed that. . . .

9. Two or more works by the same author in the same year When your list of references includes more than one work by the same author in the same year, use lowercase letters ("a," "b," and so on) with the year to order the entries in the reference list. (See item 6 on p. 558.) Use those same letters with the year in the in-text citation.

> Research by Durgin (2003b) has yielded new findings about the role of counseling in treating childhood obesity.

10. Two or more works in the same parentheses When your parenthetical citation names two or more works, put them in the same order that they appear in the reference list, separated with semicolons.

> Researchers have indicated that studies of pharmacological treatments for childhood obesity are inconclusive (Berkowitz et al., 2003; McDuffie et al., 2002).

11. Personal communication Personal interviews, memos, letters, e-mail, and similar unpublished communications should be cited in the text only, not in the reference list. (Use the first initial with the last name in parentheses.)

> One of Atkinson's colleagues, who has studied the effect of the media on children's eating habits, has contended that advertisers for snack foods will need to design ads responsibly for their younger viewers (F. Johnson, personal communication, October 20, 2009).

12. Electronic source When possible, cite electronic sources, including online sources, as you would any other source, giving the author and the year.

Atkinson (2001) found that children who spent at least four hours
a day watching TV were less likely to engage in adequate physical
activity during the week.

Electronic sources sometimes lack authors' names, dates, or page
numbers.

Unknown author

If no author is named in the source, mention the title of the
source in the signal phrase or give the first word or two of the title
in the parentheses (see also item 6). (If an organization serves as
the author, see item 7.)

The body's basal metabolic rate, or BMR, is a measure of its at-rest
energy requirement ("Exercise," 2003).

Unknown date

When the date is unknown, use the abbreviation "n.d." (for "no date").

Attempts to establish a definitive link between television programming
and children's eating habits have been problematic (Magnus, n.d.).

No page numbers

APA ordinarily requires page numbers for quotations, and it
recommends them for summaries and paraphrases from long
sources. When an electronic source lacks stable numbered pages,
include whatever information is available to help readers locate
the particular passage you are citing.

If the source has numbered paragraphs, use the paragraph
number preceded by the abbreviation "para.": (Hall, 2008, para. 5).
If the source contains headings, cite the appropriate heading in parentheses; you may also indicate the paragraph under the heading
that you are referring to, even if the paragraphs are not numbered.

Hoppin and Taveras (2004) pointed out that several other medications
were classified by the Drug Enforcement Administration as having the
"potential for abuse" (Weight-Loss Drugs section, para. 6).

NOTE: Electronic files in portable document format (PDF) often
have stable page numbers. For such sources, give the page number in the parenthetical citation.

■ **13. Indirect source** If you use a source that was cited in another source (a secondary source), name the original source in your
signal phrase. List the secondary source in your reference list and

include it in your parenthetical citation, preceded by the words "as cited in." In the following example, Satcher is the original source; Critser is the secondary source, given in the reference list.

> Former surgeon general Dr. David Satcher described "a nation of young people seriously at risk of starting out obese and dooming themselves to the difficult task of overcoming a tough illness" (as cited in Critser, 2003, p. 4).

● **14. Sacred or classical text** Identify the text, the version or edition you used, and the relevant part (chapter, verse, line). It is not necessary to include the source in the reference list.

> Peace activists have long cited the biblical prophet's vision of a world without war: "And they shall beat their swords into plowshares, and their spears into pruning hooks; nation shall not lift up sword against nation, neither shall they learn war any more" (Isaiah 2:4, Revised Standard Version).

64b APA list of references

In APA style, the alphabetical list of works cited, which appears at the end of the paper, is titled "References." For advice on preparing the list, see pages 581–82. For a sample reference list, see pages 593–94.

Alphabetize entries in the reference list by authors' last names; if a work has no author, alphabetize it by its title. The first element of each entry is important because citations in the text of the paper refer to it and readers will be looking for it in the alphabetized list. The date of publication appears immediately after the first element of the citation.

In APA style, titles of books are italicized; titles of articles are neither italicized nor put in quotation marks. (For rules on capitalization of titles in the list of references, see p. 581.)

NOTE: Many sources, both print and online, include a unique, permanent number called a digital object identifier (DOI) that allows users to access a source in a variety of ways. For a reference list entry for a print source, give all the print publication information and add the DOI, if the source has one, at the end of the entry (see item 7). For an online source, give the DOI at the end of the entry in place of a URL (see item 30).

General guidelines for listing authors (print and online)

In APA style, all authors' names are inverted (the last name comes first), and initials are used for all first and middle names.

NAME AND DATE CITED IN TEXT

Duncan (2008) has reported that. . . .

BEGINNING OF ENTRY IN THE LIST OF REFERENCES

Duncan, B. (2008).

🔲 **1. Single author**

author: last name
+ initial(s) | year | title (book)

Egeland, J. (2008). *A billion lives: An eyewitness report from the frontlines*

place of
publication | publisher

of humanity. New York, NY: Simon & Schuster.

🔲 **2. Multiple authors**   List up to seven authors by last names followed by initials. Use an ampersand (&) before the name of the last author. If there are more than seven authors, list the first six followed by three ellipsis dots and the last author's name. (See items 3–5 on pp. 552–53 for citing works with multiple authors in the text of your paper.)

Two to seven authors

all authors:
last name + initial(s) | year | title (book)

Musick, M. A., & Wilson, J. (2007). *Volunteers: A social profile.*

place of
publication | publisher

Bloomington: Indiana University Press.

all authors:
last name + initial(s)

Diessner, R., Solom, R. C., Frost, N. K., Parsons, L., & Davidson, J.

year | title (article)

(2008). Engagement with beauty: Appreciating natural, artistic, and

journal title | volume | page(s)

moral beauty. *The Journal of Psychology, 142,* 303-329.

Eight or more authors

Mulvaney, S. A., Mudasiru, E., Schlundt, D. G., Baughman, C. L., Fleming, M.,
VanderWoude, A., . . . Rothman, R. (2008). Self-management in Type 2
diabetes: The adolescent perspective. *The Diabetes Educator, 34*, 118-127.

▨ 3. Organization as author

author:
organization name · · · · · · year · · · · · · title (book)

American Psychiatric Association. (1994). *Diagnostic and statistical*

edition · · · place · · · organization as author
number · · · of publication · · · and publisher

manual of mental disorders (4th ed.). Washington, DC: Author.

If the publisher is not the same as the author, give the publisher's
name at the end as you would for any other source.

▨ 4. Unknown author   Begin the entry with the work's title.

title (book) · · · year · · · place of publication · · · publisher

New concise world atlas. (2007). New York, NY: Oxford University Press.

title (article) · · · year + month + day (for weekly publication) · · · journal title · · · volume, issue · · · page(s)

Order in the jungle. (2008, March 15). *The Economist, 386*(8571), 83-85.

▨ 5. Two or more works by the same author   Use the author's
name for all entries. List the entries by year, the earliest first.

Barry, P. (2007, December 8). Putting tumors on pause. *Science News,*
   172, 365.

Barry, P. (2008, August 2). Finding the golden genes. *Science News, 174,*
   16-21.

▨ 6. Two or more works by the same author in the same year
List the works alphabetically by title. In the parentheses, following
the year add "a," "b," and so on. Use these same letters when giving
the year in the in-text citation. (See also p. 581.)

Elkind, D. (2008a, Spring). Can we play? *Greater Good, 4*(4), 14-17.

Elkind, D. (2008b, June 27). The price of hurrying children [Web log
   post]. Retrieved from http://blogs.psychologytoday.com/blog
   /digital-children

Articles in periodicals (print)

Periodicals include journals, magazines, and newspapers. For a journal or a magazine, give only the volume number if the publication is paginated continuously throughout each volume; give the volume and issue numbers if each issue of the volume begins on page 1. Italicize the volume number and put the issue number, not italicized, in parentheses.

For all periodicals, when an article appears on consecutive pages, provide the range of pages. When an article does not appear on consecutive pages, give all page numbers: A1, A17. (See also "Online sources" beginning on p. 565 for online articles and articles accessed through a library's database.) For an illustrated citation of an article in a print journal or magazine, see page 560.

7. Article in a journal

author: last name
+ initial(s)   year   article title

Holtug, N. (2010). Immigration and the politics of social cohesion.

journal title volume   page(s)   DOI

Ethnicities, 10, 435-451. doi:10.1177/1468796810378320

8. Article in a magazine   Cite as you would a journal article, but give the year and the month for monthly magazines; add the day for weekly magazines.

McKibben, B. (2007, October). Carbon's new math. *National Geographic,*
    212(4), 32-37.

9. Article in a newspaper

author: last name   year + month + day
+ initial(s)   (for daily publication)   article title

Svoboda, E. (2008, October 21). Deep in the rain forest, stalking the next

                      newspaper title   page(s)
    pandemic. *The New York Times,* p. D5.

Give the year, month, and day for daily and weekly newspapers. Use "p." or "pp." before page numbers.

10. Article with three to seven authors

Ungar, M., Brown, M., Liebenberg, L., Othman, R., Kwong, W. M.,
    Armstrong, M., & Gilgun, J. (2007). Unique pathways to resilience
    across cultures. *Adolescence, 42,* 287-310.

Citation at a glance: Article in a journal or magazine (APA)

To cite an article in a print journal or magazine in APA style, include the following elements:

1 Author
2 Year of publication for journal; complete date for magazine
3 Title of article
4 Name of journal or magazine
5 Volume number; issue number, if required (see p. 559)
6 Page number(s) of article
7 DOI (digital object identifier), if available

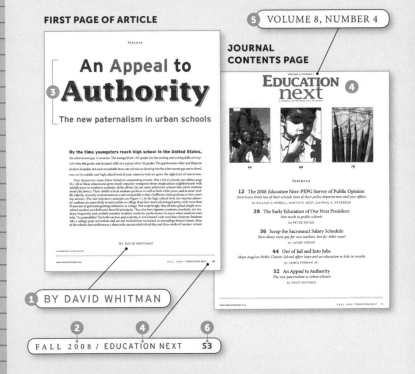

FIRST PAGE OF ARTICLE

feature

An Appeal to
③**Authority**

The new paternalism in urban schools

By the time youngsters reach high school in the United States,

BY DAVID WHITMAN

FALL 2008 / EDUCATION NEXT 53

⑤ VOLUME 8, NUMBER 4

JOURNAL CONTENTS PAGE

VOLUME 8, NUMBER 4

EDUCATION ④
next
A JOURNAL OF OPINION AND RESEARCH

44 60 70

features

12 The 2008 *Education Next*-PEG Survey of Public Opinion
Americans think less of their schools than of their police departments and post offices
by WILLIAM G. HOWELL, MARTIN R. WEST, and PAUL E. PETERSON

28 The Early Education of Our Next President
Not much in public schools
by PETER MEYER

36 Scrap the Sacrosanct Salary Schedule
How about more pay for new teachers, less for older ones?
by JACOB VIGDOR

44 Out of Jail and Into Jobs
Maya Angelou Public Charter School offers hope and an education to kids in trouble
by JAMES FORMAN JR.

52 An Appeal to Authority
The new paternalism in urban schools
by DAVID WHITMAN

www.educationnext.org FALL 2008 EDUCATION NEXT 3

① BY DAVID WHITMAN

② ④ ⑥
FALL 2008 / EDUCATION NEXT 53

REFERENCE LIST ENTRY FOR AN ARTICLE IN A PRINT JOURNAL OR MAGAZINE

┌──1──┐ ┌──2──┐ ┌────────────3────────────
Whitman, D. (2008). An appeal to authority: The new paternalism in

┌──────4──────┐ ┌─5─┐ ┌─6─┐
urban schools. *Education Next, 8*(4), 53-58.

For variations on citing articles in print journals or magazines in APA style, see pages 559–61.

■ **11. Article with eight or more authors** List the first six authors followed by three ellipsis dots and the last author.

Krippner, G., Granovetter, M., Block, F., Biggart, N., Beamish, T., Hsing, Y., . . . O'Riain, S. (2004). Polanyi Symposium: A conversation on embeddedness. *Socio-Economic Review, 2,* 109-135.

■ **12. Abstract of a journal article**

Lahm, K. (2008). Inmate-on-inmate assault: A multilevel examination of prison violence [Abstract]. *Criminal Justice and Behavior,* 35(1), 120-137.

■ **13. Letter to the editor** Follow the appropriate model for a journal, magazine, or newspaper (see items 7–9) and insert the words "Letter to the editor" in brackets after the title of the letter. If the letter has no title, use the bracketed words as the title.

Park, I. (2008, August). Defining the line [Letter to the editor]. *Scientific American, 299*(2), 10.

■ **14. Editorial or other unsigned article**

The global justice movement [Editorial]. (2005). *Multinational Monitor, 26*(7/8), 6.

■ **15. Newsletter article**

Setting the stage for remembering. (2006, September). *Mind, Mood, and Memory, 2*(9), 4-5.

■ **16. Review** Give the author and title of the review (if any) and, in brackets, the type of work, the title, and the author for a book or the year for a motion picture. If the review has no author or title, use the material in brackets as the title.

Applebaum, A. (2008, February 14). A movie that matters [Review of the motion picture *Katyn,* 2007]. *The New York Review of Books, 55*(2), 13-15.

Agents of change. (2008, February 2). [Review of the book *The power of unreasonable people: How social entrepreneurs create markets that change the world,* by J. Elkington & P. Hartigan]. *The Economist, 386*(8565), 94.

Books (print)

Items 17–29 apply to print books. For online books, see items 36 and 37. For an illustrated citation of a print book, see page 564.

Take the information about a book from its title page and copyright page. If more than one place of publication is listed, use only the first. Give the city and the state (abbreviated) for all US cities or the city and the country (not abbreviated) for all non-US cities; also include the province for Canadian cities. Do not give a state if the publisher's name includes it (as in many university presses, for example).

17. Basic format for a book

author: last name + initial(s)   year of publication   book title

McKenzie, F. R. (2008). *Theory and practice with adolescents: An applied approach.*

place of publication   publisher

Chicago, IL: Lyceum Books.

18. Book with an editor

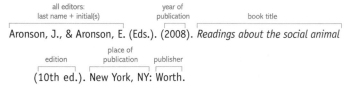

all editors: last name + initial(s)   year of publication   book title

Aronson, J., & Aronson, E. (Eds.). (2008). *Readings about the social animal*

edition   place of publication   publisher

(10th ed.). New York, NY: Worth.

The abbreviation "Eds." is for multiple editors. If the book has one editor, use "Ed."

19. Book with an author and an editor

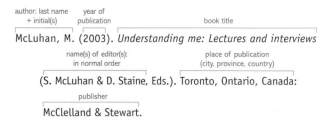

author: last name + initial(s)   year of publication   book title

McLuhan, M. (2003). *Understanding me: Lectures and interviews*

name(s) of editor(s): in normal order   place of publication (city, province, country)

(S. McLuhan & D. Staine, Eds.). Toronto, Ontario, Canada:

publisher

McClelland & Stewart.

The abbreviation "Eds." is for multiple editors. If the book has one editor, use "Ed."

book • basic format • editor • translator • edition (2nd, 3rd, etc.) • article, chapter • anthology • volumes • foreword

APA
64b   563

■ **20. Book with an author and a translator** After the title, name the translator, followed by "Trans.," in parentheses. Add the original date of publication at the end of the entry.

Steinberg, M. D. (2003). *Voices of revolution, 1917* (M. Schwartz, Trans.). New Haven, CT: Yale University Press. (Original work published 2001)

■ **21. Edition other than the first**

O'Brien, J. A. (Ed.). (2006). *The production of reality: Essays and readings on social interaction* (4th ed.). Thousand Oaks, CA: Pine Forge Press.

If the entry also requires volume numbers (see item 23), put the volume numbers after the edition number: (3rd ed., Vols. 1-3).

■ **22. Article or chapter in an edited book or an anthology**

author of chapter: last name + initial(s)   year of publication   title of chapter

Denton, N. A. (2006). Segregation and discrimination in housing.

book editor(s): in normal order   book title

In R. G. Bratt, M. E. Stone, & C. Hartman (Eds.), *A right to housing:*

page(s) for chapter   place of publication

Foundation of a new social agenda (pp. 61-81). Philadelphia, PA:

publisher

Temple University Press.

The abbreviation "Eds." is for multiple editors. If the book has one editor, use "Ed."

■ **23. Multivolume work** Give the number of volumes after the title.

Luo, J. (Ed.). (2005). *China today: An encyclopedia of life in the People's Republic* (Vols. 1-2). Westport, CT: Greenwood Press.

If the work is published in an edition other than the first (see item 21), put the edition number before the volume numbers: (3rd ed., Vols. 1-3).

■ **24. Introduction, preface, foreword, or afterword**

Gore, A. (2000). Foreword. In B. Katz (Ed.), *Reflections on regionalism* (pp. ix-x). Washington, DC: Brookings Institution Press.

Citation at a glance: Book (APA)

To cite a print book in APA style, include the following elements:

1. Author
2. Year of publication
3. Title and subtitle
4. Place of publication
5. Publisher
6. DOI (digital object identifier), if available

2 Copyright © 2008 by Thomas L. Friedman

TITLE PAGE

1 THOMAS L. FRIEDMAN

3 Hot, Flat, and Crowded
WHY WE NEED A GREEN REVOLUTION—
AND HOW IT CAN RENEW AMERICA

5 FARRAR, STRAUS AND GIROUX
4 NEW YORK

FARRAR, STRAUS AND GIROUX
NEW YORK

COPYRIGHT PAGE

Farrar, Straus and Giroux
18 West 18th Street, New York 10011

Copyright © 2008 by Thomas L. Friedman
All rights reserved
Distributed in Canada by Douglas & McIntyre Ltd.
Printed in the United States of America
First edition, 2008

Grateful acknowledgment is made for permission to reprint the following material:
Excerpts from *Three Cups of Tea* by Greg Mortenson and David Oliver Relin,
copyright © 2006 by Greg Mortenson and David Oliver Relin. Used by permission of
Viking Penguin, a division of Penguin Group (USA) Inc.
Graphs reproduced with permission from *Foreign Policy*, www.ForeignPolicy.com,
#154, May/June 2006: Copyright © 2006 by the Carnegie Endowment for International
Peace.

Library of Congress Control Number: 2008930589
ISBN-13: 978-0-374-16685-4
ISBN-10: 0-374-16685-4

Designed by Jonathan D. Lippincott

www.fsgbooks.com

1 3 5 7 9 10 8 6 4 2

FSC
Mixed Sources

This book was printed on text paper containing
30 percent post-consumer recycled content.

REFERENCE LIST ENTRY FOR A PRINT BOOK

———1——— —2— ————————3————————
Friedman, T. L. (2008). *Hot, flat, and crowded: Why we need a green*

———————4———
revolution—And how it can renew America. New York, NY:

———5———
Farrar, Straus and Giroux.

For more on citing print books in APA style, see pages 562–65.

25. Dictionary or other reference work

Leong, F. T. L. (Ed.). (2008). *Encyclopedia of counseling* (Vols. 1-4). Thousand Oaks, CA: Sage.

26. Article in a reference work

Konijn, E. A. (2008). Affects and media exposure. In W. Donsbach (Ed.), *The international encyclopedia of communication* (Vol. 1, pp. 123-129). Malden, MA: Blackwell.

27. Republished book

Mailer, N. (2008). *Miami and the siege of Chicago: An informal history of the Republican and Democratic conventions of 1968.* New York, NY: New York Review Books. (Original work published 1968)

28. Book with a title in its title   If the book title contains another book title or an article title, neither italicize the internal title nor place it in quotation marks.

Marcus, L. (Ed.). (1999). *Sigmund Freud's* The interpretation of dreams: *New interdisciplinary essays.* Manchester, England: Manchester University Press.

29. Sacred or classical text   It is not necessary to list sacred works such as the Bible or the Qur'an or classical Greek and Roman works in your reference list. See item 14 on page 556 for how to cite these sources in the text of your paper.

Online sources

When citing an online article, include publication information as for a print periodical (see items 7–16) and add information about the online version (see items 30–35).

Use a retrieval date for an online source only if the content is likely to change. Most of the examples in this section do not show a retrieval date because the content of the sources is stable; if you are unsure about whether to use a retrieval date, consult your instructor. If the source includes a DOI (digital object identifier), use the DOI in place of a URL at the end of the entry (see the note on p. 556).

If you must break a DOI or a URL at the end of a line, break it after a double slash or before any other mark of punctuation; do not add a hyphen. Do not put a period at the end of the entry.

■ **30. Article in an online journal**

author: last
name + initial(s)   year of publication   article title   journal title

Whitmeyer, J. M. (2000). Power through appointment. *Social Science Research,*
volume   page(s)   DOI

29, 535-555. doi:10.1006/ssre.2000.0680

If there is no DOI, include the URL for the journal's home page.

Ashe, D. D., & McCutcheon, L. E. (2001). Shyness, loneliness, and attitude
toward celebrities. *Current Research in Social Psychology, 6,* 124-133.
Retrieved from http://www.uiowa.edu/~grpproc/crisp/crisp.html

■ **31. Article in an online magazine** Give the author, date, article title, and magazine title. Follow with the volume, issue, and page numbers, if they are available. End with the URL for the magazine's home page.

Shelburne, E. C. (2008, September). The great disruption. *The Atlantic,*
302(2). Retrieved from http://www.theatlantic.com/

Rupley, S. (2010, February 26). The myth of the benign monopoly. *Salon.*
Retrieved from http://www.salon.com/

■ **32. Article in an online newspaper** Give the author, date, article title, and newspaper title. Follow with the page numbers, if they are available. End with the URL for the newspaper's home page.

Watson, P. (2008, October 19). Biofuel boom endangers orangutan habitat.
Los Angeles Times. Retrieved from http://www.latimes.com/

■ **33. Supplemental material published only online** If a journal, magazine, or newspaper contains extra material (an article or a chart, for example) only in its online version, give whatever publication information is available in the source and add the description "Supplemental material" in brackets after the title.

Samuel, T. (2009, March 27). Mind the wage gap [Supplemental material].

The American Prospect. Retrieved from http://www.prospect.org/

■ **34. Article from a database**   Start with the publication information for the source (see items 7–16). If the database entry includes a DOI for the article, use the DOI number at the end. For an illustrated citation of an article from a database, see page 568.

all authors:
last name + initial(s)   year   article title

Eskritt, M., & McLeod, K. (2008). Children's note taking as a mnemonic tool.

journal title   volume page(s)   DOI

Journal of Experimental Child Psychology, 101, 52-74. doi:10.1016

/jecp.2008.05.007

If there is no DOI, include the URL for the home page of the journal. If the URL is not included in the database entry, you can search for it on the Web.

Howard, K. R. (2007). Childhood overweight: Parental perceptions and

readiness for change. *The Journal of School Nursing, 23,* 73-79.

Retrieved from http://jsn.sagepub.com/

■ **35. Abstract for an online article**

Brockerhoff, E. G., Jactel, H., Parrotta, J. A., Quine, C. P., & Sayer, J.

(2008). Plantation forests and biodiversity: Oxymoron or opportunity?

[Abstract]. *Biodiversity and Conservation, 17,* 925-951. doi:10.1007

/s10531-008-9380-x

■ **36. Online book**

Adams, B. (2004). *The theory of social revolutions.* Retrieved from http://

www.gutenberg.org/catalog/world/readfile?fk_files=44092 (Original

work published 1913)

■ **37. Chapter in an online book**

Clinton, S. J. (1999). What can be done to prevent childhood obesity? In

Understanding childhood obesity (pp. 81-98). Retrieved from http://

www.questia.com/

Citation at a glance: Article from a database (APA)

To cite an article from a database in APA style, include the following elements:

1 Author(s)
2 Date of publication
3 Title of article
4 Name of periodical
5 Volume number; issue number, if required (see p. 559)

6 Page number(s)
7 DOI (direct object identifier), if available
8 URL for journal's home page (if there is no DOI)

ON-SCREEN VIEW OF DATABASE RECORD

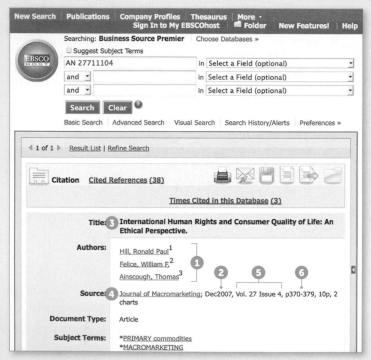

END OF DATABASE RECORD

ISSN:	0276-1467
DOI:	10.1177/027614670307128 **7**

REFERENCE LIST ENTRY FOR AN ARTICLE FROM A DATABASE

Hill, R. P., Felice, W. F., & Ainscough, T. (2007). International human

rights and consumer quality of life: An ethical perspective. *Journal*

of Macromarketing, 27, 370-379. doi:10.1177/027614670307128

For more on citing articles from a database in APA style, see item 34.

38. Online reference work

Swain, C. M. (2004). Sociology of affirmative action. In N. J. Smelser

& P. B. Baltes (Eds.), *International encyclopedia of the social and*

behavioral sciences. Retrieved from http://www.sciencedirect.com

/science/referenceworks/9780080430768

Include a retrieval date only if the content of the work is likely
to change.

39. Report or long document from a Web site

List the author's name, publication date (or "n.d." if there is no date), document title (in italics), and URL for the document. Give a retrieval date only if the content of the source is likely to change. If a source has no author, begin with the title and follow it with the date in parentheses (see item 4 on p. 558).

Source with date

Cain, A., & Burris, M. (1999, April). *Investigation of the use of mobile*

phones while driving. Retrieved from http://www.cutr.eng.usf.edu

/its/mobile_phone_text.htm

Source with no date

Archer, D. (n.d.). *Exploring nonverbal communication.* Retrieved from http://

nonverbal.ucsc.edu/

40. Section in a Web document

author (organization) year title of section

National Institute on Media and the Family. (2009). Mobile networking. In

title of Web document

Guide to social networking: Risks. Retrieved from http://www.mediafamily

URL

.org/network_pdf/MediaWise_Guide_to_Social_Networking_Risks_09.pdf

For an illustrated citation of a section in a Web document, see page 572.

41. Short work from a Web site

NATO statement endangers patients in Afghanistan. (2010, March 11).

Médecins sans frontières/Doctors without borders. Retrieved from

http://www.doctorswithoutborders.org/

42. Document from a university or government agency Web site

Cosmides, L., & Tooby, J. (1997). *Evolutionary psychology: A primer.*

Retrieved from University of California, Santa Barbara, Center for

Evolutionary Psychology website: http://www.psych.ucsb.edu

/research/cep/primer.html

43. Article in an online newsletter

Cite as an online article (see items 30–32), giving the title of the newsletter and whatever other information is available, including volume and issue numbers.

In the face of extinction. (2008, May). *NSF Current.* Retrieved from

http://www.nsf.gov/news/newsletter/may_08/index.jsp

44. Podcast

organization as producer date of posting

National Academies (Producer). (2007, June 6). Progress in preventing

podcast title descriptive label

childhood obesity: How do we measure up? [Audio podcast].

series title URL

The sounds of science podcast. Retrieved from http://media.nap.edu

/podcasts/

writer/
presenter   date of posting   podcast title

Chesney, M. (2007, September 13). Gender differences in the use of

                                    podcast number   descriptive label

complementary and alternative medicine (No. 12827) [Audio podcast].

                Web site hosting podcast

Retrieved from University of California Television website:

        URL

http://www.uctv.tv/ondemand/

45. Blog (Weblog) post Give the writer's name, the date of the post, the subject, the label "Web log post" in brackets, and the URL. For a response to a post, use the label "Web log comment."

Kellermann, M. (2007, May 23). Disclosing clinical trials [Web log post].

    Retrieved from http://www.iq.harvard.edu/blog/sss/archives/2007/05

46. Online audio or video file Give the medium or a description of the source file in brackets following the title.

writer/   no   descriptive
presenter   date   title   label

Chomsky, N. (n.d.). The new imperialism [Audio file]. Retrieved from

           URL

http://www.rhapsody.com/noamchomsky

Zakaria, F. (Host), & McCullough, C. (Writer). (2007, March 6). In focus:

    American teens, Rwandan truths [Video file]. Retrieved from http://

    www.pulitzercenter.org/showproject.cfm?id=26

47. Entry in a wiki Begin with the title of the entry and the date of posting, if there is one (use "n.d." for "no date" if there is not). Then add your retrieval date and the URL for the wiki entry. Include the date of retrieval because the content of a wiki can change frequently. If an author or an editor is identified, include that name at the beginning of the entry.

Ethnomethodology. (n.d.). Retrieved June 18, 2010, from http://stswiki

    .org/index.php?title/Ethnomethodology

48. Data set or graphic representation Give information about the type of source in brackets following the title. If there

Citation at a glance: Section in a Web document (APA)

To cite a section in a Web document in APA style, include the following elements:

1 Author
2 Date of publication or most recent update

3 Title of section
4 Title of document
5 URL of section

BROWSER PRINTOUT OF WEB SITE

2008 Minnesota Health Statistics Annual Summary – Minnesota Dept. of Health

 Minnesota Department of Health
Protecting, maintaining and improving the health of all Minnesotans   MDH

 2008 Minnesota Health Statistics Annual Summary

The Minnesota "Annual Summary" or "Minnesota Health Statistics" is a report published yearly. The most recent version of this report is *2008 Minnesota Health Statistics*, published January 2010. This report provides statistical data on the following subjects for the state of Minnesota.

To view the PDF files, you will need Adobe Acrobat Re   site).

2 published January 2010.

- Introduction, Technical Notes, Definitions (PDF: 42KB/7 pages)
- Overview of 2008 Annual Summary (PDF: 66KB/11 pages)
- Live Births (PDF: 196KB/21 pages)
- Fertility (PDF: 26KB/2 pages) ● 3
- Infant Mortality and Fetal Deaths (PDF: 188KB/15 pages)
- General Mortality (PDF: 333KB/40 pages)
- Marriage/Dissolution of Marriage Divorce (PDF: 25KB/2 pages)
- Population (PDF: 73KB/12 pages)

Note: Induced abortion statistics previously reported in this publication are now published separately.
See Report to the Legislature: Induced Abortions in Minnesota

See also Minnesota Health Statistics Annual Summary Main Page

For further information about the Annual Summary, please contact:

Center for Health Statistics
Minnesota Department of Health
Golden Rule Building, 3rd Floor
85 East Seventh Place

http://www.health.state.mn.us/divs/chs/annsum/08annsum/index.html   Page 1 of 2

⑤ [M] http://www.health.state.mn.us/divs/chs/annsum/08annsum/Fertility08.pdf

ON-SCREEN VIEW OF DOCUMENT

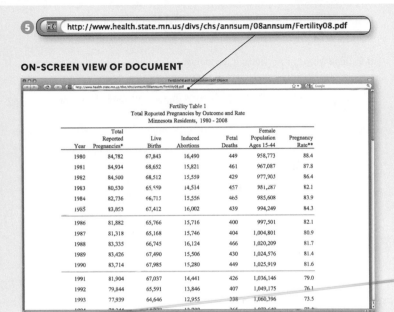

Fertility Table 1
Total Reported Pregnancies by Outcome and Rate
Minnesota Residents, 1980 - 2008

Year	Total Reported Pregnancies*	Live Births	Induced Abortions	Fetal Deaths	Female Population Ages 15-44	Pregnancy Rate**
1980	84,782	67,843	16,490	449	958,773	88.4
1981	84,934	68,652	15,821	461	967,087	87.8
1982	84,500	68,512	15,559	429	977,903	86.4
1983	80,530	65,559	14,514	457	981,287	82.1
1984	82,736	66,715	15,556	465	985,608	83.9
1985	83,853	67,412	16,002	439	994,249	84.3
1986	81,882	65,766	15,716	400	997,501	82.1
1987	81,318	65,168	15,746	404	1,004,801	80.9
1988	83,335	66,745	16,124	466	1,020,209	81.7
1989	83,426	67,490	15,506	430	1,024,576	81.4
1990	83,714	67,985	15,280	449	1,025,919	81.6
1991	81,904	67,037	14,441	426	1,036,146	79.0
1992	79,844	65,591	13,846	407	1,049,175	76.1
1993	77,939	64,646	12,955	338	1,060,396	73.5

REFERENCE LIST ENTRY FOR A SECTION IN A WEB DOCUMENT

┌────1────┐ ┌──2──┐ ┌─3─┐ ┌─4─┐
Minnesota Department of Health. (2010, January). Fertility. In *2008*

┌─5─┐
Minnesota health statistics annual summary. Retrieved from http://

www.health.state.mn.us/divs/chs/annsum/08annsum/Fertility08.pdf

For more on citing documents from Web sites in APA style, see pages
569–74.

is no title, give a brief description of the content of the source in brackets in place of the title.

U.S. Department of Agriculture, Economic Research Service. (2009). *Eating and health module (ATUS): 2007 data* [Data set]. Retrieved from http://www.ers.usda.gov/Data/ATUS/Data/2007/2007data.htm

Gallup. (2008, October 23). *No increase in proportion of first-time voters* [Graphs]. Retrieved from http://www.gallup.com/poll/111331 /No-Increase-Proportion-First-Time-Voters.aspx

49. Conference hearing

Carmona, R. H. (2004, March 2). *The growing epidemic of childhood obesity.* Testimony before the Subcommittee on Competition, Foreign Commerce, and Infrastructure of the U.S. Senate Committee on Commerce, Science, and Transportation. Retrieved from http://www.hhs.gov/asl/testify /t040302.html

50. E-mail
E-mail messages, letters, and other personal communications are not included in the list of references. (See item 11 on p. 554 for citing these sources in the text of your paper.)

51. Online posting
If an online posting is not archived, cite it as a personal communication in the text of your paper and do not include it in the list of references. If the posting is archived, give the URL and the name of the discussion list if it is not part of the URL.

McKinney, J. (2006, December 19). Adult education-healthcare partnerships [Electronic mailing list message]. Retrieved from http://www.nifl.gov /pipermail/healthliteracy/2006/000524.html

Other sources (including online versions)

52. Dissertation from a database

Hymel, K. M. (2009). *Essays in urban economics* (Doctoral dissertation). Available from ProQuest Dissertations and Theses database. (AAT 3355930)

53. Unpublished dissertation

Mitchell, R. D. (2007). *The Wesleyan Quadrilateral: Relocating the conversation*
(Unpublished doctoral dissertation). Claremont School of Theology,
Claremont, CA.

54. Government document

U.S. Census Bureau. (2006). *Statistical abstract of the United States.*
Washington, DC: Government Printing Office.

U.S. Census Bureau, Bureau of Economic Analysis. (2008, August). *U.S.*
international trade in goods and services (Report No. CB08-121,
BEA08-37, FT-900). Retrieved from http://www.census.gov
/foreign-trade/Press-Release/2008pr/06/ftdpress.pdf

55. Report from a private organization   If the publisher is
also the author, begin with the publisher's name in the author
position. For a print source, use "Author" in the publisher position at the end of the entry (see item 3); for an online source, give
the URL. If the report has a number, put it in parentheses following the title.

Ford Foundation. (n.d.). *Helping citizens to understand and influence state*
budgets. Retrieved from http://www.fordfound.org/pdfs/impact
/evaluations/state_fiscal_initiative.pdf

56. Legal source

Sweatt v. Painter, 339 U.S. 629 (1950). Retrieved from Cornell University
Law School, Legal Information Institute website: http://www.law
.cornell.edu/supct/html/historics/USSC_CR_0339_0629_ZS.html

57. Conference proceedings

Stahl, G. (Ed.). (2002). *Proceedings of CSCL '02: Computer support for*
collaborative learning. Hillsdale, NJ: Erlbaum.

58. Paper presented at a meeting or symposium (unpublished)

Anderson, D. N. (2008, May). *Cab-hailing and the micropolitics of gesture.*
Paper presented at the Arizona Linguistics and Anthropology
Symposium, Tucson, AZ.

59. Poster session at a conference

Wang, Z., & Keogh, T. (2008, June). *A click away: Student response to clickers.* Poster session presented at the annual conference of the American Library Association, Anaheim, CA.

60. Map, chart, or illustration

Ukraine [Map]. (2008). Retrieved from the University of Texas at Austin Perry-Castañeda Library Map Collection website: http://www.lib .utexas.edu/maps/cia08/ukraine_sm_2008.gif

61. Advertisement

Xbox 360 [Advertisement]. (2007, February). *Wired, 15*(2), 71.

62. Published interview

Murphy, C. (2007, June 22). As the Romans did [Interview by G. Hahn]. Retrieved from http://www.theatlantic.com/

63. Lecture, speech, or address

Fox, V. (2008, March 5). *Economic growth, poverty, and democracy in Latin America: A president's perspective.* Address at the Freeman Spogli Institute, Stanford University, Stanford, CA.

64. Work of art or photograph

Weber, J. (1992). *Toward freedom* [Outdoor mural]. Sherman Oaks, CA.

Newkirk, K. (2006). *Gainer (part II).* Museum of Contemporary Art, Chicago, IL.

65. Brochure, pamphlet, or fact sheet

National Council of State Boards of Nursing. (n.d.). *Professional boundaries* [Brochure]. Retrieved from https://www.ncsbn.org /Professional_Boundaries_2007_Web.pdf

World Health Organization. (2007, October). *Health of indigenous peoples* (No. 326) [Fact sheet]. Retrieved from http://www.who.int /mediacentre/factsheets/fs326/en/index.html

66. Presentation slides

Boeninger, C. F. (2008, August). *Web 2.0 tools for reference and instructional*
    services [Presentation slides]. Retrieved from http://libraryvoice.com
    /archives/2008/08/04/opal-20-conference-presentation-slides/

67. Film or video (motion picture)
Give the director, producer, and other relevant contributors, followed by the year of the film's release, the title, the description "Motion picture" in brackets, the country where the film was made, and the studio. If you viewed the film on videocassette or on DVD or Blu-ray Disc (BD), indicate that medium in brackets in place of "Motion picture." If the original release date and the date of the videocassette, DVD, or BD are different, add "Original release" and that date in parentheses at the end of the entry. If the motion picture would be difficult for your readers to find, include the name and address of its distributor instead of the country and studio.

Guggenheim, D. (Director), & Bender, L. (Producer). (2006). *An inconvenient*
    truth [DVD]. United States: Paramount Home Entertainment.

Spurlock, M. (Director). (2004). *Super size me* [Motion picture]. Available
    from IDP Films, 1133 Broadway, Suite 926, New York, NY 10010

68. Television program
List the producer and the date of the program. Give the title, followed by "Television broadcast" in brackets, the city, and the television network or service.

Pratt, C. (Executive producer). (2008, October 5). *Face the nation*
    [Television broadcast]. Washington, DC: CBS News.

For a television series, use the year in which the series was produced, and follow the title with "Television series" in brackets. For an episode in a series, list the writer and director and the year. After the episode title, put "Television series episode" in brackets. Follow with information about the series.

Fanning, D. (Executive producer). (2008). *Frontline* [Television series].
    Boston, MA: WGBH.

Smith, M. (Writer/producer). (2008). Heat [Television series episode]. In
    D. Fanning (Executive producer), *Frontline*. Boston, MA: WGBH.

■ **69. Sound recording**

Thomas, G. (1996). Breath. On *Didgeridoo: Ancient sound of the future*

[CD]. Oxnard, CA: Aquarius International Music.

■ **70. Computer software or video game** Add the words "Computer software" in brackets after the title of the program.

Sims 2 [Computer software]. (2005). New York, NY: Maxis.

65 APA manuscript format; sample paper

The American Psychological Association makes a number of recommendations for formatting a paper and preparing a list of references. The following guidelines are consistent with advice given in the *Publication Manual of the American Psychological Association*, 6th ed. (Washington: APA, 2010).

65a APA manuscript format

The APA manual provides guidelines for papers prepared for publication in a scholarly journal; it does not provide separate guidelines for papers prepared for undergraduate classes. The formatting guidelines in this section and the sample paper on pages 583–94 can be used for either type of paper. (See p. 595 for alternative formatting.) If you are in doubt about the specific format preferred or required in your course, ask your instructor.

Formatting the paper

Many instructors in the social sciences require students to follow APA guidelines for formatting a paper.

Materials and font Use good-quality 8½″ × 11″ white paper. If your instructor does not require a specific font, choose one that is standard and easy to read (such as Times New Roman).

Title page Begin at the top left with the words "Running head," followed by a colon and the title of your paper (shortened to no more than fifty characters) in all capital letters. Put the page number 1 flush with the right margin.

About halfway down the page, center the full title of your paper (capitalizing all words of four letters or more), your name, and your school's name. At the bottom of the page, you may add the heading "Author Note," centered, followed by a brief paragraph that lists specific information about the course or department or provides acknowledgments or contact information. See page 583 for a sample title page.

Some instructors may instead require a title page like the one on page 595. If in doubt about the requirements in your course, check with your instructor.

Page numbers and running head   Number all pages with arabic numerals (1, 2, 3, and so on) in the upper right corner about one-half inch from the top of the page. The title page should be numbered 1.

On every page, in the upper left corner on the same line as the page number, place a running head. The running head consists of the title of the paper (shortened to no more than fifty characters) in all capital letters. (On the title page only, include the words "Running head" followed by a colon before the shortened title.) See pages 583–94. (See an alternative running head on p. 595.)

Margins, line spacing, and paragraph indents   Use margins of one inch on all sides of the page. Left-align the text.

Double-space throughout the paper. Indent the first line of each paragraph one-half inch.

Capitalization, italics, and quotation marks   Capitalize all words of four letters or more in titles of works and in headings that appear in the text of the paper. Capitalize the first word after a colon if the word begins a complete sentence.

Italicize the titles of books, periodicals, and other long works, such as Web sites. Use quotation marks around the titles of periodical articles, short stories, poems, and other short works.

NOTE: APA has different requirements for titles in the reference list. See page 581.

Long quotations and footnotes   When a quotation is longer than forty words, set it off from the text by indenting it one-half inch from the left margin. Double-space the quotation. Do not use quotation marks around it. See page 591 for an example.

If you insert a footnote number in the text of your paper, place the note at the bottom of the page on which the number appears. Insert an extra double-spaced line between the last line of text on the page and the footnote. Double-space the footnote and indent the first line one-half inch. Begin the note with the superscript arabic numeral that corresponds to the number in the text. See page 585 for an example.

Abstract   If your instructor requires an abstract, include it immediately after the title page. Center the word "Abstract" one inch from the top of the page; double-space the abstract.

An abstract is a 100-to-150-word paragraph that provides readers with a quick overview of your essay. It should express your main idea and your key points; it might also briefly suggest any implications or applications of the research you discuss in the paper. See page 584 for an example.

Headings   Although headings are not always necessary, their use is encouraged in the social sciences. For most undergraduate papers, one level of heading will usually be sufficient.

In APA style, major headings are centered and boldface. Capitalize the first word of the heading along with all words except articles, short prepositions, and coordinating conjunctions. See the sample paper on pages 583–94 for the use of headings.

Visuals   APA classifies visuals as tables and figures (figures include graphs, charts, drawings, and photographs). Keep visuals as simple as possible.

Label each table with an arabic numeral (Table 1, Table 2, and so on) and provide a clear title. The label and title should appear on separate lines above the table, flush left and double-spaced.

Below the table, give its source in a note. If any data in the table require an explanatory footnote, use a superscript lowercase letter in the body of the table and in a footnote following the source note. Double-space source notes and footnotes and do not indent the first line of each note. See page 589 for an example of a table in a student paper.

For each figure, place a label and a caption below the figure, flush left and double-spaced. The label and caption need not appear on separate lines.

In the text of your paper, discuss significant features of each visual. Place the visual as close as possible to the sentences that relate to it unless your instructor prefers that visuals appear in an appendix.

Preparing the list of references

Begin your list of references on a new page at the end of the paper. Center the title "References" one inch from the top of the page, and double-space throughout. For a sample reference list, see pages 593–94.

Indenting entries Use a hanging indent in the reference list: Type the first line of each entry flush left and indent any additional lines one-half inch, as shown on page 593.

Alphabetizing the list Alphabetize the reference list by the last names of the authors (or editors); when a work has no author (or editor), alphabetize by the first word of the title other than *A*, *An*, or *The*.

If your list includes two or more works by the same author, arrange the entries by year, the earliest first. If your list includes two or more works by the same author in the same year, arrange the works alphabetically by title. Add the letters "a," "b," and so on within the parentheses after the year. Use only the year and the letter for articles in journals: (2002a). Use the full date and the letter for articles in magazines and newspapers in the reference list: (2005a, July 7). Use only the year and the letter in the in-text citation.

Authors' names Invert all authors' names and use initials instead of first names. Separate the names with commas. With two to seven authors, use an ampersand (&) before the last author's name. If there are eight or more authors, give the first six authors, three ellipsis dots, and the last author (see p. 558).

Titles of books and articles Italicize the titles and subtitles of books. Do not italicize or use quotation marks around the titles of articles. Capitalize only the first word of the title and subtitle (and all proper nouns) of books and articles. Capitalize names of periodicals as you would capitalize them normally (see 45c).

Abbreviations for page numbers Abbreviations for "page" and "pages" ("p." and "pp.") are used before page numbers of newspaper articles and articles in edited books (see item 9 on p. 559 and item 22 on p. 563) but not before page numbers of articles in magazines and scholarly journals (see items 7 and 8 on p. 559).

Breaking a URL or DOI When a URL or a DOI (digital object identifier) must be divided, break it after a double slash or before any other mark of punctuation. Do not insert a hyphen, and do not add a period at the end.

For information about the exact format of each entry in your list, consult the models on pages 557–78.

65b Sample research paper: APA style

On pages 583–94 is a research paper on the effectiveness of treatments for childhood obesity, written by Luisa Mirano, a student in a psychology class. Mirano's assignment was to write a review of the literature and to document it with APA-style citations and references. (See p. 595 for a sample of alternative formatting.)

MODELS hackerhandbooks.com/rules
> Model papers > APA papers: Mirano; Charat; Gibson; Riss; Thompson
> APA annotated bibliography: Haddad

Running head: CAN MEDICATION CURE OBESITY IN CHILDREN?   1

The header consists of a shortened title in all capital letters at the left margin and the page number at the right margin; on the title page only, the shortened title is preceded by the words "Running head" and a colon.

Can Medication Cure Obesity in Children?

A Review of the Literature

Luisa Mirano

Northwest-Shoals Community College

Full title, writer's name, and school name are centered halfway down the page.

Author Note

This paper was prepared for Psychology 108, Section B, taught by Professor Kang.

An author's note lists specific information about the course or department and can provide acknowledgments and contact information.

Marginal annotations indicate APA-style formatting and effective writing.

CAN MEDICATION CURE OBESITY IN CHILDREN?   2

Abstract

In recent years, policymakers and medical experts have
expressed alarm about the growing problem of childhood
obesity in the United States. While most agree that the
issue deserves attention, consensus dissolves around how to
respond to the problem. This literature review examines one
approach to treating childhood obesity: medication. The
paper compares the effectiveness for adolescents of the only
two drugs approved by the Food and Drug Administration
(FDA) for long-term treatment of obesity, sibutramine and
orlistat. This examination of pharmacological treatments
for obesity points out the limitations of medication
and suggests the need for a comprehensive solution
that combines medical, social, behavioral, and political
approaches to this complex problem.

Abstract appears on
a separate page.

CAN MEDICATION CURE OBESITY IN CHILDREN?   3

Can Medication Cure Obesity in Children?   Full title, centered.

A Review of the Literature

In March 2004, U.S. Surgeon General Richard Carmona called attention to a health problem in the United States that, until recently, has been overlooked: childhood obesity. Carmona said that the "astounding" 15% child obesity rate constitutes an "epidemic." Since the early 1980s, that rate has "doubled in children and tripled in adolescents." Now more than 9 million children are classified as obese.[1] While the traditional response to a medical epidemic is to hunt for a vaccine or a cure-all pill, childhood obesity is more elusive. The lack of success of recent initiatives suggests that medication might not be the answer for the escalating problem. This literature review considers whether the use of medication is a promising approach for solving the childhood obesity problem by responding to the following questions:

1. What are the implications of childhood obesity?
2. Is medication effective at treating childhood obesity?
3. Is medication safe for children?
4. Is medication the best solution?

Mirano sets up her organization by posing four questions.

Understanding the limitations of medical treatments for children highlights the complexity of the childhood obesity problem in the United States and underscores the need for physicians, advocacy groups, and policymakers to search for other solutions.

Mirano states her thesis.

What Are the Implications of Childhood Obesity?

Obesity can be a devastating problem from both an

Headings, centered, help readers follow the organization.

[1]Obesity is measured in terms of body-mass index (BMI): weight in kilograms divided by square of height in meters. A child or an adolescent with a BMI in the 95th percentile for his or her age and gender is considered obese.

Mirano uses a footnote to define an essential term that would be cumbersome to define within the text.

CAN MEDICATION CURE OBESITY IN CHILDREN?   4

individual and a societal perspective. Obesity puts children
at risk for a number of medical complications, including
Type 2 diabetes, hypertension, sleep apnea, and orthopedic
problems (Henry J. Kaiser Family Foundation, 2004, p. 1).
Researchers Hoppin and Taveras (2004) have noted that
obesity is often associated with psychological issues such as
depression, anxiety, and binge eating (Table 4).

Obesity also poses serious problems for a society
struggling to cope with rising health care costs. The cost
of treating obesity currently totals $117 billion per year—a
price, according to the surgeon general, "second only to the
cost of [treating] tobacco use" (Carmona, 2004). And as
the number of children who suffer from obesity grows, long-
term costs will only increase.

Is Medication Effective at Treating Childhood Obesity?

The widening scope of the obesity problem has
prompted medical professionals to rethink old conceptions
of the disorder and its causes. As researchers Yanovski
and Yanovski (2002) have explained, obesity was once
considered "either a moral failing or evidence of underlying
psychopathology" (p. 592). But this view has shifted: Many
medical professionals now consider obesity a biomedical
rather than a moral condition, influenced by both genetic and
environmental factors. Yanovski and Yanovski have further
noted that the development of weight-loss medications in the
early 1990s showed that "obesity should be treated in the
same manner as any other chronic disease . . . through the
long-term use of medication" (p. 592).

The search for the right long-term medication has been
complicated. Many of the drugs authorized by the Food and
Drug Administration (FDA) in the early 1990s proved to be a

In a signal phrase, the word "and" links the names of two authors; the date is given in parentheses.

Because the author (Carmona) is not named in the signal phrase, his name and the date appear in parentheses.

Ellipsis mark indicates omitted words.

CAN MEDICATION CURE OBESITY IN CHILDREN?   5

disappointment. Two of the medications—fenfluramine and dexfenfluramine—were withdrawn from the market because of severe side effects (Yanovski & Yanovski, 2002, p. 592), and several others were classified by the Drug Enforcement Administration as having the "potential for abuse" (Hoppin & Taveras, 2004, Weight-Loss Drugs section, para. 6). Currently only two medications have been approved by the FDA for long-term treatment of obesity: sibutramine (marketed as Meridia) and orlistat (marketed as Xenical). This section compares studies on the effectiveness of each.

In a parenthetical citation, an ampersand links the names of two authors.

Sibutramine suppresses appetite by blocking the reuptake of the neurotransmitters serotonin and norepinephrine in the brain (Yanovski & Yanovski, 2002, p. 594). Though the drug won FDA approval in 1998, experiments to test its effectiveness for younger patients came considerably later. In 2003, University of Pennsylvania researchers Berkowitz, Wadden, Tershakovec, and Cronquist released the first double-blind placebo study testing the effect of sibutramine on adolescents, aged 13-17, over a 12-month period. Their findings are summarized in Table 1.

Mirano draws attention to an important article.

After 6 months, the group receiving medication had lost 4.6 kg (about 10 pounds) more than the control group. But during the second half of the study, when both groups received sibutramine, the results were more ambiguous. In months 6-12, the group that continued to take sibutramine gained an average of 0.8 kg, or roughly 2 pounds; the control group, which switched from placebo to sibutramine, lost 1.3 kg, or roughly 3 pounds (p. 1808). Both groups received behavioral therapy covering diet, exercise, and mental health.

These results paint a murky picture of the effectiveness

CAN MEDICATION CURE OBESITY IN CHILDREN?   6

of the medication: While initial data seemed promising, the results after one year raised questions about whether medication-induced weight loss could be sustained over time. As Berkowitz et al. (2003) advised, "Until more extensive safety and efficacy data are available, . . . weight-loss medications should be used only on an experimental basis for adolescents" (p. 1811).

A study testing the effectiveness of orlistat in adolescents showed similarly ambiguous results. The FDA approved orlistat in 1999 but did not authorize it for adolescents until December 2003. Roche Laboratories (2003), maker of orlistat, released results of a one-year study testing the drug on 539 obese adolescents, aged 12-16. The drug, which promotes weight loss by blocking fat absorption in the large intestine, showed some effectiveness in adolescents: an average loss of 1.3 kg, or roughly 3 pounds, for subjects taking orlistat for one year, as opposed to an average gain of 0.67 kg, or 1.5 pounds, for the control group (pp. 8-9). See Table 1.

Short-term studies of orlistat have shown slightly more dramatic results. Researchers at the National Institute of Child Health and Human Development tested 20 adolescents, aged 12-16, over a three-month period and found that orlistat, combined with behavioral therapy, produced an average weight loss of 4.4 kg, or 9.7 pounds (McDuffie et al., 2002, p. 646). The study was not controlled against a placebo group; therefore, the relative effectiveness of orlistat in this case remains unclear.

Is Medication Safe for Children?

While modest weight loss has been documented for both medications, each carries risks of certain side effects. Sibutramine has been observed to increase blood pressure

For a source with six or more authors, the first author's surname followed by "et al." is used for the first and subsequent references.

CAN MEDICATION CURE OBESITY IN CHILDREN?   7

Table 1

Effectiveness of Sibutramine and Orlistat in Adolescents

Mirano uses a table
to summarize the
findings presented
in two sources.

Medication	Subjects	Treatment[a]	Side effects	Average weight loss/gain
Sibutramine	Control	0-6 mos.: placebo 6-12 mos.: sibutramine	Mos. 6-12: increased blood pressure; increased pulse rate	After 6 mos.: loss of 3.2 kg (7 lb) After 12 mos.: loss of 4.5 kg (9.9 lb)
	Medicated	0-12 mos.: sibutramine	Increased blood pressure; increased pulse rate	After 6 mos.: loss of 7.8 kg (17.2 lb) After 12 mos.: loss of 7.0 kg (15.4 lb)
Orlistat	Control	0-12 mos.: placebo	None	Gain of 0.67 kg (1.5 lb)
	Medicated	0-12 mos.: orlistat	Oily spotting; flatulence; abdominal discomfort	Loss of 1.3 kg (2.9 lb)

Note. The data on sibutramine are adapted from "Behavior
Therapy and Sibutramine for the Treatment of Adolescent
Obesity," by R. I. Berkowitz, T. A. Wadden, A. M. Tershakovec,
& J. L. Cronquist, 2003, *Journal of the American Medical
Association, 289*, pp. 1807-1809. The data on orlistat are
adapted from *Xenical (Orlistat) Capsules: Complete Product
Information*, by Roche Laboratories, December 2003, retrieved
from http://www.rocheusa.com/products/xenical/pi.pdf

[a]The medication and/or placebo were combined with
behavioral therapy in all groups over all time periods.

A note gives the
source of the data.

A content note
explains data
common to all
subjects.

CAN MEDICATION CURE OBESITY IN CHILDREN? 8

and pulse rate. In 2002, a consumer group claimed that the medication was related to the deaths of 19 people and filed a petition with the Department of Health and Human Services to ban the medication (Hilts, 2002). The sibutramine study by Berkowitz et al. (2003) noted elevated blood pressure as a side effect, and dosages had to be reduced or the medication discontinued in 19 of the 43 subjects in the first six months (p. 1809).

When this article was first cited, all four authors were named. In subsequent citations of a work with three to five authors, "et al." is used after the first author's name.

The main side effects associated with orlistat were abdominal discomfort, oily spotting, fecal incontinence, and nausea (Roche Laboratories, 2003, p. 13). More serious for long-term health is the concern that orlistat, being a fat-blocker, would affect absorption of fat-soluble vitamins, such as vitamin D. However, the study found that this side effect can be minimized or eliminated if patients take vitamin supplements two hours before or after administration of orlistat (p. 10). With close monitoring of patients taking the medication, many of the risks can be reduced.

Is Medication the Best Solution?

The data on the safety and efficacy of pharmacological treatments of childhood obesity raise the question of whether medication is the best solution for the problem. The treatments have clear costs for individual patients, including unpleasant side effects, little information about long-term use, and uncertainty that they will yield significant weight loss.

In purely financial terms, the drugs cost more than $3 a day on average (Duenwald, 2004). In each of the clinical trials, use of medication was accompanied by an expensive regime of behavioral therapies, including counseling, nutritional education, fitness advising, and monitoring. As journalist Greg

CAN MEDICATION CURE OBESITY IN CHILDREN?   9

Critser (2003) noted in his book *Fat Land,* use of weight-loss drugs is unlikely to have an effect without the proper "support system"—one that includes doctors, facilities, time, and money (p. 3). For some, this level of care is prohibitively expensive.

A third complication is that the studies focused on adolescents aged 12-16, but obesity can begin at a much younger age. Few data exist to establish the safety or efficacy of medication for treating very young children.

While the scientific data on the concrete effects of these medications in children remain somewhat unclear, medication is not the only avenue for addressing the crisis. Both medical experts and policymakers recognize that solutions might come not only from a laboratory but also from policy, education, and advocacy. A handbook designed to educate doctors on obesity called for "major changes in some aspects of western culture" (Hoppin & Taveras, 2004, Conclusion section, para. 1). Cultural change may not be the typical realm of medical professionals, but the handbook urged doctors to be proactive and "focus [their] energy on public policies and interventions" (Conclusion section, para. 1).

Mirano develops the paper's thesis.

Brackets indicate a word not in the original source.

The solutions proposed by a number of advocacy groups underscore this interest in political and cultural change. A report by the Henry J. Kaiser Family Foundation (2004) outlined trends that may have contributed to the childhood obesity crisis, including food advertising for children as well as

> a reduction in physical education classes and after-school athletic programs, an increase in the availability of sodas and snacks in public schools, the growth in the number of fast-food outlets . . . , and the increasing number of highly processed high-calorie and high-fat grocery products. (p. 1)

A quotation longer than forty words is indented without quotation marks.

CAN MEDICATION CURE OBESITY IN CHILDREN?   10

Mirano interprets the
evidence; she
doesn't just report it.

Addressing each of these areas requires more than a
doctor armed with a prescription pad; it requires a broad
mobilization not just of doctors and concerned parents but
of educators, food industry executives, advertisers, and
media representatives.

The tone of the
conclusion is
objective.

The barrage of possible approaches to combating
childhood obesity—from scientific research to political
lobbying—indicates both the severity and the complexity
of the problem. While none of the medications currently
available is a miracle drug for curing the nation's 9 million
obese children, research has illuminated some of the
underlying factors that affect obesity and has shown the
need for a comprehensive approach to the problem that
includes behavioral, medical, social, and political change.

CAN MEDICATION CURE OBESITY IN CHILDREN?   11

References

Berkowitz, R. I., Wadden, T. A., Tershakovec, A. M., & Cronquist, J. L. (2003). Behavior therapy and sibutramine for the treatment of adolescent obesity. *Journal of the American Medical Association, 289,* 1805-1812.

Carmona, R. H. (2004, March 2). *The growing epidemic of childhood obesity.* Testimony before the Subcommittee on Competition, Foreign Commerce, and Infrastructure of the U.S. Senate Committee on Commerce, Science, and Transportation. Retrieved from http://www.hhs .gov/asl/testify/t040302.html

Critser, G. (2003). *Fat land.* Boston, MA: Houghton Mifflin.

Duenwald, M. (2004, January 6). Slim pickings: Looking beyond ephedra. *The New York Times,* p. F1. Retrieved from http://nytimes.com/

Henry J. Kaiser Family Foundation. (2004, February). *The role of media in childhood obesity.* Retrieved from http:// www.kff.org/entmedia/7030.cfm

Hilts, P. J. (2002, March 20). Petition asks for removal of diet drug from market. *The New York Times,* p. A26. Retrieved from http://nytimes.com/

Hoppin, A. G., & Taveras, E. M. (2004, June 25). Assessment and management of childhood and adolescent obesity. *Clinical Update.* Retrieved from http://www.medscape .com/viewarticle/481633

McDuffie, J. R., Calis, K. A., Uwaifo, G. I., Sebring, N. G., Fallon, E. M., Hubbard, V. S., & Yanovski, J. A. (2002). Three-month tolerability of orlistat in adolescents with obesity-related comorbid conditions. *Obesity Research, 10,* 642-650.

List of references begins on a new page. Heading is centered.

List is alphabetized by authors' last names. All authors' names are inverted (last name followed by initials).

The first line of an entry is at the left margin; subsequent lines indent ½".

Double-spacing is used throughout.

CAN MEDICATION CURE OBESITY IN CHILDREN?   12

Roche Laboratories. (2003, December). *Xenical (orlistat) capsules: Complete product information.* Retrieved from http://www.rocheusa.com/products/xenical/pi.pdf

Yanovski, S. Z., & Yanovski, J. A. (2002). Drug therapy: Obesity. *The New England Journal of Medicine, 346,* 591-602.

ALTERNATIVE APA TITLE PAGE

Obesity in Children 1

Short title and page number in the upper right corner on all pages.

Can Medication Cure Obesity in Children?

A Review of the Literature

Full title, centered.

Luisa Mirano

Psychology 108, Sector B

Professor Kang

October 31, 2004

Writer's name, course, instructor's name, and date, all centered at the bottom of the page.

ALTERNATIVE APA RUNNING HEAD

Obesity in Children 5

were classified by the Drug Enforcement Administration as having the "potential for abuse" (Hoppin & Taveras, 2004, Weight-Loss Drugs section, para. 6). Currently only two medications have been approved by the FDA for long-term

---

Marginal annotations indicate APA-style formatting.

Writing about Literature

Writing about Literature, 597

All good writing about literature attempts to answer a question, spoken or unspoken, about the text:

- Why does Hamlet hesitate for so long before killing his uncle, King Claudius?

- How does street language function in Gwendolyn Brooks's "We Real Cool"?

- What does the relationship between Hana and Kip in Michael Ondaatje's novel *The English Patient* suggest about love and nationality?

- What is the connection between Latin and Gaelic in Brian Friel's play *Translations*?

- Why does Margaret Atwood make so many biblical allusions in *The Handmaid's Tale*?

- In what ways does Louise Erdrich's *Love Medicine* draw on oral narrative traditions?

- Why does it matter that Robert Hayden's poem "Those Winter Sundays" is about winter Sundays (as opposed to, say, winter Tuesdays)?

The goal of a literature paper should be to address such questions with a meaningful interpretation, presented both forcefully and persuasively.

66   Reading to form an interpretation

66a   Get involved in the work; be an active reader.

Read the work through once, closely and carefully. Think of it as speaking to you: What is it telling you? Asking you? Trying to make you feel? Then go back and read it a second time. If the work provides an introduction and footnotes, read them attentively. They may be a source of important information. Use the dictionary to look up words that are unfamiliar to you or words with subtle nuances that may affect the work's meaning.

Rereading is a central part of the process of developing your interpretation. You should read short works several times, first to get an overall impression and then again to focus on meaningful details. With longer works, such as novels or plays, read the most important chapters or scenes more than once while keeping in mind the work as a whole.

As you read and reread, interact with the work by posing questions and looking for possible answers. The chart that begins on page 602 suggests some questions about literature that may help you become a more active reader.

Annotating the work

Annotating the work is a way to focus your reading. If you own a copy of the work, you should feel free to make notes on it. If you do not, make a photocopy. The first time you read the work through, you may want to pencil a check mark next to passages you find especially significant. On a more careful rereading, pay particular attention to these passages and jot down your ideas and reactions in the margins of the page.

Here is one student's annotation of a poem by Shakespeare.

Rhyming pattern of sonnet

Shall I compare thee to a summer's day? ⟶ *Who? (Must be a loved one.)*

Thou art more lovely and more temperate: ⟶ *Pleasant-natured (like pleasant weather)?*

Rough winds do shake the darling buds of May,

And summer's lease hath all too short a date.

Sometime too hot the eye of heaven shines,

Fair = beauty, or more than beauty?

And often is his gold complexion dimmed;

And every fair from fair sometimes declines,

By chance, or nature's changing course, untrimmed.

Summer is fleeting and not always perfect. (But lover is perfect?)

What are "eternal lines to time"? Ask in class?

But thy eternal summer shall not fade,

Nor lose possession of that fair thou ow'st

Nor shall death brag thou wand'rest in his shade, ⟶ *Death would be proud to claim the lover but can't?*

When in eternal lines to time thou grow'st.

Final couplet seems to signal a shift in thought.

So long as men can breathe or eyes can see,

So long lives this, and this gives life to thee.

This = the poem? (Art, like the writer's love, is eternal.)

NOTE TAKING ON A LITERARY WORK

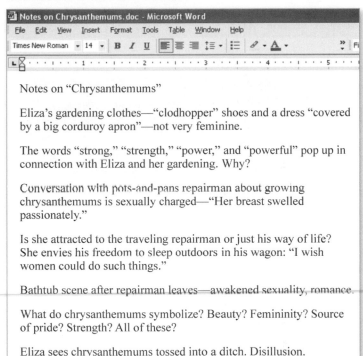

Notes on "Chrysanthemums"

Eliza's gardening clothes—"clodhopper" shoes and a dress "covered by a big corduroy apron"—not very feminine.

The words "strong," "strength," "power," and "powerful" pop up in connection with Eliza and her gardening. Why?

Conversation with pots-and-pans repairman about growing chrysanthemums is sexually charged—"Her breast swelled passionately."

Is she attracted to the traveling repairman or just his way of life? She envies his freedom to sleep outdoors in his wagon: "I wish women could do such things."

Bathtub scene after repairman leaves—awakened sexuality, romance.

What do chrysanthemums symbolize? Beauty? Femininity? Source of pride? Strength? All of these?

Eliza sees chrysanthemums tossed into a ditch. Disillusion.

Taking notes

Note taking is also an important part of rereading a work of literature. In your notes you can try out ideas and develop your perspective on the work. On this page are notes one student took on a short story, "Chrysanthemums," by John Steinbeck. Notice that some of these notes pose questions for further thought.

Discussing the work

As you may have discovered, class discussions can lead to interesting insights about a literary work, perhaps by calling attention to details that you failed to notice on a first reading. Discussions don't always need to occur face-to-face. In many classes, they happen online in discussion forums, chat rooms, blogs, or wikis. On page 600, for example, is a set of blog postings about a character in Joyce Carol Oates's short story "Where Are You Going, Where Have You Been?"

CONVERSATION ABOUT A SUBJECT

Dr. Connolly's Blog | ENG 101, Section 4

① Who is Arnold Friend?

Posted by Professor Barbara Connolly, Thu Mar 4, 2010 4:36 PM

At one point during the story Arnold Friend demands, "Don't you know who I am?" Who do you think he is? Does the reader or Connie ever really know?

View comments | Add a comment

---

4 comments on

"Who is Arnold Friend?" Original post

② Posted by Zoe Marshall, Thu Mar 4, 2010 7:23 PM

I think we're not supposed to know who Arnold Friend is. When he first arrives at Connie's house she asks him, "Who the hell do you think you are?" but Arnold ignores her question by changing the subject. He never tells her who he really is, only that he's her friend and her lover.

Posted by Mirabel Chavez, Thu Mar 4, 2010 7:47 PM

Connie is always pretending to be something else to her friends, her boyfriends, and her family. Oates describes her as having two sides: one for home and one for when she's away from home. Pretending is something Connie and Arnold have in common.

Posted by Jon Fietze, Thu Mar 4, 2010 8:04 PM

I found a lot of parallels between Arnold and the wolf in "Little Red Riding Hood." For example, Connie notices Arnold's hair, his teeth, and his grin. It reminded me of that part in "Little Red Riding Hood" when Little Red says, "Oh, Grandmother, what big teeth you have!"

Posted by Yuko Yoshikawa, Thu Mar 4, 2010 11:11 PM

I was thinking the same thing. Plus, Arnold seems like he's dressing up to hide who he is. Connie thinks that his hair is like a wig, and later that his face is a mask. It reminded me of when the wolf puts on the grandmother's clothing to trick Little Red Riding Hood, just like Arnold is trying to trick Connie.

---

1   Instructor's prompt.
2   A series of student responses to the prompt.

66b   Form an interpretation.

After rereading, jotting notes, and perhaps discussing the work, you are ready to start forming an interpretation. At this stage, try to focus on a single aspect of the work. Look through your notes and annotations for recurring questions and insights related to the aspect you have chosen.

Focusing on a central issue

In forming an interpretation, you should try to focus on a central issue. Your job is not to say everything about the work that can possibly be said. It is to develop a sustained, in-depth interpretation that illuminates the work in some specific way. You may think, for example, that *Huckleberry Finn* is an interesting book because it not only contains humor and brilliant descriptions of scenery but also tells a serious story of one boy's coming of age. But to develop this general response into an interpretation, you will have to find a focus. For example, you might address the ways in which the runaway slave Jim uses humor to preserve his dignity. Or you might examine the ironic contradictions between what Huck says and what his heart tells him.

Asking questions that lead to an interpretation

Good interpretations generally arise from good questions. What is it about the work that puzzles, intrigues, or unsettles you? What do you want to know more about? What are you uncertain about? By asking yourself such questions, you will push yourself to move beyond your first impressions to deeper insights and better ideas.

Some interpretations answer questions about literary techniques, such as the writer's handling of plot, setting, and character. Others respond to questions about social context as well — what a work reveals about the time and culture in which it was written. Both kinds of questions are included in the chart that begins on page 602.

Often you will find yourself writing about both technique and social context. For example, Margaret Peel, a student who wrote about Langston Hughes's poem "Ballad of the Landlord" (see p. 627), addressed the following question, which touches on both language and race:

> How does the poem's language—through its four voices—dramatize the experience of a black man in a society dominated by whites?

Questions to ask about literature

Questions about technique

Plot. What central conflicts drive the plot? Are they internal (within a character) or external (between characters or between a character and a force)? How are conflicts resolved? Why are events revealed in a particular order?

Setting. Does the setting (time and place) create an atmosphere, give an insight into a character, suggest symbolic meanings, or hint at the theme of the work?

Character. What seems to motivate the central characters? Do any characters change significantly? If so, what — if anything — have they learned from their experiences? Do sharp contrasts between characters highlight important themes?

Point of view. Does the point of view — the perspective from which the story is narrated or the poem is spoken — influence our understanding of events? Does the narration reveal the character of the speaker, or does the speaker merely observe others? Is the narrator perhaps innocent, naive, or deceitful?

Theme. Does the work have an overall theme (a central insight about people or a truth about life, for example)? If so, how do details in the work serve to illuminate this theme?

Language. Does language — such as formal or informal, standard or dialect, prosaic or poetic, cool or passionate — reveal the character of speakers? How do metaphors, similes, and sensory images contribute to the work? How do recurring images enrich the work and hint at its meaning? To what extent do sentence rhythms and sounds underscore the writer's meaning?

Questions about social context

Historical context. What does the work reveal about — or how was it shaped by — the time and place in which it was written? Does the work appear to promote or undermine a philosophy that was popular in its time, such as social Darwinism in the late nineteenth century or the women's movement in the mid-twentieth century?

Class. How does social class shape or influence characters' choices and actions? How does class affect the way characters view — or are viewed by — others? What economic struggles or power relationships does the work reflect or depict?

Race and culture. Are any characters portrayed as being caught between cultures: between the culture of home and the culture of work or school, for example, or between a traditional and an emerging culture? Are any characters engaged in a conflict with society because of their race or ethnic background? To what extent does the work celebrate a specific culture and its traditions?

Gender. Are any characters' choices restricted because of gender? What are the power relationships between the sexes, and do these change during the course of the work? Do any characters resist the gender roles society has assigned to them? Do other characters choose to conform to those roles?

Archetypes (or universal types). Does a character, an image, or a plot fit a pattern — or type — that has been repeated in stories throughout history and across cultures? (For example, nearly every culture has stories about heroes, quests, redemption, and revenge.) How does an archetypal character, image, or plot line correspond to or differ from others like it?

In the introduction of your paper, you will usually announce your interpretation in a one- or two-sentence thesis. The thesis answers the central question that you posed. Here, for example, is Margaret Peel's two-sentence thesis:

> Langston Hughes's "Ballad of the Landlord" is narrated through
> four voices, each with its own perspective on the poem's action.
> These opposing voices—of a tenant, a landlord, the police, and the
> press—dramatize a black man's experience in a society dominated
> by whites.

Peel's complete essay, "Opposing Voices in 'Ballad of the Landlord,'" appears on pages 623–26.

Planning the paper

67a Draft a thesis.

When planning your paper, it is good to have a working or preliminary thesis in mind. This preliminary thesis will reflect the current state of your thinking about the work and will likely change and evolve as you plan and draft. (See 1c.)

In its final form, your thesis will address the central question you asked about the work. It will likely appear at the end of your introduction and will announce your essay's main point. When drafting your thesis, aim for a strong, assertive summary of your interpretation. Here, for example, are two successful thesis statements taken from student essays, together with the central question each student had posed.

QUESTION

What does Emily Dickinson's poem "I dwell in Possibility—" tell us about the writing of poetry?

THESIS

Emily Dickinson's poem "I dwell in Possibility—" implies that poetry itself is limitless and that the role of the poet is not to create poetry but to inhabit and shape it.

QUESTION

What is the significance of the explorer Robert Walton in Mary Shelley's novel *Frankenstein*?

THESIS

Through the character of Walton, Shelley suggests that the most profound sort of knowledge is not a knowledge of nature's secrets but a knowledge of the limits of knowledge itself.

As in other writing, the thesis of a literature paper should not be too factual, too broad, or too vague (see also 2a). For an essay on Mark Twain's *Huckleberry Finn*, for example, the following would all make poor thesis statements.

TOO FACTUAL

As a runaway slave, Jim is in danger from the law.

TOO BROAD

In *Huckleberry Finn*, Twain criticizes mid-nineteenth-century American society.

TOO VAGUE

Huckleberry Finn is Twain's most exciting work.

The following thesis statement is sharply focused and presents a central idea that requires discussion and support. It connects a general point (that Twain objects to empty piety) to those specific aspects of the novel the paper will address (Huck's status as narrator, Huck's comments on religion).

EFFECTIVE THESIS

Because Huckleberry Finn is a naive narrator, his comments on conventional religion function ironically at every turn, allowing Twain to poke fun at empty piety.

67b Sketch an outline.

Your thesis may strongly suggest a method of organization, in which case you will have little difficulty jotting down your essay's key points. Consider, for example, the following informal outline, based on a thesis that leads naturally to a three-part organization.

Thesis: In Zora Neale Hurston's novel *Their Eyes Were Watching God*, Janie grows into independence through a series of marriages: first to Logan Killicks, who treats her as a source of farm labor; next to Jody Starks, who sees her as a symbol of his own power; and then to Tea Cake, with whom she shares a passionate and satisfying love that leads her to self-discovery.

—Marriage to Logan Killicks: arranged by grandmother, Janie as labor, runs away

—Marriage to Jody Starks: Eatonville, Jody as mayor, violence, Jody's death

—Marriage to Tea Cake: younger man, love, shooting, return to Eatonville

If your thesis does not by itself suggest a method of organization, turn to your notes and begin putting them into categories that relate to the thesis. For example, one student who was writing about Euripides's play *Medea* constructed the following formal outline from her notes.

Thesis: Although Medea professes great love for her children, Euripides gives us reason to doubt her sincerity: Medea does not hesitate to use the children as weapons in her bloody battle with Jason, and from the outset she displays little real concern for their fate.

I. From the beginning of the play, Medea is a less than ideal mother.

   A. Her first words about the children are hostile.

   B. Her first actions suggest indifference.

II. In three scenes Medea appears to be a loving mother, but in each of these scenes we have reason to doubt her sincerity.

III. Throughout the play, as Medea plots her revenge, her overriding concern is not her children but her reputation.

   A. Fearing ridicule, she is proud of her reputation as one who can "help her friends and hurt her enemies."

   B. Her obsession with reputation may stem from the Greek view of reputation as a means of immortality.

IV. After she kills her children, Medea reveals her real concern.

   A. She shows no remorse.

   B. She revels in Jason's agony over their death.

Whether to use a formal or an informal outline is to some extent a matter of personal preference. For most purposes, you will probably find that an informal outline is sufficient, perhaps even preferable. (See 1d and 5b.)

68 Writing the paper

68a Draft an introduction that announces your interpretation.

The introduction to a literature paper is usually one paragraph long. In most cases, you will want to begin the paragraph with a few sentences that provide context for your thesis and to end it with a thesis that sums up your interpretation. You may also want to note the question or issue that motivated your interpretation. In this way, you will help your reader understand not only what your idea or thesis *is* but also why it *matters*.

The following is an introductory paragraph announcing a student's interpretation of one aspect of the novel *Frankenstein*; the thesis is highlighted.

In Mary Shelley's novel *Frankenstein*, Walton's ambition as an explorer, to find a passage to the North Pole, mirrors Frankenstein's ambition as a scientist, to discover and master the secret of life. But where Frankenstein is ultimately destroyed by his quest for knowledge, Walton turns back from his quest when he learns of Frankenstein's fate. Walton's story might seem unimportant, but paired with Frankenstein's, it keeps us from missing one of the novel's most important themes. Through Walton, Shelley suggests that the most profound and useful sort of knowledge is not a knowledge of nature's secrets but a knowledge of the limits of knowledge itself.

68b Support your interpretation with evidence from the work; avoid simple plot summary.

Your thesis and preliminary outline will point you toward aspects of the work relevant to your interpretation. As you begin drafting the body of your paper, discuss those aspects in detail to support your ideas.

Supporting your interpretation

As a rule, each paragraph in the body of your paper should focus on some part of your overall interpretation and should include a topic sentence that states the main idea of the paragraph (see 4b). The rest of the paragraph should present details and perhaps quotations from the work that back up your interpretation. In the following paragraph, which develops part of the outline sketched on page 605, the topic sentence comes first. It sums up the significance of Janie's marriage to Logan Killicks in Zora Neale Hurston's novel *Their Eyes Were Watching God*.

Janie finds her marriage to Logan Killicks unsatisfying because she did not choose him and cannot love him. The marriage is arranged by Janie's grandmother and caretaker, Nanny, so that Janie will have a secure home after Nanny dies. When Janie objects to the marriage, Nanny tells her, "'Tain't Logan Killicks Ah wants you to have, baby, it's protection" (15). Janie marries Logan even though she does not love him. She "wait[s] for love to begin" (22), but love never comes. At first, Logan dotes on Janie, but as time passes, he demands more and more work from her. Although she works hard in the kitchen, he wants her to perform traditionally masculine tasks such as chopping wood, plowing fields, and shoveling manure. When Janie suggests that they each have their roles—"Youse in yo' place and Ah'm in mine"—Logan asserts his authority over her and doesn't seem to relate to her as family: "You ain't got no particular place. It's wherever Ah need yuh" (31). As husband and wife, Janie and Logan are estranged from each other. Janie tells him, "You ain't done me no favor by marryin' me" (31). To escape this loveless and demeaning marriage, Janie runs away with Joe Starks.

Notice that the writer has quoted dialogue from the novel to lend both flavor and substance to her interpretation (quotations are cited with page numbers). Notice too that the writer is *interpreting* the work: She is not merely summarizing the plot.

Avoiding simple plot summary

In a literature paper, it is tempting to rely heavily on plot summary and avoid interpretation. You can resist the temptation to merely list the events of the work by paying special attention to your topic sentences. The following rough-draft topic sentence, for instance, led to a plot summary rather than an interpretation.

As they drift down the river on a raft, Huck and the runaway slave Jim have many philosophical discussions.

The student's revised topic sentence, which announces an interpretation, is much better.

The theme of dawning moral awareness is reinforced by the many philosophical discussions between Huck and Jim, the runaway slave, as they drift down the river on a raft.

Usually a little thought and preparation can make the difference between a plot summary that cannot be developed and a focused, forceful interpretation. As with all writing, revision is key. To avoid simple plot summary, keep the following strategies in mind as you write.

- When you write for an academic audience, you can assume that readers have read the work. You may need to include some summary as background, but the emphasis should be on your ideas about the work.

- Pose questions that lead to an interpretation or a judgment of the work rather than to a summary. The questions in the chart that begins on page 602 can help steer you away from summary and toward interpretation.

- Read your essay out loud. If you hear yourself listing events from the work, stop and revise.

- Rather than organizing your paper according to the work's sequence of events, organize it in a way that brings out the relationships among your ideas.

 Observing the conventions of literature papers

The academic discipline of English literature has certain conventions, or standard practices, that scholars in the field use when writing about literature. These conventions help scholars communicate their ideas clearly and efficiently. If you adhere to these conventions, you will enhance your credibility and enable your readers to focus more easily on your ideas.

69a Refer to authors, titles, and characters according to convention.

The first time you refer to an author of a literary work or a secondary source, such as a critical essay, use the author's full name: *Virginia Woolf is known for her experimental novels.* In subsequent references, you may use the last name only: *Woolf's early work was largely overlooked.* As a rule, do not use personal titles such as *Mr.* or *Ms.* or *Dr.* when referring to authors.

When you mention the title of a short story, an essay, or a short or medium-length poem, put the title in quotation marks.

"The Progress of Love," by Alice Munro

"Coming Home Again," by Chang-Rae Lee

"Promises like Pie-Crust," by Christina Rossetti

Italicize the titles of novels, nonfiction books, plays, and long poems.

The Poisonwood Bible, by Barbara Kingsolver

I Know Why the Caged Bird Sings, by Maya Angelou

M. Butterfly, by David Henry Hwang

Howl, by Allen Ginsberg

Refer to each character by the name most often used for him or her in the work. If, for instance, a character's name is Lambert Strether and he is always referred to as "Strether," do not call him "Lambert" or "Mr. Strether." Similarly, write "Lady Macbeth," not "Mrs. Macbeth."

69b Use the present tense to describe fictional events.

Perhaps because fictional events have not actually occurred in the past, the literary convention is to describe them in the present tense. Until you become used to this convention, you may find yourself shifting between present and past tense. As you revise your draft, make sure that you have used the present tense consistently.

INCONSISTENT USE OF TENSES

Octavia <u>demands</u> blind obedience from James and from all of her children. When James and Ty <u>caught</u> two redbirds in their trap, they <u>wanted</u> to play with them; Octavia, however, <u>had</u> other plans for the birds (89-90).

CONSISTENT USE OF THE PRESENT TENSE

Octavia <u>demands</u> blind obedience from James and from all of her children. When James and Ty <u>catch</u> two redbirds in their trap, they <u>want</u> to play with them; Octavia, however, <u>has</u> other plans for the birds (89-90).

NOTE: When integrating quotations from the work into your own text, you will need to be alert to the problem of shifting tenses. See 70c.

69c Use MLA style to format passages quoted from the work.

Unless your instructor suggests otherwise, use MLA (Modern Language Association) style for formatting passages quoted from literary works.

MLA style usually requires that you name the author of the work quoted and give a page number for the exact location of the passage in the work. When writing about nonfiction articles and books, introduce a quotation with a signal phrase naming the author (*John Smith points out that* "...") or place the author's name and page number in parentheses at the end of the quoted passage: "... *for all time" (Smith 22)*.

When writing about a single work of fiction, however, you do not need to include the author's name each time you quote from the work. You will mention the author's name in the introduction to your paper. Then, when you are quoting from the work, you may include just the page number in parentheses following the quotation (see p. 615). You may, of course, use the author's name in a signal phrase to highlight the author's role or technique (see p. 614), but you are not required to do so. (See also 70a.)

Additional MLA guidelines for handling citations in the text of your paper appear in 70.

---

70 **Integrating quotations from the work**

Integrating quotations from a literary work can lend vivid support to your argument, but keep most quotations fairly short. You can use long quotations to present extended passages you will discuss at length, but use them sparingly. Excessive use of long quotations may interrupt the flow of your interpretation, making your paper more difficult to read and understand.

Integrating quotations smoothly into your own text can present a challenge. Because of the complexities of literature, do not be surprised to find yourself puzzling over the most graceful way to tuck in a short phrase or the clearest way to introduce a more extended passage from the work.

70a Do not confuse the work's author with a narrator, speaker, or character.

When introducing quotations from a literary work, make sure that you don't confuse the author with the narrator of a story, the speaker of a poem, or a character in a story or play. Instead of naming the author, you can refer to the narrator or speaker — or to the work itself.

INAPPROPRIATE

Poet Andrew Marvell describes his fear of death like this: "But at my back I always hear / Time's wingèd chariot hurrying near" (21-22).

APPROPRIATE

Addressing his beloved in an attempt to win her sexual favors, the speaker of the poem argues that death gives them no time to waste: "But at my back I always hear / Time's wingèd chariot hurrying near" (21-22).

APPROPRIATE

The poem "To His Coy Mistress" says as much about fleeting time and death as it does about sexual passion. Its most powerful lines are "But at my back I always hear / Time's wingèd chariot hurrying near" (21-22).

In the last example, you could mention the author as well: *Marvell's poem "To His Coy Mistress" says as much.* . . . Although the author is mentioned, readers will not confuse him with the speaker of the poem.

70b Provide context for quotations.

When you quote the words of a narrator, speaker, or character in a literary work, you should name who is speaking and provide a context for the quoted words. In the following examples, the quoted dialogue is from Tennessee Williams's play *The Glass Menagerie* and Shirley Jackson's short story "The Lottery."

> Laura is so completely under Amanda's spell that when urged to make a wish on the moon, she asks, "What shall I wish for, Mother?" (1.5.140).

> When a neighbor suggests that the lottery should be abandoned, Old Man Warner responds, "There's *always* been a lottery" (284).

70c As you integrate quotations, avoid shifts in tense.

Because it is conventional to write about literature in the present tense (see 69b) and because literary works often use other tenses, you will need to exercise care when weaving quotations into your own writing. One student's first draft of a paper on Nadine Gordimer's short story "Friday's Footprint" included the following awkward sentence, in which the present-tense main verb *sees* is followed by the past-tense verb *blushed* in the quotation.

TENSE SHIFT

> When Rita sees Johnny's relaxed attitude, "she blushed, like a wave of illness" (159).

When revising, the writer considered two ways to avoid the distracting shift from present to past tense: to paraphrase the reference to Rita's blushing and reduce the length of the quotation or to change the verb in the quotation to the present tense, using brackets to indicate the change.

REVISION 1

> When Rita sees Johnny's relaxed attitude, she is overcome with embarrassment, "like a wave of illness" (159).

REVISION 2

When Rita sees Johnny's relaxed attitude, "she blushe[s], like a
wave of illness" (159).

Using brackets around just one letter of a word can seem
fussy, so the writer chose the first revision. (See also 70d.)

70d To indicate changes in a quotation, use brackets and the ellipsis mark.

Two marks of punctuation, square brackets and the ellipsis mark
(three spaced periods), show readers that you have modified a
quoted passage in some way.

Brackets are used for additions, as in the following example
from a paper on Khaled Hosseini's novel *A Thousand Splendid
Suns*.

> Laila, fearful, confides in Tariq: "It's the whistling, the damn
> whistling [of the rockets], I hate more than anything" (156).

Because some readers might not understand the meaning of
whistling out of context, the writer has supplied a clarification in
brackets. Brackets are also used to change words or letters to keep
a quoted sentence grammatical in your context, as in the last example in 70c, or to change a capital letter to lowercase or vice
versa, as on page 619.

The ellipsis mark is used to indicate omissions. In the following example from a paper on Tim O'Brien's "How to Tell a True
War Story," the writer has omitted some words from the original
in order to keep the quoted passage brief.

> O'Brien warns his readers bluntly that they should not seek noble
> themes in war stories: "If at the end of a war story you feel
> uplifted, . . . then you have been made the victim of a very old and
> terrible lie" (347).

If you want to omit one or more full sentences from a quotation, use a period before the three ellipsis dots.

> O'Brien regards war as fundamentally immoral: "A true war story is
> never moral. . . . If a story seems moral, do not believe it" (347).

Usually you do not need an ellipsis mark at the beginning or at
the end of a quotation. But if you have dropped words at the end of

the final quoted sentence, put three ellipsis dots before the closing quotation mark and parenthetical reference, as in the example on page 619.

Remember to use brackets and ellipsis marks sparingly. The purpose of quoting is to show your readers the actual language of the work. Excessive alterations can undermine a quotation's effectiveness as evidence.

70e Enclose embedded quotations in single quotation marks.

In writing about literature, you may sometimes want to use a quotation with another quotation embedded in it—when you are quoting dialogue in a novel, for example. In such cases, set off the main quotation with double quotation marks, as you usually would, and set off the embedded quotation with single quotation marks. The following example from a student paper quotes lines from Amy Tan's novel *The Hundred Secret Senses*.

> Early in the novel the narrator's half-sister Kwan sees—or thinks she
> sees—ghosts: "'Libby-ah,' she'll say to me. 'Guess who I see yesterday,
> you guess.' And I don't have to guess that she's talking about someone
> dead" (3).

70f Use MLA style to cite passages from the work.

MLA guidelines for citing quotations differ somewhat for short stories or novels, poems, and plays.

Short stories or novels

To cite a passage from a short story or a novel, use a page number in parentheses after the quoted words.

> The narrator of Madeleine Thien's "Simple Recipes" remembers a
> conversation with her mother in which the mother described guilt
> as something one could "shrink" and "compress." After a time,
> according to the mother, "you can blow it off your body like a speck
> of dirt" (12).

If a novel has numbered divisions, give the page number followed by a semicolon; then indicate the book, part, or chapter in which the passage is found. Use abbreviations such as "bk." and "ch."

> White relies on past authors to help retell the legend of King Arthur. The narrator does not provide specifics about Lancelot's tournament at Corbin, instead telling readers, "If you want to read about the Corbin tournament, Malory has it" (489; bk. 3, ch. 39).

When a quotation from a work of fiction takes up four or fewer typed lines, put it in quotation marks and run it into the text of your essay, as in the two previous examples. When a quotation is five lines or longer, set it off from the text by indenting one inch from the left margin; when you set a quotation off from the text, do not use quotation marks. Put the parenthetical citation after the final mark of punctuation.

> Sister's tale begins with "I," and she makes every event revolve around herself, even her sister's marriage:
>
>> I was getting along fine with Mama, Papa-Daddy and Uncle Rondo until my sister Stella-Rondo just separated from her husband and came back home again. Mr. Whitaker! Of course I went with Mr. Whitaker first, when he first appeared here in China Grove, taking "Pose Yourself" photos, and Stella-Rondo broke us up. (88)

Poems

To cite lines from a poem, use line numbers in parentheses at the end of the quotation. For the first reference, use the word "lines": (lines 6-8). Thereafter, use just the numbers: (12-13).

> The opening lines of Frost's "Fire and Ice" strike a conversational tone: "Some say the world will end in fire, / Some say in ice" (lines 1-2).

Enclose quotations of three or fewer lines of poetry in quotation marks within your text, and indicate line breaks with a slash, as in the example just given. Use a space before and after the slash.

When you quote four or more lines of poetry, set the quotation off from the text by indenting one inch, and omit the quotation marks. Put the line numbers in parentheses after the final mark of punctuation.

In the second stanza of "A Noiseless Patient Spider," Whitman turns the spider's weaving into a metaphor for the activity of the human soul:

> And you O my soul where you stand,
> Surrounded, detached, in measureless oceans of
>   space,
> Ceaselessly musing, venturing, throwing, seeking the
>   spheres to connect them,
> Till the bridge you will need be form'd, till the ductile
>   anchor hold,
> Till the gossamer thread you fling catch somewhere,
>   O my soul. (6-10)

NOTE: If any line of the poem takes up more than one line of your paper, carry the extra words to the next line of the paper and indent them an additional one-quarter inch, as in the previous example. Alternatively, you may indent the entire poem a little less than one inch to fit the long line.

Plays

To cite lines from a play, include the act number, scene number, and line numbers (as many of these as are available) in parentheses at the end of the quotation. Separate the numbers with periods, and use arabic numerals unless your instructor prefers roman numerals.

Two attendants silently watch as the sleepwalking Lady Macbeth struggles with her conscience: "Here's the smell of the blood still. All the perfumes of Arabia will not sweeten this little hand" (5.1.50-51).

If no act, scene, or line numbers are available, use a page number.

When a quotation from a play takes up four or fewer typed lines in your paper and is spoken by only one character, put quotation marks around it and run it into the text of your essay, as in the previous example. If the quotation consists of two or three lines from a verse play, use a slash for line breaks, as for poetry (see p. 616). When a quotation by a single character in a play is five typed lines or longer (or more than three lines in a verse play), indent it one inch from the left margin and omit quotation marks. Include the citation in parentheses after the final mark of punctuation.

Speaking to Electra, Clytemnestra complains about the sexual double standard that has allowed her husband to justify sacrificing her other daughter, Iphigenia, to the gods. She asks what would have happened if Menelaus, and not his wife Helen, had been seized by the Trojans:

> If Menelaus had been raped from home on the sly,
> should I have had to kill Orestes so my sister's
> husband could be rescued? You think your father
> would have borne it? He would have killed me. Then
> why was it fair for him to kill what belonged to me
> and not be killed? (1041-45)

When quoting dialogue between two or more characters in a play, no matter how many lines you use, set the quotation off from the text. Type each character's name in all capital letters at a one-inch indent from the left margin. Indent subsequent lines under the character's name an additional one-quarter inch.

In the opening act of *Translations*, Friel pointedly contrasts the monolingual Captain Lancey with the multilingual Irish:

> HUGH. . . . [Lancey] then explained that he does not
> speak Irish. Latin? I asked. None. Greek? Not a
> syllable. He speaks—on his own admission—only
> English; and to his credit he seemed suitably
> verecund—James?
> JIMMY. *Verecundus*—humble.
> HUGH. Indeed—he voiced some surprise that we did not
> speak his language. (act 1)

71 | Using secondary sources

Many literature papers rely wholly on primary sources—the literary work or works under discussion. You document such papers with MLA in-text citations as explained in 70f. If a list of works cited is required, it will consist of the literary work or works (see p. 626).

In addition to relying on primary sources, some literature papers draw on secondary sources: articles or books of literary criticism, biographies of the author, the author's own essays or autobiography, or histories of the era in which the work was written. When you use secondary sources, you must document them with MLA in-text citations and a list of works cited as explained in 71a. (For an example of a paper that uses secondary sources, see pp. 628–34.)

Keep in mind that even when you use secondary sources, your main goal should be to develop and communicate your own understanding and interpretation of the literary work.

71a Use MLA style to document secondary sources.

Most writers of literature papers use the documentation system recommended by the Modern Language Association (MLA), as set forth in the *MLA Handbook for Writers of Research Papers*, 7th ed. (New York: MLA, 2009). (See 59.)

MLA recommends in-text citations that refer readers to a list of works cited. An in-text citation names the author of the source, often in a signal phrase, and gives the page number in parentheses. At the end of the paper, a list of works cited provides publication information about the sources used in the paper.

MLA IN-TEXT CITATION

Finding Butler's science fiction novel *Xenogenesis* more hopeful than *Frankenstein*, Theodora Goss and John Paul Riquelme note that "[h]uman and creature never bridge their differences in Shelley's narrative, but in Butler's they do . . ." (437).

The signal phrase names the authors of the secondary source; the number in parentheses is the page on which the quoted words appear. The in-text citation is used in combination with a list of works cited at the end of the paper. Anyone interested in knowing additional information about the secondary source can consult the list of works cited. Here, for example, is the works cited entry for the work referred to in the sample in-text citation.

ENTRY IN THE LIST OF WORKS CITED

Goss, Theodora, and John Paul Riquelme. "From Superhuman to
Posthuman: The Gothic Technological Imaginary in Mary
Shelley's *Frankenstein* and Octavia Butler's *Xenogenesis*."
Modern Fiction Studies 53.3 (2007): 434-59. Print.

As you document secondary sources with in-text citations, consult 59a; as you construct your list of works cited, see 59b.

71b Avoid plagiarism.

The rules about plagiarism are the same for literature papers as for other research writing. To be fair and ethical, you must acknowledge your debt to the writers of any sources you use. If you don't, you commit plagiarism, a serious academic offense.

In general, three different acts are considered plagiarism: (1) failing to cite quotations and borrowed ideas, (2) failing to enclose borrowed language in quotation marks, and (3) failing to put summaries and paraphrases in your own words. You may want to check out your school's plagiarism policy if you are unfamiliar with it.

If an interpretation was suggested to you by a critic's work or if an obscure point was clarified by someone else's research, it is your responsibility to cite the source (as explained in 71a). In addition to citing the source, you must place any borrowed language in quotation marks. In the following examples, the plagiarized words are underlined.

ORIGINAL SOURCE

Here again Glaspell's story reflects a larger truth about the lives of rural women. Their isolation induced madness in many. The rate of insanity in rural areas, especially for women, was a much-discussed subject in the second half of the nineteenth century.

— Elaine Hedges, "Small Things Reconsidered:
'A Jury of Her Peers,'" p. 59

PLAGIARISM

Glaspell may or may not want us to believe that Minnie Wright's murder of her husband is an insane act, but Minnie's loneliness and isolation certainly could have driven her mad. As Elaine Hedges notes, the rate of insanity in rural areas, especially for women, was a much-discussed subject in the second half of the nineteenth century (59).

BORROWED LANGUAGE IN QUOTATION MARKS

Glaspell may or may not want us to believe that Minnie Wright's murder of her husband is an insane act, but Minnie's loneliness and isolation certainly could have driven her mad. As Elaine Hedges notes, "The rate of insanity in rural areas, especially for women, was a much-discussed subject in the second half of the nineteenth century" (59).

Sometimes writers plagiarize unintentionally because they have difficulty paraphrasing a source's ideas. In the first paraphrase of the following source, the writer has copied the underlined words (without quotation marks) and followed the sentence structure of the source too closely, merely plugging in synonyms (*prowess* for *skill*, *respect* for *esteem*, and so on).

ORIGINAL SOURCE

Mothers [in the late nineteenth century] were advised to teach their daughters to make small, exact stitches, not only for durability but as a way of instilling habits of patience, neatness, and diligence. But such stitches also became a badge of one's needlework skill, a source of self-esteem and of status, through the recognition and admiration of other women.

— Elaine Hedges, "Small Things Reconsidered: 'A Jury of Her Peers,'" p. 62

PLAGIARISM: UNACCEPTABLE BORROWING

One of the final clues in the story, the irregular stitching in Minnie's quilt patches, connects immediately with Mrs. Hale and Mrs. Peters. In the late nineteenth century, explains Elaine Hedges, small, exact stitches were valued not only for their durability. They became a badge of one's prowess with the needle, a source of self-respect and of prestige, through the recognition and approval of other women (62).

ACCEPTABLE PARAPHRASE

One of the final clues in the story, the irregular stitching in Minnie's quilt patches, connects immediately with Mrs. Hale and Mrs. Peters. In the late nineteenth century, explains Elaine Hedges, precise needlework was valued for more than its strength. It was a source of pride to women, a way of gaining status in the community of other women (62).

Although the acceptable version uses a few words found in the original source, it does not borrow entire phrases without quotation marks or closely mimic the structure of the original. To write an acceptable paraphrase, resist the temptation to look at the source while you write; instead, write from memory. When you write from memory, you will be more likely to use your own words. Ask yourself, "What is the author's meaning?" and then in your own words, state your understanding of the author's basic point.

72 Sample papers

Following are two sample essays. The first, by Margaret Peel, has no secondary sources. (Langston Hughes's "Ballad of the Landlord," the poem on which the essay is based, appears on p. 627.) The second essay, by Dan Larson, uses secondary sources. (The short story on which the paper is based begins on p. 635.)

Peel 1

Margaret Peel

Professor Lin

English 102

20 April 2010

Opposing Voices in "Ballad of the Landlord"

Langston Hughes's "Ballad of the Landlord" is narrated
through four voices, each with its own perspective on
the poem's action. These opposing voices—of a tenant, a
landlord, the police, and the press—dramatize a black man's
experience in a society dominated by whites.

The main voice in the poem is that of the tenant, who,
as the last line tells us, is black. The tenant is characterized
by his informal, nonstandard speech. He uses slang ("Ten
Bucks"), contracted words ('member, more'n), and nonstandard
grammar ("These steps is broken down"). This colloquial
English suggests the tenant's separation from the world of
convention, represented by the formal voices of the police and
the press, which appear later in the poem.

Although the tenant uses nonstandard English, his
argument is organized and logical. He begins with a reasonable
complaint and a gentle reminder that the complaint is already a
week old: "My roof has sprung a leak. / Don't you 'member I told
you about it / Way last week?" (lines 2-4). In the second stanza,
he appeals diplomatically to the landlord's self-interest: "These
steps is broken down. / When you come up yourself / It's a
wonder you don't fall down" (6-8). In the third stanza, when the
landlord has responded to his complaints with a demand for rent
money, the tenant becomes more forceful, but his voice is still
reasonable: "Ten Bucks you say is due? / Well, that's Ten Bucks
more'n I'll pay you / Till you fix this house up new" (10-12).

The fourth stanza marks a shift in the tone of the argument.

Thesis states Peel's
main idea.

Details from the
poem illustrate
Peel's point.

The first citation for
lines of the poem
includes the word
"lines." Subsequent
citations from the
poem are cited with
line numbers alone.

Topic sentence
focuses on an
interpretation.

Marginal annotations indicate MLA-style formatting and effective writing.

Peel 2

At this point the tenant responds more emotionally, in reaction to the landlord's threats to evict him. By the fifth stanza, the tenant has unleashed his anger: "Um-huh! You talking high and mighty" (17). Hughes uses an exclamation point for the first time; the tenant is raising his voice at last. As the argument gets more heated, the tenant finally resorts to the language of violence: "You ain't gonna be able to say a word / If I land my fist on you" (19-20).

These are the last words the tenant speaks in the poem. Perhaps Hughes wants to show how black people who threaten violence are silenced. When a new voice is introduced—the landlord's—the poem shifts to a frantic tone:

> Police! Police!
> Come and get this man!
> He's trying to ruin the government
> And overturn the land! (21-24)

This response is clearly an overreaction to a small threat. Instead of dealing with the tenant directly, the landlord shouts for the police. His hysterical voice—marked by repetitions and punctuated with exclamation points—reveals his disproportionate fear and outrage. And his conclusions are equally excessive: this black man, he claims, is out to "ruin the government" and "overturn the land." Although the landlord's overreaction is humorous, it is sinister as well, because the landlord knows that, no matter how excessive his claims are, he has the police and the law on his side.

In line 25, the regular meter and rhyme of the poem break down, perhaps showing how an arrest disrupts everyday life. The "voice" in lines 25-29 has two parts: the clanging sound of the police ("Copper's whistle! / Patrol bell!") and, in sharp contrast, the unemotional, factual tone of a police report ("Arrest. / Precinct Station. / Iron cell.").

Peel 3

The last voice in the poem is the voice of the press, represented in newspaper headlines: "MAN THREATENS LANDLORD / TENANT HELD NO BAIL / JUDGE GIVES NEGRO 90 DAYS IN COUNTY JAIL" (31-33). Meter and rhyme return here, as if to show that once the tenant is arrested, life can go on as usual. The language of the press, like that of the police, is cold and distant, and it gives the tenant less and less status. In line 31, he is a "man"; in line 32, he has been demoted to a "tenant"; and in line 33, he has become a "Negro," or just another statistic.

Peel sums up her interpretation.

By using four opposing voices in "Ballad of the Landlord," Hughes effectively dramatizes different views of minority assertiveness. To the tenant, assertiveness is informal and natural, as his language shows; to the landlord, it is a dangerous threat, as his hysterical response suggests. The police response is, like the language that describes it, short and sharp. Finally, the press's view of events, represented by the headlines, is distant and unsympathetic.

By the end of the poem, we understand the predicament of the black man. Exploited by the landlord, politically oppressed by those who think he's out "to ruin the government," physically restrained by the police and the judicial system, and denied his individuality by the press, he is saved only by his own sense of humor. The very title of the poem suggests his—and Hughes's—sense of humor. The tenant is singing a *ballad* to his oppressors, but this ballad is no love song. It portrays the oppressors, through their own voices, in an unflattering light: the landlord as cowardly and ridiculous, the police and press as dull and soulless. The tenant may lack political power, but he speaks with vitality, and no one can say he lacks dignity or the spirit to survive.

Peel concludes with an analysis of the poem's political significance.

Peel 4

Work Cited

Hughes, Langston. "Ballad of the Landlord." *Poetry: An
Introduction*. Ed. Michael Meyer. 6th ed. Boston:
Bedford, 2010. 417-18. Print.

Ballad of the Landlord

LANGSTON HUGHES

Landlord, landlord,
My roof has sprung a leak.
Don't you 'member I told you about it
Way last week?

Landlord, landlord,
These steps is broken down.
When you come up yourself
It's a wonder you don't fall down.

Ten Bucks you say I owe you?
Ten Bucks you say is due?
Well, that's Ten Bucks more'n I'll pay you
Till you fix this house up new.

What? You gonna get eviction orders?
You gonna cut off my heat?
You gonna take my furniture and
Throw it in the street?

Um-huh! You talking high and mighty.
Talk on — till you get through.
You ain't gonna be able to say a word
If I land my fist on you.

Police! Police!
Come and get this man!
He's trying to run the government
And overturn the land!

Copper's whistle!
Patrol bell!
Arrest.

Precinct Station.
Iron cell.
Headlines in press:

MAN THREATENS LANDLORD
TENANT HELD NO BAIL
JUDGE GIVES NEGRO 90 DAYS IN COUNTY JAIL

Larson 1

Dan Larson

Professor Duncan

English 102

19 April 2010

The Transformation of Mrs. Peters:

An Analysis of "A Jury of Her Peers"

The opening lines name the story and establish context.

In Susan Glaspell's 1917 short story "A Jury of Her Peers," two women accompany their husbands and a county attorney to an isolated house where a farmer named John Wright has been choked to death in his bed with a rope. The chief suspect is Wright's wife, Minnie, who is in jail awaiting trial. The sheriff's wife, Mrs. Peters, has come along to gather some personal items for Minnie, and Mrs. Hale has joined her. Early in the story, Mrs. Hale sympathizes with Minnie and objects to the way the male investigators are "snoopin' round and criticizin'" her kitchen (191). In contrast, Mrs. Peters shows respect for the law, saying that the men are doing "no more than their duty" (191). By the end of the story, however, Mrs. Peters has joined Mrs. Hale in a conspiracy of silence, lied to the men, and committed a crime—hiding key evidence. What causes this dramatic change?

Present tense is used to describe details from the story.

Quotations from the story are cited with page numbers in parentheses.

The opening paragraph ends with Larson's research question.

One critic, Leonard Mustazza, argues that Mrs. Hale recruits Mrs. Peters "as a fellow 'juror' in the case, moving the sheriff's wife away from her sympathy for her husband's position and towards identification with the accused wom[a]n" (494). While this is true, Mrs. Peters also reaches insights on her own. Her observations in the kitchen lead her to understand Minnie's grim and lonely plight as the wife of an abusive farmer, and her identification with both Minnie and Mrs. Hale is strengthened as the men conducting the investigation trivialize the lives of women.

The thesis asserts Larson's main point.

Marginal annotations indicate MLA-style formatting and effective writing.

Larson 2

The first evidence that Mrs. Peters reaches understanding
on her own surfaces in the following passage:

> The sheriff's wife had looked from the stove
> to the sink—to the pail of water which had
> been carried in from outside. . . . That look of
> seeing into things, of seeing through a thing to
> something else, was in the eyes of the sheriff's wife
> now. (194)

Something about the stove, the sink, and the pail of water
connects with her own experience, giving Mrs. Peters a
glimpse into the life of Minnie Wright. The details resonate
with meaning.

A long quotation is
set off by indenting;
no quotation marks
are needed; ellipsis
dots indicate a
sentence omitted
from the source.

Social historian Elaine Hedges argues that such
details, which evoke the drudgery of a farm woman's work,
would not have been lost upon Glaspell's readers in 1917.
Hedges tells us what the pail and the stove, along with
another detail from the story—a dirty towel on a roller—
would have meant to women of the time. Laundry was a
dreaded all-day affair. Water had to be pumped, hauled,
and boiled; then the wash was rubbed, rinsed, wrung
through a wringer, carried outside, and hung on a line to
dry. "What the women see, beyond the pail and the stove,"
writes Hedges, "are the hours of work it took Minnie to
produce that one clean towel" (56).

Larson summarizes
ideas from a
secondary source
and then quotes
from that source; he
names the author in
a signal phrase and
gives a page number
in parentheses.

On her own, Mrs. Peters discovers clues about the
motive for the murder. Her curiosity leads her to pick up a
sewing basket filled with quilt pieces and then to notice
something strange: a sudden row of badly sewn stitches.
"What do you suppose she was so—nervous about?" asks
Mrs. Peters (195). A short time later, Mrs. Peters spots another
clue, an empty birdcage. Again she observes details on her

Topic sentences
present Larson's
interpretation.

own, in this case a broken door and hinge, suggesting that the cage has been roughly handled.

In addition to noticing details, both women draw conclusions from them and speculate on their significance. When Mrs. Hale finds the dead canary beneath a quilt patch, for example, the women conclude that its neck has been wrung and understand who must have wrung it.

As the women speculate on the significance of the dead canary, each connects the bird with her own experience. Mrs. Hale knows that Minnie once sang in the church choir, an activity that Mr. Wright put a stop to, just as he put a stop to the bird's singing. Also, as a farmer's wife, Mrs. Hale understands the desolation and loneliness of life on the prairie. She sees that the bird was both a thing of beauty and a companion. "If there had been years and years of—nothing, then a bird to sing to you," says Mrs. Hale, "it would be awful—still—after the bird was still" (198). To Mrs. Peters, the stillness of the canary evokes memories of the time when she and her husband homesteaded in the northern plains. "I know what stillness is," she says, as she recalls the death of her first child, with no one around to console her (198).

Elaine Hedges has written movingly of the isolation that women experienced on late-nineteenth- and early-twentieth-century farms of the West and Midwest:

> Women themselves reported that it was not unusual to spend five months in a log cabin without seeing another woman . . . or to spend one and a half years after arriving before being able to take a trip to town. . . . (54)

To combat loneliness and monotony, says Hedges, many women bought canaries and hung the cages outside their

Details from the story provide evidence for the interpretation.

Ellipsis dots indicate omitted words within the sentence and at the end of the sentence.

Larson 4

sod huts. The canaries provided music and color, a "spot of beauty" that "might spell the difference between sanity and madness" (60).

Mrs. Peters and Mrs. Hale understand—and Glaspell's readers in 1917 would have understood—what the killing of the bird means to Minnie. For Mrs. Peters, in fact, the act has a special significance. When she was a child, a boy axed her kitten to death and, as she says, "If they hadn't held me back I would have . . . hurt him" (198). She has little difficulty comprehending Minnie's murderous rage, for she has felt it herself.

Although Mrs. Peters's growing empathy for Minnie stems largely from her observations, it is also prompted by her negative reaction to the patronizing comments of the male investigators. At several points in the story, her body language reveals her feelings. For example, when Mr. Hale remarks that "women are used to worrying over trifles," both women move closer together and remain silent. When the county attorney asks, "for all their worries, what would we do without the ladies?" the women do not speak, nor do they "unbend" (190). The fact that the women respond in exactly the same way reveals the extent to which they are bonding.

Both women are annoyed at the way in which the men criticize and trivialize the world of women. The men question the difficulty of women's work. For example, when the county attorney points to the dirty towel on the rack as evidence that Minnie wasn't much of a housekeeper, Mrs. Hale replies, "There's a great deal of work to be done on a farm" (190). Even the importance of women's work is questioned. The men kid the women for trying to decide if Minnie was going to quilt or knot patches together for a quilt and laugh about such trivial

Transition serves as a bridge from one section of the paper to the next.

concerns. Those very quilts, of course, kept the men warm at night and cost them nothing beyond the price of thread.

The men also question the women's wisdom and intelligence. For example, when the county attorney tells the women to keep their eyes out for clues, Mr. Hale replies, "But would the women know a clue if they did come upon it?" (191). The women's response is to stand motionless and silent. The irony is that the men don't see the household clues that are right in front of them.

Larson gives evidence that Mrs. Peters has been transformed.

By the end of the story, Mrs. Peters has been so transformed that she risks lying to the men. When the county attorney walks into the kitchen and notices the birdcage the women have found, he asks about the whereabouts of the bird. Mrs. Hale replies, "We think the cat got it" (197), even though she knows from Mrs. Peters that Minnie was afraid of cats and would not have owned one. Instead of correcting the lie, Mrs. Peters elaborates on it, saying of cats, "They're superstitious, you know; they leave" (198). Clearly Mrs. Hale is willing to risk lying because she is confident that Mrs. Peters won't contradict her.

Larson draws on a secondary source that gives background on Glaspell's life.

The Mrs. Peters character may have been based on a real sheriff's wife. Seventeen years before writing "A Jury of Her Peers," Susan Glaspell covered a murder case for the *Des Moines Daily News*. A farmer's wife, Margaret Hossack, was accused of murdering her sleeping husband with two axe blows to the head. In one of her newspaper reports, Glaspell wrote that the sheriff's wife sat next to Mrs. Hossack and "frequently applied her handkerchief to her eyes" (qtd. in Ben-Zvi 30).

We do not know from the short story the ultimate fate of Minnie Wright, but Margaret Hossack, whose case inspired the story, was found guilty, though the case was later thrown out

Larson 6

by the Iowa Supreme Court. However, as Linda Ben-Zvi points
out, the women's guilt or innocence is not the issue:

> Whether Margaret Hossack or Minnie Wright
> committed murder is moot; what is incontrovertible
> is the brutality of their lives, the lack of options
> they had to redress grievances or to escape abusive
> husbands, and the complete disregard of their
> plight by the courts and by society. (38)

These are the issues that Susan Glaspell wished to stress in
"A Jury of Her Peers."

These are also the issues that Mrs. Peters comes to
understand as the story unfolds, with her understanding
deepening as she identifies with Minnie and Mrs. Hale and
is repulsed by male attitudes. Her transformation becomes
complete when the men joke that she is "married to the law"
and she responds by violating the law: hiding key evidence,
the dead canary.

Larson's conclusion
echoes his main
point without dully
repeating it.

Larson 7

Works Cited

The works cited
page lists the
primary source
(Glaspell's story) and
secondary sources.

Ben-Zvi, Linda. "'Murder, She Wrote': The Genesis of Susan
        Glaspell's *Trifles*." *Theatre Journal* 44.2 (1992): 141-62.
        Rpt. in *Susan Glaspell: Essays on Her Theater and Fiction*.
        Ed. Ben-Zvi. Ann Arbor: U of Michigan P, 1995. 19-48.
        Print.

Glaspell, Susan. "A Jury of Her Peers." *Literature and Its
        Writers: A Compact Introduction to Fiction, Poetry, and
        Drama*. Ed. Ann Charters and Samuel Charters. 5th ed.
        Boston: Bedford, 2010. 185-201. Print.

Hedges, Elaine. "Small Things Reconsidered: 'A Jury of Her
        Peers.'" *Women's Studies* 12.1 (1986): 89-110. Rpt. in
        Susan Glaspell: Essays on Her Theater and Fiction. Ed.
        Linda Ben-Zvi. Ann Arbor: U of Michigan P, 1995.
        49-69. Print.

Mustazza, Leonard. "Generic Translation and Thematic Shift in
        Susan Glaspell's *Trifles* and 'A Jury of Her Peers.'" *Studies
        in Short Fiction* 26.4 (1989): 489-96. Print.

A Jury of Her Peers

SUSAN GLASPELL

When Martha Hale opened the storm-door and got a cut of the north wind, she ran back for her big woolen scarf. As she hurriedly wound that round her head her eye made a scandalized sweep of her kitchen. It was no ordinary thing that called her away — it was probably further from ordinary than anything that had ever happened in Dickson County. But what her eye took in was that her kitchen was in no shape for leaving: her bread all ready for mixing, half the flour sifted and half unsifted.

She hated to see things half done; but she had been at that when the team from town stopped to get Mr. Hale, and then the sheriff came running in to say his wife wished Mrs. Hale would come too — adding, with a grin, that he guessed she was getting scary and wanted another woman along. So she had dropped everything right where it was.

"Martha!" now came her husband's impatient voice. "Don't keep folks waiting out here in the cold."

She again opened the storm-door, and this time joined the three men and the one woman waiting for her in the big two-seated buggy.

After she had the robes tucked around her she took another look at the woman who sat beside her on the back seat. She had met Mrs. Peters the year before at the county fair, and the thing she remembered about her was that she didn't seem like a sheriff's wife. She was small and thin and didn't have a strong voice. Mrs. Gorman, sheriff's wife before Gorman went out and Peters came in, had a voice that somehow seemed to be backing up the law with every word. But if Mrs. Peters didn't look like a sheriff's wife, Peters made it up in looking like a sheriff. He was to a dot the kind of man who could get himself elected sheriff — a heavy man with a big voice, who was particularly genial with the law-abiding, as if to make it plain that he knew the difference between criminals and non-criminals. And right there it came into Mrs. Hale's mind, with a stab, that this man who was so pleasant and lively with all of them was going to the Wrights' now as a sheriff.

"The country's not very pleasant this time of year," Mrs. Peters at last ventured, as if she felt they ought to be talking as well as the men.

Mrs. Hale scarcely finished her reply, for they had gone up a little hill and could see the Wright place now, and seeing it did not make her feel like talking. It looked very lonesome this cold March morning. It had always been a lonesome-looking place. It was down in a hollow, and the poplar trees around it were lonesome-looking trees. The men were looking at it and talking about what had happened. The county attorney was bending to one side of the buggy, and kept looking steadily at the place as they drew up to it.

"I'm glad you came with me," Mrs. Peters said nervously, as the two women were about to follow the men in through the kitchen door.

Even after she had her foot on the door-step, her hand on the knob, Martha Hale had a moment of feeling she could not cross that threshold. And the reason it seemed she couldn't cross it now was simply because she hadn't crossed it before. Time and time again it had been in her mind, "I ought to go over and see Minnie Foster" — she still thought of her as Minnie Foster, though for twenty years she had been Mrs. Wright. And then there was always something to do and Minnie Foster would go from her mind. But *now* she could come.

The men went over to the stove. The women stood close together by the door. Young Henderson, the county attorney, turned around and said, "Come up to the fire, ladies."

Mrs. Peters took a step forward, then stopped. "I'm not — cold," she said.

And so the two women stood by the door, at first not even so much as looking around the kitchen.

The men talked for a minute about what a good thing it was the sheriff had sent his deputy out that morning to make a fire for them, and then Sheriff Peters stepped back from the stove, unbuttoned his outer coat, and leaned his hands on the kitchen table in a way that seemed to mark the beginning of official business. "Now, Mr. Hale," he said in a sort of semi-official voice, "before we move things about, you tell Mr. Henderson just what it was you saw when you came here yesterday morning."

The county attorney was looking around the kitchen.

"By the way," he said, "has anything been moved?" He turned to the sheriff. "Are things just as you left them yesterday?"

Peters looked from cupboard to sink; from that to a small worn rocker a little to one side of the kitchen table.

"It's just the same."

"Somebody should have been left here yesterday," said the county attorney.

"Oh — yesterday," returned the sheriff, with a little gesture as of yesterday having been more than he could bear to think of. "When I had to send Frank to Morris Center for that man who went crazy — let me tell you. I had my hands full *yesterday*. I knew you could get back from Omaha by today, George, and as long as I went over everything here myself —"

"Well, Mr. Hale," said the county attorney, in a way of letting what was past and gone go, "tell just what happened when you came here yesterday morning."

Mrs. Hale, still leaning against the door, had that sinking feeling of the mother whose child is about to speak a piece. Lewis often wandered along and got things mixed up in a story. She hoped he would tell this straight and plain, and not say unnecessary things that would just make things harder for Minnie Foster. He didn't begin at once, and she noticed that he looked queer — as if standing in that kitchen and having to tell what he had seen there yesterday morning made him almost sick.

"Yes, Mr. Hale?" the county attorney reminded.

"Harry and I had started to town with a load of potatoes," Mrs. Hale's husband began.

Harry was Mrs. Hale's oldest boy. He wasn't with them now, for the very good reason that those potatoes never got to town yesterday and he was taking them this morning, so he hadn't been home when the sheriff stopped to say he wanted Mr. Hale to come over to the Wright place and tell the county attorney his story there, where he could point it all out. With all Mrs. Hale's other emotions came the fear now that maybe Harry wasn't dressed warm enough — they hadn't any of them realized how that north wind did bite.

"We come along this road," Hale was going on, with a motion of his hand to the road over which they had just come, "and as we got in sight of the house I says to Harry, 'I'm goin' to see if I can't get John Wright to take a telephone.' You see," he explained to Henderson, "unless I can get somebody to go in with me they won't come out this branch road except for a price I can't pay. I'd spoke to Wright about it once before; but he put me off, saying folks talked too much anyway, and all he asked was peace and quiet — guess you know about how much he talked himself. But I thought maybe if I went to the house and talked about it before his wife, and said all the women-folks liked the telephones, and that in this lonesome stretch of road it would be a good thing — well, I said to Harry that that was what I was going to say — though I said at the same time that I didn't know as what his wife wanted made much difference to John —"

Now there he was! — saying things he didn't need to say. Mrs. Hale tried to catch her husband's eye, but fortunately the county attorney interrupted with:

"Let's talk about that a little later, Mr. Hale. I do want to talk about that, but I'm anxious now to get along to just what happened when you got here."

When he began this time, it was very deliberately and carefully:

"I didn't see or hear anything. I knocked at the door. And still it was all quiet inside. I knew they must be up — it was past eight o'clock. So I knocked again, louder, and I thought I heard somebody say, 'Come in.' I wasn't sure — I'm not sure yet. But I opened the door — this door," jerking a hand toward the door by which the two women stood, "and there, in that rocker" — pointing to it — "sat Mrs. Wright."

Everyone in the kitchen looked at the rocker. It came into Mrs. Hale's mind that that rocker didn't look in the least like Minnie Foster — the Minnie Foster of twenty years before. It was a dingy red, with wooden rungs up the back, and the middle rung was gone, and the chair sagged to one side.

"How did she — look?" the county attorney was inquiring.

"Well," said Hale, "she looked — queer."

"How do you mean — queer?"

As he asked it he took out a note-book and pencil. Mrs. Hale did not like the sight of that pencil. She kept her eye fixed on her husband, as if to keep him from saying unnecessary things that would go into that note-book and make trouble.

Hale did speak guardedly, as if the pencil had affected him too.

"Well, as if she didn't know what she was going to do next. And kind of — done up."

"How did she seem to feel about your coming?"

"Why, I don't think she minded — one way or other. She didn't pay much attention. I said, 'Ho' do, Mrs. Wright? It's cold, ain't it?' And she said, 'Is it?' — and went on pleatin' at her apron.

"Well, I was surprised. She didn't ask me to come up to the stove, or to sit down, but just set there, not even lookin' at me. And so I said: 'I want to see John.'

"And then she — laughed. I guess you would call it a laugh.

"I thought of Harry and the team outside, so I said, a little sharp, 'Can I see John?' 'No,' says she — kind of dull like. 'Ain't he home?' says I. Then she looked at me. 'Yes,' says she, 'he's home.' 'Then why can't I see him?' I asked her, out of patience with her now. 'Cause he's dead' says she, just as quiet and dull — and fell to pleatin' her apron. 'Dead?' says I, like you do when you can't take in what you've heard.

"She just nodded her head, not getting a bit excited, but rockin' back and forth.

" 'Why — where is he?' says I, not knowing what to say.

"She just pointed upstairs — like this" — pointing to the room above.

"I got up, with the idea of going up there myself. By this time I — didn't know what to do. I walked from there to here; then I says: 'Why, what did he die of?'

" 'He died of a rope around his neck,' says she; and just went on pleatin' at her apron."

Hale stopped speaking, and stood staring at the rocker, as if he were still seeing the woman who had sat there the morning before. Nobody spoke; it was as if every one were seeing the woman who had sat there the morning before.

"And what did you do then?" the county attorney at last broke the silence.

"I went out and called Harry. I thought I might — need help. I got Harry in, and we went upstairs." His voice fell almost to a whisper. "There he was — lying over the —"

"I think I'd rather have you go into that upstairs," the county attorney interrupted, "where you can point it all out. Just go on now with the rest of the story."

"Well, my first thought was to get that rope off. It looked —"

He stopped, his face twitching.

"But Harry, he went up to him, and he said, 'No, he's dead all right, and we'd better not touch anything.' So we went downstairs.

"She was still sitting that same way. 'Has anybody been notified?' I asked. 'No,' says she, unconcerned.

"'Who did this, Mrs. Wright?' said Harry. He said it businesslike, and she stopped pleatin' at her apron. 'I don't know,' she says. 'You don't *know*?' says Harry. 'Weren't you sleepin' in the bed with him?' 'Yes,' says she, 'but I was on the inside.' 'Somebody slipped a rope round his neck and strangled him, and you didn't wake up?' says Harry. 'I didn't wake up,' she said after him.

"We may have looked as if we didn't see how that could be, for after a minute she said, 'I sleep sound.'

"Harry was going to ask her more questions, but I said maybe that weren't our business; maybe we ought to let her tell her story first to the coroner or the sheriff. So Harry went fast as he could over to High Road — the Rivers' place, where there's a telephone."

"And what did she do when she knew you had gone for the coroner?" The attorney got his pencil in his hand all ready for writing.

"She moved from that chair to this one over here" — Hale pointed to a small chair in the corner — "and just sat there with her hands held together and looking down. I got a feeling that I ought to make some conversation, so I said I had come in to see if John wanted to put in a telephone; and at that she started to laugh, and then she stopped and looked at me — scared."

At the sound of a moving pencil the man who was telling the story looked up.

"I dunno — maybe it wasn't scared," he hastened: "I wouldn't like to say it was. Soon Harry got back, and then Dr. Lloyd came, and you, Mr. Peters, and so I guess that's all I know that you don't."

He said that last with relief, and moved a little, as if relaxing. Everyone moved a little. The county attorney walked toward the stair door.

"I guess we'll go upstairs first — then out to the barn and around there."

He paused and looked around the kitchen.

"You're convinced there was nothing important here?" he asked the sheriff. "Nothing that would — point to any motive?"

The sheriff too looked all around, as if to re-convince himself.

"Nothing here but kitchen things," he said, with a little laugh for the insignificance of kitchen things.

The county attorney was looking at the cupboard — a peculiar, ungainly structure, half closet and half cupboard, the upper part of it being built in the wall, and the lower part just the old-fashioned kitchen cupboard. As if its queerness attracted him, he got a chair and opened the upper part and looked in. After a moment he drew his hand away sticky.

"Here's a nice mess," he said resentfully.

The two women had drawn nearer, and now the sheriff's wife spoke.

"Oh—her fruit," she said, looking to Mrs. Hale for sympathetic understanding. She turned back to the county attorney and explained: "She worried about that when it turned so cold last night. She said the fire would go out and her jars might burst."

Mrs. Peters' husband broke into a laugh.

"Well, can you beat the woman! Held for murder, and worrying about her preserves!"

The young attorney set his lips.

"I guess before we're through with her she may have something more serious than preserves to worry about."

"Oh, well," said Mrs. Hale's husband, with good-natured superiority, "women are used to worrying over trifles."

The two women moved a little closer together. Neither of them spoke. The county attorney seemed suddenly to remember his manners — and think of his future.

"And yet," said he, with the gallantry of a young politician, "for all their worries, what would we do without the ladies?"

The women did not speak, did not unbend. He went to the sink and began washing his hands. He turned to wipe them on the roller towel — whirled it for a cleaner place.

"Dirty towels! Not much of a housekeeper, would you say, ladies?"

He kicked his foot against some dirty pans under the sink.

"There's a great deal of work to be done on a farm," said Mrs. Hale stiffly.

"To be sure. And yet" — with a little bow to her — "I know there are some Dickson County farm-houses that do not have such roller towels." He gave it a pull to expose its full length again.

"Those towels get dirty awful quick. Men's hands aren't always as clean as they might be."

"Ah, loyal to your sex, I see," he laughed. He stopped and gave her a keen look. "But you and Mrs. Wright were neighbors. I suppose you were friends, too."

Martha Hale shook her head.

"I've seen little enough of her of late years. I've not been in this house — it's more than a year."

"And why was that? You didn't like her?"

"I liked her well enough," she replied with spirit. "Farmers' wives have their hands full, Mr. Henderson. And then —" She looked around the kitchen.

"Yes?" he encouraged.

"It never seemed a very cheerful place," said she, more to herself than to him.

"No," he agreed; "I don't think anyone would call it cheerful. I shouldn't say she had the home-making instinct."

"Well, I don't know as Wright had, either," she muttered.

"You mean they didn't get on very well?" he was quick to ask.

"No; I don't mean anything," she answered, with decision. As she turned a little away from him, she added: "But I don't think a place would be any the cheerfuller for John Wright's bein' in it."

"I'd like to talk to you about that a little later, Mrs. Hale," he said. "I'm anxious to get the lay of things upstairs now."

He moved toward the stair door, followed by the two men.

"I suppose anything Mrs. Peters does'll be all right?" the sheriff inquired. "She was to take in some clothes for her, you know — and a few little things. We left in such a hurry yesterday."

The county attorney looked at the two women whom they were leaving alone there among the kitchen things.

"Yes — Mrs. Peters," he said, his glance resting on the woman who was not Mrs. Peters, the big farmer woman who stood behind the sheriff's wife. "Of course Mrs. Peters is one of us," he said, in a manner of entrusting responsibility. "And keep your eye out, Mrs. Peters, for anything that might be of use. No telling; you women might come upon a clue to the motive — and that's the thing we need."

Mr. Hale rubbed his face after the fashion of a showman getting ready for a pleasantry.

"But would the women know a clue if they did come upon it?" he said; and, having delivered himself of this, he followed the others through the stair door.

The women stood motionless and silent, listening to the footsteps, first upon the stairs, then in the room above them.

Then, as if releasing herself from something strange, Mrs. Hale began to arrange the dirty pans under the sink, which the county attorney's disdainful push of the foot had deranged.

"I'd hate to have men comin' into my kitchen," she said testily — "snoopin' round and criticizin'."

"Of course it's no more than their duty," said the sheriff's wife, in her manner of timid acquiescence.

"Duty's all right," replied Mrs. Hale bluffly; "but I guess that deputy sheriff that come out to make the fire might have got a little of this on." She gave the roller towel a pull. "Wish I'd thought of that sooner! Seems mean to talk about her for not having things slicked up, when she had to come away in such a hurry."

She looked around the kitchen. Certainly it was not "slicked up." Her eye was held by a bucket of sugar on a low shelf. The cover was off the wooden bucket, and beside it was a paper bag — half full.

Mrs. Hale moved toward it.

"She was putting this in there," she said to herself — slowly.

She thought of the flour in her kitchen at home — half sifted, half not sifted. She had been interrupted, and had left things half done. What had interrupted Minnie Foster? Why had that work been left half done? She made a move as if to finish it, — unfinished things always bothered her, — and then she glanced around and saw that Mrs. Peters was watching her — and she didn't want Mrs. Peters to get that feeling she had got of work begun and then — for some reason — not finished.

"It's a shame about her fruit," she said, and walked toward the cupboard that the county attorney had opened, and got on the chair, murmuring: "I wonder if it's all gone."

It was a sorry enough looking sight, but "Here's one that's all right," she said at last. She held it toward the light. "This is cherries, too." She looked again. "I declare I believe that's the only one."

With a sigh, she got down from the chair, went to the sink, and wiped off the bottle.

"She'll feel awful bad, after all her hard work in the hot weather. I remember the afternoon I put up my cherries last summer."

She set the bottle on the table, and, with another sigh, started to sit down in the rocker. But she did not sit down. Something kept her from sitting down in that chair. She straightened — stepped back, and, half turned away, stood looking at it, seeing the woman who had sat there "pleatin' at her apron."

The thin voice of the sheriff's wife broke in upon her: "I must be getting those things from the front-room closet." She opened the door into the other room, started in, stepped back. "You coming with me, Mrs. Hale?" she asked nervously. "You — you could help me get them."

They were soon back — the stark coldness of that shut-up room was not a thing to linger in.

"My!" said Mrs. Peters, dropping the things on the table and hurrying to the stove.

Mrs. Hale stood examining the clothes the woman who was being detained in town had said she wanted.

"Wright was close!" she exclaimed, holding up a shabby black skirt that bore the marks of much making over. "I think maybe that's why she kept so much to herself. I s'pose she felt she couldn't do her part;

and then, you don't enjoy things when you feel shabby. She used to wear pretty clothes and be lively—when she was Minnie Foster, one of the town girls, singing in the choir. But that—oh, that was twenty years ago."

With a carefulness in which there was something tender, she folded the shabby clothes and piled them at one corner of the table. She looked up at Mrs. Peters, and there was something in the other woman's look that irritated her.

"She don't care," she said to herself. "Much difference it makes to her whether Minnie Foster had pretty clothes when she was a girl."

Then she looked again, and she wasn't so sure; in fact, she hadn't at any time been perfectly sure about Mrs. Peters. She had that shrinking manner, and yet her eyes looked as if they could see a long way into things.

"This all you was to take in?" asked Mrs. Hale.

"No," said the sheriff's wife; "she said she wanted an apron. Funny thing to want," she ventured in her nervous little way, "for there's not much to get you dirty in jail, goodness knows. But I suppose just to make her feel more natural. If you're used to wearing an apron—. She said they were in the bottom drawer of this cupboard. Yes—here they are. And then her little shawl that always hung on the stair door."

She took the small gray shawl from behind the door leading upstairs, and stood a minute looking at it.

Suddenly Mrs. Hale took a quick step toward the other woman.

"Mrs. Peters!"

"Yes, Mrs. Hale?"

"Do you think she—did it?"

A frightened look blurred the other thing in Mrs. Peters' eyes.

"Oh, I don't know," she said, in a voice that seemed to shrink away from the subject.

"Well, I don't think she did," affirmed Mrs. Hale stoutly. "Asking for an apron, and her little shawl. Worryin' about her fruit."

"Mr. Peters says—." Footsteps were heard in the room above; she stopped, looked up, then went on in a lowered voice: "Mr. Peters says—it looks bad for her. Mr. Henderson is awful sarcastic in a speech, and he's going to make fun of her saying she didn't—wake up."

For a moment Mrs. Hale had no answer. Then, "Well, I guess John Wright didn't wake up—when they was slippin' that rope under his neck," she muttered.

"No, it's *strange*," breathed Mrs. Peters. "They think it was such a—funny way to kill a man."

She began to laugh; at the sound of the laugh, abruptly stopped.

"That's just what Mr. Hale said," said Mrs. Hale, in a resolutely natural voice. "There was a gun in the house. He says that's what he can't understand."

"Mr. Henderson said, coming out, that what was needed for the case was a motive. Something to show anger — or sudden feeling."

"Well, I don't see any signs of anger around here," said Mrs. Hale, "I don't —" She stopped. It was as if her mind tripped on something. Her eye was caught by a dishtowel in the middle of the kitchen table. Slowly she moved toward the table. One half of it was wiped clean, the other half messy. Her eyes made a slow, almost unwilling turn to the bucket of sugar and the half empty bag beside it. Things begun — and not finished.

After a moment she stepped back, and said, in that manner of releasing herself:

"Wonder how they're finding things upstairs? I hope she had it a little more redd up there. You know," — she paused, and feeling gathered, — "it seems kind of *sneaking*: locking her up in town and coming out here to get her own house to turn against her!"

"But, Mrs. Hale," said the sheriff's wife, "the law is the law."

"I s'pose 'tis," answered Mrs. Hale shortly.

She turned to the stove, saying something about that fire not being much to brag of. She worked with it a minute, and when she straightened up she said aggressively:

"The law is the law — and a bad stove is a bad stove. How'd you like to cook on this?" — pointing with the poker to the broken lining. She opened the oven door and started to express her opinion of the oven; but she was swept into her own thoughts, thinking of what it would mean, year after year, to have that stove to wrestle with. The thought of Minnie Foster trying to bake in that oven — and the thought of her never going over to see Minnie Foster — .

She was startled by hearing Mrs. Peters say: "A person gets discouraged — and loses heart."

The sheriff's wife had looked from the stove to the sink — to the pail of water which had been carried in from outside. The two women stood there silent, above them the footsteps of the men who were looking for evidence against the woman who had worked in that kitchen. That look of seeing into things, of seeing through a thing to something else, was in the eyes of the sheriff's wife now. When Mrs. Hale next spoke to her, it was gently:

"Better loosen up your things, Mrs. Peters. We'll not feel them when we go out."

Mrs. Peters went to the back of the room to hang up the fur tippet she was wearing. A moment later she exclaimed, "Why, she was piecing a quilt," and held up a large sewing basket piled high with quilt pieces.

Mrs. Hale spread some of the blocks on the table.

"It's log-cabin pattern," she said, putting several of them together. "Pretty, isn't it?"

They were so engaged with the quilt that they did not hear the footsteps on the stairs. Just as the stair door opened Mrs. Hale was saying:

"Do you suppose she was going to quilt it or just knot it?"

The sheriff threw up his hands.

"They wonder whether she was going to quilt it or just knot it!"

There was a laugh for the ways of women, a warming of hands over the stove, and then the county attorney said briskly:

"Well, let's go right out to the barn and get that cleared up."

"I don't see as there's anything so strange," Mrs. Hale said resentfully, after the outside door had closed on the three men — "our taking up our time with little things while we're waiting for them to get the evidence. I don't see as it's anything to laugh about."

"Of course they've got awful important things on their minds," said the sheriff's wife apologetically.

They returned to an inspection of the block for the quilt. Mrs. Hale was looking at the fine, even sewing, and preoccupied with thoughts of the woman who had done that sewing, when she heard the sheriff's wife say, in a queer tone:

"Why, look at this one."

She turned to take the block held out to her.

"The sewing," said Mrs. Peters, in a troubled way. "All the rest of them have been so nice and even — but — this one. Why, it looks as if she didn't know what she was about!"

Their eyes met — something flashed to life, passed between them; then, as if with an effort, they seemed to pull away from each other. A moment Mrs. Hale sat there, her hands folded over that sewing which was so unlike all the rest of the sewing. Then she had pulled a knot and drawn the threads.

"Oh, what are you doing, Mrs. Hale?" asked the sheriff's wife, startled.

"Just pulling out a stitch or two that's not sewed very good," said Mrs. Hale mildly.

"I don't think we ought to touch things," Mrs. Peters said, a little helplessly.

"I'll just finish up this end," answered Mrs. Hale, still in that mild, matter-of-fact fashion.

She threaded a needle and started to replace bad sewing with good. For a little while she sewed in silence. Then, in that thin, timid voice, she heard:

"Mrs. Hale!"

"Yes, Mrs. Peters?"

"What do you suppose she was so — nervous about?"

"Oh, I don't know," said Mrs. Hale, as if dismissing a thing not important enough to spend much time on. "I don't know as she was — nervous. I sew awful queer sometimes when I'm just tired."

She cut a thread, and out of the corner of her eye looked up at Mrs. Peters. The small, lean face of the sheriff's wife seemed to have tightened up. Her eyes had that look of peering into something. But next moment she moved, and said in her thin, indecisive way:

"Well, I must get those clothes wrapped. They may be through sooner than we think. I wonder where I could find a piece of paper — and string."

"In that cupboard, maybe," suggested Mrs. Hale, after a glance around.

One piece of the crazy sewing remained unripped. Mrs. Peters' back turned, Martha Hale now scrutinized that piece, compared it with the dainty, accurate sewing of the other blocks. The difference was startling. Holding this block made her feel queer, as if the distracted thoughts of the woman who had perhaps turned to it to try and quiet herself were communicating themselves to her.

Mrs. Peters' voice roused her.

"Here's a bird-cage," she said. "Did she have a bird, Mrs. Hale?"

"Why, I don't know whether she did or not." She turned to look at the cage Mrs. Peters was holding up. "I've not been here in so long." She sighed. "There was a man round last year selling canaries cheap — but I don't know as she took one. Maybe she did. She used to sing real pretty herself."

Mrs. Peters looked around the kitchen.

"Seems kind of funny to think of a bird here." She half laughed — an attempt to put up a barrier. "But she must have had one — or why would she have a cage? I wonder what happened to it."

"I suppose maybe the cat got it," suggested Mrs. Hale, resuming her sewing.

"No; she didn't have a cat. She's got that feeling some people have about cats — being afraid of them. When they brought her to our house yesterday, my cat got in the room, and she was real upset and asked me to take it out."

"My sister Bessie was like that," laughed Mrs. Hale.

The sheriff's wife did not reply. The silence made Mrs. Hale turn round. Mrs. Peters was examining the bird-cage.

"Look at this door," she said slowly. "It's broke. One hinge has been pulled apart."

Mrs. Hale came nearer.

"Looks as if someone must have been — rough with it."

Again their eyes met — startled, questioning, apprehensive. For a moment neither spoke nor stirred. Then Mrs. Hale, turning away, said brusquely:

"If they're going to find any evidence, I wish they'd be about it. I don't like this place."

"But I'm awful glad you came with me, Mrs. Hale." Mrs. Peters put the bird-cage on the table and sat down. "It would be lonesome for me — sitting here alone."

"Yes, it would, wouldn't it?" agreed Mrs. Hale, a certain determined naturalness in her voice. She had picked up the sewing, but now it dropped in her lap, and she murmured in a different voice: "But I tell you what I *do* wish, Mrs. Peters. I wish I had come over sometimes when she was here. I wish — I had."

"But of course you were awful busy, Mrs. Hale. Your house — and your children."

"I could've come," retorted Mrs. Hale shortly. "I stayed away because it weren't cheerful — and that's why I ought to have come. I" — she looked around — "I've never liked this place. Maybe because it's down in a hollow and you don't see the road. I don't know what it is, but it's a lonesome place, and always was. I wish I had come over to see Minnie Foster sometimes. I can see now —" She did not put it into words.

"Well, you mustn't reproach yourself," counseled Mrs. Peters. "Somehow, we just don't see how it is with other folks till — something comes up."

"Not having children makes less work," mused Mrs. Hale, after a silence, "but it makes a quiet house — and Wright out to work all day — and no company when he did come in. Did you know John Wright, Mrs. Peters?"

"Not to know him. I've seen him in town. They say he was a good man."

"Yes — good," conceded John Wright's neighbor grimly. "He didn't drink, and kept his word as well as most, I guess, and paid his debts. But he was a hard man, Mrs. Peters. Just to pass the time of day with him —." She stopped, shivered a little. "Like a raw wind that gets to the bone." Her eye fell upon the cage on the table before her, and she added, almost bitterly: "I should think she would've wanted a bird!"

Suddenly she leaned forward, looking intently at the cage. "But what do you s'pose went wrong with it?"

"I don't know," returned Mrs. Peters; "unless it got sick and died."

But after she said it she reached over and swung the broken door. Both women watched it as if somehow held by it.

"You didn't know — her?" Mrs. Hale asked, a gentler note in her voice.

"Not till they brought her yesterday," said the sheriff's wife.

"She — come to think of it, she was kind of like a bird herself. Real sweet and pretty, but kind of timid and — fluttery. How — she — did — change."

That held her for a long time. Finally, as if struck with a happy thought and relieved to get back to everyday things, she exclaimed:

"Tell you what, Mrs. Peters, why don't you take the quilt in with you? It might take up her mind."

"Why, I think that's a real nice idea, Mrs. Hale," agreed the sheriff's wife, as if she too were glad to come into the atmosphere of a simple kindness. "There couldn't possibly be any objection to that, could there? Now, just what will I take? I wonder if her patches are in here — and her things?"

They turned to the sewing basket.

"Here's some red," said Mrs. Hale, bringing out a roll of cloth. Underneath that was a box. "Here, maybe her scissors are in here — and her things." She held it up. "What a pretty box! I'll warrant that was something she had a long time ago — when she was a girl."

She held it in her hand a moment; then, with a little sigh, opened it.

Instantly her hand went to her nose.

"Why — !"

Mrs. Peters drew nearer — then turned away.

"There's something wrapped up in this piece of silk," faltered Mrs. Hale.

"This isn't her scissors," said Mrs. Peters, in a shrinking voice.

Her hand not steady, Mrs. Hale raised the piece of silk. "Oh, Mrs. Peters!" she cried. "It's —"

Mrs. Peters bent closer.

"It's the bird," she whispered.

"But, Mrs. Peters!" cried Mrs. Hale. "*Look* at it! Its *neck* — look at its neck! It's all — other side *to*."

She held the box away from her.

The sheriff's wife again bent closer.

"Somebody wrung its neck," said she, in a voice that was slow and deep.

And then again the eyes of the two women met — this time clung together in a look of dawning comprehension, of growing horror. Mrs. Peters looked from the dead bird to the broken door of the cage. Again their eyes met. And just then there was a sound at the outside door.

Mrs. Hale slipped the box under the quilt pieces in the basket, and sank into the chair before it. Mrs. Peters stood holding to the table. The county attorney and the sheriff came in from outside.

"Well, ladies," said the county attorney, as one turning from serious things to little pleasantries, "have you decided whether she was going to quilt it or knot it?"

"We think," began the sheriff's wife in a flurried voice, "that she was going to — knot it."

He was too preoccupied to notice the change that came in her voice on that last.

"Well, that's very interesting, I'm sure," he said tolerantly. He caught sight of the bird-cage. "Has the bird flown?"

"We think the cat got it," said Mrs. Hale in a voice curiously even.

He was walking up and down, as if thinking something out.

"Is there a cat?" he asked absently.

Mrs. Hale shot a look up at the sheriff's wife.

"Well, not *now*," said Mrs. Peters. "They're superstitious, you know; they leave."

She sank into her chair.

The county attorney did not heed her. "No sign at all of anyone having come in from the outside," he said to Peters, in the manner of continuing an interrupted conversation. "Their own rope. Now let's go upstairs again and go over it, piece by piece. It would have to have been someone who knew just the —"

The stair door closed behind them and their voices were lost.

The two women sat motionless, not looking at each other, but as if peering into something and at the same time holding back. When they spoke now it was as if they were afraid of what they were saying, but as if they could not help saying it.

"She liked the bird," said Martha Hale, low and slowly. "She was going to bury it."

"When I was a girl," said Mrs. Peters, under her breath, "my kitten — there was a boy took a hatchet, and before my eyes — before I could get there —" She covered her face an instant. "If they hadn't held me back I would have" — she caught herself, looked upstairs where footsteps were heard, and finished weakly — "hurt him."

Then they sat without speaking or moving.

"I wonder how it would seem," Mrs. Hale at last began, as if feeling her way over strange ground — "never to have had any children around?" Her eyes made a slow sweep of the kitchen, as if seeing what that kitchen had meant through all the years. "No, Wright wouldn't like the bird," she said after that — "a thing that sang. She used to sing. He killed that too." Her voice tightened.

Mrs. Peters moved uneasily.

"Of course we don't know who killed the bird."

"I knew John Wright," was Mrs. Hale's answer.

"It was an awful thing was done in this house that night, Mrs. Hale," said the sheriff's wife. "Killing a man while he slept — slipping a thing round his neck that choked the life out of him."

Mrs. Hale's hand went out to the bird-cage.

"His neck. Choked the life out of him."

"We don't *know* who killed him," whispered Mrs. Peters wildly. "We don't *know*."

Mrs. Hale had not moved. "If there had been years and years of — nothing, then a bird to sing to you, it would be awful — still — after the bird was still."

It was as if something within her not herself had spoken, and it found in Mrs. Peters something she did not know as herself.

"I know what stillness is," she said, in a queer, monotonous voice. "When we homesteaded in Dakota, and my first baby died — after he was two years old — and me with no other then —"

Mrs. Hale stirred.

"How soon do you suppose they'll be through looking for the evidence?"

"I know what stillness is," repeated Mrs. Peters, in just the same way. Then she too pulled back. "The law has got to punish crime, Mrs. Hale," she said in her tight little way.

"I wish you'd seen Minnie Foster," was the answer, "when she wore a white dress with blue ribbons, and stood up there in the choir and sang."

The picture of that girl, the fact that she had lived neighbor to that girl for twenty years, and had let her die for lack of life, was suddenly more than she could bear.

"Oh, I *wish* I'd come over here once in a while!" she cried. "That was a crime! Who's going to punish that?"

"We mustn't take on," said Mrs. Peters, with a frightened look toward the stairs.

"I might 'a' known she needed help! I tell you, it's *queer*, Mrs. Peters. We live close together, and we live far apart. We all go through the same things — it's all just a different kind of the same thing! If it weren't — why do you and I *understand*? Why do we *know* — what we know this minute?"

She dashed her hand across her eyes. Then, seeing the jar of fruit on the table, she reached for it and choked out:

"If I was you I wouldn't *tell* her her fruit was gone! Tell her it *ain't*. Tell her it's all right — all of it. Here — take this in to prove it to her! She — she may never know whether it was broke or not."

She turned away.

Mrs. Peters reached out for the bottle of fruit as if she were glad to take it — as if touching a familiar thing, having something to do, could keep her from something else. She got up, looked about for something to wrap the fruit in, took a petticoat from the pile of clothes she had brought from the front room, and nervously started winding that round the bottle.

"My!" she began, in a high, false voice, "it's a good thing the men couldn't hear us! Getting all stirred up over a little thing like a — dead canary." She hurried over that. "As if that could have anything to do with — with — My, wouldn't they *laugh*?"

Footsteps were heard on the stairs.

"Maybe they would," muttered Mrs. Hale — "maybe they wouldn't."

"No, Peters," said the county attorney incisively; "it's all perfectly clear, except the reason for doing it. But you know juries when it comes to women. If there was some definite thing — something to show.

Something to make a story about. A thing that would connect up with this clumsy way of doing it."

In a covert way Mrs. Hale looked at Mrs. Peters. Mrs. Peters was looking at her. Quickly they looked away from each other. The outer door opened and Mr. Hale came in.

"I've got the team round now," he said. "Pretty cold out there."

"I'm going to stay here awhile by myself," the county attorney suddenly announced. "You can send Frank out for me, can't you?" he asked the sheriff. "I want to go over everything. I'm not satisfied we can't do better."

Again, for one brief moment, the two women's eyes found one another.

The sheriff came up to the table.

"Did you want to see what Mrs. Peters was going to take in?"

The county attorney picked up the apron. He laughed.

"Oh, I guess they're not very dangerous things the ladies have picked out."

Mrs. Hale's hand was on the sewing basket in which the box was concealed. She felt that she ought to take her hand off the basket. She did not seem able to. He picked up one of the quilt blocks which she had piled on to cover the box. Her eyes felt like fire. She had a feeling that if he took up the basket she would snatch it from him.

But he did not take it up. With another little laugh, he turned away, saying:

"No; Mrs. Peters doesn't need supervising. For that matter, a sheriff's wife is married to the law. Ever think of it that way, Mrs. Peters?"

Mrs. Peters was standing beside the table. Mrs. Hale shot a look up at her; but she could not see her face. Mrs. Peters had turned away. When she spoke, her voice was muffled.

"Not — just that way," she said.

"Married to the law!" chuckled Mrs. Peters' husband. He moved toward the door into the front room, and said to the county attorney:

"I just want you to come in here a minute, George. We ought to take a look at these windows."

"Oh — windows," said the county attorney scoffingly.

"We'll be right out, Mr. Hale," said the sheriff to the farmer, who was still waiting by the door.

Hale went to look after the horses. The sheriff followed the county attorney into the other room. Again — for one final moment — the two women were alone in that kitchen.

Martha Hale sprang up, her hands tight together, looking at that other woman, with whom it rested. At first she could not see her eyes, for the sheriff's wife had not turned back since she turned away at that suggestion of being married to the law. But now Mrs. Hale made her turn back. Her eyes made her turn back. Slowly, unwillingly, Mrs. Peters turned her head until her eyes met the eyes of the other woman. There was a moment when they held each other in a steady, burning look in which there was no evasion nor flinching. Then Martha Hale's eyes pointed the way to the basket in which was hidden the thing that would make certain the conviction of the other woman — that woman who was not there and yet who had been there with them all through that hour.

For a moment Mrs. Peters did not move. And then she did it. With a rush forward, she threw back the quilt pieces, got the box, tried to put it in her handbag. It was too big. Desperately she opened it, started to take the bird out. But there she broke — she could not touch the bird. She stood there helpless, foolish.

There was the sound of a knob turning in the inner door. Martha Hale snatched the box from the sheriff's wife, and got it in the pocket of her big coat just as the sheriff and the county attorney came back into the kitchen.

"Well, Henry," said the county attorney facetiously, "at least we found out that she was not going to quilt it. She was going to — what is it you call it, ladies?"

Mrs. Hale's hand was against the pocket of her coat.

"We call it — knot it, Mr. Henderson."

Glossary of Usage

This glossary includes words commonly confused (such as *accept* and *except*), words commonly misused (such as *aggravate*), and words that are nonstandard (such as *hisself*). It also lists colloquialisms and jargon. Colloquialisms are casual expressions that may be appropriate in informal speech but are inappropriate in formal writing. Jargon is needlessly technical or pretentious language that is inappropriate in most contexts. If an item is not listed here, consult the index. For irregular verbs (such as *sing, sang, sung*), see 27a. For idiomatic use of prepositions, see 18d.

a, an Use *an* before a vowel sound, *a* before a consonant sound: *an apple, a peach.* Problems sometimes arise with words beginning with *h* or *u*. If the *h* is silent, the word begins with a vowel sound, so use *an: an hour, an honorable deed.* If the *h* is pronounced, the word begins with a consonant sound, so use *a: a hospital, a historian, a hotel.* Words such as *university* and *union* begin with a consonant sound (a *y* sound), so use *a: a union.* Words such as *uncle* and *umbrella* begin with a vowel sound, so use *an: an underground well.* When an abbreviation or an acronym begins with a vowel sound, use *an: an EKG, an MRI, an AIDS prevention program.*

accept, except *Accept* is a verb meaning "to receive." *Except* is usually a preposition meaning "excluding." *I will accept all the packages except that one. Except* is also a verb meaning "to exclude." *Please except that item from the list.*

adapt, adopt *Adapt* means "to adjust or become accustomed"; it is usually followed by *to. Adopt* means "to take as one's own." *Our family adopted a Vietnamese child, who quickly adapted to his new life.*

adverse, averse *Adverse* means "unfavorable." *Averse* means "opposed" or "reluctant"; it is usually followed by *to. I am averse to your proposal because it could have an adverse impact on the economy.*

advice, advise *Advice* is a noun, *advise* a verb. *We advise you to follow John's advice.*

affect, effect *Affect* is usually a verb meaning "to influence." *Effect* is usually a noun meaning "result." *The drug did not affect the disease, and* *it had adverse side effects. Effect* can also be a verb meaning "to bring about." *Only the president can effect such a dramatic change.*

aggravate   *Aggravate* means "to make worse or more troublesome." *Overgrazing aggravated the soil erosion.* In formal writing, avoid the use of *aggravate* meaning "to annoy or irritate." *Her babbling annoyed* (not *aggravated*) *me.*

agree to, agree with   *Agree to* means "to give consent to." *Agree with* means "to be in accord with" or "to come to an understanding with." *He agrees with me about the need for change, but he won't agree to my plan.*

ain't   *Ain't* is nonstandard. Use *am not, are not* (*aren't*), or *is not* (*isn't*). *I am not* (not *ain't*) *going home for spring break.*

all ready, already   *All ready* means "completely prepared." *Already* means "previously." *Susan was all ready for the concert, but her friends had already left.*

all right   *All right,* written as two words, is correct. *Alright* is nonstandard.

all together, altogether   *All together* means "everyone or everything in one place." *Altogether* means "entirely." *We were not altogether certain that we could bring the family all together for the reunion.*

allude   To *allude* to something is to make an indirect reference to it. Do not use *allude* to mean "to refer directly." *In his lecture, the professor referred* (not *alluded*) *to several pre-Socratic philosophers.*

allusion, illusion   An *allusion* is an indirect reference. An *illusion* is a misconception or false impression. *Did you catch my allusion to Shakespeare? Mirrors give the room an illusion of depth.*

a lot   *A lot* is two words. Do not write *alot. Sam lost a lot of weight.* See also *lots, lots of.*

among, between   See *between, among.*

amongst   In American English, *among* is preferred.

amoral, immoral   *Amoral* means "neither moral nor immoral"; it also means "not caring about moral judgments." *Immoral* means "morally wrong." *Until recently, most business courses were taught from an amoral perspective. Murder is immoral.*

amount, number   Use *amount* with quantities that cannot be counted; use *number* with those that can. *This recipe calls for a large amount of sugar. We have a large number of toads in our garden.*

an   See *a, an.*

and etc.   *Et cetera* (*etc.*) means "and so forth"; *and etc.* is redundant. See also *etc.*

and/or   Avoid the awkward construction *and/or* except in technical or legal documents.

angry at, angry with   Use *angry with*, not *angry at*, when referring to a person. *The coach was angry with the referee.*

ante-, anti-   The prefix *ante-* means "earlier" or "in front of"; the prefix *anti-* means "against" or "opposed to." *William Lloyd Garrison was a leader of the antislavery movement during the antebellum period. Anti-* should be used with a hyphen when it is followed by a capital letter or a word beginning with *i.*

anxious   *Anxious* means "worried" or "apprehensive." In formal writing, avoid using *anxious* to mean "eager." *We are eager* (not *anxious*) *to see your new house.*

anybody, anyone   *Anybody* and *anyone* are singular. (See 21e and 22a.)

anymore   Use the adverb *anymore* in a negative context to mean "any longer" or "now." *The factory isn't producing shoes anymore.* Using *anymore* in a positive context is colloquial; in formal writing, use *now* instead. *We order all our food online now* (not *anymore*).

anyone   See *anybody, anyone.*

anyone, any one   *Anyone*, an indefinite pronoun, means "any person at all." *Any one*, the pronoun *one* preceded by the adjective *any*, refers to a particular person or thing in a group. *Anyone from the winning team may choose any one of the games on display.*

anyplace   In formal writing, use *anywhere.*

anyways, anywheres   *Anyways* and *anywheres* are nonstandard. Use *anyway* and *anywhere.*

as   Do not use *as* to mean "because" if there is any chance of ambiguity. *We canceled the picnic because* (not *as*) *it began raining. As* here could mean either "because" or "when."

as, like   See *like, as.*

as to   *As to* is jargon for *about. He inquired about* (not *as to*) *the job.*

averse   See *adverse, averse.*

awful   The adjective *awful* and the adverb *awfully* are not appropriate in formal writing.

awhile, a while   *Awhile* is an adverb; it can modify a verb, but it cannot be the object of a preposition such as *for.* The two-word form *a while* is a noun preceded by an article and therefore can be the object of a preposition. *Stay awhile. Stay for a while.*

back up, backup   *Back up* is a verb phrase. *Back up the car carefully. Be sure to back up your hard drive. Backup* is a noun meaning "a copy of electronically stored data." *Keep your backup in a safe place. Backup* can also be used as an adjective. *I regularly create backup disks.*

bad, badly   *Bad* is an adjective, *badly* an adverb. *They felt bad about ruining the surprise. Her arm hurt badly after she slid into second base.* (See 26a, 26b, and 26c.)

being as, being that   *Being as* and *being that* are nonstandard expressions. Write *because* instead. *Because* (not *Being as*) *I slept late, I had to skip breakfast.*

beside, besides   *Beside* is a preposition meaning "at the side of" or "next to." *Annie sleeps with a flashlight beside her bed. Besides* is a preposition meaning "except" or "in addition to." *No one besides Terrie can have that ice cream. Besides* is also an adverb meaning "in addition." *I'm not hungry; besides, I don't like ice cream.*

between, among   Ordinarily, use *among* with three or more entities, *between* with two. *The prize was divided among several contestants. You have a choice between carrots and beans.*

bring, take   Use *bring* when an object is being transported toward you, *take* when it is being moved away. *Please bring me a glass of water. Please take these forms to Mr. Scott.*

burst, bursted; bust, busted   *Burst* is an irregular verb meaning "to come open or fly apart suddenly or violently." Its past tense is *burst.* The past-tense form *bursted* is nonstandard. *Bust* and *busted* are slang for *burst* and, along with *bursted,* should not be used in formal writing.

can, may   The distinction between *can* and *may* is fading, but some writers still observe it in formal writing. *Can* is traditionally reserved for ability, *may* for permission. *Can you speak French? May I help you?*

capital, capitol   *Capital* refers to a city, *capitol* to a building where lawmakers meet. *Capital* also refers to wealth or resources. *The residents of the state capital protested plans to close the streets surrounding the capitol.*

censor, censure   *Censor* means "to remove or suppress material considered objectionable." *Censure* means "to criticize severely." *The administration's policy of censoring books has been censured by the media.*

cite, site   *Cite* means "to quote as an authority or example." *Site* is usually a noun meaning "a particular place." *He cited the zoning law in his argument against the proposed site of the gas station.* Locations on the Internet are usually referred to as *sites. The library's Web site improves every week.*

climactic, climatic   *Climactic* is derived from *climax,* the point of greatest intensity in a series or progression of events. *Climatic* is derived from *climate* and refers to meteorological conditions. *The climactic period in the dinosaurs' reign was reached just before severe climatic conditions brought on an ice age.*

coarse, course   *Coarse* means "crude" or "rough in texture." *The coarse weave of the wall hanging gave it a three-dimensional quality.* *Course* usually refers to a path, a playing field, or a unit of study; the expression *of course* means "certainly." *I plan to take a course in car repair this summer. Of course, you are welcome to join me.*

compare to, compare with   *Compare to* means "to represent as similar." *She compared him to a wild stallion.* *Compare with* means "to examine similarities and differences." *The study compared the language ability of apes with that of dolphins.*

complement, compliment   *Complement* is a verb meaning "to go with or complete" or a noun meaning "something that completes." As a verb, *compliment* means "to flatter"; as a noun, it means "flattering remark." *Her skill at rushing the net complements his skill at volleying. Martha's flower arrangements receive many compliments.*

conscience, conscious   *Conscience* is a noun meaning "moral principles." *Conscious* is an adjective meaning "aware or alert." *Let your conscience be your guide. Were you conscious of his love for you?*

continual, continuous   *Continual* means "repeated regularly and frequently." *She grew weary of the continual telephone calls.* *Continuous* means "extended or prolonged without interruption." *The broken siren made a continuous wail.*

could care less   *Could care less* is nonstandard. Write *couldn't care less* instead. *He couldn't* (not *could*) *care less about his psychology final.*

could of   *Could of* is nonstandard for *could have*. *We could have* (not *could of*) *taken the train.*

council, counsel   A *council* is a deliberative body, and a *councilor* is a member of such a body. *Counsel* usually means "advice" and can also mean "lawyer"; a *counselor* is one who gives advice or guidance. *The councilors met to draft the council's position paper. The pastor offered wise counsel to the troubled teenager.*

criteria   *Criteria* is the plural of *criterion*, which means "a standard or rule or test on which a judgment or decision can be based." *The only criterion for the scholarship is ability.*

data   *Data* is a plural noun technically meaning "facts or propositions." But *data* is increasingly being accepted as a singular noun. *The new data suggest* (or *suggests*) *that our theory is correct.* (The singular *datum* is rarely used.)

different from, different than   Ordinarily, write *different from*. *Your sense of style is different from Jim's.* However, *different than* is acceptable to avoid an awkward construction. *Please let me know if your plans are different than* (to avoid *from what*) *they were six weeks ago.*

differ from, differ with   *Differ from* means "to be unlike"; *differ with* means "to disagree with." *My approach to the problem differed from hers. She differed with me about the wording of the agreement.*

disinterested, uninterested *Disinterested* means "impartial, objective"; *uninterested* means "not interested." *We sought the advice of a disinterested counselor to help us solve our problem. Mark was uninterested in anyone's opinion but his own.*

don't *Don't* is the contraction for *do not. I don't want any. Don't* should not be used as the contraction for *does not,* which is *doesn't. He doesn't* (not *don't*) *want any.*

due to *Due to* is an adjective phrase and should not be used as a preposition meaning "because of." *The trip was canceled because of* (not *due to*) *lack of interest. Due to* is acceptable as a subject complement and usually follows a form of the verb *be. His success was due to hard work.*

each *Each* is singular. (See 21e and 22a.)

effect See *affect, effect.*

e.g. In formal writing, replace the Latin abbreviation *e.g.* with its English equivalent: *for example* or *for instance.*

either *Either* is singular. (See 21e and 22a.) For *either . . . or* constructions, see 21d and 22a.

elicit, illicit *Elicit* is a verb meaning "to bring out" or "to evoke." *Illicit* is an adjective meaning "unlawful." *The reporter was unable to elicit any information from the police about illicit drug traffic.*

emigrate from, immigrate to *Emigrate* means "to leave one country or region to settle in another." *In 1903, my great-grandfather emigrated from Russia to escape the religious pogroms. Immigrate* means "to enter another country and reside there." *More than fifty thousand Bosnians immigrated to the United States in the 1990s.*

eminent, imminent *Eminent* means "outstanding" or "distinguished." *We met an eminent professor of Greek history. Imminent* means "about to happen." *The snowstorm is imminent.*

enthused Many people object to the use of *enthused* as an adjective. Use *enthusiastic* instead. *The children were enthusiastic* (not *enthused*) *about going to the circus.*

etc. Avoid ending a list with *etc.* It is more emphatic to end with an example, and in most contexts readers will understand that the list is not exhaustive. When you don't wish to end with an example, *and so on* is more graceful than *etc.* (See also *and etc.*)

eventually, ultimately Often used interchangeably, *eventually* is the better choice to mean "at an unspecified time in the future," and *ultimately* is better to mean "the furthest possible extent or greatest extreme." *He knew that eventually he would complete his degree. The existentialists considered suicide the ultimately rational act.*

everybody, everyone *Everybody* and *everyone* are singular. (See 21e and 22a.)

everyone, every one *Everyone* is an indefinite pronoun. *Every one*, the pronoun *one* preceded by the adjective *every*, means "each individual or thing in a particular group." *Every one* is usually followed by *of*. *Everyone wanted to go. Every one of the missing books was found.*

except See *accept, except.*

expect Avoid the informal use of *expect* meaning "to believe, think, or suppose." *I think* (not *expect*) *it will rain tonight.*

explicit, implicit *Explicit* means "expressed directly" or "clearly defined"; *implicit* means "implied, unstated." *I gave him explicit instructions not to go swimming. My mother's silence indicated her implicit approval.*

farther, further *Farther* usually describes distances. *Further* usually suggests quantity or degree. *Chicago is farther from Miami than I thought. I would be grateful for further suggestions.*

fewer, less Use *fewer* for items that can be counted; use *less* for items that cannot be counted. *Fewer people are living in the city. Please put less sugar in my tea.*

finalize *Finalize* is jargon meaning "to make final or complete." Use ordinary English instead. *The architect prepared final drawings* (not *finalized the drawings*).

firstly *Firstly* sounds pretentious, and it leads to the ungainly series *firstly, secondly, thirdly*, and so on. Write *first, second, third* instead.

further See *farther, further.*

get *Get* has many colloquial uses. In writing, avoid using *get* to mean the following: "to evoke an emotional response" (*That music always gets to me*); "to annoy" (*After a while, his sulking got to me*); "to take revenge on" (*I got back at her by leaving the room*); "to become" (*He got sick*); "to start or begin" (*Let's get going*). Avoid using *have got to* in place of *must*. *I must* (not *have got to*) *finish this paper tonight.*

good, well *Good* is an adjective, *well* an adverb. (See 26a, 26b, and 26c.) *He hasn't felt good about his game since he sprained his wrist last season. She performed well on the uneven parallel bars.*

graduate Both of the following uses of *graduate* are standard: *My sister was graduated from UCLA last year. My sister graduated from UCLA last year.* It is nonstandard, however, to drop the word *from*: *My sister graduated UCLA last year.* Though this usage is common in informal English, many readers object to it.

grow Phrases such as *to grow the economy* and *to grow a business* are jargon. Usually the verb *grow* is intransitive (it does not take a direct object). *Our business has grown very quickly.* Use *grow* in a transitive sense, with a direct object, to mean "to cultivate" or "to allow to grow." *We plan to grow tomatoes this year. John is growing a beard.*

hanged, hung   *Hanged* is the past-tense and past-participle form of the verb *hang* meaning "to execute." *The prisoner was hanged at dawn.* *Hung* is the past-tense and past-participle form of the verb *hang* meaning "to fasten or suspend." *The stockings were hung by the chimney with care.*

hardly   Avoid expressions such as *can't hardly* and *not hardly*, which are considered double negatives. *I can* (not *can't*) *hardly describe my surprise at getting the job.* (See 26e.)

has got, have got   *Got* is unnecessary and awkward in such constructions. It should be dropped. *We have* (not *have got*) *three days to prepare for the opening.*

he   At one time *he* was commonly used to mean "he or she." Today such usage is inappropriate. (See 17e and 22a.)

he/she, his/her   In formal writing, use *he or she* or *his or her*. For alternatives to these wordy constructions, see 17e and 22a.

hisself   *Hisself* is nonstandard. Use *himself*.

hopefully   *Hopefully* means "in a hopeful manner." *We looked hopefully to the future.* Some usage experts object to the use of *hopefully* as a sentence adverb, apparently on grounds of clarity. To be safe, avoid using *hopefully* in sentences such as the following: *Hopefully, your son will recover soon.* Instead, indicate who is doing the hoping: *I hope that your son will recover soon.*

however   In the past, some writers objected to the conjunctive adverb *however* at the beginning of a sentence, but current experts allow placing the word according to the intended meaning and emphasis. All of the following sentences are correct. *Pam decided, however, to attend the lecture. However, Pam decided to attend the lecture.* (She had been considering other activities.) *Pam, however, decided to attend the lecture.* (Unlike someone else, Pam chose to attend the lecture.) (See 32f.)

hung   See *hanged, hung.*

i.e.   In formal writing, replace the Latin abbreviation *i.e.* with its English equivalent: *that is.*

if, whether   Use *if* to express a condition and *whether* to express alternatives. *If you go on a trip, whether to Nebraska or Italy, remember to bring traveler's checks.*

illusion   See *allusion, illusion.*

immigrate   See *emigrate from, immigrate to.*

imminent   See *eminent, imminent.*

immoral   See *amoral, immoral.*

USAGE   hackerhandbooks.com/rules
    > Language Debates > Sexist language
        > *however* at the beginning of a sentence

implement   *Implement* is a pretentious way of saying "do," "carry out," or "accomplish." Use ordinary language instead. *We carried out* (not *implemented*) *the director's orders.*

imply, infer   *Imply* means "to suggest or state indirectly"; *infer* means "to draw a conclusion." *John implied that he knew all about computers, but the interviewer inferred that John was inexperienced.*

in, into   *In* indicates location or condition; *into* indicates movement or a change in condition. *They found the lost letters in a box after moving into the house.*

in regards to   *In regards to* confuses two different phrases: *in regard to* and *as regards.* Use one or the other. *In regard to* (or *As regards*) *the contract, ignore the first clause.*

irregardless   *Irregardless* is nonstandard. Use *regardless.*

is when, is where   These mixed constructions are often incorrectly used in definitions. *A runoff election is a second election held to break a tie* (not *is when a second election is held to break a tie*). (See 11c.)

its, it's   *Its* is a possessive pronoun; *it's* is a contraction of *it is.* (See 36c and 36e.) *It's always fun to watch a dog chase its tail.*

kind(s)   *Kind* is singular and should be treated as such. Don't write *These kind of chairs are rare.* Write instead *This kind of chair is rare. Kinds* is plural and should be used only when you mean more than one kind. *These kinds of chairs are rare.*

kind of, sort of   Avoid using *kind of* or *sort of* to mean "somewhat." *The movie was somewhat* (not *sort of*) *boring.* Do not put *a* after either phrase. *That kind of* (not *kind of a*) *salesclerk annoys me.*

lay, lie   See *lie, lay.*

lead, led   *Lead* is a metallic element; it is a noun. *Led* is the past tense of the verb *lead. He led me to the treasure.*

learn, teach   *Learn* means "to gain knowledge"; *teach* means "to impart knowledge." *I must teach* (not *learn*) *my sister to read.*

leave, let   *Leave* means "to exit." Avoid using it with the nonstandard meaning "to permit." *Let* (not *Leave*) *me help you with the dishes.*

less   See *fewer, less.*

let, leave   See *leave, let.*

liable   *Liable* means "obligated" or "responsible." Do not use it to mean "likely." *You're likely* (not *liable*) *to trip if you don't tie your shoelaces.*

lie, lay   *Lie* is an intransitive verb meaning "to recline or rest on a surface." Its forms are *lie, lay, lain. Lay* is a transitive verb meaning "to put or place." Its forms are *lay, laid, laid.* (See 27b.)

like, as   *Like* is a preposition, not a subordinating conjunction. It can be followed only by a noun or a noun phrase. *As* is a subordinating conjunction that introduces a subordinate clause. In casual speech, you may say *She looks like she hasn't slept* or *You don't know her like I do.* But in formal writing, use *as. She looks as if she hasn't slept. You don't know her as I do.* (See also 46f and 46g.)

loose, lose   *Loose* is an adjective meaning "not securely fastened." *Lose* is a verb meaning "to misplace" or "to not win." *Did you lose your only loose pair of work pants?*

lots, lots of   *Lots* and *lots of* are informal substitutes for *many, much,* or *a lot.* Avoid using them in formal writing.

mankind   Avoid *mankind* whenever possible. It offends many readers because it excludes women. Use *humanity, humans, the human race,* or *humankind* instead. (See 17e.)

may   See *can, may.*

maybe, may be   *Maybe* is an adverb meaning "possibly." *Maybe the sun will shine tomorrow. May be* is a verb phrase. *Tomorrow may be brighter.*

may of, might of   *May of* and *might of* are nonstandard for *may have* and *might have. We might have* (not *might of*) *had too many cookies.*

media, medium   *Media* is the plural of *medium. Of all the media that cover the Olympics, television is the medium that best captures the spectacle of the events.*

most   *Most* is informal when used to mean "almost" and should be avoided. *Almost* (not *Most*) *everyone went to the parade.*

must of   See *may of, might of. Must of* is nonstandard for *must have.*

myself   *Myself* is a reflexive or intensive pronoun. Reflexive: *I cut myself.* Intensive: *I will drive you myself.* Do not use *myself* in place of *I* or *me. He gave the flowers to Melinda and me* (not *myself*). (See also 24a and 24b.)

neither   *Neither* is singular. (See 21e and 22a.) For *neither . . . nor* constructions, see 21d, 22a, and 22d.

none   *None* may be singular or plural. (See 21e.)

nowheres   *Nowheres* is nonstandard. Use *nowhere* instead.

number   See *amount, number.*

of   Use the verb *have,* not the preposition *of,* after the verbs *could, should, would, may, might,* and *must. They must have* (not *must of*) *left early.*

off of   *Off* is sufficient. Omit *of. The ball rolled off* (not *off of*) *the table.*

USAGE   hackerhandbooks.com/rules
    > Language Debates > *myself*
        > *none*

OK, O.K., okay All three spellings are acceptable, but avoid these expressions in formal speech and writing.

parameters *Parameter* is a mathematical term that has become jargon for "fixed limit," "boundary," or "guideline." Use ordinary English instead. *The task force worked within certain guidelines* (not *parameters*).

passed, past *Passed* is the past tense of the verb *pass*. *Ann passed me another slice of cake. Past* usually means "belonging to a former time" or "beyond a time or place." *Our past president spoke until past midnight. The hotel is just past the next intersection.*

percent, per cent, percentage *Percent* (also spelled *per cent*) is always used with a specific number. *Percentage* is used with a descriptive term such as *large* or *small*, not with a specific number. *The candidate won 80 percent of the primary vote. A large percentage of registered voters turned out for the election.*

phenomena *Phenomena* is the plural of *phenomenon*, which means "an observable occurrence or fact." *Strange phenomena occur at all hours of the night in that house, but last night's phenomenon was the strangest of all.*

plus *Plus* should not be used to join independent clauses. *This raincoat is dirty; moreover* (not *plus*)*, it has a hole in it.*

precede, proceed *Precede* means "to come before." *Proceed* means "to go forward." *As we proceeded up the mountain path, we noticed fresh tracks in the mud, evidence that a group of hikers had preceded us.*

principal, principle *Principal* is a noun meaning "the head of a school or an organization" or "a sum of money." It is also an adjective meaning "most important." *Principle* is a noun meaning "a basic truth or law." *The principal expelled her for three principal reasons. We believe in the principle of equal justice for all.*

proceed, precede See *precede, proceed.*

quote, quotation *Quote* is a verb; *quotation* is a noun. Avoid using *quote* as a shortened form of *quotation*. *Her quotations* (not *quotes*) *from current movies intrigued us.*

raise, rise *Raise* is a transitive verb meaning "to move or cause to move upward." It takes a direct object. *I raised the shades. Rise* is an intransitive verb meaning "to go up." *Heat rises.*

real, really *Real* is an adjective; *really* is an adverb. *Real* is sometimes used informally as an adverb, but avoid this use in formal writing. *She was really* (not *real*) *angry.* (See 26a and 26b.)

reason . . . is because Use *that* instead of *because. The reason she's cranky is that* (not *because*) *she didn't sleep last night.* (See 11c.)

reason why The expression *reason why* is redundant. *The reason* (not *The reason why*) *Jones lost the election is clear.*

relation, relationship   *Relation* describes a connection between things. *Relationship* describes a connection between people. *There is a relation between poverty and infant mortality. Our business relationship has cooled over the years.*

respectfully, respectively   *Respectfully* means "showing or marked by respect." *Respectively* means "each in the order given." *He respectfully submitted his opinion to the judge. John, Tom, and Larry were a butcher, a baker, and a lawyer, respectively.*

sensual, sensuous   *Sensual* means "gratifying the physical senses," especially those associated with sexual pleasure. *Sensuous* means "pleasing to the senses," especially those involved in the experience of art, music, and nature. *The sensuous music and balmy air led the dancers to more sensual movements.*

set, sit   *Set* is a transitive verb meaning "to put" or "to place." Its past tense is *set. Sit* is an intransitive verb meaning "to be seated." Its past tense is *sat. She set the dough in a warm corner of the kitchen. The cat sat in the doorway.*

shall, will   *Shall* was once used in place of the helping verb *will* with *I* or *we: I shall, we shall.* Today, however, *will* is generally accepted even when the subject is *I* or *we.* The word *shall* occurs primarily in polite questions (*Shall I find you a pillow?*) and in legalistic sentences suggesting duty or obligation (*The applicant shall file form A by December 31*).

should of   *Should of* is nonstandard for *should have. They should have* (not *should of*) *been home an hour ago.*

since   Do not use *since* to mean "because" if there is any chance of ambiguity. *Because* (not *Since*) *we won the game, we have been celebrating with a pitcher of root beer. Since* here could mean "because" or "from the time that."

sit   See *set, sit.*

site   See *cite, site.*

somebody, someone   *Somebody* and *someone* are singular. (See 21e and 22a.)

something   *Something* is singular. (See 21e.)

sometime, some time, sometimes   *Sometime* is an adverb meaning "at an indefinite or unstated time." *Some time* is the adjective *some* modifying the noun *time* and means "a period of time." *Sometimes* is an adverb meaning "at times, now and then." *I'll see you sometime soon. I haven't lived there for some time. Sometimes I see him at the library.*

suppose to   Write *supposed to.*

sure and   Write *sure to. We were all taught to be sure to* (not *sure and*) *look both ways before crossing a street.*

take See *bring, take.*

than, then *Than* is a conjunction used in comparisons; *then* is an adverb denoting time. *That pizza is more than I can eat. Tom laughed, and then we recognized him.*

that See *who, which, that.*

that, which Many writers reserve *that* for restrictive clauses, *which* for nonrestrictive clauses. (See 32e.)

theirselves *Theirselves* is nonstandard for *themselves. The crash victims pushed the car out of the way themselves* (not *theirselves*).

them The use of *them* in place of *those* is nonstandard. *Please take those* (not *them*) *flowers to the patient in room 220.*

then, than See *than, then.*

there, their, they're *There* is an adverb specifying place; it is also an expletive (placeholder). Adverb: *Sylvia is sitting there patiently.* Expletive: *There are two plums left. Their* is a possessive pronoun. *Fred and Jane finally washed their car. They're* is a contraction of *they are. They're later than usual today.*

they The use of *they* to indicate possession is nonstandard. Use *their* instead. *Cindy and Sam decided to sell their* (not *they*) *1975 Corvette.*

they, their The use of the plural pronouns *they* and *their* to refer to singular nouns or pronouns is nonstandard. *No one handed in his or her* (not *their*) *draft on time.* (See 22a.)

this kind See *kind(s).*

to, too, two *To* is a preposition; *too* is an adverb; *two* is a number. *Too many of your shots slice to the left, but the last two were just right.*

toward, towards *Toward* and *towards* are generally interchangeable, although *toward* is preferred in American English.

try and *Try and* is nonstandard for *try to. The teacher asked us all to try to* (not *try and*) *write an original haiku.*

ultimately, eventually See *eventually, ultimately.*

unique Avoid expressions such as *most unique, more straight, less perfect, very round.* Either something is unique or it isn't. It is illogical to suggest degrees of uniqueness. (See 26d.)

usage The noun *usage* should not be substituted for *use* when the meaning is "employment of." *The use* (not *usage*) *of insulated shades has cut fuel costs dramatically.*

use to Write *used to.*

USAGE hackerhandbooks.com/rules
> Language Debates > *that* versus *which*
> Absolute concepts such as *unique*

utilize   *Utilize* means "to make use of." It often sounds pretentious; in most cases, *use* is sufficient. *I used* (not *utilized*) *the laser printer.*

wait for, wait on   *Wait for* means "to be in readiness for" or "to await." *Wait on* means "to serve." *We're waiting for* (not *waiting on*) *Ruth to take us to the museum.*

ways   *Ways* is colloquial when used to mean "distance." *The city is a long way* (not *ways*) *from here.*

weather, whether   The noun *weather* refers to the state of the atmosphere. *Whether* is a conjunction referring to a choice between alternatives. *We wondered whether the weather would clear.*

well, good   See *good, well.*

where   Do not use *where* in place of *that. I heard that* (not *where*) *the crime rate is increasing.*

which   See *that, which* and *who, which, that.*

while   Avoid using *while* to mean "although" or "whereas" if there is any chance of ambiguity. *Although* (not *While*) *Gloria lost money in the slot machine, Tom won it at roulette.* Here *While* could mean either "although" or "at the same time that."

who, which, that   Do not use *which* to refer to persons. Use *who* instead. *That,* though generally used to refer to things, may be used to refer to a group or class of people. *The player who* (not *that* or *which*) *made the basket at the buzzer was named MVP. The team that scores the most points in this game will win the tournament.*

who, whom   *Who* is used for subjects and subject complements; *whom* is used for objects. (See 25.)

who's, whose   *Who's* is a contraction of *who is; whose* is a possessive pronoun. *Who's ready for more popcorn? Whose coat is this?* (See 36c and 36e.)

will   See *shall, will.*

would of   *Would of* is nonstandard for *would have. She would have* (not *would of*) *had a chance to play if she had arrived on time.*

you   In formal writing, avoid *you* in an indefinite sense meaning "anyone." (See 23d.) *Any spectator* (not *You*) *could tell by the way John caught the ball that his throw would be too late.*

your, you're   *Your* is a possessive pronoun; *you're* is a contraction of *you are. Is that your new bike? You're in the finals.* (See 36c and 46b.)

USAGE   **hackerhandbooks.com/rules**
> Language Debates > *who* versus *which* or *that*
> *who* versus *whom*
> *you*

Answers to Lettered Exercises

EXERCISE 7–1, page 110

a. hasty generalization; b. false analogy; c. *either . . . or* fallacy; d. faulty cause-and-effect reasoning; e. non sequitur

EXERCISE 8–1, page 115   *Possible revisions:*

   a. The Prussians defeated the Saxons in 1745.
   b. Ahmed, the producer, manages the entire operation.
   c. The tour guides expertly paddled the sea kayaks.
   d. Emphatic and active; no change
   e. Protesters were shouting on the courthouse steps.

EXERCISE 9–1, page 119   *Possible revisions:*

   a. Police dogs are used for finding lost children, tracking criminals, and detecting bombs and illegal drugs.
   b. Hannah told her rock-climbing partner that she bought a new harness and that she wanted to climb Otter Cliffs.
   c. It is more difficult to sustain an exercise program than to start one.
   d. During basic training, I was told not only what to do but also what to think.
   e. Jan wanted to drive to the wine country or at least to Sausalito.

EXERCISE 10–1, page 123   *Possible revisions:*

   a. A grapefruit or an orange is a good source of vitamin C.
   b. The women entering VMI can expect haircuts as short as those of the male cadets.
   c. Looking out the family room window, Sarah saw that her favorite tree, which she had climbed as a child, was gone.
   d. The graphic designers are interested in and knowledgeable about producing posters for the balloon race.
   e. The Great Barrier Reef is larger than any other coral reef in the sea.

EXERCISE 11–1, page 126   *Possible revisions:*

   a. Using surgical gloves is a precaution now taken by dentists to prevent contact with patients' blood and saliva.
   b. A career in medicine, which my brother is pursuing, requires at least ten years of challenging work.
   c. The pharaohs had bad teeth because tiny particles of sand found their way into Egyptian bread.
   d. Recurring bouts of flu caused the team to forfeit a record number of games.
   e. This box contains the key to your future.

EXERCISE 12–1, page 130   *Possible revisions:*

   a. More research is needed to evaluate effectively the risks posed by volcanoes in the Pacific Northwest.
   b. Many students graduate from college with debt totaling more than fifty thousand dollars.
   c. It is a myth that humans use only 10 percent of their brains.

d. A coolhunter is a person who can find the next wave of fashion in the unnoticed corners of modern society.
e. Not all geese fly beyond Narragansett for the winter.

EXERCISE 12–2, page 134 *Possible revisions:*

a. Though Martha was only sixteen, UCLA accepted her application.
b. To replace the gear mechanism, you can use the attached form to order the part by mail.
c. As I settled in the cockpit, the pounding of the engine was muffled only slightly by my helmet.
d. After studying polymer chemistry, Phuong found computer games less complex.
e. When I was a young man, my mother enrolled me in tap dance classes.

EXERCISE 13–3, page 139 *Possible revisions:*

a. An incredibly talented musician, Ray Charles mastered R&B, soul, and gospel styles. He even performed country music well.
b. Environmentalists point out that shrimp farming in Southeast Asia is polluting water and making farmlands useless. They warn that governments must act before it is too late.
c. We observed the samples for five days before we detected any growth. *Or* The samples were observed for five days before any growth was detected.
d. In his famous soliloquy, Hamlet contemplates whether death would be preferable to his difficult life and, if so, whether he is capable of committing suicide.
e. The lawyer told the judge that Miranda Hale was innocent and asked that she be allowed to prove the allegations false. *Or* The lawyer told the judge, "Miranda Hale is innocent. Please allow her to prove the allegations false."

EXERCISE 13–4, page 140 *Possible revisions:*

a. Courtroom lawyers have more than a touch of theater in their blood.
b. The interviewer asked if we had brought our proof of citizenship and our passports.
c. Reconnaissance scouts often have to make fast decisions and use sophisticated equipment to keep their teams from being detected.
d. After the animators finish their scenes, the production designer arranges the clips according to the storyboard and makes synchronization notes for the sound editor and the composer.
e. Madame Defarge is a sinister figure in Dickens's *A Tale of Two Cities*. On a symbolic level, she represents fate; like the Greek Fates, she knits the fabric of individual destiny.

EXERCISE 14–1, page 144 *Possible revisions:*

a. Williams played for the Boston Red Sox from 1939 to 1960, and he managed the Washington Senators and the Texas Rangers for several years after retiring as a player.
b. In 1941, Williams finished the season with a batting average of .406; no player has hit over .400 for a season since then.
c. Although he acknowledged that Joe DiMaggio was a better all-around player, Williams felt that he was a better hitter than DiMaggio.
d. Williams was a stubborn man; for example, he always refused to tip his cap to the crowd after a home run because he claimed that fans were fickle.
e. Williams's relationship with the media was unfriendly at best; he sarcastically called baseball writers the "knights of the keyboard" in his memoir.

EXERCISE 14–2, page 147 *Possible revisions:*

a. The X-Men comic books and Japanese woodcuts of kabuki dancers, all part of Marlena's research project on popular culture, covered the tabletop and the chairs.

b. Our waitress, costumed in a kimono, had painted her face white and arranged her hair in a lacquered beehive.

c. Students can apply for a spot in the leadership program, which teaches thinking and communication skills.

d. Shore houses were flooded up to the first floor, beaches were washed away, and Brant's Lighthouse was swallowed by the sea.

e. Laura Thackray, an engineer at Volvo Car Corporation, addressed women's safety needs by designing a pregnant crash-test dummy.

EXERCISE 14–3, page 148 *Possible revisions:*

a. These particles, known as "stealth liposomes," can hide in the body for a long time without detection.

b. Jan, a competitive gymnast majoring in biology, intends to apply her athletic experience and her science degree to a career in sports medicine.

c. Because students, textile workers, and labor unions have loudly protested sweatshop abuses, apparel makers have been forced to examine their labor practices.

d. Developed in a European university, IRC (Internet relay chat) was created as a way for a group of graduate students to talk about projects from their dorm rooms.

e. The cafeteria's new menu, which has an international flavor, includes everything from enchiladas and pizza to pad thai and sauerbraten.

EXERCISE 14–4, page 150 *Possible revisions:*

a. Working as an aide for the relief agency, Gina distributed food and medical supplies.

b. Janbir, who spent every Saturday learning tabla drumming, noticed with each hour of practice that his memory for complex patterns was improving.

c. When the rotor hit, it gouged a hole about an eighth of an inch deep in my helmet.

d. My grandfather, who was born eighty years ago in Puerto Rico, raised his daughters the old-fashioned way.

e. By reversing the depressive effect of the drug, the Narcan saved the patient's life.

EXERCISE 15–1, page 155 *Possible revisions:*

a. Across the hall from the fossils exhibit are the exhibits for insects and spiders.

b. After growing up desperately poor in Japan, Sayuri becomes a successful geisha.

c. Researchers believe that a series of nearby earthquakes contributed to the 1980 eruption of Mount St. Helens, the deadliest, most destructive volcanic eruption in US history.

d. Ice cream typically contains 10 percent milk fat, but premium ice cream may contain up to 16 percent milk fat and has considerably less air in the product.

e. If home values climb, the economy may recover more quickly than expected.

EXERCISE 16–1, page 160 *Possible revisions:*

a. Martin Luther King Jr. set a high standard for future leaders.

b. Alice has loved cooking since she could first peek over a kitchen tabletop.

    c. Bloom's race for the governorship is futile.
    d. A successful graphic designer must have technical knowledge and an eye for color and balance.
    e. You will deliver mail to all employees.

EXERCISE 17–1, page 163   *Possible revisions:*

    a. When I was young, my family was poor.
    b. This conference will help me serve my clients better.
    c. The meteorologist warned the public about the possible dangers of the coming storm.
    d. Government studies show a need for after-school programs.
    e. Passengers should try to complete the customs declaration form before leaving the plane.

EXERCISE 17–4, page 169   *Possible revisions:*

    a. Dr. Geralyn Farmer is the chief surgeon at University Hospital. Dr. Paul Green is her assistant.
    b. All applicants want to know how much they will earn.
    c. Elementary school teachers should understand the concept of nurturing if they intend to be effective.
    d. Obstetricians need to be available to their patients at all hours.
    e. If we do not stop polluting our environment, we will perish.

EXERCISE 18–2, page 173   *Possible revisions:*

    a. We regret this delay; thank you for your patience.
    b. Ada's plan is to acquire education and experience to prepare herself for a position as property manager.
    c. Peyton Manning, the ultimate competitor, has earned millions of dollars just in endorsements.
    d. Many people take for granted that public libraries have up-to-date computer systems.
    e. The effect of Gao Xinjian's novels on Chinese exiles is hard to gauge.

EXERCISE 18–3, page 175   *Possible revisions:*

    a. Queen Anne was so angry with Sarah Churchill that she refused to see her again.
    b. Correct
    c. The parade moved off the street and onto the beach.
    d. The frightened refugees intend to make the dangerous trek across the mountains.
    e. What type of wedding are you planning?

EXERCISE 18–4, page 177   *Possible revisions:*

    a. John stormed into the room like a hurricane.
    b. Some people insist that they'll always be available to help, even when they haven't been before.
    c. The Cubs easily beat the Mets, who were in trouble early in the game today at Wrigley Field.
    d. We worked out the problems in our relationship.
    e. My mother accused me of evading her questions when in fact I was just saying the first thing that came to mind.

EXERCISE 19–1, page 187   *Possible revisions:*

a. Listening to the CD her sister had sent, Mia was overcome with a mix of emotions: happiness, homesickness, and nostalgia.
b. Cortés and his soldiers were astonished when they looked down from the mountains and saw Tenochtitlán, the magnificent capital of the Aztecs.
c. Although my spoken Spanish is not very good, I can read the language with ease.
d. There are several reasons for not eating meat. One reason is that dangerous chemicals are used throughout the various stages of meat production.
e. To learn how to sculpt beauty from everyday life is my intention in studying art and archaeology.

EXERCISE 20–1, page 193   *Possible revisions:*

a. The city had one public swimming pool that stayed packed with children all summer long.
b. The building is being renovated, so at times we have no heat, water, or electricity.
c. The view was not what the travel agent had described. Where were the rolling hills and the shimmering rivers?
d. All those gnarled equations looked like toxic insects; maybe I was going to have to rethink my major.
e. City officials had good reason to fear a major earthquake: Most [*or* most] of the business district was built on landfill.

EXERCISE 20–2, page 194   *Possible revisions:*

a. Wind power for the home is a supplementary source of energy that can be combined with electricity, gas, or solar energy.
b. Correct
c. In the Middle Ages, when the streets of London were dangerous places, it was safer to travel by boat along the Thames.
d. "He's not drunk," I said. "He's in a state of diabetic shock."
e. Are you able to endure extreme angle turns, high speeds, frequent jumps, and occasional crashes? Then supermoto racing may be a sport for you.

EXERCISE 21–2, page 206

a. One of the main reasons for elephant poaching is the profits received from selling the ivory tusks.
b. Correct
c. A number of students in the seminar were aware of the importance of joining the discussion.
d. Batik cloth from Bali, blue and white ceramics from Delft, and a bocce ball from Turin have made Angelie's room the talk of the dorm.
e. Correct

EXERCISE 22–1, page 211   *Possible revisions:*

a. Every presidential candidate must appeal to a wide variety of ethnic and social groups to win the election.
b. David lent his motorcycle to someone who allowed a friend to use it.
c. The aerobics teacher motioned for all the students to move their arms in wide, slow circles.
d. Correct
e. Applicants should be bilingual if they want to qualify for this position.

EXERCISE 23–1, page 216   *Possible revisions:*

a. Some professors say that engineering students should have hands-on experience with dismantling and reassembling machines.

b. Because she had decorated her living room with posters from chamber music festivals, her date thought that she was interested in classical music. Actually she preferred rock.

c. In my high school, students didn't need to get all A's to be considered a success; they just needed to work to their ability.

d. Marianne told Jenny, "I am worried about your mother's illness." [*or* ". . . about my mother's illness."]

e. Though Lewis cried for several minutes after scraping his knee, eventually his crying subsided.

EXERCISE 24–1, page 221

a. Correct [But the writer could change the end of the sentence: . . . *than he is.*]

b. Correct [But the writer could change the end of the sentence: . . . *that she was the coach.*]

c. She appreciated his telling the truth in such a difficult situation.

d. The director has asked you and me to draft a proposal for a new recycling plan.

e. Five close friends and I rented a station wagon, packed it with food, and drove two hundred miles to Mardi Gras.

EXERCISE 25–1, page 225

a. The roundtable featured scholars whom I had never heard of. [*or* . . . scholars I had never heard of.]

b. Correct

c. Correct

d. Daniel always gives a holiday donation to whoever needs it.

e. So many singers came to the audition that Natalia had trouble deciding whom to select for the choir.

EXERCISE 26–1, page 231   *Possible revisions:*

a. Did you do well on last week's chemistry exam?

b. With the budget deadline approaching, our office has hardly had time to handle routine correspondence.

c. Correct

d. The customer complained that he hadn't been treated nicely.

e. Of all my relatives, Uncle Roberto is the cleverest.

EXERCISE 27–1, page 237

a. When I get the urge to exercise, I lie down until it passes.

b. Grandmother had driven our new hybrid to the sunrise church service on Savage Mountain, so we were left with the station wagon.

c. A pile of dirty rags was lying at the bottom of the stairs.

d. How did the game know that the player had gone from the room with the blue ogre to the hall where the gold was heaped?

e. Abraham Lincoln took good care of his legal clients; the contracts he drew for the Illinois Central Railroad could never be broken.

EXERCISE 27−2, page 242

a. The glass sculptures of the Swan Boats were prominent in the brightly lit lobby.
b. Visitors to the glass museum were not supposed to touch the exhibits.
c. Our church has all the latest technology, even a closed-circuit television.
d. Christos didn't know about Marlo's promotion because he never listens. He is [*or* He's] always talking.
e. Correct

EXERCISE 27−3, page 250   *Possible revisions:*

a. Correct
b. Watson and Crick discovered the mechanism that controls inheritance in all life: the workings of the DNA molecule.
c. When city planners proposed rezoning the waterfront, did they know that the mayor had promised to curb development in that neighborhood?
d. Correct
e. Correct

EXERCISE 28−1, page 257

a. In the past, tobacco companies denied any connection between smoking and health problems.
b. There is nothing in the world that TV has not touched on.
c. I want to register for a summer tutoring session.
d. By the end of the year, the state will have tested 139 birds for avian flu.
e. The benefits of eating fruits and vegetables have been promoted by health care providers.

EXERCISE 28−2, page 258

a. A major league pitcher can throw a baseball more than ninety-five miles per hour.
b. The writing center tutor will help you revise your essay.
c. A reptile must adjust its body temperature to its environment.
d. Correct
e. My uncle, a cartoonist, could sketch a face in less than two minutes.

EXERCISE 28−3, page 264   *Possible revisions:*

a. The electrician might have discovered the broken circuit if she had gone through the modules one at a time.
b. If Verena wins a scholarship, she will go to graduate school.
c. Whenever there is a fire in our neighborhood, everybody comes out to watch.
d. Sarah did not understand the terms of her internship.
e. If I lived in Budapest with my cousin Szusza, she would teach me Hungarian cooking.

EXERCISE 28−4, page 267   *Possible answers:*

a. I enjoy riding my motorcycle.
b. The tutor told Samantha to come to the writing center.
c. The team hopes to work hard and win the championship.
d. Ricardo and his brothers miss surfing during the winter.
e. The babysitter let Roger stay up until midnight.

EXERCISE 29–1, page 275

a. Doing volunteer work often brings satisfaction.
b. As I looked out the window of the plane, I could see Cape Cod.
c. Melina likes to drink her coffee with lots of cream.
d. Correct
e. I completed my homework assignment quickly. *Or* I completed the homework assignment quickly.

EXERCISE 30–1, page 280

a. There are some cartons of ice cream in the freezer.
b. I don't use the subway because I am afraid.
c. The prime minister is the most popular leader in my country.
d. We tried to get in touch with the same manager whom we spoke to earlier.
e. Recently there have been a number of earthquakes in Turkey.

EXERCISE 30–2, page 282   *Possible revisions:*

a. Although freshwater freezes at 32° Fahrenheit, ocean water freezes at 28° Fahrenheit.
b. Because we switched cable packages, our channel lineup has changed.
c. The competitor confidently mounted his skateboard.
d. My sister performs the *legong*, a Balinese dance, well.
e. Correct

EXERCISE 30–3, page 284

a. Listening to everyone's complaints all day was irritating.
b. The long flight to Singapore was exhausting.
c. Correct
d. After a great deal of research, the scientist made a fascinating discovery.
e. Surviving that tornado was one of the most frightening experiences I've ever had.

EXERCISE 30–4, page 285

a. an intelligent young Vietnamese woman; b. a dedicated Catholic priest;
c. her old blue wool sweater; d. Joe's delicious Scandinavian bread; e. many beautiful antique jewelry boxes

EXERCISE 31–1, page 287

a. Whenever we eat at the Centerville Café, we sit at a small table in the corner of the room.
b. Correct
c. On Thursday, Nancy will attend her first home repair class at the community center.
d. Correct
e. We decided to go to a restaurant because there was no fresh food in the refrigerator.

EXERCISE 32–1, page 294

a. Alisa brought the injured bird home and fashioned a splint out of Popsicle sticks for its wing.
b. Considered a classic of early animation, *The Adventures of Prince Achmed* used hand-cut silhouettes against colored backgrounds.

c. If you complete the evaluation form and return it within two weeks, you will receive a free breakfast during your next stay.
d. Correct
e. Roger had always wanted a handmade violin, but he couldn't afford one.

EXERCISE 32–2, page 294

a. J. R. R. Tolkien finished writing his draft of *The Lord of the Rings* trilogy in 1949, but the first book in the series wasn't published until 1954.
b. In the first two minutes of its ascent, the space shuttle had broken the sound barrier and reached a height of over twenty-five miles.
c. German shepherds can be gentle guide dogs, or they can be fierce attack dogs.
d. Some former professional cyclists claim that the use of performance-enhancing drugs is widespread in cycling, and they argue that no rider can be competitive without doping.
e. As an intern, I learned most aspects of the broadcasting industry, but I never learned about fundraising.

EXERCISE 32–3, page 297

a. The cold, impersonal atmosphere of the university was unbearable.
b. An ambulance threaded its way through police cars, fire trucks, and irate citizens.
c. Correct
d. After two broken arms, three cracked ribs, and one concussion, Ken quit the varsity football team.
e. Correct

EXERCISE 32–4, page 297

a. NASA's rovers on Mars are equipped with special cameras that can take close-up, high-resolution pictures of the terrain.
b. Correct
c. Correct
d. Love, vengeance, greed, and betrayal are common themes in Western literature.
e. Many experts believe that shark attacks on surfers are a result of the sharks' mistaking surfboards for small injured seals.

EXERCISE 32–5, page 302

a. Choreographer Alvin Ailey's best-known work, *Revelations*, is more than just a crowd-pleaser.
b. Correct
c. Correct
d. A member of an organization that provides job training for teens was also appointed to the education commission.
e. Brian Eno, who began his career as a rock musician, turned to meditative compositions in the late seventies.

EXERCISE 32–6, page 307

a. Cricket, which originated in England, is also popular in Australia, South Africa, and India.
b. At the sound of the starting pistol, the horses surged forward toward the first obstacle, a sharp incline three feet high.
c. After seeing an exhibition of Western art, Gerhard Richter escaped from East Berlin and smuggled out many of his notebooks.

d. Corrie's new wet suit has an intricate blue pattern.

e. The cookies will keep for two weeks in sturdy, airtight containers.

EXERCISE 32–7, page 307

a. On January 15, 2008, our office moved to 29 Commonwealth Avenue, Mechanicsville, VA 23111.

b. Correct

c. Ms. Carlson, you are a valued customer whose satisfaction is very important to us.

d. Mr. Mundy was born on July 22, 1939, in Arkansas, where his family had lived for four generations.

e. Correct

EXERCISE 33–1, page 313

a. Correct

b. Tricia's first artwork was a bright blue clay dolphin.

c. Some modern musicians (trumpeter John Hassell is an example) blend several cultural traditions into a unique sound.

d. Myra liked hot, spicy foods such as chili, kung pao chicken, and buffalo wings.

e. On the display screen was a soothing pattern of light and shadow.

EXERCISE 34–1, page 317

a. Do not ask me to be kind; just ask me to act as though I were.

b. When men talk about defense, they always claim to be protecting women and children, but they never ask the women and children what they think.

c. When I get a little money, I buy books; if any is left, I buy food and clothes.

d. Correct

e. Wit has truth in it; wisecracking is simply calisthenics with words.

EXERCISE 34–2, page 318

a. Strong black coffee will not sober you up; the truth is that time is the only way to get alcohol out of your system.

b. Margaret was not surprised to see hail and vivid lightning; conditions had been right for violent weather all day.

c. There is often a fine line between right and wrong, good and bad, truth and deception.

d. Correct

e. Severe, unremitting pain is a ravaging force, especially when the patient tries to hide it from others.

EXERCISE 35–1, page 320

a. Correct [Either *It* or *it* is correct.]

b. If we have come to fight, we are far too few; if we have come to die, we are far too many.

c. The travel package includes a round-trip ticket to Athens, a cruise through the Cyclades, and all hotel accommodations.

d. The news article portrays the land use proposal as reckless, although 62 percent of the town's residents support it.

e. Psychologists Kindlon and Thompson (2000) offer parents a simple starting point for raising male children: "Teach boys that there are many ways to be a man" (p. 256).

EXERCISE 36–1, page 325

a. Correct
b. The innovative shoe fastener was inspired by the designer's young son.
c. Each day's menu features a different European country's dish.
d. Sue worked overtime to increase her family's earnings.
e. Ms. Jacobs is unwilling to listen to students' complaints about computer failures.

EXERCISE 37–1, page 331

a. As for the advertisement "Sailors have more fun," if you consider chipping paint and swabbing decks fun, then you will have plenty of it.
b. Correct
c. After winning the lottery, Juanita said that she would give half the money to charity.
d. After the movie, Vicki said, "The reviewer called this flick 'trash of the first order.' I guess you can't believe everything you read."
e. Correct

EXERCISE 39–1, page 339

a. A client left his or her [*or* a] cell phone in our conference room after the meeting.
b. The films we made of Kilauea on our trip to Hawaii Volcanoes National Park illustrate a typical spatter cone eruption.
c. Correct
d. Correct
e. Of three engineering fields — chemical, mechanical, and materials — Keegan chose materials engineering for its application to toy manufacturing.

EXERCISE 40–1, page 344

a. Correct
b. Some combat soldiers are trained by government diplomats to be sensitive to issues of culture, history, and religion.
c. Correct
d. How many pounds have you lost since you began running four miles a day?
e. Denzil spent all night studying for his psychology exam.

EXERCISE 41–1, page 346

a. The carpenters located three maple timbers, twenty-one sheets of cherry, and ten oblongs of polished ebony for the theater set.
b. Correct
c. Correct
d. Eight students in the class had been labeled "learning disabled."
e. The Vietnam Veterans Memorial in Washington, DC, had 58,132 names inscribed on it when it was dedicated in 1982.

EXERCISE 42–1, page 349

a. Howard Hughes commissioned the *Spruce Goose*, a beautifully built but thoroughly impractical wooden aircraft.

b. The old man screamed his anger, shouting to all of us, "I will not leave my money to you worthless layabouts!"

c. I learned the Latin term *ad infinitum* from an old nursery rhyme about fleas: "Great fleas have little fleas upon their back to bite 'em, / Little fleas have lesser fleas and so on *ad infinitum*."

d. Correct

e. Neve Campbell's lifelong interest in ballet inspired her involvement in the film *The Company*, which portrays a season with the Joffrey Ballet.

EXERCISE 44–1, page 361

a. Correct

b. The swiftly moving tugboat pulled alongside the barge and directed it away from the oil spill in the harbor.

c. Correct

d. Your dog is well known in our neighborhood.

e. Roadblocks were set up along all the major highways leading out of the city.

EXERCISE 45–1, page 365

a. Assistant Dean Shirin Ahmadi recommended offering more world language courses.

b. Correct

c. Kalindi has an ambitious semester, studying differential calculus, classical Hebrew, brochure design, and Greek literature.

d. Lydia's aunt and uncle make modular houses as beautiful as modernist works of art.

e. We amused ourselves on the long flight by discussing how spring in Kyoto stacks up against summer in London.

EXERCISE 46–1, page 368

a. stage, confrontation, proportions; b. courage, mountain (noun/adjective), climber, inspiration, rescuers; c. need, guest, honor, fog; d. defense (noun/adjective), attorney, appeal, jury; e. museum, women (noun/adjective), artists, 1987

EXERCISE 46–2, page 371

a. his; b. that, our (pronoun/adjective); c. that, he, himself, some, his (pronoun/adjective); d. I, my (pronoun/adjective), you, one; e. no one, her

EXERCISE 46–3, page 373

a. told; b. were, killed; c. brought down; d. Stay, 'll [will] arrive; e. struggled, was trapped

EXERCISE 46–4, page 375

a. Adjectives: weak, unfocused; b. Adjectives: The (article), Spanish, flexible; adverb: wonderfully; c. Adjectives: The (article), fragrant, the (article), steady; adverb: especially; d. Adjectives: hot, cold; adverbs: rather, slightly, bitterly; e. Adjectives: The (article), its (pronoun/adjective), wicker (noun/adjective); adverb: soundly

EXERCISE 47–1, page 383

a. Complete subjects: The hills and mountains, the snow atop them; simple subjects: hills, mountains, snow; b. Complete subject: points; simple subject:

points; c. Complete subject: (You); d. Complete subject: hundreds of fire-flies; simple subject: hundreds; e. Complete subject: The evidence against the defendant; simple subject: evidence

EXERCISE 47–2, page 387

a. Subject complement: expensive; b. Direct object: death; c. Direct object: their players' efforts; d. Subject complement: the capital of the Russian Empire; e. Subject complement: bitter

EXERCISE 47–3, page 387

a. Direct objects: adults and children; object complement: weary; b. Direct object: community service; object complement: her priority; c. Direct object: the work; object complement: finished; d. Indirect objects: the agent, us; direct objects: our tickets, boarding passes; e. Indirect object: students; direct object: healthy meal choices

EXERCISE 48–1, page 391

a. In northern Italy, as their first language (adverb phrases modifying *speak*); b. through the thick forest (adjective phrase modifying *hike*); with ease (adverb phrase modifying *completed*); c. To my boss's dismay (adverb phrase modifying *was*); for work (adverb phrase modifying *late*); d. of Mayan artifacts (adjective phrase modifying *exhibit*); into pre-Columbian culture (adjective phrase modifying *insight*); e. In 2002, in twelve European countries (adverb phrases modifying *became*)

EXERCISE 48–2, page 394

a. Updating your software (gerund phrase used as subject); b. decreasing the town budget (gerund phrase used as object of the preposition *in*); identifying nonessential services (gerund phrase used as subject complement); c. to help her mother by raking the lawn (infinitive phrase used as direct object); raking the lawn (gerund phrase used as object of the preposition *by*); d. Understanding little (participial phrase modifying *I*); passing my biology final (gerund phrase used as object of the preposition *of*); e. Working with animals (gerund phrase used as subject)

EXERCISE 48–3, page 397

a. so that every vote would count (adverb clause modifying *adjusted*); b. that targets baby boomers (adjective clause modifying *campaign*); c. After the Tambora volcano erupted in the southern Pacific in 1815 (adverb clause modifying *realized*); that it would contribute to the "year without a summer" in Europe and North America (noun clause used as direct object of *realized*); d. that at a certain point there will be no more oil to extract from the earth (noun clause used as direct object of *implies*); e. when you are rushing (adverb clause modifying *are overlooked*)

EXERCISE 49–1, page 400

a. Complex; that are ignited in dry areas (adjective clause); b. Compound; c. Simple; d. Complex; Before we leave for the station (adverb clause); e. Compound-complex; when you want to leave (noun clause)

Acknowledgments

Scott Adams, "Dilbert and the Way of the Weasel." Copyright © 2000 by United Feature Syndicate. Reprinted with permission of United Media.

Jonathan Adler, excerpt from "Little Green Lies." Copyright © 1992 *Policy Review*. Reprinted by permission.

Nelson W. Aldrich, Jr., excerpt from "Old Money."

American Heritage Dictionary, definition for "regard" from *The American Heritage Dictionary of the English Language, Fourth Edition*. Copyright © 2010 by Houghton Mifflin Harcourt Publishing Company. Reproduced by permission from The American Heritage Dictionary of the English Language, Fourth Edition.

Linda Ben-Zvi, excerpt from "'Murder, She Wrote': The Genesis of Susan Glaspell's *Trifles*." *Theatre Journal* 44.2 (1992): 141–62. Copyright © 1992 The Johns Hopkins University Press. Reprinted with permission of The Johns Hopkins University Press.

Eugene Boe, excerpt from "Pioneers to Eternity: Norwegians on the Prairie" from *The Immigrant Experience*, edited by Thomas C. Wheeler. Copyright © 1971 by Doubleday, a division of Random House, Inc. Used by permission of Doubleday, a division of Random House, Inc.

Carl Botan and Mihaela Vorvoreanu, excerpt from "What Do Employees Think about Electronic Surveillance at Work?" p. 126.

Jane Brody, excerpt from *Jane Brody's Nutrition Book*. Copyright © 1981 W. W. Norton & Company.

Bruce Catton, excerpt from "Grant and Lee: A Study in Contrasts."

Napolean A. Chagnon, excerpt from *Yanomamo: The Fierce People*. Copyright © 1992 Harcourt Brace College Publishers.

Barnaby Conrad III, excerpt from "Train of Kings."

Earl Conrad, excerpt from *Harriet Tubman*. Copyright © 1943 Associated Publishers.

James Crocket et al., excerpt from *Wildflower Gardening*. Copyright © 1977 Time-Life Education.

EBSCO Information Services, various screen shots. Reprinted with permission of EBSCO Information Services.

Equal Exchange, Inc., coffee advertisement. Copyright © Equal Exchange, Inc. Reprinted by permission.

Thomas L. Friedman, screen shots of the copyright page and title page from *Hot, Flat, and Crowded: Why We Need a Green Revolution — And How It Can Renew America*. Copyright © 2008 by Thomas Friedman. Reprinted by permission of Farrar, Straus & Giroux, LLC.

Brian Friel, excerpt from *Translations: A Play*. Copyright © 1995 Faber & Faber. Reprinted by permission.

Robert Frost, excerpt from "Fire and Ice," from *Robert Frost: Collected Poems, Prose, and Plays*. Copyright © 1995 Library of America: Collector's Edition.

Gale, screen shot from Academic OneFile. Reprinted with permission from Cengage Learning.

Susan Glaspell, "A Jury of Her Peers." Copyright © 2005 Digireads.com Publishing. Reprinted by permission.

Jane Goodall, excerpt from *In the Shadow of Man.* Copyright © 2010 Mariner Books, 50th Anniversary of Gombe Edition.

Stephen Jay Gould, excerpt from "Were Dinosaurs Dumb?" *Natural History* 87.5: 9–16. Reprinted by permission of Rhonda R. Shearer.

Dan Gutman, excerpt from "The Way Baseball Works."

Hillary Hauser, excerpt from "Exploring a Sunken Realm in Australia."

Elaine Hedges, "Small Things Reconsidered: 'A Jury of Her Peers,'" in *Susan Glaspell: Essays on Her Theater and Fiction*, edited by Linda Ben-Zvi, The University of Michigan Press, 1995, pp. 49–67. Reprinted by permission.

Richart Hofstadter, excerpt from "America at 1750."

Khaled Hosseini, excerpt from *A Thousand Splendid Suns.* Copyright © 2008 Riverhead Trade.

Langston Hughes, "Ballad of the Landlord" from *The Collected Poems of Langston Hughes* by Langston Hughes, edited by Arnold Rampersad with David Roessel, Associate Editor. Copyright © 1994 by the Estate of Langston Hughes. Used by permission of Alfred A. Knopf, a division of Random House, Incorporated and Harold Ober Associates, Incorporated.

Lynn Hunt et al., map, "Castile and Portugal" from *The Making of the West, Volume II.* Copyright © 2005 by Bedford/St. Martin's. Reprinted by permission of Bedford/St. Martin's.

International Monetary Fund, graph "Wishing-well," GDP forecasts, percentage increase on previous year. Source: International Monetary Fund

Shirley Jackson, excerpt from *The Lottery and Other Stories.* Copyright © 2005 Farrar, Straus & Giroux. Reprinted by permission.

Henry J. Kaiser Family Foundation, excerpt from "The Role of Media in Childhood Obesity" (2004), p. 1 (#7030). Copyright © 2004 by The Henry J. Kaiser Family Foundation. This information was reprinted with permission from the Henry J. Kaiser Family Foundation. The Kaiser Family Foundation is a non-profit private operating foundation, based in Menlo Park, California, dedicated to producing and communicating the best possible analysis and information on health issues.

Dorling Kindersley, excerpt from *Encyclopedia of Fishing.* Copyright © 1994 by DK Publishing.

Frederic Lane, excerpt from *The Naked Employee: How Technology Is Compromising Workplace Privacy*, p. 142. Copyright © AMACOM.

Shirley Geok-lin Lim (book), Mitsuye Tamada (selection), screen shots of the title page and first page of selection, "Guilty on Both Counts" from *Asian American Literature, An Anthology.* Copyright © 2000 NTC/Contemporary Publishing Company; Teachers Edition.

Robert MacNeil and William Cran, excerpt from *Do You Speak American?* Copyright © 2004 by Neely Productions, Inc. and William Cran. Used by permission of Doubleday, a division of Random House, Inc.

Margaret Mead, excerpt from "New Superstitions for Old."

Chris Meleksi, excerpt from student essay.

US Department of Energy, Hybrid electric vehicle sales by year in the United States, data from http://www1.eere.energy.gov/vehiclesandfuels/facts/ 2009_fotw598.html.

Olivia Vlahos, excerpt from "Human Beginnings." Copyright © 1970 Penguin Books Group.

Eudora Welty, excerpt from "Why I Live at the P.O." from *The Collected Stories of Eudora Welty.* Copyright © 1982 Harcourt Brace.

David Whitman, "An Appeal to Authority: The New Paternalism in Urban Schools." Screen shots of article page and table of contents from *Education Next* 8.4 (Fall 2008): 53.

Walt Whitman, excerpt from "A Noiseless Patient Spider."

Tennessee Williams, excerpt from *The Glass Menagerie.* Copyright © 1999 New Directions.

Garry Wills, excerpt from "Two Speeches on Race," from *The New York Review of Books* 55.7 (May 1, 2008).

Brenda Wineapple, screen shots of copyright page and title page from *White Heat: The Friendship of Emily Dickinson and Thomas Wentworth Higginson.* Copyright © 2008 by Brenda Wineapple. Used by permission of Alfred A. Knopf, a division of Random House, Inc.

Fred Zwicky, "Tornado Touch." Copyright © Fred Zwicky. Reprinted by permission.

Index

verbs
active voice, 253–54
conditional, 261–63
forms of, 252–57
with gerunds or infinitives, 264–67
modals (*can*, *might*, *should*, etc.),
258–60
negative forms, 261
passive voice, 255–57
tenses, 252–57, 261–63
must, as modal verb, 258, 260, 372
must of (nonstandard). See *may of*,
might of, 662
myself, 219, 662

N

namely, and sentence fragments, 185
Narration, as pattern of organization, 56
Narrowing a subject, 3, 5, 422–23
N.B., 343
nearly, placement of, 127–28
Needed words, 119–23
articles (*a*, *an*, *the*), 122–23, 267–76
in comparisons, 121–22
in compound structures, 120
it, 277–78
in parallel structures, 118
subjects, 277–78
that, 121
there, 278
verbs, 242, 277
Negatives
double, avoiding, 231, 261
forming, 261
not and *never*, 375
neither (singular), 200–01, 208–09, 662
neither . . . nor
and parallel structure, 117–18
and pronoun-antecedent
agreement, 211
and subject-verb agreement, 200
never
as adverb, 375
in double negatives, avoiding, 231
nevertheless
comma with, 302–03
semicolon with, 315–16
news (singular), 205
Newspapers. See Periodicals
News sites, 434–35

no
comma with, 304–05
in double negatives, avoiding, 231, 261
nobody (singular), 200–01, 208–09
Noncount nouns, 268–74
none, 200–01, 662
Nonrestrictive (nonessential) elements,
commas with, 298–302
Non sequitur, 106
Nonsexist language, 167–70, 208–09, 210
Nonstandard English, avoiding, 165–66
no one (singular), 200–01, 208–09
nor
comma with, 292–93
as coordinating conjunction, 117, 377
parallelism and, 117–18
and pronoun-antecedent
agreement, 211
and subject-verb agreement, 200
not
as adverb, 261, 375
in double negatives, avoiding, 231,
261
in forming negatives, 261
placement of, 127–28
Notes. See Footnotes or endnotes;
Information notes (MLA)
Note taking
for analysis, 70–73
and avoiding plagiarism, 451–56
on drafts, 41
to generate ideas, 14
for literature papers, 599
sample notes, 72–73
nothing (singular), 200–01, 208–09
not only . . . but also, 377
and parallel structure, 117–18
and pronoun-antecedent
agreement, 211
and subject-verb agreement, 200
Noun/adjectives, 368, 374
Noun clauses, 396–97
words introducing, 396–97
Noun markers, 267–76
Nouns. See also Nouns, types of
adjectives with, 374
articles with, 267–76
capitalizing, 362–63
defined, 368
of direct address, comma with, 304–05
plural form, singular meaning
(*athletics*, *economics*, etc.), 205

Multilingual/ESL Menu

Revision Symbols

Boldface numbers refer to sections of the handbook.

abbr	faulty abbreviation **40**	p	error in punctuation
adj/adv	misuse of adjective or adverb **26**	ʌ̦	comma **32**
add	add needed word **10**	no ,	no comma **33**
agr	faulty agreement **21, 22**	;	semicolon **34**
appr	inappropriate language **17**	:	colon **35**
art	article (*a, an, the*) **29**	꣐̌	apostrophe **36**
awk	awkward	" "	quotation marks **37**
cap	capital letter **45**	. ?	period, question mark,
case	error in case **24, 25**	!	exclamation point **38**
cliché	cliché **18e**	— ( )	dash, parentheses,
coh	coherence **4d**	[ ] ...	brackets, ellipsis mark,
coord	faulty coordination **14a**	/	slash **39**
cs	comma splice **20**	¶	new paragraph **4e**
dev	inadequate development **4b, 6e**	pass	ineffective passive **8**
		pn agr	pronoun agreement **22**
dm	dangling modifier **12e**	proof	proofreading problem **3c**
-ed	error in -*ed* ending **27d**	ref	error in pronoun reference **23**
emph	emphasis **14**	run-on	run-on sentence **20**
ESL	English as a second language **28–31**	-s	error in -*s* ending **21, 27c**
exact	inexact language **18**	sexist	sexist language **17e, 22a**
frag	sentence fragment **19**	shift	distracting shift **13**
fs	fused sentence **20**	sl	slang **17c**
gl/us	see Glossary of Usage	sp	misspelled word **43**
hyph	error in use of hyphen **44**	sub	faulty subordination **14a**
idiom	idioms **18d**	sv agr	subject-verb agreement **21, 27c**
inc	incomplete construction **10**	t	error in verb tense **27f**
irreg	error in irregular verb **27a**	trans	transition needed **4d**
ital	italics **42**	usage	see Glossary of Usage
jarg	jargon **17a**	v	voice **8a**
lc	lowercase letter **45**	var	lack of variety in sentence structure **14, 15**
mix	mixed construction **11**	vb	verb problem **27, 28**
mm	misplaced modifier **12a–d**	w	wordy **16**
mood	error in mood **27g**	//	faulty parallelism **9**
nonst	nonstandard usage **17c, 27**	ʌ	insert
num	error in use of numbers **41**	x	obvious error
om	omitted word **10, 30b**	#	insert space
		⌒	close up space

Detailed Menu

When you have questions as you write, *Rules for Writers*, Seventh Edition, offers quick, practical advice in language you can understand and in a format that's easy to use. What's more, it's already priced lower than almost every other college handbook. When you think about it, hanging on to *Rules* after your writing class — and continuing to use it in business, psychology, or literature — makes the handbook an even better value.

"If you are a college student, you need *Rules for Writers*. It'll be the best reference on your shelf, and **it'll save you hours of Web surfing** to find an answer to a writing question."
— Darrell L. Smith, former student

"We like *Rules* because it's affordable, easy to use, and **flexible enough for multiple courses**." — Anne Helms, *Alamance Community College*

"This handbook has **everything student writers need in one place**, which can't be said for any single site on the Web."
— Wendy Perkins, *Prince George's Community College*

"To be honest, my students love the low price of *Rules for Writers*."
— Heidi Marshall, *Florida State College, Jacksonville*

Bedford Media adds value. For free resources to support your writing, visit the companion Web site for *Rules for Writers* for exercises, model papers, videos, reliable research help, and more: **hackerhandbooks.com/rules**. Want to go completely digital? For a handbook that can be used on a computer, tablet, or e-reader, see **bedfordstmartins.com/ebooks**.

ISBN-13: 978-0-312-64795-7
ISBN-10: 0-312-64795-6

90000

9 780312 647957

BEDFORD/ST. MARTIN'S
bedfordstmartins.com